Criminal Justice

CRIMINAL JUSTICE

Volume 2

Firearms—Race riots in the twentieth century

Edited by
Phyllis B. Gerstenfeld
California State University, Stanislaus
Department of Criminal Justice

Salem Press, Inc.
Pasadena, California   Hackensack, New Jersey

Editor in Chief: Dawn P. Dawson

Editorial Director: Christina J. Moose   *Editorial Assistant:* Dana Garey
Project Editor: R. Kent Rasmussen   *Photo Editor:* Cynthia Beres
Production Editor: Joyce I. Buchea   *Acquisitions Editor:* Mark Rehn
Manuscript Editor: Elizabeth Ferry Slocum   *Graphics and Design:* James Hutson
Assistant Editor: Andrea Miller   *Layout:* William Zimmerman

Cover photo: Brand-X Pictures/Bill Fritsch

Library of Congress Cataloging-in-Publication Data

Criminal justice / edited by Phyllis B. Gerstenfeld.
    p. cm.
Includes bibliographical references and index.
ISBN-10: 1-58765-218-8 (set : alk. paper)
ISBN-13: 978-1-58765-218-9 (13-digit set : alk. paper)
ISBN-10: 1-58765-220-X (vol. 2 : alk. paper)
ISBN-13: 978-1-58765-220-2 (vol. 2 : alk. paper)
1. Criminal law—United States—Encyclopedias. 2. Criminal justice, Administration of—United States—Encyclopedias. 3. Crime—United States—Encyclopedias. 4. Criminal procedure—United States—Encyclopedias. I. Gerstenfeld, Phyllis B.

KF9214.5.C75 2006
345.75′05—dc22

2005017803

First Printing

Contents

Contents

Complete List of Contents

Volume I

Volume II

Complete List of Contents

Volume III

Criminal Justice

Firearms

Definition: Small arms weapons that use gun-powder to fire lethal projectiles

Criminal justice issues: Constitutional protections; federal law; law codes

Significance: Most U.S. states permit private owners of most types of firearms; however, increasing numbers of states and some cities have started prohibiting certain types of firearms.

Throughout U.S. history, private ownership of most types of firearms was legal. Since the last decades of the twentieth century, however, there have been increasing challenges to private gun ownership. By the year 2005, a significant number of states and cities had laws prohibiting possession of certain types of firearms.

Classifications of Firearms

Throughout the United States, it is lawful to own rifles and shotguns. The former have barrels with twisting grooves (the rifling) that make their bullets spin, thereby imparting greater stability and accuracy in their trajectories. In contrast, ordinary shotguns are smooth-bored weapons that fire bunches of small lead pellets (shot), which are held in plastic shells, with gunpowder and primers, until they are fired. Ordinary rifles and shotguns are the firearms most commonly used by hunters, whose activities are considered a form of sport.

Handguns are legal almost everywhere in the United States. In 2004, about three-quarters of the states allowed all adults who passed background checks and, in most states, completed safety training classes to obtain permits to carry handguns in public for protection. Such restrictions as have been placed on handgun ownership have generally been enacted by municipal governments. For example, in 1976, Washington, D.C., banned acquisition of new handguns. Chicago did the same in 1982. However, both cities allowed residents who already owned registered handguns to keep them. During the 1970's and 1980's, several Chicago suburbs also enacted bans, all of which applied retroactively to handguns already possessed by residents. Several other Illinois towns have banned handgun sales but not handgun possession. Other states that place bans on small handguns include California, Hawaii, Maryland, Massachusetts, and Minnesota.

Several states and cities prohibit the possession of handguns of certain sizes. These small handguns are often derided as "junk guns" or "Saturday night specials." Definitions of outlawed guns vary widely. Some are based on the melting points of the guns, because the less-expensive guns most often used in crimes are typically made from metal alloys that melt at lower temperatures than more expensive guns. Other laws focus on the sizes of the guns or their barrels. Still others are based on the presence or absence of certain features of the guns.

The Debate Over Handgun Ownership

Legal challenges to municipal bans on handgun ownership have been repeatedly rejected by the courts. Most challenges have been based on the Second Amendment to the U.S. Constitution, which states that "the right of the people to keep and bear Arms, shall not be infringed." A challenge to a San Francisco handgun prohibition did succeed in 1982. In that case, however, a court struck down the city's ordinance because it conflicted with a state law explicitly forbidding local governments from banning guns.

Advocates of handgun prohibition point out that while handguns constitute only about one-third of all guns in the United States, they are involved in a greatly disproportionate share of crimes that involve firearms. They also note that because handguns are small and easily concealed, they are easier for criminals to carry. Prohibitionists argue that the banned handguns are worthless for sports or self-defense, are dangerous to the user, and are preferred by criminals. Prohibition opponents contest all these claims and note that the prohibitions always include exemptions for police, which implies that the guns can, in fact, be used for self-defense.

Opponents of prohibition argue that if handguns were banned, many criminals would simply use hacksaws to shorten the barrels of rifles and shotguns. Then, because rifles and shotguns are more powerful weapons, the number of deaths from firearms might increase. Prohibition opponents also argue that because handguns are portable and concealable, they are the best guns for carrying in public for self-defense.

There have also been efforts to ban rifles that fire the comparatively large .50 caliber bullets. However, in early 2005, California was the only state to ban such rifles. Supporters of such legislation emphasize that the power and long-distance capability of .50 caliber rifles are inherently dangerous. Prohibition opponents argue that .50 caliber rifle shooting is an expensive hobby whose participants are no threat to anyone. They also contend that gun-control laws should concentrate on disarming dangerous people, rather than ban particular models of guns.

Federal Laws

There is no federal ban on small gun ownership, but the federal Gun Control Act of 1968 gave the Bureau of Alcohol, Tobacco, Firearms and Explosives the authority to prohibit importation of guns that were not suited for sporting purposes. The bureau used this authority to halt the importation of inexpensive foreign handguns. During the 1970's, legislation to ban Saturday night specials received a great deal of attention in Congress, but no bill was passed. One bill would have banned two-thirds of all handguns; another would have banned 90 percent of all handguns by classifying them as Saturday night specials.

In 1988, Congress responded to new developments in plastic firearm technology by passing legislation requiring that all guns include at least four ounces of metal and that the guns' metal must show recognizable gun profiles. The legislation was intended to prevent the invention of guns that could be sneaked through metal detectors and X-ray machines. The legislation did not affect any guns then in existence, including the Glock pistol.

No one has yet manufactured an all-plastic gun. During the 1980's, the Glock Company began using plastic polymers for the frames of its handguns. The plastic frames made the guns more durable and lighter in weight and thus more suitable for frequent carrying. During the 1990's, many other manufacturers started making plastic frames. By the early twenty-first century, plastic frames were common in new handgun design and were also appearing in some long guns.

Automatic and Semiautomatic Firearms

Automatic guns are models that fire continuously, as their triggers are pressed. These guns are also commonly known as machine guns.

In 1934, Congress responded to the criminal violence that had surged during the Prohibition era by passing the National Firearms Act (NFA). That law required owners of automatic guns to pay one-time federal taxes of two hundred dollars on their guns and to register them. The law also imposed a similar requirement on short-barreled rifles and shotguns.

In 1986, Congress outlawed the manufacture of new automatic firearms for the nongovernment market. The law allowed owners to keep the estimated 200,000 automatic guns then in private hands. Those guns could also be bought and sold, pursuant to the registration and tax requirements.

Firearm Use by Convicted Felons

These figures reflect the firearm use of only those felons in federal and state prisons in the year 1997 who actually used firearms while committing their crimes. For example, 49.1 percent of state prisoners who used firearms in their crimes fired their weapons during their crimes, against only 12.8 percent of firearm-using federal prisoners who did so.

	Percentage of total firearm users	
Use of weapons	*state*	*federal*
Fired their weapons	49.1	12.8
Killed or injured victims	22.8	5.0
Other results	26.3	7.8
Brandished weapons	73.2	46.2
to scare someone	48.6	29.3
to defend themselves	41.1	24.9

Source: U.S. Bureau of Justice Statistics, Firearm Use by Offenders, 2001.

In 2004, Delaware, Hawaii, Iowa, Illinois, Kansas, New York, Rhode Island, and Washington did not allow private ownership of automatic firearms. California required permits that were considered nearly impossible to obtain, except by film producers. In all other states, possession of automatic firearms remained lawful, within the bounds of the National Firearms Act.

Semiautomatic firearms are guns that automatically reload as each round is fired. Energy from each round's gunpowder explosions is used to move the next round into the firing chamber. Users of semiautomatic weapons do not have to perform additional actions, such as operating a lever or pump, to place the next round in firing position. However, unlike automatic guns, semiautomatic guns fire only one round at a time when their triggers are pressed. All semiautomatics fire at essentially the same rate.

In the United States, the term "assault weapon" is usually applied to semiautomatic firearms. No bans in the United States apply to every semiautomatic. In countries such as Germany and Australia, however, all semiautomatic rifles and shotguns are prohibited. Germany also prohibits pump-action guns.

American lawmakers who wish to ban some, but not all, semiautomatics have often faced a difficult task in defining exactly what is to be prohibited. Some assault weapon prohibitions are simply lists of specific gun models. Other prohibitions look to the design history of the guns. Still others are based on the presence or absence of certain accessories, such as bayonet lugs and folding stocks, or the types of grips the guns have.

A federal prohibition on the manufacture of new assault weapons was enacted in 1994 and expired in September, 2004. Several states have bans on assault weapons that are unaffected by the expiration of the federal law. California's law is the most restrictive, followed by those of New

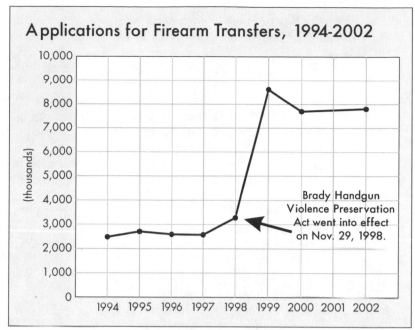

Applications for Firearm Transfers, 1994-2002

(thousands)

Brady Handgun Violence Preservation Act went into effect on Nov. 29, 1998.

Source: U.S. Bureau of Justice Statistics, 2002.

Jersey, Connecticut, Massachusetts, and New York. Bans on "assault pistols" that do not apply to rifles or shotguns are enforced in Maryland and Hawaii. All these state bans have grandfather clauses that allow existing owners of the banned guns to keep them, provided the guns are properly registered. Some cities, especially in New York and Ohio, have local bans.

Almost all semiautomatic handguns, as well as many semiautomatic rifles, store their ammunition in rectangular magazines that can be replaced within seconds. Assault weapon laws often include restrictions on the permissible sizes of detachable magazines. Gun-control advocates have proposed limits of six rounds of ammunition. The 1994 federal law had outlawed manufacture of magazines holding more than ten rounds. Some state and local laws have limits of fifteen to twenty rounds.

Prohibition advocates argue that the banned guns are of no value except for killing many people quickly. Prohibition opponents argue that the guns are useful for all sporting purposes, and in particular that some of the banned rifles are used in elite target-shooting competitions. They also contend that the guns are useful for lawful defense—especially since assault weapon laws always allow the police to possess such guns, and the only purpose of police gun possession is for lawful defense.

David B. Kopel

Further Reading

Cramer, Clayton E. *For the Defense of Themselves and the State: The Original Intent and Judicial Interpretation of the Right to Keep and Bear Arms*. Westport, Conn.: Praeger, 1994. The best legal history of the right to bear arms and related gun-control cases in both federal and state courts.

Halbrook, Stephen P. *Firearms Law Deskbook: Federal and State Criminal Practice*. St. Paul, Minn.: Thomson/West, 2003. Annual handbook for attorneys that is also accessible to lay readers. Focuses mainly on federal law but includes some state issues, particularly assault weapons. A useful appendix summarizes the gun laws of each state.

Hemenway, David. *Private Guns, Public Health*. Ann Arbor: University of Michigan Press, 2004. Treatise by the director of the Harvard Injury Control Research Center, who argues that guns should be treated as a public health issue, and that reduced gun availability would decrease firearms injuries. Written in part as a rebuttal to Gary Kleck's *Targeting Guns*.

Kleck, Gary. *Targeting Guns: Firearms and Their Control*. Hawthorne, N.Y.: Aldine de Gruyter, 1997. Presents the author's social science research about the efficacy of various gun controls, including the prohibition of handguns and assault weapons.

Korwin, Alan. *Gun Laws of America: Every Federal Gun Law on the Books, with Plain English Summaries*. 3d ed. Phoenix, Ariz.: Bloomfield Press, 1999. Collection of all federal gun laws in one volume, with summaries for general readers. Free updates are available at the publisher's Web site, at www.bloomfieldpress.com.

Ludwig, Jens, and Philip J. Cook. *Evaluating Gun Policy: Effects on Crime and Violence*. Washington, D.C.: Brookings Institution Press, 2003. Collection of social science research papers that are generally supportive of restrictions and prohibitions.

State Laws and Published Ordinances: Firearms. 25th ed. Washington, D.C.: Bureau of Alcohol, Tobacco, Firearms and Explosives, 2004. Federal compendium of all state laws on firearms. Formerly printed, the publication is now available only through the Bureau of Alcohol, Tobacco, Firearms and Explosives's Web site, www.atf.gov. The same Web site also contains many other useful publications about federal firearms laws.

See also Bill of Rights, U.S.; Bureau of Alcohol, Tobacco, Firearms and Explosives; Deadly force; Gun laws; Omnibus Crime Control and Safe Streets Act of 1968; Right to bear arms; Special weapons and tactics teams (SWAT); Violent Crime Control and Law Enforcement Act.

Ford v. Wainwright

The Case: U.S. Supreme Court ruling on capital punishment
Date: Decided on June 26, 1986
Criminal justice issues: Capital punishment; defendants; mental disorders
Significance: This case forced the criminal justice system to examine controversies surrounding mental illness and the death penalty, in particular what types of mental conditions should spare condemned prisoners from execution.

On July 19, 1974, Alvin Bernard Ford was convicted of first-degree murder after shooting a Fort Lauderdale police officer in a robbery attempt. Ford was sentenced to death by electric chair in the Florida court system. During his trial and sentencing, Ford appeared to be mentally competent. After his first year of prison, Ford received only one disciplinary report for his behavior. In 1982, his mental condition gradually began to decline, and he started having delusions. For example, Ford thought that his family was being held hostage at the prison and that the Ku Klux Klan had made him a target of conspiracy. Ford's communication skills deteriorated; his writing and speaking became incoherent.

Florida law stipulated that if the governor is informed that a death-row inmate may be insane, a commission of psychiatrists must be appointed to examine the person. The examiners must determine whether the person understands the consequences of the death penalty and why it is being imposed. After a thirty-minute interview, two of the three psychiatrists diagnosed Ford as psychotic, yet all three determined that Ford was competent enough to be executed. Relevant testimony of two psychiatrists who had worked with Ford over time, however, was not included in the fact-finding process. They concluded that Ford was severely psychotic and not competent to be executed. No opportunity was given to other knowledgeable experts to dispute the findings of the state-appointed commission. Based on the commission's results, the governor found Ford to be competent and issued a death warrant for his execution.

Florida's Eleventh Circuit Court of Appeals stayed the execution to hear the issues. The court decided against Ford. The U.S. Supreme Court agreed to hear Ford's appeal. In a 5-4 decision, the Supreme Court overturned the decision of the Florida court and ordered that the case be remanded to federal district court for a full hearing. Justice Thurgood Marshall wrote the majority opinion of the Supreme Court. He concluded that the Eighth Amendment prohibits the states from imposing the death penalty on prisoners who are insane. The court found that Florida's process of evaluating condemned prisoners did not provide adequately for deciding whether Ford was competent to be executed.

Before the federal district court could determine Ford's competency, Alvin Ford died in prison. His death left issues unresolved, such as how competency is defined, what should be done in cases where the inmate wavers between stages of competency and incompetence, whether medication should be used to restore an inmate's mental health before execution, and whether mentally retarded inmates are competent for execution.

Michelle R. Royle

Further Reading

Conley, R., R. Luckasson, and G. N. Bouthilet. *The Criminal Justice System and Mental Retardation: Defendants and Victims.* Baltimore: Brookes, 1992.

Fabrega, H. "Culture and Formulation of Homicide: Two Case Studies." *Psychiatry* 67 (2004): 178-196.

Lewis, Dorothy Otnow. *Guilty by Reason of Insanity: A Psychiatrist Explores the Minds of Killers.* New York: Ivy Books, 1999.

Monahan, J. *Mental Illness and Violent Crime.* Washington, D.C.: U.S. Department of Justice, 1996.

Whitlock, Francis Antony. *Criminal Responsibility and Mental Illness.* London: Butterworths, 1963.

See also Capital punishment; Cruel and unusual punishment; Insanity defense; Supreme Court, U.S.

Forensic accounting

Definition: Integration of accounting, auditing, and investigative skills to assist in legal investigations of possible fraud and other white-collar crimes

Criminal justice issues: Business and financial crime; evidence and forensics; fraud; white-collar crime

Significance: The specialized field of forensic accounting deals with the discovery, analysis, interpretation, summary, and presentation of financial issues or economic analysis. It involves looking beyond the numbers to detect improper, unethical, or illegal activities. Another term for forensics accounting is fraud accounting.

Forensic accounting encompasses both litigation support and investigative accounting. Litigation support is the factual presentation of economic issues related to litigation. It deals primarily with issues related to quantifying economic damages. A typical litigation support case is the calculation of economic loss resulting from a breach of contract. In these types of cases, forensic accounting professionals quantify the damages sustained by parties who are involved in legal disputes to help resolve the disputes. When unresolved disputes go to court, forensic accountants may testify as expert witnesses.

Auditing is the systematic process of objectively obtaining and evaluating evidence regarding financial matters. Investigation is the process of determining whether criminal matters, such as intellectual property theft, employee theft, identity theft, securities fraud, falsification of financial statements, or insurance fraud have occurred. As part of investigations, forensic accountants may recommend actions that can be taken to minimize risks of future losses.

Investigations may also occur in civil matters. For example, forensic accountants may search for hidden assets in divorce cases. However, investigative accounting is mostly associated with investigations of criminal matters.

When Forensic Accounting Is Needed

Forensic accountants search for evidence of criminal conduct or assist in determinations of claimed damages or rebuttals of such claims. As such, forensic accounting is required in situations needing high levels of detail or precision that are sustainable in adversarial legal proceedings. It provides an accounting analysis that is suitable to courts, thereby forming the basis for dispute resolution. Typical situations requiring forensics accounting involve white-collar crimes, insurance and securities fraud, employee theft, kickbacks, business disputes, and impaired or lost income-generating cases,

Most forensic accounting investigations involve financial theft, economic crime, bankruptcy, mergers, personal injury, and matrimonial divorce valuations. In addition, a wide range of noncriminal cases rely on forensic accounting; these include investment analyst research, litigation support, underwriting due diligence, and enterprise risk management.

Business Disputes and Fraud Investigations

The primary business disputes requiring forensic accounting investigations are professional negligence, breach of contract, warranty and products liability, patent infringements, construction claims, business valuation or dissolution, and property and income losses for insurance claim purposes, such as business interruption.

The most common investigations deal with fraud- and theft-related matters that are criminal, civil, or insurance remedies. Since the widespread corporate scandals of 2000-2004 and terrorist threats, there have been numerous investigations of financial statement manipulation, shareholder and partnership disputes, stock market fraud, supplier kickbacks, computer crime, and money laundering. Other investigations involve the search for hidden assets or unreported income for income tax, matrimonial, or related disputes.

When conducting investigations, one of the first steps that forensic accountants take is to learn as much as possible about matters such as target computers and their networks, peripheral devices, and telecommunication devices, including electronic mail, voice mail, and instant-messaging systems. Forensic accountants frequently interview information technology (IT) staff members so they can identify how and where data are stored. This part of investigations is critical to gain clear understandings of how data files, transaction data, electronic mail, and voice mail are archived. After understanding and documenting the data and telecommunication systems, forensic accountants know the dates of complete data backups. This knowledge is used to select and restore the backups most likely to contain information related to the investigation of suspected fraud.

An example of the value of forensic accounting is the case of HealthSouth Corporation, which is based in Birmingham, Alabama. Forensic accountants determined that the corporation's executives and others had committed massive accounting fraud. They discovered fraudulent entries made between 1992 and 2003 that overstated earnings by more than four billion dollars. As a result of their investigation and evidence, HealthSouth, its former investment bank, and its former audit company faced a class-action lawsuit from shareholders and bondholders. In addition, fifteen former executives pleaded guilty to taking part in the fraud scheme. HealthSouth founder Richard Scrushy faced criminal charges but was acquitted on all charges in June, 2005—possibly because the government failed to make its complex case understandable to the jury.

As a result of its effectiveness in business cases, personal injury cases are increasingly using forensic accounting to evaluate issues such as loss of earnings as well as pension or dependency claims.

Forensic accounting crosses over into criminology by the way it investigates suspicious activities. It requires special expertise, similar to the investigative skill of being able to tell when someone is being deceptive. Forensic accountants must know and be able to follow generally accepted principles, have the credentials to qualify as experts, and be competent in written and oral communications, logical reasoning, problem solving, critical thinking, and computer skills.

Linda Volonino
George F. Kermis

Further Reading

Albrecht, W. Steve, and Chad Albrecht. *Fraud Examination and Fraud Prevention*. Hoboken, N.J.: John Wiley & Sons, 2003. Discusses all phases of forensic accounting using actual examples. Explains critical accounting principles and how to implement fraud investigation processes.

Anastasi, Joe. *The New Forensics: Investigating Corporate Fraud and the Theft of Intellectual Property*. Hoboken, N.J.: John Wiley & Sons, 2003. Discusses how computers can detect fraud and other corporate criminal activities.

Crumbley, D. Larry, Lester E. Heitger, and G. Stevenson Smith. *Forensic and Investigative Accounting*. Chicago: Commerce Clearing House, 2003. Explains issues and practices associated with forensics accounting, including uncovering accounting fraud, courtroom procedures, litigation support, and cybercrime.

Friedman, Jack P., and L. Weil Roman. *Litigation Support Report Writing: Accounting, Finance, and Economic Issues*. Hoboken, N.J.: John Wiley & Sons, 2003. A collection of effective litigation reports on financial and accounting subjects. Each chapter is an actual litigation report that was submitted to court.

Silverstone, Howard, and Michael Sheetz. *Forensic Accounting and Fraud Investigation for Non-Experts*. Hoboken, N.J.: John Wiley & Sons, 2003. General guide for detecting, preventing, and prosecuting financial fraud.

See also Cold cases; Confessions; Consent searches; Conspiracy; Corporate scandals; Document analysis; Embezzlement; Forensics; Forgery.

Forensic anthropology

Definition: Analysis and identification of human skeletal remains that sometimes uses archaeological methods to recover buried remains

Criminal justice issues: Evidence and forensics; investigation; medical and health issues; technology

Significance: Anthropologists participate in the criminal justice system by assisting in the identification of human remains, particularly in cases in which decomposition is far advanced and when significant bone trauma is associated with death.

The field of forensic anthropology may be said to have begun in 1939, when W. M. Krogman published an article in the *FBI Law Enforcement Bulletin* that was the first attempt to synthesize data used in the identification of a human skeleton. Thereafter, forensic anthropology was associated with the medicolegal identification of human skeletal remains, a skill first put to use at the end of World War II to identify bodies of soldiers killed in battles in the South Pacific. In 1947, the U.S. Army established a central identification laboratory in Hawaii. Its facilities were also used to help identify remains from the Korean and Vietnam Wars and other conflicts. The work done in that lab created the data, methods, and training techniques for modern anthropologists who use their skills in the identification of missing persons and victims of crimes.

The American Academy of Forensic Sciences (AAFS) formed in 1948. It now has ten subsections, including a physical (biological) anthropology section that was established in 1972. With the support of the AAFS, the American Board of Forensic Anthropology was organized in 1978. It certifies physical anthropologists who specialize in forensic work. In 2005, more than fifty certified physical anthropologists worked in the United States.

Identifying Human Remains

When skeletal remains need to be identified, forensic anthropologists begin their work by determining if the remains are human. Once that

Sculptor Eileen Barrow (left) and forensic anthropologist Mary Manhein (right) pose with the bust of a woman's head that they made at Louisiana State University in 2004. They created the bust from the skull of an unknown murder victim whose body had been discovered and then buried in Louisiana in 1986. Law-enforcement officials hoped to use the bust to identify the woman and catch her killer. *(AP/Wide World Photos)*

determination is made, they establish whether the remains come from more than one individual. In some cases, the state of the remains—that is, the extent of their decomposition and their insect infestations—provides clues to how long it has been since the person died. Anthropologists then attempt to determine the age, sex, height, approximate weight, general physique, and race of the deceased. Their success in these endeavors depends on how complete the remains are and their condition. Age estimates for children can be relatively precise because of clear patterns in the developmental sequences of teeth and bones. After people reach eighteen to twenty-five years of age, the physical deterioration that accompanies their aging becomes more variable, making assessments of their ages more difficult.

The sex of adults can be readily determined from size and shape differences, particularly in the pelvis bones, as the configurations of women's hips are affected by childbearing. However, determining the sexes of preadolescent children whose remains are decomposed is almost impossible because young bodies are unaffected by the physical changes that follow the release of adolescent hormones. Height can be estimated from measurements of either partial or complete long bones of the limbs.

Some bodies have unusual skeletal characteristics or indications of prior diseases or injuries that are unique to the individuals. When such characteristics are identifiable, they can provide positive identifications of the decedents after comparisons are made to medical records, such as X rays of bones and teeth. Gunshot and blunt trauma wounds, severe disease, and other forms of trauma may point to the causes or manners of death.

Recovery of Remains

Forensic anthropologists are particularly helpful in the recovery of remains. Those who are trained in physical anthropology are usually bone specialists, and some physical anthropologists are also trained in DNA analysis. Other anthropologists have training in archaeology that makes them experts in recovery. Some are trained in both subdisciplines. Anthropologists generally know when body parts are missing during searches. Those with archaeological training are experienced in mapping and recovery of physical evidence and in excavating graves. The more information that can be retrieved from sites, the more likely it is that the dead can be identified and the circumstances of their death be accurately reconstructed.

Skeletal remains that are unearthed during construction projects or accidentally through natural processes can be identified as recent or older. In the United States, the remains of early Native Americans are often uncovered. Such remains are not connected with contemporary crimes, but they may, on occasion, become the focus of litigation by representatives of modern Native American tribes. An example is the remains of so-called Kennewick Man, who was found in the state of Washington in 1996. That nearly ten-thousand-year-old body is believed to come from the earlier group of humans to enter the Americas. For this reason, the body is of great interest to scientists. However, members of Washington Indian tribes wanted to rebury the man's remains.

Mass Fatalities

Forensic anthropologists are also consulted when human remains are disarticulated, burned, or otherwise severely damaged, as in the cases of fires and mass disasters. Clyde Snow, perhaps the best-known modern forensic anthropologist, assisted in the identification of victims of serial killers and at plane crashes, particularly after 1979.

During the 1980's, the Disaster Mortuary Operational Response Team (DMORT) was organized by volunteers to coordinate an optimal response to mass disasters such as plane crashes. DMORT is now a program within the U.S. Department of Homeland Security that steps into situations that are too big to be handled by local resources, but only when requested by local municipalities. Physical anthropologists are among the volunteers.

In 1984, Snow was part of a team that flew to Argentina to help in the identification of victims of the ousted government's campaign of mass murder, torture, summary executions, and political "disappearances" of Argentine citizens. He helped train a local team, oversaw recovery, and testified as an expert witness in Argentinean courts of law. The precedent he established led to human rights organizations establishing multidisciplinary scientific teams that include forensic anthropologists working in countries around the world. Meanwhile, unprecedented terrorist activities have created new needs for forensic anthropologists within the United States.

After the terrorist attacks of September 11, 2001, the World Trade Center Human Identification Project was organized to identify the remains of victims of the World Trade Center tower collapses. Its work has been particularly challenging to forensic specialists. After the disaster, there was no definitive list of victims, and the remains of many victims were highly fragmented and often mixed together. In some cases, minute fragments represented the only remains of the nearly three thousand victims. Forensic specialists, including both DNA and bone specialists, reviewed nineteen thousand separate pieces of human remains. DNA testing alone was not enough to resolve some of the cases. The anthropologists were able to determine the sex, ancestry, and ages of many victims and used their findings to separate many incorrectly associated remains.

Joan C. Stevenson

Further Reading

Bass, William M., and Jon Jefferson. *Death's Acre: Inside the Legendary Lab—the Body Farm—Where the Dead Do Tell Tales*. New York: Putnam, 2003. Bass describes challenging cases as well as his research at the University of Tennessee's "Body Farm."

Benedict, Jeff. *No Bone Unturned: The Adventures of the Smithsonian's Top Forensic Scientist and the Legal Battle for America's Oldest Skeleton*. New York: HarperCollins, 2003. One of many books detailing forensic cases. In this book are the cases of forensic anthropologist Doug Owsley.

Byers, Steven N. *Introduction to Forensic Anthropology*. Boston: Allyn and Bacon, 2002. Solid overview of the standard methods used in forensic anthropology.

Rhine, Stanley. *Bone Voyage: A Journey in Forensic Anthropology*. Albuquerque: University of New Mexico Press, 1998. Very readable description of forensic anthropologist Rhine's experiences.

Steadman, Dawnie W., ed. *Hard Evidence: Case Studies in Forensic Anthropology*. Upper Saddle River, N.J.: Prentice Hall, 2003. Case studies in how anthropological methods are applied in specific instances by forensic scientists.

See also Crime labs; Crime scene investigation; DNA testing; Espionage; Expert witnesses; Forensic entomology; Forensic odontology; Forensic psychology; Forensics; Homeland Security Department; Missing persons; War crimes.

Forensic entomology

Definition: Use of insects and their by-products as evidence in legal investigation, prosecution, and defense

Criminal justice issues: Criminology; evidence and forensics; investigation

Significance: Corpse-eating insects can aid criminal investigations, especially those concerning homicide.

It is well known that corpses draw flies and other insects, including spiders and mites. A human body may also be infested while alive, for example by lice. Insects can become evidence in criminal cases involving corpses. Insect evidence is also used in other cases, from civil suits over termite damage to prosecution of poachers who leave animal evidence that gathers insects.

Insect evidence was considered in criminal cases in China as early as 1235 C.E. The term "forensic entomology" was coined in 1855, although during the following century many still doubted that it qualified as a science. During the 1980's, the area of study burgeoned; its professional jour-

nals include the *Journal of Entomological Science*, *Journal of Forensic Science*, and *Journal of Medical Entomology*. During the early twenty-first century, forensic entomology became almost popular—albeit still a specialized discipline—gaining exposure both from television shows such as *CSI: Crime Scene Investigation* and real-life advances resulting from growing knowledge and more detailed methodology. The journal *Forensic Science International* issued a special forensic entomology issue, and the University of California, Davis held a forensic entomology conference in 2004.

One well-known laboratory for forensic entomology is the Body Farm at the University of Tennessee, Knoxville, featured in a novel by Patricia Cornwell. William M. Bass III developed this facility in which insect behavior and reproduction, in various venues which include human corpses, can be studied under many conditions.

Uses of Forensic Entomology

The most common use of entomological evidence in homicide or murder investigation is to determine the time of death. Changes undergone by the body itself help only to determine the postmortem interval (PMI) within the first forty-eight or seventy-two hours after death, but insect evidence can establish the PMI after weeks or even months have passed. The two primary clues as to time of death are the kinds of insects present and their stages of development. For example, blowflies find a body quickly, while beetles usually arrive much later. Then, over time, there is a sequence of eggs, larvae, pupae, and empty pupa cases. Many insects lay eggs only at certain times of the year, or only during the day or the night; these facts can help establish parameters as to the time of death.

Insects can also help preserve chemical evidence. Laboratories have discovered drugs, poisons, and other chemicals in dead flies after the chemicals were no longer detectable in the body in which the flies fed. Crab lice have even given up samples of human DNA.

Interpretation of such evidence in a corpse requires not only detailed entomological knowledge but also knowledge of the environment. Temperature, especially, can greatly affect insect development, as can the natural population in the environment at the time. Studies by Melanie Archer, published in journals in 2003 and 2004, challenged the usefulness of insect data because her experiments over two years found unexpectedly wide variations in insect evidence. However, most forensic entomologists see this only as a call for more research. They generally do not propose one interpretation of the evidence anyway but state what is possible or impossible based on the range of scenarios. This may be enough to single out or eliminate a suspect.

Conversely, insect evidence can help establish some facts about the scene of death. A contrast between local fauna and those in the corpse can show that a body has been moved from the death site. Water insects, such as midge larvae, can help indicate where, when, and how deep a body has lain underwater. Because blowflies lay eggs in moist areas, a cluster of maggots may indicate the sites of open wounds, even after decomposition has blurred evidence in the body's flesh. If the time of death is known, the type and number of insects present can show whether the corpse was hidden in a closed room, buried, or even frozen for part of the time since demise.

Drawbacks

Clearly, forensic entomology can provide useful data for legal investigations concerning the time and place and even the nature of the death. It can also lead to misinterpretations. For example, insect activity can disturb clothing on the body in a way that can be confused with evidence of sexual assault. Insects can also seem to mimic mutilation and may mislead investigators concerning wound patterns or blood evidence.

Crime Scene Investigation Procedure

Most police and crime investigators are not educated in how to interpret insect evidence, which requires a lengthy and detailed background in entomology. They are, however, now trained in how to collect such evidence, preserve it (alive or dead), and label it, including at what exact time and place (in or near the body) it was found. The recording of data about the scene, such as whether it was in a sunny or shaded area, is also important. Then the evidence is interpreted by specialists, who often act as expert witnesses at trials.

Bernadette Lynn Bosky

Further Reading

Bass, William M., and Jon Jefferson. *Death's Acre: Inside the Legendary Lab—the Body Farm—Where the Dead Do Tell Tales*. New York: Putnam, 2003. Tells the story of the Body Farm at the University of Tennessee, with only a bit too much about Bass's own life apart from forensic entomology.

Byrd, Jason H., and James L. Castner, eds. *Forensic Entomology*. Boca Raton, Fla.: CRC Press, 2000. Offers many essays that examine vital issues but assumes more knowledge of insects than a novice may have.

Erzclioglu, Zakaria. *Maggots, Murder, and Men*. New York: Thomas Dunne Books, 2002. Offer case studies, basic entomological information, and considerations of how forensic entomology is used, and misused, in court.

Goff, M. Lee. *A Fly for the Prosecution: How Insect Evidence Helps Solve Crimes*. Cambridge, Mass: Harvard University Press, 2001. Similar to the Erzclioglu book listed above.

Greenberg, Bernard, and John Charles Kunich. *Entomology and the Law*. New York: Cambridge University Press, 2002. A comprehensive textbook, academic and thorough. May entertain the novice and will be needed by any professional.

See also Autopsies; Bloodstains; Crime labs; Crime scene investigation; DNA testing; Expert witnesses; Forensic anthropology; Forensic psychology; Forensics; Latent evidence; Television crime dramas.

Forensic odontology

Definition: Examination of teeth to identify human remains, or to match bite marks to the teeth of an individual

Criminal justice issues: Criminology; evidence and forensics; investigation; medical and health issues

Significance: Jaws and teeth are important in forensic science because sometimes they are the only identifiable part of a decomposed or mutilated human body. Also, unique dental characteristics can allow the use of bite marks as evidence in criminal cases.

Forensic odontology (dentistry) is often used to identify people killed in large-scale disasters such as plane crashes, fires, or earthquakes, but is also important for identifying victims, attackers, and missing persons in criminal investigations. Forensic dentists match dental records to the jaws and teeth of human remains. They may also be called upon to match bite marks to a living person's teeth.

Teeth and jaws are more durable than other body parts and can remain intact even when the rest of a body is too decomposed for visual identification. Teeth may be matched to dental records for identification of remains that are burned or otherwise too damaged to view by relatives or others who knew the deceased, or when there is no one available to identify a body. Forensic dentistry may also be used to confirm the identity of a decomposed or damaged body believed to be that of a specific person.

An individual's teeth and jaws are affected over time by aging, diet, medical conditions, and daily activities. Forensic dentists may be able to give law-enforcement officials information about an unidentified person based upon these effects. In addition, most Americans receive professional dental care during their lives, generating a record of procedures such as fillings and extractions. Naturally occurring dental characteristics, combined with dental work, will usually result in a unique dental profile which can be matched to the teeth of a decomposed or otherwise unidentifiable body.

Forensic dentistry is also used to match bite marks to the teeth of criminal suspects. If the victim of an attack was bitten, the bite marks are measured, photographed, and documented so they can be matched later to an impression of a suspect's teeth. The size of a bite and other specific characteristics, such as missing teeth, can be used to match a bite mark to an alleged attacker. Bite marks found on substances at a crime scene (usually food) can also be preserved and matched to suspects' teeth.

Identification through dental records can be faster and less expensive than DNA analysis, but not all dentists are trained to deal with identification of human remains or bite marks. In criminal cases, law-enforcement officials work with dentists who specialize in forensics.

Maureen Puffer-Rothenberg

Further Reading

Fixott, Richard H. *Forensic Odontology*. Philadelphia: W. B. Saunders, 2001.

Genge, N. E. "Working the Scene of the Body Human: Forensic Odontology." In *The Forensic Casebook: The Science of Crime Scene Investigation*. New York: Ballantine Books, 2002.

See also Crime labs; Crime scene investigation; Forensic anthropology; Forensics; Missing persons.

Forensic palynology

Definition: Use of pollen and spore data to help solve crimes

Criminal justice issues: Criminology; evidence and forensics; investigation

Significance: In cases where other evidence may be lacking, inconclusive, or unbelievable, forensic palynology data may prove to be the relevant link in solving a crime.

The word "forensic" is applied to the scientific methods of crime investigation and the resulting evidence being used in courts of law, while "palynology" pertains to the study of pollen, spores, algal cysts, and a broad variety of acid-resistant microscopic plant cells. Forensic palynology probably emerged in the 1950's, with two of the earliest cases reported in 1959. During the 1960's and 1970's, the well-known Swiss criminologist Max Frei used forensic palynology data to link suspects to crime scenes and criminal activities. In nature, each plant type has distinctive pollen or spores that distinguish it from other plants, thus acting like a set of "fingerprints."

Despite its success in helping solve a number of crime cases, by 2004 forensic palynology was not extensively used in the United States for a variety of reasons. First, there are few palynologists in the world with forensic training or expertise. Even for those with appropriate credentials, personal liability associated with testifying in court is an issue, as is the stress associated with cross-examination procedures. Sample collection is another major issue. Samples must be carefully extracted in order to avoid contamination. In some crime investigations, there just is not enough sample material available to provide any for palynology studies. When samples are available for palynology studies, specially equipped, contaminant-free laboratories are needed in which to do the analysis. In addition, pollen and spore databases used for making comparisons and identifications were still being assembled and made accessible to forensic palynologists. Finally, there was little funding available for forensic palynology work.

Given the above constraints, forensic palynology has most often been used as a tool in crime investigations in New Zealand and Australia, where it is approved and court-tested. Due to personal liability issues and a lack of knowledge about how pollen data can play a vital role in solving certain crimes, forensic palynology has been used only minimally in the United States. Efforts are being made by many forensic scientists to increase its acceptance and usage in the United States and other countries.

Alvin K. Benson

Further Reading

Genge, Ngaire E. *The Forensic Casebook: The Science of Crime Scene Investigation*. New York: Ballantine, 2002.

Nickell, Joe, and John F. Fischer. *Crime Science: Methods of Forensic Detection*. Lexington: University of Kentucky Press, 1999.

Pearsall, Deborah M. *Paleoethnobotany: A Handbook of Procedures*. New York: Academic Press, 2000.

See also Crime labs; Forensics; Latent evidence; Toxicology; Trace evidence.

Forensic psychology

Definition: Application of psychology to legal issues

Criminal justice issues: Criminology; evidence and forensics; interrogation; investigation

Significance: Forensic psychology has become an increasingly popular discipline since the mid-1980's, thanks to media exposure and advances in the discipline. As a consequence, psychology is having a greater and greater impact in criminal justice and the law.

Forensic psychology is sometimes confused with criminal psychology; however, the former is actually a much broader field. Criminal psychology is limited to criminal applications, most specifically personality. Forensic psychology encompasses not only criminal applications but also civil applications. In fact, more forensic psychologist work is done on the civil side of the law than on the criminal side. That is in keeping with the fact that the bulk of court work is in the field of civil, not criminal, law.

The intersection of such vastly different fields as psychology and the law poses certain difficulties. Few lawyers have an understanding of psychology, and few psychologists understand the law. Law students generally do not take psychology courses, and only a minority of psychology students—even forensic psychology students—take courses in the law. Moreover, psychologists and lawyers function in very different ways. The goal of psychologists is to seek the truth about certain matters. The goal of attorneys is to provide the best possible cases for their clients. The

Media Perceptions of Forensic Psychology

If media images are to be believed, forensic psychologists spend most of their time constructing criminal personality profiles and tracking serial killers. There can be no doubt that much of the popularity of forensic psychology has been driven by news media and popular films and television series. Although criminal personality profiling makes up only a slim segment of forensic psychology work, it is the most common theme for the media to highlight.

two goals may be at odds. While attorneys must be advocates for their clients, professional forensic psychologists rarely advocate anything. Instead, they present their interpretations of the psychological data they collect.

History of Forensic Psychology

Forensic psychology traces its roots back to around the turn of the twentieth century, when only a few people were working in the field of psychology. Psychologists such as Wilhelm Wundt, Alfred Binet, and Sigmund Freud contributed bits and pieces from their areas of specialization that would later become important to forensic psychology. Hugo Munsterberg is generally recognized as the founder of forensic psychology. Although his interests were not confined to that field, he made significant contributions in the areas of memory and eyewitness accuracy, confessions, hypnosis, crime detection, and suggestibility. Munsterberg's 1908 book *On the Witness Stand* addressed these areas, but it was not until the 1940's and 1950's that forensic psychology began to gain acceptance, first in civil courts, later in criminal courts. In a notable early example, forensic psychologists testified about the effects of segregation on schoolchildren in the U.S. Supreme Court's landmark *Brown v. Board of Education* (1954) case.

Forensic Psychologists on the Job

Forensic psychologists work in several broad areas: as trial consultants; with police departments; in correctional settings; in mental health; in family courts; in tort, personal injury, and malpractice litigation; assessing civil competency; and in education. As trial consultants, forensic psychologists assist attorneys in preparing for

trial, including alternative dispute resolution, jury selection, evaluating eyewitness testimony, and making determinations on competency (competency to enter a plea, competency to stand trial) and insanity. Forensic psychologists also evaluate and testify in court regarding the presence or absence of psychological disorders such as posttraumatic stress syndrome, battered woman syndrome, rape trauma syndrome, and antisocial personality disorder.

Forensic psychologists also work with law enforcement in a variety of ways, from assisting during selection of officers (by administering psychological tests and conducting interviews), to working on negotiations teams during hostage crises, to counseling individual officers after stressful incidents. Forensic psychologists assist in the criminal investigation process by constructing criminal personality profiles, administering lie detector tests, and consulting on interrogation interviews. In a correctional setting, a forensic psychologist may assess prisoners during the intake process and treat a variety of offenders (sex offenders, drug offenders) on an ongoing basis.

In civil courts, forensic psychologists work in a variety of settings. For example, in mental health settings, they may assess individuals for the presence or absence of specific disorders. In family courts, forensic psychologists perform custody evaluations. They also assess and testify regarding tort, personal injury, and malpractice litigation. Forensic psychologists may assess civil competency pertaining to making wills or entering into contracts. They may also work in education, assessing the presence or absence of educational disabilities.

Training of Forensic Psychologists

As late as the 1970's, people who wanted to become forensic psychologists were pretty much left to their own devices to define their own educational and professional paths, as there were no graduate programs in the field. Those who wanted to become forensic psychologists generally obtained master's degrees and doctorates in subareas of psychology, such as clinical, school, and counseling. They often worked in mental health or corrections or with children and families.

During the 1970's, a handful of psychology and law programs existed, and during the 1980's, graduate programs in forensic psychology began to appear. By the early twenty-first century, many fine programs in forensic psychology throughout the United States were offering a variety of degrees focusing on forensic psychology and psychology and the law. However, no standard curriculum has emerged, and there is considerable variation in courses offered in programs. It is generally agreed, however, that internships should be a part of all forensic psychology training. Forensic psychology itself remains an unlicensed field, but many professionals in the field are licensed in other areas, such as clinical psychology and mental health.

Ayn Embar-Seddon
Allan D. Pass

Further Reading

Bartol, C., and A. Bartol. *Psychology and Law.* 3d ed. Belmont, Calif.: Wadsworth/Thomson Learning, 2004.

Hess, A., and I. Weiner. *The Handbook of Forensic Psychology.* 2d ed. New York: John Wiley & Sons, 1999.

Wrightsman, L. *Forensic Psychology.* Belmont, Calif.: Wadsworth/Thomson Learning, 2001.

See also Competency to stand trial; Criminals; Forensics; Insanity defense; Latent evidence; Mental illness; Motives; Police psychologists; Psychological evaluation; Psychological profiling.

Forensics

Definition: Applications of science to the legal arena, particularly criminal investigations

Criminal justice issues: Evidence and forensics; investigation; technology

Significance: Forensic science and forensic medicine, as they relate to the processing of crime scene evidence, have become increasingly important to the resolution of cases

within the criminal justice system, particularly as evolving technologies have allowed forensics to make ever greater contributions to criminal investigations.

Forensic science broadly encompasses the use of science in both criminal and civil courts. The types and variety of forensic evidence that can be presented in courtrooms are almost limitless. In criminal courts, forensic evidence is essential in drug cases. Forensic medicine is especially valuable in the handling of evidence relating to bodies in homicide and rape cases. In civil courts, forensic evidence is often presented in product-liability and injury cases.

Forensic Specialties

The field of forensic science includes a variety of subdisciplines. These include forensic medicine, forensic anthropology, forensic entomology, forensic odontology, forensic palynology, forensic serology, and criminalistics. Forensic medicine is further divided into the areas of forensic pathology, forensic toxicology, forensic odontology, and forensic psychiatry.

Forensic pathology studies how and why people die and concentrates on sudden, unexpected, and violent deaths. During homicide investigations, forensic pathologists frequently perform autopsies. Forensic toxicology is concerned with chemicals—especially drugs and poisons—found in human bodies. During death investigations, forensic toxicologists may make determinations on whether victims have been killed by poisons, such as lead. Toxicology analyses can also be used to determine whether a drug such as rohypnol—the so-called "date-rape" drug—has been used in sexual assaults.

Forensic odontology, which is also known as forensic dentistry, deals with dental evidence. It is usually used to identify bodies or to link bite marks on victims to dental impressions of suspects. Forensic psychiatrists combine knowledge and practical experience in medicine, mental health, and the neurosciences and are called upon to testify in the courtroom regarding psychological disorders and disabilities.

Forensic anthropologists are most frequently called upon when human skeletal remains are found. Anthropologists use the remains to assist in identifying victims. They may also provide approximate dates and causes of death. Forensic entomology studies how insects colonize dead bodies. On the basis of examination of insects, estimates of times of death can be made. Forensic serologists specialize in identifying and processing blood, semen, saliva, and other bodily fluids. They may also be involved in analyses of bloodstains, blood spatters, and DNA specimens. Such evidence is often crucial in sexual assault cases and homicide investigations.

Criminalistics

Criminalistics is a broad area of forensics that is concerned with analyses of a wide variety of evidence. It encompasses questioned documents, voice examinations; ballistics and firearms; tool marks; fingerprints; tire-tracks and shoe prints; paint and glass fragments; hair, fibers, and soil; and arson and explosives. The area of questioned documents includes all types of possible forgeries of documents, papers, inks, computer copies, and handwriting analysis. Voice examination is employed to identify speakers and to ascertain whether speakers are telling the truth.

Ballistics is the study of the physics of objects in flight. In forensics, it is primarily concerned with bullets and other projectiles used as weapons. Ballistics experts can determine the angles at which projectiles strike surfaces and the damage that the projectiles cause.

Experts in firearms study all types of guns, shotguns, bullets, cartridges, and cases. Tool marks are most often found at the scenes of burglaries and other crimes at which criminals gain forcible entry into secured areas. Fingerprint experts dust for, lift, and interpret fingerprint evidence left at crime scenes. Tire-tracks and shoe prints, like fingerprints, are impressions that are often left at crime scenes and can be lifted or copied in castings made with plaster-like materials.

Many experts deal with fragment and fiber evidence and examine the microscopic differences in paints, glass, hairs, fibers, and soils. For example, through thorough examination, it may be possible to match minute samples from a crime scene with the paint or glass on a suspect's car.

"Criminalistics" vs. "Forensic Science"

It is common for the terms "criminalistics" and "forensic science" to be used interchangeably. Although there is considerable overlap between the terms, they do not mean exactly the same thing. Criminalistics is used specifically for those areas that deal with the processing of crime scene evidence, such as fingerprinting, ballistics, and tool-mark investigation. Forensic science encompasses criminalistics but also encompasses other, more general, scientific knowledge that has become useful to the legal system, such as DNA analysis.

Paint and glass examination are frequently important in the prosecution of hit-and-run cases.

Affiliated Fields

Areas related to forensic science include forensic psychology, forensic nursing, forensic accounting, forensic engineering, and forensic computer analysis. Forensic psychology includes such activities as criminal personality profiling, child custody evaluations, and litigation consultation. Forensic nursing is an emerging specialization within nursing that concentrates on working with sexual assault and domestic violence victims. It also contributes to evidence collection for law enforcement.

Forensic accounting utilizes accounting principles to evaluate the financial paperwork of organizations to determine if fraud is present. This specialization within accounting has become increasingly important due to highly publicized increases in financial wrongdoing among large corporations. Forensic engineering studies how structures respond to stresses. Forensic engineers explained how and why the Twin Towers of the World Trade Center collapsed during the terrorist attacks of September 11, 2001. Forensic computer analysis is the specialty within computer science that deals with analyses of computer evidence for the prosecution of individuals who steal or alter computer data.

History of Forensic Science

There are two distinct historical threads within forensic science. The first is the history of the development of law enforcement and investigation techniques. The second is the history of a variety of scientific advances that have been useful to solve cases.

The techniques used by investigators and detectives to solve cases have traditionally been called criminalistics. Has Gross, who is credited as the founder of modern criminalistics, worked as a prosecutor and judge in Austria. He was responsible for publishing the first professional paper on the application of the sciences to criminal investigation during the 1890's.

Locard's Exchange Principle, named for the French criminalist Edmond Locard, is the guiding principle behind all forensic science. It states that whenever two objects come into contact with each other, there is an exchange of materials between them. In other words, when crimes are committed and the offenders are at the crime scenes, the offenders invariably leave behind material—which may be microscopic—that can be traced back to them. Locard established an early crime laboratory in Lyons, France, in 1910.

Alphonse Bertillon developed the first system of person identification, based on body measurements, in Paris during the mid-nineteenth century. His system was soon replaced by fingerprints, which were found to be more individual than the body measurements.

The first forensic laboratory in the United States was opened by the Los Angeles Police Department during the early 1920's. During the 1930's, several state laboratories were set up throughout California. California's early start in forensics gave it an edge in the field that it retained into the twenty-first century. Meanwhile, the Federal Bureau of Investigation established its first forensic laboratory in 1932.

Since the field of forensics was founded, it has been advanced by numerous scientific advances. These include developments in microscopy—from Galileo's invention of the first microscope in the sixteenth century to the invention of the electron microscope during the 1930's—chemistry, biology, biochemistry, optics, microbiology, molecular biology, and DNA analysis.

Forensic Medicine

Forensic medicine—the use of medicine to determine cause and manner of death—dates back to ancient Greece and the birth of medicine. From the inception of this discipline, medical practitioners have mastered techniques for determining the time and manner of human deaths. Forensic medical testimony is one of the oldest forms of scientific testimony and has been widely accepted in courts and legal systems across the world. With the advent of modern medicine in the sixteenth and seventeenth centuries, forensic

After sealing off access to crime scenes, one of the first things that police investigators do is photograph evidence. Photography is important not only for preserving the positions of evidence for later study but also for capturing transitory evidence, such as wet prints and liquid spills, before they disappear. *(Brand-X Pictures)*

medicine became irrevocably entrenched in the investigative process. In modern criminal justice, forensic medicine is a necessary part of any death investigation. Medical examiners oversee death investigations and may be called upon to testify in court regarding the facts surrounding deaths.

The Importance of Crime Scenes

The role of forensic science and medicine in the criminal justice system is to aid in the arrest and prosecution of criminals. When law-enforcement officers witness crimes, making arrests is easy. However, in real life, that rarely happens. Arrests that lead to successful convictions are dependent upon three things: witnesses who can testify well, crime scene evidence that can be processed and presented at court, and voluntary confessions by perpetrators. Not all three components need be present for convictions, but each component helps build the state's case against criminal defendants.

Forensic science is most concerned with the processing of crime scenes. The importance of this work cannot be overstated. Criminal investigations begin at crime scenes; if they are not handled properly, the investigations may not progress any further. All the modern scientific advances available to law enforcement cannot make up for what is lost when crime scenes are not been properly guarded and preserved for forensic analysis. Crime scenes must be kept and processed in as pristine a condition as possible.

Depending upon the size of the law-enforcement departments responding to crimes, the responsibility for collecting evidence from crime scenes may fall to the responding officers, the lead detectives, or crime scene technicians. In large jurisdictions, specialists may collect different types of evidence. For example, fingerprint specialists dust for and lift fingerprints.

Evidence from crime scenes may be examined in three different ways. Physical methods, which are often used, include measuring sizes of objects and where they are in relation to each other; physical matching and comparisons—which are common with glass fragments—and photography. Since the advent of digital photography, the first responders have been able to photograph evidence and make prints quickly and easily, thereby helping to ensure that even transitory evidence, such as wet shoe prints, can be preserved.

Chemical methods are often used—especially in the processing of drug evidence. Before convictions can be obtained in drug cases, techniques such as chromatography and spectrography are employed to determine the chemical makeups of evidence at the scenes. Chemical analyses are also performed on blood-alcohol evidence. Biological methods, including microscopy, may also be used, especially when the evidence consists of minute fibers and fragments.

Training

Training within forensic medicine and forensic science is very diverse, depending upon the particular job descriptions. Forensic medicine requires medical degrees and advanced training. Crime scene technicians generally have college degrees or certificate training. Police officers who work at crime scenes may have on-the-job-training or take specific classes. Individuals who work in crime labs generally have either master's or doctoral degrees in chemistry, biology, or other natural sciences.

Ayn Embar-Seddon
Allan D. Pass

Further Reading

Bass, William M., and Jon Jefferson. *Death's Acre: Inside the Legendary Lab—the Body Farm—Where the Dead Do Tell Tales*. New York: Putnam, 2003. Tells the story of the Body Farm at the University of Tennessee, with only a bit too much about Bass's own life apart from forensic entomology.

Ellen, David. *The Scientific Examination of Documents: Methods and Techniques*. 2d ed. Boca Raton, Fla.: CRC Press, 1997. Guide to methods of examining handwritten, printed, typed, and photocopied documents. Written for lawyers, law-enforcement professionals, and others who investigate the authenticity of documents but accessible to general readers.

Evans, C. *The Casebook of Forensic Detection: How Science Solved One Hundred of the World's Most Baffling Crimes*. New York: John Wiley & Sons, 1998. Fascinating account of some of the most interesting and sensational achievements of forensic science and medicine.

Genge, N. *The Forensic Casebook: The Science of Crime Scene Investigation*. New York: Ballantine Books, 2002. Exploration of forensics for lay readers.

Lee, Henry C., Timothy M. Palmbach, and Marilyn T. Miller. *Henry Lee's Crime Scene Handbook*. New York: Academic Press, 2001. Lee is the most widely recognized crime scene expert in the world. This book is a hands-on guide that covers in detail how to manage crime scenes; collect information; find, collect, and preserve physical evidence; conduct field tests; and reconstruct the sequences of events.

Owen, David. *Hidden Evidence*. Willowdale, Ontario, Canada: Firefly Books, 2000. Another popular treatment of the contributions of forensics to criminal investigations.

See also Autopsies; Bloodstains; Circumstantial evidence; Cold cases; Coroners; Crime labs; Crime scene investigation; DNA testing; Document analysis; Fingerprint identification; Forensic accounting; Forensic anthropology; Forensic entomology; Forensic odontology; Forensic palynology; Forensic psychology; Latent evidence; Medical examiners; Shoe prints and tire-tracks; Toxicology; Trace evidence.

Forestry camps

Definition: Minimum-security facilities in which low-risk adult and juvenile offenders work with local, state, and federal forestry departments to maintain public forests

Criminal justice issues: Prisons; punishment; rehabilitation

Significance: Forestry camps have become an attractive alternative to prison incarceration for both adult and juvenile low-risk offenders. Not only are they less costly to operate than prisons, they also provide valuable services to states and the nation as a whole and are often effective in providing rehabilitative training for inmates.

Forestry camps are therapeutic alternative correctional facilities and programs in which inmates work as members of fire squads, create fire breaks, thin forests, participate in reforestation projects, assist local communities with forestry beautification projects, and work in such support positions as food preparation and housekeeping.

Forestry camp programs began during the Depression years of the 1930's with the implementation of the medical model of rehabilitation in an effort to alleviate prison overcrowding. Usually located in state and federal forests, the camps provided cheap labor to forestry departments experiencing budget shortages due to the depressed economy. By the 1940's, the camps were becoming popular sites for placement of offenders convicted of evading the military draft. At that time, camp inmates were required to perform hard labor, while paying their states fees for the privilege of working in camps instead of being sent to prisons. The rehabilitative characteristics of most forestry camps included behavior-modification programs based on individual counseling and group therapy.

Inmates of forestry camps have always been mostly low-risk adult and juvenile offenders. In the beginning, adults convicted of lesser property crimes or nearing the ends of prison sentences after proving themselves trustworthy were the most likely candidates for forestry camps. By the 1950's, some states were beginning to experiment with forestry camps for juvenile offenders. However, it was not until 1974 that forestry camps were recognized nationally as alternative punishments for low-risk juveniles. This change was a direct result of the Juvenile Justice and Delinquency Prevention Act of that same year.

Forestry camps are now so diverse that it is difficult to describe them in general terms. For example, some camps have military-type boot camp facilities, while others reflect the more relaxed therapeutic medical model. In some facilities, inmates engage in hard labor, while in others they participate in activities such as gardening classes taught by members of gardening clubs.

Forestry camps were originally designed only for adult men. Camps for juveniles opened later, and now forestry camps exist for female offenders. One such program is located in the Federal Bureau of Prisons' facility for women at Bryan, Texas. Based on the boot camp model, that program began during the early 1990's. Women in the program are a mixture of volunteers from the general prison population and women who enter the program through plea agreements.

Some of the positive accomplishments of forestry camps include the protection of habitats for an endangered woodpecker species in the Sam Houston National Forest, clearing brush for the public park at the George Bush Presidential Library, and maintenance of public parks at Lake Summerville in Bryan, Texas.

Elizabeth H. McConnell

Further Reading

Rojek, J. E., and G. G. Jensen. *Exploring Delinquency: Causes and Control*. Los Angeles: Roxbury Publishing, 1996.

Selke, W. A. *Prisons in Crisis*. Bloomington: Indiana University Press, 1993.

See also Boot camps; Bureau of Prisons; Community-based corrections; Pleas; Prison escapes; Rehabilitation; Work camps.

Forgery

Definition: Illegal alteration of documents
Criminal justice issues: Business and financial crime; fraud
Significance: Forgery cheats individuals, corporations, and nations in a number of ways, including major losses of personal property.

Forgery is often defined as any deliberate tampering with a written legal paper for the purpose of deceit or fraud. It may start with a blank piece of paper and involve the production of entire forged documents. In most cases, however, forgery involves merely the signing of another person's name to a check or other legal document, such as a contract or a will. In some cases, it also entails altering the language or monetary values on such documents. Forgery is a close cousin of counterfeiting, the wholesale manufacture of imitation documents—most often currency.

Laws against forgery date back to the Rome of the first century B.C.E. More recent attempts to

codify such law arose in Elizabethan England during the late sixteenth century. By the middle of the eighteenth century, William Blackstone had declared that all forgery in England was a capital crime. In the United States, federal law codifies forgery; however, it may be handled by either state or federal courts, depending on its substance.

Forged items are not considered illegal until their possessors attempt to use them. When caught, perpetrators may invoke any of several lines of defense against the charges brought against them. The first is that authority was granted to them to sign documents for other persons. Another is that the alterations performed were genuine efforts to correct perceived errors in the documents. Yet another argument frequently invoked is that the accused did not forge the items in question. Forgers have even been known to insist that their forged documents are genuine and to attempt to impeach the experts brought in to verify their forgeries. This approach sometimes works, as even the most advanced modern techniques of scientific document examination are not infallible.

In the United States, forgery is punished by fines or by imprisonment, the extent of which depends on local and federal laws. However, intent to defraud must be proved before sentences can be passed.

Sanford S. Singer

Further Reading

Brayer, Ruth. *Detecting Forgery in Fraud Investigations: The Insider's Guide*. Alexandria, Va.: ASIS International, 2000.

Dines, Jess E. *Document Examiner Textbook*. Irvine, Calif.: Pantex International, 1998.

Ellen, David. *The Scientific Examination of Documents: Methods and Techniques*. 2d ed. Boca Raton, Fla.: CRC Press, 1997.

Slyter, Steven A. *Forensic Signature Examination*. Springfield, Ill.: C. C. Thomas, 1996.

See also Counterfeiting; Document analysis; Embezzlement; Forensic accounting; Fraud; Identity theft; Money laundering.

Fourth Amendment

The Law: Amendment to the U.S. Constitution that limits the power of government officials to search for or seize evidence from individuals

Date: Ratified in 1791

Criminal justice issues: Constitutional protections; police powers; search and seizure

Significance: The Fourth Amendment checks the power of the police to conduct searches. It requires police to obtain a warrant before searching for or seizing evidence and protects private property by requiring a neutral judge to approve the warrant's issuance.

The Fourth Amendment to the Constitution was passed by Congress and ratified by the states in 1791 as part of the package of amendments known as the Bill of Rights. The Fourth Amendment was written to prevent the type of abuses that had occurred in the British colonies. The British had used general warrants to conduct house-to-house searches for contraband and fugitives from justice. These warrants did not specify the place to be searched or limit the lengths to which officials could go in seizing private property. With the independence of the United States and the writing of a new constitution, the founders of the new nation sought to limit the ability of government officials to invade the private property of citizens.

Unreasonable Search and Seizure

The words of the Fourth Amendment are vague and flexible, allowing judges to interpret them to meet changes in police procedures and technology. The amendment prohibits unreasonable searches and seizures, rather than all searches and seizures by police. According to the amendment, people are to be safe in their persons, houses, papers, and effects, protecting the individual from personal search and the individual's property from improper searches or seizures by officials. While prohibiting unreasonable searches and seizures, the amendment does allow for reasonable types of searches. Under the amendment, police can search or seize property if they obtain a warrant that spells out what evidence they are seeking and what area they will be searching. The warrant must be approved by a neutral magistrate or judge who is a member of the judicial branch of government. The police cannot go outside the limits of the warrant to search other buildings or people not specifically mentioned in the warrant.

Exclusionary Rule

Although the Fourth Amendment prohibits unreasonable searches and seizures, it does not provide a means to enforce the amendment. The courts have created a tool known as the exclusionary rule to prevent the use in trial of illegally seized evidence. In the case of *Weeks v. United States* (1914), the U.S. Supreme Court ruled that because police had not obtained a warrant before seizing papers belonging to Weeks, the papers could not be introduced as evidence against Weeks in his trial and must be returned. The *Weeks* decision only applied to evidence seized by federal officials and used in federal courts. It was not until *Mapp v. Ohio* (1961) that the Court ruled that evidence seized by state officials without benefit of a warrant could also be excluded from state courts.

Exceptions to the Exclusionary Rule

The *Mapp* decision was controversial. By throwing out evidence that could have been used to prosecute a criminal defendant, the courts appeared to be allowing criminals to go free. The public outcry against the rule eventually led the justices to create exceptions allowing the use of some evidence in trials even if seized without a warrant.

The courts have identified a broad public safety exception to the exclusionary rule that allows searches of bags and persons before boarding an airplane or entering a government building such as a courthouse. Every person entering the building is searched without a warrant being issued or without probable cause to suspect that the person has committed or is prepared to commit a crime.

Another exception to the exclusionary rule involves vehicle searches. Courts have recognized that the mobility of cars would allow for the destruction of evidence before police could obtain a

Text of the Fourth Amendment

The right of the people to be secure in their persons, houses, papers, and effects, against unreasonable searches and seizures, shall not be violated, and no Warrants shall issue, but upon probable cause, supported by Oath or affirmation, and particularly describing the place to be searched, and the persons or things to be seized.

warrant. Beginning with the case of *Carroll v. United States* (1925), the Supreme Court has allowed searches of automobiles without warrants if the police had suspicion that the vehicle was being used for illegal purposes. In *Michigan v. Sitz* (1990), the Supreme Court also allowed police to stop vehicles at checkpoints to see if the driver is impaired by alcohol or drugs.

Police also do not need a warrant to enter a building if they are engaged in hot pursuit. In *Warden v. Hayden* (1967), the police were chasing a fleeing suspect who had just robbed a store. When the suspect fled into a house, the police followed, arrested him, and searched the building, finding evidence of the crime. The Supreme Court ruled that the evidence could be used in trial even though the police lacked a warrant because they were engaged in hot pursuit of a fleeing suspect.

New Technology and the Fourth Amendment

The Fourth Amendment has been interpreted to apply to new technologies that did not exist when the amendment was written. Wiretapping of phone lines was introduced as the telephone became a widely used technology. In *Olmstead v. United States* (1928), the Supreme Court ruled that wiretapping was not covered under the Fourth Amendment and police did not need a warrant before tapping a line because it was not a search. In *Katz v. United States* (1967), the Supreme Court overturned *Olmstead* and ruled that warrants were required before police could tap a phone and listen in on conversations because wiretapping was considered a search if the suspect had a reasonable expectation of privacy.

In *California v. Ciraolo* (1986), police used a plane to look into Ciraolo's backyard, which was surrounded by a 10-foot-high fence. The police found evidence of marijuana and used what they saw to obtain a warrant to search Ciraolo's house. The Court upheld the conviction because the marijuana plants were in plain sight, and police could seize evidence in plain sight without a warrant.

In *Kyllo v. United States* (2001), however, the Supreme Court ruled that police need to obtain a warrant before using a thermal imaging device to detect heat leaving a building. The device detected heat that was not in plain sight, and the use of the device was a search that required a warrant.

Douglas Clouatre

Further Reading

Franklin, Paula. *The Fourth Amendment*. New York: Silver Burdett Press, 2001. Describes the origins of the Fourth Amendment as a check on police abuses.

Greenhalgh, William W. *The Fourth Amendment Handbook: A Chronological Survey of Supreme Court Decisions*. 2d ed. Chicago: Criminal Justice Section, American Bar Association, 2003. Professional handbook for lawyers on the Fourth Amendment.

LaFave, W. R. *Search and Seizure: A Treatise on the Fourth Amendment*. 3d ed. St. Paul, Minn.: West Publishing, 1995. Standard work on the Fourth Amendment's search and seizure clause.

Wetterer, Charles M. *The Fourth Amendment: Search and Seizure*. Springfield, N.J.: Enslow, 1998. Discusses the various aspects of search and seizure law and how the courts have interpreted the amendment.

See also Automobile searches; *California v. Greenwood*; Consent searches; Electronic surveillance; Exclusionary rule; *Illinois v. McArthur*; *Illinois v. Wardlow*; *Knowles v. Iowa*; No-knock warrants; *Olmstead v. United States*; Privacy rights; Search and seizure; Search warrants; Supreme Court, U.S.; *Weeks v. United States*; *Whren v. United States*; *Wilson v. Arkansas*; Wiretaps.

Fraud

Definition: Intentional deceptions or misrepresentations undertaken to deprive others of money, property, or other valuable assets

Criminal justice issues: Business and financial crime; computer crime; fraud; white-collar crime

Significance: Although frauds are by their nature difficult to identify and quantify, it is clear that fraud constitutes one of the most pervasive and costly crime problems in the United States.

Throughout history, the term "fraud" has undergone a series of transformations. The earliest recorded definition of fraud was made during the early fourteenth century, when it was defined as deceit, trickery, or intentional perversion for the purpose of inducing others to part with something of value. During the eighteenth century, England's Parliament added the concept of false pretenses to the definition of fraud in cover an area of law previously untouched by larceny statutes. The modern American definition of fraud, as used in the Uniform Crime Reports and local law-enforcement agencies throughout the country, calls it deceitful conversion and the obtaining of money or property by false pretenses. Despite disparities in definitions of fraud, it generally is agreed that four elements must be present for fraud to occur: a material false statement, knowledge of the statement's falsity, reliance on the false statement by a victim, and damages suffered by the victim.

Prevalence

Collectively, fraud costs Americans hundreds of billions of dollars every year, and fraud, by its very nature, presents difficult challenges for law enforcement. One of the difficulties in countering fraud is that there are no discernible typologies among either its perpetrators or its victims. Perpetrators range from lower- and middle-class persons to corporate titans. In addition, fraud is rarely perpetrated by lone offenders; it generally relies on collusion between two or more parties.

Among victims, the only distinguishable characteristics of victims are age and levels of educa-tion. The young, the elderly, and persons with at least some college education are the most likely targets of fraud. The average victim spends in excess of 150 hours and nearly $800 repairing the damage caused by fraud. Most victims are unaware of how perpetrators of the frauds against them get their information about them. However, they generally know a few things about the perpetrators themselves, such as names, addresses, and phone numbers. Law enforcement uses such information to apprehend the perpetrators.

Consumer reporting agencies such as the Federal Trade Commission and Social Security Administration and federal law-enforcement report an estimated 125,000 to 175,000 victims annually. Approximately 15 percent of the victims of fraud have reported that the suspects are persons whom they personally know, such as relatives, friends, neighbors, and coworkers. Roughly the same percentage of victims believe they have been victims of fraud because of lost or stolen purses and wallets, mail theft, or telephone solicitations.

Fraud takes many forms but is generally divided into three basic categories: fraud against the government, corporate and financial fraud, and consumer fraud.

Fraud Against the Government

Among the most common forms of fraud perpetrated against the government are tax fraud, health care fraud, child-support fraud, bankruptcy fraud, social security fraud, and housing and welfare fraud. Of these types, the most important are tax and health care fraud. Simple tax evasion is the most costly type of fraud against the government. It is practiced in a variety of ways—through deliberate underreporting of income, keeping multiple sets of account books, maintaining false records, claiming personal expenditures as business expenses, and concealing assets and income. One of the challenges faced by agencies responsible for combating such frauds is separating honest errors from willful violations. During the first years of the twenty-first century, the Internal Revenue Service estimated that it was losing about $28 billion per year in uncollected taxes.

Since the early 1990's, health care fraud, which includes frauds against Medicare and Medicaid, has reached epidemic proportions. It usually takes the form of submission of deliberately claims to tax-funded health insurance programs. Several million health insurance benefit transactions every year are believed to be fraudulent.

Examples of health care fraud include billing for medical services never rendered, billing for services or procedures that are more expensive than those actually performed, double billing by misrepresenting uncovered treatments as covered ones, falsifying patient diagnoses, promoting of fraudulent and unproven devices for treatment, and misrepresentations of identity by switching identification cards.

Health care fraud has drawn many criminals away from other types of crime because it is viewed as both safer and more lucrative. After tax evasion, health care fraud is the second most costly white-collar crime in the United States, costing citizens an average of more than $50 billion per year. However, the impact of health care fraud extends far beyond its purely financial costs. Falsifying patient diagnoses and histories for financial gain also poses physical risks to patients as well as theft of benefits for those who have lifetime limits on their insurance. Despite the magnitude of health care fraud on a variety of levels, the government has been reluctant to prosecute this type of fraud, thereby perpetuating the problem.

Corporate and Financial Fraud

A host of subcategories can be identified under the guise of corporate crime. These include secu-

Evangelists Tammy Faye Bakker and Jim Bakker during a broadcast of their widely syndicated *PTL Club* (Praise the Lord) television program in 1986. Three years after this picture was taken, Jim Bakker was convicted of defrauding contributors of millions of dollars in one of the most celebrated scandals of the late twentieth century. For years, Bakker had used his television "ministry" to solicit donations, which at their peak exceeded one million dollars a week. Meanwhile, he paid himself and his wife large salaries and multimillion-dollar bonuses until his empire collapsed in the late 1980's. Among the frauds that Bakker perpetrated was selling more "exclusive" partnerships in a hotel than could be accommodated. To cover his frauds, Bakker kept two sets of books. *(AP/Wide World Photos)*

rities, mail, wire, bank, mortgage, loan, check, credit card, and private health care fraud. Securities and credit card fraud are the most common types of corporate and financial fraud.

Securities frauds include the deliberate falsifying of statements or omission of documents filed with the Securities and Exchange Commission (SEC), insider trading, buying and selling of securities that are not registered with the SEC, and engaging in interstate communications with potential buyers. Securities fraud has been statutorily regulated since the passage of the federal Securities Act of 1933. That law was enacted to prohibit deceit, misrepresentation, and fraud in the sale of securities, and to require that investors receive financial and other information regarding the sale of public securities. The National White Collar Crime Center has estimated that securities and commodities fraud totals $40 billion annually.

Credit card frauds include unauthorized use of credit cards, reproduction of credit card strips, and reproduction of credit cards to utilize the balances for the purpose of obtaining financial gain. In 2005, about 1.2 billion credit cards were in circulation in the United States, and nearly 190 million Americans were credit card holders. Card issuers lose about $1 billion annually to credit card fraud, and merchants lose significantly more.

Consumer Fraud

Consumer fraud's main components include telemarketing fraud, Internet fraud, and identity theft. The latter two are the most common types of consumer fraud. Consumer Sentinel is an investigative cyber tool, created by various public and private partners to collect and share information pertaining to fraud with all law-enforcement agencies. Its database is maintained by the Federal Trade Commission, which received 516,740 fraud complaints in 2003 alone. Identity theft constituted 214,905 of those complaints. These figures include only the incidents of fraud reported by consumers during that year. Unknown numbers of fraudulent incidents go unreported.

Internet fraud is becoming increasingly common as the World Wide Web emerges as a powerful medium for conducting business. This type of fraud encompasses all schemes using components of the Internet to conduct fraudulent transactions, such as work-at-home schemes, phony credit card offers, fraudulent investment opportunities, electronically mailed advertisements known as "spam," and the use of legitimate business names to persuade computer users to disclose passwords to obtain financial information.

The single largest category of Internet-related complaints—80 percent—is online auction fraud. This occurs when victims win auctions but either never receive the products for which they pay or find that the quality of the goods they receive has been misrepresented. There are many completely honest dealers on the Internet, but it is almost impossible for buyers to distinguish between them and the criminals who use the Internet for exploitation.

Although current research indicates that incidents of fraud are declining, an important new type of fraud, identity theft, is rapidly expanding. One-half of all fraud complaints reported to the Federal Trade Commission relate to identity theft. A 2003 survey found that over the previous five years, one in eleven people fell victim to identity theft. However, it is difficult to quantify this crime accurately because it is estimated that more than 60 percent of its victims fail to report their bad experiences.

Identity theft involves the taking of personal information to use for some type of financial gain. Such information can be taken from many different sources, ranging from the contents of mailboxes and garbage cans to utility bills and even eavesdropping on conversations. Occasionally, employees of banks, retails stores, and restaurants take account numbers from credit card strip readers. Some perpetrators get information by telephoning their victims and pretending to be representatives of legitimate businesses who are asking to verify information. With the personal information they collect, criminals can apply for credit cards or make withdrawals from bank accounts in their victims' names.

Investigation

Fraud investigations are both unusually time-consuming and labor-intensive. The nature of frauds and their ability to remain undetected for extended periods post special hurdles to investigators, and partly for this reason, law-enforcement agencies make fraud investigations a low priority and focus their resources on investigations of other types of crime. The reluctance of law enforcement to go after perpetrators of fraud has reinforced the perception among criminals that fraud is safer and more lucrative to practice than other crimes, such as drug trafficking.

According to the Federal Bureau of Investigation's Uniform Crime Report, the number of arrests for fraud in 2002 was 233,087—up from the previous year's 211,177 cases. Since these numbers are based upon the numbers of cases that law-enforcement agencies actually report to the FBI, the increase may be due, in part, simply to an increase in the number of agencies reporting fraud. For example, 9,511 agencies reported their arrest rates in 2001, and 10,372 agencies reported their arrest rates in 2002. The majority (54 percent) of fraud offenders in 2002 were men between the ages of 25 and 29. There were no demonstrable differences in race or ethnicity among offenders.

Prosecution

The main law-enforcement agency responsible for protecting U.S. financial institutions is the Federal Bureau of Investigation, which is charged with identifying and disassembling criminal organizations and individuals that target financial institutions. Between 2000 and 2004, FBI investigations led to more than eleven thousand convictions for fraud and more than $8 billion in restitution orders.

Multiagency task forces have been established in the hope that collaborative efforts will aid in capturing, prosecuting, and punishing fraud offenders. Operation Continued Action, created in 2004, marked the beginning of the largest nationwide law-enforcement initiative in history. The program was initiated by the FBI and involved the U.S. Attorney's Office, as well as many federal, state, and local law-enforcement agencies. Its main goal was to counter financial frauds, such as mortgage and loan fraud, identity theft, check kiting, insider trading, and internal theft.

Another effort to foster national cooperation among law-enforcement entities is the Internet Fraud Complaint Center (IFCC). This came about as part of the initiative by the U.S. Department of Justice in combating the problem of Internet fraud. This joint venture between the FBI, Internal Revenue Service, and Postal Inspection Service was designed to provide law enforcement with a single point of contact for identifying Internet fraud schemes. As strides in technological advancements continues, Internet fraud is expected to continue to soar.

Punishment

The Department of Justice prosecutes cases of identity theft under a wide array of federal statutes, including the Identity Theft and Assumption Deterrence Act of 1998. In most instances. identity theft convictions carry maximum sentences of fifteen years imprisonment, fines, and forfeiture of any personal property used to commit the offenses. It should be noted that identity theft is often coupled with violations of other forms of fraud, including computer, mail, wire, and financial fraud. Those offenses are felonies, and convictions can carry penalties as high as thirty-years prison sentences.

In 1996, the Health Insurance Portability and Accountability Act made health care fraud a federal criminal offense. In addition to substantial fines, convictions for this crime can carry sentences to federal prisons of up to ten years. Moreover, the sentences can be doubled when fraudulent acts result in harm to patients. When patients die as a direct result of health care fraud, offenders can be sentences to life in prison.

Lisa Landis Murphy

Further Reading

Abagnale, Frank. *The Art of the Steal: How to Protect Yourself and Your Business from Fraud, America's Number-One Crime*. New York: Broadway, 2002. Authoritative guide to fraud prevention by the former check forger and hoaxer whose career was dramatized in the 2002 film *Catch Me If You Can*, in which Leonardo DiCaprio played Abagnale.

Albrecht, W. Steve, and Chad Albrecht. *Fraud Examination and Prevention*. Mason, Ohio: South-Western Educational Publishing, 2003. Examination of methods of detecting, investigating, and preventing fraud.

Anastasi, John. *The New Forensics: Investigating*

Corporate Fraud and the Theft of Intellectual Property. Hoboken, N.J.: John Wiley & Sons, 2003. Using actual case studies, Anastasi describes the use of computer forensics to detect and prosecute a multitude of different types of fraud.

Friedrichs, David O. *Trusted Criminals: White Collar Crime in Contemporary Society*. 2d ed. Belmont, Calif.: Wadsworth, 2004. Comprehensive overview of ways to control white-collar crime, including fraud.

Identity Theft: How to Protect Your Name, Your Credit Card, Your Virtual Information, and What to Do When Someone Hijacks Any of These. Ada, Ohio: Silver Lake Publishing, 2004. Combines law-enforcement and security personnel interviews with case studies to provide practical advice on avoiding identity theft.

Pickett, K. H. Spencer, and Jennifer Pickett. *Financial Crime Investigation and Control*. Hoboken, N.J.: John Wiley & Sons, 2002. Useful handbook for law-enforcement personnel involved in financial crime investigations.

Swierczynski, Duane. *Complete Idiot's Guide to Frauds, Scams, and Cons*. Indianapolis, Ind.: Alpha Books, 2003. Simplified and entertaining guide to the elements of confidence games, consumer scams, and popular frauds.

Wells, Joseph. *Corporate Fraud Handbook: Prevention and Detection*. Hoboken, N.J.: John Wiley & Sons, 2004. Examines an array of fraud schemes and provides insights on prevention and detection.

_____. *Principles of Fraud Examination*. Hoboken, N.J.: John Wiley & Sons, 2004. Employs the use of actual case studies to examine fraud schemes by employees, owners, managers, and executives, and how to develop preventive measures.

See also Bigamy and polygamy; Cable and satellite television signal theft; Computer crime; Consumer fraud; Embezzlement; Forgery; Identity theft; Insurance fraud; Mail fraud; Tax evasion; Teapot Dome scandal; Telephone fraud; Theft; Voting fraud; White-collar crime.

Freedom of assembly and association

Definition: Right of the people to be active in self-government and to associate with those who hold similar values

Criminal justice issues: Civil rights and liberties; constitutional protections

Significance: Freedoms such as that of assembly and association are ends in themselves. Additionally, people who are not allowed a voice in their government and an opportunity for the redress of grievances will necessitate the use of force to maintain civil order.

Freedom of assembly is a right guaranteed in the First Amendment to the Constitution of the United States. The entire First Amendment could rightly be said to guarantee the freedom of association, although that right is one inherent in the right of a free people to own property, conduct business, and engage in the political process. The First Amendment says in its entirety, "Congress shall make no law respecting an establishment of religion, or prohibiting the free exercise thereof; or abridging the freedom of speech, or of the press; or the right of the people peaceably to assemble, and to petition the Government for a redress of grievances."

The denial of this freedom of petition for redress was given in the Declaration of Independence as being present in all the grievances which had been denied by the English Crown. Under U.S. law, this right is inviolable. It is only the absence of a peaceable nature, as exhibited in actual criminal behavior or in incitement to criminal behavior, that can justify dispersing an assembly.

In *United States v. Cruikshank et al.*, heard in 1875, U.S. Supreme Court chief justice Morrison R. Waite wrote:

> The right of the people peaceably to assemble for lawful purposes existed long before the adoption of the Constitution of the United States. In fact, it is, and always has been, one of the attributes of citizenship under a free government. It "derives

its source," to use the language of Chief Justice John Marshall, in *Gibbons v. Ogden*, "from those laws whose authority is acknowledged by civilized men throughout the world." It is found wherever civilization exists. It was not, therefore, a right granted to the people by the Constitution. The government of the United States when established found it in existence, with the obligation on the part of the States to afford it protection.

This right is, therefore, a part of the original law of nature and of nature's god acknowledged in the Declaration of Independence and throughout the other founding documents.

Some confusion has arisen throughout American history as to the extent of freedom of assembly. One of the problems that came about was that some of the states saw this amendment as ensuring only protection from abridgement by the federal government of this right. The assertion made was that states and local governments could abridge these rights. However, the Supreme Court eventually found that the Fourteenth Amendment, ratified in 1868, settled the issue, requiring that "No State shall make or enforce any law which shall abridge the privileges or immunities of Citizenship of the United States; nor shall any state deprive any person of life, liberty, or property, without due process of law; nor deny to any person within its jurisdiction the equal protection of the laws."

Mark W. Rizzo

Further Reading

Blackstone, William. *Of the Nature of Laws in General*. Vol. 1 in *Commentaries on the Laws of England*. Chicago: University of Chicago Press, 1979.

_____. *Of Offences Against the Public Peace*. Vol. 4 in *Commentaries on the Laws of England*. Chicago: University of Chicago Press, 1979.

See also Bill of Rights, U.S.; Conspiracy; Constitution, U.S.; Due process of law; Equal protection under the law; September 11, 2001, attacks; Supreme Court, U.S.

Furman v. Georgia

The Case: U.S. Supreme Court ruling on capital punishment
Date: Decided on June 29, 1972
Criminal justice issues: Capital punishment; civil rights and liberties; constitutional protections
Significance: Ruling that existing laws for imposing capital punishment were unconstitutional because of their random and unpredictable application, the Court appeared to imply that any capital punishment laws might be found unconstitutional.

William Furman, Lucious Jackson, and Elmer Branch were convicted and sentenced to death in the states of Georgia and Texas. After the three defendants were unsuccessful in their appeals to the supreme courts of the two states, their attorneys appealed to the U.S. Supreme Court, which granted review and consolidated the cases into one decision.

The majority of the Court voted 5 to 4 to strike down Georgia's and Texas's laws for imposing the death penalty, and the effect was to nullify all death-penalty statutes in the United States. With the justices sharply divided, the majority announced the ruling in a short, unsigned *per curiam* opinion, followed by 231 pages of individual opinions by the nine justices. The majority agreed that existing laws allowed judges and juries so much discretion on whether to impose the death sentence that the result was arbitrary, irrational, and contrary to due process of law. Two members of the majority argued in concurring opinions that capital punishment was always unconstitutional, one concurring opinion emphasized the equal protection clause of the Fourteenth Amendment, and two other concurring opinions addressed only the arbitrary, unpredictable application of the penalty.

Justice William Brennan's concurrence presented a vigorous argument for the idea that capital punishment always was "cruel and unusual punishment." Like others of the majority, he quoted statements (called *dicta*) in *Trop v. Dulles* (1958) that the Eighth Amendment draws its meaning "from the evolving standards of decency that mark the progress of a maturing society" and that the amendment prohibited "inhuman treatment." From this perspective Brennan severely criticized capital punishment for four reasons: that it violated human dignity, that it was applied arbitrarily, that its declining use showed that it was increasingly unacceptable to contemporary society, and that it was excessive since it was not more effective than a less severe punishment.

In contrast, Justice William Rehnquist and the other dissenters emphasized that capital punishment was envisioned by the Framers of the Constitution. They argued that it was undemocratic for judicial authority to strike down legislative enactments without being able to point to explicit statements in the Constitution.

Since *Furman* ruled that all existing laws providing for capital punishment were unconstitutional, the decision escalated controversy about capital punishment. Although the decision left the constitutionality of capital punishment unclear, thirty-five states soon enacted new legislation that took the concerns of *Furman* into account. Portions of these laws would later be declared unconstitutional, but in *Gregg v. Geor-*

gia (1976) the majority of the Court would decide that capital punishment is constitutional so long as there are proper procedures and regulations.

Thomas Tandy Lewis

Further Reading

Bohm, Robert M. *Deathquest: An Introduction to the Theory and Practice of Capital Punishment in the United States*. Cincinnati: Anderson Publishing, 2003.

Carter, Linda E., and Ellen Krietzberg. *Understanding Capital Punishment Law*. Newark, N.J.: LexisNexis, 2004.

Latzer, Barry, ed. *Death Penalty Cases: Leading Supreme Court Cases on Capital Punishment*. 2d ed. Burlington, Mass.: Butterworth Heinemann, 2002.

Sarat, Austin. *When the State Kills: Capital Punishment and the American Condition*. Princeton, N.J.: Princeton University Press, 2001.

See also Bill of Rights, U.S.; Capital punishment; *Coker v. Georgia*; Cruel and unusual punishment; Death-row attorneys; *Gregg v. Georgia*; *Tison v. Arizona*; *Witherspoon v. Illinois*; Supreme Court, U.S.

G

Gag orders

Definition: Declarations by trial judges forbidding everyone involved in trial proceedings from discussing the cases with the media

Criminal justice issues: Judges; legal terms and principles; media; trial procedures

Significance: Gag orders help courts to conduct their business without having information relating to cases be improperly released to the public. Judges implement the orders to protect the actors in the cases from being overwhelmed by the media and to protect the cases themselves from being tainted by false or exaggerated information that finds its way into the news.

Courts and judges impose gag orders during trials to limit the information presented to the public about court proceedings. Such orders are most commonly used in high-profile cases to limit information access by the media to actual court proceedings, case evidence, and testimony. Gag orders also restrict the access of jury members to information about their trials when they are not sequestered.

Gag orders are imposed not only on attorneys and their staffs but also on witnesses and potential witnesses, law-enforcement officers, and any other persons who participate in court proceedings. Orders are imposed to make sure there are no leaks of unauthorized material to the press or public. If only attorneys were under the orders, they might speak with staff members who, in turn, could release information if they were not also covered by the orders. Any person who violates a gag order can be held in contempt of court and punished as a result.

An example of a high-profile case in which a gag order was imposed was the California trial of Scott Peterson for the murder of his wife and her unborn child that concluded with Peterson's conviction in December, 2004. That trial was subjected to saturation media coverage, and the presiding judge in the case imposed a gag order throughout the full duration of Peterson's trial. The order was imposed during the preliminary stages of the trial to protect ongoing investigations and to protect witnesses and others presenting testimony.

Jenephyr James

Further Reading

Chermak, Steven M. *Victims in the News: Crime and the American News Media*. Boulder, Colo.: Westview Press, 1995.

Chiasson, Lloyd, ed. *The Press on Trial: Crimes and Trials as Media Events*. Westport, Conn.: Greenwood Press, 1997.

Surette, Ray. *Media, Crime, and Criminal Jus-*

Gagging Jay Leno

In March, 2005, early in singer Michael Jackson's child-molestation trial in California's Santa Barbara County, trial judge Rodney Melville placed a gag order on talk-show host Jay Leno, who had been making many jokes about Jackson on *The Tonight Show*. At the request of Leno's attorneys, the judge clarified his order. He explained that the order was not intended to stop Leno from making jokes about Jackson's case on his show, but merely to prevent him from saying anything relating to his own personal involvement in the case. Leno had been subpoenaed as a witness by the defense, which was expected to question him on a communication he had received from the family of Jackson's accuser. In fact, the judge even said of Leno, "I'd like him to tell good jokes, rather than bad."

Before the judge clarified his gag order, Leno carefully avoided saying anything about Jackson on his show. At the same time, however, he used his celebrity guests to deliver the jokes that he himself refrained from using. After the judge clarified his order, Jackson's attorneys complained that it was insufficient to protect their client from what they regarded as the excessive cruelty of Leno's jokes.

tice. 2d ed. Pacific Grove, Calif.: Brooks/Cole Publishing, 1998.

See also Contempt of court; Judges; Print media; Television courtroom programs; Television news; Trial publicity.

Gambling

Definition: Playing of games and placing of bets to win money or other prizes

Criminal justice issues: Morality and public order; organized crime; victimless crime

Significance: American attitudes toward gambling have shifted back and forth throughout history; however, since the mid-twentieth century, all forms of gambling, including state-run lotteries, have spread throughout the United States. By late 2004, Hawaii and Utah were the only remaining states that prohibited all forms of gambling.

Gambling appears to have existed as long as civilization itself. Archaeologists have uncovered objects used in gambling games that date back as 2,300 B.C.E. in China. Additionally, anthropologists and archaeologists have found evidence of gambling in almost all ancient cultures. However, although gambling has always been a part of human civilization, it has not always been an accepted practice. During the fourteenth century, for example, England's King Henry VIII criminalized gambling when he found that the men in his armies were spending more time playing games of chance than they were in their studies and training. The history of gambling in the United States has followed a similar course. Although gambling clearly is an integral part of American culture, public acceptance of gambling and gamblers has historically been at the whim of ever-changing social and political winds and influences.

Gambling in Early North America

The first American settlers had divergent views on the appropriateness of gambling in the New World. As would come to be a common conflict regarding many social issues, English set-

tlers to North America brought with them English traditions and beliefs and viewed gambling primarily as harmless entertainment. The Puritans, on the other hand, viewed gambling in a much less benign manner and enacted prohibitory laws to reflect their beliefs. Thus, while gambling was primarily considered a proper gentleman's diversion in most English colonies, it was strictly forbidden in the Puritan settlements.

Despite the toleration of gambling among early English colonists, many colonists came to blame gambling for the ills of colonial life. In addition, monetary interests in Great Britain began to blame gambling for the perceived laziness and idleness of colonial settlers. During the early eighteenth century, Britain was still financially supporting its colonies, and its leaders were growing impatient waiting for the colonies to become self-sustaining. Although the monetary interests viewed gambling as a problem in the English settlements, they did not disregard the potential to raise revenue through gambling. By the time of the American Revolution in the 1770's, all thirteen British colonies had instituted government-run lotteries to raise revenue. Lottery revenue contributed to the establishment of some of the most prestigious institutions of higher learning—Columbia, Yale, Harvard, Princeton, and Dartmouth. During the Revolution itself, the Continental Congress voted to hold a $10 million lottery to fund the war; however, the lottery was never held.

After the Revolution, extravagant casinos arose throughout the new country. As the United States expanded west, so did gambling. Gambling houses and establishments were started in the river towns of the South, and gambling moved west as the nation expanded to the Pacific Ocean. However, due to lottery scandals and public disdain for the professional gamblers who preyed on the weak, public attitudes toward gambling gradually shifted. This shift led to changes in many state gambling laws. By 1840, most U.S. states had banned the lotteries, gaming houses, and riverboats that had come to represent gambling in the young nation.

The Next Wave

In many ways, the frontier spirit of American settlers paralleled the spirit of gaming enthusiasts. Similar to California gold prospectors, gamblers sought adventure and quick wealth. It was thus no surprise that gambling followed the mass movement to the West. During the California gold rush of 1849, San Francisco became the new capital of gambling in the country. Throughout California, gambling thrived among those seeking adventure and fortune in a still untamed territory. Meanwhile, public feeling against gambling—and particularly professional gamblers—spread in the West. Leaders of the new settlements desired national respectability, which the wild nature of the frontier gambling culture did not provide. As in the East, gambling was increasingly blamed for social ills, such as drug abuse, drunkenness, and sexual promiscuity. By the 1860's, professional gamblers were being lynched in San Francisco. By 1910, gambling was largely outlawed throughout the United States.

Antigambling laws sent an official message of morality and abstinence to the citizenry but did little to curb actual gambling. From private games of poker and craps to illegal lotteries and "numbers game" rackets and illegal casinos and gambling houses, gambling continued to flourish within the United States. Whether through paying protection money to law-enforcement officers or simply keeping illegal gambling activities sufficiently quiet, gambling remained integral to American culture.

The Twentieth Century and Beyond

The Great Depression of the 1930's ravaged both the U.S. economy and the morale of American citizens. As public officials became desperate to stimulate the economy, attitudes toward legalized gambling again shifted. During the 1930's, legal horse racing returned to twenty-one states.

Gambling machines in an Indian-operated casino in Palm Springs, California. By 2004, the rapid expansion of Indian casinos among California's many tribes poised California to overtake neighbor Nevada in total gambling revenue. *(AP/Wide World Photos)*

By the 1950's, bingo was legal in eleven states, and the public sentiment again approved some certain levels of legalized gambling.

As public officials changed their views on certain types of legalized gambling, law-enforcement agencies in the eastern United States began cracking down hard on illegal private casinos, sports betting, and numbers games controlled by organized crime groups. Crime families then began seeking more hospitable locations for their gambling operations. They initially turned to California, where they opened floating casinos in the Pacific Ocean, just beyond the three-mile limit of government jurisdiction. While organized crime groups were making money off the coast of California, a neighboring state, Nevada, was struggling with its recent decision to legalize gambling.

In 1931, partially as a result of flourishing illegal gambling and the view that anti-gambling laws were unenforceable, Nevada legalized most forms of gambling. However, cutbacks in consumer spending caused by the Great Depression caused Nevada's new gaming industry to struggle. It was only after California began suppressing gambling within its borders that Nevada's modern legal gambling empire began to grow. Intensified enforcement of gambling laws in California pushed organized crime groups to Nevada, where they financed most of the early casinos. Though these people remained criminals, they also had well-developed business skills and access to large sums of money—both of which were scarce in Depression-weary Nevada.

By the 1950's, gambling was flourishing in Nevada, particularly in Las Vegas. However, it was dominated by organized crime families. This fact was well known to anyone with even a passing knowledge of the industry. As its illegitimacy was again becoming a blight on respectable society, the authorities began once more to crackdown on the criminal underbelly of the gambling world. During the 1950's, the U.S. Senate found rampant levels of criminality within the hierarchy of the Las Vegas casinos. Such activities included money laundering, prostitution, and sheltering profits from taxes and led to a federal crackdown on gaming interests. As a result of

Gross Legal Gambling Revenue in the United States in 2003

Industry	Gross revenue (billions of dollars)
Card rooms	0.85
Commercial casinos*	28.69
Charitable games and bingo	2.67
Indian casinos	16.82
Legal bookmaking	0.13
Lotteries	19.93
Pari-mutuel wagering	3.79
Total	$72.88

*Figure for commercial casino gambling includes deepwater cruise ships, cruises-to-nowhere, and noncasino devices.
Source: Christiansen Capital Advisors LLC. Figures are for most recent year available. Gross gambling revenue (GGR) is the amount wagered minus winnings returned to players; it is the figure used to determine what a casino, racetrack, lottery, or other gaming operation earns before taxes, salaries, and other expenses are paid out.

federal and state pressures, organized crime families were forced to sell off their Nevada casino interests. Nevada's casinos are now highly regulated and closely scrutinized by both federal and state authorities. Nevertheless, organized crime remained involved in many of the casino world's satellite activities, such as prostitution.

Lotteries

At the end of the nineteenth century, no state-sponsored lotteries existed in the United States. This fact, however, did not stop most Americans from participating in such games of chance. With millions of Americans playing various forms of illegal lotteries on a weekly basis, several problems arose. First, law-enforcement officers did not want, and did not have the ability to enforce, laws against lotteries. With so many Americans playing the numbers, few officers wanted to be involved in restricting such a popular entertainment source.

Whether buying tickets in legal lotteries in other nations—such as the Irish Sweepstakes—or playing illegal numbers games, many otherwise law-abiding Americans were knowingly breaking the law regularly. This led to another

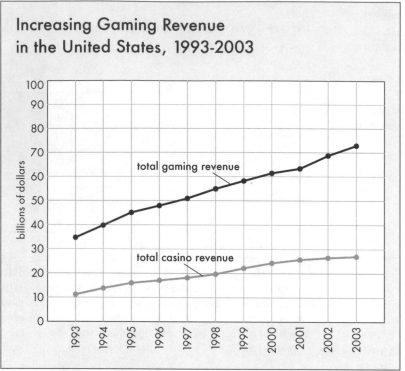

Increasing Gaming Revenue in the United States, 1993-2003

Sources: American Gaming Association, Christiansen Capital Advisors LLC. All dollar amounts are billions. Casino totals for 2000-2003 do not include deepwater cruise ships, cruises-to-nowhere, or noncasino devices.

run lotteries. In 1974, Massachusetts became the first state to offer "scratcher" lottery tickets. In 1978, New Jersey went a step further by legalizing casino gambling in its then-dilapidated resort town of Atlantic City.

These developments were merely the beginning of major changes, and gambling has developed into a growth industry in the United States. By the year [District of Columbia were operating state-sponsored lotteries, and that number continued to grow.

Additionally, casino gambling has also rapidly expanded. In 1993, only ten states allowed any form of legal casino gambling. By the late 1990's, that number had grown to twenty-seven states. In addition, Indian reservations have been permitted to make their own laws regarding gambling on their lands because of their sovereign status. By 2002, 330 of the 558 recognized reservations in the United States were operating casinos in twenty-eight different states. Indian casinos have expanded so rapidly in California that by 2004 the state was poised to pass Nevada in total gambling revenues. In 2003 alone, the gambling industry in the United States took in revenues of over $72 billion, including a significant amount of money that is now generated via Internet gambling.

Theodore Shields

problem: If playing in illegal lotteries was a crime, then the country was teeming with criminals. Moreover, there was the danger that the disrespect showed for lottery prohibition could develop into general disrespect for the law. Such problems led to the general acceptance of numbers games by local authorities and law-enforcement officers. When law-enforcement officers cracked down on numbers games, they did so mostly to send warnings to criminals about their other illegal activities. The first half of the twentieth century saw a thriving numbers industry in the United States. However, government needs for new sources of revenue soon changed that situation.

By the 1960's, the public's growing opposition to rising taxes and state needs for new sources of funding combined with the unenforceability of laws against numbers games led to reconsideration of state-sponsored lotteries. By 1971, New Hampshire, New York, and New Jersey had state-

Further Reading

Cook, Philip J., and Charles T. Clotfelter. *Selling Hope: State Lotteries in America.* Cambridge, Mass.: Harvard University Press, 1991. Comprehensive study of the history and current state of government-run lotteries. Contains extensive statistical data.

Fromson, Brett Duval. *Hitting the Jackpot: The Inside Story of the Richest Indian Tribe in History.* New York: Grove Press, 2004. Fascinating account of how Connecticut's nearly extinct Mashantucket Pequot Indians parlayed their legal status as an Indian tribe into a major land-owning community with a casino that generates more than one billion dollars a year in revenue.

Gordon, John S. "Born in Iniquity." *American Heritage* 45, 1 (February-March, 1994): 14-16. Survey of the history of gambling in the United States.

International Gaming Institute. *The Gaming Industry: Introduction and Perspectives.* New York: John Wiley & Sons, 1996. Industry-sponsored book on all aspects of gambling, from its history to inside looks at how casinos are operated and explanations of the technology of the games.

Mason, W. Dale. *Indian Gaming: Tribal Sovereignty and American Politics.* Norman: University of Oklahoma Press, 2000. Scholarly study of the rise of Indian casinos.

O'Brien, Timothy L. *Bad Bet: The Inside Story of the Glamour, Glitz, and Danger of America's Gambling Industry.* New York: Random House/Times Business, 1998. The nature of compulsive gambling and its regulation. Includes bibliography and index.

Pavalko, Ronald M. *Risky Business: America's Fascination with Gambling.* New York: Wadsworth, 1999. Sober, unbiased, and comprehensive study of the social, economic, and legal impacts of gambling in the past and present.

Walker, Michael B. *The Psychology of Gambling.* New York: Pergamon Press, 1997. Broad examination of the behavior of gamblers, with some attention to the treatment of problem gambling, which the author, a psychologist, sees as a function of irrational thinking that can be corrected.

See also Commercialized vice; Cybercrime; Gangsters of the Prohibition era; Lynching; Mafia; Organized crime; Police corruption; Public-order offenses; Sports and crime; Sting operations; Victimless crime.

Gangsters of the Prohibition era

Identification: Criminals who profited by meeting the popular demand for illegal alcoholic beverages
Date: 1920's through the early 1930's
Criminal justice issues: Organized crime; substance abuse; violent crime
Significance: Criminal organizations replaced the unruly street gangs of the past

During the early decades of the twentieth century, Congress passed much reform legislation. The 1910 Mann Act was designed to stop the movement of prostitutes across state lines. The 1914 Harrison Narcotic Act outlawed such drugs as opium, heroin, and morphine. These acts were followed by the Eighteenth Amendment and the Volstead Act, which created Prohibition. Prohibition laws unintentionally led to unprecedented profits for criminals. The illegal, wide-scale distribution of alcohol demanded abilities beyond those of most urban gangsters. Just as the legislation was, in part, a reaction to new technology—first telegraphs and trains, later telephones and automobiles—that freed crime from narrow urban limits, so gangsters needed new skills to take advantage of this technology.

Urban Gangs

Criminal gangs developed as cities grew. Most gangs were ethnic, uniting young people from slums such as New York's Five Points or Chicago's Bloody Maxwell. Gangs terrorized their neighborhoods, killed opponents, and battled each other for territory. Relying more on muscle than intelligence, they nonetheless established complex and corrupt relationships with politicians, police officers, and, later, businessmen and some labor unions. Politicians hired gang thugs to intimidate voters, steal ballot boxes, and otherwise influence elections. In turn, to avoid arrest, gangs paid protection money to politicians and police. By the end of the nineteenth century, labor unions and business leaders alike hired gang members to interfere in labor disputes. Under increasingly complex conditions, a new kind of leadership developed. Monk Eastman and Paul Kelly in New York and Jim Colosimo in Chicago were transitional figures between the unruly gang activities of earlier days and the organized crime of the Prohibition era.

The New Criminals

The four Prohibition-era leaders with the most lasting influence on American culture were Arnold Rothstein, Johnny Torrio, Meyer Lansky, and Al Capone. They had in common an unusual degree of organizational and administrative ability. Commentators then and later repeatedly remarked that these men could have succeeded in any business. Rothstein was an excellent mathematician; Capone briefly worked as a bookkeeper. To market illegal alcohol, these abilities were necessary. These men directly or indirectly coordinated the work of thousands of employees, including operators of illegal breweries and distilleries, attorneys, accountants, truck drivers, warehouse workers, and seamen. Some maintained their own fleets of ships and trucks. They maintained relationships with the politicians, police, judges, police officers, and Prohibition agents who were on their payrolls. They established affiliations with gangs in other cities, such as the Purple Gang in Detroit and Egan's Rats in St. Louis. They crossed ethnic, racial, and geographical lines.

Rothstein was the dominant New York figure at the beginning of Prohibition. Operating from

Film actor Edward G. Robinson gained fame during the Prohibition era by playing a number of gangster roles, including "Little Rico" Cesare Enrico Bandello in 1931's *Little Caesar*. At a time when real-life gangster violence dominated national headlines, film producers adhered to a code that would not allow characters firing guns and their victims to appear on the screen at the same moments. *Little Caesar* got around that limitation in this scene by showing Robinson shoot a man and the clear silhouette of his victim's shadow at the same moment. *(Museum of Modern Art, Film Stills Archive)*

Lindy's Restaurant in New York's Times Square, he was a gambler, a fixer, and a banker as well as part owner of Harlem's famous Cotton Club. He mediated territorial battles among other gangsters. With Prohibition, he established a system for the importing of high-quality alcohol. Realizing that narcotics were easier to smuggle than liquor, he used his delivery system to found the modern international narcotics trade. Among those he mentored was Meyer Lansky. After Rothstein's 1928 murder, Frank Costello of the Unione Siciliana became the most powerful figure in New York.

In Chicago, Torrio, a graduate of New York's Five Points gang, assisted Colosimo until the latter's murder in 1920, probably authorized by Torrio. Colosimo had been unwilling to enter the illegal liquor business. With Colosimo's murder, Torrio expanded the empire that Capone was to inherit, establishing power in Indiana and Illinois cities near Chicago. Torrio invented roadhouses, rural drinking spots accessible only to those with automobiles. In 1925, Capone took over when Torrio, after an attempt on his life, retired to Italy. Capone's reign was brief and bloody, but his flair for public relations, his flamboyant style, and his ability to manipulate the media caused him to capture the popular imagination.

Lansky, who began in bootlegging, chartered his own ships to import liquor and bragged about his highly successful shipping industry. He later used his wealth to fund gambling operations from Saratoga Springs, New York, to Las Vegas and Havana. Like Rothstein, he tried to teach his men, sometimes successfully, to talk, look, and behave like members of legitimate corporate culture. He did not allow flashy clothes or public brawls. At the same time, understanding the legitimate corporate culture, he offered high payment and rewarded good work with bonuses.

Surrounding and sometimes opposing these men were a galaxy of criminal figures whose volatile, violent natures and shifting allegiances often generated more headlines than did any leaders except Capone. They included Charles "Lucky" Luciano, Ben "Bugsy" Siegel, "Dutch" Schultz (born Arthur Flegenheimer), Louis "Lepke" Buchalter, Albert Anastasia, Irving "Waxey" Gordon, Owen "Owney" Madden, Frankie Uale (or Yale or Ioele), and John Thomas "Legs" Diamond, among many others. In Chicago, Dean ("Dion") O'Banion was a major figure whose 1924 murder triggered the gang wars of the 1920's. These men dominated headlines, but similar gang behavior occurred in cities across the United States. As profits increased, so did violence.

Gangsters and the Law

Law-enforcement authorities using traditional methods were overwhelmed. Corruption of police, politicians, and Prohibition officers was widespread; gangsters bragged that they controlled police departments. Many people, including officials and jury panel members, opposed the law, especially in urban centers. As speakeasies sprang up for the sale of illegal alcohol, the gangster became a public figure. In New York by 1927, an estimated thirty thousand speakeasies were in business. There, gangsters mingled with the elite of show business, government, and the arts. Beginning in 1923, some states simply refused to allocate resources to fight alcohol violations; the rebellion began in New York and included New Jersey, Montana, Nevada, and Wisconsin. This placed the burden of enforcement on understaffed, undertrained, underpaid, and often corrupt federal agents, while bootleggers delivered liquor to congressmen and President Warren G. Harding served liquor in the private quarters of the White House.

Even with limited enforcement, violations overwhelmed the criminal justice system. As early as 1920, Americans consumed an estimated 25 million gallons of illegal liquor. That year, about thirty illegal breweries were operating in Chicago alone. Chicago gangsters were supplying beer to more than twenty thousand outlets. In 1928, Mabel Willebrandt, deputy attorney general in charge of Prohibition and once a strong speaker in favor of Prohibition, resigned her post. In 1929, she published a book, *The Inside of Prohibition*. Claiming that it was impossible to prevent importation of vast amounts of liquor, she reported that, in 1924 alone, federal courts were swamped, with more than twenty-two thousand liquor cases pending at the end of that fiscal year.

In an attempt to control alcohol-related crime, the federal government used new technology. Wiretapping became legal. In Seattle, where Prohibition had been law since 1916, Roy Olmstead, a young police lieutenant and millionaire bootlegger, was caught in 1920. His trial judge allowed what had formerly been illegal wiretapping evidence. The Supreme Court, in *Olmstead v. United States* (1928), upheld the legality of this evidence.

Federal income tax laws offered another new way to trap criminals. After the Supreme Court decision in *United States v. Sullivan* (1927), gangsters had to file income tax reports, even on illegal income. The court refused to permit gangsters to plead the Fifth Amendment against self-incrimination in order to protect themselves against evasion charges. The Internal Revenue Service had authority to investigate these men for income tax evasion. By tracking expenditures, Internal Revenue Service agents proved that vast sums of money had passed through the hands of Capone and others.

Aftermath

Vast sums remained. In the Great Depression that followed the 1929 stock market crash, banks failed across the United States; gangsters, however, could provide the sums that legitimate businesses and organizations needed. The new, organized gangs were not destroyed by loss of a leader; as in industry, a new executive officer could promptly step into the vacated place. Thus, Prohibition-era gang activities had far-reaching consequences.

Betty Richardson

Further Reading

Asbury, Herbert. *The Gangs of New York: An Informal History of the Underworld*. New York: Thunder's Mouth Press, 2001. Basic source about gangs since its original 1927 publication.

Behr, Edward. *Prohibition: Thirteen Years That Changed America*. New York: Arcade, 1996. Extensive treatment of gangster-related corruption in government.

Downey, Patrick. *Gangster City: The History of the New York Underworld 1900-1935*. Fort Lee, N.J.: Barricade Books, 2004. Study of lesser-known crime figures.

Keefe, Rose. *Guns and Roses: The Untold Story of Dean O'Banion, Chicago's Big Shot Before Al Capone*. Nashville, Tenn.: Cumberland House, 2003. Study of a central figure in early Chicago Prohibition-era crime.

Lacey, Robert. *Little Big Man: Meyer Lansky and the Gangster Life*. New York: Little, Brown, 1991. Lengthy study of bootlegging and gambling figure.

Pietrusza, David. *Rothstein: The Life, Times, and Murder of the Criminal Genius Who Fixed the 1919 World Series*. New York: Carroll & Graf, 2003. Biography of man who manipulated and funded much Prohibition-era gang activity.

Reppetto, Thomas. *American Mafia: A History of Its Rise to Power*. New York: Henry Holt, 2004. Study of twentieth century gangs.

See also Alcohol use and abuse; Capone, Al; Commercialized vice; Criminals; Drugs and law enforcement; Federal Bureau of Investigation; Gambling; Internal Revenue Service; *Olmstead v. United States*; Organized crime; Political corruption; Prohibition; Saint Valentine's Day Massacre; Wiretaps.

Gault, In re

The Case: U.S. Supreme Court ruling on court procedures in juvenile cases
Date: Decided on May 15, 1967
Criminal justice issues: Evidence and forensics; juvenile justice; trial procedures
Significance: This Supreme Court decision established the principle that juvenile court procedures must include the most basic procedural rights and evidentiary rules.

The *In re Gault* case arose from the 1964 arrest of Gerald Gault in Gila County, Arizona, for making a lewd telephone call to a neighbor. Gault, who was then fifteen years old, was on probation for an earlier minor offense. Although the state produced no evidence at Gault's hearing, the juvenile judge found him to be delinquent. The basis of the finding was evidently police rumors about him and statements elicited from him in the absence of his parents or his lawyer. He was committed to a state industrial school until his eighteenth birthday. Had an adult committed the same crime, the maximum penalty that could have been assessed under Arizona law would have been a fifty-dollar fine and two months' imprisonment. Gault's appeal to the Arizona Supreme Court was unsuccessful, and he brought the case to the U.S. Supreme Court.

Gault argued that the Arizona juvenile code was unconstitutional on its face because it gives the judge almost unlimited discretion to take juveniles from their parents and commit them to an institution without notice of the charges, the right to counsel, the right to confront and cross-examine witnesses, the right to a transcript of the proceedings, or the right to an appeal. Arizona argued that because the main purpose of juvenile proceedings is to protect juvenile defendants from the full rigor and consequences of the criminal law, informal procedures are required. In Arizona's view, Gault's commitment to a state institution was protective rather than punitive.

The Supreme Court decided for Gault by a vote of 8 to 1. In an opinion by Justice Abe Fortas, the Court held that the due process clause of the Fourteenth Amendment requires that juvenile defendants are at least entitled to notice of the charges, right to counsel, right to confrontation and cross-examination of witnesses, the privilege against self-incrimination, a transcript of the proceedings, and appellate review. Justice Fortas insisted that these are the minimal guarantees necessary to assure fairness. He argued that the guarantees would not unduly interfere with any of the benefits of less formal procedures for juveniles. Justice John M. Harlan wrote a separate concurrence agreeing with the result but suggesting that the crucial minimum guarantees should be limited to notice of the charges; the right to counsel, including assigned counsel for indigent families; a transcript; and the right to appeal. In dissent, Justice Potter Stewart argued that because juvenile proceedings are not adversary criminal actions, the court is unwise to fasten procedural guarantees upon them.

In re Gault forces states to provide juvenile defendants with the central procedural guarantees of the Fifth Amendment. The possibility that young defendants will be unfairly judged to have committed crimes or been delinquent was substantially reduced.

Robert Jacobs

Further Reading

Champion, Dean John. *The Juvenile Justice System: Delinquency, Processing, and the Law*. 4th ed. Upper Saddle River, N.J.: Prentice-Hall, 2003.

Cox, Steven M., John J. Conrad, and Jennifer M. Allen. *Juvenile Justice: A Guide to Theory and Practice*. 5th ed. New York: McGraw-Hill, 2003.

Feld, Bary C. *Cases and Materials on Juvenile Justice Administration*. St. Paul, Minn.: West Publishing, 2000.

See also Criminal justice system; Criminal procedure; Due process of law; Evidence, rules of; Juvenile courts; Juvenile justice system; Juvenile waivers to adult courts; *Parens patriae*; Supreme Court, U.S.; Uniform Juvenile Court Act.

Geographic information systems

Definition: Systems used to plot and analyze geographic locations of such data as crimes

Criminal justice issues: Crime statistics; investigation; technology

Significance: Improvements in the collection, mapping, and analysis of geographic data are making geographic data increasingly valuable tools for crime prevention, crime investigation, and law-enforcement resource allocation.

Geographic information systems (GIS) are methods of plotting geographically defined locations of various phenomena on maps of areas such as cities, counties, and states. Plotting was originally done by hand, but since the late twentieth century it has been done digitally on computers. Now, incidents such as burglaries, murders, and traffic accidents can be precisely located with geographic global positioning system coordinates. Incidents plotted on digitized maps can be displayed on computer screens or printed on paper.

The field of geographic information systems has existed since at least 1916, when Ernest Burgess reported the results of a study of crimes reported to the Chicago police. During the 1920's, Clifford Shaw and Henry McKay reported on the distribution of adjudicated juvenile delinquents living in Chicago and other cities in the United States. Peter and Patricia Brantingham later revolutionized the use of GIS for law enforcement and crime prevention. The computerization of GIS began around 1975 in an industry dominated by the ArcViewGIS and MapInfo software programs.

GIS is becoming an increasingly useful tool for law-enforcement agencies. For example, a police department can use GIS to plot the distribution of residential burglaries in a city, along with the characteristics of each offense, and then analyze the data to create a burglary-prevention plan. Kim Rossmo, a Vancouver, British Columbia, police officer who holds a doctorate in criminology, developed a GIS-based program to track the crimes of mobile serial offenders, particularly murderers. Rossmo's system has been used to pinpoint probable locations of serial offenders' homes to within four-square-block areas.

Lawrence M. Salinger

Further Reading

La Vigne, Nancy G., and Julie Wartell, eds. *Crime Mapping Case Studies: Successes in the Field.* Washington, D.C.: Police Executive Research Forum, 1998.

Rossmo, D. Kim. *Geographic Profiling.* New York: CRC Press, 2000.

Vann, Irvin B., and G. David Garson. *Crime Mapping: New Tools for Law Enforcement.* New York: P. Lang, 2003.

Weisburd, David, and Tom McEwen, eds. *Crime Mapping and Crime Prevention.* Monsey, N.Y.: Criminal Justice Press, 1997.

See also Computer information systems; Criminal history record information; Criminal records; Homeland Security Department; Law enforcement; Police; Violent Criminal Apprehension Program.

Gideon v. Wainwright

The Case: U.S. Supreme Court ruling on right to counsel

Date: Decided on March 18, 1963

Criminal justice issues: Attorneys; defendants

Significance: The Supreme Court ruled that states must provide legal counsel to poor defendants in criminal trials because the right to counsel guaranteed by the Sixth Amendment applies without reservation to the states.

Prior to this case, considerable confusion existed as to whether the Sixth Amendment's "right to counsel" provision applied to the states as well as to the federal government. In 1932, in the famous "Scottsboro" case of *Powell v. Alabama*, the Supreme Court had stressed the vulnerability of the accused and concluded that their conviction transgressed the fair trial provisions of the Sixth Amendment because they had not benefited from

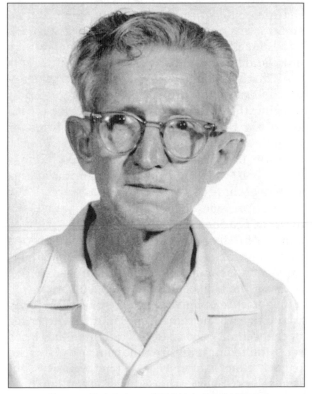

Clarence Earl Gideon. *(AP/Wide World Photos)*

legal representation. That case, however, teemed with qualifying circumstances. The accused were a half dozen young, transient black defendants with little education and, in some instances, with diminished intelligence, who were tried without effective counsel and sentenced to death for raping two white women. Nevertheless, it was believed that the Supreme Court had, in *Powell*, made the right-to-counsel provision of the Sixth Amendment applicable to the states.

This conclusion prevailed for a decade before the Supreme Court explicitly corrected that misunderstanding in *Betts v. Brady* (1942). Stressing the exceptional circumstances involved in the Scottsboro cases, a majority concluded in *Betts* that the right to a fair trial does not require that the criminally accused be represented by an attorney under ordinary circumstances in state proceedings, even in capital cases. Following the *Betts* decision, it was generally supposed that the accused could adequately represent themselves, especially if they had previously witnessed the judicial system at work. Remarkable circumstances such as those of the *Powell* case were an exception to the rule.

Gideon v. Wainwright challenged this assumption. Clarence Gideon fit the *Betts* test. He had been on the wrong side of the bar more than once, and he had actively represented himself in his trial. In accepting the case on appeal, the Supreme Court committed itself to determining whether the concept of a fair trial requires counsel as a general proposition. No other basis existed for deciding the case.

From the outset it appeared that *Gideon* would be a landmark case. Abe Fortas, one of Washington, D.C.'s most celebrated lawyers and later a Supreme Court justice, represented Gideon on a *pro bono* basis. In Fortas's view, Gideon had repeatedly made errors in defending himself that most first-year law students would have avoided. The Supreme Court agreed, overturning *Betts* on the basis of the complex and often confusing nature of judicial proceedings to the ordinary citizen. "The right of one charged with crime to counsel may not be deemed fundamental and essential to fair trials in some countries," Justice Hugo L. Black summarized for the majority, "but it is in ours." Shortly thereafter, the right to counsel was extended to pretrial accusatory proceedings and custodial arrests (*Escobedo v. Illinois*, 1964; *Miranda v. Arizona*, 1966). Meanwhile, in his retrial, with a qualified attorney representing him, Gideon was acquitted of the crime for which he had been previously convicted.

Joseph R. Rudolph, Jr.

Further Reading

Lewis, Anthony. *Gideon's Trumpet*. New York: Vintage Books, 1989.

Reiman, Jeffrey. *The Rich Get Richer and the Poor Get Prison: Ideology, Crime and Criminal Justice*. Boston: Allyn & Bacon, 2004.

Smith, Christopher E. *Courts and the Poor*. Chicago: Nelson-Hall, 1991.

Taylor, John B. *Right to Counsel and Privilege Against Self-Incrimination: Rights and Liberties Under the Law*. Santa Barbara, Calif.: ABC-Clio, 2004.

Tomkovicz, James J. *The Right to the Assistance of Counsel: A Reference Guide to the United States Constitution*. Westport, Conn.: Greenwood Press, 2002.

See also *Argersinger v. Hamlin*; Bill of Rights, U.S.; *Certiorari*; Counsel, right to; Death-row attorneys; Defendant self-representation; Due process of law; Equal protection under the law; *Habeas corpus*; Incorporation doctrine; Public defenders; Supreme Court, U.S.

Good time

Definition: Reduction of prison sentences based on good behavior or participation in some kind of program by inmates

Criminal justice issues: Legal terms and principles; prisons; rehabilitation

Significance: Inmates may reduce the lengths of time they serve in prison based on their good behavior. This policy has the additional effect of freeing up needed space in penal institutions.

Good time allows correctional officials to reduce days, months, and years from inmates' sentences if the inmates behave well in prison. Correctional officials utilize the policy of good time to maintain institutional order and to reduce crowding. The first such statute was passed in New York in 1817, implementing good time at Newgate prison in Greenwich Village. The statute permitted a sentence reduction of up to 25 percent for first-time offenders.

There are different forms of good time. Statutory good time is given automatically when inmates serve their time without incident. Meritorious good time is given to inmates who perform exceptional acts. Earned good time allows inmates to receive time off their sentence for participation in some kind of work, education, or rehabilitation program. The amount of good time varies by state. Usually, five to ten days can be accrued for behaving well for one month. In some states, when an inmate earns a certain amount of good time, say ninety days, the time can be vested. Then the days cannot be taken away for poor behavior. In some states, good time is subtracted from the minimum sentence. As a result of good time, some inmates are eligible for parole before the minimum sentence is served.

Good time is not a right of all inmates. The policy must be state-created, and some states eliminated good time during the "get-tough-on-crime" era. Wisconsin has adopted "bad time" to allow time to be added, delaying an inmate's release date. There has been controversy about good time. The pressures in favor of increasing the amount of good time a prisoner can earn come from overcrowded prison populations and court decrees ordering states to place limits on prisoners. It is relatively straightforward for a legislature to shave days off prison sentences by increasing good-time credits that can be earned. This type of reform avoids the negative publicity that can accompany a parole release. When good-time credits lead to very early releases, however, the policy receives criticism as being "soft" on crime, and some believe it creates the possibility of placing the community in danger.

Harry R. Dammer

Further Reading

Abadinsky, Howard. *Probation and Parole*. 7th ed. Upper Saddle River, N.J.: Prentice-Hall, 2000.

Glaze, Lauren, and Seri Pella. *Probation and Pa-*

role in the United States, 2003. Washington, D.C.: Bureau of Justice Statistics, 2004.

Petersilia, Joan, ed. *Community Corrections: Probation, Parole, and Intermediate Sanctions*. New York: Oxford University Press, 1998.

Travis, Jeremy, and Sarah Lawrence. *Beyond the Prison Gates: The State of Parole in America*. Washington, D.C.: Urban Institute, 2002.

See also Indeterminate sentencing; Pardons; Prison escapes; Prison overcrowding; Rehabilitation.

Graffiti

Definition: Unauthorized drawing, writing, or painting on a surface in a public space

Criminal justice issues: Juvenile justice; vandalism

Significance: There is considerable disagreement about the damage to society caused by graffiti. Some argue that graffiti is simply a form of vandalism whose appearance erodes public perception of an area in a manner similar to that of abandoned buildings, outward prostitution, drug use, and other incivilities. Others contend that many forms of graffiti can be classified as significant pieces of artwork and add to the culture of an area.

Graffiti is drawing, writing, or painting on a public surface without permission of the owner of the object or surface. By 2004, graffiti had become common in nearly all major urban areas throughout the world. Although many consider it vandalism, the creation of graffiti is a complex phenomenon that is difficult to encompass with one simple label. There are noticeable differences not only among the different groups or people who create graffiti but also in their artistic abilities and the motives behind their graffiti.

Graffiti's existence may parallel the origins of human existence, as cave drawings and paintings can be traced back to the earliest known communication between humans. This provides evidence for the historical nature of public self-

Before New York City undertook a massive cleanup effort, its subway cars were literally covered with graffiti. *(AP/Wide World Photos)*

expression through drawing, writing, and painting and suggests that graffiti is a more deeply rooted movement than the mere rebellious destruction of property. Indeed, the use of caves, walls, or other surfaces to describe political ideology and to identify boundaries of territory seems to be a natural part of human existence.

Modern graffiti can be traced to urban areas in the northeastern United States. During the 1960's and 1970's, graffiti became a popular method by which urban youth in Philadelphia and New York left their marks or identification around their neighborhoods. This process quickly became known as "tagging" or leaving one's signature or initials in as many places as possible. Tagging eventually became a competition between individuals and gangs, and the sophistication of the tags grew with the competition.

Graffiti tags have caused graffiti to develop a negative stereotype with many today, and they are often viewed as senseless vandalism and a sign of urban decay. Some criminological theories have depicted graffiti as incivilities that increase the amount of crime in an area as well as the perception of crime. Accordingly, graffiti signifies a competition for territory between gangs, vandalism created by rebellious and misguided youth, and an overall breakdown in the values and organization of the community.

Graffiti as Art

Other sociologists contend that some graffiti has artistic value and actually adds to the cultural backdrop of a community. Accordingly, much of the graffiti in an area represents a yardstick of artistic acceptance and ability in the community and a tolerance of the diversity and free speech within. Although graffiti may be considered a sign of urban decay by some, it can also be seen as an extension of the artistic community and a complex device through which nonconventional artists speak to one another. Whether it is a political statement, an artistic message, or some other form of communication, many argue that graffiti should have a welcomed and natural place in society.

The contradicting views surrounding graffiti are understandable considering the diverse nature of graffiti itself. Although many serious artists do create graffiti, particularly the multicolored pieces by hip-hop artists, there are undoubtedly many whose markings have less artistic value and are performed with an intention to destroy property. Moreover, the surfaces on which graffiti is placed differ greatly, and all present different challenges. Graffiti is often found on buildings, billboards, subway cars, and subway station walls. Graffiti artists have even begun to target trains that travel to other cities and states in an attempt to extend their messages beyond their local communities.

Responses to graffiti have depended largely on the type of graffiti and the policymakers' perspectives on graffiti. Some communities have treated graffiti as a vandalism or crime problem and have relied solely on traditional law-enforcement strategies. Popular law-enforcement methods include greater numbers of real and simulated patrols, increased lighting, and surveillance cameras in the areas of concern. Along with increasing the certainty of capture for undertaking graffiti, increases in the severity of sentences for those apprehended are common.

Graffiti Removal

Graffiti removal procedures are critical to any graffiti reduction plan. Because most removal chemicals have difficulty avoiding a "ghosting effect" whereby the old image is still slightly visible after removal, more focus is being placed on the production of paints that are easy to remove. In addition, antigraffiti surfaces are becoming more popular in areas where graffiti is a known problem. These surfaces often employ special paints on which paint used to create graffiti has difficulty sticking.

Finally, because police and removal efforts often fail to decrease graffiti, some communities work with graffiti artists in an attempt to strike a middle ground. A number of communities provide areas for legal graffiti in a manner similar to "tolerance zones" for drug use in some European countries. The rationale is that the respect and attention shown toward the work of graffiti artists will result in a mutual benefit to both the artists and the community. Ideally, the artists will enjoy the attention to their work and will, in turn, place their art in areas that are less destructive to the property and natural beauty of the community.

Brion Sever

Further Reading

Coffield, F. *Vandalism and Graffiti: The State of the Art.* London: Calouste Gulbenkian Foundation, 1991.

Leet, D., G. Rush, and A. Smith. *Gangs, Graffiti, and Violence: A Realistic Guide to the Scope and Nature of Gangs in America.* 2d ed. Incline Village, Nev.: Copperhouse, 2000.

MacDonald, N. *The Graffiti Subculture: Youth, Masculinity and Identity in London and New York.* Basingstoke, England: Palgrave, 2001.

Phillips, S. *Wallbangin': Graffiti and Gangs in L.A.* Chicago: University of Chicago Press, 1999.

See also Criminology; Cruel and unusual punishment; Juvenile delinquency; Vandalism; Youth gangs.

Grand juries

Definition: Legal bodies formally charged with determining if there is sufficient evidence in criminal investigations to proceed to trials
Criminal justice issues: Investigation; prosecution; trial procedures
Significance: Arrest and arraignment; prosecution; trial procedures

Grand juries, unlike trial juries, do not determine the guilt or innocence of the accused but assess whether the government has enough evidence to advance to a criminal trial (grand juries do not operate in civil proceedings). In this way the grand jury is intended, in the words of the Supreme Court, to "serve as a buffer or referee between the government and the people who are charged with crimes."

The grand jury was imported to the American context as part of English law and was originally meant to protect the colonies against capricious actions of royalist courts. Grand juries were explicitly recognized in the U.S. Constitution's Fifth Amendment, which specifies that "No person shall be held to answer for a capital, or otherwise infamous crime, unless on a presentment or indictment of a Grand Jury" while laying out a limited number of exceptions for those engaged in military or militia service.

Operation and Composition

Grand jury proceedings, which occur as part of the criminal process at both the state and federal levels, usually begin when a "bill of indictment," a written accusation of a crime, is submitted to the jury by a prosecutor. The grand jury then examines the government's case, conducting hearings in which witnesses are called and evidence presented. Again, in contrast with trial proceedings, these hearings are conducted in secret, the public is excluded from attendance, and the accused has no right to present evidence, although the jury may grant this right. Grand juries operate without the direct supervision of a judge—who still exercises some oversight outside the jury chamber—and proceedings are usually dominated by the prosecution, in part because defense attorneys are generally excluded from participation. Although grand juries are normally formed to assess evidence presented by prosecutors, at times they are constituted as independent investigative bodies, the basic function of which is to determine whether there is enough evidence of a crime to proceed to trial.

Federal grand juries have twenty-three members, while state grand juries vary in size from five to twenty-three members. If a legally specified number of jurors from this group believes that the evidence is sufficient to continue prosecution, the grand jury issues an indictment, also known as a "true bill," to the court with jurisdiction over the case. If a true bill is not returned, the case is dismissed and a "no bill" or "ignoramus" rendered. At the federal level, twelve jurors are needed to return an indictment or ignoramus, and in the states the number varies depending on the juries' overall size. In any event, unanimity is not required; by some estimates

grand juries issue indictments 95 percent of the time.

Grand jury members are usually selected at random from voting rolls, although the process varies somewhat at the state level. Grand jurors generally serve for three to eighteen months, although the terms of service can run shorter or longer. Thus, a single grand jury typically reviews a large number of cases.

Powers of the Grand Jury

Witnesses who appear before grand juries possess few procedural rights. Prosecutors are not required to consider or present evidence that might demonstrate the innocence of the accused. In *Williams v. United States* (1992), the U.S. Supreme Court ruled that federal prosecutors need not present evidence favorable to the defense in seeking indictments. Moreover, although the accused may know the names of those testifying before the grand jury, they have no right to confront and cross-examine them. Some evidence inadmissible before trial juries is acceptable in the context of a grand jury inquiry, including hearsay. Those appearing before a grand jury have no right to representation by counsel, although they may request to consult with an attorney outside the grand jury chamber. Some states permit attorneys to be brought into the jury room.

The courts have consistently upheld the broad powers and prerogatives of the grand jury, including the secrecy of its proceedings and its power to compel witnesses to appear, testify, and provide evidence. However, in *Kastigar v. United States* (1972), the U.S. Supreme Court found that grand juries' power to subpoena witnesses and compel testimony must be balanced against constitutional protections against self-incrimination found in the Fifth Amendment to the U.S. Constitution. The Court ruled that compelled testimony and any information or evidence directly derived therefrom cannot be used in subsequent criminal proceedings against the testifying individual—who might still be prosecuted through evidence obtained independently from the grand jury. The Court has consistently avoided insisting that the grand jury is constitutionally required at the state level, making the grand jury provisions of the Fifth Amendment one of the few portions of the Bill of Rights that have not been applied to the states. In *Hurtado v. California* (1884), the Court held that the grand jury protections of the Fifth Amendment need not be extended to the states.

Informations and Presentments

While numerous states authorize the grand jury system, many others use an alternate process known as an "information" to determine whether the prosecution's case should proceed to trial. In an information, a prosecutor provides a written accusation of a crime to the court with the initial authority to hear the case. Usually the prosecution's accusation is initially inspected by a magistrate to ensure its propriety.

On occasion, grand juries go beyond simply determining the sufficiency of the evidence before them by offering "presentments." Although not quite indictments, presentments draw attention to alleged illegal or corrupt activities. In 1974, for example, a grand jury presentment identified President Richard M. Nixon as an "unindicted co-conspirator" for his role in the Watergate scandal.

Grand juries are used in most federal felony prosecutions, although the information is employed in noncapital criminal cases at the district court level and in some civil cases. The state use of grand juries varies widely, with some states employing them optionally and others relegating them to certain classes of investigations, such as in the event of corruption charges against public officials. Grand juries are no longer employed in England; their importance in the U.S. legal system is unique.

The grand jury has been the object of frequent criticism, both from those who find it a cumbersome element of the legal system and from those who consider it a menace to criminal rights and civil liberties in general. The former critics often point to the "information" as a preferable, more efficient procedure for advancing the course of a criminal investigation. Those who object that grand juries have great potential for abuse argue that prosecutors' unbridled authority within the grand jury chamber allows them to intimidate witnesses and cajole jurors, so that the indictment becomes more of a foregone conclusion than an actual check against improper investigations. Defenders of the existing grand jury insist that it serves a critical function in ensuring that the charges against a suspect stem from well-considered evidence rather than from malice, haste, or expedience.

Bruce G. Peabody

Further Reading

Abraham, Henry J. *The Judicial Process*. 6th ed. New York: Oxford University Press, 1993. Includes a concise account of the historical roots of the grand jury.

Clark, Leroy D. *The Grand Jury: The Use and Abuse of Political Power*. New York: Quadrangle, 1975. Critical examination of problems in the grand jury system arising from political influences.

Del Carmen, Rolando V. *Criminal Procedure: Law and Practice*. 6th ed. Belmont, Calif.: Thomson/Wadsworth, 2004. Comprehensive and readable review of criminal procedure that includes a solid discussion of the grand jury in the broader context of criminal procedure.

Frankel, Marvin E., and Gary P. Naftalis. *The Grand Jury: An Institution on Trial*. New York: Hill & Wang, 1977. Another critical study of grand juries in practice.

Younger, R. D. *The People's Panel: The Grand Jury in the United States, 1634-1941*. Providence, R.I.: Brown University Press, 1963. Detailed study of grand juries in U.S. legal history.

See also Criminal procedure; Criminal prosecution; Fifth Amendment; *Hurtado v. California*; Indictment; Information; Jury duty; Jury system; Organized crime; Preliminary hearings; Public prosecutors; Testimony; Trials.

Gregg v. Georgia

The Case: U.S. Supreme Court ruling on capital punishment

Date: Decided on July 2, 1976

Criminal justice issues: Capital punishment; constitutional protections; punishment

Significance: The Court ruled that the death penalty itself was not a cruel and unusual punishment but that procedural safeguards were required to prevent its use in an arbitrary and unpredictable manner.

At the trial stage of bifurcated proceedings, a jury found Troy Gregg guilty of the murder of two men while engaged in armed robbery. In the penalty stage of proceedings, the judge instructed the jury to consider both mitigating and aggravating circumstances and not to impose the death penalty unless it found aggravating circumstances to exist beyond a reasonable doubt. Based on these instructions, the jury returned a verdict of death. The Georgia Supreme Court, which was required by law to review the record, upheld the sentence as not excessive or disproportionate to penalties in similar cases. Gregg and his lawyer then petitioned the U.S. Supreme Court for review.

A few years earlier, in *Furman v. Georgia* (1972), the Supreme Court had ruled that all existing laws allowing capital punishment were in violation of the Eighth Amendment because they failed to prevent arbitrary and unpredictable application. Many observers thought that it would be impossible to devise new laws that would satisfy the concerns expressed in the *Furman* decision, but between 1972 and 1976, thirty-five states, including Georgia, had passed new statutes authorizing the death penalty. With this background, observers were keenly interested in whether the Court would strike down Georgia's new legislation.

In *Gregg*, the Court voted 7 to 2 to uphold the statutory system under which Troy Gregg had been sentenced. The major idea in Justice Potter Stewart's majority opinion was that capital punishment is not unconstitutional per se. Stewart referred to the historical acceptance of capital punishment in American history and to the fact that the majority of state legislatures had recently indicated that they did not consider the punishment to be cruel and unusual. The death penalty, moreover, appeared to be a "significant deterrent" for some people, and the notion of retribution, while not the dominant goal in criminal law, was not forbidden or inconsistent with the recognition of human dignity. Stewart found that Georgia's laws prevented death from being imposed in an arbitrary or capricious manner, and

he specifically endorsed three elements: first, the bifurcated proceedings; second, the judge's instructions to consider the defendant's character and the nature of the circumstances; and third, mandatory review by Georgia's high court to determine whether the death sentence was disproportionate.

Two liberal dissenters on the Court, Justices William Brennan and Thurgood Marshall, argued that capital punishment was always excessive, was not a significant deterrent, and was inconsistent with the concept of human dignity.

The *Gregg* decision indicated that in the foreseeable future the Supreme Court would allow capital punishment, but that its application would be slow, expensive, and rare because of the Court's insistence on procedural safeguards to prevent arbitrary or disproportionate sentencing. *Gregg* appeared to reflect the complex views of a public that was increasingly concerned about the growth of violent crime. By 1991 some twenty-five hundred persons were under sentence of death in the United States, but during that year there were only fourteen executions.

Thomas Tandy Lewis

Further Reading

Bohm, Robert M. *Deathquest: An Introduction to the Theory and Practice of Capital Punishment in the United States.* Cincinnati: Anderson Publishing, 2003.

Carter, Linda E., and Ellen Krietzberg. *Understanding Capital Punishment Law.* Newark, N.J.: LexisNexis, 2004.

Latzer, Barry, ed. *Death Penalty Cases: Leading Supreme Court Cases on Capital Punishment.* 2d ed. Burlington, Mass.: Butterworth Heinemann, 2002.

Sarat, Austin. *When the State Kills: Capital Punishment and the American Condition.* Princeton, N.J.: Princeton University Press, 2001.

See also Bill of Rights, U.S.; Capital punishment; *Coker v. Georgia*; Cruel and unusual punishment; Death-row attorneys; *Furman v. Georgia*; Supreme Court, U.S.; *Tison v. Arizona*; *Witherspoon v. Illinois*.

Gun laws

Definition: State and federal laws regulating the private ownership and use of firearms

Criminal justice issues: Constitutional protections; law codes

Significance: The numbers of federal, state, and local criminal laws and regulations pertaining to firearms increased substantially during the late twentieth century.

The constitutional basis for gun ownership in the United States lies in the Second Amendment to the Constitution, whose origins can be found in English common law. It uses language that is clear but general, and there is considerable disagreement as to how it should be interpreted. Firearms are controversial, and gun laws are reflective of a polarization of opinion between pro- and antigun views among the electorate.

Many gun laws—for example, those that prohibit felons and the insane from buying guns—serve logical purposes. The polarization of the gun debate, however, has resulted in many inconsistencies. For example, federal law bans assault weapons because of their lack of sporting purpose while the Second Amendment makes clear reference to the military purpose of firearms ownership, and one state law makes it a felony to carry a tear gas sprayer while it is a misdemeanor to carry a gun.

During the eighteenth, nineteenth, and early twentieth centuries, many gun laws were created for explicitly racist or classist reasons, prohibiting or preventing African Americans and immigrants from having guns. During the late twentieth century, many federal, state, and local gun laws were passed, which—like three-strikes criminal laws, zero-tolerance drug laws, and laws against selling alcohol on Sunday—have been criticized as having more emotional than

---

The Second Amendment

A well regulated Militia, being necessary to the security of a free State, the right of the people to keep and bear Arms, shall not be infringed.

---

practical appeal. Few people, after all, are willing to challenge in public debate a law against carrying a gun at or near a school.

In contrast, in 1987 Florida liberalized its concealed carry law, and other states later followed suit, leading to an increase in concealed weapons among ordinary citizens. It is a reflection of the polarization of the firearms controversy that as laws instituting waiting periods, background checks, bans, and stiffer sentences for criminal use of guns went into effect, various states began to allow average citizens to carry guns. What these two contrary trends have in common is public fear of criminal violence.

Supreme Court Cases

In *Cruikshank v. United States* (1876), the Supreme Court ruled that the Second Amendment did not oblige the state of Louisiana to allow two lynching victims to defend themselves with guns. In *Miller v. Texas* (1894), the Supreme Court declined to decide whether the Second Amendment applied to states. In *United States v. Miller* (1939), which challenged the ban established by the National Firearms Act (NFA) of 1934 on shotguns with barrels less than eighteen inches long, the Court declined to make a broad ruling on the application of the Second Amendment to the states, instead focusing on whether a short-barreled shotgun was of much use as a military weapon and hence deserving of legal protection. The Court ruled that a short-barreled shotgun was of no military use and that the government could therefore legally ban such a weapon.

In *Verdugo-Urquidez v. United States* (1990), the Court ruled that private individuals have the right to keep and bear arms. In *Printz v. United States* (1994) and *Mack v. United States* (1994), the Court ruled unconstitutional a portion of the Brady Handgun Violence Prevention Act (1993), a federal law mandating that chief law-enforcement officers conduct background checks on all purchasers of handguns in the officers' jurisdictions. A nationwide, computerized background check system, a provision of the Brady law that became operational in November, 1998, does not impose the same federally mandated burden on local law enforcement as did the part of the Brady law that was ruled unconstitutional.

Federal Laws

The federal agency charged with the enforcement of federal firearms laws is the Bureau of Alcohol, Tobacco, Firearms and Explosives (ATF). This agency has its origins during the early days of the federal government, when federal agents pitted themselves against traders in illegal whiskey and tobacco who defended their shipments with firearms.

The first wide-reaching federal gun law, the National Firearms Act (NFA), arose out of public reaction to the gangster violence of the Prohibition era. The NFA banned, with few exceptions, civilian ownership of fully automatic guns (which continue to fire as long as the trigger is held back), silencers, shotguns with barrels less than eighteen inches long, and rifles with barrels less than sixteen inches long. The Federal Firearms Act of 1938 regulated interstate commerce of firearms, notably by requiring licenses for manufacturers and dealers in firearms. Those who wish to buy wholesale, sell guns, make guns, or ship them across state lines must have a federal firearms license (FFL). Those with FFLs must also keep detailed records of their transactions involving firearms. It is a crime to misuse or steal an FFL, and FFL holders are required to comply with federal, state, and local regulations regarding the sale and transfer of guns. The serial numbers of guns are recorded when they are transferred, allowing a gun recovered from a crime to be traced back to its last legal owner.

The 1968 Gun Control Act is the primary federal gun control law. It prohibits convicted felons, fugitives, persons who have been ruled mentally defective or been committed to a mental institution, persons dishonorably discharged from the armed services, illegal aliens, and persons who have renounced their U.S. citizenship from owning guns. The act also schedules FFL license fees, prohibits mail-order sales of firearms, and allows persons to buy handguns only in the states in which they reside.

The Violent Crime Control and Law Enforcement Act of 1994 banned assault weapons. This act specifically lists various guns as assault weapons and describes features that qualify other weapons not on the list as assault weapons. A firearm may be classified as an assault weapon if it is semiautomatic and has two or more of the following features: a folding stock, a pistol grip (on a long gun), a magazine attachment point outside the grip (on a handgun), a threaded barrel, or a bayonet lug. This act also banned magazines with a capacity greater than ten rounds. Continued ownership and trade in banned weapons and magazines that were in existence before the ban was imposed are permitted. Federal gun laws have generally allowed people to keep guns made illegal by new laws. For example, persons who legally owned magazines in 1994 with a capacity greater than ten rounds did not have to surrender them in 1995.

State Laws

In addition to federal gun laws, all fifty U.S. states have their own gun laws. Some federal laws deal with hunting, especially on federal land, but most hunting laws pertaining to firearms have been enacted by the states. Typical hunting laws specify hunting seasons, require persons to purchase hunting licenses, impose ammunition capacity limitations on firearms used in hunting, and establish rules about the use of bait, aiming devices, and clothing. Guns may not be used in traps, and guns used for poaching may be confiscated.

Vermont allows concealed carry of a firearm

Finding Up-to-Date Information on Gun Laws

Because the numbers of federal, state, and local gun laws have increased rapidly during recent decades, books about gun laws have short shelf lives. Books that summarize specific gun laws—rather than Second Amendment issues—are often more easily found where guns are sold than in libraries.

The Bureau of Alcohol, Tobacco, Firearms and Explosives (www.atf.gov/firearms/index.htm), the National Rifle Association (nra.org), and Handgun Control Inc. (www.handguncontrol.org), among other institutions, maintain Internet Web sites that include practical information about gun laws. Federal, state, and local laws may be accessed directly on the Internet and in law libraries.

without a permit, and Utah has a concealed carry law that is recognized only by Arkansas. All but seven other states (in which carrying concealed weapons is prohibited) require people to have permits to carry concealed guns. Thirty states are known as "shall issue" states, because local law-enforcement heads routinely issue concealed carry permits to applicants who meet the requirements. Twelve states are known as "may issue" states, because local law-enforcement heads may (or, more likely, may not) issue concealed weapons permits to applicants.

States usually do not honor one another's permits. Thus, people who may be able to carry guns legally in one state may not be able to carry their guns legally in another state. Sworn police officers are generally exempt from laws against concealed carry of firearms. Private security guards, while on duty and in uniform, generally may carry exposed firearms, but they typically must pass firearms safety tests and background checks. Although in some states it is technically legal for civilians to carry guns exposed, their doing so would almost certainly be considered a breach of the peace.

In most jurisdictions, it is illegal to carry a firearm in an automobile. It may be legal, however, to transport a firearm in a vehicle if the gun is fully unloaded and locked in a container (other than the glove compartment) that is inaccessible to the driver (in the trunk, for example). Loaded or unloaded guns may not be carried, for example, in purses or briefcases next to the driver.

Other Laws

Hunting is well established as a lucrative form of tourism, and hunting tours to almost any country can be arranged. It is illegal simply to transport guns across national borders; those engaging in hunts need to obtain all necessary permits before leaving the United States. Hunting with

---

Typical State Gun-Permit Requirements

Specific rules vary among the states. However, most states require applicants to

- ✓ be at least twenty-one years old
- ✓ be residents of the states in question
- ✓ provide fingerprints
- ✓ submit to criminal and mental health background checks
- ✓ pass firearms safety courses
- ✓ pay application fees

Applicants must also not belong to any category of persons forbidden to own guns. Such categories typically include

- ✓ convicted felons
- ✓ persons convicted of misdemeanors punishable by more than one year's imprisonment
- ✓ persons convicted of misdemeanor firearms misuse
- ✓ fugitives from justice
- ✓ undocumented aliens
- ✓ illegal drug users
- ✓ persons under restraining orders
- ✓ persons under indictment for crimes that would render them ineligible for permits if convicted
- ✓ persons ineligible to own guns under federal and local laws

---

handguns is prohibited in Mexico and Canada.

Guns may be checked as baggage on commercial air flights as long as they are unloaded, in a locked case, and kept in a storage compartment not accessible to passengers. Additionally, a person transporting a firearm on a commercial flight must inform the carrier of its presence.

Those under twenty-one may not purchase handguns, and those under eighteen may not purchase long guns. Many state and federal laws further restrict the access of minors to guns and ammunition. Often, minors may not shoot guns except under the direct supervision of an adult. Parents may be held liable under civil law, and in some cases criminal law, if their children cause harm with a gun.

Eric Howard

Further Reading

Bijlefeld, Marjolijn, ed. *The Gun Control Debate: A Documentary History*. Westport, Conn.: Greenwood Press, 1997. Collection of more than two hundred historical documents, covering the full sweep of U.S. history.

Cottrol, Robert J., ed. *Gun Control and the Constitution: Sources and Explanations on the Second Amendment*. New York: Garland Publishing, 1994. One-volume paperback edition (and a longer, three-volume hardback) collecting major court cases and scholarly articles on both sides of the debate.

Halbrook, Stephen P. *That Every Man Be Armed: The Evolution of a Constitutional Right*. 2d ed. Oakland, Calif.: Independent Institute, 1994. Examines the origins and interpretations of the Second Amendment.

Kopel, David B., Alan Korwin, and Stephen P. Halbrook. *Supreme Court Gun Cases*. Phoenix, Ariz.: Bloomfield Press, 2003. Contains all the relevant text of every Supreme Court case involving the Second Amendment, gun control laws, and self-defense.

Korwin, Alan, and Michael P. Anthony. *Gun Laws of America: Every Federal Gun Law on the Books, with Plain English Summaries.* Phoenix, Ariz.: Bloomfield Press, 1997. Does an admirable job of listing and condensing the federal gun laws.

Machtinger, John. *How to Own a Gun and Stay Out of Jail* (California edition). Los Angeles: Gun Law Press, 1995. Summarizes California's gun laws and how they apply to typical gun owners. Other titles in the publisher's series cover the laws of other specific states.

Malcolm, Joyce Lee. *To Keep and Bear Arms: The Origins of an Anglo-American Right*. Cambridge, Mass.: Harvard University Press, 1994. Exceptionally well-researched examination of the Second Amendment's origins in English law.

See also Background checks; Bureau of Alcohol, Tobacco, Firearms and Explosives; Common law; Constitution, U.S.; Criminal history record information; Criminal law; Drive-by shootings; Firearms; Right to bear arms; Self-defense.

Habeas corpus

Definition: Court order, or writ, to bring a person being detained before a court or judge to determine whether the person's imprisonment is lawful

Criminal justice issues: Appeals; arrest and arraignment; jurisdictions; legal terms and principles

Significance: *Habeas corpus* has long been part of the common law to protect people from unlawful imprisonment; the judicial branch of government has authority over the executive police power in this regard. When prisoners' appeals are exhausted, the writ of *habeas corpus* provides an avenue through which they can request reviews of their convictions.

Petitions for writs of *habeas corpus*, also known as the Great Writ, are among the most commonly used proceedings to test the constitutionality of detentions and imprisonments. *Habeas corpus* is a Latin phrase that translates as "that you have the body." Prisoners or detainees who apply for the writ are usually known as petitioners, and the named respondents are the persons who have legal custody of them. Petitions may be brought either under state law or, if certain conditions have been met, under federal law. Although persons who are being detained pending trials or other proceedings can also petition for the writs, by far the largest category of petitioners includes those who have already been convicted of crimes.

Procedures

The procedures used to petition for state writs of *habeas corpus* vary from state to state and are governed by state statutes and court rules. In the federal system, petitions for writs of *habeas corpus* by state prisoners and detainees cannot be filed until all available remedies under state law have been exhausted. This exhaustion rule is based upon the concept of comity, which requires the courts of one jurisdiction to avoid interfering in the affairs of other jurisdictions unless absolutely necessary.

The exhaustion requirement gives the states the opportunity to address constitutional issues raised by their own prisoners and detainees, perhaps avoiding the need for the federal courts to become involved. Federal writs of *habeas corpus* are further limited by the requirement that federal petitions be filed within one year after convictions, or other actions, become final. This limit was imposed by the Antiterrorism and Effective Death Penalty Act of 1996. Finally, in order to prevent abuse of the writ, there are stringent requirements on the filing of second or successive writs addressing the same issues.

Federal writs of *habeas corpus* are used by detainees and prisoners who claim that their continued detention or imprisonment violates the U.S. Constitution. Errors of state law do not support *habeas* relief, unless those errors also violate a federal constitutional provision. Detainees usually complain that they are being held without probable cause in violation of the Fourth Amendment, or that they have not been provided with speedy trials, as guaranteed by the Sixth Amendment.

Petitions of convicted prisoners often raise numerous points attacking their state convictions on federal constitutional grounds. However, *habeas corpus* does not constitute an appeal and is governed by different standards from those that

---

Habeas Corpus in the U.S. Constitution

The common-law principle of *habeas corpus* is clearly acknowledged in Article I, section 9 of the Constitution:

> The Privilege of the Writ of Habeas Corpus shall not be suspended, unless when in Cases of Rebellion or Invasion the public Safety may require it.

govern essentially the same grounds in direct appeals. For example, a state court error—even an error that violates the federal Constitution—will not support relief unless the state court has also acted unreasonably. In other words, the state court must not only be wrong but must also have been unreasonable in reaching its incorrect decision. The federal courts must also presume that a state court's factual findings are correct, unless a prisoner can prove that the findings are incorrect by clear and convincing evidence.

Former professional boxer Rubin "Hurricane" Carter at a 2004 news conference holding the writ of *habeas corpus* that had freed him from prison in 1986 after he had spent nearly twenty years in prison on false murder charges. *(AP/Wide World Photos)*

Grounds for *Habeas Corpus*

The grounds urged by prisoners in federal *habeas* petitions fall into two general categories. The first contains errors relating to conduct of trials that do not relate to particular constitutional rights. Such trial errors support *habeas* relief only when they are so grossly prejudicial that they fatally infect the trials and deny the fundamental fairness that is the essence of due process. Federal courts approach such grounds with considerable self-restraint, and it is usually only the most egregious of errors that entitle state prisoners to federal *habeas* relief.

The second category contains grounds based upon violations of particular constitutional rights, such as the right to effective counsel or the right against self-incrimination. When state prisoners can prove violations of such fundamental rights, it is more likely that relief will be granted.

Petitions for *habeas corpus* can also be used by prisoners to attack the execution of their sentences rather than the convictions themselves. In other words, prisoners can use writs to complain that their sentence have not been computed correctly or that their earned sentence credits have been lost. However, just as with petitions attacking convictions, petitions attacking execution of sentences must allege violation of the federal Constitution. Such petitions are usually based upon the due process clause of the Fourteenth Amendment. When petitions are granted, the prisoners are not set free unless corrections of the errors result in enough sentence credits to entitle them to immediate release.

Most petitions for *habeas corpus* in noncapital cases are filed by prisoners *pro se*, that is, without legal representation. Prisons ordinarily provide preprinted forms to be used by prisoners who wish to file petitions for *habeas corpus*. They also provide law libraries for them to do legal research. When a court determines that a hearing should be conducted on a prisoner's petition, counsel is usually appointed to assist the prisoner. However, most petitions are resolved without the need for hearings.

Sharon K. O'Roke

Further Reading

Barnes, Patricia G. *CQ's Desk Reference on American Criminal Justice: Over Five Hundred Answers to Frequently Asked Questions from Law Enforcement to Corrections.* Chicago: University of Chicago Press, 2000. Features answers to frequently asked questions about the U.S. legal system. Reference materials include significant laws and court decisions, and a glossary of common legal terms.

Hanson, Roger A. *Federal Habeas Corpus Review: Challenging State Court Criminal Convictions*. Washington, D.C.: U.S. Department of Justice, Bureau of Justice Statistics, 1995. Statistical study of *habeas corpus* petitions in eighteen federal district courts in nine states.

Lewis, Anthony. *Gideon's Trumpet*. New York: Vintage Books, 1989. History of the landmark 1963 U.S. Supreme Court decision in *Gideon v. Wainwright* that follows James Earl Gideon's handwritten *habeas corpus* petition for the right to legal counsel in criminal proceedings. Includes notes, table of cases leading up to the final verdict, and index.

Schmalleger, Frank. *Criminal Justice Today: An Introductory Text for the Twenty-first Century*. 8th ed. Upper Saddle River, N.J.: Pearson/Prentice-Hall, 2005. Introductory textbook on the U.S. criminal justice system.

See also Antiterrorism and Effective Death Penalty Act; Appellate process; Bill of Rights, U.S.; *Certiorari*; Cruel and unusual punishment; Defendant self-representation; Effective counsel; False convictions; *Gideon v. Wainwright*; Judicial review; Magna Carta; *Mandamus*; Martial law.

Halfway houses

Definition: Use of supervised living arrangements, usually in urban areas, as an alternative to prisons

Criminal justice issues: Probation and pretrial release; punishment; rehabilitation

Significance: The use of halfway houses as an alternative to incarceration is on the rise.

Halfway houses have many different forms and treatment philosophies and serve different populations. Offenders on probation and those facing potential prison sentences are referred to as "halfway in," while offenders planning to be released into the community soon after serving prison time are referred to as "halfway out."

A structured living environment is provided to halfway-in offenders in the attempt to remove bad influences that may lead to more criminal behavior. Residents are held accountable for their time. Frequently, they are required to work or at least look for a job, be drug free, obey curfew hours, and perform duties around the halfway house. Offenders create a life for themselves in a community, but they are also held accountable for their activities and are supervised under specific house rules. In addition to room and board, they are frequently given vocational training, treatment for substance abuse, anger management therapy, and other assistance.

Leaving prison may lead to the so-called revolving door of recidivism because former convicts often lack social support and ties to conventional society. For the halfway out, halfway houses are successful at offering support for individuals lacking family and friends willing to support and sponsor them as they return from prison.

Halfway house programs are frequently criticized for coddling inmates and for punishing them too lightly for their crimes. Observers frequently criticize the nature of room and board, which is less institutional than that of a jail, and the benefits offenders receive of free education, vocational training, and health care.

Most often, halfway houses are located in urban settings where there are increased access to public transportation, flexible job opportunities, social services, and health care facilities. In order to keep costs down, the homes are usually located in lower-income neighborhoods. Residents of neighboring communities are frequently concerned that the residents of halfway houses are criminal offenders living in neighborhoods already facing significant crime and declining property values. The phrase "not in my backyard" has been popularized to describe a situation in which citizens see the overall benefit of specific programs such as halfway houses but claim that those programs should exist in some other community.

Zoning boards and town councils frequently attempt to stifle the growth of local halfway houses by refusing accommodations for building changes or creating rules that limit the number of unrelated individuals residing in one residence. This leads to communities getting several smaller operations housing five to eight people instead of a larger operation with many people under one roof.

It is difficult to assess the success or failure of halfway houses as a general concept because there is a great deal of variability among the services offered, types of staffing, rules, location of the building, and general community support for the house residents. This variability results in ample support for and against the development of these facilities. However, the number of halfway houses is expected to increase because of a number of factors including substantial overcrowding in prisons and jails, cost savings of halfway houses over traditional incarceration, the popular acceptance of alternative sanctions for nonviolent offenders, and the promise of greater reintegration into the community.

John C. Kilburn, Jr.

Further Reading

Clear, Todd, and Harry Dammer. *The Offender and the Community*. Belmont, Calif.: Wadsworth, 1999.

Petersilia, Joan, ed. *Community Corrections: Probation, Parole, and Intermediate Sanctions*. New York: Oxford University Press, 1998.

See also Community-based corrections; Criminal justice system; House arrest; "Not-in-my-backyard" attitudes; Prison escapes; Prison industries; Prison overcrowding; Recidivism; Rehabilitation; Work camps; Work-release programs.

Harmelin v. Michigan

The Case: U.S. Supreme Court ruling on mandatory sentences

Date: Decided on June 27, 1991

Criminal justice issues: Punishment; substance abuse

Significance: Upholding a Michigan drug possession law that carried a mandatory term of life imprisonment, the Supreme Court rejected the plaintiff's argument that the sentence was "cruel and unusual punishment" and therefore in violation of the Eighth Amendment.

Under Michigan law, the petitioner, Ronald Allen Harmelin, was convicted of possessing 672 grams of cocaine and sentenced to mandatory life imprisonment because the amount was in excess of the 650-gram threshold specified in the law for imposing the mandatory sentence. The Michigan State Court of Appeals upheld the sentence, rejecting Harmelin's claim that the sentence violated the protection against "cruel and unusual punishment" guaranteed by the Constitution. Harmelin argued that the sentence violated that restriction because it was "disproportionate" to his crime and, further, that because it was mandatory it provided for no "mitigating circumstances" that would allow a judge any latitude in sentencing.

Harmelin's appeal to the U.S. Supreme Court was denied and his sentence upheld. Justice Antonin Scalia delivered the Court's principal opinion. It concluded that because there is no proportionality provision in the Eighth Amendment, a sentence cannot be deemed cruel or unusual on the basis that it is disproportionate to the crime involved. Furthermore, it argued that Harmelin's claim that his mandatory sentence deprived him of his right to a consideration of mitigating circumstances had no precedent in constitutional law. It observed that mandatory penalties, though they could be harsh or extreme, were common enough in the history of the United States and had never been construed as cruel and unusual in the constitutional sense of that phrase. While granting that Harmelin's argument had support in the so-termed individualized capital-sentencing doctrine of the Court's death-penalty legal theory, the majority dismissed Harmelin's claim because of the qualitative difference between execution and all other forms of punishment.

Justice Anthony Kennedy, joined by Justices Sandra Day O'Connor and David Souter, although concurring with the judgment against Harmelin, claimed that the Eighth Amendment's cruel and unusual punishment provision does encompass "a narrow proportionality principle that applies to noncapital sentences." Citing various precedents, these justices argued that the Court, though not clearly or consistently, had previously determined the constitutionality of noncapital punishments based on that principle, although said precedents had taken under review only the length of a punishment's term, not its type.

Having again broached the issue of proportionality, the Supreme Court was likely to face more challenges to mandatory sentencing. From state to state, in statutes imposing mandatory sentences, there is no uniform-sentencing code governing types of punishment or their length. Although in *Harmelin* the Court argued that state legislatures must retain the prerogative of establishing their own penal codes, where there is a wide discrepancy between mandatory penalties imposed for the same crime by one state and another, plaintiffs may seek relief from enforcement of the more severe penalty.

John W. Fiero

Further Reading

Gaines, Larry K., and Peter B. Kraska, eds. *Drugs, Crime, and Justice*. Prospect Heights, Ill.: Waveland Press, 2003.

Tonry, Michael. *Reconsidering Indeterminate and Structured Sentencing*. Washington, D.C.: U.S. Department of Justice, Office of Justice Programs, National Institute of Justice, 1999.

_____. *Sentencing Matters*. New York: Oxford University Press, 1996.

United States Sentencing Commission. *Federal Sentencing Guidelines Manual 2003*. St. Paul, Minn.: West Group, 2004.

See also Cruel and unusual punishment; Drugs and law enforcement; Mandatory sentencing; Punishment; *Rummel v. Estelle*; Supreme Court, U.S.

Harmless error

Definition: Legal mistake made during the course of a defendant's progress through the justice system that is not considered to be damaging to the defendant's case

Criminal justice issues: Appeals; convictions; legal terms and principles; prosecution

Significance: The principle of harmless error holds that mistakes made by prosecutors should not be the basis of reversing trial results on appeal, if those mistakes do not significantly alter court proceedings or outcomes or substantially violate the constitutional rights of the parties.

If a legal mistake, or error, is made during a trial, the results of the trial often may be reversed on appeal. For example, a conviction may be overturned by an appellate court for such a prosecutorial error as admitting illegally seized evidence into trial. However, if the error is a minor mistake that can be proven beyond a reasonable doubt not to influence the outcome of the trial or create prejudice against the defendant, the error may be considered "harmless," and the trial result will be allowed stand. The principle of harmless error prevents appellate courts from overturning judicial decisions for unimportant courtroom mistakes.

During the early twentieth century, convictions were sometimes reversed for errors as trivial as omitting the word "the" from "peace and dignity of the state" at the end of an indictment. Recognizing the need for "harmless error," the U.S. Congress began including it in legislation in 1911. In 1948, harmless error was added to procedural law.

Jennifer C. Gibbs

Further Reading

Garner, Bryan A., ed. *Black's Law Dictionary*. 8th ed. St. Paul, Minn.: Thomson/West, 2004.

"Harmless Constitutional Error: A Reappraisal." *Harvard Law Review* 83, no. 4 (February, 1970).

See also Appellate process; *Arizona v. Fulminante*; Attorney ethics; Case law; Criminal procedure; Criminal prosecution; Exclusionary rule; Judicial review; Reversible error; Search and seizure.

Harris v. United States

The Case: U.S. Supreme Court ruling on search and seizure

Date: Decided on March 5, 1968

Criminal justice issues: Police powers; search and seizure

Significance: This case established the principle that if evidence of crimes is in "plain view" of law-enforcement officers while the officers are fulfilling their authorized duties, its use in criminal proceedings does not violate a defendant's constitutional protection against unlawful search and seizure.

James H. Harris, the petitioner, prior to his appeal to the U.S. Supreme Court, was tried for robbery in the U.S. District Court for the District of Columbia. Evidence used against him included his victim's automobile registration card, which the police found on the metal strip under the door of Harris's car after it had been impounded for its protection while Harris was being held as the robbery suspect. During his trial, Harris moved to have that evidence suppressed on the grounds that it was obtained through unlawful search. The district court denied the request, and Harris was convicted and sentenced to prison. Thereafter, a panel of the Court of Appeals for the District of Columbia reversed the conviction, concluding that the registration card had been obtained by unlawful search; however, it also granted the government's petition for a rehearing before the full court of appeals, which subsequently overturned the panel's determination, ruling that the conviction did not violate the petitioner's rights.

On *certiorari*, the U.S. Supreme Court upheld the decision, affirming the admissibility of the questionable evidence. Seven justices concurred in the majority opinion, arguing that nothing in the Fourth Amendment protects a suspect from the use of incriminating evidence found as a result of normal safeguards taken while a suspect's property is in police custody. According to the opinion, objects in the "plain view" of police officers authorized to be in a position to view the objects cannot be construed as the products of a search, are therefore subject to seizure, and may be introduced as evidence.

Various Supreme Court cases, including *Ker v. California* (1963), had established the right of law-enforcement agents to seize objects in plain view to be used as criminal evidence, but none addressed the issue of whether securing of evidence from a defendant's property while it was in police custody constituted an illegal search. Jurists concerned with the protection of an accused individual's rights argue that the *Harris* decision erodes the Fourth Amendment guarantees against illegal search and seizure. Because

the circumstances were somewhat unusual, however, the application of *Harris* to other attempts to suppress evidence is likely to be fairly limited. Nevertheless, the ruling does reflect the Supreme Court's increasing unwillingness to broaden its interpretation of constitutional guarantees in favor of the accused to the disadvantage of criminal investigators and prosecutors.

John W. Fiero

Further Reading

Dash, Samuel. *The Intruders: Unreasonable Searches and Seizures from King John to John Ashcroft*. New Brunswick, N.J.: Rutgers University Press, 2004.

Del Carmen, Rolando V. *Criminal Procedure: Law and Practice*. 6th ed. Belmont, Calif.: Thomson/Wadsworth, 2004.

LaFave, W. R. *Search and Seizure: A Treatise on the Fourth Amendment*. 3d ed. St. Paul, Minn.: West Publishing, 1995.

McWhirter, Darien A. *Search, Seizure, and Privacy*. Phoenix, Ariz.: Oryx Press, 1994.

See also *Chimel v. California*; Criminal procedure; Due process of law; Evidence, rules of; Search and seizure; Supreme Court, U.S.

Hate crime

Definition: Crime committed because of the victims' race, ethnicity, religion, sexual orientation, or other group characteristic

Criminal justice issues: Civil rights and liberties; constitutional protections; hate crime

Significance: Hate crime is not new, but it has only been since the late decades of the twentieth century that it has received extensive scholarly and legal attention. Studying and preventing hate crime has proved to be a challenging task.

During the 1980's states began passing laws against what became known as hate, or bias, crimes. Although these laws differed considerably from jurisdiction to jurisdiction, most of them worked by adding additional penalties

Characteristics of Hate Crime Offenders

Many people assume that those who commit hate crimes belong to organized hate groups such as the Ku Klux Klan or "skinhead" gangs. In fact, only 5-14 percent of offenders are believed to belong to such groups. Nevertheless, most offenders share a number of characteristics.

✓ Most are male.
✓ Most are white.
✓ Most are young—in their late teens or early twenties.
✓ Most have brief or no previous arrest records.
✓ Most commit their crimes with small groups of friends.
✓ Contrary to popular assumptions, not all offenders are uneducated; many are high school and college students.
✓ Most are motivated to commit their crimes not because of passionate hatred for their victims, but because they want to experience excitement or impress their peers.

when offenders chose their victims because of their membership, or presumed membership, in certain racial, ethnic, religious, or sexual orientation groups. By the end of the twentieth century, nearly every state had some form of hate crime law, as did many nations. The U.S. federal government also passed a law requiring the Department of Justice to collect hate crime data from local law-enforcement agencies.

Proponents of hate crime laws argued that special legislation was needed for several reasons. Existing laws, such as those in some states that prohibited desecrating cemeteries and places of worship, covered only a small proportion of bias-motivated crime. Many people and groups believed that the frequency of hate crimes was increasing. Furthermore, it was argued, hate crimes are worse than "ordinary" crimes because they have a greater impact on victims and communities.

Hate crime laws have been challenged on a number of constitutional grounds. The U.S. Supreme Court has ruled on them in such cases as *Wisconsin v. Mitchell* (1993), *R.A.V. v. City of St. Paul* (1992), and *Virginia v. Black* (2003). These rulings have made it permissible to punish offenders when their crimes are motivated by their victims' group membership. Moreover, bias may be considered as an aggravating circumstance in death penalty cases. However, laws that seek to punish expressions of bias, such as cross burning, must be drafted carefully so as to avoid infringing on First Amendment rights.

Aside from the constitutional issues, the other major debate concerning hate crimes has centered on what kind of groups to include within the protection of the laws. All hate crime statutes include race, religion, and ethnicity, but other categories have been more controversial. Many hate crime laws do not include crimes on the basis of sexual orientation, even though gays and lesbians are frequent targets. States are also split as to whether they include gender and disability.

Police and Hate Crimes

It has proven to be difficult to enforce hate crime laws effectively. Few of these crimes—probably less than one-third—are reported to police. This is due to a number of factors, including victims' fears and lack of understanding of the law, as well as poor relations between some communities and their police. Attempts have been made to improve police handling of hate crimes. Some states, such as California, require training on hate crimes in their police academies. Many jurisdictions have created special bias crime units, although the effectiveness of these units varies widely.

Despite these efforts, arrests for hate crimes remain uncommon, and successful prosecutions are even rarer. This is because convicting offenders on hate crime charges requires proving their biased motive beyond a reasonable doubt, which is often difficult. Even California, which has the largest number of reported hate crimes in the nation—around one-quarter of the total—usually has only about two hundred hate crime convictions a year.

The Impact of Hate Crimes

The most common victims of hate crimes in virtually every jurisdiction are African Americans. Gays and lesbians and Jews are also frequent targets. However, members of virtually every ethnic group, including whites, experience hate crimes to some extent. Homicides are rarely connected with hate crimes, although they tend to garner media attention. Much more common are assaults and vandalism.

It is difficult to assess the full impact of hate crimes upon victims and communities. Only a handful of studies have carefully examined whether hate crime victims were more psychologically damaged than victims of what are considered "ordinary" crimes. The studies do suggest that hate crimes might be more harmful in some cases, but more research must be done before firm conclusions can be drawn.

Even fewer studies have looked at the impact of hate crimes on communities at large. Certainly some of the more egregious incidents have received extensive media attention. These have included the killing of gay college student Matthew Shepard in Wyoming, the dragging murder of James Byrd in Texas, and the murder of transgendered teenager Gwen Araujo in California. The term "hate crime" is certainly one with which most members of the public have become familiar. Whether these crimes have a greater ripple effect than other kinds of crimes, however, is unknown.

One thing that does appear clear is that, contrary to popular belief, the number of hate crimes in the United States has not been increasing. Some events have certainly led to an increase in hate crime against certain people, such as crimes

The suspects in the brutal killing of University of Wyoming student Matthew Shepard awaiting arraignment in October, 1998. After changing their pleas to guilty to avoid capital punishment, the two men were sentenced to double life terms without parole, and the woman was sentenced to a brief term for her role as an after-the-fact accessory. *(AP/Wide World Photos)*

against Muslims after the terrorist attacks of September 11, 2001. However, the overall number of hate crimes reported to the police has remained relatively constant, with about nine thousand crimes reported throughout the United States during the first years of the twenty-first century.

Organized Hate

To many people thinking of hate crime, the first image that leaps to mind is that of organized hate groups, such as the Ku Klux Klan and other white supremacist bodies. The numbers of these groups vary from year to year. In 2003, it was estimated that approximately seven hundred hate groups were active in the United States. Another thing that tends to vary over time is the types of groups that are active.

There are many different branches of organized hate in the United States. The oldest of these is the Ku Klux Klan, which has existed in various incarnations since the Civil War. At the start of the twenty-first century, there were actually numerous Klan organizations, many of which were in conflict with one another. Other types of hate groups that remain active include racist skinheads, militias and extremist patriot groups, and white nationalist organizations. There are also a smaller number of nonwhite extremist groups, such as black nationalists and Jewish extremists.

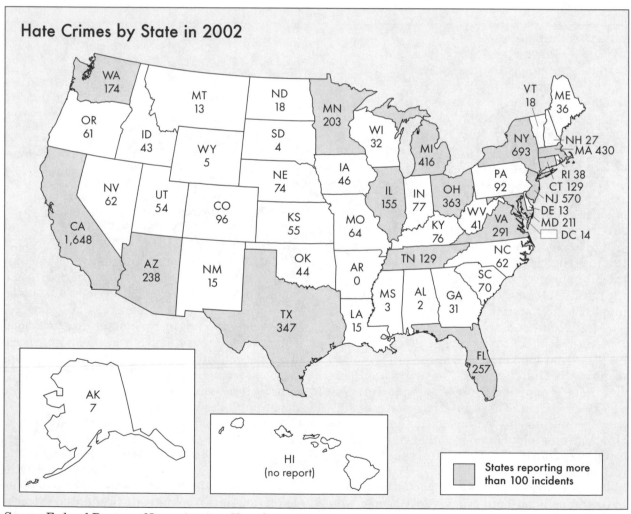

Hate Crimes by State in 2002

Source: Federal Bureau of Investigation, *Hate Crime Statistics.* Data are based on reports made by the individual states, whose hate-crime criteria and reporting methods may differ.

It is difficult for law-enforcement agencies to track hate groups for several reasons. Group memberships and leaders tend to be fluid, and the groups tend to form and dissolve quickly. By the beginning of the twenty-first century, many of these groups had abandoned their traditional military-style uniforms and were attempting to appear less extremist and more mainstream. Furthermore, in part to avoid legal liability for the acts of their members, many groups began officially disclaiming criminal acts. Some even claimed to be "love" groups rather than hate groups. When their members do commit violent acts, the groups with which they are affiliated typically claim to have nothing to do with the crimes. Some hate group leaders have also encouraged "lone wolf activism," telling their followers to act as individuals or in small cells, rather than in large groups.

Another law-enforcement difficulty in dealing with hate groups is that everyone in the United States is protected by the First Amendment, which guarantees citizens the freedom to join organizations—even hate groups—and to create, distribute, and possess bias-filled literature or symbols, so long as no criminal acts are committed.

The United States probably has a greater diversity of hate groups than any other nation, but other countries have their own hate groups. Around the turn of the twenty-first century, hate groups in the United States were increasing their ties to groups abroad. This trend has been facilitated by the growing ease of communication on the Internet. It has been estimated that there are hundreds, and perhaps even thousands, of Web sites with content devoted to hate. Although the content of some of these sites is illegal in other countries, most are protected by the First Amendment in the United States. For this reason, foreign hate groups often use American Internet service providers. These international ties further complicate law enforcement, both in the United States and abroad. Another complication is the often thin line between hate crimes and terrorism.

It is unclear what the full impact of organized hate groups is on hate crime. Most people who commit hate crimes do not belong to such groups, but it is possible that the groups' rhetoric and lit-

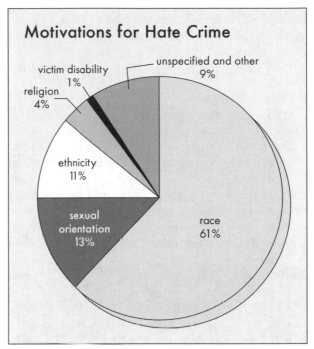

Source: U.S. Bureau of Justice Statistics, 2005. Data are based on nearly 3,000 incidents of hate crime reported to the National Incident-Based Reporting System (NIBRS) in 1997-1999. Because of rounding, percentages do not add up to 100.

erature may motivate unaffiliated people to commit hate crimes.

Combating Hate Crimes

Hate crime laws are not the only method that has been created to combat hate crimes. In some communities, task forces and other organizations have been created to improve hate crime responses and to improve communications among community groups and government agencies. These organizations typically involve representatives from law enforcement, government prosecutors, educational institutions, and other community-based groups.

Many organizations make fighting hate crimes a primary part of their mission. Some are large, such as the Jewish Anti-Defamation League and the National Gay and Lesbian Task Force. Others are grassroots groups, sometimes run by as few as one or two volunteers. In addition to tracking hate groups and lobbying for hate crime legislation, these groups' activities have included educating young people, adults, and police officers; victims' advocacy; and counseling and treatment of offenders.

Phyllis B. Gerstenfeld

Further Reading

Anti-Defamation League. *Hate Hurts: How Children Learn and Unlearn Prejudice*. New York: Chicken House, 2000. Guidebook to the development and reduction of prejudice in children.

Bell, Jeannine. *Policing Hatred: Law Enforcement, Civil Rights, and Hate Crime*. New York: New York University Press, 2002. Examination of how police departments deal with hate crimes.

Gerstenfeld, Phyllis B. *Hate Crimes: Causes, Controls, and Controversies*. Thousand Oaks, Calif.: Sage Publications, 2004. Comprehensive textbook on all aspects of hate crimes.

King, Joyce. *Hate Crime: The Story of a Dragging in Jasper, Texas*. New York: Pantheon, 2002. Vivid account of James Byrd's savage murder by white racists in Texas.

Levin, Jack. *The Violence of Hate: Confronting Racism, Anti-Semitism, and Other Forms of Bigotry*. Boston: Allyn & Bacon, 2002. Broad overview of hate crimes, with particular attention to crimes against members of racial, ethnic, and religious groups.

Neiwert, David. *Death on the Fourth of July: The Story of a Killing, a Trial, and Hate Crime in America*. New York: Palgrave Macmillan, 2004. True story of a hate crime in Washington that led to a death.

Perry, Barbara. *In the Name of Hate: Understanding Hate Crimes*. New York: Routledge, 2001. Sociological explanation of why hate crimes occur.

Streissguth, Thomas. *Hate Crimes*. New York: Facts On File, 2003. Overview and bibliography of hate crimes.

See also *Bowers v. Hardwick*; Computer crime; Ku Klux Klan; Lynching; *R.A.V. v. City of St. Paul*; September 11, 2001, attacks; Sexual harassment; Victimology; *Virginia v. Black*; *Wisconsin v. Mitchell*.

Hearings

Definition: Formal meetings used for inquiries, examinations, and determinations of issues arising within legal actions

Criminal justice issues: Investigation; trial procedures

Significance: Hearings often play important roles in deciding procedural and substantive issues before legal actions go to trial.

Hearings are formal or quasi-formal proceedings used by courts, legislatures, administrative agencies, and government departments to address specific issues. Judicial hearings normally focus an individual issues, or groups of issues, arising from larger cases. Hearings may be used as procedural tools to guarantee that due process rights are being protected. Examples of common hearings held in criminal cases include arraignments, which are used to enter initial pleas, review bail, and protect due process rights; preliminary hearings, in which probable cause in felony cases is examined; and motion hearings, in which procedural and substantive legal issues are considered.

As a rule, hearings before a court require the attendance of all parties to the cases. In most hearings, every party has a right to be heard regarding the issues at hand. An *ex parte* hearing is one in which only one party to a case is present. Such hearings are generally reserved to matters of an emergency nature, when notice and opportunity to be heard cannot reasonably be given to all parties.

Some hearings, such as preliminary hearings, may also require the attendance and testimony of witnesses and the presentation of evidence. Other hearings focus on legal questions only and typically provide the parties or their attorneys opportunities to address the courts on specific issues. In the most formal hearings, court reporters or other court officers preserve records of the matters discussed. In less formal hearings, no recording is done and the only record is the order entered by the judge following the hearing.

In criminal matters the most common hearings are preliminary hearings, in which questions of probable cause are examined by courts. Other hearing types include hearings on motions, evidence, and arraignment. Hearings *in camera* are held in the privacy of judges' chambers or anterooms, outside the normal confines of courtrooms.

Hearings are also used by legislative bodies to make inquiries into factual or legal issues of interest to the legislature. Such hearings are commonly conducted by committees or subcommittees of the entire legislature. In many instances, the legislative bodies or committees may possess the power of subpoena to compel witnesses to appear and testify. Such power affords legislative bodies the authority to investigate, normally a government action reserved to the executive branch, and to make inquiries into matters affecting legislation.

Government administrative agencies also use hearings as quasi-judicial exercises of their power. Such agencies are generally afforded this power through the legislation that creates them, and the purposes of such hearings are to take enforcement, corrective, or investigative action into matters arising under the agencies' authority. A common example can be found in many cases arising from charges of driving under the influence. The criminal charges are handled by the courts, but the question of how such crimes affect the offenders' driving privileges is normally handled through the administrative procedures of state driver's license bureaus.

Carl J. Franklin

Further Reading

Acker, J. R., and D. C. Brody. *Criminal Procedure: A Contemporary Perspective*. 2d ed. Sudbury, Mass.: Jones and Bartlett, 2004.

LaFave, Wayne R., Jerold H. Israel, and Nancy J. King. *Criminal Procedure*. 4th ed. St. Paul, Minn.: Thomson/West, 2004.

See also Arraignment; Criminal procedure; Inquests; Parole; Preliminary hearings; Testimony; Witnesses.

Hearsay

Definition: Out-of-court statements offered in evidence at trial to prove the truth of the matter asserted

Criminal justice issues: Evidence and forensics; legal terms and principles; witnesses

Significance: Generally if testimony is based on hearsay and no exception applies, it must be excluded from evidence at trial.

The procedural rule requiring the exclusion of hearsay is one of the central rules of evidence. For a statement to be considered hearsay, it must meet two requirements. First, it must be an assertive oral or written statement or act of conduct. Second, it must be offered at trial to prove the truth of the matter asserted. If the statement is offered for a purpose other than proving the truth of the matter asserted, for example to show the statement's effect on the hearer's state of mind, then it is not hearsay.

Hearsay is generally inadmissible at trial because opposing parties in cases cannot cross-examine the persons who made the original statements. However, there are several standard sets of exceptions, often based on necessity or reliability factors, to the hearsay exclusion rule. For example, when the original maker of the statement is unavailable to testify, perhaps because of death or lack of memory, certain hearsay statements can be admitted into evidence. Also, when out-of-court statements can be considered more reliable as evidence than in-court testimony of those who made the original statement, certain types of hearsay statements can be allowed. In addition, some types of statements, although they fit the traditional definition of hearsay, are considered to be exempt from the hearsay definition.

Mahalley D. Allen

Further Reading

Binder, David F. *Hearsay Handbook*. 4th ed. St. Paul, Minn.: West Publishing, 2001.

Fenner, G. Michael. *The Hearsay Rule*. Durham, N.C.: Carolina Academic Press, 2003.

Fisherman, Clifford S. *A Student's Guide to Hearsay*. 2d ed. New York: Matthew Bender, 1999.

See also Cross-examination; Evidence, rules of; Grand juries; Testimony; Witnesses.

High-speed chases

Definition: Vehicular pursuits by law-enforcement officers of suspected or known criminals or traffic law violators

Criminal justice issues: Police powers; traffic law

Significance: Police high-speed pursuits raise important legal and safety issues for both law-enforcement organizations and the public.

Vehicular pursuits have grown into a major social problem, as pursuit litigation costs taxpayers millions of dollars annually. In addition, such pursuits raise concerns regarding the safety of the officers and of the public. Officers' actions during a vehicular pursuit can have far-reaching implications for law-enforcement agencies as well as the officers involved. If an officer is found to have been negligent during the course of the

pursuit, subsequent litigation can be financially devastating for both department and officer.

Although the safety risk is not exorbitantly high, there is little doubt that high-speed chases can become dangerous quite quickly in some circumstances. Research has demonstrated that approximately half of all pursuit crashes occur within the first two minutes of a chase.

Despite varying rates of crashes, injuries, and fatalities, police pursuits have been supported by researchers and officers alike as a necessary component of police work. Officers believe that felony offenses are the most likely to result in a high-speed chase. Officers have also indicated that their approval or tolerance for a pursuit increases in proportion to the seriousness of the crime committed. When asked about the abolishment of pursuits, officers generally respond that the police, as a law-enforcement institution, would suffer a loss of respect from the public as well as potential offenders. Most police officers have indicated a belief that the danger to the pub-

An Iowa state police officer inspects the results of a high-speed chase that ended when the white car being pursued pulled into highway lanes moving traffic in the opposite direction and collided head-on with the second car, which was carrying a woman and two small children. *(AP/ Wide World Photos)*

Hot Pursuit

When deciding whether to pursue suspects, law-enforcement officers must weigh the benefits against the risks of engaging in what become dangerous chases. The use of high-speed, or hot, pursuits to apprehend fleeing suspects has received increased interest from the public and legal practitioners alike. As the result of high-profile pursuits that resulted in deaths and injuries, police pursuit policy has been called into question increasingly. A study published in 2002 estimated that police pursuits led to approximately 350 deaths per year and that the number of pursuits was increasing.

Most police pursuits tend to begin with stops for traffic violations and then escalate into chases. According to one study, 50 percent of all pursuit collisions occur within the first two minutes of the pursuits, and more than 70 percent of collisions occur within six minutes.

In response to the dangers of pursuits, rights organizations and interest groups have lobbied for law-enforcement departments to update their pursuit policies and change the ways they handle pursuits. An increasing number of police departments have prohibited officers from initiating chases of suspects who are suspected of committing only minor offenses. Critics contend that these new policies restrict officers from doing their jobs, especially when suspects who are stopped for minor offenses may actually be guilty of major crimes.

The debate continues between those who want to curtail pursuits to almost nonexistence and those who want to allow police the discretion to initiate and continue chases. Suggested compromises include better training for officers rather than policies that stop officers from chases and allow criminals possibly to go free. By training officers to respond more efficiently to pursuits, the dangers posed to the public, the officers, and the suspects may be reduced, while allowing officers to use their discretion to initiate and continue pursuits.

Jenephyr James

lic would increase, as would crime in general, if pursuits were eliminated as an acceptable means of apprehending suspects.

During the early twenty-first century, the Chicago and Los Angeles police departments developed new written policies to aid officers in instances of high-speed pursuit, in an effort to decrease threats to public safety. The new policies prohibit pursuits following most routine traffic violations and place tighter controls on officers in unmarked vehicles. The more restrictive policies are designed to increase police accountability and public safety, while simultaneously reducing the dangerousness of vehicular pursuits.

Data from the National Highway Traffic Safety Administration (NHTSA) and the Fatality Analysis Reporting Systems (FARS) have been used in an effort to come to terms with disparities observed among research studies concerning the precise number of fatalities occurring as a result of police pursuits. There have been discrepancies between many research endeavors and official data as to the exact number of individuals killed or injured as a result of police pursuits.

In spite of the perceived danger posed by pursuits, many scholars have noted a trend in the underreporting of police pursuits. A dramatic disparity between the official record of pursuits and those in which officers actually engage has emerged. It has been estimated that for every fourteen vehicular pursuits, as few as five are reported. This has been termed the "dark figure" of pursuits.

Legal Issues

Police pursuits have involved the legal system to a large extent. The Supreme Court, as well as district courts, has been called upon to rule on issues such as Fourth Amendment seizure considerations, Fourteenth Amendment due process concerns, and the use of force in pursuits.

The Supreme Court refuses to detail specifically the circumstances under which a pursuit amounts to a Fourth Amendment seizure, but it has suggested that a pursuit communicates to reasonable persons that they are not at liberty to ignore the police and go about their business. Originally, the Court agreed with the district courts by stating that a pursuit alone did not constitute a seizure protected under the Fourth Amendment. Later, this decision was overturned as justices deemed a pursuit an actual seizure applicable under the Fourth Amendment.

Additionally, the Court has ruled on issues related to the Fourteenth Amendment's guarantee of substantive due process. Justices have decided that only arbitrary conduct shocking to the conscience and unrelated to the legitimate object of arrest satisfies the requirements of the Fourteenth Amendment's guarantee of due process.

Twenty-first Century Developments

Many police departments have experimented with strategies to reduce, and possibly eliminate, the need for high-speed vehicular pursuits. Aerial pursuit is a tactic used by many larger urban departments. Aircraft such as helicopters can hover and maneuver in ways that can safely track a suspect fleeing on foot or in a vehicle. The use of aircraft is an effective, albeit costly, method of pursuing suspects safely and with minimal danger to bystanders. Ideally, costs saved in decreasing litigation arising from vehicular chases could be put to good use in increased air patrol and pursuit.

Larger metropolitan agencies are also experimenting with "stop" techniques, such as so-called sticky foam, pulse guns, and road spikes, in an effort to decrease the need for vehicular pursuits in apprehending suspects. The added degree of safety to the general population has motivated departments to increase funding for these new tools, and many new devices have a great deal of potential in this regard.

Wendy L. Hicks

Further Reading

Alpert, Geoffrey, and Lorie A. Fridell. *Police Vehicles and Firearms: Instruments of Deadly Force*. Prospect Heights, Ill.: Waveland Press, 1992. A broad overview of negligence and liability issues concerning vehicular pursuits and police shootings.

Burns, Ronald, G., and Charles E. Crawford. *Policing and Violence*. Upper Saddle River, N.J.: Prentice-Hall, 2001. An extensive treatment of many forms of violence affecting law-enforcement officers, including vehicular pursuits.

Kappeler, Victor E. *Critical Issues in Police Civil Liability*. Prospect Heights, Ill.: Waveland Press, 1993. A comprehensive look at the many varieties of civil liability affecting police agencies.

Palacios, William, Paul Cromwell, and Roger G. Dunham. *Crime and Justice in America—A Reader: Present Realities and Future Prospects*. 2d ed. Upper Saddle River, N.J.: Prentice-Hall, 2001. A reader designed to provide students with a glimpse into a variety of issues relevant to modern law enforcement in the United States.

Roberts, Albert, ed. *Critical Issues in Crime and Justice*. 2d ed. Thousand Oaks, Calif.: Sage, 2003. An edited book containing brief essays related to many contemporary law-enforcement issues.

Wrobleski, Henry M., and Karen M. Hess. *Introduction to Law Enforcement and Criminal Justice*. New York: Wadsworth, 2003. An introductory text designed to provide readers with a general overview of the function of police in a democratic government.

See also Deadly force; Highway patrols; Hit-and-run accidents; Police; Police academies; Proximate cause; Search and seizure; Speeding detection; Supreme Court, U.S.; Traffic law; Vicarious liability.

Highway patrols

Definition: State government law-enforcement agencies whose primary responsibilities are traffic management and traffic law enforcement

Criminal justice issues: Law-enforcement organization; traffic law

Significance: The two kinds of primary state law-enforcement agencies, highway patrols and state police, represent a departure from the American tradition of local control of police.

Like state police, highway patrols are state government law-enforcement agencies that are responsible for policing the highways within a state. The principal duty of highway patrols is to support the safe and efficient use of the highways by enforcing traffic laws, investigating traffic crashes, directing and controlling traffic, and promoting traffic safety. Highway patrol officers, sometimes called state traffic officers or state troopers, are generally not responsible for investigating crimes and enforcing criminal laws, except for those offenses that occur in their presence, are encountered incident to the performance of their traffic responsibilities, or as may be specifically authorized by state statute.

State governments generally began to establish law-enforcement agencies during the early twentieth century as a result of concerns with urban police corruption, ineffectiveness of rural sheriffs' departments, and the inability or unwillingness of both municipal and rural police to deal with violent labor disputes. As automobile use increased and highway systems expanded in the 1910's and 1920's, the need for motor vehicle regulation and law enforcement became apparent, further influencing the development of state law-enforcement agencies.

The state of Maryland is credited with establishing the first "highway patrol" in 1914, when the state commissioner of motor vehicles was authorized to appoint "motorcycle deputies" to enforce the motor vehicle laws. Most state law-enforcement agencies created after 1920 were essentially highway patrols, and the authority of these agencies has been expanded over time beyond strictly motor vehicle law enforcement, with some being reorganized as state police agencies.

In 2000, there were fifteen primary state law-enforcement agencies officially named "highway patrol" and twenty-two called "state police," but other agencies are named "state patrol" and "department of public safety," so it is not always possible to determine the type of agency from its name alone.

The traffic safety mission of highway patrols is an important responsibility, and highway patrols prioritize the apprehension of persons who drive under the influence of alcohol or drugs, utilizing a number of tactics including sobriety checkpoints to identify impaired drivers. Speeding is a major contributing factor in traffic crashes, and speed limit violations are a top enforcement priority. Highway patrols use radar and laser speed detection devices, as well as aircraft and other visual methods of detecting speeders. Highway patrols also focus on hazardous moving violations, vehicle equipment violations, and driver license and vehicle registration violations.

Preventable Deaths

In 2002, 42,815 people were killed in traffic crashes in the United States (41 percent of these crashes involved alcohol consumption). That figure was two and one-half times the number of murder victims (c. 16,204) during that same year. The crime of murder is often difficult for law-enforcement agents to prevent, but police can prevent many traffic crashes, saving lives and preventing injuries, by preventing or stopping unsafe driving behavior.

Other Traffic-Law Enforcers

Highway patrols and state police departments are not the only types of police agencies that are responsible for traffic-law enforcement. Many municipal police departments and sheriffs' departments also have traffic units. The New York City Police Department is unique because it has a unit within its Traffic Control Division called the "Highway Patrol" that is responsible for traffic management on the city's limited-access highways.

In most states, highway patrols have been statutorily assigned additional responsibilities, such as commercial vehicle safety, auto theft investigation, and security of state officials and buildings. Some highway patrols may provide services such as radio dispatch, crime laboratory, and criminal history records systems for other law-enforcement agencies. After the terrorist attacks of September 11, 2001, highway patrols have often been assigned homeland security responsibilities.

Raymond L. Sparks

Further Reading

Bechtel, H. Kenneth. *State Police in the United States: A Socio-Historical Analysis.* Westport, Conn.: Greenwood Press, 1995.

Torres, Donald A. *Handbook of State Police, Highway Patrols, and Investigative Agencies.* Westport, Conn.: Greenwood Press, 1987.

See also High-speed chases; Hit-and-run accidents; International Brotherhood of Police Officers; Law enforcement; Mothers Against Drunk Driving; Police; Sobriety testing; Speeding detection; State police; Traffic law.

Hit-and-run accidents

Definition: Vehicular accidents in which involved drivers leave the scene prior to the arrival of police

Criminal justice issues: Substance abuse; traffic law

Significance: Hit-and-run accidents pose serious concerns for law enforcement, insurance companies, and criminologists studying determinants of automobile accidents.

In managing traffic accidents, law-enforcement agencies rely primarily on citizen reporting and cooperation surrounding automobile accidents. When drivers disobey these laws and flee the scenes of accidents, they pose a fundamental threat to the system in place for traffic control, which is dependent on courteous and reliable drivers. Moreover, hit-and-run accidents limit investigations into accident causes that are necessary for proper liability and insurance purposes as well as the assessment of cause.

The proclivity of drivers to leave the scene of accidents has been a problem since the origins of organized transportation. The use of automobiles increased greatly during the late twentieth century, and problems caused by hit-and-run accidents have increased proportionately. Indeed, the increasing severity of punishments for drunk driving—the leading cause of motor vehicle accidents—has given drivers an added incentive to leave accident scenes.

Because data on accidents, as with all data on crime, are largely reliant on reporting by victims, it is difficult to document the exact number of accidents in which drivers leave the scene. Since a high percentage of serious accidents come to the attention of police, however, there is much existing evidence suggesting a high frequency of hit-and-run accidents. Indeed, studies have found that drivers leave the scene in 11 percent of serious accidents nationally and in 20 percent of all accidents involving fatalities.

Hit-and-run accidents have created various issues for those involved in defining, refining, and studying the phenomenon. In fact, there has been substantial debate over exactly what constitutes a hit-and-run accident. Should the term be applied only to motor vehicle accidents, or should it be extended to include situations in which objects fly off vehicles and hit other vehicles? Moreover, hit-and-run accidents provide a quandary for insurance agencies, with legal debates surrounding the type of uninsured protection that should be provided for victims of hit-and-run drivers.

Since people who are badly hurt in hit-and-run accidents may not receive the timely medical help they need when drivers leave the scene, many believe that hit-and-run accidents crimes should be punished more severely. In this regard, leaving the scene of an accident is deemed a criminal offense and generally receives a punishment even when the fleeing driver is not at fault in the accident.

Brion Sever

Further Reading

Broughton, J. *Hit and Run Accidents, 1990-2002.* Washington D.C.: Road Safety Division, Department of Transportation, 2004.

Druker, Linda. *The Hit and Run Accident: It's a Crime.* Boston: Massachusetts Office of the Commissioner of Probation, 1986.

Solnick, Sara, and David Hemenway. "Hit the Bottle and Run: The Role of Alcohol in Hit-and-Run Pedestrian Fatalities." *Journal of Studies on Alcohol* 55 (1994): 679-684.

See also Drunk driving; High-speed chases; Highway patrols; *Illinois v. Wardlow*; Manslaughter; Mothers Against Drunk Driving; Nonviolent resistance; Sobriety testing; Speeding detection; Traffic courts; Traffic law.

Hobbs Act

The Law: Federal law—also known as the Anti-Racketeering Act of 1946—that outlaws interference with interstate commerce through robbery or extortion

Date: Enacted on July 3, 1946

Criminal justice issues: Federal law; robbery, theft, and burglary

Significance: In addition to protecting interstate commerce from criminal activities, the Hobbs Act limited the ability of labor unions to enforce the interests of their constituencies within the boundaries of the law.

The bill that became the Hobbs Act was introduced by Alabama congressman Carl Hobbs on January 3, 1945, in response to a 1942 Supreme Court decision in favor of Local 807 of the Teamsters Union of New York. The Court's ruling had essentially nullified the Anti-Racketeering Act of 1934, and the purpose of the Hobbs Act was to put new antiracketeering legislation on the books by amending the 1934 act. Title I, section 2 of the Hobbs Act stated that it was a felony to obstruct, delay, or affect interstate commerce "in any way or degree" through robbery or extortion. To make the act effective, it redefined the key terms "commerce," "robbery," and "extortion."

Debate over the bill centered on its effect on workers and organized labor. Supporters of the bill argued that it protected farmers from harassment by the Teamsters Union and pointed out that Title II of the bill upheld previous laws guaranteeing labor's rights. Foes of the bill nevertheless questioned whether the bill was merely an antiracketeering measure or was also intended to be antilabor. They pointed out that the Hobbs Act would make it difficult for a union to picket a company effectively during a strike.

Thomas Winter

Further Reading

Smith, Richard W. "Interpreting the Constitution from Inside the Jury Box: Affecting Interstate Commerce as an Element of the Crime." *Washington and Lee Law Review* 55, no. 2 (Spring, 1998): 615-658.

Thierer, Adam D. *The Delicate Balance: Federalism, Interstate Commerce, and Economic Freedom in the Technological Age*. Washington, D.C.: Heritage Foundation, 1998.

Yarbrough, Steven C. "The Hobbs Act in the Nineties: Confusion or Clarification of the Quid pro Quo Standard in Extortion Cases Involving Public Officials." *Tulsa Law Review* 31 (1995).

See also Anti-Racketeering Act of 1934; Antitrust law; Blackmail and extortion; Conspiracy; Organized crime; Organized Crime Control Act; Racketeer Influenced and Corrupt Organizations Act.

Homeland Security Department

Identification: Federal cabinet-level department that coordinates the work of twenty-two separate agencies

Date: Established on March 1, 2003

Criminal justice issues: Federal law; law-enforcement organization; terrorism

Significance: The Homeland Security Department encourages active communication and collaboration among its numerous agencies and organizations to meet the department's primary goal of improving the security of the United States against possible terrorist attacks and natural disasters.

After the terrorist attacks of September 11, 2001, in New York City, Washington, D.C., and Pennsylvania, a massive reorganization of 180,000 federal employees from twenty-two different agencies was proposed by President George W. Bush and authorized by the Homeland Security Act of 2002. This controversial restructuring unified a sprawling federal network of institutions and organizations into the Homeland Security Department in order better to protect against terrorist threats, as well as natural and accidental disasters throughout the United States and its territories. The enormous consolidation merged major agencies such as the U.S. Border Patrol, Immigration and Naturalization Service, Secret

Service, Coast Guard, Customs Service, Federal Emergency Management Agency (FEMA), and Transportation Security Administration under a single cabinet-level department on March 1, 2003.

With a proposed budget in 2005 of more than $40 billion, the department was tasked with overseeing and managing the daily operations of protecting national targets, coordinating domestic intelligence, preparedness, research initiatives, and monitoring the flow of trade and legal immigration across all U.S. ports of entry. Agencies in the Homeland Security Department are divided among four major divisions: Border and Transportation Security, Emergency Preparedness and Response, Science and Technology, and Information Analysis and Infrastructure Protection.

Borders, Transportation, and National Preparedness

The Homeland Security Department's Border and Transportation directorate oversees security and management of immigration, borders, and transportation operations in the United States. Its Citizenship and Immigration Services branch (USCIS) provides all services and benefits relating to immigration. Customs and Border Protection (CBP) serves as the enforcement agency and oversees the legal entry of goods, services, and persons into and out of ports of entry.

The Federal Protective Service is charged with protecting all federal buildings and installations. Another major responsibility of this directorate includes the monitoring of transportation systems by the Transportation Security Administration (TSA). With an estimated 11 million trucks, 2 million road cars, and 55,000 calls on ports per year, the TSA has the enormous task of protecting and monitoring all forms of transit, including air travel, across the country. Also working closely with other agencies in this directorate are the Animal and Plant Health Inspection Service, the Office of Domestic Preparedness, and the Federal Law Enforcement Training Center (FLETC).

The seal of the Department of Homeland Security contains a shield with images of the land, sea, and air to represent the scope of the department's responsibilities, and twenty-two stars for the twenty-two agencies absorbed by the new department. (AP/Wide World Photos)

The federal Emergency Preparedness and Response directorate combines agencies from the Departments of Justice and Health and Human Services with FEMA. These agencies now collectively deal with emergency disaster planning and response. Through grants provided to state and local response personnel such as police, fire, rescue, and medical response teams, this division ensures adequate training, equipment, and planning for emergencies.

A central component of preparedness planning involves coordinating large-scale hypothetical disaster drills across communities to test their readiness for attacks using nuclear and biological weapons and attacks with weapons of mass destruction. Other agencies under this directorate focus on the stockpiling of drugs to treat biochemical assaults and training medical workers on how to treat victims. Domestic Emergency Response Teams and the National Domestic Preparedness Office work with FEMA and other agencies to develop comprehensive strategies for planning, prevention, response to and recovery from acts of terrorism and to assist when natural disasters strike.

Scientific Advancement and Threat Assessment

All available technological and scientific anti-terrorism groups across the federal government were combined under the Science and Technology directorate of the Homeland Security Department. These organizations work together and provide states with federal guidelines regarding responses to weapons of mass destruction. By merging resources, labs, and scientific knowledge formerly scattered across the Departments of Energy, Agriculture, and Defense, the Homeland Security Department tries to assist local and state public safety officials in developing sound plans to monitor and defend their communities.

The final group included in the Homeland Security Department is that of the Information Analysis and Infrastructure Protection directorate. Its agencies gather and analyze information from many national agencies and then issue threat assessment warnings to U.S. citizens and targets. The Homeland Security Advisory System issues these warnings to specific and general targets and encourages continuous public vigilance. The Advisory System also provides information to local and state authorities, the private sector, and international partners as intelligence is received.

A color-coded threat level system is used to communicate the perceived danger to the public and has been activated when threats have been discovered. These warnings attempt to protect important infrastructure systems that are most prone to attack, including food, water, health, emergency, and telecommunications systems. Using a federal television campaign, the Homeland Security Department has also encouraged Americans to make family emergency plans in the case of a terrorist attack or natural disaster.

Additional Agencies and Initiatives

In addition to Homeland Security Department's four directories, the U.S. Coast Guard and Secret Service are also part of the Homeland Security Department. The Coast Guard monitors the coastal and interstate waters of the United States and its territories, assists other agencies in the prevention of the illegal entry of aliens and contraband, and provides rescue missions and aid to vessels in distress.

The Secret Service also remains intact under the Homeland Security Department and reports directly to the secretary of Homeland Security. First established in 1865, the Secret Service was initially created to protect against counterfeit currency. Perhaps the service's most visible role includes its responsibility for protecting former, current, and elected presidents and vice presidents, along with their immediate families. The service also protects major political candidates, visiting diplomats, and other high-ranking government officials. The Secret Service Uniformed Division has also guarded the grounds of the White House since 1860. Other initiatives of the department focus on potential threats to banking and finance systems, health and safety of citizens, and the monitoring of potential targets and intelligence across the world.

In an attempt to expand collaboration among federal, state, and local governments, as well as organizations in the private sector, the Homeland Security Department is building a coalition of organizations that are linked together by a computer-based counterterrorism communications network. In 2005, the Homeland Security Information Network linked agencies in more than fifty major cities, all fifty states, Washington, D.C., and five U.S. territories through a state-of-the-art computer communication system. This system relays sensitive, nonclassified information to more than one hundred different agencies and approximately one thousand users who share a joint counterterrorism mission.

Future expansion of this project targets including smaller agencies at county levels and private businesses and sharing classified information among cleared parties. This system aims to offer real-time information across geographical regions and between public and private sectors in order better to identify, share, and respond to terrorist threats.

Future Challenges

With the massive integration of numerous agencies across departments, the transition of key personnel, services, and cross-authorized duties has not been accomplished without difficulties. Audits of the department's financial statements are used to determine what corrective measures are necessary to streamline government spending and identify potential wastes of taxpayer funds. Dramatic changes within the agencies consolidated into the department are expected to continue as the agencies are studied and redundant jobs and assignments are eliminated. Budgetary and human resource management has been a critical area of concern from the inception of the integration of so many independent agencies under one umbrella department.

The changing of employee benefits, the cutting of automatic overtime pay for personnel, the elimination of seniority and rank for those persons being adopted into new agencies, and the potential loss of trained employees to the private sector are all challenging issues that the department will address in the years to come. With so many important responsibilities concerning national defense, homeland security, disaster preparedness, and transportation and border protections resting on the shoulders of the Homeland Security Department, this fledgling department is expected to remain in the public eye and front and center on the war on terrorism in post-September 11, 2001, America.

Denise Paquette Boots

Further Reading

Brzezinski, Matthew. *Fortress America: On the Frontline of Homeland Security—An Inside Look at the Coming Surveillance State*. New York: Bantam Books, 2004. Offering both hypothetical and real stories about the war on terror since September 11, 2001, this book takes a critical look at the Department of Homeland Security, the sacrificing of civil liberties, and damage done to international alliances.

Flynn, Stephen. *America the Vulnerable: How Our Government Is Failing to Protect Us*. New York: HarperCollins, 2004. A former Coast Guard commander offers compelling evidence of the continued threats to soft and hard targets in the United States and argues that much more should be done by the govern-ment and private sector to fight against terrorists.

Kettl, Donald F. *Department of Homeland Security's First Year: A Report Card*. New York: Century Foundation Books, 2004. This directory offers job descriptions in depth that are available through Homeland Security. It also includes relevant Web sites, phone contacts, hiring information, and advice for interviewing and preparing for a variety of careers through the Homeland Security Department.

Mena, Jesus. *Homeland Security: Techniques and Technologies*. Hingham, Mass.: Charles River Media, 2004. Examination of the efforts related to cyberterrorism and what systems and artificial intelligence are used to aggregate, integrate, and assimilate data that is integral to business, government, and individuals.

White, Jonathan R. *Defending the Homeland: Domestic Intelligence Law Enforcement and Security*. Stamford, Conn.: Wadsworth, 2003. Law-enforcement perspective provided that details how the criminal justice system as changed since September 11.

See also Attorney general of the United States; Border patrols; Coast Guard, U.S.; Computer information systems; Deportation; Drugs and law enforcement; Immigration and Naturalization Service; Law enforcement; Patriot Act; President, U.S.; Secret Service, U.S.; September 11, 2001, attacks; Skyjacking; Terrorism.

Hoover, J. Edgar

Identification: Director of the Federal Bureau of Investigation (FBI), 1924-1972
Born: January 1, 1895, Washington, D.C.
Died: May 2, 1972, Washington, D.C.
Criminal justice issues: Federal law; government misconduct; law-enforcement organization
Significance: J. Edgar Hoover built the FBI into the world's foremost scientific law-enforcement agency, but his personal abuse of his virtually unregulated power precipitated a decline in his reputation.

A lawyer at the age of twenty-two, Hoover entered the Justice Department in 1917, investigating aliens and communists during and after World War I. In 1924 he became director of the Bureau of Investigation, then under the cloud of Harding administration scandals. Hoover upgraded recruiting and training standards and in 1935 renamed it the Federal Bureau of Investigation (FBI). With its extensive fingerprint file, crime-detection laboratory, training academy, and Crime Information Center (created in 1967) to assist state and local police, the FBI gained a worldwide reputation for scientific law enforcement.

These achievements were enhanced by skillful public relations. During the Depression, Hoover and his agents became national heroes—glamorized through films and radio programs as well as Hoover's own books and articles—for hunting down criminals such as John Dillinger.

During World War II, the FBI guarded against enemy agents and saboteurs. After the war, the target became American communism. Much publicized was the FBI's association with the House Committee on Un-American Activities, which convicted Alger Hiss and Julius and Ethel Rosenberg of espionage for the Soviet Union. Later, FBI files assisted Senator Joseph R. McCarthy's communist witch-hunts.

Hoover's writings—*Persons in Hiding* (1938), *Masters of Deceit* (1958), and *A Study of Communism* (1962)—consistently gave the impression that he alone was America's bulwark against every evil, from internal radicals to foreign agents. Beyond such self-aggrandizement, however, Hoover's personal life was well hidden. His own voyeuristic obsession with spying on others and amassing damaging information on their private lives undoubtedly made him acutely conscious of protecting his own privacy. A 1991 biography by Curt Gentry, *J. Edgar Hoover: The Man and the Secrets*, includes descriptions of Hoover as a secret transvestite.

From the 1950's into the 1970's, Hoover's Counter-Intelligence Program (COINTELPRO) investigated individuals and organizations con-

J. Edgar Hoover during his early years as director of the Federal Bureau of Investigation. *(AP/Wide World Photos)*

sidered dangerous: Martin Luther King, Jr., the Communist Party, the Ku Klux Klan, the Black Panthers, labor unions, student Vietnam War protesters, and civil rights organizations. Many legitimately feared the FBI's power and its stated mandate to investigate any radical opposition to conventional political beliefs. FBI agents were to act on the side of national security, needing only the "smoking gun" rule to burglarize organizations' offices. FBI wiretaps were coded and indexed in a top-secret "electronic surveillance card file."

Hoover consistently denied the existence of organized crime, despite its exposé by the Kefauver Senate committee, perhaps because his gambling in Mafia clubs made him vulnerable to the mob. The stormy relationship between Hoover and Attorney General Robert F. Kennedy stemmed from Kennedy's investigation of Mafia activities and from the FBI's laxity in enforcing federal civil rights laws.

By the 1970's demands for Hoover's resignation had become widespread. After his death, his reputation was tarnished by information published through 1967's Freedom of Information Act and contained in a 1976 Senate study of intelligence activities. Hoover was found to have abused his power and, beginning in 1925, to have accumulated damaging files on twenty-five million people, including presidents and members of Congress. Even before Hoover's death, legislation limited FBI "information fishing expeditions" that placed Hoover beyond the control of the attorney general and the president. So great was his prestige and power that no president dared remove him from his position.

To some, Hoover was a symbol of law enforcement, patriotism, and anticommunism; to others he symbolized government repression and persecution of dissenters and reformers. All agree that he was one of the most controversial figures in American history.

Daniel C. Scavone

Further Reading

Churchill, Ward, and Jim Vander Wall. *The COINTELPRO Papers: Documents from the FBI's Secret Wars Against Dissent in the United States*. 2d ed. Cambridge, Mass.: South End Press, 2002. Documentary history of the COINTELPRO program initiated by Hoover.

De Loach, Cartha "Deke." *Hoover's FBI: The Inside Story by Hoover's Trusted Lieutenant*. Washington, D.C.: Regnery, 1995. Sympathetic first-person account by one of Hoover's top aides. The book is particularly interesting in its story of the efforts to remove Hoover from office.

Kessler, Ronald. *The Bureau: The Secret History of the FBI*. New York: St. Martin's Press, 2002. Critical history of the bureau emphasizing its abuses under Hoover.

See also Bank robbery; COINTELPRO; Espionage; Federal Bureau of Investigation; Organized crime; Prohibition; Ten-most-wanted lists.

House arrest

Definition: Intermediate form of sanction that allows offenders to remain in their homes under specific restrictions

Criminal justice issues: Probation and pretrial release; punishment; sentencing

Significance: House arrests are an alternative to incarceration, one often used in order to help manage the strained resources of correctional facilities

House arrest is a punitive sanction that allows convicted offenders to remain in their homes instead of going to prison. There are three levels of house arrest: curfew, home detention, and home confinement. Specific restrictions are imposed at all three levels. Curfew, the mildest version of house arrest, is frequently used for juveniles and requires that the offender be home by a certain time each day. The next level, home detention, is more restrictive in that it limits the amount of time that offenders may be away from their homes and also dictates where they may go. For example, travel is usually prohibited except for that which involves work, medical treatment appointments, or church. The most restrictive level of house arrest is home incarceration, calling for offenders to remain at their homes the majority of the time, with allowances only to attend specific and limited appointments.

House arrest can be used as a stand-alone sanction, however, it is commonly used in conjunction with probation. For house arrest to be effective, there must be an organized and well-equipped system to monitor offenders. House arrest has been touted as an effective response to prison overcrowding by allowing nonviolent offenders and offenders convicted of minor offenses to serve their correctional time within their own community.

House arrest has also been considered an effective way to reduce the increasing costs of corrections. The average annual amount spent monitoring an offender on house arrest was $5,000, compared to a cost of $35,000 to incarcerate an offender. In some jurisdictions, certain expenses associated with house arrest are passed to the offender, making the financial aspect an attractive one to proponents of house arrest. Other benefits associated with house arrest extend beyond the offender and may positively affect the stability of the offender's family. Because the offender is allowed to maintain employment, that person is better able to contribute to the family's well-being.

Just as there are perceived benefits of using house arrest as an intermediate sanction, there are perceived problems. Although offenders may be ordered to be home daily by a prescribed time, opportunities exist for the offender to get around the mandate, particularly when telephone calls are used for tracking the offender's compliance. Also, offenders are often admonished to refrain from socializing with known felons, but this mandate is difficult to monitor and control when the offender is under house arrest. Difficulties also arise when the monitoring of offenders is contracted to outside vendors who use rotating staff who have little personal knowledge of the offender.

Tonya Y. Willingham

Further Reading

Del Carmen, A. *Corrections*. St. Paul, Minn.: Coursewise, 2000.

McShane, M., and W. Krause. *Community Corrections*. New York: Macmillan, 1993.

Rackmill, S. J. "An Analysis of Home Confinement as a Sanction." *Federal Probation* 58, no. 1 (1994): 45-53.

See also Community-based corrections; Electronic surveillance; Halfway houses; Parole; Prison overcrowding; Probation; Suspended sentences; Work camps.

Hung juries

Definition: Juries that are unable to reach innocent or guilty verdicts by the required voting margin

Criminal justice issues: Juries; trial procedures; verdicts

Significance: The controversy over the phenomenon of hung juries has been the catalyst for empirical research and jury reform.

The occurrence of hung juries within the criminal justice system has long been a controversial and intriguing phenomenon. Hung juries have remained an issue of concern over time because of their potential negative consequences, which include the emotional impact on the victims and families and the costs of retrying cases.

There are many explanations as to why jury members fail to convict or acquit a defendant. A hung jury may be the result of individual, group, or evidentiary factors. Many critics of the jury trial propose that hung juries result from failures within the group interaction during deliberation. Hung juries have been attributed to jurors' poor intelligence, personality eccentricities, corruption, difficulty with evidence comprehension, and outright refusal to follow the law (such as jury nullification). In addition, ambiguous or inadequate evidence presentation by the attorneys may also result in a jury deadlocking.

Understanding the actual factors contributing to hung juries is challenging. For example, many jurisdictions do not maintain systematic records of jury trials that hang because they occur so infrequently. More specifically, jury deliberations have long been viewed as a "black box" demanding absolute confidentiality. As a result, early research on juries, and more specifically on hung juries, was scarce before the mid-1970's. Groundbreaking and early empirical research was conducted on the American jury by Harry Kalven, Jr., and Hans Zeisel. Their study briefly addressed the issue of hung juries and found that hung juries occurred at a rate of 5.5 percent, or roughly one in twenty.

The catalyst for empirical research on the jury system and hung juries was the U.S. Supreme Court decision in *Apodaca v. Oregon* (1972). In *Apodaca*, the Court decided unanimous verdicts were not constitutionally mandated in noncapital cases and that a majority vote by jurors could convict or acquit a defendant. The Court's reasoning was that allowing majority-rule verdicts would increase the efficiency of the court process and decrease the cost of a jury trial, with little or no negative consequences on the quality of jury deliberations.

Subsequent research confirmed that the rate of hung juries and the length of jury deliberations decreased when majority-rule verdicts were used. However, empirical research also revealed that nonunanimous verdicts decreased the quality of deliberation and decreased juror satisfaction with the deliberation process. For example, once a majority verdict was met, the minority or dissenting opinions no longer needed to be considered.

Erin J. Farley

Further Reading

Abramson, Jeffery. *We, the Jury: The Jury System and the Ideal of Democracy.* Cambridge, Mass.: Harvard University Press, 1994.

Hannaford-Agor, Paula L., Valerie P. Hans, Nicole L. Mott, and G. Thomas Munsterman. *Are Hung Juries a Problem?* Williamsburg, Va.: National Center for State Courts, 2002.

Kalven, Harry, and Hans Zeisel. *The American Jury.* Boston: Little, Brown, 1966.

See also *Baker v. Wingo*; Dismissals; Jury duty; Jury nullification; Jury sequestration; Jury system; Mistrials; Trials.

Hurtado v. California

The Case: U.S. Supreme Court ruling on due process

Date: Decided on March 3, 1884

Criminal justice issues: Constitutional protections; testimony; trial procedures

Significance: For the first time, the Supreme Court indicated that the due process clause of the Fourteenth Amendment might apply some provisions of the Bill of Rights to the states.

After Joseph Hurtado learned that his wife was having an affair, he shot and killed his rival. California authorities charged him with murder by filing an information—a formal accusation by a public prosecutor—in a state court. He was tried, convicted, and sentenced to death.

Hurtado appealed to the U.S. Supreme Court. He noted that the Fifth Amendment would have prevented the federal government from putting him on trial unless he had been indicted by a grand jury. He claimed that the Fourteenth Amendment's prohibition against a state's depriving "any person of life, liberty, or property without due process of law" meant that the state of California was bound to observe the same procedural limitations imposed on the federal government by the Fifth Amendment. The Supreme Court rejected his claim.

The Fifth Amendment contains a list of specific prohibitions on the federal government. It may not subject anyone to double jeopardy, self-incrimination, or trial without prior indictment by a grand jury. In addition, it prohibits the federal government from depriving anyone of "life, liberty, or property without due process of law." Noting that the Constitution contained no superfluous language, the Court reasoned that had the framers of the Fifth Amendment meant "due process of law" to include the right to be indicted before trial, they would not have listed indictment as a separate, additional requirement.

The Fourteenth Amendment protects against state deprivation of due process of law. The Court ruled that the phrase has the same limitations it had in the Fifth Amendment. Consequently, the Fourteenth Amendment due process clause does not prohibit the state's use of an information instead of an indictment.

Due process of law means that states cannot impose "arbitrary power" on their subjects. "Law," said the Court, "is something more than mere will exerted as an act of power." It excludes "acts of attainder, bills of pains and penalties, acts of confiscation . . . and other similar special, partial, and arbitrary exertions of power."

Justice John Harlan disagreed with the majority's interpretation of the due process clauses. He said that the framers of the Fifth Amendment listed certain prohibitions not because they were something other than due process of law but because they were essential to it.

Hurtado v. California is important for two reasons. Though the Court ruled that the due process clause of the Fourteenth Amendment did not incorporate the indictment requirement of the Fifth Amendment, it opened the door to incorporation by stating that certain standards of justice—some of which might be found in the Bill of Rights—did apply against the states. In addition, the majority opinion is a classic statement distinguishing the rule of law from the arbitrary exercise of power.

William H. Coogan

Further Reading

Berger, Raoul. *The Fourteenth Amendment and the Bill of Rights.* Norman: University of Oklahoma Press, 1990.

Curtis, Michael Kent. *No State Shall Abridge: The Fourteenth Amendment and the Bill of Rights.* Durham, N.C.: Duke University Press, 1990.

Lewis, Thomas T., ed. *The Bill of Rights.* 2 vols. Pasadena, Calif.: Salem Press, 2002.

Orth, John V. *Due Process of Law: A Brief History.* Lawrence: University Press of Kansas, 2003.

See also Bill of Rights, U.S.; Due process of law; Grand juries; Incorporation doctrine; Indictment; Information; Supreme Court, U.S.

Identity theft

Definition: Crime of wrongfully obtaining and using personal data of others for one's own profit

Criminal justice issues: Business and financial crime; fraud; robbery, theft, and burglary

Significance: Every year, nearly ten million Americans lose access to personal accounts and lose assets when they have their identities stolen in what the federal government has called the nation's-fastest growing crime.

Criminal identity theft occurs when individuals, without permission, transfer, take, or use for their own benefit the personal and financial information of others. The types of information sought by identity thieves include social security numbers, driver's license information, passport and citizenship paperwork, financial account numbers and passwords, insurance records, tax returns, and credit card numbers and account information.

Types of Identity Theft

Five main categories of identity theft have been reported in the United States since the early 1990's. These categories serve as benchmarks for the numerous subvarieties of identity theft. They fall under the broad headings of true name, or cloning, identity theft; account takeovers; criminal identity theft; Internet and telecommunications fraud; and professional identity theft.

True name, or cloning, identity theft occurs when offenders use other people's personal information to open new accounts in the victims' own names. The information sought by this type of identity thief usually focuses on social security numbers, which are used to establish lines of credit in the potential victims' names. Once thieves gain access to their victims' social security numbers, they literally begin to take over their victims' full identities.

Account takeover occurs when criminals gain access to other persons' existing accounts and use them to make fraudulent transactions. This type of identity theft is most often used to purchase merchandise, to lease cars and dwellings, and to manipulate and bleed savings accounts, retirement portfolios, and other assets.

Criminal identity theft occurs when criminals give to law-enforcement officials the identifying data of other persons in place of their own and when the impostors present counterfeit documents containing other persons' personal data. Such impostors often fraudulently obtain driver's licenses and social security cards in their victims' names and provide these false identification documents to law enforcement. When impostors lack the appropriate visual identification cards, they give law enforcement the names of friends or relatives.

Internet and telecommunications identity theft may be the fastest-growing type of identity theft in the world. Internet and telecommunications technologies allow offenders more quickly and efficiently to open new accounts, strike online merchant sites, sell and share information electronically with other criminals, and then simply disappear into the dark confines of cyberspace. Telemarketing schemes, electronic mail and regular mail offers, site cloning, using chatrooms from public lists, and various forms of fraudulent sweepstakes and prize giveaways are the most common techniques used to carry out this type of identity theft.

Professional identity theft usually consists of concerted efforts of two or more professional thieves who work together to amass as much money and merchandise as possible by stealing and using others' identities before being detected. These criminals sometimes pose as representatives of charitable organizations; volunteers in community-affiliated groups; members of social associations; and representatives of known professional organizations, such as state police or local fire department unions. In all cases, their sole purpose is to gain their potential victims' personal and financial information. In some extreme cases, these criminals create false merchant sites to elicit personal information or employ hacking and cracking methods to infiltrate directly the valid organizations they claim to represent in order to gather personal information about the organizations' donors.

Identity Theft Techniques

Several common techniques are used to conduct identity theft. Some criminals conduct what is known as "dumpster diving" expeditions, in which they literally rummage through business and residential trash cans and dumpsters to search for copies of checks, credit card and bank statements, credit card solicitations, or other records that contain personal information. After the thieves harvest such information, it becomes possible for them to assume the identities of other persons and take control of the latters' active accounts or even establish new accounts in their victims' names.

A second technique used by identity thieves has been dubbed "shoulder surfing." In this technique, offenders literally look over the shoulders of their potential victims as the latter enter personal information into telephones, computers, and automatic teller machines (ATMs). They may also wait for potential victims to leave credit card receipts on restaurant tables or in trash receptacles near automatic teller machines, banks, and residences. After the offenders get hold of codes, passwords, and account information, they begin the process of victimization.

Among the newest techniques for stealing identity information are those known as "under the color of authority" and "skimming." Thieves using the former technique fraudulently obtain credit reports by using their employers' authorized access to credit report companies without authorization and by posing as landlords, employers, and other persons who may have legitimate rights to see people's personal information. Skimming occurs when thieves steal credit and debit card account numbers when the cards are processed at restaurants, retail stores, and other business

locations. Thieves employing this technique use using a special data-collecting device known as a "skimmer."

One of the newest and most innovative techniques used by identity theft criminals is called "phishing"—a technique used on the Internet that plays on the word "fishing." Phishing identity thieves send out large volumes of unsolicited electronic mail messages that appear to be from legitimate companies requesting personal account information. Criminals then use the data they harvest to their own advantage by robbing the unsuspecting victims' accounts.

History

Identity theft is not a new crime phenomenon. Criminals have been committing similar offenses for centuries. Classic examples are petty thieves who steal wallets and purses and use the credit cards in them to go on shopping sprees. Until recent years, such crimes were categorized simply as fraud and petty theft. However, with vast advances in computing and telecommunication technologies of the late 1990's, a new wave of identity thieves emerged who were skilled at concealing both their true identities and their illicit behavior.

Fraudulent transactions on the Internet are the most common form of identity theft crimes.

States and Districts with Highest Identity-Theft Rates in 2003

Rank	District or state	Victims	Victims per 100,000 residents
1	District of Columbia	704	123.1
2	California	30,738	90.7
3	Arizona	4,517	88.0
4	Nevada	1,705	85.3
5	Texas	14,357	68.9
6	Florida	10,898	68.2
7	New York	12,698	66.9
8	Washington	3,894	66.1
9	Maryland	3,497	66.0
10	Oregon	2,200	64.3

Source: National and State Trends in Identity Fraud and Identity Theft, January-December 2003. Washington, D.C.: Federal Trade Commission, 2004.

Before the rise of the Internet, identity theft criminals had to appear in person at banks and lending institutions to apply for accounts and faced a high risk of being caught. However, with the instant credit accounts now available on the Internet, the likelihood of identity theft criminals being caught has been significantly reduced, while the potential rewards for thievery have increased greatly.

It was not until 1998 that the federal government finally acknowledged the threat posed by identity theft and enacted legislation against it. The first federal law of its kind, the Identity Theft and Assumption Deterrence Act of 1998 served as a model for the individual states to follow in drafting their identity theft legislation.

Prevalence

The full damage done by identity theft is difficult to measure since identity theft is often the means by which criminals commit other crimes. Moreover, victims may not even know they have been victimized for more than a full year after the fact. It has been estimated that average identity theft victims do not know they have been victimized until fourteen to sixteen months after the crimes occur. Because of their consequent embarrassment or shame, they often do not file criminal complaints.

In fiscal year 2003, the federal government estimated that American financial and business institutions lost about $48 billion to identity theft, and individual citizens lost about $5 billion to the crime. The federal government now admits that identity theft is the fastest-growing category of crime in the United States. According to the Federal Trade Commission, in 2003 an estimated 10 million Americans had been victims of identity theft during the previous year; 27 million had been victims during the previous five years; and

During a February, 2005, news conference, Senator Charles Schumer of New York, the chairman of a committee investigating identity theft and information brokers, calls attention to posters displaying personal information on film stars Brad Pitt and Jennifer Aniston that was taken from a databank on the World Wide Web. Schumer wished to dramatize the ease with which identity thieves could collect information. *(AP/Wide World Photos)*

Most Common Forms of Identity Theft

Rank	Type	Percentage of victims
1	Credit card: establishing new accounts & defrauding existing accounts	33%
2	Phone or utilities: establishing new telecommunications accounts & defrauding existing accounts	21%
3	Other: includes medical, internet related, rental, bankruptcy, and insurance fraud	19%
4	Bank: establishing new accounts & defrauding existing accounts	17%
5	Employment related: taking of confidential personal and or corporate identities	11%
6	Loans: includes fraudulent business, personal, student, and auto loans	6%

Source: Federal Trade Commission, 2003. Percentages based on 500,000 complaints received. Percentages add up to more than 100 because some victims reported more than one type of identity theft.

close to 35 million had been victims during the previous ten years.

Investigation

The need for stronger law enforcement against identity theft is evident in the fact that only about one in seven hundred cases results in capture and successful prosecution of offenders by federal authorities. The rate is even smaller for local and state authorities. One of the most pressing issues facing law enforcement is how to investigate and successfully prosecute the often complex identity theft cases. Since the year 2000, all fifty U.S. states have enacted identity theft laws.

Many federal, state, and local law-enforcement agencies and private institutions participate in the identity theft investigation and prosecution. These range from such federal regulatory agencies as the Federal Trade Commission to nonprofit organizations, such as the Identity Theft Resource Center in California, that work closely with law enforcement.

Section 5 of the federal Identity Theft Act makes the Federal Trade Commission (FTC) a central clearinghouse for identity theft complaints. The law requires the FTC to log and acknowledge complaints, provide victims with relevant information, and refer their complaints to such entities as major national consumer reporting agencies and other state and local law-enforcement agencies.

The U.S. Department of Justice encourages federal prosecutors to make greater use of the resources on identity theft provided by regulatory agencies and nonprofit watchdog groups. The FTC's Consumer Sentinel database, for example, is an invaluable resource for federal agents and prosecutors; it provides instant access to thousands of complaints filed about possible identity thefts. In addition, the Internet Fraud Complaint Center—a joint project of the Federal Bureau of Investigation (FBI) and the National White Collar Crime Center—provides investigators with information about Internet fraud schemes in which identity theft may figure.

The Department of Justice recognizes that all identity theft victimizations are serious offenses, even when no money is actually taken. Identity theft demands a comprehensive response that involves prosecution for identity theft and other offenses as appropriate laws prescribe. This holistic approach requires legitimate and continual cooperation among federal, state, and local law-enforcement agencies.

On the federal investigative level, violations of the Identity Theft Act are examined by such investigative agencies as the U.S. Secret Service, the Federal Bureau of Investigation, and the U.S. Postal Inspection Service. They are then prosecuted directly by the Department of Justice.

The Department of Justice prosecutes identity theft and fraud cases under a variety of federal statutes, while also assisting various state and local district attorneys in preparing and prosecuting their cases. Federal prosecutors in various states also make use of multiagency task forces that share resources to investigate identity theft and other related white-collar offenses. The Secret Service in particular recognizes the exponential growth of the electronic and computer world and developed a plan of action in late 1995 to create nontraditional task forces to assist in combating such crimes as identity theft.

In the past, traditional task forces consisted largely of law-enforcement officers and investigators to the exclusion of other parties that could make considerable contributions. This new type of nontraditional task force evolved into what the Secret Service named the Electronic Crimes Task Force. The first of its kind was established in the state of New York in 1995 and consisted of not only law-enforcement officers and analysts from various different levels, but also prosecutors, private industry professionals, and academics. By establishing new relationships with private sector organizations and numerous university scholars, the task force opened itself up to sources of information and communication lines with limitless potential. Now, task forces in every region of the United States deal with identity theft and related crimes. Although the victimization rate continues to increase, the efforts of both investigators and prosecutors continue to grow stronger and more effective, with hopes of eventually winning the war against identity thieves.

Since 1999, the U.S. Department of Justice has chaired the Identity Theft Subcommittee of the Attorney General's Council on White-Collar Crime. The subcommittee brings together representatives from federal, state, and local law-enforcement and regulatory agencies on a monthly basis. They share data about identity theft developments and promote interagency cooperation and coordination on identity theft enforcement and prevention efforts.

Prosecution and Punishment

Since Congress's enactment of the Identity Theft Act in 1998, federal prosecutors have made increasing use of the law's power and have issued sentences to convicted offenders that have ranged as high as fifteen years in prison, along with substantial fines, for offenses that net at least one thousand dollars during any twelve-month period. In July of 2004, President George W. Bush signed the Identity Theft Penalty Enhancement Act, which expanded maximum penalties for identity theft. The new legislation also defined a new offense, "aggravated identity theft," as a charge that can be added to other criminal charges in crimes that employ stolen identities, such as terrorist acts and various forms of fraud.

In addition, to ensure that persons convicted under the federal identity theft statutes receive appropriately tough sentences, the United States Sentencing Commission, with unwavering support from the Department of Justice, issued new guidelines for identity theft crimes. Now, even cases in which there is no monetary loss or that involve first-time offenders may result in prison sentences. The guidelines also encourage harsher penalties for more severe offenses, such as those that seriously affect their victims' lives.

Paul M. Klenowski

Further Reading

General Accounting Office. *Identity Theft: Prevalence and Cost Appear to Be Growing.* Washington, D.C.: General Printing Office, 2002. Federal government report on identity theft based on interviews and quantitative research. Perhaps the most accurate picture of the nature of identity victimization to date.

Hage, Brian S., et al. *Identity Theft in the United States.* Morgantown, W.Va.: National White Collar Crime Center, 2001. Excellent explanation of what the crime of identity theft is, who tends to be targeted, profound statistics on the extent of the problem, and steps for dealing with the crime.

Hammond, Robert J., Jr. *Identity Theft: How to Protect Your Most Valuable Asset.* Franklin Lakes, N.J.: Career Press, 2003. General guide to identity theft protection strategies.

Hayward, Claudia L., ed. *Identity Theft.* Hauppauge, N.Y.: Novinka Books, 2004. Brief collection of articles on various aspects of identity theft.

Jasper, Margaret C. *Identity Theft and How to Protect Yourself.* Dobbs Ferry, N.Y.: Oceana Publications, 2002. Practical guide to lay readers on methods of avoiding identity theft victimization.

Sullivan, Bob. *Your Evil Twin : Behind the Identity Theft Epidemic.* New York: John Wiley & Sons, 2004. Comprehensive examination of the scope of identity theft crimes and methods of prevention, with many examples of real cases by an identity theft expert. Also discusses the failure of law enforcement to attack the problem more aggressively.

Vacca, John R. *Identity Theft.* Upper Saddle River, N.J.: Prentice Hall, 2003. Comprehensive textbook on legal aspects of identity theft.

Welsh, Amanda. *The Identity Theft Protection Guide: Safeguard Your Family, Protect Your Privacy, Recover a Stolen Identity.* New York: St. Martin's Press, 2004. Detailed manual offering advice on countering identity theft.

See also Computer fraud; Criminals; Cybercrime; Forensic accounting; Forgery; Fraud; Private detectives; Telephone fraud; Theft; White-collar crime.

Ignorance of the law

Definition: Criminal defense based on defendants' claims to have been ignorant of the laws they have broken

Criminal justice issues: Defendants; pleas

Significance: Ignorance of the law by a person committing an offense is not an excuse for committing the offense.

The maxim that "ignorance of the law excuses not" was a Roman law principle assimilated into the common law. The Anglo-American common law restates this ancient maxim as "ignorance of the law is no excuse" or "everyone is presumed to know the law." The common-law justification of the rule was to encourage citizens to learn the law. Failure to comprehend the legal effect of making an admission provides no excuse for a defendant. As one court put it, "Ignorance of the law excuses no one." The modern trend of the law is a steady erosion of the ignorance of the law doctrine.

The common-law position was based on the fact that most common-law crimes were *malum in se*, or inherently evil. The "ignorance of the law" maxim is less compelling for complex statutes that criminalize conduct that is not inherently evil. Many activities in the modern regulatory state are wrong simply because a legislature defines them as wrong. Regulatory offenses are often referred to as *malum prohibitum*, or public welfare crimes. The "ignorance of the law" defense has a continuing vitality for many public welfare offenses. Nevertheless, persons may be prosecuted for violation of a water pollution statute, for example, even if they profess to having been ignorant that the activity is illegal.

Criminal defendants may be prosecuted for receiving stolen goods even if they did not know that such receipt is illegal. The fact that the U.S. Congress used the adverb "knowingly" to authorize punishment of those not having a permit for firearms does not lead to the conclusion that there is an exception to the ignorance of the law defense. Similarly, ignorance is no defense in other substantive fields of the law. Employers are not excused for failing to maintain a safe workplace simply because they were unaware of occupational safety laws. Ignorance of the law does not excuse public officials from requirements imposed upon them by sunshine, or open government, laws.

The ignorance of the law doctrine is inapplicable to offenses that are defined with a state-of-mind requirement. However, the U.S. Congress or a state may define knowledge of the law as an element of an offense. In such statutes, a willful violation requires some mental state more culpable than mere intent to perform a forbidden act. Courts often rule that the word "willfully" requires knowledge of the law, which is an exception to the presumed knowledge principle. Likewise, mistake of fact or the law may be an excuse or defense if it negates the mental state that is the element of a crime.

The willfulness required for criminal contempt is the knowledge that one is violating a court order, not the knowledge that the violation of the order is a crime. A mistake of fact is a misapprehension of a fact that, if true, would have justified the act or omission. Mistake of law or ignorance of the law is a defense when a defendant's willfulness or knowledge is an element of the defense. Another exception to the no-excuse doctrine occurs when a defendant has relied on an interpretation of law given by a public official. Courts are more receptive to the "mistake of law" defense if the statute is complex or ambiguously worded. If there is a complex business, environmental, or other complex statute, courts sometimes permit ignorance of the law to excuse a violation. The policy justification for this exception to the general rule is the danger of convicting individuals involved in apparently innocent activity.

Michael L. Rustad

Further Reading

Abramson, Leslie, with Richard Flaste. *The Defense Is Ready: Life in the Trenches of Criminal Law*. New York: Simon & Schuster, 1997.

Acker, J. R., and D. C. Brody. *Criminal Procedure: A Contemporary Perspective*. 2d ed. Sudbury, Mass.: Jones and Bartlett, 2004.

Ingram, Jefferson L. *Criminal Procedure: Theory and Practice*. Upper Saddle River, N.J.: Prentice-Hall, 2005.

See also Criminal intent; Criminal law; Criminal liability; Criminal prosecution; Cultural defense; Defenses to crime; Excuses and justifications; Mitigating circumstances.

Illegal aliens

Definition: Colloquial term for foreign-born persons who enter the United States without legal authorization and those who enter legally but violate the terms of their admission or fail to acquire permanent residence status

Criminal justice issues: Civil rights and liberties; federal law; international law; terrorism

Significance: The steady increase in the population of undocumented aliens in the United States presents a variety of challenges to the American criminal justice system. In addition to the federal government's monumental problem of enforcing the nation's immigration laws, state and local law-enforcement agencies face a growing problem of criminal activities by illegal aliens.

In 1994, the U.S. Immigration and Naturalization Service (INS) produced the first detailed national estimates of the numbers of illegal aliens in the United States. The INS estimated that 3.4 million unauthorized residents were in the country in October, 1992. Later, the INS estimated the number to be about 7 million in the year 2000. The U.S. Census Bureau's estimate for that same year was 8 million. Since the early 1990's, the annual growth rate of the illegal alien population has ranged between 350,000 and 500,000. At that rate, the number of illegal residents in the United States was about 9 million in 2004. That figure is roughly equivalent to the *combined* populations of the eleven smallest U.S. states, and some researchers believe that the actual number of illegal aliens is even significantly higher.

Mexico, the United States' southern neighbor, is the single largest source of illegal immigrants. Of the more than 8 million illegal aliens residing in the United States in 2004, about 5.3 million—well more than half—came from Mexico. Undocumented Mexican workers in the United States are an important part of the Mexican national economy. They send home an estimated $20 billion to $30 billion a year.

An additional 2 million illegal aliens were born in other parts of Latin America, primarily Central American nations. Taken together, Mexicans and other Latin Americans make up more than three-fourths of all illegal aliens in the United States. About 10 percent of illegal aliens originate in Asia, while Europe and Canada supply about 5 percent. The rest come from Africa and other parts of the world.

Illegal Aliens and the Criminal Justice System

The standard American response to illegal immigration has been increased border enforcement through the authority of the federal government. Throughout the 1990's, the numbers of both illegal border crossings and illegal aliens in the United States increased incrementally. Among the strategies to stem illegal immigration were Operation Gatekeeper in California, Operation Hold-the-Line in Texas, and Operation Safeguard in Arizona. All were attempts to deter illegal border crossings.

The U.S. Department of Justice allocated unprecedented resources to these innovative strategies, including additional Border Patrol agents; advanced computer systems; and improved security fences, lighting, and support vehicles. As a result, by 1998, the numbers of attempted border

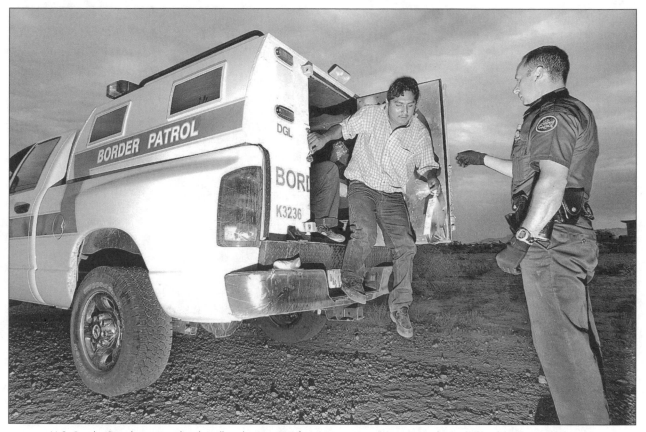

U.S. Border Patrol agents unloading illegal immigrants for processing in Arizona in mid-2004. *(AP/Wide World Photos)*

crossings and apprehensions dropped to their lowest levels in almost twenty years. However, human rights activists and researchers criticized these efforts and argued that increased surveillance along the border was not preventing illegal entries but instead was forcing undocumented immigrants to seek riskier methods of entering the United States. In response to these charges, U.S. president George W. Bush and Mexican president Vicente Fox later pledged to pursue immigration reform policies to address border enforcement and human rights concerns.

The fact that the terrorist attacks on the United States of September 11, 2001, were perpetrated by illegal aliens made countering illegal immigration a top priority of the Bush administration. After that date, new federal laws and policies were adopted, including the Patriot Act of 2001, the Homeland Security Act of 2002, and the Enhanced Border Security and Visa Entry Reform Act of 2002. In March, 2003, the Immigra-

tion and Naturalization Service was divided into three bureaus within the newly created Department of Homeland Security: the Bureau of Immigration and Customs Enforcement (ICE), the Bureau of Customs and Border Protection (CBP), and U.S. Citizenship and Immigration Services (USCIS).

Although the federal government is primarily responsible for securing the nation's borders, the impact of illegal aliens on the criminal justice system reaches far beyond the federal system. Indeed, the problem and its required solutions may have an even deeper impact on state and local jurisdictions. At state and local levels, the costs of arresting, prosecuting, sentencing, and supervising illegal aliens who commit criminal offenses have become a major issue. Some states have filed suits to force the federal government to reimburse them for the costs of criminal justice actions against aliens for whom the federal government is responsible.

The federal government does reimburse states for some costs associated with criminal acts by illegal aliens. Section 510 of the Immigration Reform and Control Act of 1986 (IRCA) authorizes the U.S. attorney general to reimburse states for the criminal justice costs attributable to undocumented persons. The Bureau of Justice Assistance, a branch of the Office of Justice Programs, administers the State Criminal Alien Assistance Program (SCAAP), in conjunction with the Bureau of Immigration and Customs Enforcement (ICE) of the Department of Homeland Security. SCAAP provides federal payments to states and localities that incur correctional officer salary costs for incarcerating undocumented aliens who have been convicted of at least one felony or two misdemeanors for violations of state or local law and are incarcerated for at least four consecutive days during a reporting period. During the fiscal year 2004, the total appropriation was approximately $297 million. SCAAP payments are calculated with a formula that provides pro-rata shares of the funds to jurisdictions that apply, based on the total number of eligible criminal aliens as determined by ICE.

Criminal illegal aliens pose considerable challenges to law-enforcement efforts in part due to the highly criticized stance of many cities and counties that have adopted "sanctuary laws." Such laws are local ordinances adopted in attempts to reduce victimizations of aliens and to improve crime reporting rates among immigrant populations. The National Council of La Raza and other advocacy groups have defended sanctuary laws by arguing that they promote community-oriented policing efforts and protect against racial profiling, police misconduct, and civil rights violations. Critics against the policy contend that such laws allow illegal aliens who commit crimes to circumvent federal law and avoid identification and deportation.

Future Trends

The number of illegal aliens residing in the United States grew steadily throughout the 1990's. More than half of all unauthorized visitors in the country were born in Mexico. According to the Center for Immigration Studies, about

Foreign-born Residents of the United States in 2002

County of birth	Total residents (millions)	Percentage of all foreign born
Mexico	9.8	30
Other Latin America	7.3	23
Asia	8.5	26
Europe and Canada	5.4	17
Africa and other countries	1.4	4
Totals	32.4	100

Source: U.S. Census Bureau, Current Population Survey, March, 2002.

9 percent of living people born in Mexico now reside in the United States. Additional resources to deter illegal border crossings as a result of laws implemented following the September 11, 2001, attacks have done little to slow the influx of illegal aliens, and there is no evidence to suggest that current levels of illegal entry into the United States will decrease significantly.

Barring major changes in the nation's legal immigration policy or enforcement strategies, it is likely that immigration will continue at roughly current levels. More and more people will continue to enter this country lawfully. At the same time, however, it can be expected that many will enter the United States illegally. Controlling the national borders, thwarting organized alien smuggling rings, and identifying and deporting people who are in the United States illegally, especially those who commit crimes, will be priorities.

Wayne J. Pitts

Further Reading

Daniels, Roger. *Guarding the Golden Door: American Immigration Policy and Immigrants Since 1882*. New York: Hill & Wang, 2004. Study of the impact of ignorance, partisan politics, and unintended consequences in immigration policy during the post-9/11 war on terrorism.

Hing, Bill Ong. *Defining America Through Immigration Policy*. Philadelphia: Temple University Press, 2004. Broad survey of federal immigration policies and their impact on the social structure of the United States.

Nevins, Joseph. *Operation Gatekeeper: The Rise of the "Illegal Alien" and the Making of the U.S.-Mexico Boundary*. New York: Routledge, 2002. Critical history of federal efforts to control the influx of undocumented immigration across the border with Mexico.

Ngai, Mae M. *Impossible Subjects: Illegal Aliens and the Making of Modern America*. Princeton, N.J.: Princeton University Press, 2004. History of immigration that emphasizes the place of illegal aliens in the construction of modern American society and nationality.

Williams, Mary E., ed. *Immigration: Opposing Viewpoints*. San Diego: Greenhaven Press, 2004. Collection of essays by experts and observers familiar with immigration, presenting diverse social, political, and legal views on U.S. immigration policy.

See also Border patrols; Coast Guard, U.S.; Deportation; Identity theft; Immigration and Naturalization Service; Justice Department, U.S.; Mexican justice system; Organized crime; Palmer raids; Patriot Act.

Illinois v. Gates

The Case: U.S. Supreme Court ruling on search warrants

Date: Decided on June 8, 1983

Criminal justice issue: Search and seizure

Significance: This case overruled the stringent standards of the "two-prong" test—also known as the *Aguilar-Spinelli* test—in favor of the "totality of the circumstances" test. In so doing, law-enforcement officers were given more flexibility in establishing probable cause when requesting a search warrant.

On May 3, 1978, the police in Bloomington, Illinois, received an anonymous letter stating that Lance and Susan Gates were involved in illegal drug trafficking. The letter delineated how the Gateses allegedly transported narcotics from Florida to Illinois. Specifically, Susan drove their car to Florida so the trunk could be loaded with drugs. Lance flew to Florida a few days later and drove the car back to Illinois. The letter also stated that the defendants had approximately $100,000 worth of drugs in their basement.

Subsequently, the police found the Gateses' home address and verified that Lance had recently made a plane reservation for May 5, a few days after the police received the letter. Investigators later confirmed Lance had flown to Florida and stayed overnight in a hotel room registered in Susan's name. Based upon the anonymous letter and the information gathered by the police, a judge issued a search warrant. When the Gateses returned to Illinois, their car and home were searched, and large amounts of drugs and weapons were seized. The Illinois Supreme Court suppressed the evidence by ruling sufficient probable cause had not been established because the police could not verify whether the author of the anonymous letter was both reliable and credible, thus satisfying analytical standards established in *Aguilar v. Texas* and *Spinelli v. United States*, known as the *Aguilar-Spinelli* test. The state of Illinois appealed to the U.S. Supreme Court.

In the *Gates* case, the U.S. Supreme Court ruled that the *Aguilar-Spinelli* test was excessively rigid in that it failed to incorporate the basis of knowledge that law-enforcement agents possessed when applying for a warrant. The Court determined that although the letter itself could not establish probable cause, the fact that law-enforcement agents were able to confirm some of the activity described in the letter to be accurate was sufficient to establish probable cause and justify issuance of a search warrant. The Court reversed the lower court ruling and established that the test for probable cause would be based upon the "totality of the circumstances."

Heidi Jo Blair-Esteves

Further Reading

Horwitz, Morton J. *The Warren Court and the Pursuit of Justice*. New York: Hill and Wang, 1998. Examines segregation, the Civil Rights movement, McCarthyism, and other issues of democratic culture.

Schwartz, Bernard, ed. *The Burger Court: Counter-Revolution or Confirmation?* New

York: Oxford University Press, 1998. Essays included are written by justices, journalists, feminists, and lawyers.

Yarbrough, Tinsley E. *The Burger Court: Justices, Rulings, and Legacy.* Santa Barbara, Calif.: ABC-Clio, 2000. Describes major decisions rendered by Warren E. Burger's court and their impact.

See also Drugs and law enforcement; *Leon, United States v.*; Police powers; Probable cause; Search warrants; Supreme Court, U.S.

Illinois v. Krull

The Case: U.S. Supreme Court ruling on search and seizure

Date: Decided on March 9, 1987

Criminal justice issue: Search and seizure

Significance: In this case, the Supreme Court held that the "good-faith exception," sometimes allowing the courtroom use of evidence seized illegally, could apply to certain warrantless searches.

Illinois businesses that buy and sell used automobile parts or that process automobile scrap metal were required by a 1981 statute to obtain a business license, maintain detailed records of their transactions, and make these records and the business premises available to the state for inspection at any reasonable time to determine the accuracy of the records. On July 5, 1981, the Chicago police entered the premises of Action Iron & Metal, Inc., an automobile wrecking yard, to inspect its records and examine the vehicle identification numbers of cars in the yard. The clerk at the wrecking yard was unable to produce any records other than a paper pad on which approximately five vehicle purchases were listed. The inspection of the wrecking yard disclosed that three of the cars were stolen and a fourth car had no vehicle identification number. Two men (Krull, who held the license for Action Iron & Metal, Inc., and the clerk) were charged with various criminal violations of the Illinois motor vehicle statutes.

On July 6, 1981, a federal court held that the Illinois statute was an unconstitutional administrative search law. Based on this decision, the Illinois trial court held that the search was illegal. The Illinois trial court also held that the *United States v. Leon* (1984) good-faith exception to the exclusionary rule did not apply because it was limited to circumstances in which a warrant was issued by a neutral magistrate. The Illinois Supreme Court affirmed the trial court's decision. The U.S. Supreme Court, however, in a 5-4 vote, reversed the decision. It stated that the *Leon* good-faith exception to the exclusionary rule could apply when a police officer's reliance on the constitutionality of a statute authorizing the search was objectively reasonable, even though the statute is subsequently declared unconstitutional.

In Justice Harry Blackmun's majority opinion, the Court noted that *Leon* had reaffirmed that the purpose of the exclusionary rule is to deter future unlawful police conduct, not to provide a cure for past unlawful police conduct. Because the exclusion of evidence undermines the truth-finding process of a criminal trial, the exclusionary rule remedy should be imposed only when the likelihood of deterring future unlawful police conduct outweighs the cost to the criminal justice system's primary purpose: determining the guilt or innocence of a defendant.

The statutory authorization for the warrantless search functions like the warrant for three reasons, the Court said. First, there is no evidence that legislators ignored the requirements of the Fourth Amendment in passing such legislation. Second, members of the legislature, like neutral magistrates, have no direct stake in the day-to-day conduct of law enforcement, so there is little incentive for them to overstep the limits of the Fourth Amendment. Third, no proof was offered that the application of the exclusionary rule would deter legislators from enacting statutes that may be declared unconstitutional or that exclusion of evidence in these cases will significantly deter future unlawful police conduct. Therefore, any marginal deterrent benefit in applying the exclusionary rule to cases such as this is outweighed by the cost of excluding reliable and relevant evidence from the process of determining guilt.

In this case, the police acted in a reasonable manner in relying on the statute as authorizing a lawful search, because the Supreme Court had approved warrantless administrative searches in similar cases. In closing, the Court limited its decision by noting that if there was proof that the legislature wholly abandoned its responsibility to enact constitutional laws under the Fourth Amendment, or if a reasonable officer should have known the statute was unconstitutional, then the exclusionary rule should apply. Despite the caveat at the close of the opinion, the *Krull* case significantly expanded the scope of the decision in *Leon* by leaving open the possibility that it could be applied to other warrantless search circumstances.

Johnny C. Burris

See also Evidence, rules of; Search and seizure; Supreme Court, U.S.

Illinois v. McArthur

The Case: U.S. Supreme Court ruling defining powers of police officers when obtaining a warrant

Date: Decided on February 20, 2001

Criminal justice issues: Police powers; search and seizure

Significance: The decision in *Illinois v. McArthur* allows police officers with probable cause to believe that criminal evidence is located in a private home to use reasonable means to prevent destruction of that evidence while they are waiting for a search warrant.

In *Illinois v. McArthur*, Tesa McArthur requested and received police protection when she moved out of the trailer where she had been living with her husband, Charles McArthur. After relocating, she informed officer John Love that she had seen her husband hide marijuana under the sofa. When Charles McArthur refused to consent to a search of the trailer, Love instructed his colleague to obtain a search warrant. While waiting for the warrant, Love refused to allow McArthur, who was standing on the front porch,

to reenter the trailer, except under supervision. Whenever McArthur went into the trailer, Love stood in the doorway, where he could see the sofa. About two hours later, armed with a warrant, police officers found and seized a small amount of marijuana and a marijuana pipe.

When Charles McArthur was prosecuted for misdemeanor possession of an illegal drug and paraphernalia, his attorneys moved to suppress the evidence. They argued that the porch constituted part of the trailer home and that the refusal to allow McArthur free access to his home was inconsistent with a primary purpose of the Fourth Amendment—to secure the privacy of persons in their homes. The trial court granted the motion, and an appellate court upheld the judgment. The state's supreme court denied the petition for a review.

The U.S. Supreme Court, however, by an 8-1 vote, held that the restriction on McArthur had been reasonable in the light of the circumstances. Writing for the Court, Justice Stephen Breyer balanced privacy considerations with concerns of law enforcement and made six points. First, the police had probable cause to believe that criminal evidence existed in a particular place. Second, there was good reason to expect that McArthur, unless supervised, would destroy the evidence. Third, the officers did not violate McArthur's personal privacy beyond the extent necessary to secure the evidence. Fourth, the restraint did not continue any longer than necessary. Fifth, earlier precedents had recognized that a person standing in an open doorway was in a "public place." Sixth, in contrast to *Welsh v. Wisconsin* (1984), the offenses at issue in this case were jailable crimes.

In a concurring opinion, Justice David Souter wrote that if Charles McArthur had not stepped outside the trailer, the threat of his destroying evidence would have constituted exigent circumstances to justify a prompt, warrantless search of the trailer. In a dissenting opinion, Justice John Paul Stevens argued that the majority struck the wrong balance, and he praised the Illinois jurists for placing a higher value on the sanctity of a private home than on the prosecution of a petty offense.

The *McArthur* decision did not break any new ground, but it helped clarify the extent to which police officers, when acting reasonably and with sensitivity, might intrude into the privacy of a home in order to prevent the destruction of criminal evidence.

Thomas Tandy Lewis

Further Reading

Epstein, Lee, and Thomas Walker. *Constitutional Law for a Changing America*. 5th ed. Washington, D.C.: Congressional Quarterly, 2003.
O'Brien, David M. *Constitutional Law and Politics*. 6th ed. New York: W. W. Norton, 2005.

See also Fourth Amendment; Privacy rights; Probable cause; Search and seizure; Search warrants; Supreme Court, U.S.

Illinois v. Wardlow

The Case: U.S. Supreme Court ruling on reasonable suspicion
Date: Decided on January 12, 2000
Criminal justice issues: Arrest and arraignment; police powers; search and seizure
Significance: This Supreme Court decision expanded the powers of police to stop and frisk suspects by holding that taking flight in high-crime areas gives police enough evidence to undertake such actions.

In 1995, two police officers were working in a special operations unit of the Chicago Police Department going into an area of the city known for high drug trafficking. There they noticed a man named Wardlow, who was carrying an opaque bag. After looking in their direction, Wardlow immediately fled. The officers then gave chase and eventually caught him. On the basis of his belief that people in high-crime neighborhoods often carry arms, one of the officers conducted a patdown search of Wardlow and found a gun.

Wardlow was later convicted of unlawful possession of a firearm by a felon. Prior to his trial, Wardlow moved to suppress having his gun submitted as evidence, arguing that the officers had no basis for pursuing him in the first place. Since their chase was illegal, he argued, so, too, was their frisking of him. Thus, the evidence should be suppressed because of the exclusionary rule.

Wardlow lost his argument at the trial level, but his conviction was overturned by the Illinois Supreme Court, which held his contention that his gun should have been suppressed as evidence, because his actions did not give the officers reasonable suspicion to stop him. After the state appealed this ruling, the case went to the U.S. Supreme Court, which overruled Illinois's supreme court.

Writing in the majority opinion for the Court, Chief Justice William H. Rehnquist contended that while an individual's presence in a high-crime area was not by itself sufficient to justify the arresting officer's reasonable suspicion, it was a factor that could be considered. Moreover, the chief justice noted, the defendant's "unprovoked flight" in that area should also be considered a factor in determining whether reasonable suspicion existed. In short, while neither flight nor presence in a high-crime area by itself was sufficient to constitute reasonable suspicion, the two combined were sufficient.

Wardlow was one of a series of cases in which the Supreme Court sought to define what constituted a level of evidence sufficient to form the "reasonable suspicion" to permit officers to stop and frisk. In its earlier decision in *Brown v. Texas* (1979), the Court held that the mere presence of an individual in a high-crime area was not enough to create a reasonable suspicion of criminal activity. In *Florida v. Royer* (1983), the Court had ruled that refusal of a citizen to stop to talk to police did not create the necessary reasonable suspicion to validate a stop. In the view of many, the Supreme Court's decision in *Wardlow* broadened the definition of "reasonable suspicion" and, hence, expanded law enforcement's right to stop individual citizens.

David M. Jones

Further Reading

Amar, Akhil Reed. *The Constitution and Criminal Procedure*. New Haven, Conn.: Yale University Press, 1997.
Bloom, Robert M. *Searches, Seizures, and Warrants*. Westport, Conn.: Praeger Publishing, 2003.

Yarborough, Tinsley. *The Rehnquist Court and the Constitution.* Oxford, England: Oxford University Press, 2000.

See also Due process of law; Fourth Amendment; Hit-and-run accidents; Probable cause; Racial profiling; Reasonable suspicion; Search and seizure; Stop and frisk; Supreme Court, U.S.; *Terry v. Ohio.*

Immigration and Naturalization Service

Identification: Federal government agency that until 2003 administered laws relating to the admission, exclusion, and deportation of aliens and the naturalization of aliens lawfully residing in the United States

Date: Established in 1891; functions transferred to Department of Homeland Security in 2003

Criminal justice issues: International law; law-enforcement organization; terrorism

Significance: For more than a century, the Immigration and Naturalization Service (INS) was the primary federal agency responsible for enforcing laws pertaining to legal and illegal immigration and naturalization.

Since the ratification of the U.S. Constitution in 1789, American citizens have struggled to reconcile sometimes conflicting ideas of a nation open to all comers as a land of opportunity, against the goal of preserving the prosperity and well-being of those already settled and the definition of how one becomes an American. Immigration was viewed as an issue concerning the ethnic makeup of the United States and how foreign arrivals were assimilated into American society.

Historically, federal immigration policies have been shaped by public attitudes toward the race, ethnicity, and social class of newcomers to the nation. The late nineteenth century was a golden era for immigrants when, with few exceptions (mainly the Chinese and certain types of laborers), virtually all persons not afflicted with

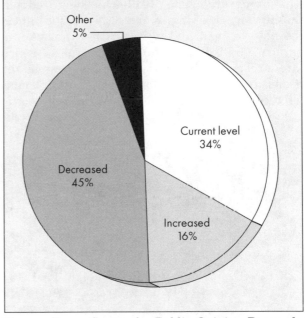

Public Opinion on U.S. Immigration Levels in 2004

In January, 2004, a CBS News/*New York Times* poll asked a cross-section of Americans whether legal immigration into the United States should be kept at its current level, increased, or decreased.

Other 5%

Current level 34%

Decreased 45%

Increased 16%

Source: Roper Center for Public Opinion Research. Figures reflect responses of 1,022 adults surveyed in January, 2004.

chronic or mental illnesses could come to stay in the United States. By the 1880's, state boards or commissions under the direction of the U.S. Treasury Department were administering immigration laws.

Creation of the INS

To help monitor this great wave of immigration and to centralize the enforcement of immigration laws, Congress passed the Immigration Act of 1891, which created the Immigration and Naturalization Service to administer federal laws relating to the admission, exclusion, and deportation of aliens and the naturalization of aliens lawfully residing in the United States. In 1892, the INS opened an immigrant screening station at Ellis Island in New York Harbor. From then until 1954, when the station closed, approximately twelve million immigrants entered the United States through Ellis Island. Additional immigrant stations were opened at other principal ports of entry during the early twentieth century.

Congress continued to exert federal control over immigration with the passage of a series of laws in the early twentieth century, most notably the Immigration Act of 1917, which required that immigrants wishing to enter the United States be able to read and write in their native language. The federal naturalization rules—which are a responsibility assigned to Congress by the Constitution—were enforced by a host of courts of record until the Basic Naturalization Act of 1906 was passed; that law codified the rules for

naturalization still in effect in the twenty-first century.

Mass immigration slowed during World War I but resumed in 1920. Congress responded with a new immigration policy of national origins quotas. Immigration was limited by assigning each nationality a quota based on its representation in past U.S. census figures. The U.S. State Department distributed a limited number of visas each year through U.S. embassies abroad, and the INS admitted only immigrants who arrived with valid visas.

These new restrictions led to increased illegal immigration and alien smuggling. In 1924, Congress created the U.S. Border Patrol, and immigration laws were more rigorously enforced. The resulting increase in appeals under the law led to creation of the Immigration Board of Review that eventually became the Executive Office of Immigration Review. During the Great Depression of the 1930's, the volume of immigration dropped significantly, and in 1940 the INS was moved from the Department of Labor to the Department of Justice.

During World War II, immigration was viewed as a national security matter, rather than an economic issue. Among other duties, the INS recorded and fingerprinted every alien in the United States through the Alien Registration Program, operated internment camps and detention facilities for enemy aliens, and assisted in guarding national borders. After the war, Congress recodified and combined all previous immigration and naturalization law into the Immigration and Nationality Act of 1952. Cold War concerns about criminal aliens within the United States prompted INS investigation and deportation of suspected communists, subversives, and organized crime figures.

U.S. Customs and Immigration and Naturalization Service agents checking vehicles entering the United States from Canada on September 12, 2001—one day after the terrorist attacks on the United States. Security measures were extremely tight immediately after the terrorist attacks and remained tighter than ever before through the years that followed. (AP/Wide World Photos)

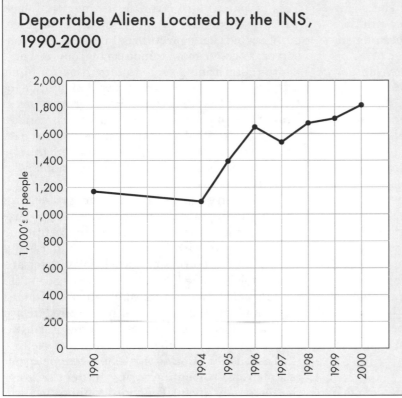

Deportable Aliens Located by the INS, 1990-2000

Source: U.S. Bureau of Citizenship and Immigration Services, *Statistical Yearbook*.

Modern Immigration Reforms

In 1965, Congress replaced the national origins system with a preference system designed to reunite families of immigrants and to attract more skilled immigrants to the United States. This new policy was a response to changes in the sources of immigration. The majority of applicants for immigration visas no longer came from Europe but from Asia and Latin America. The preference system continued to limit the number of immigration visas available each year, however.

During the late twentieth century, changes in world migration patterns, the ease of international travel, and a growing emphasis on controlling illegal immigration fostered the growth of the INS. Following the terrorist attacks of September 11, 2001, the INS was one of several existing federal agencies that were incorporated into the new U.S. Department of Homeland Security, a cabinet department of the federal government that is concerned with protecting the American homeland and the safety of American citizens.

Since the creation of the Department of Homeland Security, most INS functions have been divided into two bureaus: the U.S. Citizenship and Immigration Services (USCIS) and the Bureau of Immigration and Customs Enforcement. The Executive Office for Immigration Review and the Board of Immigration Appeals, which review decisions made by the USCIS, remain under jurisdiction of the Department of Justice.

Immigration officers now specialize in inspection, examination, adjudication, legalization, investigation, patrol, and refugee and asylum issues. The USCIS continues to enforce laws providing for selective immigration and controlled entry of temporary visitors such as tourists and business travelers. It does so by inspecting and admitting arrivals at land, sea, and airports of entry, administering benefits such as naturalization and permanent resident status, and apprehending and removing aliens who enter illegally or violate the requirements of their stay. Like its predecessor, the INS, the USCIS has been criticized for downplaying its mission of social service and cultural assimilation while overemphasizing its law-enforcement role in ways that may produce human rights abuses.

Theodore M. Vestal

Further Reading

Daniels, Roger. *Guarding the Golden Door: American Immigration Policy and Immigrants Since 1882*. New York: Hill & Wang, 2004. Study of the impact of ignorance, partisan politics, and unintended consequences in immigration policy during the post-9/11 war on terror.

Fiss, Owen, Joshua Cohen, and Joel Rogers. *A Community of Equals: The Constitutional Protection of New Americans*. Boston: Beacon

Press, 1999. Analysis of the major social disabilities immigrants face and the legal acts and amendments that deny them these constitutional rights.

Jacoby, Tamar, ed. *Reinventing the Melting Pot: The New Immigrants and What It Means to Be American.* New York: Basic Books, 2004. Collection of twenty-two essays from a diverse assortment of writers about the "melting pot" as both ideal and reality.

Ngai, Mae M. *Impossible Subjects: Illegal Aliens and the Making of Modern America.* Princeton, N.J.: Princeton University Press, 2003. History of immigration that emphasizes the place of illegal aliens in the construction of modern American society and nationality.

Welch, Michael. "The Role of the Immigration and Naturalization Service in the Prison-Industrial Complex." *Social Justice* 27 (Fall, 2000): 73-89. Critical analysis of the INS in administering policies that produce human rights abuses rather than cultural assimilation.

See also Attorney general of the United States; Border patrols; Criminal records; Deportation; Drugs and law enforcement; Homeland Security Department; Illegal aliens; Justice Department, U.S.; Terrorism.

Immunity from prosecution

Definition: Legally binding promise not to prosecute a potential defendant, typically offered in exchange for testimony

Criminal justice issues: Defendants; immunity; trial procedures

Significance: Offering immunity from prosecution permits the government to compel testimony that might otherwise be blocked by the Fifth Amendment right against self-incrimination.

A successful prosecution sometimes depends upon testimony by an accomplice of the accused.

This is particularly true for crimes that lack witnesses external to the criminal enterprise, such as a specific victim or a third-party observer. These crimes include conspiracy, bribery, white-collar crimes such as securities fraud, or organized crimes involving the distribution of forbidden goods or services such as drugs or prostitution. Although testimony can ordinarily be compelled, that of an accomplice, who is also guilty of criminal activity, is shielded by the self-incrimination clause of the Fifth Amendment to the U.S. Constitution.

To circumvent this impediment, prosecutors offer a binding promise of nonprosecution in exchange for the testimony. Because prosecution is now foreclosed, witnesses' interests in not being turned into the tool of their own legal undoing are adequately satisfied. Even if witnesses deem the bargain a bad one, they may not refuse the immunity, and testimony may now be required before any compulsory forum, including grand juries, trials, or legislative investigations.

"Transactional immunity" offers complete protection from prosecution on any matter related to the testimony given. The more limited "use immunity" bans future prosecution based upon the witness's testimony or on leads developed as a result of the testimony but does not bar prosecution based upon evidence acquired wholly independently of the witness's testimony. The latter, as an equivalent for the right against self-incrimination, was upheld by the U.S. Supreme Court in 1972, in *Kastigar v. United States.*

John C. Hughes

Further Reading

Amar, Akhil Reed. *The Constitution and Criminal Procedure.* New Haven, Conn.: Yale University Press, 1997.

Taylor, John B. *Right to Counsel and Privilege Against Self-Incrimination.* Santa Barbara, Calif.: ABC-Clio, 2004.

See also Amnesty; Background checks; Conspiracy; Criminal liability; Diplomatic immunity; International tribunals; Police civil liability; Self-incrimination, privilege against; Witness protection programs.

Impeachment of judges

Definition: Procedure for removing from office judges who engage in serious misconduct

Criminal justice issues: Government misconduct; judges

Significance: Impeachment of federal officials is uncommon. Most impeachment proceedings against federal officials have been against judges, but even these are relatively rare.

The closing years of the twentieth century witnessed the impeachment of three federal judges: Harry Claiborne, Alcee Hastings, and Walter Nixon. Frequently, but not inevitably, judicial impeachment follows a criminal conviction for some offense. Judge Claiborne was impeached during the 1980's after being convicted of tax fraud, and Judge Nixon was impeached after his conviction for perjury. Judge Hastings, on the other hand, was acquitted of criminal charges but was subsequently impeached by the Senate.

One might imagine that impeachment proceedings would be unnecessary in cases in which judges have been convicted of crim-

Newspaper illustration of Chief Justice Salmon Chase (right) being sworn in before testifying at his own impeachment trial. *(Library of Congress)*

Impeachment

Impeachment is a stage in the process of removing public officials from their posts before their normal terms of duty expire. It is normally reserved for serious misconduct on the part of public officials, including judges. Under the U.S. Constitution, federal officials, including federal judges, may be impeached upon a showing that they have engaged in acts of treason, bribery, or "other high crimes and misdemeanors." In its narrow sense, impeachment is merely the formal bringing of charges against an official, who is then tried. Impeachment by itself does not remove a person from office. In the federal government, the House of Representatives initiates impeachment proceedings against officials, while the Senate conducts the ensuing trials and votes on whether to convict.

inal violations. In fact, judges so convicted frequently resign and thus escape the further indignity of impeachment. However, such resignations are not inevitable and certainly not always quickly accomplished. Federal judge Robert Collins was imprisoned in 1991 but continued to draw his annual salary until his resignation in August, 1993. Harry Claiborne, unwilling to consider resignation, drew his judicial salary for two years while he served a prison term in the 1980's, until Congress finally impeached him.

Attempts to impeach judges have not been reserved simply for the rank and file of the judiciary. Even judicial luminaries, such as Supreme Court justices, have sometimes had to endure the stern gaze of a Congress willing to consider their impeachment. In 1805, for example, Justice Samuel Chase faced impeachment proceedings against him but ultimately prevailed, causing

Thomas Jefferson to grouse that the prospect of impeachment was "not even a scarecrow." In the twentieth century, Justice William O. Douglas had to fend off impeachment charges led by then-House minority leader Gerald R. Ford. Douglas was ultimately vindicated when the House Judiciary committee refused to recommend impeachment articles to the House.

Timothy L. Hall

Further Reading

Black, Charles Lund, Jr. *Impeachment: A Handbook*. New Haven: Yale University Press, 1998.

Kuo, M. E., ed. *Impeachment: An Overview of Constitutional Procedures and Practices*. New York: Nova Science Publishers, 2003.

Trial of Samuel Chase, an Associate Justice of the Supreme Court of the United States, Impeached by the House of Representatives for High Crimes and Misdemeanors Before the Senate of the United States. Reprint. 2 vols. New York: Da Capo Press, 1970.

See also Judges; Political corruption; Supreme Court, U.S.

In forma pauperis

Definition: Latin phrase, meaning "as a poor pauper," that is applied to legal matters involving poor persons

Criminal justice issues: Defendants; legal terms and principles

Significance: The legal principle of *in forma pauperis* allows poor defendants to file motions or complaints in courts without cost. The purpose of this provision is to make courts accessible to all citizens, regardless of their means.

When a person seeking help from a court cannot afford to pay the standard fees, the costs are covered by the state or federal government. In such cases, the normal costs are waived by the court, which might also provide an indigent person assistance of an attorney. *In forma pauperis* petitions are available at both the state and federal levels. *In forma pauperis* filings are generally considered to be confidential. When trial courts accept them, the applicants' eligibility for relief continues through any appellate proceedings that follow the initial court actions.

Eligibility for *in forma pauperis* help is based on income, and the standards may vary widely. However, in most states, persons receiving public assistance or using food stamps are generally eligible to file *in forma pauperis*. The principle also applies to state and federal prisoners who are without resources.

The best-known *in forma pauperis* criminal case was the U.S. Supreme Court's *Gideon v. Wainwright* ruling in 1963. The case originated when Clarence Gideon was tried for burglary. He asked for an attorney at his trial but was denied and was eventually convicted. While in prison, he filed an appeal with the U.S. Supreme Court, arguing that he had been denied his Sixth Amendment right to an attorney. The Court accepted his *in forma pauperis* petition and heard the matter. In a 9-0 vote, the justices agreed with Gideon and reversed his conviction. The Court stated that the issue Gideon's case raised was of such broad significance that it made its ruling retroactive—something virtually unheard of.

Lawrence C. Trostle

Further Reading

Galloway, Russell W. *Justice for All? The Rich and Poor in Supreme Court History, 1790-1990*. 2d ed. Charleston, N.C.: Carolina Academic Press, 1991.

Lewis, Anthony. *Gideon's Trumpet*. New York: Vintage Books, 1989.

Reiman, Jeffrey. *The Rich Get Richer and the Poor Get Prison: Ideology, Class, and Criminal Justice*. 7th ed. Boston: Allyn & Bacon, 2004.

See also *Argersinger v. Hamlin*; *Certiorari*; Counsel, right to; Equal protection under the law; *Gideon v. Wainwright*; *Miranda v. Arizona*; Public defenders.

Incapacitation

Definition: Aim or rationale of punishment that seeks to control crime by rendering criminals unable, or less able, to commit crimes, such as by incarceration of the offenders

Criminal justice issues: Crime prevention; legal terms and principles; punishment

Significance: Incapacitation provides a justification for certain forms of punishment as well as a strategy for crime control.

Incapacitation refers to the idea that certain forms of punishment are effective means of reducing crime if they restrict the abilities and opportunities of criminals to commit crimes. For example, confining offenders in prison removes them from society and renders them unable to commit further crimes against the general public. Execution has the ultimate incapacitating effect. Even parole may help to incapacitate criminals by limiting their movement and thus restricting their opportunities for committing crimes.

The nineteenth century British utilitarian philosopher Jeremy Bentham discussed incapacitation in a treatment of the ends of punishment. Bentham regarded the principal end of punishment as control of conduct, and he used the term "disablement" to refer to the effect of punishment on the offender's "physical power." This was contrasted with reformation, which refers to the use of punishment to control conduct by influencing the offender's will, and with deterrence, whereby punishment sets an example and thus controls the conduct of people besides the offender. Contemporary discussions of the aims and effects of punishment follow Bentham, at least roughly, in distinguishing among reform or rehabilitation, incapacitation, and general deterrence by example or threat of punishment.

Incapacitation is an expected, or at least hoped for, effect of punishment. Incapacitative effects, however, do not occur in two types of situations. The first is cases in which offenders would not have committed any additional crimes even if they had not been punished. The second is situations in which other individuals take the place of the incarcerated criminals, taking advantage of the opportunities that have opened. This often occurs in the case of criminal activity related to gangs, when the arrest and imprisonment of one member may not result in a decrease in crime. Other gang members or new recruits often fill the positions vacated by the arrest of fellow gang members.

Studies have not established that a strict incapacitation approach to crime control is likely to lead to a significant reduction in the rate of crime. Skeptics point to periods during which crime rates have risen despite increased use of imprisonment. Studies have yielded mixed estimates of any incapacitative effect, with some research projecting a slight increase in crime (4 or 5 percent) with a reduction in prison use. Other research has projected a substantial decrease in crime if the prison population were increased. There is some evidence that the effect of incapacitation varies with types of criminal behavior. Some criminologists have recommended a policy of selective incapacitation—for example, of "career criminals" or violent criminals. Some states have enacted laws imposing life sentences on persons convicted three times of violent or serious crimes; these are sometimes colloquially called "three-time loser" laws or "three strikes and you're out" policies.

Mario F. Morelli

Further Reading

Foucault, Michel. *Discipline and Punish: The Birth of the Prison*. Translated by Alan Sheridan. New York: Vintage Press, 1995.

Garland, David. *Punishment and Modern Society*. Chicago: University of Chicago Press, 1990.

Honderich, T. *Punishment: The Supposed Justifications*. Harmondsworth: Penguin, 1984.

Zimring, Franklin, and Gordan Hawkins. *Incapacitation: Penal Confinement and the Restraint of Crime*. New York: Oxford University Press, 1995.

See also Auburn system; Community-based corrections; Criminology; Deterrence; Just deserts; Mandatory sentencing; Psychological evaluation; Punishment; Recidivism; Rehabilitation; Solitary confinement; Supermax prisons; Three-strikes laws.

Inchoate crimes

Definition: Crimes related to the planning of criminal acts, or activities preceding criminal acts that encourage or facilitate criminal acts

Criminal justice issues: Crime prevention; legal terms and principles

Significance: Inchoate crimes are behaviors intended to lead to crimes. They are criminalized to prevent the subsequent criminal act and also to punish those who plan, discuss, encourage, facilitate, threaten, or prepare for criminal acts.

Inchoate crimes include preparatory or uncompleted acts, including intent or attempt to commit a crime, even if the attempt is not completed; verbal crimes, including solicitation or conspiracy to commit a crime; and pre-criminal acts that imply that a crime is likely to be committed, such as possession of the instruments of crime (like pry bars, offensive weapons, or master keys), possession of items in areas where they are prohibited (like firearms in schools or airports, where the items could be used to commit a crime); and purchasing and stockpiling weapons and other material items that subsequently could be used to commit a crime (for example, explosive materials or hordes of cash).

The inchoate crime is attached to the intended crime. Examples of inchoate crimes include attempted murder, solicitation of prostitution, conspiracy to commit fraud, possession of the instruments of burglary, possession of weapons with the intent to commit an act of terror, or stockpiling cash with the intent of purchasing drugs. The inchoate crime may be prosecuted whether or not the actual crime occurred. The inchoate crime is usually considered to be of the same grade and degree as the most serious offense being prepared to commit. For example, if the completed act would have been murder in the first degree, then the charge is attempted murder in the first degree, and those found guilty are sentenced accordingly.

In many cases, the defendant is charged and the material items are seized or forfeited as a precaution against their use by others in the commission of a crime, or as a preconviction punitive act permitted by law. Seized cash, vehicles, real estate, computers, firearms, and other material items make their way into police custody and are sold, distributed, or used as allowed by law.

Legal Issues Related to Enforcement

Because the crimes are either verbal crimes or the possession of otherwise legal materials, there are serious free speech, search and seizure, due process, and other constitutional issues involved in investigation and prosecution. Police sometimes engage in entrapment behaviors to encourage potential criminal actors to reveal their intentions; this raises questions about due process, admissibility of evidence, police corruption and culpability, and the rights of otherwise law-abiding citizens. Clandestine police involvement with suspect groups changes the group dynamics and creates a new and larger critical mass, making possible inchoate crimes far beyond the group's original capabilities, further raising questions about police culpability.

Gordon Neal Diem

Further Reading

Adams, David. "The Problem of Incomplete Attempt." *Social Theory and Practice* 24 (1998): 317-343.

Gillies, Peter. *The Law of Criminal Conspiracy.* Sydney: Federation Press, 1990.

Hasnas, John. *Attempting the Impossible: The Conditions for Culpability.* Durham, N.C.: Duke University Press, 1988.

Lassiter, G. Daniel, ed. *Interrogations, Confessions, and Entrapment.* New York: Kluwer Academic/Plenum, 2004.

Marcus, Paul. *The Entrapment Defense.* Newark, N.J.: LexisNexis, 2002.

See also Accomplices and accessories; Attempt to commit a crime; Conspiracy; Criminal intent; Criminal law; Due process of law; Entrapment; *Mens rea*; Patriot Act; Privacy rights; Search and seizure; Solicitation to commit a crime.

Incorporation doctrine

Definition: Process through which the U.S. Supreme Court has extended U.S. Bill of Rights protections to the states

Criminal justice issues: Constitutional protections; courts

Significance: When the Bill of Rights was added to the U.S. Constitution in 1791, its provisions applied only to the federal government, not to the states. However, since the 1920's, the U.S. Supreme Court has, through the incorporation doctrine, gradually extended almost all criminal justice provisions of the Bill of Rights to the states.

When the Bill of Rights was framed in 1789, the rights and protections it conferred applied only to the federal government—a principle that the Supreme Court affirmed in its 1833 *Barron v. Baltimore* ruling. In that case, Barron argued that the due process clause of the Fifth Amendment of the Bill of Rights should be applied to state governments after the city of Baltimore had deprived him of his property without due process of law. However, the Supreme Court held that the protections of the Bill of Rights did not apply to the states.

In 1868, when the Fourteenth Amendment was ratified, it added another due process clause to the Constitution. At the time, it was widely believed that this new provision would extend Bill of Rights protections to the states. However, in 1873, the Supreme Court again ruled that the Bill of Rights did not apply to the states in the so-called *Slaughterhouse* cases.

Finally, in its 1925 *Gitlow v. State of New York* ruling, the Supreme Court held, for the first time, that a portion of the Bill of Rights applied to the states through the due process clause of the Fourteenth Amendment. This case concerned the First Amendment's freedom of speech and the press clause. Gitlow himself lost his case, but the Court's ruling opened the door for what was to become known as the incorporation doctrine, or selective incorporation of Bill of Rights protections into state law. After *Gitlow*, the states joined the federal government in guaranteeing that government would not interfere with free expression.

In 1932, the Supreme Court began extending Bill of Rights protections to the states on a case-by-case basis. In *Powell v. Alabama* (1932), for example, the Court held that an Alabama state court had violated the rights of several young black men on trial for rape when it denied them the right to be represented by an attorney—a Sixth Amendment protection. This right to an attorney was applied to Alabama under the due process provision of the Fourteenth Amendment. The Court used the due process clause again in 1936 in *Brown v. Mississippi*, in which it held that Mississippi had tortured a confession out of a defendant and then convicted him, a violation of the Fifth Amendment.

Since the 1930's, the Supreme Court has continued to incorporate the protections of the Bill of Rights, applying them to the states on a case-by-case basis. The U.S. Bill of Rights now affords all citizens the same criminal law protections at the state level as they enjoy at the national level. The only Bill of Rights clauses remaining to be incorporated in the early years of the twenty-first century were the Seventh Amendment's right to jury trials in civil cases and the Fifth Amendment's right to be indicted by a grand jury.

Lawrence C. Trostle

The Fourteenth Amendment's Due Process Clause

All persons born or naturalized in the United States and subject to the jurisdiction thereof, are citizens of the United States and of the State wherein they reside. No State shall make or enforce any law which shall abridge the privileges or immunities of citizens of the United States; nor shall any State deprive any person of life, liberty, or property, without due process of law; nor deny to any person within its jurisdiction the equal protection of the laws.

Further Reading

Campbell, Andrea. *Rights of the Accused*. Philadelphia: Chelsea House, 2001.

Curtis, Michael Kent. *No State Shall Abridge: The Fourteenth Amendment and the Bill of Rights.* Durham, N.C.: Duke University Press, 1990.

Lewis, Thomas T., ed. *The Bill of Rights.* 2 vols. Pasadena, Calif.: Salem Press, 2002.

See also Bill of Rights, U.S.; Constitution, U.S.; Due process of law; *Escobedo v. Illinois*; Exclusionary rule; *Gideon v. Wainwright*; *Hurtado v. California*; *Mapp v. Ohio*; *Miranda v. Arizona*; *Palko v. Connecticut*; *Powell v. Alabama*; Supreme Court, U.S.; *Weeks v. United States*.

Indecent exposure

Definition: Unlawful and intentional exposure in public places of one's normally covered body parts

Criminal justice issues: Deviancy; morality and public order; sex offenses

Significance: Most indecent exposure cases involve men exposing themselves to women. A large majority of these cases of indecent exposure remain unreported to law enforcement, however, because of the victims' tendency to be embarrassed about the situations.

Indecent exposure is generally understood to be the intentional public exposure of such human body parts as the genital regions and female breast nipples in public places for the purpose of arousing sexual desire in others or shocking viewers. It may encompass a variety of acts, including lewd behavior, exhibitionism, public indecency, and any other acts that members of a community would regard as obscene. Generally regarded as offensive to established standards of decency, indecent exposure is proscribed by the laws of every state.

Laws against indecent exposure have a deep history that goes back to early English common

The "Wardrobe Malfunction"

Public concern over indecent exposure rose dramatically in early 2004, after an estimated 140 million people saw singer Janet Jackson expose one of her breasts during the halftime show of the Super Bowl football game. While Jackson was singing a duet with Justin Timberlake, Timberlake reached across the bodice of her costume, seized the material, and pulled it back, revealing Jackson's bare right breast. Jackson remained exposed only a few seconds, but that was long enough for millions of television viewers to see what had happened. In the public outcry that followed, Timberlake apologized for the incident, stating that it was an accident, a "wardrobe malfunction." Questions about whether the incident was planned and who was responsible remained unanswered. There was some evidence that the Music Television Channel (MTV)—which produced the halftime show—planned the incident.

CBS-TV, which broadcast the game, reported that it received more than 540,000 complaints from viewers. The Federal Communications Commission (FCC) later fined Viacom, Inc., the owner of CBS-TV, a total of $550,000 for the incident—$27,500 for each of the twenty network affiliates that broadcast the game. The fine was the largest ever levied by the FCC, but it would have paid for only 7.3 seconds of commercial broadcast time during the Super Bowl.

(AP/Wide World Photos)

law. In England, it was linked to notions of modesty, immodesty, privacy, and sexuality. England's Vagrancy Act of 1824 provided that any person who deliberately, openly, lewdly, and obscenely exposed his body with the intent of insulting female viewers was deemed a scoundrel and a vagabond.

Indecent exposure can be conceptualized in several ways. It may be seen as a reflection of a lack of self-control, or as merely a temporary behavior that manifests itself only in special situations, such as during New Orleans's boisterous Mardi Gras celebrations. It may also be a behavior that a person exhibits only when under the influence of alcohol, drugs, or peer influences, when people—especially young people—are more likely to engage in public indecencies.

Some researchers have argued that indecent exposure may reflect underlying disorders that may eventually be manifest in much more serious criminal acts, such as rape—especially if incidents are not reported or punished. Some studies have shown that what may begin as an "innocent" acts of exposure progress into violent sex-related crimes.

Charges for indecent exposure vary from state to state, but it is considered a misdemeanor in all fifty states. In some jurisdictions, persons convicted of indecent exposure may be required to register as sex offenders on a national database. Although such lewd behavior may seem a minor offense, convictions can be extremely damaging to offenders' reputations and social standing in their communities.

Bernadette Jones Palombo

Further Reading

Morneau, R. H., Jr., and R. R. Rockwell. *Sex, Motivation, and the Criminal Offender*. Springfield, Ill.: Charles C Thomas, 1980.

Riordan, S. "Indecent Exposure: The Impact upon the Victim's Fear of Sexual Crime." *The Journal of Forensic Psychiatry* 10 (1999): 309-316.

See also Contributing to delinquency of minors; Misdemeanors; Pedophilia; Pornography; Public-order offenses; Rape and sex offenses; Sex offender registries; Sexual harassment.

Indeterminate sentencing

Definition: System of awarding prison sentences whose terms are defined by minimum and maximum lengths

Criminal justice issues: Punishment; rehabilitation; sentencing

Significance: Federal and most state courts no longer use the once universal system of awarding prison terms of indeterminate length; the change has reduced the role of discretion in all parts of the criminal justice system.

As recently as the mid-1970's, the judicial systems of every U.S. state, the District of Columbia, and the federal government had indeterminate sentencing systems. Under those systems, legislature set statutory maximums on authorized prison sentences. In awarding sentences, judges could choose between prison, probation, and fines and set maximum prison terms. Corrections officials could determine good time and early releases; and parole boards could set release dates, Virtually all those decisions were free from appellate review. By 2004, most states and the federal government had systems with structured sentencing.

Indeterminate sentencing takes its name from the fact that at the time convicted offenders are sentenced, they do not know exactly how long they will be in prison or under supervision. Under that kind of system, the sentences that judges award to offenders are defined by ranges of years, usually divided into "low" and "upper" ranges. In most states, offenders are required to serve at least 100 percent of their low range and not more than 100 percent of their upper range.

The goal of indeterminate sentencing was to allow sentencing decisions to be based on the individual characteristics of the cases and offenders. At every stage of the sentencing and corrections process, officials had the authority to tailor punishments and treatments to the needs of individual offenders. By the mid-1970's, indeterminate sentencing systems were beginning to erode. Civil and prisoner rights activists claimed that the broad discretion afforded by indeterminate sentencing systems produced arbitrary and unpredictable decisions that were often racially biased. Opponents of indeterminate sentencing also claimed that standardless discretion denied offenders constitutional due process.

Critics also claimed that indeterminate sentencing removed links between the seriousness of crimes and the sentences that were awarded. They argued that offenders should receive specific punishments for specific crimes so that nothing depreciates the seriousness of the crimes. Detractors also argued that indeterminate sentencing allows judges and other officials involved in sentencing decisions to negate public perceptions and views of punishments.

There are many arguments in support of indeterminate sentencing as well. One argument is exactly the reverse of the argument that the indeterminate process insulates the public from the punishment process. Proponents of indeterminate sentencing argue that leaving punishment decisions to criminal justice experts, such as judges, rather than to legislatures, is more likely to result in rehabilitation of the offenders.

Proponents would also argue that indeterminate sentencing does a better job of taking into account rehabilitation and public safety goals than is the case in determinate sentencing systems. At the heart of indeterminate sentencing is the idea that humans are malleable and redeemable and that if they are given the opportunity to better themselves in exchange for earlier release dates, they will reform. Indeterminate sentencing allows judges and correctional officials, professionals who routinely work with offenders, to determine the risk factors and recommend release dates and plans. By giving professionals who know the individual offenders the opportunity to determine their release date, public safety concerns are given top priority.

Jennifer R. Albright

Further Reading

Krantz, Sheldon, and Lynn Branham. *The Law of Sentencing, Corrections, and Prisoners' Rights*. St. Paul, Minn.: West Publishing, 1997.

Tonry, Michael. *Reconsidering Indeterminate and Structured Sentencing*. Washington, D.C.: U.S. Department of Justice, Office of Justice Programs, National Institute of Justice, 1999.

Tonry, Michael, and Richard Fraser. *Sentencing and Sanctions in Western Countries*. New York: Oxford University Press, 2001.

Ulmer, Jeffery T. *Social Worlds of Sentencing: Court Communities Under Sentencing Guidelines*. Albany: State University of New York Press, 1997.

See also Blended sentences; Concurrent sentences; Good time; Just deserts; Mandatory sentencing; Presentence investigations; Rehabilitation; Sentencing; Sentencing guidelines, U.S.

Indictment

Definition: Formal criminal charges issued by grand juries

Criminal justice issues: Pleas; prosecution; trial procedures

Significance: American federal law and the laws of many states provide that no one may be held for trial for a crime without being indicted by a grand jury.

In some states, a defendant may be bound over for trial by a judge after a preliminary hearing without being indicted by a grand jury. The purpose of indictments is to prevent arbitrary arrest. Before arrests are made (except in a few cases of hot pursuit), impartial grand juries must secretly consider the evidence and decide whether an arrest would be justified. The indictment requirement grew out of the tendency of English officials, including the English Parliament itself, to simply arrest persons they did not like.

An indictment by a grand jury does not mean that a person is guilty. It means only that the grand jury finds compelling evidence of two things: that a crime has been committed and that there is good reason to believe that the defendant in question might have committed the crime. A regular trial before a jury or a judge, a plea of guilty, or a decision to dismiss the case must follow before the action is complete. Indictments may be sealed and opened at a later date, such as when an arrest is made.

Indictments by grand juries are not required by the U.S. Constitution in state criminal justice systems, although many states use them. The U.S. Supreme Court so ruled in the 1884 case of *Hurtado v. California*. In that case, the Court said that whatever procedure is used must afford the defendant as much protection as was provided under the old common law of England. In English common law, informations rather than indictments were used. Informations are accusations by a public official that an individual has committed a crime. The common law is no longer used as justification, but "settled usage" is, and information is "settled usage." In 1937, Justice Benjamin Cardozo wrote that the Bill of Rights injunction to use indictments at the federal level was not extended to the states by the Fourteenth Amendment as many sections of the Bill of Rights were, because the Fourteenth Amendment extended only those portions of the Bill of Rights that "are of the very essence of a scheme of ordered liberty," such as freedom of speech. Cardozo wrote that the right to indictment by a grand jury is not of that nature.

Therefore, states may and often do use informations rather than indictments to bring persons to court, and in many states it is customary for a judge at a preliminary hearing, rather than for a grand jury, to determine whether a crime has been committed and whether the defendant ought to be summoned to a trial for that crime.

Dwight Jensen

Further Reading

Abraham, Henry J. *The Judicial Process*. 6th ed. New York: Oxford University Press, 1993.

Del Carmen, Rolando V. *Criminal Procedure: Law and Practice*. 6th ed. Belmont, Calif.: Thomson/Wadsworth, 2004.

Frankel, Marvin E., and Gary P. Naftalis. *The Grand Jury: An Institution on Trial*. New York: Hill & Wang, 1977.

Garcia, Alfredo. *The Fifth Amendment: A Comprehensive Approach*. Westport, Conn.: Greenwood Press, 2002.

Neubauer, David W. *America's Courts and the Criminal Justice System*. 8th ed. Belmont, Calif.: Wadsworth/Thomson Learning, 2005.

See also Bill of particulars; Criminal prosecution; Defendants; Fifth Amendment; Grand juries; *Hurtado v. California*; Information; Judges; Jury system; Misdemeanors; Public prosecutors; Speedy trial right; Trials.

Information

Definition: Written accusation by a prosecutor that an individual has committed a crime

Criminal justice issues: Arrest and arraignment; legal terms and principles; prosecution

Significance: Information is an example of how court procedures require different criminal justice actors, such as the police and the prosecutor, to work together.

Once a person is arrested, a prosecutor must decide whether or not to file charges. The prosecutor may base this decision on several different factors, including evidence in the case. For the suspect to be tried, the evidence must indicate that there is at least probable cause to believe a crime has been committed and that the suspect is the perpetrator. Prosecutors must rely on law-enforcement agencies to gather and present evidence supporting such a belief. Without sufficient or proper evidence, prosecutors will be unable to bring a case to trial.

One way for prosecutors to initiate charges is by filing an information. An information is a document formally listing the charges against a suspect. This document, signed by the prosecutor, is required in felony prosecutions in most states that do not use a grand jury to initiate charges.

This process highlights how actors in the criminal justice system depend on one another to ensure that the system works. Each step in the process is controlled by a different legal actor. For example, charges cannot be initiated without a police investigation. Trials cannot begin without a prosecutor demonstrating to a judge that there is probable cause to believe a crime was committed and that the accused was involved.

Jenifer A. Lee

Further Reading

Rabe, Gary A., and Dean John Champion. *Criminal Courts: Structure, Process, and Issues*.

Upper Saddle River, N.J.: Prentice Hall, 2002.
Stolzenberg, Lisa, and Stewart J. D'Alessio. *Criminal Courts for the Twenty-first Century*. 2d ed. Upper Saddle River, N.J.: Prentice Hall, 2002.

See also Arrest; Bill of particulars; District attorneys; Felonies; Grand juries; *Hurtado v. California*; Indictment; Judges; Preliminary hearings; Probable cause; Trials.

Inquests

Definition: Formal government inquiries into legal matters, particularly homicides

Criminal justice issues: Homicide; investigation; medical and health issues

Significance: Inquests are used as judicial inquiries or official examinations to gather evidence before trials begin.

The purpose of a legal inquest is to obtain information to determine whether a crime has been committed or not. Inquests are solely investigatory and are most commonly used in murder cases. During the inquests, judges oversee all judicial procedures related to the cases in question before actual trial dates are set. In state courts, assistant district attorneys represent the government and present all evidence having any legal bearing on the cases.

All forms of evidence gathered during inquests help determine whether criminal charges should be filed. The evidence gathered is then presented to the courts under sworn testimony. This includes any physical evidence, such as firearms or other weapons that might be involved with the alleged crimes. At this time, witness testimony is also presented to the courts under oath. Results of any autopsies completed by county coroners are also presented, as well as results of any ballistic testing and any other medical tests relevant to the cases.

Inquest hearings themselves are closed to both the public and the media. Only persons having personal interests in the outcomes of the cases may attend the initial hearings. These people may include legal representation of any suspects under investigation. After an inquest is completed, the presiding judge forwards all the evidence submitted to the relevant court, which is likely to be a superior court. At that time, evidence gathered through the inquest is accessible only to attorneys general, district attorneys, and defendant counsel.

After reviewing all information on a case, a district attorney or an attorney general decides whether charges should be filed. If no charges are found and it is determined that there will be no criminal trial, the information and evidence gathered by the inquest are opened to the public. After an open finding is reported to the public, an inquest can be reopened if new evidence is presented to the coroner.

The most common types of inquest are medical examinations into the causes of suspicious deaths. County coroners normally perform these duties. The requirements for qualified coroners are vast and vary from jurisdiction to jurisdiction. However, most jurisdictions require their coroners to have legal training. Other examples of inquests include inquiries into environmental disasters and cases of severe corruption resulting in possible impeachment or incarceration.

Emily I. Troshynski

Further Reading

Blanche, Tony, and Brad Schreiber. *Death in Paradise: An Illustrated History of the Los Angeles County Department of Coroner*. New York: Four Walls Eight Windows, 2001.

Schneir, Walter, and Miriam Schneir. *Invitation to an Inquest*. New York: Pantheon, 1983.

See also Autopsies; Coroners; Grand juries; Preliminary hearings; Trial publicity; Trial transcripts; Trials; Verdicts.

Insanity defense

Definition: Defense tactic used to reduce the culpability of a criminal defendant

Criminal justice issues: Defendants; medical and health issues; pleas

Significance: When the insanity defense is invoked, or when one pleads guilty but men-

The Insanity Defense and Attorney Ethics

Director Otto Preminger's 1959 film *Anatomy of a Murder* is the story of a legal case involving an army officer (Ben Gazzara) accused of murder. Declaring that he killed his alleged victim because the man raped his wife, the officer claims to have acted under the influence of an "irresistible impulse," which made him temporarily insane at the time of the murder. In fact, during an initial interview with his client, the lawyer (Jimmy Stewart) as much as tells his client that the "irresistible impulse" defense is his only chance of an acquittal. The client accordingly frames his account of the killing in such a way as to take advantage of that defense. In real life, similar conduct on the part of an attorney would be regarded as unethical in most states. Lawyers, even criminal defense lawyers, are not permitted to offer evidence at trials that they know to be false. They may not simply invent stories designed to win their clients' acquittal, which appears to be what the lawyer does in *Anatomy of a Murder*.

Timothy L. Hall

tally ill, it is the burden of the defense to show that at the time of the crime, the defendant was unable to know right from wrong, that the defendant was unable to resist an impulse, or that the defendant's actions were a product of a mental defect or disease.

The insanity defense is often known as the not guilty by reason of insanity (NGRI) plea. Individuals invoking the NGRI plea at trial acknowledge that the acts they committed were criminal but contend that an intentional state of mind was lacking. The insanity defense is rooted in the concept that persons may lack moral blameworthiness because mental illness absolves them of guilty intent for their actions. Determining the individual's state of mind at the time of the criminal act becomes a central issue in the consideration of an NGRI plea.

The defense must convince the jury that the defendant was mentally ill at the time of the act. In order to accomplish this conclusion, defendants are often portrayed as having been victims of unusual trauma in their lives that leads to a mental illness. Critics of the NGRI plea suggest that defendants may pretend to have a mental illness and then profit from presenting the fraudulent claim. Because of the difficulties inherent in the NGRI plea, it is used infrequently and in only approximately 2 percent of capital cases.

Identifying Mental Illness

Historically, a number of guiding principles have been used to consider the state of mind of a defendant at the time of the criminal act. One of the first was the M'Naughten Rule that was established in 1843. This principle is often known as the "knowing right from wrong" rule, and it stated that persons are considered sane unless it can be proved that at the time of the criminal act they were laboring under a defect of reason caused by a disease of the mind so that they did not know the nature and quality of the acts. If the individuals knew they were committing the act, they did not understand that was a wrongdoing. The M'Naughten Rule is related to the cognitive aspects of understanding about right and wrong and how it relates to an individual's behavior. It is sometimes called the right-wrong test.

A principle from 1887 was known as the doctrine of the irresistible impulse. This concept suggested that defendants may not be responsible for their actions even if there was understanding of the wrongful nature of the act. In the circumstance that the person had no power to choose between right and wrong because of an irresistible impulse that compelled the person to act beyond reason, the individual would be held blameless. The doctrine of irresistible impulse has been the foundation for the volitional aspects of an insanity defense. This principle addresses the question of whether persons were unable to control their behavior sufficiently to prevent the criminal act.

Twentieth century applications of these principles include the Durham rule, established through a U.S. Court of Appeals decision in 1954. The Durham rule expanded the insanity defense to include the scientific findings regarding mental illness and developed a "product test." Using the Durham rule, an accused person is not deemed criminally responsible for unlawful acts if the actions were the product of the mental disease or a mental defect.

The American Law Institute proposed a further refinement to the insanity defense in 1962, called the substantial capacity test for insanity. This combined both the cognitive aspects of the M'Naughten Rule and the volitional component of the doctrine of irresistible impulse. The substantial capacity test of insanity held that a defendant is not legally responsible for an act if, at the time of commission, the person lacked a substantial capacity either to appreciate the action's criminal character or to conform behavior to the law's requirement of right and wrong.

Within the federal court system, the Federal Insanity Defense Reform Act (IDRA) of 1984 applies. This act abolished the volitional element of the substantial capacity test and narrowed the cognitive component to only "unable to appreciate." This IDRA also specified two important requirements for the presentation of an insanity defense. First, the mental disorder must be a severe condition that impedes functioning. Second, the burden of proof was shifted from the prosecution to the defense. With the IDRA, the defense must convincingly establish the state of mind of the defendant at the time of the criminal act to have been mentally ill. Previously, the prosecution had to show that the defendant was sane when the crime was committed.

Applications of the Insanity Defense

Reforms in the insanity defense as illustrated in the IDRA came about in response to extensive protest following the outcome of the trial of John Hinckley. In 1981, Hinckley attempted to assassinate U.S. president Ronald Reagan. In 1982, Hinckley was acquitted on the grounds that he was acting outside of reason and not guilty by reason of insanity. Since that trial, reforms in the insanity defense have tried to discourage its use and make its success unlikely when and if used.

In 2004, a majority of states adhered to some revised version of the substantial capacity test or the M'Naughten Rule. Various jurisdictions require a pretrial screening of the defendant that includes psychiatric evaluation and appraisal of criminal responsibility. Research has shown that the vast majority of insanity defense pleas were withdrawn after the screening process. Of those defendants most frequently successful in insanity defense pleas, the following characteristics have been present: woman defendant, one who had a previously diagnosed severe mental illness, one whose crime was not murder, and one who had prior hospitalizations.

Many critics of the insanity defense argue that it requires an impossible task to be completed, as psychiatric testimony often fails to agree on the mental state of a defendant. In 2004, some states had abolished the insanity defense for criminal acts, and others had established the plea of guilty but mentally ill as an alternative. This plea prevents a defendant from being acquitted for a criminal act and then being turned over to a mental health facility, from which the person could be released at any time.

Frank J. Prerost

Further Reading

Fabrega, H. "Culture and Formulation of Homicide: Two Case Studies." *Psychiatry* 67 (2004): 178-196. This article shows how culture influences the evaluation of a defendant's mental health.

Nicholson, R. A., et al. "A Comparison of Instruments for Assessing Competency to Stand Trial." *Law and Human Behavior* 12 (1988): 313-322. Provides examples of the techniques used to screen for mental disorders.

Simon, Robert. "Legal Issues in Psychiatry." In *Comprehensive Textbook of Psychiatry*, edited by B. Sadock and V. Sadock. 7th ed. Baltimore: Lippincott, Williams & Wilkins, 2000. Detailed presentation of the legal aspects of the insanity defense from the perspective of professionals completing the evaluations for the court system.

Szegedy-Maszak, M. "The Brainwashing Defense." *U.S. News and World Report* (December 22, 2003): 135. Example of how a person who has experienced brainwashing may not be competent to stand trial.

Weiss, K. "Confessions and Expert Testimony." *Journal of the American Academy of Psychiatry and Law* 31 (2003): 451-458. Good discussion of the problems in establishing mental illness through the inconsistencies of expert testimony.

See also Bifurcated trials; Competency to stand trial; Comprehensive Crime Control Act; Criminal intent; Criminal law; Defendant self-representation; Defenses to crime; Diminished capacity; Excuses and justifications; Forensic psychology; Malice; *Mens rea*; Mental illness.

Insider trading

Definition: Purchase or sale of securities by persons who have access to information that is not available to those with whom they deal or to traders generally

Criminal justice issues: Business and financial crime; fraud; white-collar crime

Significance: Under federal law, corporate "insiders" are discouraged from taking advantage of their unique access to information by engaging in short-term trading in the corporation's securities. Laws regulating insider trading are designed to create equal opportunities for all investors, on the theory that for the stock market to be fair it must in principle be equally accessible and equally unpredictable for all participants.

Insider trading is prohibited in the United States by Section 10(b) of the Securities and Exchange Act of 1934. Federal securities regulations are designed to prevent corporate executives, directors, attorneys, accountants, investment bankers, and other so-called "insiders" from using their positions to gain unfair advantages in the market trading of their corporations' securities. To buy or sell securities on the basis of confidential information or to recommend trading to others on that basis constitutes a violation of federal securities regulations, potentially subjecting the insider to criminal prosecution by the Securities and Exchange Commission (SEC) and civil lawsuits by injured investors. Insider trading first became widely publicized during the 1980's, when two prominent financiers, Ivan Boesky and Michael Milken, were convicted of numerous securities violations, sentenced to prison, and fined more than $700 million.

The 1934 Securities and Exchange Act was a response to a variety of fraudulent activities during the 1920's that manipulated stock prices and misled investors. For example, investment pools would "bid up" prices of selected stocks, often by trading the stocks back and forth among members of the pool, and then sell them to investors lured by the stocks' upward movements. Spreading of false rumors was another popular tactic.

The Insider Trading Act of 1984 extended the general rule against insider trading beyond narrow categories of "insiders." It stated that *any* person with nonpublic information who appeared to use that information while buying or selling securities might be prosecuted. Anyone aiding or abetting such a person might also be subject to penalties. Court decisions have prohibited the spreading of inside information to others who may trade in securities.

Those who oppose insider trading laws argue that the practice is unavoidable because some people will always have greater knowledge than others about financial affairs. Moreover, they argue that capitalism benefits when those who gain information from their labor are allowed to profit from it. Advocates of insider trading argue that knowledge is an individual possession, not a collective one.

High-Profile Cases

Whatever the philosophical arguments in favor of or against insider trading laws, the fact is that juries consistently find against persons charged with breaking those laws. Since the turn of the twenty-first century, a number of insider trading cases have been highly publicized. For example, in 2004, media tycoon Martha Stewart was tried on four counts of obstruction of justice that arose from charges that she had used insider information to sell stock in ImClon Systems in 2001. After a five-week trial, her jury deliberated for three days before reaching a verdict. It held that Stewart and her broker had obstructed justice and then lied about the conditions of her sale of the ImClone stock.

Earlier, the former chief executive officer of ImClone Systems, Samuel Waksal, pleaded guilty to charges of insider trading. In October, 2003, he admitted in court that he had tipped off family members and friends that the Food and Drug Administration had not reviewed ImClone's new cancer drug, allowing his family members and friends to sell their company shares before the stock's price went down.

In another major case involving insider trading, the chief financial officer of the credit card company Capital One, David M. Willey, resigned in 2003 after learning that the SEC was investigating him for insider trading. He and his wife had sold a large block of their shares in the company just before its stock fell dramatically on the announcement of its decision to increase its reserves. Wiley was being investigated for acting on knowledge not available to the public.

The key to insider trading is in the phrase "knowledge not available to the public." Simply because of their positions in the business world, certain people are privy to information not readily available to the public or even general shareholders. That knowledge gives them unfair advantages over others, enabling them to maximize their profits while other investors lose money through no fault of their own. Sharing inside information with others, for profit or for friendship, is also prohibited as a logical extension of the insider trading laws. Although those who are strong supporters of free enterprise may argue that insider trading laws punish those who have earned the right to acquire and benefit from special knowledge, most prosecutors and the general public disagree.

Frank A. Salamone
Updated by the Editors

Further Reading

Dalley, Paula J. "From Horse Trading to Insider Trading: The Historical Antecedents of the Insider Trading Debate." *William and Mary Law Review* 39 (1998): 1289-1353. Brief scholarly overview of the history of insider trading.

Lu Shen-Shin. *Insider Trading and the Twenty-four Hour Securities Market: A Case Study of Legal Regulation in the Emerging Global Economy*. Hanover, Mass.: Christopher, 1999. Examination of the application of federal regulations on the securities markets.

Reiman, Jeffrey H. *The Rich Get Richer and the Poor Get Prison: Ideology, Class and Criminal Justice*. Boston: Allyn and Bacon, 2004. Critical assessment of the failure of government to control white-collar crime.

Rosoff, Stephen M., and Henry N. Pontell. *Looting America: Greed, Corruption, Villains, and Victims*. Upper Saddle River, N.J.: Prentice Hall, 2003. Comprehensive overview of white-collar crime in the corporate world.

See also Consumer fraud; Corporate scandals; Fraud; Insurance fraud; Theft; White-collar crime.

Insurance fraud

Definition: Willful misrepresentations or fabrications by claimants or providers of facts concerning accidents, injuries, or thefts for the purpose of monetary gain

Criminal justice issues: Business and financial crime; fraud; medical and health issues; white-collar crime

Significance: Insurance fraud has been rated as the second-most costly crime in the United States. Heightened awareness of the many forms that insurance fraud can take and collaborative efforts among medical service providers, insurance companies, and law-enforcement agencies are essential to combating the crime.

Since its inception in the early seventeenth century, the insurance industry has thrived. Now, more than five thousand insurance companies operate in the United States and control more than $1.8 trillion in assets. However, both the nature and the prosperity of the industry have invited criminal enterprise. Insurance fraud is rated as the second-most costly crime in the United States, after tax evasion. Its average annual costs have been estimated at $115-120 billion. These costs are ultimately passed along to American consumers, whose average annual insurance premiums are about one thousand dollars per year higher for every family.

The complex nature of insurance fraud and the vast number of subcategories it encompasses make a comprehensive definition of the term nearly impossible. In general, insurance fraud constitutes falsification of facts for the purpose of deceiving insurance providers, with the intent to obtain money to which one is not entitled.

Types of Insurance Fraud

Insurance fraud falls into two distinct categories: opportunistic fraud and hard fraud. Also known as soft fraud, opportunistic fraud is the more common type. A simple example is a car owner who lies about the number of miles the vehicle is driven each year in order to pay lower premiums on auto insurance. Most people who engage in opportunistic fraud do not regard their acts as fraud, instead dismissing their behavior as inconsequential "white lies."

Hard fraud is the intentional misrepresentation of facts to win large monetary settlements. It is a lucrative field for organized crime rings that organize lavish schemes to misappropriate millions of dollars. Many types of insurance are targets of hard fraud, but three types stand out as the most common: auto insurance fraud, workers' compensation fraud, and health care fraud.

It has been estimated that more than one-third of all auto insurance injury claims contain some type of fraud; 90 percent of these are instances of opportunistic fraud. The most common forms of these frauds are falsifying information on auto mileage and inflating repair costs to cover deductibles—a scam known as padding. Other forms of auto insurance fraud include staged accidents that involve vehicle damage and medical claims, exaggerations and falsifications of injuries, abandonment of vehicles for the purpose of filing stolen-vehicle claims, false hit-and-run claims in one-car accidents, and claiming injuries to persons not actually involved in accidents.

Lawrence, Massachusetts, a town about twenty-five miles north of Boston, has won such notoriety for staged automobile accidents and insurance fraud that it has been dubbed the "insurance fraud capital" of the state. *(AP/Wide World Photos)*

According to the U.S. Chamber of Commerce, 25 percent of all workers' compensation claims are fraudulent. This type of fraud takes three forms: claimant fraud, provider fraud, and premium fraud. In claimant fraud, the most common form, employees often fake or exaggerate injuries in order to collect greater compensation awards. Another form of claimant fraud is claiming on-the-job injuries when the injuries actually occur elsewhere.

Provider fraud is perpetrated by medical professionals who do such things as report false or exaggerated injuries among their patients, submit false charges for services, itemize fees for single procedures, and withhold information on insurance coverage. Premium fraud is perpetrated by employers who intentionally mislead insurance carriers about the nature of their companies and employees in order to pay lower premiums. Employers may understate their payrolls, misclassify their employees' job titles, or list salaried employees as independent contractors.

The health care industry is one of the hardest hit by insurance fraud and deals with millions of fraudulent transactions annually. Health care fraud is committed, in varying degrees, by claimants and service providers alike. Claimant frauds include patients forging receipts, requesting doctors to falsify reports to cover desired procedures, and petitioning doctors to waive co-payments.

Provider frauds include billing for services never rendered, providing procedures that are not medically necessary, accepting kickbacks for referrals, billing for services costing more than those actually provided, misrepresenting non-covered treatments as covered treatments, and misrepresenting patients' identities by the falsification of medical cards.

Medicare and Medicaid fraud is a particularly large area that provides enormous opportunities for organized crime. An example would be the creation of a phony clinic that generates fraudulent claims using authentic patient insurance and provider billing information that has been bought or stolen. Such schemes are sustained by teams of doctors and lawyers.

Investigation

Despite the growing magnitude of insurance fraud, law-enforcement agencies were long reluctant to pursue this type of crime. That fact has encouraged many criminals to switch from other types of crime to insurance fraud, which is typically both safer and more lucrative. The attitude of law enforcement toward insurance fraud began to change during the mid-1980's, when insurance premiums started rising rapidly. Public concern prompted lawmakers to begin developing plans to help keep health care costs under control.

Most states have created fraud bureaus, and insurance companies have their own special investigation units. Although some states still list insurance fraud as a misdemeanor, the majority rate it as a felony, with punishments of up to seven years in prison and fifteen thousand dollars in fines.

Insurance companies and law-enforcement officials face innumerable challenges in averting insurance fraud. While the public clamors for lower health care costs, most Americans believe it is acceptable to do such things as exaggerate their insurance claims to cover deductibles. In order to strengthen the effectiveness of the criminal justice system's handling of insurance fraud, it is important that the crime be listed as a felony offense in every state penal code. Otherwise, it will fall under the general category of fraud by deception and will hold lower penalties.

Lisa Landis Murphy

Further Reading

Albrecht, W. S., and C. Albrecht. *Fraud Examination and Prevention*. Mason, Ohio: South-Western Educational Publishing, 2003. Broad study of various forms of fraud, including insurance fraud, that illustrates how frauds are detected, investigated, and prevented.

Dorstein, K. *Accidentally or on Purpose: The Making of a Personal Injury Underworld in America*. New York: St. Martin's Press, 1996. Study of personal injury fraud based on the author's extensive interviews of people in the industry.

Lichtor, J. *Personal Injury Insurance Fraud: The Process of Detection—a Primer for Insurance and Legal Professionals*. Tucson, Ariz.: Lawyers and Judges Publishing, 2002. Handbook for people in the insurance and legal professions that includes a history of personal injury and workers' compensation fraud and practical advice on investigation and prevention.

Tillman, Robert. *Global Pirates: Fraud in the Offshore Insurance Industry*. Boston: Northeastern University Press, 2002. Study of insurance fraud throughout the world. Uses a multitude of case studies and offers recommendations for preventing fraud.

Torras, H. W., and H. Torras. *Health Care Fraud and Abuse: A Physician's Guide to Compliance*. Chicago: American Medical Association, 2002. Handbook on insurance fraud for medical professionals that explains methods for detecting and avoiding fraud.

Whitlock, C., and Ben Chandler. *MediScams: How to Spot and Avoid Health Care Scams, Medical Frauds, and Quackery from the Local Physician to the Major Health Care Providers and Drug Manufacturers*. New York: St. Martin's Press, 2001. Practical advice for consumers on insurance fraud that contains an inside look into the many schemes that plague the health-care industry.

See also Consumer fraud; Corporate scandals; Fraud; Insider trading; Insurance fraud; Money laundering; Tax evasion; Telephone fraud; White-collar crime.

Internal affairs

Definition: Units within police departments that investigate charges of police misconduct

Criminal justice issues: Government misconduct; police powers; professional standards

Significance: Internal affairs units provide citizens with avenues for reporting police misconduct and seeking redress.

Individuals and governments that have control over people are often abusive. The same may be said of police personnel. Since the inception of formalized policing during the first half of the nineteenth century, police misconduct and misbehavior have often occurred in policing agencies. The early decade of the twenty-first century does not appear to be any closer to eliminating this problem. This may be due to the very nature of police work.

Police in American society have legal and recognized positions of authority and power. Their primary mission is to maintain social order through their legitimate authority. However, police periodically misuse their authority and have confrontations with citizens. Confrontations can occur, for example, when citizens challenge police officers' authority or do not obey officers' commands as quickly as the officers would like. Confrontations between citizens and police may leave the impression that the police often overstep their authority in enforcing social order.

Human rights groups as well as many members of minority groups believe that the police have often denied citizens their civil rights. In actuality, American police officers have the responsibility to protect the constitutional rights of all citizens. However, there are police officers and officials who do not believe that their responsibility extends to all citizens equally.

The police have the responsibility to maintain the trust of the community. When there are reports of inappropriate behavior and actions performed by police officers, then citizens lose confidence in the police. If police even give the appearance of wrongdoing, citizens lose respect for them. Without community support, the police will have difficulties in maintaining order and solving crimes.

Police misconduct includes any wrongdoing by officers who commit acts that violate criminal laws or departmental regulations or policies. Actions such as excessive use of force, corruption, use of drugs on duty, and rudeness to citizens are examples of behaviors that cannot be condoned. When police are charged with misconduct, the departmental branches responsible for investigating the charges are internal affairs units.

Purpose of Internal Affairs

The goal of internal affairs units is to protect both communities and their police departments from inappropriate police behavior by investigating citizen allegations of misconduct. Most departments have structured complaint procedures. Citizens can file their complaints in person, by telephone, or by mail. It is generally preferable that complainants identify themselves, as anonymous complaints lack the impact of identifiable complaints.

Ideally, all complaints, regardless of their nature, are impartially investigated. Most complaints are minor and are handled by supervisors. For example, a rudeness complaint—which is common—would be handled by the offending officer's immediate supervisor. Serious allegations are handled by the formal internal affairs units. Their investigations can lead to officers being reprimanded, suspended, or even terminated. In a formal investigation, all witnesses to the alleged misconduct are interviewed, and all relevant physical evidence is collected and examined. This evidence includes information submitted by the officers under investigation.

Investigations

Police officers under investigation may not wish to cooperate but are required to do so. When they are interviewed by internal affairs investigators, the investigators must follow guidelines established by the U.S. Supreme Court's 1967 ruling in *Garrity v. New Jersey*. These guidelines include a statement that investigators read to officers under investigation that is known as the "Garrity warning." (It is also sometimes called the "Garrity law" or "Garrity rule.")

Similar to the Miranda warning that police officers read to suspects whom they arrest, the Garrity warning advises officers under investigation that they must answer all questions asked by investigators or face disciplinary action, including possible termination. However, the Garrity warning also requires that officers being questioned be advised that their responses to questions cannot be used in criminal prosecutions. Officers who may face criminal prosecution are informed that they are not required to answer the questions, but if they do, then their responses may be used against them in criminal proceedings.

Upon completion of internal affairs investigations, the findings are submitted to the departments' police chiefs or other high-ranking administrators. The investigations can have several possible outcomes. They may sustain the allegations or rule them "not sustained" for lack of evidence to prove or disprove the allegations. Exoneration is the finding in cases in which the

investigators conclude that the alleged acts did occur but were justified, lawful, and proper. When investigators find sufficient evidence to conclude that the alleged misconduct did not occur, they rule the case closed, with "no finding."

When allegations against officers are sustained, disciplinary action is taken against the officers. Such discipline varies with the seriousness of the misconduct and the officers' prior service records. Punishment can range from formal letters of reprimand to suspensions from duty without pay and termination. Letters reporting the investigations' findings are sent to the complainants.

Michael J. Palmiotto

Further Reading

Bennet, W., and Karen Hess. *Management and Supervision in Law Enforcement*. 4th ed. Belmont, Calif.: Wadsworth, 2004. Comprehensive textbook on all aspects of local police work, including community-oriented policing.

Fyfe, James, et al. *Police Administration*. 5th ed. New York: McGraw-Hill, 1997. Comprehensive textbook on all aspects of police administration, including internal affairs investigations.

Palmiotto, Michael J. *Community Policing: A Policing Strategy for the Twenty-first Century*. 2d ed. Boston: Jones and Bartlett, 2005. Comprehensive and up-to-date survey of all aspects of community-oriented policing.

Thrasher, Ronald. "Internal Affairs: The Police Agencies' Approach to the Investigation of Police Misconduct. In *Police Misconduct*, edited by Michael J. Palmiotto. Upper Saddle River, N.J.: Prentice Hall, 2001. College-level course reader that covers many aspects of police misconduct, including brutality and corruption.

Walker, Samuel, and Charles M. Katz. *The Police in America: An Introduction*. 5th ed. New York: McGraw-Hill, 2005. Up-to-date textbook covering all aspects of police work in the United States.

See also Bill of Rights, U.S.; International Brotherhood of Police Officers; King beating case; Knapp Commission; Miranda rights; Police brutality; Police civil liability; Police dogs; Police ethics.

Internal Revenue Service

Identification: Federal agency responsible for enforcing income and excise tax laws, and investigating criminal violations of the Internal Revenue Code and related financial crimes

Date: Established in 1862

Criminal justice issues: Business and financial crime; computer crime; federal law; fraud

Significance: The Internal Revenue Service (IRS) is the only federal agency commissioned to investigate criminal violations of the U.S. Internal Revenue Code.

The IRS, a branch of the Department of the Treasury, was established in 1862 by President Abra-

ham Lincoln to enact a tax to compensate for the expense of the Civil War. As a direct result of the IRS Restructuring and Reform Act of 1998, the IRS was reorganized into four major operating divisions, corresponding to various categories of taxpayers. The four divisions are the Wage and Investment division, the Small Business/Self-Employed division, the Large and Mid-Size Business division, and the Tax-Exempt and Government Entities division. There are three additional divisions: Communications and Liaison, Appeals, and Criminal Investigation. This discussion will focus on the Criminal Investigation division.

The predecessor of the Criminal Investigation division was created in 1919, when an IRS intelligence unit was assembled to investigate tax fraud. This unit attained much notoriety in the summer

Internal Revenue Service data transcribers entering information from individual income tax returns into computers at the Cincinnati Service Center, which alone processes more than six million returns a year. (AP/Wide World Photos)

of 1930, when world-renowned gangster Al Capone saw his deviant career brought to an end by the IRS, not for his violent criminal activity but for income tax evasion. In 1978, the unit was named Criminal Investigation when its jurisdiction was expanded to include activities violating the Money Laundering Act and Bank Secrecy Act of 1970. This division is identified as the law-enforcement aspect of the Internal Revenue Service. From 1919 to 2004, the conviction rate for federal tax prosecutions was 90 percent or better, the highest among all federal law-enforcement agencies.

The Criminal Investigation division comprises twenty-nine hundred special agents performing a combination of accounting and law-enforcement duties in the investigation of financial crimes. Its operations include surveillance and undercover work, intelligence, strike forces, and the organized crime drug task force. Six areas categorize financial crimes in a diverse combination of industries and professions for which this division is responsible: tax return preparer fraud, real estate fraud, automotive industry fraud, construction industry fraud, restaurant industry fraud, and medical fraud. In the wake of the September 11, 2001, terrorist attacks on the United States, as well as myriad technological advancements in the use of computers to commit crime, the Criminal Investigation division has augmented its financial skills and law-enforcement resources to create several task forces to combat terrorism.

Lisa Landis Murphy

Further Reading

Plan Your IRS Career. Washington, D.C.: U.S. Department of Treasury, Internal Revenue Service, 1997.

Schmalleger, F. *Your Criminal Justice Career: A Guidebook*. Englewood Cliffs, N.J.: Prentice-Hall, 2002.

Territo, L., J. B. Halsted, and M. Bromley. *Crime and Justice in America: A Human Perspective*. 6th ed. Englewood Cliffs, N.J.: Prentice-Hall, 2003.

See also Fraud; Gangsters of the Prohibition era; Internal Revenue Service; Money laundering; Tax evasion; Treasury Department, U.S.

International Association of Chiefs of Police

Identification: Professional law-enforcement organization

Date: Founded in 1893

Place: Chicago, Illinois

Criminal justice issues: Crime statistics; law-enforcement organization; professional standards

Significance: Throughout its long history, the International Association of Chiefs of Police (IACP) has supported police training, education, innovative technology, and modernization with an international outreach to all world police agencies.

The original name of the IACP when it was founded in 1893 was National Chiefs of Police Union. Its founders were police chiefs who wanted to share information on wanted suspects and criminal activity among law-enforcement agencies throughout the United States. The association's members shared the belief that if any jurisdiction was unaware of criminal activities in other geographical areas, that lack of information was of benefit only to criminals.

The association's original goal of sharing criminal information developed into the Uniform Crime Reports during the 1920s. Published annually by the Federal Bureau of Investigation (FBI) since 1930, this publication now serves as the official source of crime statistics for the United States. The IACP was also responsible for creating the FBI's Identification Bureau during the mid-1920's.

The association has made numerous contributions to the field of law enforcement during its century-plus history. It has fostered police professionalism, law-enforcement ethics, and technological advancement. In 1934, the association published a newsletter that subsequently evolved into the modern organization's *Police Chief* magazine, which continues to serve as the professional voice of the law-enforcement community today. In 1955, the IACP established an International Police Academy and continued to advocate the development of standards for police training throughout the United States. Since then, basic standards have been adopted nationally and now serve as an international model for police standards and training. The IACP was also responsible for establishing the Commission on Accreditation for Law Enforcement Agencies during the 1980's. The organization continues to be the leading advocate for law-enforcement training and professionalism worldwide.

Lawrence C. Trostle

Further Reading

Bennet, W., and Karen Hess. *Management and Supervision in Law Enforcement*. 4th ed. Belmont, Calif.: Wadsworth, 2004.

Fyfe, James, et al. *Police Administration*. 5th ed. New York: McGraw-Hill, 1997.

Kenny, Dennis J., and Robert P. McNamara, eds. *Police and Policing: Contemporary Issues*. 2d ed. Westport, Conn.: Praeger, 1999.

See also Canadian justice system; Law enforcement; Peace Officers Standards and Training; Police academies; Police chiefs; Police ethics.

International Brotherhood of Police Officers

Identification: Large, multijurisdictional union of law-enforcement officers

Date: Founded in 1964

Criminal justice issues: Civil rights and liberties; law-enforcement organization; professional standards

Significance: The International Brotherhood of Police Officers, or IBPO, is one of the leading organizations serving as a legal watchdog for the rights of police officers. It works to win police officers fair and equitable contracts and better working conditions, and it lobbies for legislation that assists police work.

The IBPO is one of the largest police officer unions in the United States. It is presently affiliated with two other large unions, the Service Employees International Union (SEIU) and the AFL-CIO. Affiliated with the National Association of Government Employees since 1970, the IBPO was founded after seven Rhode Island police officers were fired in 1964 when they protested a promotional examination for which answers had been previously circulated. The fired officers succeeded in persuading the Rhode Island legislature to allow police officers in the state to organize for the purpose of collective bargaining. The first local was formed, and other affiliates for officers in different states followed soon thereafter. By 2004, the organization claimed a national membership of approximately 14,000 officers.

The union focuses on several specific services that it provides its members. It negotiates contracts, and attorneys are provided who have successfully represented members before civil service commissions and all levels of courts and labor-relations boards. The union's full-time lobbying staff in Washington, D.C., and state capitals has had many notable achievements, including Senate approval of a death benefit presently set at $250,000 for family members of officers killed in the line of duty. The lobbying arm of the IBPO has also begun an initiative called the Committee on Political Education (COPE), funded by IBPO members and designed to fight anti-employee legislation.

Eric W. Metchik

Further Reading

Bennet, W., and Karen Hess. *Management and Supervision in Law Enforcement*. 4th ed. Belmont, Calif.: Wadsworth, 2004.

Miller, L., and Karen Hess. *Police in the Community: Strategies for the Twenty-first Century*. 3d ed. Belmont, Calif.: Wadsworth, 2002.

See also Deadly force; Highway patrols; Internal affairs; Peace Officers Standards and Training; Police; Police Activities League; Police chiefs; Police civil liability; Police ethics; Reasonable force; State police.

International law

Definition: Body of international norms and practices established by national governments to deter and to punish criminal acts of international consequence

Criminal justice issues: International law; law codes; terrorism

Significance: International criminal law punishes major crimes against persons by coordinating national legislative and enforcement activities at the international level.

International customary law has long recognized that dangerous and despicable criminal acts can be committed by individuals in ways that threaten other people as well as the interests and order of governments and of the international community. Under international law, individuals are primarily situated within the domestic and territorial jurisdiction of a particular country, and every country has the right to establish systems of criminal as well as civil law. In this sense, individuals are directly and firstly subject to the criminal laws of the countries in which they live or that they travel through, and they can be arrested, tried, and punished under national criminal statutes. Governments are free to punish violators of their domestic criminal statutes as well as those who have violated crimes of an international nature. Indeed, governments have long recognized that certain kinds of harmful activities transcend domestic enforcement, requiring international regulation and cooperation so that law and order is kept not only within but also among nations.

In modern times, the number and scope of criminal acts by individuals that threaten the interests of governments and the international community have increased. Piracy at sea is a historical example of an international crime. More recently, slavery and the international slave trade came to be regarded as international criminal acts requiring international attention. Modern international criminal law embraces many other acts that threaten international stability and justice, including skyjacking, hostage taking, war crimes, crimes against humanity, genocide, and terrorism, among others.

Early Developments

As mentioned, a classic example of an international criminal act is piracy at sea. For many centuries, customary international law treated piracy as a threat to the safety of maritime trade. Those who engaged in plunder and pillage at sea were seen as criminals, and their unregistered vessels were regarded as pirate ships. Persons engaging in piratical acts made themselves international outlaws by violating the rules of civilized nations, which included an obligation to refrain during time of peace from detaining, pillaging, or destroying the ships, crew, passengers, and cargo of vessels engaged in peaceable commerce. Pirates were seen by governments as criminals who were *hostes humani generis*, that is, "the enemies of all humankind." Any government could apprehend, try, and punish pirates under a principle of universal jurisdiction. The pirate did not need to be a citizen or subject of the state taking punitive action. Pirates were considered international criminals, and all persons had a duty to refrain from piratical acts. This demonstrates the earliest development of what is now called an international crime; governments perceived an interest in regulating a common threat to their peaceable interaction that required the development of common norms and procedures for punishing and deterring the criminal behavior.

During the nineteenth century, slavery and the slave trade were gradually added to the list of international criminal activities, as governments began to take steps both in their domestic legislation and enforcement as well as in their international relations. A nation could outlaw slavery within its own territory, but interdiction and prohibition of the slave trade required international cooperation. Great Britain took the lead in this endeavor in the 1830's by outlawing slavery in its domains. It followed up by using British naval power to interdict slave trade and by pressuring other nations to join it in the endeavor. Momentum to classify slave trading as criminal gathered steam during the late nineteenth century, leading up to the promulgation of the 1919 Convention of St. Germain, which was the first international treaty to outlaw the slave trade on land and sea. Numerous subsequent treaties built on the St. Germain Treaty, and the slave trade entered the class of international criminal acts.

War Crimes

Governments have long acknowledged limits on the behavior of armed forces during war, breaches of which could be punished by a soldier's national state or by any other state that might gain custody over military personnel suspected of egregious violations of customary norms of war, such as the willful massacre of civilian populations; the murder of unarmed, wounded, or sick soldiers; or the killing of prisoners of war. However, prosecutions for such war crimes were infrequent in the practice of nations, and thus such crimes often went unpunished.

In 1899 and 1907, world governments met to negotiate the Hague Conventions as an attempt to codify the international customary norms of war. These treaties failed to win enough ratification to enter into force, but they did largely enter into the actual practice of nations and thus did express the prevailing customs of war acknowledged by governments. Various Geneva Red Cross Conventions dating from 1864, 1929, and 1949 clarified state obligations toward prisoners of war and toward sick and wounded soldiers as well as civilian populations, thus contributing to the further development of international humanitarian law.

After World War II and the egregious crimes of Germany's Nazi regime, the trials at Nuremberg constituted a visible international attempt to punish war criminals. The tribunal introduced two new international crimes, namely crimes against peace and crimes against humanity. Soldiers could no longer claim immunity from punishment for violating the laws of war by invoking the defense of superior orders. Similarly, high-ranking military officers and government officials implicated in crimes against humanity could no longer claim sovereign immunity. Although the Nuremberg tribunal sparked controversy as a form of "victor's justice" and complaints of unfair ex post facto application of punishment for actions not previously considered criminal, the principles invoked at Nuremberg have entered into state practice.

The movement to make crimes against peace a whole new classification of crime was criticized, given the fact that war and planning for war were routine aspects of state practice prior to World War II. However, very few German officials were convicted of crimes against peace alone; most of those sentenced to long prison sentences or to execution were guilty of more flagrant war crimes violations or of crimes against humanity. Definition of the so-called crime of aggression continues to elude full international consensus.

The new class of criminal acts, referred to as crimes against humanity, was introduced at Nuremberg to address the unprecedented and shocking acts perpetrated under the Nazi regime, which exterminated six million Jews and an equal number of non-Jewish people in Germany and various countries under German occupation during the Holocaust. The discovery of a vast network of extermination and concentration camps shocked the international community. Thus, while no international law existed prior to World War II forbidding such acts of mass murder and genocide, their very outrageous character cried out for justice.

Among civilized nations and peoples, it should not be necessary to prohibit unthinkable crimes. The historical experience of the twentieth century suggests that it was necessary to do so and that even the articulation of crimes against humanity would not be sufficient to deter subsequent grave violations against human dignity on a vast scale, as genocides in Cambodia, Rwanda, and Sudan would continue to demonstrate. In the wake of World War II the United Nations (U.N.) began the process of drafting human rights declarations and treaties to protect individuals from persecution and to declare as criminal various acts such as genocide, torture, and, eventually, after long and controversial debate, terrorism.

Genocide

The shock of the Nazi-perpetrated Holocaust led to the perceived need for specific action against mass murder and the extermination of peoples. War crimes could be punished by governments through their own administrative machinery or by special tribunals, such as those set up following World War II at Nuremberg and in the Far East. A government's crimes against its own people or against occupied civilian populations required wider legal action and political willingness to act.

In 1948, the United Nations promulgated the Genocide Convention to prohibit any government

Inmates in a German concentration camp during World War II. The egregious crimes committed by the Nazi regime under German chancellor Adolf Hitler changed the way the world looked at international law and gave rise to a postwar tribunal at Nuremberg at which surviving Nazi leaders were called to account for their violations of human rights. *(National Archives)*

or person from the planning or the carrying out of plans to destroy a people. This treaty protects ethnic, racial, religious, and national groups from destruction. It forbids not only their killing in whole or part but also other measures meant to eliminate groups of people through policies of abortion, sterilization, seizure of children, separation of families, forced deportation, and depopulation. Persons guilty of planning or executing such policies may be tried by a court in the state where the act was committed or by international bodies recognized by treaty members. An example of such an international tribunal includes the recently established International Criminal Court (ICC), which may take legal action against persons, including heads of state, accused of genocide.

The existence of modern law and tribunals has

not prevented war crimes, genocide, and other inhumane criminal activity. Genocidal activities in the Korean War as well as the slaughter of Ugandans under Idi Amin, of Cambodians under Pol Pot, and of Christians in the Arab-dominated country of the Sudan all took place without full justice for the perpetrators. Saddam Hussein's extermination of Shiite Muslims and Kurds in Iraq and the "ethnic cleansing" policies so widely practiced in Bosnia and Herzegovina and Kosovo, along with the genocidal policies pursued by extremist Hutus against Tutsis in Rwanda, illustrated the need for more determined international action to prevent and punish genocide. In these latter cases, national and international tribunals were established to bring perpetrators of such crimes to justice, and legal action against many of them was still pending in 2004.

United Nations secretary general Kofi Annan views the skulls of some of the victims of the 1994 genocide in Rwanda, where more than one-half million people were killed during an outburst of ethnic rage and as many as two million Rwandans may have fled into neighboring countries to escape the violence. The failure of the outside world to intervene led to new calls for international mechanisms to prevent future genocides. (AP/Wide World Photos)

New Tribunals

The many modern examples of state-sponsored genocide pushed the international community to take steps in the 1990's to strengthen international procedures and mechanisms to punish international crimes of genocide. The U.N. Security Council established an International Criminal Tribunal for Yugoslavia in 1993 and an International Criminal Tribunal for Rwanda in 1994. The government of Rwanda has taken steps through its own court systems to punish offenders as well.

During the 1990's, international efforts to replace such ad hoc tribunals with a more permanent and global criminal court led to the negotiation and establishment of the ICC. Under the statute of this court, international criminal acts include not only traditional war crimes but also torture, terrorism, and the undefined crime of

aggression. The ICC prosecutor has the authority to indict any individual whose country of nationality or jurisdiction has been unable or unwilling to take legal action against a suspected war criminal.

By establishing a universal jurisdiction, the ICC should, theoretically, deter international criminal activity. During the 1990's and the early twenty-first century, the United States indicated that it would not ratify the ICC. Its objections to the treaty included the refusal by member states to include provisions to account for American constitutional practice as well as concerns about American military personnel, especially those serving in international peacekeeping missions, being subjected to hostile and frivolous charges and actions under the ICC statute. Differences in American and European legal philosophies became apparent during the drafting stage and deepened during the implementation of the statute.

Other International Criminal Acts

Various treaties have been promulgated that have established a variety of additional international criminal laws, apart from those addressing war crimes and genocide. The old concern about piracy at sea gave way during the 1960's and 1970's to concern about air piracy and skyjacking. Treaties declaring such actions criminal have variously given jurisdiction for punishment of such crimes to countries of nationality, countries of landing, or countries of registry. As with genocide, persons guilty of skyjacking may also be extradited for trial and punishment to any state making a legitimate extradition request under bilateral or multilateral treaties.

Another crime that has been increasingly prohibited under both regional and international treaties is that of torture. The difficulty in gaining full international consensus on this issue centered on the definition of torture, which may include less objectionable acts of high-pressure interrogation, such as sleep deprivation, as well as clearly inimical practices of inflicting bodily pain or mutilation. Exactly where legitimate interrogation ends and torture begins is a debated question. Still, clear examples of torture are widely reviled, and few governments are willing openly to justify them, although many governments continue to practice the clearly more objectionable forms of torture, despite all international efforts to eliminate such practices.

Terrorism

Of special interest in the twenty-first century is the need to prevent and punish acts of terrorism, which, by definition, represent arbitrary crimes of violence, including hostage taking, murder, and bombings aimed at killing and intimidating innocent civilian populations. Under the traditional laws of war, terrorists are regarded as war criminals, and several international treaties of recent origin attempt to encourage the prevention of terrorist bombings and the apprehension, extradition, and punishment of those guilty of terrorist acts. From the early 1970's into the mid-1990's, the United Nations

had a difficult time even defining terrorism, owing to the political claims of national liberation movements that employed terrorist tactics. In 1997, the United Nations finally settled on a definition of terrorism that specifically forbade arbitrary acts of criminal violence aimed at instilling terror among innocent civilian populations for any political purposes. With the increase of terrorist acts in rich and poor countries alike, international tolerance of terrorism declined, and steps to uncover terrorist organizations and to punish those guilty of terrorist acts intensified, especially in the wake of the terrorist attacks of September 11, 2001.

Exercising Jurisdiction

As international law stood in 2004, any country may, on its own authority and initiative, take action to apprehend, indict, detain, try, convict, and punish individuals guilty of international crimes. Most guilty individuals are likely to face the domestic criminal justice systems of countries whose law, safety, security, and good order have been disturbed by the international criminal activity. International action also is possible and raises the prospect of concurrent jurisdiction, whereby more than one country and more than one court at the national, regional, or global level may exercise the right to jurisdiction.

This national and international action will address not only the more visible and well-known crimes of genocide, war crimes, torture, terrorism, and skyjacking but also other international criminal activity such as trafficking in women and children, counterfeiting, money laundering, unlawful experimentation on human beings, destruction and theft of national treasures and antiquities, international prostitution, drug trafficking, and trafficking in child pornography. An increasing array of such activities are perpetrated not only within but also between and among countries.

Thus, although domestic action against such crimes can be expected to continue, countries increasingly enter into bilateral and multilateral cooperative agreements to regulate, eliminate, and punish such crimes. Domestic action against such crimes often requires extradition agreements to ensure either that criminals fleeing from punishment in one country are returned to it for trial or that accused persons face trial in the country to which they have escaped.

As the ad hoc criminal tribunals for Yugoslavia and Rwanda illustrate, further steps at the regional and global levels can be taken to spread a wider net of cooperation to ensure that justice is meted out to international criminals. Finally, the ICC represents the most global endeavor to prevent and punish various international crimes. Ultimately, however, the success of all such efforts depends upon the will and ability of governments to follow through on the punishment of those persons guilty of crimes against human dignity and decency. Treaties are rarely self-enforcing. Rather, governments, in countless decisions and actions, determine day by day whether such criminals are brought before the bar of justice.

Robert F. Gorman

Further Reading

Broomhall, Bruce. *International Justice and the Criminal Court: Between Sovereignty and the Rule of Law*. New York: Oxford University Press, 2003. Solid assessment of the prospects for the development of an international justice system in which the ICC is situated. Examines traditional elements of international criminal law, the Nuremberg principles, and the scheme and the viability of the ICC in the light of various obstacles, including American objections.

Cassese, Antonio. *International Criminal Law*. New York: Oxford University Press, 2003. Readable introduction to international criminal law examining the substantive aspects of the law and the procedural dimensions of state practice.

Gardam, Judith, ed. *Humanitarian Law*. Brookfield, Vt.: Ashgate, 1999. Collection of previously published articles by distinguished scholars on human rights, humanitarian law, the Geneva conventions, and the laws of war.

Levie, Howard S. *Terrorism in War: The Law of War Crimes*. New York: Oceana, 1992. Extensive collection of documents and commentary on the modern development of the laws of war and war crimes from the late nineteenth century into the early twentieth century, with special emphasis on developments since World War II.

Proust, Jordan J., and Bassiouni M. Cherif, et al. *International Criminal Law: Cases and Materials*. 3 vols. Durham, N.C.: Carolina Academic Press, 1996. Thorough and systematic exegesis of the history, principles, scope, and practice of international criminal law. A valuable source of materials and commentaries for serious students.

Sands, Philippe, ed. *From Nuremberg to the Hague: The Future of International Criminal Justice*. Cambridge, England: Cambridge University Press, 2003. Collection of five thoughtful essays on the evolution of the Nuremberg law, the application of the Nuremberg experience to the ICC, the drafting of the ICC statute, and lessons drawn from the Yugoslavia and Rwanda tribunals.

Von Glahn, Gerhardt. *Law Among Nations: An Introduction to Public International Law*. 7th ed. New York: Longman, 1996. Widely used standard text of international law containing useful chapters on international criminal law, human rights, and war crimes. A thoughtful and balanced classic in the field of international law.

See also Antiterrorism and Effective Death Penalty Act; Canadian justice system; Criminology; Diplomatic immunity; *Ex post facto* laws; Extradition; International tribunals; Interpol; Skyjacking; Terrorism; War crimes; World Court.

International tribunals

Definition: Courts established by countries at the regional or global level to try war criminals

Criminal justice issues: Courts; international law; military justice; terrorism

Significance: International tribunals enable countries to cooperate in bringing to justice perpetrators of such crimes as genocide and terrorism.

Although governments are free to prosecute individuals accused of various war crimes within their own domestic jurisdictions, many have decided on various occasions to establish international tribunals for this purpose. Reasons for this vary. Sometimes governments desire to place pressure on particular governments to desist from commission of war crimes, as was the case in the former Yugoslavia. Sometimes the deeds committed by governments and their officials are so grave and outrageous that other governments wish to make an example of them by attracting more widespread publicity and thereby promoting a climate conducive to future deterrence. This happened after World War II in the Nuremberg Trials. As the International Criminal Court (ICC) illustrates, governments may wish to establish a more effective global mechanism to deter and punish war crimes. The existence of international tribunals does not prevent governments from taking decisive domestic action to try and punish war crimes, but it does offer them some flexibility in determining when, where, and how to bring accused war criminals to justice.

The Nuremberg Experience

Following World War I, the Treaty of Versailles provided for the possibility of extensive trials of German officials accused of violating the customs and laws of war. Of the nearly nine hundred persons originally listed for trial, only a dozen were actually tried, and only half of them received sentences upon conviction. However, the nature and scope of atrocities committed during World War II by Germany's Nazi regime dwarfed those committed during World War I, and a horrified international community took determined steps to ensure that high-ranking Nazi government officials would face international justice for their crimes.

Agreement was reached in London to establish the International Military Tribunal, which came to be known as the Nuremberg tribunal. Three classes of crimes were outlined, including the uncontroversial class of war crimes—which were widely accepted by governments as part of international customary law—and the more controversial crimes against peace and crimes against humanity, which represented new laws which could only give rise to *ex post facto* punishment. The vast majority of individuals sentenced under the Nuremberg Trials were convicted of traditional war crimes, while only two were convicted for crimes against humanity alone.

With regard to war crimes, the Nuremberg trials set aside sovereign immunity claims by government officials, and it revoked the traditional defense by which soldiers could claim immunity from prosecution under the principle of following superiors' orders. Trials were also held in the Far East, using the same threefold classification of crimes. More than seven thousand persons were arrested under the terms of the two tribunals, around forty-six hundred persons were tried, and nearly thirty-seven hundred were convicted, more than one thousand of whom received death sentences.

Post-World War II Trends

Following World War II, governments returned to the more traditional practice of dealing with war crimes within their own military justice systems or by their own national courts, includ-

Former Yugoslav president Slobodan Milošević, who was charged with sixty-six counts of war crimes. *(AP/Wide World Photos)*

ing such famous trials as those involving Nazi criminal Adolf Eichmann, who was tried and convicted to a death sentence in an Israeli court. The United States Army tried six of its own military personnel for the My Lai massacre during the Vietnam War, but only Lieutenant William L. Calley, Jr., was convicted. National tribunals and courts also dealt with increasing numbers of skyjacking attempts through extradition agreements and domestic trials. Similarly, terrorists could also be subjected to domestic legal action even though their crimes took on an increasingly international character.

As the range of criminal activities grew, along with the civil wars that produced many grossly inhumane situations, the international community once again took steps to highlight the gravity of various war crimes and to pursue trials in international settings. The first international tribunal following Nuremberg was created by the United Nations Security Council in 1993 to address the problem of so-called ethnic cleansing during the Balkan Wars in the former Yugoslavia. The International Criminal Tribunal for Yugoslavia (ICTY) eventually tried and sentenced war criminals on all sides of the Bosnian civil war, including Bosnian Muslims and Croats, as well as Serbs, with the most celebrated example being Slobodan Milošević, the former president of Yugoslavia.

In 1994, the U.N. Security Council established a second regional tribunal, the International Criminal Tribunal for Rwanda (ICTR), to bring to justice extreme Hutus in Rwanda who were responsible for the ruthless massacres of hundreds of thousands of Tutsis and moderate Hutus. Many prosecutions were secured under the ICTR, where the death penalty does not apply, while the Rwandan government tried and convicted hundreds more, many of whom were executed.

The International Criminal Court

With egregious abuses of human rights burgeoning in dozens of civil wars around the world, and with the sense that regional tribunals for each would be a cumbersome approach, momentum grew in the 1990's to establish an International Criminal Court (ICC), which would have a universal jurisdiction to try individuals who es-

cape national legal action. Disputes arose during the negotiation of the ICC statute owing to differing American and European constitutional and legal approaches. Thus, when the ICC statute was opened for ratification, the United States sought revisions, many of which were ignored. The United States then announced that it would not ratify the statute. This raised controversy, but both the Clinton and George W. Bush administrations expressed concerns that American military personnel could be subjected to frivolous suits under the ICC statute.

Conclusion

Whether by international, regional, or ad hoc tribunals, or by national action, governments have shown an increasing desire to take action against individuals who are accused of major war crimes. The crimes themselves, as well as the efforts to implement international justice, nevertheless remain charged with controversy.

Robert F. Gorman

Further Reading

Bassiouni, M. Cherif, and Peter Manikas. *The Law of the International Criminal Tribunal for the Former Yugoslavia*. Irvington-on-Hudson, N.Y.: Transnational, 1996. An extensive collection of documents with background and commentary on the negotiation, establishment, and operation of the Tribunal for Yugoslavia.

Politi, Mauro, and Giuseppe Nesi, eds. *The Rome Statute of the International Criminal Court: A Challenge to Impunity*. Burlington, Vt.: Ashgate, 2001. A collection of essays by noted legal and human rights specialists concerning the Rome Statute.

Schabas, William. *An Introduction to the International Criminal Court*. 2d ed. New York: Cambridge University Press, 2004. Historical assessment of the formation of the ICC and the Rome Statute.

Sewall, Sarah B., and Carl Kaysen, eds. *The United States and the International Criminal Court: National Security and International Law*. Lanham, Md.: Rowman & Littlefield, 2000. A collection of essays by distinguished academics and practitioners concerning the complications of U.S. participation in the ICC.

Von Glahn, Gerhardt. *Law Among Nations: An Introduction to Public International Law*. New York: Longman, 1996. Chapters in this standard text provide background to the development of international criminal law and the punishment of war crimes by national courts and international tribunals.

See also Courts-martial; Diplomatic immunity; Extradition; International law; Military justice; War crimes; World Court.

Interpol

Identification: More formally known as the International Criminal Police Organization, the largest international police organization in the world

Date: Founded in 1923

Criminal justice issues: Law-enforcement organization; international law; terrorism

Significance: The increasing internationalization of crime—particularly in the areas of drug trafficking, arms dealing, money laundering, human trafficking, high-tech crime, and terrorist activities—has heightened the importance of cooperation among police and law-enforcement officers around the world.

The International Criminal Police Organization, or Interpol, was founded in 1923 to facilitate cross-border police cooperation and in 2004 had a membership of 181 nations. Differences in cultures, languages, and legal systems can cause difficulties in cooperation among police of different nations. Interpol's mission is to help police and law-enforcement officers from around the world cooperate with one another to prevent and solve international crimes. Interpol addresses only international crimes involving two or more member countries, and thus much of its work is focused on crimes such as drug trafficking, arms dealing, money laundering, counterfeiting, human trafficking, information technology crimes, and—strongly emphasized—terrorism. Interpol does not engage in casework that is political, military, or religious in character.

Interpol Services and Organization

Interpol provides three basic services for member nations. First, its global communications system allows police from member nations to store and exchange information. Member countries are thereby connected and are able to access police information around the clock, including data regarding persons being sought by police forces worldwide. Second, Interpol makes its information available to law-enforcement agencies within numerous databases: Fingerprints, pictures, and even DNA profiles can be accessed by computer. Third, Interpol provides support for police operations throughout the world.

The General Assembly is Interpol's governing body and is composed of delegates appointed by the governments of member states. It meets once a year and decides issues of general policy, resources, programs, and operations. Each member country has one vote, and decisions are made by a simple majority in the form of resolutions. The General Assembly also elects the organization's Executive Committee, which supervises the execution of the decisions of the General Assembly and prepares the agenda for its sessions. The Executive Committee has thirteen members, a president, three vice presidents, and nine delegates. Interpol is funded from the member countries, with contributions based on each nation's ability to pay.

National Central Bureaus

Each member country has its own Interpol office, or National Central Bureau (NCB). These bureaus form a point of contact for any foreign agency or government wishing to exchange or gather information on international criminal activities. The U.S. National Central Bureau (USNCB) operates within the guidelines prescribed by the Department of Justice, in conjunction with the Department of Homeland Security. It is an office under the control and direction of the Departments of Justice and Treasury.

The threat of terrorist activities, the increasing internationalization of crime, and the large number of foreign nationals residing in or visiting the United States have increased the importance of the USNCB and its relationship to Interpol. USNCB assistance is given not only to authorities in Interpol member countries but also to all U.S. federal, state, and regional enforcement agencies. Each state has an Interpol contact, and nine metropolitan areas now have direct access to Interpol's resources; in 2004, Seattle joined New York, Washington, D.C., Los Angeles, San Francisco, Chicago, Boston, San Diego, and Miami.

One important Interpol service is helping member countries' police communicate critical crime-related information to one another using Interpol's international notices, a system that helps the world's law-enforcement community exchange information about missing persons, unidentified bodies, and persons who are wanted in connection with serious crimes. These notices, color-coded to designate their purposes, are published at the request of a member country by the Interpol General Secretariat in the organization's four official languages. The NCB of a country receives the notices and distributes them among appropriate law-enforcement authorities. Ten different types of notices exist to communicate various kinds of criminal information.

Interpol's Role in Combating Terrorist Activities

In the wake of the terrorist attacks in the United States on September 11, 2001, Interpol underwent substantial change in order to combat terrorism better. New, more efficient systems of information exchange have been developed to facilitate international police cooperation in combating terrorist activities. Interpol has also attempted to avoid politically sensitive aspects of terrorism by focusing on such criminal aspects as murder, kidnapping, and illegal weapons trade.

On May 6, 2004—in association with the U.S. National Central Bureau of Interpol, the U.S. Department of Justice, and the Interpol General Secretariat in Lyon, France—the U.S. Department of State announced that the United States is joining many other countries in providing current information on passports reported lost or stolen. It is thought this program will contribute substantially to worldwide travel document security and impede the movement of terrorists and other criminals across international borders.

Jerome L. Neapolitan

Further Reading

Anderson, M. "Interpol and the Developing System of International Police Cooperation." In *Crime and Law Enforcement in the Global Village*, edited by W. F. McDonald. Cincinnati: Anderson Publishing, 1997.

Bresler, F. *Interpol.* New York: Penguin Press, 1992.

Deflem, M. *Policing World Society: Historical Foundations of International Police Cooperation.* New York: Oxford University Press, 2002.

Imhoff, J. J., and S. P. Cutler. *Interpol: FBI Law Enforcement Bulletin* 67, no. 12. Chapel Hill, N.C.: Academic Search Elite, University of North Carolina Academic Affairs, 1998.

See also Attorney general of the United States; Canadian justice system; Computer information systems; Drug Enforcement Administration; Federal Bureau of Investigation; International law; Marshals Service, U.S.; Money laundering.

J

Jaywalking

Definition: Crossing of public streets at illegal locations

Criminal justice issue: Traffic law

Significance: By crossing thoroughfares at unmarked locations and at unexpected moments, jaywalkers endanger their own lives and can create traffic hazards and liability issues that affect others.

As American city streets grow ever more congested with vehicles, pedestrians become increasingly restricted in where they are permitted to cross streets. The marked crosswalks established at most intersections and other places allow pedestrians to cross streets as safely as possible, particularly when they are combined with lighted traffic signals designed to stop vehicular traffic. However, the forced channeling of pedestrians into marked crossing zones has given rise to the phenomenon of jaywalkers—people who cross streets without regard for marked crossing zones and lighted signals. They cross where and when they wish, often with only casual regard for their own safety.

Crossing streets, especially in busy urban areas, involves more than merely stepping off curbs and walking. Most municipalities designate crosswalks for pedestrians to cross streets. Many are marked, especially at corners and mid-block locations, but some are unmarked. Many marked zones are in special locations, such as school crosswalks and busy shopping areas. Given the full range of pedestrian crossing zones, crossing the street has become a very regulated business.

Many people prefer to choose when and where to cross streets, and different municipalities have developed innovative ways to limit their movements. Hong Kong, for example, has erected fences along the edges of sidewalks that have openings only at crosswalks. Streets in the busiest parts of downtown Las Vegas have pedestrian overpasses to separate people from vehicles. The overpasses permit pedestrians to walk freely, but only over roads, not through them.

Many cities have created four-way crossings in their busy downtown areas. In these places, when traffic lights turn red, all vehicular traffic, in all directions, stops, and pedestrians can cross any direction, even diagonally. Some municipalities have installed sound signals and ramped curbs so that visually impaired individuals or individuals in wheelchairs or walkers may safely cross streets in marked zones.

Despite all these innovations designed for safety, many people continue to jaywalk. When police officers give tickets to offenders, the fines typically range from $40 to $100 for each offense. However, fines in special places in some cities can run as high as $750. Moreover, in some municipalities, convicted jaywalkers are required to attend "walking schools" to learn how to cross streets safely. In the East Asian nation of Singapore, jaywalkers can be fined the equivalent of three hundred U.S. dollars and be sentenced to two months in jail.

Most jaywalking offenses are settled with payments of fines. However, when jaywalkers are involved in accidents that result in court cases, the courts consistently rule that fault lies with them, not the drivers of vehicles. Jaywalkers are almost always held responsible for their own injuries and also any damage they cause to the vehicles involved in their accidents.

Robert Stewart

The First "Jaywalkers"

The slang term "jaywalking" appears to have originated in New England during the early twentieth century. At that time, the word "jay" was a slang term for a stupid, dull, or unsophisticated person. Thus, people stupid or foolish enough to disregard traffic laws designed for their own safety by crossing streets recklessly were dubbed "jaywalkers."

Further Reading

Evans, Leonard. *Traffic Safety*. Bloomfield, Mich.: Science Serving Society, 2004.

Holt, Daniel J., ed. *Pedestrian Safety*. Warrendale, Pa.: Society of Automotive Engineers, 2004.

See also Citations; Fines; Misdemeanors; Nonviolent resistance; Traffic fines; Traffic schools.

Jim Crow laws

Definition: Discriminatory laws designed to disfranchise and segregate African Americans in the South

Criminal justice issues: Civil rights and liberties; constitutional protections; government misconduct; political issues

Significance: Jim Crow laws established a system of white supremacy and discrimination in the United States that lasted from the end of Reconstruction until well into the 1960's. Although virtually all Jim Crow laws are now off the books, their legacy has left African Americans politically and economically disadvantaged.

The term "Jim Crow" is thought to have originated in the song "Jump Jim Crow," which a white minstrel performer in blackface made famous during the 1830's. His exaggerated mimicking of African American stereotypes may have caused the term to become associated with southern stereotypes of presumed black inferiority. After the end of Reconstruction in the South in the late 1870's, southern states began passing legislation to take away the rights that former slaves had enjoyed after the Civil War. By the turn of the twentieth century, the term Jim Crow became synonymous with discrimination and particularly racial segregation.

Development of Segregation

The first segregation laws actually originated in the North before the Civil War. In some northern states, African Americans were segregated in railway cars, theaters, schools, prisons, and hospitals. They were also frequently barred from restaurants and hotels and were excluded from jury service. Some northern states had constitution provisions restricting the admission of African Americans to their states.

After the Civil War, the states of the defeated Confederacy adopted laws known as "black codes" that restricted the rights of new freed slaves and created a system similar to slavery. However, Reconstruction soon brought in Union troops and forced the creation of new governments. African American men were given the same voting rights as white men, and many African Americans were elected to political office for the first time. This overturning of the southern order naturally angered many white southerners and engendered resentments that would later be expressed in vengeful legislation.

During the 1870's, the U.S. Supreme Court began to issue rulings that limited federal protections of the civil rights guaranteed by the equal protection and privileges and immunities clauses of the Fourteenth Amendment, which had been ratified in 1868. These rulings had the effect of contributing to the later development of legally mandated racial segregation. In 1877, for example, the Court ruled in *Hall v. de Cuir* that states could not prohibit segregation on common carriers. In 1883, the Court declared unconstitutional the Civil Rights Act of 1875, and ruled that the Fourteenth Amendment gave Congress the power to restrain states but not individuals from racial discrimination and segregation. In 1890, in *Louisville, New Orleans and Texas Railroad v. Mississippi*, the Court ruled that states could constitutionally require segregation on carriers.

The Supreme Court's landmark *Plessy v. Ferguson* decision of 1896 established the principle of separate-but-equal in a ruling upholding a Louisiana law that required segregation on railroad cars. The separate-but-equal doctrine would serve as the constitutional underpinning of legal segregation until the mid-1950's. Finally, in 1898, the Court upheld the new Mississippi constitution that effectively disfranchised African Americans. The Court also ignored its separate-but-equal principle in public education when it ruled in 1899 in *Cumming v. County Board of Education* that statutes establishing separate schools for whites were valid even if they provided no comparable schools for African Americans.

Jim Crow Laws

Jim Crow laws generally consisted of statutes that disfranchised and segregated African Americans. The most common disfranchising device was the use of literacy tests, which required prospective voters to read, write, and interpret passages from the U.S. and state constitutions. In theory, the tests applied equally to all citizens, but in practice they were gimmicks designed to take away the vote from former slaves, few of whom had had opportunities to learn to read. At the same time, the states' so-called grandfather clauses restored the vote to many illiterate white southerners by exempting from the literacy test requirement citizens whose grandfathers had been eligible to vote—a loophole of no benefit to former slaves. Some states also provided exemptions for illiterate citizens judged to be of "good moral character"—a subjective evaluation made by biased white registrars. Moreover, even if black would-be voters could read, they still had to get past the registrars' subjective evaluations of their interpretations of constitutional texts.

Another common disfranchising device was the use of poll taxes, which affected both poor blacks and poor whites. These taxes were generally payable six to eighteen months prior to elections. Would-be voters who failed to pay them by deadlines could not vote. Some states also required voters to pay the taxes not only for forthcoming elections but for all previous elections to retain their eligibility to vote.

A final disfranchising technique was the so-called white primary, which thirteen southern states used to prevent African Americans from having meaningful voices in the electoral process. Because most white southerners were Democrats during the Jim Crow era, Democratic Party primaries were the most important elections. Candidates who won the Democratic primaries were virtually assured of victory in the general elections, which Republican Party candidates occasionally did not even bother to contest. Since political parties were regarded as private clubs, they remained exempt from government anti-discrimination laws until well into the twenti-

"White only," "Colored only," and similar signs were common sights in the South and some northern cities during the Jim Crow era. *(Library of Congress)*

eth century, allowing local Democratic Party branches legally to exclude African Americans from voting in party primaries—which were the only elections that mattered.

The disfranchisement of African Americans gave white southerners total control over political processes and allowed them to enact discriminatory laws. As the U.S. Supreme Court diluted the provisions of the Fourteenth Amendment and federal civil rights laws, southern states moved quickly to segregate African Americans. Mandatory segregation on public transportation was followed by segregated waiting rooms and ticket windows. Local ordinances segregated almost everything that might mix members of different racial groups, from theaters, swimming pools, and restaurants to parks, phone booths, elevators, and even public benches and water fountains. At the state level, schools, mental institutions, homes for the aged, and prisons were segregated. Florida even required that school textbooks used by black and white students be stored separately when classes were not in session. Eventually, the Jim Crow system governed nearly every aspect of daily life, and white supremacy was the norm in the South.

Challenges to Segregation

As early as 1915, the Supreme Court began overturning Jim Crow laws. During that year, the Court declared grandfather clauses unconstitutional in *Guinn v. United States.* Many other antidiscriminatory decisions followed, such as the Court's 1944 banning of white primaries in *Smith v. Allwright.* The Court's most important ruling, however, came in 1954, when its justices unanimously declared racial segregation in public schools unconstitutional in *Brown v. Board of Education.* That landmark decision was the beginning of the end of the separate-but-equal doctrine. In his opinion on the *Brown* ruling, Chief Justice Earl Warren wrote that in the matter of education, "separate" could never be "equal."

The 1950's also brought the Civil Rights movement and a new anti-Jim Crow attitude in federal government. In 1964, the U.S. Congress passed the Civil Rights Act, a far-reaching law that ended segregation in many public accommodations, outlawed employment discrimination, and anticipated further major civil rights legislation.

The following year, Congress passed the first Voting Rights Act. It eliminated literacy tests as a voting requirement. During that same year, the Supreme Court declared poll taxes unconstitutional in *Harper v. Virginia.* These developments did not end all Jim Crow laws immediately, but they set the United States on a course that would, in fact, lead to the abolition of legally mandated segregation and discrimination. The changes wrought by the end of Jim Crow meant that African Americans could, for the first time, become full participants in the American political process.

William V. Moore

Further Reading

Litwack, Leon. *Trouble in Mind: Black Southerners in the Age of Jim Crow.* New York: Alfred A. Knopf, 1998. Account of the history and impact of segregation on African Americans.

Rasmussen, R. Kent. *Farewell to Jim Crow: The Rise and Fall of Segregation in America.* New York: Facts On File, 1997. History of segregation laws and the long struggle to overturn them. Written for young-adult readers.

Williamson, Joel. *The Crucible of Race: Black-White Relations in the American South Since Emancipation.* New York: Oxford University Press, 1984. Examination of the role race has played in the South since the Civil War.

Woodward, C. Vann. *The Strange Career of Jim Crow.* 3d ed. New York: Oxford University Press, 1974. Classic study of the origins of segregation in the United States.

See also Civil disobedience; Equal protection under the law; Hate crime; Ku Klux Klan; Lynching; Marshals Service, U.S.; Race riots in the twentieth century; Scottsboro cases.

Judges

Definition: Appointed and elected public officials who are charged with authoritatively and impartially resolving disputes presented in courts of law

Criminal justice issues: Judges; jurisdictions; professional standards; verdicts

In the American system of justice, judges do not decide criminal cases unless defendants ask for bench trials. In jury trials, the main function of judges is to act as referees by making sure that correct procedures are followed, that both prosecution and defense are able to present their cases, and that the juries understand their responsibilities. *(Brand-X Pictures)*

Significance: Judges play a critical role in the criminal justice system, both as authoritative managers of courtroom proceedings and often as the impartial arbiters of facts, guilt, and sentences. Judges are therefore expected to possess a number of valuable qualities that equip them to meet the high standards and demanding tasks of their office.

The United States tends to employ what is known as an adversary system in courtrooms, which means that the parties in legal disputes are expected to present their cases in their own best interests. In such settings, judges are not expected to assist either side to make its case or even to seek out evidence and facts. Instead, it is expected that such evidence will be made available by the parties either through deliberately presenting pertinent facts or through cross-examination. The judge's role thus becomes one of enforcing the rules and ensuring that a fair trial takes place. Some describe this role as akin to that of a

referee enforcing the rules of a game. However, the judge's role typically goes beyond the tasks implied by this analogy.

The complexities of U.S. law, coupled with the sometimes tense emotions and deliberate deceptions in the courtroom, can conspire to make the judge's task of ensuring a fair trial extremely difficult. The judge can be expected to exercise an almost superhuman combination of wisdom, compassion, logic, circumspection, integrity, and objectivity. While they may fall short of this ideal, judges typically are better trained and more disciplined than the general population. Almost all federal and state judges have law degrees and extensive courtroom experience, often as attorneys. Standards for municipal judges are usually less demanding. However, the respect accorded to the profession overall is valuable to judges in maintaining authority in the courtroom.

Deciding Verdicts and Imposing Sentences

In addition to managing courtroom proceedings, judges frequently must pass judgment at the conclusion of a trial. This function is sometimes served partly or wholly by juries. Judges can be called upon to determine guilt or innocence, to pass sentences in criminal trials, and to ascertain damages in civil trials.

In determining guilt or assigning blame, judges often must choose between two well-presented and plausible arguments. Sometimes, however, they are faced with two problematic and poorly presented arguments. Either way, they are frequently forced to make a definitive decision based on conflicting and incomplete information. In doing this, they must draw on a thorough knowledge of the law and a keen understanding of human nature while being familiar with the facts of a case.

Once guilt is determined, sentencing remains a difficult and complex task faced by judges. Most crimes can warrant a range of penalties, depending on the particular circumstances. Judges are expected to weigh such matters as the violence or damage caused by the crime, personal information about the defendant (such as age, criminal record, and evident contrition), and the conclusiveness of the conviction. This last point is especially relevant when a jury, rather than the judge, decides the matter of guilt.

Judges are usually constrained in their sentencing decisions by statutes that limit the types and lengths of sentences. In some cases their sentencing discretion is broad. In others the range of permissible sentences is quite narrow. For example, judges are often bound by mandatory sentencing guidelines for certain crimes. Many of these guidelines were enacted in the 1970's and 1980's by legislative bodies that were frustrated by the wide divergence of sentences for essentially the same crimes handed down by different judges. Some judges lost their jobs because of their alleged unwillingness to mete out suitably harsh penalties. During the 1980's, for example, several California supreme court justices lost their reelection bids in the wake of public anger that they repeatedly overturned death-penalty convictions. During the late 1990's the federal government and many state governments passed "three-strikes" laws, which required that persons convicted of three felonies be sentenced to life imprisonment. Thus, judges are subjected to legal and political constraints in their sentencing duties that can limit judicial independence.

Judicial Independence

Of all the qualities judges must have, impartiality is perhaps the most important. If a judge possesses personal interests linked to the outcome of a trial or if a judge is subject to political pressure, then the entire criminal justice system can be undermined. Different jurisdictions promote judicial independence in a variety of ways: by establishing lifetime (or at least long-term) judicial appointments, by requiring that judges recuse themselves from cases in which they have a personal interest, by paying them generous salaries to reduce their susceptibility to bribes, or by prohibiting them from practicing law while in office.

Federal judges in the United States are appointed by the president of the United States and confirmed by the U.S. Senate. Similarly, judges in many state systems are appointed by the governor and confirmed by the state legislature, although in many other states judges are elected or periodically reaffirmed through a popular vote. In a small number of states judges are nominated by a special nominating commission appointed by a state officer, serve for a fixed "probationary" period, and are then subjected to a popular confirmation vote to earn a full term. In each system of judicial appointment, there is some effort to balance the competing needs of independence and accountability.

The legitimacy of the judiciary relies not only on judicial objectivity and independence but also on the public perception of these qualities. Governments therefore make deliberate efforts to symbolically illustrate judicial independence: Courts and judicial chambers are usually separated from executive and legislative buildings; judges wear somber, ecclesiastical-looking black robes; judicial elections are studiously nonpartisan; and courtrooms are frequently adorned with images of scales, swords, and other symbols of justice.

As either a supplement or alternative to the principle of impartiality, the notion of judicial balance is sometimes put forward as an important factor in ensuring justice. That is, multimember courts (such as supreme courts and many appeals courts) are sometimes composed of judges with a range of ideological backgrounds. The idea is that both "liberal" and "conservative" views should be represented on the bench. During the late twentieth century more controversial efforts were undertaken to ensure that the judges of a given jurisdiction reflect the ethnic, racial, and gender diversity of the populations they serve. These and other efforts to achieve balance among judges challenge the notion of justice as an absolute quality to be sought in each judge's actions and decisions.

Steve D. Boilard

Further Reading

Coffin, Frank M. *On Appeal: Courts, Lawyering, and Judging.* New York: W. W. Norton, 1994. Insider's view of the appellate process in a federal appeals court. Coffin reveals tells exactly how his court processes appeals, from receipt of briefs, through oral arguments, and on to final decisions.

Gunther, Gerhard. *Learned Hand: The Man and the Judge.* New York: Alfred A. Knopf, 1994. Study of the judicial career of a man who may have been the most influential judge in America not to sit on the Supreme Court, by his former clerk.

Kelly, Zachary A. *Judges and Lawyers*. Vero Beach, Fla.: Rourke Corp., 1999. Explains the roles of lawyers and judges within the court system and defines terminology related to their functions.

McIntosh, Wayne V., and Cynthia L. Cates. *Judicial Entrepreneurship: The Role of the Judge in the Marketplace of Ideas*. Westport, Conn.: Greenwood Press, 1997. Broad discussion of judges in the criminal justice system.

O'Brien, David M., ed. *Judges on Judging: Views from the Bench*. 2d ed. Washington, D.C.: CQ Press, 2004. Collection of personal reflections written by judges about the issues they face and their philosophies of jurisprudence.

Philips, Susan U. *Ideology in the Language of Judges: How Judges Practice Law, Politics, and Courtroom Control*. New York: Oxford University Press, 1998. Analytical treatment of judicial thought and behavior.

Vile, John R., ed. *Great American Judges: An Encyclopedia*. 2 vols. Santa Barbara, Calif.: ABC-Clio, 2003. Comprehensive reference work on American judges, with articles on one hundred judges who figure prominently in criminal justice studies.

See also *Amicus curiae* briefs; Appellate process; Case law; Change of venue; Clerks of the court; Contempt of court; Gag orders; Impeachment of judges; Judicial system, Objections; Opinions; Plea bargaining; Sentencing; Sentencing guidelines, Summonses; Three-strikes laws; Trials; *Voir dire*.

Judicial review

Definition: Power of the courts to examine laws to determine their constitutionality and to declare null and void laws failing to meet that standard

Criminal justice issues: Appeals; constitutional protections; courts

Significance: The power of judicial review is a significant and controversial power of the U.S. federal and state judicial system. Although the power to create laws belongs to the legislative branch of government (and to the executive branch through the power of executive order), the courts, given their power of judicial review, have the final say in declaring what is the law.

The broad power of judicial review was not explicitly assigned to the judicial branch of government by the Constitutional Convention of 1787. Rather, its creation can be traced to the judicial branch itself—in particular, to the 1803 decision in *Marbury v. Madison* by the U.S. Supreme Court led by Chief Justice John Marshall. This decision opened the way for the judicial branch, in interpreting the law, to become at least as powerful as the legislative and executive branches.

Controversy over the principle of judicial review does not, however, stem from questions about its historical legitimacy but rather from the processes by which justices acquire their positions in the courts. While many judges at the state level are elected to their positions, the justices of the U.S. Supreme Court are appointed to their positions for life. This causes many to worry that the power of judicial review, at least at the federal level, is undemocratic in its very nature, granting such power to the judicial branch that it threatens the balance of power among the three branches of government.

The concern that the principle of judicial review unduly extends the power of the courts and "politicizes" the power of the judiciary is shared by both conservatives and liberals alike. Liberals worry that in the hands of a conservative Supreme Court the power of judicial review could be used to overturn progressive social legislation, such as affirmative action laws. Around the turn of the twentieth century new laws creating more favorable working conditions for laborers were deemed invalid in the case of *Lochner v. New York* (1905) and other decisions. Conservatives worry that in the hands of a liberal Supreme Court the power of judicial review could be used by justices to promote social change. As an example of so-called judicial activism they point to *Roe v. Wade* (1973), which, on the basis of an implicit constitutional right to privacy, overturned a statute making abortions illegal in the state of Texas. Controversy over the power of judicial review aside, the existence of this power exerts an influence over lawmakers that many would claim is beneficial, as the knowledge that laws are subject to judicial review can lead to greater care and conscientiousness on the part of lawmakers in crafting legislation.

Diane P. Michelfelder

Further Reading

Baum, Lawrence. *The Supreme Court*. 8th ed. Washington, D.C.: CQ Press, 2003.

Greenberg, Ellen. *The Supreme Court Explained*. New York: W. W. Norton, 1997.

Lewis, Thomas T., and Richard L. Wilson, eds. *Encyclopedia of the U.S. Supreme Court*. 3 vols. Pasadena, Calif.: Salem Press, 2001.

McGuire, Kevin. *Understanding the U.S. Supreme Court*. New York: McGraw-Hill, 2002.

Neubauer, David W. *America's Courts and the Criminal Justice System*. 8th ed. Belmont, Calif.: Wadsworth/Thomson Learning, 2005.

See also Appellate process; Bill of attainder; Case law; *Certiorari*; Constitution, U.S.; Court types; Due process of law; *Habeas corpus*; Harmless error; Jurisdiction of courts; *Stare decisis*; Supreme Court, U.S.

Judicial system, U.S.

Definition: One of the three co-equal branches of American state and federal governments that provides forums for applying laws and resolving civil and criminal cases

Criminal justice issues: Courts; federal law; law codes

Significance: The American court system embodies the adversary system of justice, in which it is the role of all parties in cases to take the lead in investigating the facts, presenting evidence, and formulating legal arguments to demonstrate why they, and not their adversaries, should prevail, within the settings of neutral forums.

The U.S. judicial system is actually made up of fifty-two distinct and separate judicial systems: the federal court system and fifty-one autonomous systems for each of the U.S. states and the federal District of Columbia. Moreover, the military forces and U.S. territories also have their own separate systems. However, the federal and state court systems share the same basic structures and follow similar procedures in their proceedings. Also, both types of court systems contain trial and appellate courts, though the individual courts may function somewhat differently.

Trial and Appellate Courts

Trial courts are courts of the first instance; they hear evidence, determine the facts, and make initial decisions in cases. In addition, trial court proceedings are conducted by judges who sit alone, without other judges, and decide the applicable legal principles and make initial rulings as to issues of procedure and admission of evidence. When cases are being tried by juries, the presiding judges' roles are usually limited to those functions, and the trial juries have responsibility for deciding the facts and reaching verdicts.

In bench trials, which have no juries, the judges alone make findings on the facts and pronounce verdicts. Although trial courts are situated at the base of the judicial system, the fact-finding roles of these courts often have greater importance than the courts' ultimate decisions because determinations as to the facts cannot be re-argued when cases are appealed.

On the level above trial courts are appellate courts, which hear and decide appeals of decisions made below by the trial courts. Depending on the courts and their jurisdictions, the losing parties' ability to bring appeals may be automatic or may be solely at the discretion of the appellate courts. The main function of appellate courts is to review decisions of the trial courts below them and to resolve questions of law, regardless of whether the original cases were decided by judges or juries.

The facts of cases that are found by the trial courts are accepted as "given" on appeal, and panels of judges instead hear arguments about whether the trial courts have made errors in applying the law. For example, a losing party at trial may argue on appeal that the factual evidence does not support an ultimate judgment of liability in a civil case, that a judge was mistaken in admitting certain witness testimony into evidence in a criminal case, or that a judge or jury misinterpreted the law. These examples demonstrate that the main benefit of appellate review is to create opportunities to have second looks at disputed aspects of cases in order to correct errors that may have affected their outcomes.

Procedures in trial and appellate courts differ significantly. In trial courts, in which evidence of facts is admitted, the trial judges preside over processes in which attorneys representing opposing sides call witnesses to testify and answer questions. The judges resolve issues as to the admissibility of the evidence, ensure that both sides in cases have fair opportunities to argue their sides, and then instruct the juries on the laws that should guide their decisions when they consider the evidence and endeavor to reach verdicts.

Proceedings in appellate courts are less complex. No testimony or other evidence is accepted. Rather, panels of appellate judges allot each attorney certain amounts of time to argue the legal issues orally on behalf of their clients and to answer questions posed by the judges. Additionally, the attorneys submit written arguments or "briefs" to elaborate their arguments further. Afterward, the appellate judges consider the cases and decided either to affirm (agree with) or reverse (disagree with) the trial court decisions, based on applicable laws. On occasion, appellate courts reverse and remand cases back to the trial courts for reconsideration of specified aspects of the cases.

State Courts

Judges in state courts are usually elected or appointed. At the base of state court systems are courts that possess special or limited authority. For example, suits involving small amounts of money or highly particular legal matters may be resolved in small-claims courts or traffic courts or before magistrates or justices of the peace. Some states require that small claims be submitted first to arbitration before panels of lawyers. In most of these courts, the litigating parties represent themselves, without professional counsel, and the proceedings are less formal than in trial courts. Losing parties in these proceedings usually have the right to bring their cases before trial courts for new hearings.

State court systems are geographically divided into subdivisions or judicial districts. Most state trial courts have general authority to hear wide ranges of civil and criminal cases. Some trial courts may be large enough to be subdivided into sections based on the types of cases they hear, such as civil, criminal, and domestic-relations divisions.

Whether general or specific, a court's authority to hear a particular type of case is referred to as its subject-matter jurisdiction. Trial courts have authority to decide criminal prosecutions against defendants who commit crimes within their states. In addition, trial courts in civil cases must have jurisdiction over either the persons or the property involved in disputes. For example, when a dispute is about title to, or rights in, property located within the state, the court has *in rem* jurisdiction to decide the case.

By contrast, personal jurisdiction is based on the locations, residences, or activities of the parties within the state. Even defendants who do not reside with a state may be subject to the jurisdiction of its courts if they have been doing business in the state or have established other significant connections to the state. Cases that are filed in trial courts, or that are brought to trial courts from small-claims courts or magistrates, are decided in the manner described earlier. Once final decisions are reached in the trial courts, the losing parties may appeal.

Most state court systems have intermediate appellate courts, in which losing parties have a guaranteed right to bring appeals, and supreme court, in which the ability to bring appeals rests at the discretion of the courts' judges. A few states have no intermediate appeals courts. In such states, appeals from trial courts go directly to their supreme courts. Unless a case involves only state-law issues, the U.S. Supreme Court sometimes agrees to hear appeals from decisions of state supreme courts, particularly when aspects of federal law are at issue or when a party's U.S. constitutional rights are involved. For example, defendants who are found guilty of crimes in state courts but who believe that their federal constitutional right to due process was violated by police during their arrests may petition the U.S. Supreme Court to review their cases.

Federal Courts

Judges in the federal system are appointed by the U.S. president and confirmed by the U.S. Senate. In the federal court system, lawsuits begin in district courts, which are the federal equivalents of state trial courts. Every state has at least one federal district court within its boundaries that operates separately, but alongside the state's trial courts. As in state trial courts, proceedings in federal district courts are presided over by judges who decide questions of applicable law. Determinations of facts may be made by either jurors or judges. As in state trial courts, federal district courts must have jurisdiction over the subject matter of the cases they try.

Federal district courts have jurisdiction over defendants charged with federal crimes. The courts have authority to hear civil cases as matters of either diversity jurisdiction or federal question jurisdiction. Diversity jurisdiction exists when the opposing parties in a case are citizens of different states, or when at least one party is a citizen of a foreign nation, and when the amounts in dispute exceed $75,000. Federal question jurisdiction exists when the claims arise under issues pertaining to the U.S. Constitution or federal statutes or treaties of the United States. There is no required amount in controversy for federal question jurisdiction.

There are also a few more specialized types of federal courts. Bankruptcy courts hear petitions under the federal bankruptcy law. The Court of International Trade hears cases involving customs and import or export of goods. The Court of Federal Claims decides cases brought against the U.S. government.

As in many state court systems, losing parties in federal district courts have an automatic right to appeal. Thus, defendants who have been convicted of crimes in federal district courts may file appeals as a matter of right in order to challenge their convictions. The U.S. courts of appeal operate as all appellate courts do, typically with panels of three judges reviewing cases for errors of law and accepting the facts as decided in the district courts.

The U.S. judicial system comprises thousands of courts under federal, state, and territorial jurisdictions, but all the courts are ultimately answerable to the Supreme Court of the United States, whose seat is in Washington, D.C. *(Library of Congress)*

The United States is divided into thirteen circuits, each with its own court of appeals. Eleven circuits cover several states and hear appeals from criminal and civil cases decided by federal district courts sitting within those states. The District of Columbia has its own circuit court of appeals, and a federal circuit court of appeals exists to hear specific appeals involving patents, claims against the federal government, and customs and international trade matters.

U.S. Supreme Court

The U.S. Supreme Court is the highest court for both federal and state court systems. Except in rare circumstances, the Supreme Court functions as an appellate court, hearing appeals from the federal courts of appeal and state supreme courts. The Court comprises eight associate justices and a chief justice, whose official title is "chief justice of the United States." All the justices are appointed by the president and confirmed by the Senate.

In almost all cases, the Supreme Court has discretion as to whether to hear specific appeals and agrees to hear only a small fraction of the cases submitted for its consideration. The Court usually defers to state supreme courts on matters of state law or in interpreting a state's constitution. Most appeals heard by the Supreme Court involve significant questions of federal law or constitutional rights or issues of national importance that are subjects of disagreement among various circuit courts of appeal.

Kurt M. Saunders

Further Reading

Abraham, Henry J. *The Judicial Process*. New York: Oxford University Press, 1998. Provides an introductory description and analysis of American courts.

Hall, Timothy L., ed. *The U.S. Legal System*. 2 vols. Pasadena, Calif.: Salem Press, 2004. Comprehensive survey of the American legal system whose articles emphasize basic legal concepts and offer a practical guide to how the federal and state legal systems work. Particular attention is paid to the workings of the courts.

Janosik, Robert J., ed. *Encyclopedia of the American Judicial System: Studies of the Principal*

Institutions and Processes of Law. New York: Charles Scribner's Sons, 1987. Comprehensive reference on the American court system.

Kelly, Zachary A. *Judges and Lawyers*. Vero Beach, Fla.: Rourke, 1999. Explains the roles of lawyers and judges within the court system and defines terminology related to their functions.

Meador, Daniel J. *American Courts*. St. Paul, Minn.: West Publishing, 1991. Presents a succinct and straightforward description of the American judicial process.

Meador, Daniel J., and Jordana S. Bernstein. *Appellate Courts in the United States*. St. Paul, Minn.: West Publishing, 1994. Contains a complete and concise description of state and federal appellate court systems.

Smith, Christopher E. *Courts and Trials: A Reference Handbook*. Santa Barbara, Calif.: ABC-Clio, 2003. Reference guide for information about the judicial process and its component parts.

See also Appellate process; Court types; Criminal justice in U.S. history; Criminal justice system; Criminal procedure; Discretion; Judges; Judicial review; Jurisdiction of courts; Jury system; Justice; Opinions; *Stare decisis*; Supreme Court, U.S.; Trials.

Jurisdiction of courts

Definition: Authority of different types of courts to hear and decide cases
Criminal justice issues: Courts; jurisdictions
Significance: Jurisdiction is a complicated but important issue. In criminal matters, a court is without authority to decide a criminal case unless it has both the jurisdiction to decide the particular kind of criminal case and jurisdiction over the defendant.

One of the most important issues facing a court in any case is whether it has jurisdiction over the case. In its broadest sense, "jurisdiction" is the authority of any branch of the justice system to interpret or apply the law. For example, the jurisdictions of federal law-enforcement agencies are explicitly defined by law. Within the court system, however, jurisdiction refers to the authority of courts to hear and decide cases. A court cannot decide a case unless it exercises authority that is appropriate to its own jurisdiction.

Both federal and state courts face limitations in the kinds of cases they can decide. The U.S. Constitution, state constitutions, and federal and state laws grant and limit the jurisdiction of courts. A court must have both subject-matter jurisdiction and personal jurisdiction to make legally valid decisions.

Subject-matter Jurisdiction

Subject-matter jurisdiction refers to the *kinds* of cases that a specific type of court is authorized to hear. In criminal cases, subject-matter jurisdiction refers to whether particular courts can hear and decide criminal cases, and if so, what kinds of criminal cases the courts can decide. Most criminal matters fall under the subject-matter jurisdiction of state courts because the U.S. Constitution explicitly provides that the states have the duty of protecting the general welfare of the people. This duty includes deciding what acts should be criminal and what punishments should be awarded for committing specific crimes. A state's criminal laws, known as a penal or criminal code, and its criminal procedure law, define the subject-matter jurisdiction for that state's courts.

The U.S. Constitution and laws enacted by the U.S. Congress provide the subject-matter jurisdiction of federal courts. In criminal matters, federal courts have subject-matter jurisdiction over cases concerning violations of federal criminal laws. In addition, federal courts can review convictions from state courts when defendants raise constitutional issues. In some instances, state and federal courts have concurrent jurisdiction over the same actions. Concurrent jurisdiction refers to the authority of different courts to decide the same case that occurs within the same territory, and over the same subject matter. For example, state criminal laws define robbery as a crime. Therefore, a state court would have subject-matter jurisdiction over a defendant charged with robbing a bank in its state. However, robbery of a bank that is federally insured is also a violation of federal law. Consequently, a federal court would have subject-matter jurisdiction over the same defendant under applicable federal law.

Courts also differ in terms of whether their subject-matter jurisdiction is limited or general. Limited jurisdiction courts can decide only specific matters, while general jurisdiction courts are not so limited. Each state has courts of general jurisdiction that can hear both civil and criminal matters. However, states also have lower-level courts that can decide specific kinds of cases.

Limited Jurisdiction Courts

While there is enormous variation among state court systems, some examples will illustrate the idea of limited jurisdiction. Many state laws provide that family courts have jurisdiction over matters such as child abuse, domestic violence, child custody, and child support. States often give surrogate courts the authority to adjudicate matters concerning wills, trusts, and estates. In criminal matters, town and justice courts frequently have jurisdiction over misdemeanors, while higher-level courts have jurisdiction over felonies. Thus, a court of limited criminal jurisdiction does not have the authority to hear and decide a murder case.

In the federal court system, the issue of subject-matter jurisdiction is more complex. Federal courts are courts of limited subject-matter jurisdiction that are divided into three separate areas: diversity jurisdiction (suits between citizens of different states), ancillary jurisdiction (matters not ordinarily under federal jurisdiction that are associated with federal offenses), and federal-question jurisdiction. Federal criminal cases usually do not involve either diversity jurisdiction or ancillary jurisdiction. However, federal-question jurisdiction can involve criminal matters. Federal courts can hear two types of matters that fall under federal-question jurisdiction: violations of federal law and issues arising under the U.S. Constitution. Federal-question jurisdiction explains why federal courts can decide cases concerning violations of federal criminal law as well as cases from state courts in which defendants raise constitutional issues.

Finally, subject-matter jurisdiction concerns the ideas of original and appellate jurisdiction. A court has original jurisdiction when it can hold trials and rule on matters directly while appellate jurisdiction refers to courts that rule on matters previously decided by other courts. All states specify the courts that have original jurisdiction and appellate jurisdiction. In federal courts, U.S. District Courts exercise original jurisdiction, while U.S. Courts of Appeal and the U.S. Supreme Court exercise appellate jurisdiction. However, there are certain cases in which the U.S. Supreme Court can exercise original jurisdiction. These kinds of cases do not involve criminal matters.

Personal Jurisdiction

Also called *in personam* jurisdiction, personal jurisdiction refers to the authority that courts have over persons who are subjects of cases. Personal jurisdiction is sometimes confused with venue, a term for the location of a trial or proceeding. Personal jurisdiction concerns the question of whether a court has the authority to make a determination concerning a particular defendant.

For a court to exercise personal jurisdiction over a defendant, the defendant must have some contact with the state that is to hear the case. In civil matters, the issue of personal jurisdiction is often a complicated question, especially when a defendant lives out of state. In criminal proceedings, a defendant's contact with a state merges with the idea of territoriality. Therefore, personal jurisdiction exists over persons who commit offenses that affect the interests of that state. In federal criminal matters, personal jurisdiction exists over persons who commit offenses within the territory of the particular federal judicial district.

Patricia E. Erickson

Further Reading

Barkan, Steven E., and George Bryjak. *Fundamentals of Criminal Justice.* Boston: Allyn & Bacon, 2003. Basic overview of criminal justice in the United States.

Latzer, Barry. *State Constitutions and Criminal Justice.* Westport, Conn.: Greenwood Press, 1991. Examination of the constitutional bases of criminal justice as reflected in the widely differing constitutions of the various states, with attention to state court systems.

Meyer, Jon'a, and Diana R. Grant, eds. *The Courts in Our Criminal Justice System.* Upper Saddle River, N.J.: Prentice Hall, 2002. Textbook on the role that the courts play within the criminal justice system as a whole.

Miller, William S. *A Primer on American Courts.* New York: Longman, 2004. Up-to-date survey of the various types of U.S. courts for lay readers.

Neubauer, David W. *America's Courts and the Criminal Justice System.* 8th ed. Belmont, Calif.: Wadsworth/Thomson Learning, 2005. Comprehensive analysis of the dynamics of criminal justice in action as seen in the relationship of judge, prosecutor, and defense attorney.

Stolzenberg, Lisa, and Stewart J. D'Alessio. *Criminal Courts for the Twenty-first Century.* 2d ed. Upper Saddle River, N.J.: Prentice Hall, 2002. Up-to-date textbook on the criminal court system.

See also Appellate process; Change of venue; Court types; Criminal procedure; Criminal prosecution; Judicial review; Judicial system, U.S.; Multiple jurisdiction offenses; Precedent; Supreme Court, U.S.; Trials; World Court.

Jury duty

Definition: Obligation of citizens to respond to summonses to serve the legal system by hearing evidence and rendering decisions in trials

Criminal justice issues: Juries; trial procedures; verdicts

Significance: Because jury service entrusts ordinary citizens with the responsibility of decision making, it is the most direct means through which ordinary citizens can participate in the judicial process.

Juries play a critical role in the American system of justice, and service as a juror is considered both a duty and a privilege. The selection process begins with juror qualification, which is initiated when local court administrator offices mail out questionnaires requesting the information necessary to determine whether recipients are qualified to serve as jurors. The traditional sources for selecting names for jury pool have been voter-registration lists. However, many jurisdictions supplement those lists with other source lists, such as telephone directories, tax-assessment rolls, censuses, and lists of licensed drivers. When recipients complete and return the questionnaires, the court administrators eliminate those who are unqualified. For example, some jurisdictions require that jurors understand English or that they have not been convicted of felonies.

After pools of qualified prospective jurors are determined, the next phase involves the random selection of names to whom are sent summonses for jury service. Random selection is important to ensure racial, ethnic, gender, and economic diversity in the pools. When summoned, recipients receive instructions as to where and when to appear for service. Persons summoned for jury duty have a legal duty to report. Failure to do so can, in some cases, result in arrest or fines.

Certain persons may be excused from jury duty. For example, federal law exempts public officials and police and fire department employees. Many states excuse persons in active military service or those who have recently served as jurors. In addition, it is possible to be excused from service, or have service postponed, for reasons of family, medical, or financial hardship. Written requests and proof are required to support such excusals or postponements.

The selection of jurors for trials begins when panels of prospective jurors are called into courtrooms and sworn to answer truthfully questions posed by the attorneys about their qualifications to hear and decide the cases. This questioning process, known as *voir dire*, is done to ensure that the only jurors selected are those who have no conflicts of interest or biases that might compromise their ability to render fair and impartial verdicts.

Attorneys representing opposing sides in cases may challenge the ability of individual panel members to serve on juries. A person may be challenged for cause if the *voir dire* examination reveals a possible prejudice

---

Jury Exemptions and Disqualifications in Texas

These rules for exempting and disqualifying prospective jurors in the state of Texas are representative of rules in others states. However, every state has its own unique combination of rules.

Exemptions

✓ all persons over seventy years of age
✓ all persons who have legal custody of children younger than ten years of age and jury service would require leaving the children without adequate supervision
✓ students of high schools and colleges
✓ officers or employees of the state's legislative bodies or any of those bodies' affiliated departments and agencies
✓ primary caretakers of persons with disabilities who cannot care for themselves (this exemption does not apply to health care workers)
✓ all persons who have been summoned for service in counties with populations of at least 250,000 and have served as petit jurors in those counties during the previous three years
✓ members of the U.S. military forces serving on active duty and deployed to locations away from the members' home stations and out of their county of residence

Disqualifications

✓ all persons who are not at least eighteen years of age
✓ all persons who are not of sound mind and good moral character
✓ all persons who are not able to read and write
✓ all persons who are not citizens of the counties in which they are asked to serve as jurors
✓ all persons who are not qualified to vote in the counties in which they are asked to serve
✓ all persons who have recently served as jurors in other specified courts
✓ all persons who have been convicted of felonies
✓ all persons who are under indictment or other legal accusations of misdemeanor theft or any felony charges
✓ all persons who are not citizens of the United States

Prospective jurors entering an Alabama courthouse. Until jurors are called to courtrooms for impanelling, they are unlikely to know anything at all about the cases they are to try, unless the cases have been in the news. *(AP/Wide World Photos)*

against one of the parties. In addition, each party has a right to a limited number of peremptory challenges for which no explanations need be given. Those not eliminated through use of these challenges are seated as jurors to hear the cases. Additional panelists are reserved as alternate jurors in case any of the seated jurors must be excused due to illness or other reasons during the course of the trials.

Kurt M. Saunders

Further Reading

Abramson, Jeffrey. *We, the Jury: The Jury System and the Ideal of Democracy*. Cambridge, Mass.: Harvard University Press, 2000.

Jonakait, Randolph N. *The American Jury System*. New Haven, Conn.: Yale University Press, 2003.

Schwartz, Victor E., et al. *Safeguarding the Right to a Representative Jury: The Need for Improved Jury Service Laws*. Washington, D.C.: National Legal Center for the Public Interest, 2003.

Stanley, Jacqueline. *Jurors' Rights*. Naperville, Ill.: Sourcebooks, 1998.

See also *Batson v. Kentucky*; Grand juries; Hung juries; Jury nullification; Jury sequestration; Jury system; Trials; *Voir dire*.

Jury nullification

Definition: Power of juries to change, alter, or modify the law or facts in cases they are considering in trials

Criminal justice issues: Juries; legal terms and principles; trial procedures; verdicts

Significance: Jury nullification presupposes a jury's inherent power to either disregard a judge's instructions on the law, or, in addition, disregard some or all of the evidence presented in litigation. Although it is difficult to establish just how much jury nullification takes place, many experts on jury behavior believe it is on the rise.

It is argued that the jury, as the community's conscience, must be allowed to operate as a brake on the misapplication of the law in particular circumstances. Criminal cases, in particular, offer a fertile field for the application of the nullification principle. For example, verdicts in so-called "mercy killing" trials, trials involving politically charged issues, and trials of battered women charged with spousal killing often exhibit jury nullification at work. Likewise, many Americans have taken the position that the O. J. Simpson acquittal by a predominantly African American jury in 1995 was a clear example of jury nullification premised on race.

There is an on-going debate in American criminal justice about whether or not jury nullification, if carried too far, will lead to a lawless society. On the other hand, if no discretion were allowed a jury to nullify what it believed to be an oppressive rule of law, the outcome might be technically legal but morally outrageous. All the nation's Founding Fathers were in favor of the trial jury's discretionary power to nullify. John Adams, Alexander Hamilton, and Thomas Jefferson were robustly in favor of granting to the trial jury the power to determine both the law and the facts, unburdened by either a judge's instructions or the rules of evidence.

In both theory and practice it is assumed that at the end of judicial proceedings the judge instructs the jury on the rules of law to be applied to the case at hand. Using these instructions, the jury applies the law to the facts they find during their deliberations. However, since no two cases are alike and since every case is infected, to a greater or lesser extent, with both legal and factual ambiguity, the jury is often left to view the law and the facts through its own peculiar prism. It is at this point that the cry of jury nullification is often heard by the losing side.

Most American trial and appellate judges are not in favor of instructing the jury on its power to disregard the law or the facts in a particular case. Judges arguably fear a total disregard for both le-

gal principles and relevant facts if juries are simply left to their own devices. Thus, while a jury still holds a sort of veto power over the rigidity and inaptness of certain legal principles, trial judges and their appellate counterparts are generally content to remain silent on a jury's power to nullify.

John C. Watkins, Jr.

Further Reading

Abramson, Jeffery. *We, the Jury: The Jury System and the Ideal of Democracy.* Cambridge, Mass.: Harvard University Press, 1994.

Conrad, Clay S. *Jury Nullification: The Evolution of a Doctrine.* Durham, N.C.: Carolina Academic Press, 1998.

Jonakait, Randolph N. *The American Jury System.* New Haven, Conn.: Yale University Press, 2003.

See also Hung juries; Jury duty; Jury sequestration; Jury system; Miscarriage of justice; Simpson trials; Trials; Verdicts.

Jury sequestration

Definition: Isolation of jurors from the public during trials

Criminal justice issues: Juries; media; trial procedures; verdicts

Significance: Impartiality is essential to jurors, and sequestration prevents them from being improperly influenced by news reports, family members, friends, or other sources of information.

A paramount concern for judges during jury trials is ensuring that jurors' decisions are based on properly presented evidence. In controversial cases there are fears that jurors' exposure to news reports or opinionated acquaintances will improperly affect jury deliberations and the verdict. In such cases judges may order the jury to be sequestered in order to shield jurors from improper sources of information. Because jurors must live together in a hotel away from their friends and family, jury sequestration imposes significant costs on the personal lives of jurors. Sequestration also generates significant expenses for the court, which must pay for the jurors' food and lodging throughout the course of the trial.

Sequestration may occur in cases involving highly publicized crimes or well-known defendants. Sequestration may be particularly appropriate when the news media informs the public about information and evidence that is not admissible in court. For example, if the police found a bloody weapon in the defendant's home but that weapon could not be presented at trial because it was found during an illegal search, the judge may sequester the jury to prevent the jurors from reading about the weapon in the newspapers.

Because of the cost and inconvenience of jury sequestration, judges rarely order it. Judges must often make a decision about sequestration at the beginning of a trial. If sequestration is possible, judges may ask potential jurors during jury selection if sequestration would create special hardships that would make it exceptionally unfair or difficult for them to serve. For example, the mother of a young child may be excused from jury duty if the judge agrees that sequestration would pose an exceptional hardship for the mother and child.

When jurors are sequestered, bailiffs must monitor their contact with the outside world. In some situations, bailiffs cut out and destroy all newspaper articles about the trial before the newspapers are given to the jurors. Bailiffs also monitor television programs watched by jurors to make sure that they do not watch news stories about the trial. Judges also instruct jurors on the importance of their responsibilities and warn them to avoid all news reports and conversations about the trial. If the bailiffs or other jurors inform the judge that a specific juror has read prohibited newspaper articles, talked about the case with outsiders, or otherwise undertaken forbidden behavior, the judge may dismiss the juror from the case and seat an alternate. In major cases, alternate jurors are sequestered along with the regular jurors and hear the same evidence presented in court, even if they are not ultimately permitted to participate in deliberating the verdict.

Christopher E. Smith

Further Reading

Abramson, Jeffery. *We, the Jury: The Jury System and the Ideal of Democracy*. Cambridge, Mass.: Harvard University Press, 1994.

Jonakait, Randolph N. *The American Jury System*. New Haven, Conn.: Yale University Press, 2003.

Schwartz, Victor E., et al. *Safeguarding the Right to a Representative Jury: The Need for Improved Jury Service Laws*. Washington, D.C.: National Legal Center for the Public Interest, 2003.

Stanley, Jacqueline. *Jurors' Rights*. Naperville, Ill.: Sourcebooks, 1998.

See also Bailiffs; Hung juries; Jury duty; Jury nullification; Jury system; Trial publicity; Trials.

Jury system

Definition: System in which groups of citizens who are representative of their communities hear testimony and assess evidence in court cases to determine the truth or falsehood of such testimony and evidence

Criminal justice issues: Courts; juries; trial procedures; verdicts

Significance: A right guaranteed by the U.S. Constitution, trial by jury is a central component of Anglo-American justice and is especially important in criminal trials. The jury system affords those accused of crimes to receive a hearing by a cross section of ordinary citizens in whose hands the determination of guilt or innocence rests.

During the late twentieth century, four of every five jury trials in the world was conducted in the United States. Despite the inadequacies to which legal scholars, criminologists, and legislators have repeatedly pointed in the jury system, the system is more securely entrenched in the American justice system than in any other system in the world. Moreover, despite modifications that various state governments have made in it, one can safely predict that the jury system will remain intact in the United States for many years to come.

The jury system is a fundamental part of the American justice system largely because the authors of the Declaration of Independence listed as one of their major complaints against the British crown government that it was "depriving us, in many Cases, of the Benefits of Trial by Jury." Given this background, the nation's founders made provision for the jury system when they drew up the U.S. Constitution.

Constitutional Mandates

Article III of the U.S. Constitution promises those accused of any federal crimes—except for impeachment—the right to trial by jury. The Fifth Amendment specifies that no citizen shall be answerable for the commission of any capital or "otherwise infamous crime, unless on a presentment or indictment of a Grand Jury," thereby placing the judgment of testimony and evidence in the hands of a representative body of the citizenry.

The Sixth Amendment guarantees a speedy public trial "by an impartial jury of the State and district wherein the crime shall have been committed." The word "impartial" is particularly important in this amendment and has been the basis for empaneling disinterested jurors to hear both criminal and civil cases. The Seventh Amendment states that "in suits of common law, where the value in controversy shall exceed twenty dollars, the right of trial by jury shall be preserved, and no fact tried by a jury, shall be otherwise reexamined in any Court of the United States, than according to the rules of the common law." This amendment, which firmly establishes the right to trial by jury, also establishes the all-important guarantee against double jeopardy.

The Fourteenth Amendment guarantees the right of a jury trial to any defendant accused of a crime, federal or state, that carries a penalty of more than six months' imprisonment. The protection of this amendment, which has been tested in the courts, is not extended to those accused of minor offenses.

Given constitutional guarantees that resulted from zealous reactions to widespread dissatisfaction with Great Britain's governance of the colonies, the American judicial system could not easily be moved to abandon the jury system. For all the faults jurists have found with the system, it is so fundamentally a part of American justice that it is inconceivable to envision the American justice system without it.

Grand Juries

Grand juries are bodies that usually consist of between sixteen and twenty-three jurors. They are subdivided into two types of juries, those that charge defendants and those that investigate. The first of these examines evidence brought forth against suspects to determine whether it is sufficient to warrant formal charges that will lead to court trials by other, smaller juries. If the evidence suggests that there is probable cause for trials, indictments are issued that set in motion the machinery for jury trials.

Investigatory grand juries examine evidence against public officials suspected or accused of criminal misconduct in office. They also investigate alleged criminal activity in other segments of society, such as organized crime. They, too, can issue indictments if the testimony and evidence suggest probable cause.

Hearings held by grand juries are closed to the public. The rights of those suspected of violations are protected meticulously, and all suspects enjoy the presumption of innocence. Indictments are not declarations of guilt; they merely indicate the need for further investigation.

Petit Juries

The type of jury with which most Americans are familiar is the petit, or petty, jury, so designated because of its comparatively small size. In the United States, petit juries generally contain twelve jurors and some alternates. However, in some states juries may range in size from six to ten members.

In criminal cases, petit juries decide whether defendants are guilty or innocent of the crimes of which they have been accused. In civil cases, juries establish liability and determine the damages awarded to successful complainants. The courtrooms in which cases are tried by petit juries are generally open to the public. However, judges may limit the numbers of observers and are empowered, under certain circumstances, to clear their courtrooms of spectators when they believe that their presence is disrupting proceedings. All defendants in criminal cases that petit juries hear are deemed innocent until their guilt is proved to the jury beyond a reasonable doubt. Presumption of innocence is the keystone of the American justice system. If a reasonable doubt exists about any defendant's guilt, a verdict of acquittal must be returned.

Coroners' Juries

In most jurisdictions, coroners' juries are composed of six members. It is their purpose to hold investigations, termed inquests, into causes of death in cases in which doubt exists. They are frequently called upon, for example, to determine whether deaths are the result of murder or suicide. They work closely with forensic pathologists, who perform autopsies that provide the juries with the information they need to make reasonable judgments.

The Making of Juries

Stringent rules govern how juries are constituted. To begin with, pools of jurors must be representative of the general population of the United States. Moreover, no U.S. citizen may be excluded from a pool of jurors on such arbitrary

grounds as race, gender, or class. Furthermore, jurors drawn from the jury pool to judge specific cases must also be representative of the community wherein the indictment has been issued.

In the distant past, juror pools were drawn only from members of communities who owned property. However, that method of selection was successfully challenged by those who contended that it imposed a class distinction upon jury selection. Eventually, jury pools came to be drawn from voting rolls. Before ratification of the Nineteenth Amendment guaranteed women the right to vote in all states in 1920, however, women were excluded from the voting rolls in most states. Until the Voting Rights Act of 1965, voting rolls in many southern states held the names of few black voters, making it impossible to impanel truly representative juries in those states.

Toward the end of the twentieth century, other methods began to be employed to develop pools of jurors. The most common of these draws pools from lists of licensed drivers as well as registered voters. This method broadened substantially the composition of jury pools and constituted a major advance toward making juries more representative of the general population than they had previously been.

In deciding who will serve on juries slated to hear specific cases, in a process known as *voir dire*, attorneys for both defense and prosecution question potential jurors drawn from the pool. The selection of appropriate juries is essential to the successful defense or prosecution of any case. Effective attorneys select juries with great care and deliberation, sometimes employing consultants specially trained in jury selection to guide them toward the best choices. When attorney questioning uncovers obvious biases that might cloud jurors' objectivity or give reason to suspect that potential jurors have already reached conclusions about the cases to be tried, attorneys on either side may reject them as jurors. Such dismissals are called objections for cause. Attorneys are permitted an unlimited number of such objections.

The most dramatic moment in every jury trial comes when the foreperson rises to read the jury's verdict. (Brand-X Pictures)

Attorneys are also allowed limited numbers of peremptory challenges. These challenges do not require them to offer any explanations or justifications to the courts. For example, an attorney may legitimately issue a peremptory challenge to exclude a retiree dependent upon investment income in a trial of a stockbroker accused of fraudulent dealings with elderly clients. Likewise, an attorney might exclude the president of a local temperance organization from serving on a jury in a drunk driving case. However, peremptory challenges that are clearly made on the basis of race or gender may lead to mistrials.

Jury Verdicts

In most jurisdictions, decisions to find defendants guilty in criminal cases must be unanimous. If even a single juror votes against conviction and cannot be persuaded in subsequent jury balloting to change the vote, a deadlock is declared in the trial and a hung jury is said to exist. There are no official limits on how many ballots juries may take during their deliberations.

When jury deliberations result in hung juries, defendants in the cases are still presumed innocent. However, the accusations against them remain intact. Prosecutors may later elect to reopen their cases and hold new trials. However, in many instances the press of other cases makes prosecutors reluctant to do so. Prosecutors may also come under administrative pressures to consider costs to the government over the pursuit of justice. Some jurisdictions have sought to overcome the problem of hung juries by allowing specified majority votes of guilty—often ten out of twelve—to produce convictions. In Scotland, it has long taken only a simple majority vote to convict.

The secrecy of what goes on in jury rooms generally remains sacrosanct after trials. Although jurors may be individually polled after their foreperson announces their verdict, they are under no obligation to explain their votes to anyone at any time.

One of the jurors in California's highly publicized murder trial of Scott Peterson speaks to the press after Peterson was sentenced to death for killing his pregnant wife, Laci, in March, 2005. Although jurors are forbidden to discuss cases outside the courtroom during trials, they are free to speak their minds the moment that the trials end. *(AP/ Wide World Photos)*

Roots of the Jury System

The American jury system is a product of a millennium of English and American history. It originated in medieval England and grew out of the development of codified laws and statutes that came to be accepted by society to replace or at least supplement many of the controls that earlier resided in the family, whose eldest male member usually served a judicial function. The rules that governed such a system were often capricious, whereas law as society conceives it is meant to be uniform, and justice as society conceives it is ideally blind.

When the Norman ruler William the Conqueror invaded England in 1066, right (which was often determined by combat) did not always triumph over might. Persons who accused others of crimes besmirched the integrity of the other persons, who then might feel honor-bound to engage in combat with their accusers to avenge the insults. In such situations, might was right. The stronger combatants won, regardless of whose case was more valid in their disputes.

In many societies, trial by ordeal was a popular form of determining guilt or innocence until three or four centuries ago. Accused persons who

587

could walk over glowing embers without blistering their feet or carry several pounds of hot coals in their hands without injury were considered innocent of all charges against them. Innocence, needless to say, was seldom the outcome in such primitive judicial procedures.

Before the year 1000, England's King Ethelred I, recognizing that the English system of justice was deficient, appointed twelve of his most trusted followers to investigate illegal activities and make formal accusations against suspects, much as grand juries do in modern society. After their evidence was heard, guilty votes by at least eight of the twelve resulted in convictions. It is probably this early English model of twelve-man juries that eventually led to twelve members being the standard for modern petit juries in the United States.

In the Anglo-Saxon era, with society centered in small villages or feudal keeps, people knew one another well. As early as 850, England's King Alfred divided every community in his domain into units of ten families that were mutually responsible for one another's behavior. Each ten groups of such families, or "tithings," constituted a judicial unit called a "hundred." County courts run by sheriffs met twice a year to hear cases brought by

---

A Realistic Hollywood Film

The 1962 film *To Kill a Mockingbird*, in which Gregory Peck plays Atticus Finch, a white lawyer in a small southern town during the 1930's, is sometimes studied by law students because of its realistic depiction of trial procedures. In the film, Finch risks becoming a social pariah by agreeing to defend Tom Robinson (Brock Peters), a poor African American man accused of raping a white woman. Despite Finch's careful and impassioned defense, an all-white jury convicts Robinson. At the time in which the film is set, the U.S. Supreme Court had already ruled that African Americans could not be explicitly excluded from jury service. Nevertheless, southern jurisdictions continued to employ a variety of strategies to keep black citizens off juries. The film thus offers a realistic portrayal of the hopelessness of Finch's defense case.

Timothy L. Hall

---

the "hundredors," as they were called. Cases were heard by twelve members of the hundredors who were selected because of their personal knowledge of each case being tried.

Among the early British, reputation carried great weight and honor was valued above all else. If people well respected in the community were accused of crimes by others, they either owned up to the accusations and made amends or, upon their honor, vowed innocence. Such vows were readily accepted from people who were known to be honest. However, strangers who vowed innocence were often subjected to ordeals to prove their claims.

When groups of people made accusations, the accused were expected to find eleven thanes who would swear to their honesty and honor. If they could not persuade that many to testify, they were usually subjected to physical ordeals and, predictably, adjudged guilty. These earliest juries of thanes selected by the accused were quite opposite to the impartial juries that are fundamental to modern jury systems. They were selected because they had already made up their minds and were predisposed in favor of the defendants. Under modern judicial systems, when prospective jurors are found to have any bias for or against defendants, they are precluded from serving. Studies of judicial decisions in England between 1550 and 1750 reveal that during those two centuries, juries consistently voted to acquit people they knew and voted to convict people they did not know.

Objections to the Jury System

The jury system has been tried and abandoned in many countries. Generally it has been observed that whenever a nation attempts to impose such a jury system upon its established judicial system, the attempt soon fails. In such situations, modifications in the system are usually so great as to make it almost unrecognizable as a jury system. For example, in France, Germany, and Denmark, experiments with juries were eventually replaced by trial systems that involve judges and lay assessors who help to weigh evidence.

Outside the United States, the jury system seems most firmly entrenched in Great Britain, where it was originally established and refined quite early. In Australia, New Zealand, and Canada, jury systems are strong because they were established as the original system in those countries—all of which inherited the British legal system.

A major objection to trial by jury is that many jurors lack the intelligence, backgrounds, or stamina to assess effectively evidence given within a legal context. This objection has been heard increasingly as law cases have placed increasing demands on jurors, expecting them to understand highly technical evidence, such as the results of polygraph tests, DNA (deoxyribonucleic acid) testing, and other modern laboratory procedures that are now applied to gathering and evaluating evidence.

Another type of complaint about the jury system is the proven fact that some jurors can be bribed by parties to the cases being tried. This problem can be largely eliminated by sequestering juries, which is sometimes done in highly publicized trials. In such trials, juries are sometimes cut off from communication with the outside world for periods lasting several months. In cases that involve organized crime, jurors may have ample cause to fear for their physical welfare and safety during and after trials. On the other hand, jurors assigned to high-profile cases are occasionally eager to serve because they have ulterior motives, such as plans to profit from their experience after the trials by writing books or taking to the television talk-show circuit.

Sometimes, potentially competent jurors are excused because of the disruptions to their lives that long sequestration might cause them. Occasionally, members of sequestered juries finish their service and find that they have lost their jobs or that their marriages or other personal relationships are foundering.

Criticism has also been directed toward juries in civil cases that award unrealistically high settlements to complainants whose cases succeed. Appellate courts have often reduced or eliminated some of the most unrealistic settlements, but appealing a verdict is a cumbersome process that is costly to the complainants, the defendants, and the government.

R. Baird Shuman

Further Reading

Abramson, Jeffrey. *We, the Jury: The Jury System and the Ideal of Democracy*. Cambridge, Mass.: Harvard University Press, 2000. Objective and comprehensive overview of the jury system.

Guinther, John. *The Jury in America*. New York: Facts On File, 1988. Balanced review of the American jury system.

Holland, Barbara. "Do You Swear that You Will Well and Truly Try . . . ?" *Smithsonian* 25 (March, 1995). Clear and concise article that presents an accurate historical account of the American jury system in a lively and engaging style.

Lesser, Maximus A., and William S. Hein. *The Historical Development of the Jury System*. Buffalo, N.Y.: W. S. Hein, 1992. Exhaustive study of the jury system focusing on its roots and historical development.

Schwartz, Victor E., et al. *Safeguarding the Right to a Representative Jury: The Need for Improved Jury Service Laws*. Washington, D.C.: National Legal Center for the Public Interest, 2003. Up-to-date critique of the jury system, with suggestions for improvements.

See also *Batson v. Kentucky*; Burden of proof; Criminal procedure; Fourth Amendment; Grand juries; Hung juries; Judicial system, U.S.; Jury duty; Jury nullification; Jury sequestration; Verdicts; *Voir dire*; *Witherspoon v. Illinois*.

Just deserts

Definition: The concept that punishments for crimes should match the severity of the crimes themselves

Criminal justice issues: Crime prevention; legal terms and principles; punishment; sentencing

Significance: The concept of just deserts, related to the retributive philosophy of criminal justice, has gained in popularity as the crime problem in the United States has grown.

In a 1976 report entitled *Doing Justice*, criminologist Andrew von Hirsch and other members of the Committee for the Study of Incarceration called for a turning away from the then-prevailing philosophy of rehabilitation of offenders and moving toward a sentencing model that emphasizes giving criminals what they "deserve" for the particular crimes they have committed. Under the rehabilitative model, indeterminate sentencing and wide discretion on the part of sentencers are viewed as desirable. The so-called just deserts model (the term is from the French, hence the unusual spelling of "deserts"), by contrast, shifts the focus in sentencing to the seriousness of the offender's crime. Proponents of this approach generally favor reducing sentencing disparities and using guidelines that prescribe standardized sentences. The general aim is to give the same punishment to all individuals who commit the same crime.

The just deserts model draws some inspiration from the classical retributivist theory of punishment, such as that of the eighteenth century German philosopher Immanuel Kant. According to Kant, judicial punishment "must in all cases be imposed on [the criminal] only on the ground that he has committed a crime." It is a matter of opinion and the subject of much debate what the appropriate punishment is for any given crime. Among the factors usually considered are the seriousness of the crime, the criminal's previous record, and the amount of harm done to the criminal's victim.

Mario F. Morelli

Further Reading

Cooper, Alison. *A Punishment to Fit the Crime?* North Mankato, Minn.: Sea to Sea Publications, 2005.

Davis, Michael. *To Make the Punishment Fit the Crime: Essays in the Theory of Criminal Justice*. Boulder, Colo.: Westview Press, 1992.

Friedman, Lawrence M. *Crime and Punishment in American History*. Portland, Oreg.: Basic Books, 1994.

Garland, David. *Punishment and Modern Society*. Chicago: University of Chicago Press, 1990.

See also Community-based corrections; Criminal justice system; Deterrence; Discretion; Incapacitation; Mandatory sentencing; Probation, adult; Punishment; Recidivism; Rehabilitation; Sentencing; Sentencing guidelines, U.S.; United States Sentencing Commission; Victimology.

Justice

Definition: The administration of rewards and punishments according to rules and principles that society considers fair and equitable

Criminal justice issues: Constitutional protections; legal terms and principles

Significance: Generally considered the most fundamental purpose of government and civil society, justice encompasses criminal law and the criminal justice system, civil law and civil courts, and social justice.

In writing for the Federalist Papers in 1788, future president James Madison called justice "the end of government . . . the end of civil society. It ever has been and ever will be pursued until it be obtained, or until liberty be lost in the pursuit." For Madison and the other founders, justice meant a society in which people were secure in their persons and property, in which all enjoyed the rights to "life, liberty, and the pursuit of happiness," and in which citizens were governed only with their consent. In the American political tradition, the Declaration of Independence is the single best articulation of the principles of justice that animated the nation's founding. While other nations embraced other notions of justice, such as the rule of the wealthy or the promotion of a specific religion, these were not to be the foundation of American government and civil society. American justice falls into three categories: criminal, civil, and social.

Criminal Justice

Encompassing the laws, procedures, and institutions that communities employ to apprehend, prosecute, and punish those who violate the property or persons of others, criminal justice is primarily a state and local concern in the United States. The federal government plays a minor role because the most typical crimes—such as theft, burglary, robbery, assault, and murder—violate state, not federal, law. The agencies charged with bringing offenders "to justice" are usually local police departments and municipal or county prosecutors. The courts, though established under state law, are commonly organized and run at the county level. Criminals punished by incarceration normally serve terms of less than a year in county jails or more than a year in state prisons.

The federal government actively investigates and prosecutes violations of federal law, such as counterfeiting, interstate drug trafficking, immigration violations, assaults on federal officials, violations of federal regulations governing such activities as environmental pollution and commercial transactions, terrorism, and espionage.

Key justice issues in prosecuting criminal defendants include how suspects or their homes are searched, how evidence is seized, the nature of interrogations, the admissibility of confessions, the provision of legal assistance to the indigent, and the number and types of appeals—particularly from state to federal courts.

There are many similarities among the criminal laws of the fifty states—in all of which murder, rape, robbery, burglary, and certain other negative behaviors are illegal. Nevertheless, disputes occasionally arise over whether governments even should prohibit certain behaviors. This is especially true of so called victimless crimes, such as the personal use of illicit drugs, unauthorized gambling, and prostitution. Opponents of laws against such activities often argue that consenting adults should have the right to engage in any activities that do not directly harm others and that it is "unjust" for a state to limit personal choices in such ways. Defenders of such laws emphasize the function of the law and of government as a moral teacher. Upholders of the latter position maintain, for example, that a government's legalization of cocaine use would send a signal to the people that the community approves such behavior; the inevitable result would be an increase in harmful behavior and grave social costs.

Civil Justice

Generally less controversial than criminal justice, civil justice covers a wide range of legal matters governing the relations among individuals in civil society. These include contracts between private parties, marriage and divorce, parents' responsibility for their children's welfare, harms done without criminal intent, licensing of commercial or professional activities, and health and safety regulations. Civil courts provide forums for aggrieved parties to assert and vindicate their rights.

Perhaps the most controversial aspect of the civil justice system is the dramatic late twentieth century increase in awards to plaintiffs for harms done by government agencies or corporations. Proponents of "tort reform" have called for limits to "punitive damages" (those awarded to punish transgressors) and ceilings on attorney contingency fees.

Social Justice

In contrast to criminal and civil justice, social justice is a twentieth century concept. Embracing the idea that the government has an obligation to promote economic and social well-being, it is strongly associated with the administration of President Franklin D. Roosevelt, who broadly expanded the notion of rights contained in the Declaration of Independence. "Life, liberty, and the pursuit of happiness" were reinterpreted to encompass the "right" to be protected from hunger, unemployment, or the disabilities of sickness and old age. It thus became the task of government to correct inequities in the social and economic systems, to redistribute income and wealth from those who had more to those who had less.

Another component of the movement for social justice was the Civil Rights movement, which peaked in the 1960's. Under such leaders as Martin Luther King, Jr., this movement sought to extend the promises of the Declaration of Independence and the Constitution to Americans of all races. It led to a national commitment in the landmark Civil Rights Acts of 1964 and 1965 to prohibit state and local discrimination in public facilities and employment and to enforce vigorously the right to vote. King summed up the aim of the movement in his famous "I Have a Dream" speech: "Now is the time to make justice a reality for all of God's children."

Joseph M. Bessette

Further Reading

Abadinsky, H. *Law and Justice: An Introduction to the American Legal System*. Upper Saddle River, N.J.: Prentice-Hall, 2003. General survey of American justice with an emphasis on law.

Barak, Gregg, Jeanne M. Flavin, and Paul S. Leighton. *Class, Race, Gender and Crime: Social Realities of Justice in America*. Los Angeles: Roxbury, 2002. Broad overviews of justice issues.

Cohen, William, and David J. Danelski. *Constitutional Law: Civil Liberty and Individual Rights*. New York: Foundation Press, 2002. Casebook on three hundred Supreme Court decisions relating to the most basic issues of justice.

Hamilton, Alexander, James Madison, and John Jay. *The Federalist Papers*. Edited by Maria Hong. New York: Pocket Books, 2004. Any study of American justice should begin with the documents on which the nation was founded, such as these essays written by Hamilton, Madison, and Jay to promote the ratification of the Constitution. Hong's edition is one of the most recent of many editions. An updated edition of a classic version is that edited by Clinton Rossiter (New York: Signet Books, 2003).

McClellan, James. *Liberty, Order, and Justice: An Introduction to the Constitutional Principles of American Government*. Cumberland, Va.: James River Press, 1989. Another excellent general overview of justice in the United States.

Siegel, Larry J., ed. *American Justice: Research of the National Institute of Justice*. St. Paul, Minn.: West, 1990. Excellent introduction to the subject of American justice.

See also Bill of attainder; Constitution, U.S.; Criminal justice system; Due process of law; Equal protection under the law; False convictions; Judicial system, U.S.; Just deserts; Miscarriage of justice; National Institute of Justice; Obstruction of justice; Restorative justice; Supreme Court, U.S.

Justice Department, U.S.

Identification: Federal cabinet-level department that investigates, prosecutes, and punishes offenses against the United States, makes national criminal justice policy, and provides financial, training, and other forms of support to state and municipal law-enforcement agencies

Date: Established in 1870

Criminal justice issues: Federal law; law-enforcement organization

Significance: The largest and most influential law-enforcement entity in the U.S. criminal justice system, the federal Justice Department serves as a link between the court system and the executive branch of the federal government. It also brings suit against violators of federal law and defends the U.S. government against claims brought by persons, organizations, and local and state governments.

In 1789, the first U.S. Congress laid the foundations of the federal justice system by creating both the federal court system and the office of U.S. attorney general. The legislation creating the office of attorney general empowered the holder of that office to appear on behalf of the United States in Supreme Court cases in which the United States was concerned and to give advice and legal opinions when required by the president or heads of any of the executive departments.

Working with only small staffs, the attorneys general carried out their duties without the aid of a bureaucratic department until 1870, when Congress established the Department of Justice. From that modest beginning, the department grew to its twenty-first century position as the largest investigative, prosecutive, and punishment entity in the United States. In 2003, its budget exceeded $22 billion, and it employed almost 106,000 persons—a figure almost exactly the same as the entire population of Washington, D.C., in 1870.

Organization

The modern Justice Department contains dozens of offices, sections, agencies, and other entities that carry out a broad variety of functions related to the criminal justice system. Its law-enforcement agencies include the Federal Bureau of Investigation (FBI), the Drug Enforcement Administration (DEA), and the Bureau of Alcohol, Tobacco, Firearms and Explosives (ATF). These agencies investigate crimes against the United States and threats to national security. They also coordinate with state and local law-enforcement offices and provide training and expertise in nonfederal cases.

The Justice Department also is responsible for conducting all litigation—except as otherwise authorized by statute—in which the United States is a party. Its lawyers include U.S. attorneys and assistant U.S. attorneys, who represent the federal government within assigned districts, and so-called "main justice" prosecutors. Based in Washington, D.C., these prosecutors travel outside the national capital to handle cases throughout the nation. They present criminal matters to federal grand juries and prosecute criminal cases in federal court.

Justice Department lawyers also appear on behalf of the United States in appellate courts and before the U.S. Supreme Court. They may also testify in trials to present the government's views in cases to which the United States itself is not a party. They also handle international criminal matters on behalf of federal, state, or municipal governments and in cases in which foreign fugitives flee to the United States to avoid prosecution in other countries. In U.S. extradition cases, Justice Department lawyers represent the governments of the foreign nations involved.

The U.S. Marshals Service protects federal courts, parties to criminal cases, witnesses, and criminally used or obtained property forfeited to the United States. The department's Bureau of Prisons maintains custody of persons convicted of crimes against the United States. Finally, various offices within the Justice Department provide training, technical assistance, financial aid, and coordination to state and local investigative and prosecution offices.

In a series of statutes, Congress specifically authorized the positions of attorney general, deputy attorney general, assistant attorney general, solicitor general, ten assistant attorneys general, and ninety-three U.S. attorneys. Congress also created the investigative, protective, and prison entities and directed that they be integrated into the Justice Department.

Distinctions Between Federal and State Offenses

Under the nation's federal system of government, responsibility to enforce the law is divided between the federal, state, and local governments. A curious and primary distinction between the federal and state governments is that whereas the powers of the former are few and narrowly defined, those of the latter are both numerous and indefinite. The federal Justice Department can prosecute only offenses that violate federal law, such as statutes enacted by Congress. Some crimes are uniquely federal, some are uniquely subject to state jurisdiction, and some are concurrently proscribed by both state and federal law.

Uniquely federal crimes, which are prosecuted and punished only by the U.S. Justice Department, include such offenses as counterfeiting U.S. currency, treason, espionage and other national security related offenses, immigration fraud, federal tax offenses, federal program fraud, and other crimes that are directed solely against the interests of the national government. The Justice Department may also prosecute crimes within "the special maritime and territorial jurisdiction of the United States," which includes federal enclaves such as Army bases, as well as places and vessels outside the territorial jurisdiction of any state.

Criminal acts that are subject to the concurrent criminal jurisdiction of both state and federal authorities include the manufacture and distribution of drugs; kidnapping; gun offenses and other crimes that also involve interstate activity; frauds in which instrumentalities of interstate or foreign commerce are used; and other crimes that harm federally protected institutions, such as robberies of banks that are federally insured.

The range of offenses that are exclusively within the reach of state authorities and thus not subject to federal prosecution is large. They include purely regional crimes that have no connections with interstate or foreign commerce or do not implicate instrumentalities or other legitimate interests of the federal government. Murder, for example, is ordinarily not a federal crime, but it may be prosecuted by the Justice Department when its victims are federal government officials or foreign diplomats or when it occurs on military bases or other federal property.

In the late twentieth century, federal law criminalized a broad range of conduct that traditionally had been addressed by state laws, in part because of congressional dissatisfaction with local prosecution efforts and state-ordered sentences on convicted offenders. The U.S. Supreme Court's 1995 decision in *United States v. Lopez* reinvigorated federal principles and rebuffed federal prosecutions of crimes that are subject to state jurisdiction and do not reflect constitutionally sanctioned federal interests.

Authority for the prosecution of federal offenses resides primarily with the U.S. attorneys, who are distributed throughout the country, and with "main justice," the assistant attorneys general who head the criminal divisions and their attorneys. Prosecutive authority for tax, antitrust, and environmental matters is assigned to other divisions within the Justice Department. Those divisions are also headed by presidentially appointed assistant attorneys general.

The Attorney General

The attorney general ordinarily does not appear personally in pending cases, though it is not unusual for one to argue a case before the U.S. Supreme Court. However, attorneys general and their subordinates have the power to set national priorities and to issue guidelines to Justice Department prosecutors on a broad variety of litigation matters. Attorneys general must also approve the issuance of federal grand jury or trial subpoenas.

Because attorneys general are political appointees who serve at the pleasure of the presidents, it is an inherent conflict of interest to give the attorney general responsibility for investigating and prosecuting the president or other top executive branch officials. Accordingly, Congress created independent counsels, who are appointed by judges when it is necessary to conduct politi-

At the start of his second term in 2005, President George W. Bush (left) appointed Alberto Gonzales attorney general of the United States. In that office, Gonzales became the head of the U.S. Department of Justice and oversaw all its diverse functions. *(AP/Wide World Photos)*

cally sensitive investigations. On June 30, 1999, the independent counsel statute expired, and investigations and prosecutions of top executive branch officials once again became the responsibility of the attorney general. In practice, attorneys general appoint "special prosecutors" to conduct such investigations or prosecutions when the attorney general cannot do so.

United States Attorneys

Ninety-three U.S. attorneys are stationed throughout the United States, Puerto Rico, the Virgin Islands, Guam, and the Northern Mariana Islands. Each U.S. attorney is appointed by the president, with the U.S. Senate's advice and consent, and serves at the pleasure of the president. Each attorney serves within one of the ninety-four congressionally established judicial districts, with the exception that a single U.S. attorney serves for the District of Guam and the District of the Northern Mariana Islands. The U.S. attorneys are the chief federal law-enforcement officers in their own districts. By law, the

U.S. attorneys and assistant U.S. attorneys are empowered to prosecute criminal cases brought by the federal government.

U.S. attorneys have considerable discretion in determining priorities and in deciding whether to present cases to federally impaneled grand juries and, when indictments are returned, to prosecute cases. They also have broad discretion in choosing and pursuing investigative and litigation techniques. However broad though, this discretion is not unlimited. The attorneys general set national priorities and retain the right to approve certain litigation and investigative decisions of the U.S. attorneys. Main justice must authorize the initiation of criminal charges under the Racketeer Influenced and Corrupt Organizations (RICO) Act of 1970. Main justice must also approve requests for judicial orders conferring immunity on prospective witnesses when judicially conferred immunity is necessary to compel the witnesses to give evidence that might be self-incriminatory. U.S. attorneys may not appeal district court decisions without approval from the solicitor general in the Justice Department.

Congress can also restrict the discretion of U.S. attorneys by requiring approval by main justice of certain actions. For example, the federal wiretap statute requires that U.S. attorneys who seek judicial orders authorizing wiretaps or other electronic surveillance receive authorization from main justice.

Criminal Division and Other Enforcement Divisions

The Criminal Division of the Justice Department also has significant prosecution authority. It comprises multiple sections, with particular responsibility for prosecuting a variety of offenses including narcotics, organized crime, terrorism, money laundering, white-collar fraud, bribery of public officials and other forms of public corruption, computer crimes, criminal copyright offenses, violation of child exploitation and obscenity statutes, certain violent crimes, and alien smuggling.

The Criminal Division also operates as the central authority in international treaty matters concerning criminal law enforcement. Treaties for extradition and mutual legal assistance (the process by which the judicial or prosecution authorities in one country seek assistance in securing important evidence located in another country) generally are negotiated by attorneys of the Department of State and the Criminal Division. After treaties are negotiated, ratified, and entered into force, the Criminal Division makes and receives international requests for extradition or mutual legal assistance, even when fugitives or evidence are sought by state or local prosecutors.

Although the primary responsibility for criminal prosecutions lies within the Criminal Division, other litigation divisions within the department have limited criminal law-enforcement authority. For example, the Antitrust Division prosecutes criminal antitrust violations. The Tax Division prosecutes major tax offenses, such as the promotion of fraudulent tax shelters, and is also involved in the prosecution of terrorist financing cases. The Civil Rights Division prosecutes slavery, voter fraud, and criminal civil rights violations. The Environmental and Natural Resources Division prosecutes environmental offenses, such as criminal violations of the Clean Air Act of 1970.

The Federal Bureau of Investigation

Several entities under the umbrella of the Justice Department have exclusively or primarily investigative functions. The FBI, the DEA, and the ATF are the primary investigative agencies. In addition, the department participates in international criminal investigations and cooperation, primarily through Interpol.

Established as the Bureau of Investigation in 1908, the Federal Bureau of Investigation has the broadest responsibility of all federal investigative agencies, with authority to investigate more than 180 kinds of federal crimes. During the first years of the twenty-first century, its official top priority was counterterrorism. The FBI is also the primary domestic agency responsible for the investigation of espionage, treason, and other related national security matters. In addition, the FBI has responsibility for investigating cybercrime and cyber-based attacks, public corruption, civil rights offenses, transnational and national organized crime, white-collar crime, and significant violent crime in violation of U.S. law.

The FBI has other criminal justice functions as well. For example, it maintains a computerized database of fingerprint records in its Integrated Automated Fingerprint Identification System, whose data are available to other federal and state law-enforcement agencies. Its profiling unit and laboratories also assist in federal and state investigations and prosecutions. Thomas Harris's novel *Silence of the Lambs* (1988) and novels by author Patricia Cornwell have portrayed the profiling unit in some detail.

The FBI Academy in Quantico, Virginia, trains federal, state, local, and international police officers. The FBI's National Crime Information Center (NCIC) maintains databases containing a wide variety of information; its databases are accessed approximately two million times a day by federal, state, and local police agencies.

The director of the FBI is appointed by the president, with Senate approval, for a term of ten years. His or her resignation can, however, be requested by the sitting president. FBI agents are based in fifty-six field offices and four hundred satellite offices within the United States, and FBI legal attachés (called legats) in forty-five offices outside the United States support investigations and operations around the world.

U.S. Marshals Service

The Justice Department's U.S. Marshals Service is the oldest of the U.S. law-enforcement agencies. The Marshals Service was created to provide security and protection for federal courts. The service now has myriad law-enforcement functions. Its protective functions include protection of courthouses and courtrooms and, as necessary, federal prosecutors and judges. It also transports and maintains the security of federal witnesses and prisoners. It runs the federal Witness Protection Program, which protects, relocates, and provides new identities to people—and sometimes their family members—who are in jeopardy on account of their testimony in criminal trials. Between 1970 and 2004, more than 7,500 people were enrolled in the program.

The U.S. Marshals Service also has a significant police function. It executes arrest warrants issued for fugitives who are accused of violating federal laws. In fact, federal marshals arrest more people than all other federal law-enforcement agencies combined. The service also is responsible for apprehending foreign fugitives

sought for extradition and believed to be in the United States. It also is the primary agency for tracking U.S. fugitives charged by federal, state, or regional authorities when those fugitives are believed to have fled to points outside the United States.

The Marshals Service is responsible for the housing and transportation of persons charged with federal crimes (from point of arrest to the date of sentencing) and of internationally wanted fugitives. It houses more than forty-seven thousand federal prisoners (prior to conviction and sentencing) each day, in federal facilities or, through contract arrangements, in jails maintained by state and local authorities. It operates the Justice Prisoner and Alien Transportation System (JPATS), which transports prisoners and criminal aliens between judicial districts and correctional institutions and even to and from foreign countries. It manages and disposes of properties acquired by criminals through illegal activities after those properties have been seized and forfeited to the United States. Under the auspices of the Justice Department Asset Forfeiture Program, the Marshals Service in 2004 managed nearly $1 billion worth of property, proceeds of which are designed for federal, state, local, and foreign law-enforcement purposes.

Other Investigative and Protective Agencies

The Drug Enforcement Administration enforces U.S. laws concerning controlled substances. It investigates organizations and persons involved in the importation, growing, manufacture, and distribution of controlled substances in the United States. DEA agents are based throughout the United States as well as abroad, where they support investigations and international operations.

Formerly a branch of the U.S. Treasury Department, the Justice Department's Bureau of Alcohol, Tobacco, Firearms and Explosives (ATF) enforces federal firearms laws and investigates violent crimes involving guns and explosives. The ATF also investigates offenses involving the smuggling of contraband untaxed alcohol and tobacco, but they form a small part of its overall work.

The National Central Bureau (NCB) of Interpol, the International Criminal Police Organization that is headquartered in Lyon, France, is the U.S. point of contact for international law enforcement. The NCB facilitates U.S. participation in international law-enforcement cooperation by transmitting requests and information to and from Interpol member states and domestic law-enforcement agencies and coordinating information in international investigations. Among other key functions, Interpol facilitates efforts to locate internationally wanted fugitives and property that has been stolen and transported across national borders.

U.S. Bureau of Prisons

Offenders convicted of federal crimes and sentenced to prison terms are remanded to the custody of the Bureau of Prisons (BOP). The bureau has wide discretion to designate their places of imprisonment and then to regulate the conduct of the prisoners within that penal institution.

Sara Criscitelli

Further Reading

Clayton, Cornell C. *The Politics of Justice: The Attorney General and the Making of Legal Policy*. Armonk, N.Y.: M. E. Sharpe, 1992. Scholarly examination of the role of the attorney general in the shaping of national legal policies.

Cole, George F., and Christopher Smith. *American System of Criminal Justice*. 10th ed. Belmont, Calif: Thompson/Wadsworth, 2004. Standard textbook that covers all aspects of criminal justice in the United States, with extensive attention to the Justice Department and its branches.

Earley, Pete, and Gerald Shur. *WITSEC: Inside the Federal Witness Protection Program*. New York: Bantam Books, 2002. Inside view of the federal witness protection program, based on Shur's twenty-five-year career as a Justice Department attorney.

Johns, Margaret, and Rex R. Perschbacher. *The United States Legal System: An Introduction*. Durham, N.C.: Carolina Academic Press, 2002. Broad survey of the American justice system, with considerable attention to the Justice Department.

Kessler, Ronald. *The Bureau: The Secret History of the FBI*. New York: St. Martin's Press, 2002.

Critical assessment of the Federal Bureau of Investigation that focuses on allegations that the bureau often abused its power.

Littman, Jonathan. *The Fugitive Game*. New York: Little, Brown, 1996. Inside look at the U.S. Marshals Service's work in tracking fugitives from justice.

Reebel, Patrick A., ed. *Federal Bureau of Investigation: Current Issues and Background*. New York: Nova Science, 2002. Collection of essays on the FBI with attention to some of its most publicized investigations, including those into the 1995 Oklahoma City bombing, the 1996 Montana "Freemen" standoff, and the 1993 Branch Davidian siege.

Stroud, Carsten. *Deadly Force: In the Streets with the U.S. Marshals*. New York: Bantam Books, 1996. Exploits of modern federal fugitive hunters.

See also Attorney general of the United States; Attorneys, U.S.; Criminal justice system; Federal Bureau of Investigation; Immigration and Naturalization Service; Marshals Service, U.S.; National Institute of Justice; Omnibus Crime Control and Safe Streets Act of 1968; Organized crime; Secret Service, U.S.; Solicitor general of the United States.

Juvenile courts

Definition: Courts specializing in cases involving juvenile offenders

Criminal justice issues: Courts; juvenile justice; rehabilitation

Significance: Relative to adult criminal courts, juvenile courts provide a more rehabilitative and prevention-oriented approach to defendants, while observing the specific legal rights of juveniles.

In 1899, Illinois established the first juvenile court in the United States, marking a significant change in the way society dealt with youthful offenders. Prior to that time, criminal courts treated juveniles and adults similarly, and they often convicted and sentenced children as young as seven. Throughout the nineteenth century, individuals and organizations advocated for reforms in the criminal justice system. They argued that juveniles are developmentally different from adults and that the justice system should recognize this difference in its treatment and punishment of juveniles. The juvenile court was a product of these reforms.

A guiding principle of the early juvenile courts was *parens patriae*, which refers to the state acting in a parental role to care for the protection and welfare of juveniles. Under this principle, the courts treated juvenile offenders as delinquents, not criminals, and they used a variety of noncriminal sanctions in an effort to rehabilitate delinquent juveniles. Relative to criminal courts, juvenile court proceedings were less adversarial, and judges considered a larger variety of extralegal factors in making decisions. Every state had some form of juvenile court legislation by 1945, established on the premise that juveniles could be rehabilitated through appropriate treatment programs and services.

Changes in Juvenile Courts

While the early reforms fostered a more benevolent and humane system of juvenile justice, they also produced a system in which juveniles lacked many due process rights afforded to adults charged with crimes, including access to counsel. With the state acting in a parental role, these rights seemed unnecessary for juveniles. This lack of rights and protections was frequently challenged, however, and as the twentieth century progressed, juvenile courts experienced several procedural changes stemming from decisions of the U.S. Supreme Court.

Some of the most significant changes came from the Supreme Court's 1967 decision in the case *In re Gault*, in which, among other things, the Court ruled that a juvenile has a constitutional right to a notice of charges, a right to counsel, and a protection against self-incrimination. These and other Supreme Court rulings created a juvenile court that was more formal procedurally but still focused on the unique developmental capacities and needs of juveniles.

Legislative changes also affected juvenile courts in the latter half of the twentieth century. During the 1950's and 1960's, the public became concerned with the large number of juveniles

detained or imprisoned for rehabilitative treatment, especially as treatment programs generally failed to demonstrate effectiveness in reducing delinquent behavior. In 1974, Congress passed the Juvenile Justice and Delinquency Prevention Act, which required the deinstitutionalization of juvenile detention facilities. As part of this process, detention and correctional facilities began to remove status offenders and to separate juvenile and adult offenders.

During the 1980's, the public's perception that juvenile crime rates were rapidly increasing led to a second wave of significant legislative changes. Several states enacted punitive laws and limited the discretion and jurisdiction of the juvenile court. Some states identified certain offenses for which juveniles would be automatically transferred to adult criminal court, and other states established mandatory minimum sentences for serious offenses. In sum, these changes produced a juvenile court system that more closely resembled the adult criminal court system.

In 2004, juvenile courts varied widely from state to state. As a group, however, juvenile courts continued to reflect the public and legislative intent to get "tough on crime." During the 1990's, almost all state juvenile court systems became more punitive in their procedures regarding transfers to adult court, sentencing, and confidentiality of juvenile court records and hearings.

The Juvenile Court Process

Juvenile courts typically follow a similar pattern in processing delinquency cases. When a juvenile is accused of breaking the law, the prosecution, typically referred to as the district attorney or state attorney, must decide whether to pursue the case in court, to handle it informally, or to dismiss the case altogether. Informal processing usually involves diverting the juvenile's case to community service or to some type of counseling or education program. These services and programs are often designed to prevent future delinquent behavior.

If the prosecution formally processes the case by filing a delinquency petition, the judge is then responsible for adjudicating the case. The adjudication process often requires a trial, at which the judge will determine if the juvenile is delinquent or is responsible for the offense. At the disposition stage, the judge typically has the discretion to place a delinquent juvenile on probation or in a commitment facility for a specified length of time. The juvenile court also handles cases in which delinquent juveniles violate conditions of their probation, and it determines the need to hold juveniles in secure detention during the adjudication process.

Christopher M. Hill

Further Reading

Champion, Dean John. *The Juvenile Justice System: Delinquency, Processing, and the Law.* 4th ed. Upper Saddle River, N.J.: Prentice-Hall, 2003. Broad overview of delinquency and the juvenile justice system response, including police, prosecutorial, and judicial decision making. It examines juvenile legal rights and the courts' decisions regarding adjudication, disposition, and sanctions.

Humes, Edward. *No Matter How Loud I Shout: A Year in the Life of Juvenile Court.* Reprint ed. New York: Touchstone, 1997. Humes writes about the day-to-day operation of the Los Angeles juvenile court as he observes the lives of five juveniles progressing through the court system.

McCord, Joan, Cathy Spatz Widom, and Nancy Crowell, eds. *Juvenile Crime, Juvenile Justice.* Washington, D.C.: National Academy Press, 2001. In addition to a historical perspective, this book describes how cases move through juvenile courts and how recent legislation has affected court procedures, including transfers to criminal court and sentencing.

Tanenhaus, David S. *Juvenile Justice in the Making.* New York: Oxford University Press, 2004. The author examines three thousand juvenile case files from Chicago during the early twentieth century to provide an updated historical perspective on the origins of juvenile courts. This book addresses the fundamental question of how juveniles should be treated under the law.

Watkins, John C., Jr. *The Juvenile Justice Century: A Sociolegal Commentary on American Juvenile Courts.* Durham, N.C.: Carolina Academic Press, 1998. Watkins examines histori-cal and current changes to juvenile law that impact the operations of juvenile courts.

See also Blended sentences; Court types; Diversion; *Gault, In re*; Juvenile delinquency; Juvenile Justice and Delinquency Prevention Act; Juvenile justice system; Juvenile waivers to adult courts; *Parens patriae*; Probation, juvenile; Restitution; Status offenses; Uniform Juvenile Court Act; Vandalism; Youth authorities.

Juvenile delinquency

Definition: Adolescent criminal behavior

Criminal justice issues: Crime prevention; juvenile justice; rehabilitation; violent crime

Significance: Juvenile delinquency is a major social concern in the United States. Every year, millions of juveniles are arrested on charges ranging from minor status offenses, such as truancy, to such serious crimes as burglary, robbery, rape, auto theft, aggravated assault, larceny, and homicide. Moreover, juvenile delinquency often carries over into adult criminal behavior.

Widely publicized school shootings during the late 1990's and early years of the twenty-first century have raised public concerns about rising adolescent violence and created the perception that juvenile delinquency is increasing. However, statistical studies show that juvenile crime rates are actually declining. In 2001, the total number of juvenile arrests was 2.3 million—a figure 4 percent below the total for 2000 and 20 percent below the 1997 total. Nevertheless, public pressures have been mounting for wholesale reforms in the juvenile justice system, including calls for abandoning the system and treating adolescent offenders as adults. In order to understand the role of juveniles in the American criminal justice system, it is necessary to examine the root causes of juvenile delinquency.

Patterns of Delinquency

A common assumption about adolescent crime is that juveniles from lower-class families are more apt to be delinquent than those from middle- and upper-class families. However, this view has been disputed by some researchers, who claim that no connections between social class and delinquency exist, and that to infer otherwise borders on racism. Furthermore, while some scholars see connections between race and delinquency (African American juveniles are arrested more often than are white or Hispanic adolescents), other researchers disagree, stating that while black juveniles are arrested at a higher frequency, the reason is that crimes committed by African Americans are more likely to come to the attention of the police.

There are also connections between age arrests. For example, the ages of juvenile property crime offenders peak at sixteen and then decline sharply thereafter. Arrest rates for violent crimes peak at age eighteen, followed by a much slower decline. Likewise, there are also connections between gender and delinquency, with boys having higher rates of delinquency than girls. Gender differences are most evident in violent and property crimes, with boys committing most of the most serious offenses. Girls do commit similar types of crimes, but less frequently. Statistics show that boys are more likely than girls to be arrested for every category of crime except prostitution and running away.

Individual juvenile offenders tend to differ from adult offenders in the varieties of crimes that they commit. Only a small number of juvenile offenders specialize in specific crimes. A large majority of them commit a wide range of minor offenses, such as truancy, disorderly conduct, loitering, and curfew violations. However, only a small percentage commit mixtures of both minor and serious offenses.

The ages at which juveniles begin their delinquent behavior are strong indicators in predicting their future criminal behavior. The term "early onset" is applied to juveniles who begin behaving delinquently in their early childhood. Early onset delinquents usually continue their delinquent behavior into adulthood. Moreover, they commit delinquent acts at higher rates, and the crimes they commit are more often violent. The term "adolescent onset" applies to juveniles who do not begin their delinquent behavior until they reach adolescence. Adolescent onset delinquents are more common than early onset delin-

quents, and the crimes they commit are, on average, less serious. Adolescent onset delinquents are also more likely to stop their delinquent activities in late adolescence.

General Risk Factors

One point about juvenile delinquency that is almost undisputed is that there is a strong correlation between poverty and criminal behavior. Most scholars and juvenile justice professionals agree that adolescent violence and aggression is strongly linked to socioeconomic status, for several primary reasons. Families living in poverty often have parents who are less nurturing and less apt to monitor their children's activities closely. Poverty makes it difficult for parents and communities to provide the needed guidance and supervision juveniles need. Also, unemployed men in rough inner-city environments have a greater tendency than men living comfortably in middle- and upper-class communities to behave aggressively in order to assert their power and strength. Violence tends to beget violence. Juveniles growing up in dysfunctional environments in which aggressive behavior is praised are apt to engage in violence themselves.

A more controversial subject that has received major media coverage concerns biological factors: the question of how heredity, or genetics, influences antisocial behavior. Studies of genetically identical twins and biologically unrelated adopted siblings have shown that links do exist between genetics and delinquency. However, most researchers agree that criminal behavior is more likely when there are matches between juveniles' genetic predispositions toward lawbreaking and living in environments conducive to such activity.

Individual traits have also been found to correlate with delinquency, especially for high-rate and serious offenders. Studies have shown that juveniles with low verbal intelligence quotas—those who have trouble with self-expression, remembering information, and thinking abstractly—have an increased probability for delinquency. Lack of verbal skills contribute to difficulties in attaining goals in a positive manner. Juveniles suffering from attention deficit hyperactivity disorder (ADHD) are more likely to exhibit symptoms of juvenile delinquency.

A primary concern about ADHD adolescents is

the hyperactivity/impulsivity continuum of the disorder. Common ADHD behaviors include being overly active for one's age, acting impulsively, focusing only on immediate events, and engaging in generally reckless behavior. ADHD also creates a greater need for stimulation that makes adolescents seek excitement, an impulse that easily bored juveniles may satisfy by turning to crime, which they may even regard as fun. Other manifestations of ADHD included reduced ability to learn from punishment, insensitivity to others, poor interpersonal problem-solving skills, and drug and alcohol use.

Family and School Factors

Family factors that play a role in breeding juvenile delinquency include having criminal parents, living in large families, growing up with little discipline, parental rejection, low socioeconomic status, and frequent changes of residence. Parents who exhibit hyper-aggressive behavior teach their children, by example, to be "strong" and "tough."

A factor that inhibits delinquent tendencies is having parents who express their love openly and take active interests in their children's daily lives. Other protective factors include attachment to parents, lack of serious family conflicts, church attendance, community support, and emphasis on academic achievement. Parental socialization is crucial, as parents teach their children not to engage in criminal behavior. When parents are indifferent to their children's development, the likelihood of delinquency increases.

School experiences correlate with juvenile delinquency as well. Low academic performance, misbehavior in and out of classrooms, weak attachments to teachers and principals, and lack of involvement in school activities are all associated with delinquency. Some schools have proven themselves successful in dealing with juvenile delinquents. Small schools with high teacher-pupil ratios and adequate supplies of needed materials, such as computers and overhead projectors, can be protective factors against adolescent criminality. Other desirable qualities in schools include clear and concise rules, absence of corporal punishment, enjoyable working conditions for both faculty and students, and, most important, teachers who care about their students.

Youth Gangs

The old adage "Birds of a feather flock together" accurately sums up the impact of youth gangs on juvenile delinquency. Gangs are perceived as distinct groups of individuals within communities. Their members see themselves as unique and different and worthy of commanding respect. A central hallmark for gang involvement, however, is myriad criminal acts leading to negative responses from both the police and community residents. Youth gangs are common throughout the United States and can be found in virtually every city, including small towns and rural communities.

Many arrests for violent acts of juvenile delinquency are gang related, and most serious juvenile violence occurs in encounters between members of rival gangs. As a means of protection, gang members frequently carry guns, which range from small handguns and shotguns to automatic assault rifles and machine guns.

Most gang members are young African Americans between the ages sixteen and twenty. Some gangs are highly organized structures, while others have little structure. Individual gang members may be classified as instigators and followers; instigators are mostly boys, and girls are mostly followers. Delinquent peers tend to reinforce each other's maladaptive behavior and allay one another's concerns about police and societal sanctions.

Reasons for joining gangs include possessing poor social skills that prohibit the delinquent from affiliating with nondelinquent adolescents, which may result from negative experiences at school. Quests for excitement can make gang activity appealing to bored adolescents. Quests for money are also strong motivators, as most gang members come from poor families and see few alternative prospects for making money. Stressful living conditions in homes also promote gang involvement.

Illegal drugs play an important role in youth gangs, many of whose members use drugs and traffic in them. The need for money to buy drugs tends to lead gang members into other types of crime. Addicted gang members who cannot find the money to support their drug habits may even be driven to more serious crimes, including murder, to find ways to obtain their drugs. Moreover,

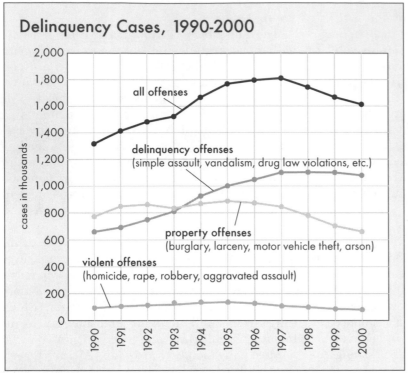

Delinquency Cases, 1990-2000

all offenses

delinquency offenses
(simple assault, vandalism, drug law violations, etc.)

property offenses
(burglary, larceny, motor vehicle theft, arson)

violent offenses
(homicide, rape, robbery, aggravated assault)

Source: National Center for Juvenile Justice. Figures reflect delinquency offenses receiving judicial action.

studies have shown that many juvenile offenders are under the influence of drugs when they commit crimes. It is possible that the majority of violent crimes committed by delinquents are drug related.

Theories About Delinquency

Many theories have been advanced over the years that attempt to explain why some juveniles become delinquent while others do not. During the 1950's, Albert Bandura, a psychologist at Stanford University, formulated what he called social learning theory as a means for understanding how people learn new behaviors. In essence, his theory posits that people are more likely to repeat behaviors for which they receive positive reinforcement, while avoiding those for which they receive nothing or negative reinforcement. For a given behavior to be learned, all that is needed is the requisite level of reinforcement applied at the appropriate time. By contrast, for a behavior to be unlearned, all reinforcement should be withheld.

Bandura's theory posits that crime is a learned behavior and that what is learned can be unlearned by using sound psychological principles. According to social learning theory, the behavior of delinquent juveniles results from exposure to people with maladaptive values and attitudes toward crime. Over time, juveniles in such environments become socialized to accept antisocial behavior.

Rational choice theory is another method that attempts to understand what makes juveniles delinquent. It argues that juvenile delinquency should be viewed from the perspectives of the individuals who choose to engage in criminal activity. Before initiating illegal acts, individuals weigh the chances of succeeding versus failing and being caught by authorities. After they make up their minds, they decide on courses of action, thus making logical decisions. A hallmark of antisocial behavior is lack of empathy for victims. Rational theory holds that to ameliorate juvenile delinquency, adolescents must be taught how to emphasize with others.

According to rational choice theory, people capable of choosing bad behaviors are equally capable of choosing legal behaviors. Social strain theory argues that when juveniles experience mental stress or conflict, they become upset and engage in delinquent behavior because they are being inundated by negative thoughts and feelings.

Social strain theory holds that there are two major "strain" categories: failing to achieve one's goals and loss of positive stimuli or presentations of negative stimuli. The first type of strain generally centers on obtaining money, winning status and respect, and seeking personal autonomy. The second category deals with adolescents' loss of things that they value, as well as the presentation of noxious stimuli. Examples of the former might include being insulted before one's peers or becoming a victim of a crime. Examples of the latter include learning that one's parents are divorcing, having a romantic relationship end, or being arrested by police. Treatment methods involve various behavioral techniques such as self-talk, self-management, anger management, and relaxation therapy.

Punishment and Prevention

Many "get-tough" advocates feel that juvenile delinquency can be reduced if delinquents have a greater fear of being incarcerated, especially if they realize how harsh incarceration can be. However, studies of the deterrent effect of harsher punishments do not support such views. Increasing the harshness of incarceration has not been reflected in reductions of delinquent behavior, even of juveniles released from incarceration.

Among the reasons advanced for why punitive measures do not reduce delinquency is that punishments do not address the underlying causes of delinquent behavior. Moreover, while punishment might cause offenders mental and physical distress, it may also contribute to their social learning by teaching them how not to get caught. Finally, it is pointed out that the notion of deterrence is based on assumptions of rational behavior, while most juvenile delinquents, as well as their adult counterparts, do not always think rationally.

The concept of incapacitation has been promoted heavily in the media as a strategy for controlling delinquency. The principle behind incapacitation is that the best method for combating criminal behavior is to lock up the perpetrators for long periods. Delinquents who are locked up cannot cause society any further trouble. However, studies of the effectiveness of incapacitation on reducing delinquency have shown that incapacitation achieves only nominal reductions.

Prevention programs attempt to prevent juveniles from becoming delinquents in the first place. Federal legislation funding juvenile justice programs has tended to favor proven prevention programs over more expensive deterrence and incapacitation programs. Well-designed programs that emphasize treating problems over punishing behavior have been found to reduce delinquency significantly. By intensively targeting the causes of delinquency, the programs often have effects that last for long periods. Their in-

structors rely heavily on cognitive behavioral techniques and stress changing the juveniles' ways of thinking, since a major premise in cognitive behaviorism is that one's thought processes are echoed in behavior. For example, juveniles who come into the programs thinking that the only way they can make decent livings is by engaging in criminal activity are taught how to eradicate negative cognition, replacing it with positive problem-solving skills. Research thus far indicates that the prevention programs are indeed helping juvenile delinquents.

Cary Stacy Smith

Further Reading

Bernard, Thomas J. *The Cycle of Juvenile Justice*. New York: Oxford University Press, 1992. Very readable review of the changing historical conceptions of justice and legal rights regarding children. The author shows how the breakdown of traditional social controls led to the social creation of juvenile delinquency.

Binder, Arnold, Gilbert Geis, and Dickson Bruce. *Juvenile Delinquency: Historical, Cultural and Legal Perspectives*. New York: Macmillan, 1988. Well-written text that provides useful information on the historical conceptions of children and the social construction of "child deviance."

Champion, Dean John. *The Juvenile Justice System: Delinquency, Processing, and the Law*. 4th ed. Upper Saddle River, N.J.: Prentice-Hall, 2003. Broad overview of delinquency and the stages through which offenders are processed in the juvenile justice system. Examines legal rights of juveniles and court decisions on adjudication, disposition, and sanctions.

Cox, Steven M., John J. Conrad, and Jennifer M. Allen. *Juvenile Justice: A Guide to Theory and Practice*. 5th ed. New York: McGraw-Hill, 2003. Comprehensive examination of the juvenile justice system that connects theory and practice.

Feld, Barry C. *Cases and Materials on Juvenile Justice Administration*. St. Paul, Minn.: West Group, 2000. Compilation of court cases, statutes, and articles on juvenile administrative procedures in the United States.

Jonson-Reid, M. "Child Welfare Services and Delinquency: The Need to Know More." *Child*

Welfare 83, no. 2 (2004): 157-174. Examination of juvenile delinquency from the perspective of social services providers.

Malmgren, K. W., and S. M. Meisel. "Examining the Link Between Child Maltreatment and Delinquency for Youth with Emotional and Behavioral Disorders." *Child Welfare* 83, no. 2 (2004): 175-189. Examination of one cause contributing to juvenile delinquency.

Paternoster, R., S. Bushway, R. Brame, and R. Apel. "The Effects of Teenage Employment on Delinquency and Problem Behaviors." *Social Force* 82, no. 1 (2003): 297-336. Sociological treatment of one contributing factor in juvenile delinquency—the ability of adolescents to earn money honestly.

Rosenheim, Margaret K., et al., eds. *A Century of Juvenile Justice*. Chicago: University of Chicago Press, 2002. Comprehensive and broad-ranging collection of essays on the history of juvenile justice. The majority of the volume focuses on twentieth century U.S. history, but individual essays also treat the nineteenth century, Japan, and Great Britain.

Shoemaker, D. J. *Theories of Delinquency: An Examination of Explanations of Delinquent Behavior*. 4th ed. New York: Oxford University Press, 2000. Survey of theoretical approaches to explaining delinquent behavior. Clearly written evaluations of the various individualistic and sociological theories.

Siegel, L. J., Brandon C. Welsh, and Joseph J. Senna. *Juvenile Delinquency: Theory, Practice, and Law*. 8th ed. New York: Wadsworth, 2002. Comprehensive examination of juvenile justice along with policies, theories, landmark court decisions, and contemporary issues. The eighth edition of this perennial textbook pays special attention to multimedia and Web resources.

See also Contributing to delinquency of minors; Juvenile courts; Juvenile Justice and Delinquency Prevention, Office of; Juvenile Justice and Delinquency Prevention Act; Juvenile justice system; Juvenile waivers to adult courts; *Parens patriae*; Probation, juvenile; Status offenses; Uniform Juvenile Court Act; Vandalism; Wickersham Commission; Youth authorities; Youth gangs.

Juvenile Justice and Delinquency Prevention, Office of

Identification: Branch of the U.S. Department of Justice that provides support to states, local communities, and Native American tribal jurisdictions in an effort to treat and prevent serious juvenile delinquency, child abuse, and child neglect

Criminal justice issues: Juvenile justice; law-enforcement organization

Date: Established in 1974

Significance: The Office of Juvenile Justice and Delinquency Prevention, or OJJDP, was created to provide federal aid to states and local communities in a continued and comprehensive initiative to deinstitutionalize and decentralize the practices of juvenile justice throughout the United States.

A semiautonomous branch within the federal Department of Justice's Law Enforcement Administration Agency (LEAA), the OJJDP provides information and funding to local, state, and tribal juvenile justice agencies. Through this provision, the OJJDP aids these agencies in child service provisions, public protection, research initiatives, and specialized training for justice system officials interacting with youth.

The OJJDP was established when the U.S. Congress passed the Juvenile Justice and Delinquency Prevention Act in 1974. Initial motivation for the creation of the office was the provision of funding to state and local jurisdictions involved in continued efforts to develop alternatives to confinement for juvenile offenders. This primary goal persisted throughout the 1980's.

During the 1990's, the OJJDP embraced a comprehensive approach to the study and treatment of juvenile delinquency, stressing prevention, assessment of risk and need, family factors, and graduated sanctions for youth. In 2002, Congress reauthorized the Juvenile Justice and Delinquency Prevention Act, which provided for continued support of the OJJDP's initial goals while increasing funding opportunities for communities and states, as well as placing a renewed focus on research, training, technical assistance, and the dissemination of information.

Courtney A. Waid

Further Reading

Champion, Dean John. *The Juvenile Justice System: Delinquency, Processing, and the Law.* 4th ed. Upper Saddle River, N.J.: Prentice Hall, 2003.

Olson-Raymer, Gayle. *Criminology: The Role of the Federal Government in Juvenile Delinquency Prevention—Historical and Contemporary Perspectives.* Evanston, Ill.: Northwestern School of Law Journal of Criminal Law and Criminology, 1983.

Tanenhaus, David S. *Juvenile Justice in the Making.* New York: Oxford University Press, 2004.

See also Contributing to delinquency of minors; DARE programs; Juvenile delinquency; Juvenile Justice and Delinquency Prevention Act; Juvenile justice system; Probation, juvenile; Restorative justice; Uniform Juvenile Court Act; Youth authorities.

Juvenile Justice and Delinquency Prevention Act

The Law: Federal law that was the U.S. Congress's first major attempt to unify the treatment of juvenile offenders throughout the United States

Date: Became effective on September 7, 1974

Criminal justice issues: Juvenile justice; morality and public order

Significance: This landmark federal legislation created the Office of Juvenile Justice and Delinquency Prevention and recommended major changes to state juvenile justice systems.

The Juvenile Justice and Delinquency Prevention Act of 1974 (JJDPA) was enacted by the U.S. Congress to provide juvenile offenders uniform treatment in every state's justice system. The act was passed with strong support from both Democrats and Republicans and a wide range of special interest groups.

One of the most significant components of the JJDPA was the creation of the Office of Juvenile Justice and Delinquency Prevention. Because each state has independent jurisdiction over its juvenile court system, participation in the JJDPA was made optional, and the act made federal funds available to states that chose to participate. This federal funding served as strong motivation for the individual states to bring their juvenile justice systems into compliance with the new federal requirements. Under the JJDPA, states were mandated to remove status offenders from secure and correctional facilities. This movement is often referred to as the deinstitutionalization of status offenders. Another significant requirement placed on states by JJDPA was a prohibition against placing juveniles in any institutions in which they might have regular contacts with adult offenders.

Since 1974, Congress has periodically reauthorized the Juvenile Justice and Delinquency Prevention Act and appropriated funds to support the programs it created. Furthermore, Congress has responded to trends in juvenile crime by reevaluating and amending the act. For example, during the late 1980's, rising violent juvenile crime rates prompted Congress to refocus the Juvenile Justice and Delinquency Prevention Act on serious and chronic juvenile offenders, allowing states to prosecute certain juvenile offenders as adults.

The 2004 version of the Juvenile Justice and Delinquency Prevention Act established two primary goals for the law. First, states were required to provide high-quality prevention programs that work with juveniles, their families, and communities to prevent delinquent behavior. Second, states were required to hold juveniles accountable for their actions by providing opportunities to make restitution to victims, perform community service, and develop the character qualities necessary to become productive members of their communities.

Laurie M. Kubicek

Further Reading

Champion, Dean John. *The Juvenile Justice System: Delinquency, Processing, and the Law.* 4th ed. Upper Saddle River, N.J.: Prentice-Hall, 2003.

Cox, Steven M., John J. Conrad, and Jennifer M. Allen. *Juvenile Justice: A Guide to Theory and Practice.* 5th ed. New York: McGraw-Hill, 2003.

Hess, Karen M., and Robert W. Drowns. *Juvenile Justice.* 4th ed. Belmont, Calif.: Wadsworth/Thomson Learning, 2004. Comprehensive overview of the juvenile justice system that connects theory and practice.

Olson-Raymer, Gayle. *Criminology: The Role of the Federal Government in Juvenile Delinquency Prevention—Historical and Contemporary Perspectives.* Evanston, Ill.: Northwestern School of Law Journal of Criminal Law and Criminology, 1983.

See also Contributing to delinquency of minors; Diversion; Juvenile courts; Juvenile delinquency; Juvenile Justice and Delinquency Prevention, Office of; Juvenile justice system; Juvenile waivers to adult courts; Status offenses; Uniform Juvenile Court Act; Youth authorities.

Juvenile justice system

Definition: Separate justice system developed for minors

Criminal justice issues: Crime prevention; courts; juvenile justice; rehabilitation

Significance: Since the turn of the twentieth century, one of the most significant developments in the American justice system has been a trend away from treating juvenile offenders in the adult justice system by developing a largely autonomous system of justice designed for the special needs of adolescents.

The origins of America's separate juvenile justice system go back to 1899, when the state of Illinois created the first juvenile courts in Cook County, which includes Chicago. That first system had a special juvenile court and associated clinics staffed with experts in social services. Compared to traditional adult courts, that juvenile court was informal. Focusing on rehabilitating minors, it operated under the philosophy of *parens patriae*, which means the state playing the role of parent. That principle gave Illinois's court the power to intervene in the lives of any juvenile under the age of sixteen who committed delinquent or criminal acts or was thought to be in need of state help. Since then, *parens patriae* has been the cornerstone of the juvenile justice system in the United States.

The special clinics that opened in conjunction with the first juvenile court system employed experts in psychology and sociology to treat and punish juveniles. During the nineteenth century, troubled minors who were taken from their homes were generally confined in so-called houses of refuge, which attempted to reeducate youths using indeterminate sentencing, education, skills training, physical labor, religious training, parental discipline, and apprenticeships. In reality, the houses of refuge resembled harsh military training camps, in which minors were ill-treated and overworked in overcrowded conditions.

New reformatories were developed after problems with houses of refuge became apparent. Reformatory facilities were systems of cottages that resembled traditional family homes. Most of the reformatories were located in rural areas, where physical labor was emphasized. Like the houses of refuge, the reformatories tried to teach minors skills they could use to become law-abiding and contributing adults. Foster parent arrangements were also made for some juveniles, and probation became popular for juveniles during the early twentieth century.

The Philosophy of *Parens Patriae*

The principle of *parens patriae* has had a profound impact on the development of juvenile justice in the United States. Under that philosophy, minors can be confined in houses of refuge or reformatories for being incorrigible and unruly, regardless of their parents' wishes. The constitutionality of the broad government power was challenged on numerous occasions. The first challenge came as early as in 1838, when the case of *Ex parte Crouse* reached the Supreme Court of Pennsylvania. In that case, a father challenged the constitutionality of *parens patriae* through a writ of *habeas corpus* after his daughter, Mary Ann, was sent to a house of refuge against his will. Although Mary Ann was described by her mother as wayward and disobedient, she had not actually committed a crime. Nevertheless, the courts upheld the state's decision, holding that confinement was in Mary Ann's best interests.

In 1870, an Illinois court limited *parens patriae* in *People v. Turner*. In that case, another minor was confined for a noncriminal action against the will of both of his parents. In that case, however, the court ruled that the son should be released to the care of his parents. The case was significant because it went against common practice of the day. However, it did not set a widely followed precedent and was largely ignored by other courts. *Parens patriae* was challenged again in 1905 in *Commonwealth v. Fisher*. In this case, a juvenile was sentenced to seven years confinement for a minor crime that would have received a much less severe sentence in an adult court. A court held that state intervention was necessary and in the best interests of the child. In essence, this opinion gave the courts even more discretion.

Beginning in 1966, the U.S. Supreme Court began limiting how *parens patriae* could be practiced. In *Kent v. United States* (1966) a sixteen-year-old boy was waived to an adult jurisdiction, without a hearing in juvenile court, to be tried on robbery and rape charges. As a result, the juvenile received a sentence that was harsher than he would have received if he had been tried in a juvenile jurisdiction. The case was appealed to the U.S. Supreme Court on grounds that his Sixth Amendment rights had been violated. The Court agreed, holding that the state was not acting in the boy's best interests.

In 1967, the Supreme Court handed down a landmark decision in another challenge to *parens patriae* in the case of *In re Gault*. That case originated in Arizona when fifteen-year-old Gerald Gault was taken into custody by police after allegedly making lewd phone calls and was confined in a detention facility for one week before he was granted a hearing before a juvenile court judge. Meanwhile, his parents were not even informed of the charges against him. There was no record of the hearing, and Gault's alleged victim did not make a court appearance. Nevertheless, Gault was sentenced to confinement in a reform school until he reached legal majority.

Lower courts in Arizona that heard the Gault case upheld the doctrine of *parens patriae*. On appeal, the case eventually reached the U.S. Supreme Court, whose ruling changed the way juveniles are treated in the juvenile justice system. The Court held that juveniles are entitled to due process and fair treatment and that notices of charges against them must be sent to their parents or guardians in a timely manner. The Court also held that juveniles are entitled to be represented by attorneys, and, finally, they must be interviewed in the presence of their parents or guardians. The *In re Gault* decision severely limited the power of *parens patriae* by giving juvenile offenders and their parents more rights.

The Juvenile Justice Process

The workings of the juvenile justice system differ from those of the adult justice system in processing of cases. When juveniles are detained or arrested, decisions are made whether to process their cases formally in the juvenile justice system or to divert them to less formal proceedings. Cases that are diverted may be handled by parents, school administrators, or others.

Diversion is a common practice in juvenile justice and in some instances is mandatory, particularly in cases involving status offenses. Decisions to divert cases are usually made by the arresting officers, but sometimes intake officers may be consulted. Intake officers typically work on behalf of state prosecutors. Both police and intake officers have the authority to talk to juvenile offenders' family members, examine their criminal records, and talk to their teachers and others before making diversion decisions.

Juveniles who are not diverted are formally charged in petitions, the juvenile justice version of arrest warrants. In addition to specifying charges, the petitions also serve as informing documents to the juveniles' parents and guardians. Finally, the petitions specify the court jurisdictions in which the cases are to be adjudicated.

The matter of what jurisdiction in which juveniles are tried is a controversial subject in the field of juvenile justice. Juveniles may be tried in juvenile court or waived to adult jurisdictions.

There are three mechanisms with which juvenile cases can be waived to adult jurisdictions. The one most commonly used is statutory exclusion. This type of waiver is used for certain serious offenses that are automatically excluded from juvenile jurisdiction. Such offenses include, most notably, murder. Most states have statutory exclusions.

The second mechanism used to waive juvenile cases to adult jurisdictions is the judicial waiver, which is simply the use of judicial discretion. Some states set lower age limits for this type of waiver. The third type of waiver is the concurrent jurisdiction, or prosecutorial, waiver. In some states, prosecutors have the authority to file cases in both juvenile and adult jurisdictions concurrently because of the nature of the offenses and ages of the offenders. However, the U.S. Supreme Court's ruling in *Breed v. Jones* (1975) ensured that juveniles cannot be tried in a juvenile court and then be waived and tried in an adult jurisdiction. This protection is the juvenile equivalent of the Fifth Amendment's double jeopardy protection.

After juveniles have been tried or adjudicated, their records are usually sealed and can be expunged when the offenders reach legal majority. The rationale behind this principle is that juveniles should be allowed to enter adulthood with clean records and not have juvenile criminal records that may impede their educational or employment opportunities. Expungement is not automatic, however, and is usually dependent upon the offenders demonstrating good behavior. Moreover, in some instances, juvenile records can be unsealed. Such a situation might arise in the case of a former juvenile offender who commits a violent crime as an adult, leading a prosecutor to suspect that his juvenile record may be relevant to his later acts.

Juvenile Dispositions

Disposition is the term given to juvenile sentencing. Dispositions for juveniles are based on

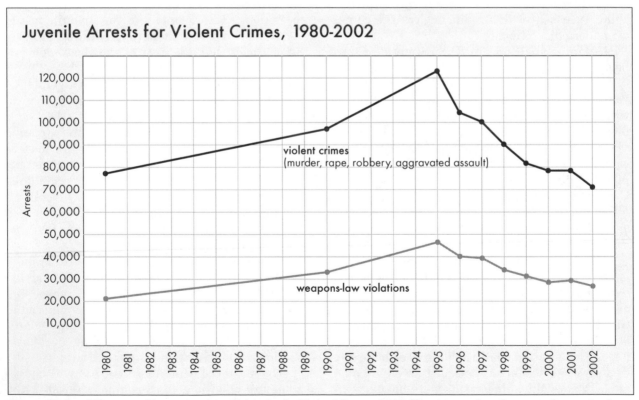

Juvenile Arrests for Violent Crimes, 1980-2002

violent crimes
(murder, rape, robbery, aggravated assault)

weapons-law violations

Arrests

Source: Federal Bureau of Investigation, *Crime in the United States*, 2003. Figures are for all reported arrests of persons under 18 years of age.

the principle of least detrimental alternative, that is, what is in the best interest of the juvenile. Dispositions should also be part of an overall treatment plan for the juveniles and are based largely on predispositional reports prepared by prosecutors or intake officers. Predispositional reports contain information about such matters as the juveniles' criminal records, family backgrounds, and their academic progress. Judges consult these reports to determine what are the best sentences for the juveniles.

In addition to traditional dispositions, such as confinement and probation, a number of alternative dispositions are available for juveniles. One type that began being used widely during the mid-1980's, but that is less used now, is juvenile boot camps. Boot camps, also known as shock incarceration, are viewed as intermediate forms of punishment. Stays are usually brief and seem to be most effective for juveniles who need more structure in their lives and are able to retain what they learn after their release. Modeled on military boot camps, juvenile justice boot camps are based on the notion that sending troubled juveniles into the military may straighten them out.

Another alternative form of disposition is wilderness programs. Like boot camps, these programs are comparatively brief in duration and are considered a form of shock incarceration. Current wilderness programs have evolved from such well-established programs as Outward Bound. Wilderness programs teach youths basic survival and dispute-resolution skills and promote self-esteem and confidence.

States that administer creative juvenile justice systems have additional alternative strategies that are implemented even before the dispositions stage. For example, during the late 1990's, Washington State began a special juvenile gun court. Although that court is technically part of the state's adult system, juveniles who are charged with certain first-time handgun-related offenses are processed through gun court and participate in the Handgun Intervention Program, which teaches them about gun safety. Numerous other states have used Washington's gun court as models for their own gun courts. Other states have drug courts for juveniles whose guidelines are similar to those of gun courts.

Washington is also known for other innovations in juvenile justice. In 1977, for example, the state passed the Juvenile Justice Reform Act, which required that all adjudicated juveniles between the ages of eight and seventeen spend at least some time in institutions. Many other states have adopted similar legislation. Experts have argued that the rationale behind such legislation was to scare juveniles straight.

Other examples of dispositions for juveniles include court-ordered school attendance, financial restitution, fines, community service, outpatient psychotherapy, drug and alcohol treatment, residential community programs, tattoo removal programs, foster home placement, sentencing circles, shaming, and restorative justice. Dispositions for juveniles may involve either indeterminate or determinate sentences. Indeterminate sentencing allows judges to order detention for indefinite periods, within certain parameters. When it is judged that the juveniles are rehabilitated, they may be released before serving the maximum periods of their indeterminate sentences.

Juvenile Appeals

Appeal is not a constitutionally guaranteed right for juveniles; however, most states provide for juvenile appeals by statute. Appeals may be made directly to appellate courts, asking them to review the facts of the cases. If successful, they result in complete retrials of the original cases. Collateral appeals use legal writs to challenge lower court decisions. Writs of *habeas corpus* are orders issued by courts to examine whether persons being held in custody are being lawfully detained. Writs of *certiorari* are orders from the U.S. Supreme Court requiring lower courts to forward the records of cases for review.

Monica L. P. Robbers

Further Reading

Champion, Dean John. *The Juvenile Justice System: Delinquency, Processing, and the Law.* 4th ed. Upper Saddle River, N.J.: Prentice-Hall, 2003. Broad overview of juvenile delinquency and the juvenile justice system response that considers juvenile legal rights and court decisions regarding adjudication, disposition, and sanctions.

Hess, Karen M., and Robert W. Drowns. *Juvenile Justice*. 4th ed. Belmont, Calif.: Wadsworth/Thomson Learning, 2004. Comprehensive overview of the juvenile justice system that connects theory and practice.

McCarthy, F. B., W. W. Patton, and J. G. Carr. *Juvenile Law and Its Processes: Cases and Materials*. 3d ed. Cincinnati: Anderson Publishing, 2003. Textbook providing both historical and contemporary overviews of juvenile justice, with attention to specific cases and statutes.

Siegel, L. J. *Juvenile Delinquency: The Core*. Belmont, Calif.: Wadsworth/Thomson Learning, 2001. Broad overview of topics in juvenile justice that discusses government policies, theories, landmark court decisions, and contemporary issues.

Tanenhaus, David S. *Juvenile Justice in the Making*. New York: Oxford University Press, 2004. Study of three thousand juvenile case files from Chicago during the early twentieth century to provide an updated historical perspective on the origins of juvenile courts. This book addresses the fundamental question of how juveniles should be treated under the law.

Watkins, John C., Jr. *The Juvenile Justice Century: A Sociolegal Commentary on American Juvenile Courts*. Durham, N.C.: Carolina Academic Press, 1998. Watkins examines historical and current changes to juvenile law that impact the operations of juvenile courts.

Whitehead, J. T., and S. P. Lab. *Juvenile Justice: An Introduction*. 4th ed. Cincinnati: Anderson Publishing, 2003. Introductory textbook examining the history of juvenile justice in the United States, from its nineteenth century roots to the early twenty-first century.

See also Boot camps; Criminal history record information; Criminal justice system; Diversion; *Gault, In re*; Juvenile courts; Juvenile delinquency; Juvenile Justice and Delinquency Prevention, Office of; Juvenile Justice and Delinquency Prevention Act; Juvenile waivers to adult courts; *Parens patriae*; Probation, juvenile; School violence; Status offenses; Uniform Juvenile Court Act; Youth authorities.

Juvenile waivers to adult courts

Definition: Formal processes of moving cases from juvenile to adult courts

Criminal justice issues: Courts; juvenile justice

Significance: Minors may be tried as adults in a number of ways, and the frequency with which this happens is on the increase.

At one time, the United States had no separate court system for juveniles, and all minors tried on criminal charges were tried as adults. However, within a few years of the establishment of the juvenile court system in 1899, virtually every U.S. state had a separate juvenile justice system. In contrast to the adult criminal justice systems, the systems for juveniles were meant to emphasize rehabilitation rather than punishment. Eventually, however, many people agreed that there were some cases in which it was desirable to try certain minors as adults, and so several systems evolved that allowed juvenile cases to be waived, or transferred, to adult courts.

A juvenile case can be waived through any of three major processes. The first of these is statutory waiver. For statutory exclusion, a state law specifies that for cases involving minors over a certain age who commit certain offenses, the case must be heard in adult court. In California, for example, juveniles over the age of fourteen who are accused of certain kinds of murders must be tried as adults. In 2004, about twenty-nine states had similar forms of statutory exclusion.

The second type of waiver is judicial waiver. Under this system, if a person over a certain age is accused of certain offenses, a hearing (often called a "fitness hearing") is held. The judge considers several factors to determine whether the minor is amenable to treatment by the juvenile justice system. These factors might include the minor's age and intelligence, as well the degree of complexity and sophistication of the offense committed by the minor. All but four states allowed judicial waivers in 2004.

The third type, prosecutorial waiver, is also known as direct file. In states that permit this form of waiver, prosecutors may choose to file the

Cell block of a new juvenile correctional facility that opened in Michigan in 1999. Only the most dangerous juvenile offenders are incarcerated in prison facilities, but because of the need to separate juvenile from adult offenders, they must be housed in separate facilities, such as this one. (AP/Wide World Photos)

cases of juveniles of specified ages who are accused of certain crimes in adult, rather than juvenile, courts. No hearings are required. The number of states allowing direct file is steadily increasing.

Modern Trends

In response to a publicly perceived upswing in juvenile violent crime during the early 1990's, many states began increasing the number of offenses for which juvenile cases could be waived to adult courts. They also lowered minimum ages for waivers and added additional types of waivers. As a result, increasing numbers of youths were being tried as adults. However, studies of juvenile justice have raised questions about the wisdom of this trend, as juveniles who are waived to adult courts have shown increased tendencies to become repeat offenders.

This trend also raises questions of racial justice. Cases of juveniles belonging to racial and ethnic minorities have been far more likely to be waived to adult courts than those of white juve-

niles—a trend that has been increasing disparities within the American justice system. Moreover, many critics believe that it is unethical to expose any youths to adult penalties and adult correctional facilities and to abandon rehabilitative attempts among young offenders.

Phyllis B. Gerstenfeld

Further Reading

Fagan, Jeffrey, and Frank E. Zimring, eds. *The Changing Borders of Juvenile Justice: Transfer of Adolescents to the Criminal Court*. Chicago: University of Chicago Press, 2000.

Williams, Frank P., III, and Marilyn D. McShane, eds. *Encyclopedia of Juvenile Justice*. Thousand Oaks, Calif.: Sage, 2002.

See also Blended sentences; Criminal history record information; *Gault, In re*; Juvenile courts; Juvenile delinquency; Juvenile Justice and Delinquency Prevention Act; Juvenile justice system; Probation, juvenile; Uniform Juvenile Court Act; Violent Crime Control and Law Enforcement Act.

K

Katz v. United States

The Case: U.S. Supreme Court ruling on electronic surveillance

Date: Decided on December 18, 1967

Criminal justice issues: Privacy; search and seizure; technology

Significance: This Supreme Court case established the principle that electronic surveillance constitutes a search subject to the Fourth Amendment's warrant and probable cause provisions.

Charles Katz was convicted of transmitting wagering information over the telephone on the basis of information he gave over a public telephone which he habitually used. The Federal Bureau of Investigation gained access to this information by attaching an external listening device to the telephone booth. The lower court concluded that since the booth had not been physically invaded, this investigative method did not constitute a "search" within the meaning of the Fourth Amendment, which requires an antecedent showing of probable cause and the issuance of a warrant. The Supreme Court, however, finding that the government had violated Katz's "legitimate expectation" of privacy, declared that the government's methods did indeed constitute a search and reversed the ruling.

Katz v. United States substituted a "reasonable expectation of privacy" test for the physical intrusion test the Court had previously used to determine if a police search and seizure was constitutional. This new test was cogently phrased in Justice John M. Harlan's concurring opinion: There "is a twofold requirement, first that a person have exhibited an actual (subjective) expectation of privacy and, second, that the expectation be one that society is prepared to recognize as 'reasonable.'" Harlan's opinion was used by lower courts to parse the meaning of *Katz*, but as he himself later recognized in *United States v. White* (1971), any evaluation of a questionable search must of necessity "transcend the search for subjective expectations." The government could, for example, defeat any expectation of privacy in telephone conversations by issuing a declaration that all such conversations are subject to third-party eavesdropping.

The reasonableness requirement may mean that an expectation of privacy in a particular realm must be shared by a majority of Americans. Yet it might also mean that although there are areas in which reasonable individuals might legitimately expect to maintain their privacy, such expectations can be superseded by more important policy considerations, such as the need for railroad engineers to give blood and urine specimens for purposes of drug testing (see *Skinner v. Railway Labor Executives Association*, 1989).

In *White*, Harlan defined searches as "those more extensive intrusions that significantly jeopardize the sense of security which is the paramount concern of Fourth Amendment liberties," but the Supreme Court has applied the *Katz* doctrine narrowly. In *United States v. Miller* (1976), for example, the Court ruled that persons do not have a reasonable expectation of privacy as to bank records of their financial transactions. In *Smith v. Maryland* (1979), the Court found that while individuals might reasonably expect the content of their telephone conversations to remain private, they cannot entertain a similar expectation as to the telephone numbers they call. In both cases, the Court based its decision on the fact that the information plaintiffs claimed to be off limits to police was already accessed by others—bank employees and telephone companies, respectively.

Lisa Paddock

Further Reading

Adams, James A., and Daniel D. Blinka. *Electronic Surveillance: Commentaries and Statutes*. Notre Dame, Ind.: National Institute for Trial Advocacy, 2003.

McGrath, J. E. *Loving Big Brother: Performance, Privacy and Surveillance Space*. New York: Routledge, 2004.

Stevens, Gina Marie, and Charles Doyle. *Privacy: Wiretapping and Electronic Eavesdropping.* Huntington, N.Y.: Nova Science, 2002.

See also Bill of Rights, U.S.; *Chimel v. California*; Electronic surveillance; Evidence, rules of; Fourth Amendment; Privacy rights; Search and seizure; Stakeouts; Supreme Court, U.S.; Wiretaps.

Kevorkian, Jack

Identification: Pioneer physician in the field of assisted suicide

Born: May 28, 1928; Pontiac, Michigan

Criminal justice issues: Civil rights and liberties; homicide; medical and health issues

Significance: Kevorkian's persistent efforts to assist terminally ill patients to commit suicide kept him in constant legal trouble and drew national attention to right-to-die questions.

Jack Kevorkian studied medicine at the University of Michigan medical school, where he graduated in 1952 with a specialty in pathology. By the 1970's, he was working as a pathologist in Michigan and California. During the late 1980's, he began advertising as a death counselor and built a suicide machine, which he called the Mercitron. In 1990, Janet Adkins, a women suffering from Alzheimer's disease, became the first person to use the machine to kill herself. Kevorkian eventually claimed that he assisted in more than one hundred suicides and earned the nickname "Dr. Death" from his critics.

In 1998, Kevorkian sent a videotape of an assisted suicide to *60 Minutes*, a widely viewed television news program. The tape showed Kevorkian administering a lethal injection to Thomas Youk, a man in his fifties who suffered from Lou

Dr. Jack Kevorkian demonstrating his "suicide machine." *(AP/Wide World Photos)*

No Regrets

In a telephone interview with a Pontiac, Michigan, reporter in April, 2004, Dr. Jack Kevorkian said, "There is no doubt that I expect to die in prison." Although he reaffirmed a promise that he had made earlier in affidavits, that he would assist in no more suicides if he were to be released, he expressed no regrets for what he had done or what had happened to him, saying, "I knew what I was doing."

In response to a letter-writing campaign to secure Kevorkian's early release, prosecutor David Gorcyca, who had led Oakland County's successful prosecution of Kevorkian in 1999, said that Kevorkian should be treated no differently than any other convicted prisoner. "He flouted the law and baited, no, begged me, on national TV to prosecute him. . . . Now he has to suffer the penalty."

Source: Detroit Free Press, April 11, 2004.

Gehrig's disease. Three days later, Kevorkian was charged with the murder of Youk. He represented himself in a Michigan court and was convicted in April, 1999, of second-degree murder. He received a ten- to twenty-five-year prison sentence and was incarcerated at the Thumb Correctional Facility in Lapeer, Michigan. A federal appeals court later rejected his appeal for a new trial, despite Kevorkian's signing an affidavit promising that if he were released, he would not assist in more suicides.

Much of the controversy surrounding Kevorkian was focused on the suicides of patients who were not terminally ill but who nevertheless requested his services. Through the years that he assisted patients with their suicides, numerous disability rights advocates campaigned to stop him and opposed all efforts to legalize assisted suicide and mercy killings. These advocates argued that so-called mercy killings target people with disabilities, the elderly, and members of groups considered to place burdens on society.

Alison S. Burke

Further Reading

Betzold, Michael. *Appointment with Doctor Death*. Troy, Mich.: Momentum Books, 1993.

Brovins, Joan M., and Thomas Oehmke. *Dr. Death: Dr. Jack Kevorkian's RX—Death*. Hollywood, Fla.: Lifetime Books, 1993.

Loving, Carol. *My Son, My Sorrow: The Tragic Tale of Dr. Kevorkian's Youngest Patient*. Far Hills, N.J.: New Horizon Press, 1998.

See also Murder and homicide; Suicide and euthanasia.

Kidnapping

Definition: Abduction of persons by force, threats of force, or trickery, with the intent of holding them against their will for indefinite periods

Criminal justice issues: Domestic violence; federal law; juvenile justice; kidnapping

Significance: Kidnapping is an age-old crime and one that now commands wide public attention. However, the full extent of kidnapping in the United States is not clearly understood, partly because of confusion over definitions of the crime and seriously discrepant incidence statistics that have been disseminated.

Although kidnapping knows no age boundaries, those most vulnerable to becoming victims are children. In 1932, a sensational kidnapping case captured national attention when the twenty-month-old son of the famed aviator Charles A. Lindbergh was abducted from his home. Although the family paid a ransom of fifty thousand dollars and cooperated with their son's unknown kidnappers, the baby was eventually found in a shallow grave near his home. He had apparently been murdered and buried the same night he was abducted. More than three years later, a German immigrant named Bruno Hauptmann was arrested for the crime; he was convicted and sentenced to death.

Questions surrounding Hauptmann's possible innocence and Lindbergh's possible involvement in his own son's death remain ongoing sources of controversy and debate in the twenty-first century. More important, however, was the fact that the Lindbergh case provided the impetus for the

Congress making kidnapping a federal crime in 1934 with its passage of what became known as the Lindbergh law. That federal statute authorized severe punishments for all convicted kidnappers who transport their victims across state or national borders.

National interest in kidnapping waned after the 1930's but the crime regained notoriety during the early 1980's. New interest in the crime was aroused by another sensational case. In 1981, the beheaded body of a kidnapped six-year-old boy named Adam Walsh was found in Florida, and several kidnapped children were murdered in Atlanta, Georgia.

Kidnapping offenses pose unique challenges for the criminal justice system. One of these challenges is a general lack of awareness and understanding about the true magnitude and nature of the problem. Public debate on the subject has been confused by public hysteria, inaccurate statistics, and misinformation about the characteristics of primary offenders and the types of children who are most at risk.

The Nature of Kidnapping Crimes

Multiple disparities in definitions of kidnapping have clouded the reliability and validity of the statistics associated with the crime. The public has adopted a stereotypical definition of kidnapping based on individual perceptions and media portrayals. In the public mind, kidnapping is a heinous crime that includes lengthy or permanent removals of children from homes for reasons such as ransom, sexual assault, and murder. However, those types of crime do not occur nearly as frequently as they are portrayed in the media.

Another definition of kidnapping is the legal definition as defined by the Federal Bureau of Investigation (FBI). The National Crime Information Center (NCIC) has three categories under which the FBI files missing persons cases: juvenile, endangered, and involuntary. The vast majority of missing children fall under the juvenile category, which covers situations in which there is no evidence of foul play. The endangered category covers children who are missing and in the company of other persons in circumstances that suggest their physical safety is in danger. In 2001, the number of kidnappings rated in the endangered category increased by nearly 6 percent, whereas, those in the involuntary category dropped 1 percent. The involuntary category covers situations in which children are missing under circumstances that suggest their disappearances are not voluntary.

In an effort to clear up confusion over the term "kidnapping," the U.S. Department of Justice issued its first National Incidence Study of Missing, Abducted, Runaway, and Thrownaway Children in 1990. This study describes three basic types of abduction: nonfamily abduction, stereotypical abduction, and family abduction. The researchers defined nonfamily abductions to include abductions by friends, acquaintances, and strangers. Most children taken under this form of abduction are missing for only about one hour.

Stereotypical kidnapping is nonfamily abduction committed by acquaintances or strangers, who keep the abducted children overnight and take them a minimum of fifty miles away from their homes. Most such abductors kidnap children with the intent of permanently removing or killing them.

Family abduction generally occurs when relatives of the abducted children, or persons acting on their behalf, remove the children for the purpose of concealing them or taking them out of state. Such cases usually involve violations of parental custody orders with the intent of depriving the children's legal caretakers of their custodial rights, either permanently or for extended periods of time.

Prevalence

Confusion over the prevalence of child kidnapping has been exacerbated by the publicizing of unsubstantiated statistics to legitimize child abduction as a serious problem. When the missing children's movement first began to attract public attention during the mid-1980's, figures as high as 50,000 abductions per year in the United States were initially reported. Professional researchers, however, countered that such statistics were greatly overstated and that more accurate figures were between 70 and 600 abductions per year. Exaggeration of kidnapping statistics reflects the need of some to establish child abduction as a major social problem. Nevertheless, since Congress's passing of the Missing Children's Act of 1982, the numbers of missing persons reported to police have tended to rise annually.

The National Incidence Study of Missing, Abducted, Runaway, and Thrownaway Children, or NISMART, which was initiated by the Department of Justice, marked a preliminary effort to accurately measure the scope of child abduction. NISMART blended several sources of data, such as telephone surveys, analyses of law-enforcement records, and homicide data to generate more accurate figures of both actual and attempted abductions throughout the country. The 1990 report indicated that more than 800,000 children were reported missing annually—a figure that equates to more than 2,000 missing person reports daily. Of those, more than 58,000 children were abducted by nonfamily members. Serious long-term stranger abductions accounted for more than 100 children, of whom 40 percent were killed. The staggering figure that emerged from the NISMART findings was that, while activists estimated the number of family abductions was relatively low in comparison to nonfamily abductions, the study found that more than 200,000 children were victims of family abductions.

Characteristics and Correlates of Kidnapping

Correlates of child kidnapping are complex to identify. Apparent discrepancies in statistical data that have been collected may stem from subjective interpretations of what constitutes family abduction on the part of parents participating in

Amber Alert message posted on electronic signs on a New Jersey turnpike in March, 2003. The sign advises passing motorists to be on the lookout for a gray Daewoo automobile with the New Jersey license plate "NHD 73F." The suspect in this case was a father who abducted his two-year-old daughter. *(AP/Wide World Photos)*

the survey. What some parents may consider to be abduction, others may consider to be exercises of their right to be with their own children. Many questions about the findings of NISMART studies confound their meaning. Such questions include the extent of underreporting of family abduction by police and the breadth of the definition of kidnapping used in the studies.

No reliable national data are available to provide a basis of measuring the true extent of child abduction. However, several studies have attempted to identify victim and perpetrator paradigms. These studies have found that most child abductors are male strangers between the ages of twenty and twenty-nine, and that they generally abduct victims from the latters' homes.

Grassroots Action and Publicity

The 1980's saw the creation of numerous organizations dedicated to raising public awareness of child abduction and lobbying for legislative action. Some of these were founded by the parents of abducted children. For example, in 1984, John Walsh founded the National Center for Missing and Exploited Children (NCMEC), which offers services to families of kidnapped, sexually exploited, and endangered children. The organization also helps coordinate efforts of local law-enforcement personnel, all facets of the criminal justice system, as well as members of public and private sectors to safeguard children. The NCMEC and other child advocacy organizations, such as the Polly Klaas Foundation, have been instrumental in obtaining stronger child protection laws and publicizing incidences of missing and endangered children.

One of the earliest efforts of the NCMEC was the implementation of missing-children clearinghouses in every state. In the twenty-first century, the organization expanded its work to address the problem of preventing international abductions. Additionally, in 1990, Congress passed the National Child Search Assistance Act, which mandated an immediate police report and NCIC entries for every case. After the act was passed, the numbers of missing persons reported annually increased more than 32 percent.

The highly publicized personal tragedies of families who had lost children to abduction generated widespread fears among American families concerned about protecting their own children. Local television stations began broadcasting photographs of missing children, dairies printed photos of missing children on milk cartons, utility companies included pictures of missing children in their monthly billings, and child-fingerprinting campaigns began in shopping malls. American society became convinced that there was a kidnapping epidemic.

Amber Alerts

In the fall of 2001, the NCMEC launched the national Amber Plan to assist cities and towns across the country with creating local plans for issuing missing-child alerts. The name has dual significance. "Amber" is an acronym for "America's Missing: Broadcast Emergency Response." The NCMEC created the first Amber Plan in 1996 in response to the kidnapping and brutal murder of nine-year-old Amber Hagerman in Arlington, Texas.

Amber Hagerman's body was found only four days after her abduction. A neighbor who saw her abduction provided details of the kidnapping but no system was in place to disseminate that information quickly. Afterward, outraged members of Amber's community proposed that the broadcasting media issue emergency alerts to the public immediately after children are kidnapped, providing all available details to enable members of the public to assist in apprehending offenders. The first Amber Plan was then instituted in the state of Texas. The plans are voluntary partnerships among law-enforcement agencies and broadcasters to transmit emergency signals via radio and television broadcasts, electric highway signs, electronic mail, and lottery terminals to notify the public quickly when children are abducted.

The U.S. Department of Justice has estimated that 74 percent of children who are kidnapped and found murdered are killed within the first three hours of their abductions. That astonishing statistic points up the importance of disseminating information on abductions as quickly as possible. However, Amber Alerts are not automatically activated when children are reported missing. Four criteria must first be met. The missing children must be under the age of seventeen and in danger of serious bodily harm, and law enforcement must suspect that the children have actually been kidnapped. Finally, there must be enough information on the children's disappearance to make it possible for members of the public to aid in their recovery.

Prosecution and Punishment

Because kidnapping is not listed among the index offenses on the FBI's Uniform Crime Reports (UCR), it is difficult to obtain accurate data on rates of prosecution and punishment. Acts of kidnapping are often associated with other criminal offenses such as sexual assault and homicide. UCRs list only the most serious offenses committed in crimes involving multiple offenses. Under common law, the crime of kidnapping was considered a misdemeanor. Now, there is agreement among the states that it should be considered a felony. However, the states disagree on what type of felony it should be called. Most states list kidnapping as a first-degree felony that is punishable by life imprisonment. The circumstances surrounding specific offenses determine the degree of the felony and length of punishment imposed.

Lisa Landis Murphy

Further Reading

Fass, Paula S. *Kidnapped: Child Abduction in America.* Cambridge, Mass.: Harvard University Press, 1999. Comprehensive history of kidnapping in the United States, with particular attention to the role of the media in kidnapping cases over the last century.

Finkelhor, D., G. Hotaling, and A. Sedlak. *Missing, Abducted, Runaway, and Thrownaway Children in America: First Report, Numbers, and Characteristics, National Incidence Studies.* Washington, D.C.: U.S. Department of Justice, Office of Justice Program, Office of Juvenile Justice and Delinquency Prevention, 1990. First NISMART report.

Gardner, Lloyd C. *The Case That Never Dies: The Lindbergh Kidnapping.* New Brunswick, N.J.: Rutgers University Press, 2004. One of the most thorough and up-to-date studies of the famous Lindbergh baby kidnapping case of the early 1930's. Pays particular attention to Bruno Hauptmann's trial.

Haberman, Maggie, and Jeane MacIntosh. *Held Captive: The Kidnapping and Rescue of Eliza-*

beth Smart. New York: Avon, 2003. Journalistic depiction of a highly publicized kidnapping investigation in 2002-2003.

Newton, Michael. *The Encyclopedia of Kidnappings.* New York: Facts On File, 2002. Comprehensive guide to more than eight hundred kidnapping cases, ranging from ancient times to the early twenty-first century.

Roensch, Greg. *The Lindbergh Baby Kidnapping Trial: A Primary Source Account.* New York: Rosen Publishing Group, 2003. Another up-to-date and detailed examination of what has been dubbed the "crime of the century."

Smart, Ed, L. Smart, and L. Morton. *Bringing Elizabeth Home: A Journey of Faith and Hope.* New York: Doubleday, 2003. One family's personal account surrounding the abduction, captivity, search for, and safe return of their daughter, Elizabeth Smart.

See also *Brady v. United States*; Carjacking; Child abduction by parents; Child abuse and molestation; Lindbergh law; Missing persons.

King beating case

The Event: Arrest and beating of Rodney King and subsequent criminal trial of the arresting officers

Date: March 3, 1991-June 1, 1994

Place: Los Angeles and Simi Valley, California

Criminal justice issues: Arrest and arraignment; government misconduct; police powers

Significance: The trial of four white policemen following the arrest and beating of Rodney King, a black man, sparked a major investigation of police brutality in Los Angeles and violent race riots after a California court acquitted the police.

Following a high-speed chase along a Los Angeles highway that ended just after midnight on March 3, 1991, California Highway Patrol officers Timothy and Melanie Singer stopped driver Rodney Glen King and his two passengers, Bryant Allen and Freddie Helms, for questioning. More than twenty Los Angeles Police Department (LAPD) officers soon arrived on the scene in

Los Angeles's Lake View Terrace neighborhood. Police sergeant Stacey Koon, assisted by officers Theodore Briseno, Laurence Powell, and Timothy Wind, took over the investigation. The police quickly subdued and handcuffed Allen and Helms without incident. Their encounter with King, however, caused a controversy with far-reaching legal and social consequences.

King's Arrest

According to the four white police officers who arrested Rodney King, a black man, King refused at first to leave the car and then resisted arrest with such vigor that the officers had to apply two jolts from a Taser electric stun gun, fifty-six blows from aluminum batons, and six kicks (primarily from Briseno) to subdue King before they successfully handcuffed and cordcuffed him to restrain his arms and legs. The event probably would have gone unnoticed had not George Holliday, an amateur cameraman who witnessed the incident, videotaped the arrest and sold the tape to a local television station news program. The videotape became the crucial piece of evidence that the state of California used to charge the four LAPD arresting officers with criminal assault and that a federal grand jury subsequently used to charge the officers with civil rights violations.

Broadcast of Holliday's tape on national news programs elicited several responses from the LAPD. On March 6, 1991, the LAPD released King from custody and admitted that officers failed to prove that King had resisted arrest. On March 7, Los Angeles police chief Daryl Gates announced that he would investigate King's arrest and, if the investigation warranted it, would pursue criminal assault charges against the arresting officers. On March 14, a Los Angeles County grand jury indicted Sergeant Koon and officers Briseno, Powell, and Wind for criminal assault, and they subsequently pleaded not guilty.

Investigation of Police Brutality

Overwhelming public sympathy for King following the national broadcast of Holliday's videotape prompted Los Angeles mayor Tom Bradley to investigate charges that instances of police brutality motivated by racism were commonplace during LAPD arrest operations. On April 1,

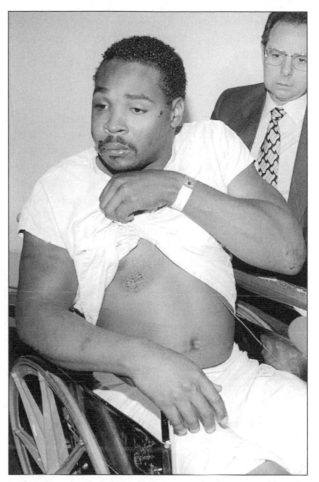

Rodney King showing reporters the injuries that he received from his beating. *(AP/Wide World Photos)*

1991, Mayor Bradley appointed a nonpartisan commission, headed by Warren Christopher (who had formerly served as President Jimmy Carter's deputy secretary of state), to study the LAPD's past record of complaints regarding police misconduct. On April 2, Bradley called on Police Chief Gates, who had served on the LAPD since 1949 and had been police chief since 1978, to resign. In May, the LAPD suspended Sergeant Koon and officers Briseno and Powell without pay and dismissed officer Timothy Wind, a rookie without tenure, pending the outcome of their criminal trial. King then filed a civil rights lawsuit against the city of Los Angeles.

Several significant developments occurred as the officers awaited trial. On July 9, 1991, the Christopher Commission released the results of its investigation and its recommendations to the five-member Los Angeles Police Commission. The Police Commission employed the police chief and was responsible for the management of the LAPD. The Christopher Commission found that the LAPD, composed of 67.8 percent white officers in 1991, suffered from a "siege mentality" in a city where 63 percent of the population were people of color. The commission also found that a small but significant proportion of officers repeatedly used excessive force when making arrests and that the LAPD did not punish those officers when citizens filed complaints. Finally, the commission recommended measures to exert more control over the LAPD's operations, including limiting the police chief's tenure to a five-year term, renewable by the Police Commission for one additional term only. After the release of the Christopher Commission report, Police Chief Gates announced his retirement, effective in April, 1992 (which he later amended to July, 1992). On July 23, 1991, a California court of appeal granted the police defendants' request for a change of venue for the upcoming criminal trial.

The State of California Court Trial

The trial of the four officers began on March 4, 1992, in the new venue—the primarily white community of Simi Valley in Ventura County. The jury who heard the state of California's case against the four officers consisted of ten whites, one Latino, and one Asian. The officers' defense lawyers presented Holliday's videotape broken down into a series of individual still pictures. They asked the jury to judge whether excessive force—that is, force that was not warranted by King's "aggressive" actions—was employed at any single moment during the arrest. Referring often to the "thin blue line" that protected society from the "likes of Rodney King," the defense built a case that justified the police officers' actions. King's lawyer, Steven Lerman, a personal injury specialist, advised King not to testify at the trial out of concern that King's "confused and frightened" state of mind since the beating might impair his memory of events and discredit his testimony. The Simi Valley jury acquitted the four officers of all charges of criminal assault, with the exception of one count against officer Laurence Powell on which the jury was deadlocked.

The acquittal of the four police officers on April 29, 1992, ignited widespread and destructive riots led by poor and angry black Angelenos. The riots affected areas throughout Los Angeles but particularly devastated parts of impoverished South Central Los Angeles. Fifty-three people died during the riots, which raged until May 2, and more than one billion dollars' worth of property was damaged. There had long been friction between Los Angeles's neighboring Korean and black communities, and the Korean American community bore the brunt of the rioters' destructive attacks.

The Federal Court Civil Rights Trial

On August 5, 1992, a federal grand jury indicted the four officers for violating King's civil rights. The grand jury charged Sergeant Koon with violating the Fourteenth Amendment, which obligated Koon, as the officer in charge of the arrest, to protect King while he was in police custody. Officers Briseno, Powell, and Wind were charged with violating the Fourth Amendment in using more force than necessary, and using that excessive force willfully, when they arrested King. King testified during the federal trial. On April 17, 1993, a jury of nine whites, two African Americans, and one Latino found Koon and Powell guilty and Briseno and Wind not guilty. On August 4, 1993, Koon and Powell were sentenced to two-and-one-half-year prison terms. In May, 1994, a Los Angeles jury awarded King $3.8 million in compensatory damages in his civil rights lawsuit against the city, but on June 1, 1994, the jury denied King's request for additional punitive damages.

Karen Garner

Further Reading

Gooding-Williams, Robert, ed. *Reading Rodney King/Reading Urban Uprising*. New York: Routledge, 1993. Collection of essays that place the King incident in the broader context of race relations in late twentieth century America.

Khalifah, H. Khalif, ed. *Rodney King and the L.A. Rebellion: Analysis and Commentary by Thirteen Best-Selling Black Writers*. Hampton, Va.: U.B. & U.S. Communications Systems, 1992. Collection of African American perspectives that tend to be sympathetic to King.

Koon, Stacey, with Robert Deitz. *Presumed Guilty: The Tragedy of the Rodney King Affair*. Washington, D.C.: Regnery Gateway, 1992. Firsthand account by one of the police officers involved in King's beating.

Owens, Tom, with Rod Browning. *Lying Eyes: The Truth Behind the Corruption and Brutality of the LAPD and the Beating of Rodney King*. New York: Thunder's Mouth Press, 1994. Severely critical analysis of the Los Angeles police department focusing on the King incident.

Roth, Mitchel P. *Historical Dictionary of Law Enforcement*. Westport, Conn.: Greenwood Press, 2000. Viewing policing from an international perspective, this volume covers the history of law enforcement from early accounts of policing under Caesar Augustus to such present-day events as Rodney King and the LAPD.

Thrasher, Ronald. "Internal Affairs: The Police Agencies' Approach to the Investigation of Police Misconduct." In *Police Misconduct*, edited by Michael J. Palmiotto. Upper Saddle River, N.J.: Prentice Hall, 2001. Chapter in a college-level reader that covers many aspects of police misconduct, including brutality and corruption.

See also Change of venue; Civilian review boards; Double jeopardy; Due process of law; Internal affairs; Police brutality; Police ethics; Race riots in the twentieth century; Reasonable force.

Knapp Commission

Identification: Body established to investigate allegations of widespread corruption among New York City police

Date: Established in 1970; issued report in 1972

Criminal justice issues: Government misconduct; police powers

Significance: This commission investigated and substantiated unprecedented levels of

> ## *Serpico* and the Knapp Commission
>
> The Knapp Commission won additional fame in the 1973 feature film *Serpico* in which Al Pacino played Frank Serpico, a real-life New York City policeman who turned whistle-blower. During the Knapp Commission investigation, the real Serpico received death threats for "ratting-out" his fellow officers. While working as an undercover drug agent, Serpico was shot in the face. Afterward, he alleged that his fellow officers refused to call an ambulance for him because they viewed him as a traitor. Serpico survived the shooting and shortly afterward quit the police department, but not before testifying against corrupt police officers.

police corruption, resulting in the dismissal and prosecution of police officers and a massive restructuring of New York City's police department.

Named after its appointed leader, Whittman Knapp, the Knapp Commission was charged with the responsibility of investigating allegations of extreme police corruption among officers within the New York City Police Department (NYPD). The commission was impaneled in 1970 by Mayor John Lindsay after he learned that *The New York Times* was preparing to publish a major exposé of rampant police misconduct in the city's police department. The newspaper's primary informants were NYPD officers Sergeant David Durk and Detective Frank Serpico, both of whom agreed to talk to the newspaper after their police supervisors and the mayor's office ignored their concerns about corruption in the department.

The commission held public hearings to investigate the behavior of police officers alleged to be "dirty cops"; it also examined the organizational structure of the police department. The hearings were contentious, with police officers testifying against fellow officers about their involvement in bribery, prostitution, drug rings, and illegal gambling.

The commission eventually found that there was, indeed, widespread corruption within the police department. In its report, it classified corrupt officers as "meat-eaters" and "grass-eaters." The former were officers who aggressively sought out bribes or other corrupt activity; the latter were officers who accepted bribes or partook in unethical behavior when opportunities were presented to them.

The commission's findings led to a massive restructuring of the police department, dismissals of many officers and supervisors, and criminal prosecutions of dirty cops. In response to controversies surrounding the commission, the mayor abolished it in 1972. A year later, the problem of corruption in the NYPD received new national attention with the release of the film *Serpico*, which was based on Peter Maas's book about the Knapp Commission's star witness.

Rachel Bandy

Further Reading

City of New York. *The Knapp Commission Report on Police Corruption.* New York: George Braziller, 1972.

Delattre, Edwin J. *Character and Cops: Ethics in Policing.* 4th ed. Washington, D.C.: American Enterprise Institute Press, 2002.

Sherman, Lawrence W., ed. *Police Corruption: A Sociological Perspective.* Garden City, N.Y.: Anchor Books, 1974.

See also Civilian review boards; Internal affairs; Law enforcement; Police; Police corruption; Police ethics; Police powers.

Chief Justice William H. Rehnquist. *(Supreme Court Historical Society)*

Knowles v. Iowa

The Case: U.S. Supreme Court ruling on vehicle searches

Date: Decided on December 8, 1998

Criminal justice issues: Police powers; search and seizure

Significance: This decision limited the authority of police to search cars while conducting routine traffic stops. Police could no longer search cars after traffic stops without either consent or probable cause.

Starting with its decision in *Carroll v. United States* (1925), the U.S. Supreme Court recognized that police can stop and search vehicles without the benefit of a warrant. The mobility of automobiles would allow for the destruction of evidence before the police could obtain a lawful warrant. Police do not, however, have a free hand in searching cars, as seen in *Knowles v. Iowa.*

A man named Knowles was pulled over for speeding by an Iowa state policeman. The officer wrote Knowles a citation for speeding, then conducted a search of Knowles's car without his consent. The officer did not have probable cause for conducting the search and had not arrested Knowles. The search turned up drug paraphernalia, and Knowles was arrested and convicted on drug charges in Iowa state court. Knowles appealed, claiming the search of his car violated the Fourth Amendment's ban on unreasonable search and seizure. Knowles's appeals were denied by Iowa appellate courts, and he appealed the case to the U.S. Supreme Court.

The Supreme Court overturned the conviction. In writing the opinion for a unanimous court, Chief Justice William Rehnquist noted that police could search automobiles either with the consent of the owner during a lawful arrest or to protect evidence of a crime. Rehnquist stated that the officer had only conducted a routine traffic stop and had not suspicion nor probable cause to believe Knowles was engaged in illegal activity.

Without such cause, the officer had no reason to search the car.

According to Rehnquist, after writing the traffic citation for speeding, the officer was required to allow Knowles to continue on his way without a search. Conducting a routine traffic stop did not provide the officer with the basis for a full search of the automobile. Because the search was illegal under the Fourth Amendment, the drug evidence was to be excluded from any trial of Knowles.

The Knowles decision cut back on the authority of police to search cars on public highways. The Rehnquist court, which usually ruled for police in such cases, instead noted that the Fourth Amendment did prohibit searches that were not linked to an arrest or some probable cause. The ruling created a clearer definition of the circumstances under which police could use traffic stops as a reason for conducting full-blown searches of automobiles and people.

Douglas Clouatre

Further Reading

Franklin, Paula. *The Fourth Amendment*. New York: Silver Burdett Press, 2001. Study of the limitations placed on police powers by the Fourth Amendment.

Wetterer, Charles M. *The Fourth Amendment: Search and Seizure*. Springfield, N.J.: Enslow, 1998. Discusses the various aspects of search and seizure law and how the courts have interpreted the amendment.

See also Automobile searches; Consent searches; Exclusionary rule; Fourth Amendment; *Mapp v. Ohio*; Search and seizure; Supreme Court, U.S.; *Whren v. United States*.

Ku Klux Klan

Identification: White supremacist organization

Date: Founded in 1866

Place: The South

Criminal justice issues: Civil rights and liberties; hate crime; terrorism

Significance: Ku Klux Klan terrorism was instrumental in preventing African Americans in the South from gaining their civil rights after the Civil War; in a later incarnation, the Klan terrorized and propagandized against African Americans, Roman Catholics, Jews, and Asian Americans.

The original Ku Klux Klan was organized in the South after the Civil War in order to "keep the Negro in his place"—in the fields and subordinated to whites. It was founded in 1866 by former Confederate general Nathan Bedford Forrest, and it disbanded in 1871-1872. It has been estimated that the Klan murdered four hundred African Americans between 1866 and 1872; none of the people responsible was given more serious punishment than fines.

In 1915 William Joseph Simmons chartered the second version of the Klan, "The Invisible Empire, Knights of the Ku Klux Klan, Inc.," in Atlanta, Georgia. The new Klan was a tightly integrated secret fraternal organization dedicated to the "American" ideals of racial purity and traditional morality. Heavy initial recruitment coincided with the Atlanta filming of D. W. Griffith's *The Birth of a Nation* (1915), which glorified the Ku Klux Klan of post-Civil War Reconstruction.

After World War I, African Americans returned home proud of their distinguished service and filled with high expectations. Their hopes for full citizens' rights and status were similar to the dreams of the newly freed slaves which had called forth the original Klan. The Klan depicted African Americans as seeking to "intermingle" the races.

The 1920's was the peak of the Klan's popularity. New immigrants (notably Italian, Irish, and Polish Catholics; Russian and Slavic Jews; and Asians) were altering the white Anglo-Saxon Protestant profile of the American population. The Klan's hate literature depicted Roman Catholics and Jews as racial and religious threats to traditional American values. Asians were easy to stereotype and denigrate; like African Americans, they simply looked different. Klan propaganda against these groups attracted millions of members. Membership was strong across the southern United States from Florida to Texas and in the Midwest, especially in Indiana. Members came from all strata of white male society. In fact, the Klan's program reflected the feelings of many Americans in the 1920's. In 1924 the Klan helped elect eleven governors and sixteen congressmen, and in 1928 it helped defeat presidential candidate Al Smith.

Violence was perpetrated by only a minority of the group's members. In 1921, the exposure of Klan violence by *The New York World* and the ensuing congressional investigation of the Klan actually caused membership to burgeon. Under Hiram Wesley Evans, who replaced Simmons by a coup in 1922, the Klan renounced violence and worked more in the open arena of political lobbying and propaganda. In 1925, however, the murder conviction of David C. Stephenson, Grand Dragon of the Indiana Klan, and numerous other Klan outrages that made headlines diminished the Klan's popularity and effectiveness. Most Americans became disgusted with the Klan as an extremist group whose claims to protect American values proved false when it trampled on individual freedom and rights. In 1939, Evans sold the Klan to James A. Colescott, who dissolved the organization in 1944 rather than pay its back taxes.

The modern Ku Klux Klan began in the 1940's, its primary purpose being to oppose any civil rights gains by African Americans. Although it was organized nationally in 1956, it has typically been highly fragmented. The main result of its activities and headlines was to add impetus to the Civil Rights movement in the 1950's and 1960's, as people all over the country were outraged by the Klan's violent tactics. In 1991, Louisiana gubernatorial candidate David Duke was controversial because he had formerly been a Grand Wizard in the Klan; he was defeated.

Daniel C. Scavone

Further Reading

Chalmers, David Mark. *Hooded Americanism: The History of the Ku Klux Klan*. New York: F. Watts, 1981. Standard history of the Klan that has seen numerous editions and updates.

Randel, William. *The Ku Klux Klan: A Century of Infamy*. Philadelphia: Chilton Books, 1965. Excellent history of origins and events that also uses a moral perspective.

Stanton, Bill. *Klanwatch: Bringing the Ku Klux Klan to Justice*. New York: Weidenfeld, 1991. The former Klanwatch director explains new initiatives to disable the Klan, most of which have been effective.

Wade, Wyn Craig. *The Fiery Cross: The Ku Klux Klan in America*. New York: Simon & Schuster, 1987. Wade recounts the Klan's history and episodes of violence, revealing its legacy of race hatred.

See also COINTELPRO; *Ford v. Wainwright*; Hate crime; Jim Crow laws; Lynching; Slave patrols; Terrorism; Vigilantism; *Virginia v. Black*.

Kyllo v. United States

The Case: U.S. Supreme Court ruling on warrantless searches

Date: Decided on June 11, 2001

Criminal justice issues: Search and seizure; substance abuse

Significance: This case established that government use of technology not commonly employed by the public to sense images, sounds, or smells coming from homes is a form of search and thus requires a warrant.

In 1991, Agent William Elliott of the U.S. Department of the Interior suspected that Danny Kyllo was growing marijuana in his Florence, Oregon, residence. Initially, Elliott believed that Kyllo resided with his estranged wife, Luanna, who had recently been arrested on drug charges. Additionally, known drug dealers occupied two of the units in the triplex in which Kyllo resided. Further, Kyllo allegedly advised a police informant that both he and his wife could supply marijuana. Elliott also reviewed Kyllo's electrical utility records and found that his home's power usage was unusually high.

Based on this information, Elliott and Dan Haas, a member of the Oregon National Guard, used an Agema Thermovision 210 thermal imager to scan the triplex in which Kyllo lived on January 16, 1992. The device was used to determine whether the amount of heat emanating from Kyllo's home was consistent with the amount of power used by the types of high-intensity lamps often associated with indoor marijuana growing. Within minutes, the scan revealed that the garage roof and one wall were noticeably hotter than the rest of Kyllo's home and the other parts of his triplex.

Producing the results of the scan, the information provided by the informant, and Kyllo's subpoenaed utility bills, Elliott obtained a warrant from a federal magistrate judge to search Kyllo's home. The search found weapons, illegal drug paraphernalia, and more than one hundred marijuana plants.

After he was indicted on a federal drug charge, Kyllo unsuccessfully moved to suppress the evidence seized from his home. He conditionally pleaded guilty to the charge of producing marijuana and was subsequently sentenced to five and one-half years in prison. The district court considering Kyllo's appeal decided that the warrantless thermal imaging scan of Kyllo's home was permissible under the Fourth Amendment. The court reasoned that the thermal imager did not reveal any intimate details of Kyllo's home, and that only the heat being emitted from the home was recorded. Additionally, the court concluded that there was sufficient probable cause to issue the search warrant.

Kyllo next appealed the district court's decision. Ultimately, an appeals court upheld the decision of the lower court, maintaining that use of the device revealed nothing more than the amount of heat rising from the home and that Kyllo had not attempted to conceal the heat.

The U.S. Supreme Court heard Kyllo's case on February 20, 2001, and released its decision on June 11, 2001. Five of the nine justices ruled in favor of Kyllo, thus reversing the decision of the appellate court. The opinion, delivered by Justice Antonin Scalia, stated that exploration of the details of the home that would have been "unknowable without physical intrusion" qualifies as a search and is unreasonable without a warrant.

Christine Ivie Edge

Further Reading

Katsh, M. Ethan. *Clashing Views on Controversial Legal Issues.* Guilford, Conn.: McGraw-Hill/Dushkin, 2004.

LaFave, Wayne R. *Search and Seizure: A Treatise on the Fourth Amendment.* 3d ed. St. Paul, Minn.: West Publishing, 1996.

See also *Chimel v. California;* Fourth Amendment; *Illinois v. Krull; Maryland v. Buie;* Probable cause; Search and seizure; Search warrants; Stakeouts; Supreme Court, U.S.

L

Latent evidence

Definition: Evidence—which is typically biological material—that is left behind by fingers or other body parts that come into contact with surfaces

Criminal justice issues: Evidence and forensics; investigation; technology

Significance: Modern techniques of recovering latent evidence offer law-enforcement personnel increased opportunities to find evidence that can be used to solve crimes.

Fingerprints, palm prints, and sole prints are examples of latent evidence composed of naturally secreted materials, such as sweat, lipids, and sebum (skin oil) that human hands and feet may deposit on surfaces with which they come into contact. Latent evidence may be deposited on both porous surfaces, such as fabrics, and nonporous surfaces, such as glass. However, evidence on porous surfaces is generally likely to last longer than that on nonporous surfaces because it may soak into the porous surfaces.

Latent prints may be distinguished from visible prints, such as bloodstains that are transferred from nonporous sources to materials such as carpeting. Latent evidence also is distinguished from what are known as plastic, or three-dimensional, prints, which are created when friction ridges come into contact with softer surfaces and make three-dimensional impressions into the softer surfaces.

Collection Techniques

Latent prints are enhanced or visualized, prior to collection, using physical, chemical, or instrumental methods. All prints are photographed prior to performing other visualization techniques. Physical methods of collection include the use of certain colored powders and brushes. Prior use of cyanoacrylate (chemical adhesives such as superglue) fuming enhances the effectiveness of physical visualization methods. Physical methods are used for dry nonporous surfaces.

Once visualized, the latent prints are photographed a second time. The latent prints are then lifted, placed on backing cards and documented.

Chemical methods can be used for processing prints on both dry and wet surfaces. For dry surfaces, certain dye-staining techniques, using substances such as gentian violet, fluorescent materials, and other laser-excitable materials, are used, followed by lighting or laser excitation, followed by photography of the developed prints. On wet surfaces, small-particle reagent sprays or physical developers are used. On porous surfaces, the chemicals react with the biological evidence, not with the surfaces. Numerous techniques and substances are used, including silver nitrate and ninhydrin.

Latent prints even can be lifted from the skin of homicide victims. Such prints are collected using glue fuming, with or without the transfer lift technique using magnetic fingerprint powder. This technique involves directing the fumes from heated glue onto the skin.

Ronna F. Dillon

Further Reading

Cole, Simon A. *Suspect Identities: A History of Fingerprinting and Criminal Identification.* Cambridge, Mass.: Harvard University Press, 2001.

Gilbert, James N. *Criminal Investigation.* New York: Prentice Hall, 2004.

James, Stuart H., and Jon J. Nordby. *Forensic Science: An Introduction to Scientific and Investigative Techniques.* Boca Raton, Fla.: CRC Press, 2003.

Lee, Henry C., T. Palmbach, and M. T. Miller. *Henry Lee's Crime Scene Handbook.* New York: Academic Press, 2001.

See also Bloodstains; Circumstantial evidence; Crime scene investigation; DNA testing; Document analysis; Fingerprint identification; Forensic entomology; Forensic psychology; Forensics; Shoe prints and tire-tracks; Toxicology; Trace evidence.

Law enforcement

Definition: Component of the criminal justice system that is responsible for such functions as crime prevention and fighting, order maintenance, conflict management, and other services

Criminal justice issues: Law-enforcement organization; police powers

Significance: American law enforcement encompasses approximately 17,500 different public agencies at the local, state, and federal levels of government that employ about 750,000 sworn officers. Primary law enforcement is performed at the local level, which includes cities, municipalities, and counties. State and federal law-enforcement officials enforce laws at their levels of government and also assist local law-enforcement agencies with their functions.

Depending on the local jurisdiction, law-enforcement officers may serve as police officers or deputy sheriffs. The United States has a mixture of police departments and sheriff offices/departments which serve a variety of different functions.

History

American law enforcement has its roots in English history. Modeled on the principles and structure of the London Metropolitan Police Force of the early nineteenth century, early American policing began in earnest during the mid-nineteenth century in response to the urban problems brought on by the Industrial Revolution, as increasing numbers of people lived and worked together in densely populated and racially and ethnically diverse communities. Early American policing was tainted by the significant influences of politics and local politicians who sought to gain control of the police for political purposes. Appointments and promotions were based largely on the value of individual officers to the local political authorities responsible for administering police departments. Corruption and political patronage were very common in departments.

From the mid-nineteenth century through the early twentieth century the functions of law enforcement in the United States included not only the traditional crime-fighting roles but also social services that complemented local social service agencies in assisting the poor and disadvantaged. As law enforcement entered the twentieth century and technology advanced, political pressures on police lessened, and departments became more professional. Among the changes taking place during this era of professionalization, or reform, included the adoption of motorized patrol using automobiles and motorcycles, the application of civil service system hiring processes, improved training, forensic science improvements, and a general increased profile with the public.

The Prohibition era of the 1920's elevated the influence of organized crime, placing the Federal Bureau of Investigation in the media spotlight and cementing the "crime-fighting" image of law enforcement for several decades. By contrast, the social turmoil of the 1960's soiled the reputation of local law enforcement as a result of direct confrontations between police and war protesters, civil rights demonstrators, and drug users. Many

The nation's state police forces perform many functions that were previously performed by National Guard units under the direction of the state governments. *(Brand-X Pictures)*

of these confrontations provoked police to use excessive force, thereby damaging their image among the citizens whom they were sworn to serve and protect. This era of policing resulted in a number of significant changes within the law-enforcement community.

In 1968, the U.S. Congress enacted the Omnibus Crime Control and Safe Streets Act, which created the Law Enforcement Assistance Administration. This agency was created to improve police professionalism and increase the capacity to fight crime. It provided federal grants to local police to improve their crime-fighting technology and subsidize the education of police officers who wanted to make law enforcement their careers.

Efforts were also made to improve police-community relationships with the intent to forge partnerships with the community to fight crime and improve the quality of life. This eventually evolved into a philosophical change in policing from a primarily reactive response to problems to a combination reactive/proactive response in which problem solving became the primary focus of law enforcement through the implementation of a community policing strategy. This strategy has carried into the twenty-first century.

Organizational Structure

Law-enforcement agencies typically include operational and administrative, or support services, components. The offices of police chief, police commissioner, and police superintendent are generally separate components. Operational components usually include basic patrol operations and criminal-investigation branches. They often also include traffic enforcement and special operations divisions.

The administrative components typically encompass the more purely administrative, or "business," functions of the agencies, such as human resources offices, training divisions, crime laboratories, fleet management, information management, and other support services.

The offices of police chiefs normally include the chiefs' administrative staffs; internal affairs, or investigative, components; and inspections components, which handle internal audits. Public affairs, or media offices, are also placed under the chiefs' offices.

Federal Law-Enforcement Officers	
Criminal investigation/enforcement	37,208
Police response and patrol	20,955
Corrections	16,915
Noncriminal investigation/inspection	12,801
Court operations	4,090
Security/protection	1,320
Other	156
Total	93,445

Source: U.S. Bureau of Justice Statistics, 2005. Table includes all nonmilitary federal officers authorized to carry firearms and make arrests in June, 2002. The agencies employing the largest numbers of officers were the Immigration and Naturalization Service (19,101), Federal Bureau of Prisons (14,305), U.S. Customs Service (11,634), and Federal Bureau of Investigation (11,248).

Local Police Functions

The primary functions of local law-enforcement agencies revolve around basic law enforcement and crime fighting. These functions include the enforcement of state laws and local ordinances and codes. Law-enforcement officers arrest violators and often testify in trials. Officers are also responsible for order and conflict management. They break up fights, intervene in violent domestic disputes, and other conflicts, which often include disagreements between landlords and their tenants and merchants and their consumers.

Local agencies' crime prevention responsibilities include helping to educate the public on how to reduce opportunities for crime and initiating local plans to prevent terrorist activities. The intelligence responsibilities of law enforcement require officers to gather information that may assist their agencies to reduce crime and improve the quality of life in the local communities.

Local agencies are also usually responsible for enforcing traffic laws and investigating accidents. Their mission is to help reduce both the frequency of traffic accidents and their severity through systematic evaluations of problem areas. Local law enforcement also provides a vast array of other services, which include investigating animal complaints and handling juvenile and administrative matters.

State and Federal Law-Enforcement Agencies

Every U.S. state but Hawaii has a primary state law-enforcement agency. Most have similar responsibilities. All state law-enforcement agencies are committed to working with myriad local law-enforcement agencies within their jurisdictions. The cooperative relationships between state and local agencies typically include memoranda of understanding (MOU) that spells out the duties and functions of the state and local agencies.

State law-enforcement agencies coordinate statewide criminal investigations, provide statewide forensic services and crime laboratory assistance, and enforce traffic laws on interstate highway systems.

Well over one hundred different departments and agencies have their own law-enforcement services. Of these, by far the largest and best known are the Federal Bureau of Investigation, the U.S. Secret Service, the Bureau of Alcohol, Tobacco, Firearms and Explosives (ATF), and the Drug Enforcement Administration (DEA). These agencies investigate specifically federal crimes, coordinate investigations with state and local law-enforcement agencies, and assist in homeland security activities.

Law-Enforcement Standards

During the 1970's, it was widely recognized that there was a need to improve professionalism of law enforcement in agencies throughout the United States. To help achieve that goal, four prestigious law-enforcement organizations came together and developed professional standards in law enforcement. These groups included the International Association of Chiefs of Police (IACP), the National Sheriffs' Association (NSA), the National Organization of Black Law Enforcement Executives (NOBLE), and the Police Executive Research Forum (PERF). Their work led to the creation of the Commission on Accreditation for Law Enforcement Agencies (CALEA) in 1979. A private commission, it comprises private and public sector executives who are dedicated to improving law-enforcement services in the United States.

The standards defined by the new commission covered many critical areas in law enforcement, including the use of deadly force, high-speed pursuit driving, prisoner processing and detention, hiring practices, training, patrol and investigative procedures, and handling of juvenile matters. By 2003, more than six hundred separate law-enforcement agencies in the United States had been accredited by the commission for meeting its standards.

Community Policing

The vast majority of law-enforcement agencies in the United States engage in some form of community policing. This philosophy of policing was initiated in the 1970's as a result of a fundamental evaluation of how law-enforcement services were being provided and how well they worked. A philosophical switch from reactive to reactive/proactive policing made its debut.

The fundamental emphasis in community policing is developing active partnerships with communities to enhance mutual trust. After relationships are developed, the emphasis switches to problem solving and improving the quality of life

Law-Enforcement Agencies and Personnel in 2000

Type of agency	Number of agencies	Number of employees full-time			part-time		
		sworn	civilian	total	sworn	civilian	total
Local police	12,666	440,920	124,995	565,915	27,351	34,853	62,204
Sheriff offices	3,070	164,711	129,112	293,823	10,426	12,599	23,025
State police	49	56,348	30,680	87,028	95	722	817
Totals	15,785	661,979	284,787	946,766	37,872	48,174	86,046

Source: U.S. Bureau of Justice Statistics, Law Enforcement Management and Administrative Statistics, 2000.

within the communities. In contrast to earlier eras, when police felt that they could handle crime problems without active community involvement, the modern community-oriented policing era emphasizes the mutual benefits to be gained by police-community cooperation.

Modern police officers train in police academies that encourage critical thinking and train officers to see themselves as "project managers" within their beats. It is no longer acceptable for officers to be simply "report writers" who place bandages on problems and are content to let the next shifts deal with the same kinds of problems at the same locations. Officers are encouraged to think more creatively and to solicit assistance in problem solving from other governmental agencies, community groups, private sector groups, and the media.

Challenges

Law enforcement faces many new challenges in the twenty-first century. A primary challenge comes from new threats of terrorism, especially since the terrorist attacks on the United States of September 11, 2001. Police in every jurisdiction must now be alert to the danger signs of possible terrorist training and activity and know how to deal with the new threats. The challenge of facing the terrorism threat cannot be overestimated.

Shrinking law-enforcement budgets present another serious challenge. Agencies must continuously look at ways to carry out their functions in the most cost-efficient manner possible. Likewise, the recruitment, retention, scheduling, and deployment of police officers will continue to require innovative thinking and approaches on the part of police executives.

As modern technologies continue to change and grow more complex, so, too, do the challenges to law enforcement to keep up with the changes. Computerization of all aspects of law enforcement and improvements in communication—especially in dispatching centers—are now permanent priorities. Modernizing forensic services, such as DNA analysis, is also a critical concern.

Finally, there is an unprecedented need for interagency communication and cooperation. With criminal mobility increasing at an unprecedented pace, police must develop significant relationships with all levels of law enforcement and allied agencies in order to improve information sharing.

Jay Zumbrun

Further Reading

Lardner, James, and Thomas A. Reppetto. *NYPD: A City and Its Police: The Inside Story of New York's Legendary Police Department.* New York: Henry Holt, 2000. Inside look at the operations of the biggest police force in the United States.

Lee, Henry C., Timothy M. Palmbach, and Marilyn T. Miller. *Henry Lee's Crime Scene Handbook.* New York: Academic Press, 2001. Henry Lee is the most widely recognized crime scene expert in the world. This book is a hands-on guide that covers in detail how to manage a crime scene; collect information; search for, collect, and preserve physical evidence; conduct field tests; and reconstruct sequences of events.

Lesce, Tony. *Cops! Media vs. Reality.* Port Townsend, Wash.: Loompanics, 2001. Exploration of the many different ways in which law enforcement is depicted in the media. Lesce analyzes the reasons behind these differences and discusses how law enforcement really operates.

Morash, Merry, and Kevin J. Ford. *The Move to Community Policing.* Thousand Oaks, Calif.: Sage Publications, 2002. Community policing continues to be of great interest to policy makers, scholars, and local police agencies. Successfully achieving the transformation from a traditional policing model to community policing can be difficult, and this tries to show how transitions can be made smoothly.

Perlmutter, David D. *Policing the Media: Street Cops and Public Perception of Law Enforcement.* Thousand Oaks, Calif.: Sage Publications, 2001. Report on the ethnography of a police department, derived from the author's experience riding on patrol with officers and joining the department as a reserve police officer.

Roth, Mitchel P. *Historical Dictionary of Law Enforcement.* Westport, Conn.: Greenwood Press, 2000. Viewing policing from an international perspective, this volume covers the history of law enforcement from the days of the ancient Roman Empire to such present-day events as the Rodney King beating.

Stevens, Dennis J. *Policing and Community Partnerships.* Upper Saddle River, N.J.: Prentice Hall, 2002. Virtual manual on how community-oriented policing can be used to raise the quality of life in communities.

See also Campus police; Coast Guard, U.S.; Community-oriented policing; Criminal justice system; Federal Bureau of Investigation; Highway patrols; Homeland Security Department; Marshals Service, U.S.; Police; Police chiefs; President's Commission on Law Enforcement and Administration of Justice; Sheriffs; Strategic policing; Women in law enforcement and corrections.

Law Enforcement Assistance Administration

Identification: Federal agency created to assist local law-enforcement bodies to combat civil unrest

Date: Created in 1968; abolished in 1982

Criminal justice issues: Federal law; law-enforcement organization; morality and public order

Significance: This short-lived federal agency was given responsibility for developing state and local law-enforcement agencies' riot control capabilities following massive urban riots during the mid-1960's, but the infusions of federal dollars were principally used for police equipment rather than broader programs to reduce violence.

The Law Enforcement Assistance Administration (LEAA) was created by Title I of the Omnibus Crime Control and Safe Streets Act of 1968. In response to a series of studies of urban violence in the 1960's and a growing fear of riots in more cities, the agency was established to provide federal funds and technical assistance to state and local law-enforcement agencies. Its mandates

were to encourage state and local officials to adopt comprehensive plans to deal with the specific kinds of urban violence they might encounter and to build local capacities to respond effectively to the violence. In support of that activity, LEAA provided block grants to state and local law-enforcement agencies and undertook research on how to reduce the levels of violence and to improve the effectiveness of law-enforcement efforts. The clear priority in the grant program was to expand state and local capabilities in riot control, although relatively small amounts were also allocated to improve police-community relations and other programs to reduce racial conflict in some cities.

LEAA became a symbol of the "law and order" orientation of the federal government during the late 1960's and, later, of the ineffectiveness of that approach in reducing violence. Over the life of the agency, $5 billion was provided to state and local governments to respond to the threat of riots. The block-grant funding permitted local authorities to spend the money where they believed it was most needed, within the broad guidelines of the Omnibus Crime Control and Safe Streets Act. Most of the money was spent to improve policing capabilities rather than to address the causes of the violence or to reduce the level of tension between police and communities. In fact, so many local governments invested their LEAA grant money in police cars that the program was sometimes referred to as federal funding for "car buying." Money was also spent on communications equipment and weaponry for special weapons and tactics (SWAT) teams.

For the most part, the expenditures did little to reduce tension and violence. Subsequent studies of civil disorders even indicated that the police themselves tended to increase the levels of tension and often caused outbreaks of violence because of their poor training and insensitivity to community concerns. During the 1970's, studies by the Office of Management and Budget and other agencies severely criticized LEAA for not addressing the root causes of urban violence or improving relationships between police and other city officials and African American communities. The agency was eliminated in 1982.

William L. Waugh, Jr.

Further Reading

Button, James W. *Black Violence: Political Impact of the 1960's Riots*. Princeton, N.J.: Princeton University Press, 1978.

Connery, Robert, ed. *Urban Riots*. New York: Vintage Books, 1969.

Higham, Robin, ed. *Bayonets in the Streets: The Use of Troops in Civil Disturbances*. Lawrence: University of Kansas Press, 1969.

Report of the National Advisory Commission on Civil Disorders. New York: Bantam Books, 1968.

See also Law enforcement; Omnibus Crime Control and Safe Streets Act of 1968; President's Commission on Law Enforcement and Administration of Justice.

Leon, United States v.

The Case: U.S. Supreme Court ruling on search and seizure

Date: Decided on July 5, 1984

Criminal justice issues: Search and seizure; substance abuse

Significance: This Supreme Court ruling created a "good-faith" exception to the exclusionary rule in search and seizure cases.

In August, 1981, an extensive drug investigation began in Burbank, California, based originally on tips received from an informant of unproven reliability. Search warrants were issued for the search of three homes in the area, including the house of Alberto Leon. The ensuing search resulted in the seizure of large quantities of cocaine and methaqualone. After the seizure, the defendants challenged the validity of the warrants. They argued that the state's affidavits had not presented the issuing magistrate—a California Superior Court judge—with appropriate evidence to establish probable cause. The reliability of the informant had not been properly established, and the information presented by the police was stale.

A federal district court and the United States Court of Appeals for the Ninth Circuit both agreed with the defendants and ordered the evidence suppressed. The court of appeals rejected the government's suggestion that the Fourth Amendment exclusionary rule should not apply where evidence is seized in reasonable, good-faith reliance on a search warrant. The government asked the Supreme Court to reverse the decision of the court of appeals and establish such a good-faith exception.

Justice Byron R. White, writing for the majority of seven members of the Court, held that there is a good-faith exception. He argued that the exclusionary rule is not required by the text of the Fourth Amendment. It is a judge-made rule, whose purpose, as established in *Mapp v. Ohio* (1961), is to deter police misconduct. The rule discourages unlawful police searches by denying the investigating officers the "fruits" of their misconduct. In this case, however, there was no police misconduct. The officers relied on the warrant, believing it to be valid. To refuse to admit the evidence, Justice White argued, would have no deterrent effect on law-enforcement personnel at all. Consequently the evidence should be admitted and Leon's conviction should stand.

Justices William Brennan and Thurgood Marshall dissented. Justice Brennan's opinion insisted that the exclusionary rule is required by the Fourth Amendment and that its purpose is to deter all official lawlessness, whether of police or courts. He charged that the majority had adopted a "crabbed" view of the amendment in order to limit its application and to do away with the exclusionary rule altogether. Once an unlawful search has taken place, the Fourth Amendment has been violated, whether or not evidence is found and whether or not evidence is admissible. Brennan concluded that the broader interpretation of the exclusionary rule should be adopted in order to prevent all invasions of people's privacy by government.

United States v. Leon is important because the good-faith exception to the exclusionary rule that it established remains valid and has become settled doctrine. The Court, however, has not been inclined to curtail the application or efficacy of the exclusionary rule beyond *Leon*. The decision may have been the high-water mark for that wing of the court which was anxious to restrict the scope of the exclusionary rule.

Robert Jacobs

Further Reading

Bloom, Robert M. *Searches, Seizures, and Warrants*. Westport, Conn.: Praeger, 2003.

LaFave, W. R. *Search and Seizure: A Treatise on the Fourth Amendment*. 3d ed. St. Paul, Minn.: West Publishing, 1995.

McWhirter, Darien A. *Search, Seizure, and Privacy*. Phoenix, Ariz.: Oryx Press, 1994.

Wetterer, Charles M. *The Fourth Amendment: Search and Seizure*. Springfield, N.J.: Enslow, 1998.

See also Bill of Rights, U.S.; Exclusionary rule; *Illinois v. Gates*; *Mapp v. Ohio*; Perjury; Search and seizure; Supreme Court, U.S.

Lesser-included offenses

Definition: Elements of lower-level crimes that are contained within higher crimes

Criminal justice issues: Legal terms and principles; pleas; trial procedures

Significance: Lesser-included crimes are used in proving the higher crime as well as in determination of appropriate level of charging and plea bargains.

All the elements of lesser-included crimes are found within the elements of the higher crime. For example, the misdemeanor crime of battery is commonly defined as the harmful or offensive touching of another. The higher crime of aggravated battery includes the same elements but is differentiated from battery by the addition of an element requiring use of a dangerous weapon. Thus, the lesser crime of battery is merged with the higher crime of aggravated battery when the harmful or offensive touching is accomplished by way of a dangerous weapon such as a knife. In this way, the elements of a criminal act may be shared between crimes at different levels.

Lesser-included offenses can be found in a variety of criminal laws such as those against murder, rape, robbery, burglary, and similar crimes. In each instance, the elements of a lesser crime are found within the elements of the higher crime. As an example, in many jurisdictions the lesser crime of trespassing is a part of the higher

crime of burglary. Likewise, the crime of theft is a lesser crime of the crime of robbery.

In three significant areas of procedural law, lesser-included offenses become very important. First, when dealing with any plea bargain, the lesser-included offense is commonly used in reducing the crime or potential punishment. Second, when evaluating a criminal act for liability, the courts will consider the crime that is most appropriate for the facts given. Third, the issue of double jeopardy arises when the independent lesser offense is charged after a person has been convicted of the higher crime. As a rule, the government may not charge a person with both the lesser and higher crime.

Carl J. Franklin

Further Reading

Cammack, M., and N. M. Garland. *Advanced Criminal Procedure in a Nutshell*. Eagan, Minn.: West, 2001.

LaFave, Wayne R., Jerold H. Israel, and Nancy J. King. *Criminal Procedure*. 4th ed. St. Paul, Minn.: Thomson/West, 2004.

See also Concurrent sentences; Crime; Criminal liability; Criminal procedure; Discretion; Misdemeanors; Multiple jurisdiction offenses.

Lindbergh law

The Law: Congressional legislation making kidnapping for ransom and carrying victims across state lines a federal crime

Date: Passed on June 22, 1932

Criminal justice issues: Federal law; jurisdictions; kidnapping

Significance: This law was one of many enacted during the 1930's that made crimes that transcend state borders federal offenses and thus placed them under Federal Bureau of Investigation (FBI) jurisdiction.

During the late 1920's and early 1930's, kidnapping had become more prevalent as gangs often resorted to the crime for ransom. Congress had begun investigating measures to intensify penalties for the crime, and several citizens' groups

Lindbergh family home from which the baby was kidnapped. Investigators believed that the ladder was used by the kidnapper to remove the baby from his upstairs nursery. *(AP/Wide World Photos)*

from Chicago and St. Louis testified in front of the House Judiciary Committee seeking federal intervention. Despite these endeavors, the movement to pass a bill to make kidnapping a federal offense punishable by death was slow. It would be the kidnapping and murder of a small child that would move a nation to change the laws regarding kidnapping.

On March 1, 1932, Charles A. Lindbergh, Jr., the infant son of Charles and Anne Lindbergh, was kidnapped and subsequently found murdered. Charles Lindbergh, the first person to fly solo across the Atlantic Ocean, was a beloved national hero, and the public outcry resulted in a massive police investigation to find the perpetrator. While police forces in New Jersey and New

York focused on the crime, Congress worked to pass a federal kidnapping law.

At the time of the kidnapping, there were no federal statutes or a national agency charged with combating kidnapping. To compound the problem, interstate cooperation was minimal. Sentencing varied tremendously, with the death penalty used in seven states, life imprisonment in sixteen states, and prison terms ranging from one to ninety years in the remaining states. To further confuse the situation, only twenty-five states had laws specifically dealing with kidnapping for ransom.

Buoyed by public support, Congress passed a kidnapping bill, widely referred to as the "Lindbergh law," on June 22, 1932. The new law made kidnapping for ransom a federal offense when the victim was transported across state lines or to another country. Further, if the victim was not returned within twenty-four hours, there was a rebuttable presumption that the transportation had occurred. Initially, the maximum penalty for this crime was life imprisonment. Amended in 1933, the Lindbergh law made harming the kidnapping victim a capital offense punishable by death and allowed the Federal Bureau of Investigation to enter and oversee the investigation within twenty-four hours. (In 1968, the U.S. Supreme Court ruled that the death penalty was unconstitutional in Lindbergh law cases.) Subsequent congressional measures during the mid-1930's enlarged the jurisdiction of the FBI and the definition of federal offenses to include other interstate crimes.

Ironically, Bruno Hauptmann, who was arrested for the kidnapping and murder of Charles Lindbergh, Jr., could not be punished under the new law, under the principle of *ex post facto* laws, because the law was passed after the crime occurred. Instead, the only charge available was statutory felony murder in the course of a burglary. Thus, the state of New Jersey convicted and executed Hauptmann on April 3, 1936, for committing a murder in the course of stealing the infant's pajamas.

Jennifer Davis

Further Reading

Campbell, Geoffrey A. *The Lindbergh Kidnapping*. San Diego, Calif.: Lucent Books, 2003.

Fass, Paula S. *Kidnapped: Child Abduction in America*. Cambridge, Mass.: Harvard University Press, 1999.

Gardner, Lloyd C. *The Case That Never Dies: The Lindbergh Kidnapping*. New Brunswick, N.J.: Rutgers University Press, 2004.

Hixson, Walter L. *Murder, Culture, and Injustice: Four Sensational Cases in American History*. Akron, Ohio: University of Akron Press, 2001.

Roensch, Greg. *The Lindbergh Baby Kidnapping Trial: A Primary Source Account*. New York: Rosen Publishing Group, 2003.

See also Child abuse and molestation; Federal Bureau of Investigation; Kidnapping.

Literature about criminal justice

Criminal justice issues: Media; investigation
Significance: The conflicts between criminals and society are frequent subjects of both serious and popular literature, and fiction with criminal justice themes has shown steady advances in both its realism and the variety of subject matter and characters that it depicts.

The punishment of criminal acts is an enduring feature of social life. Consequently, it is not surprising to find that crime and its punishment are recurring backgrounds for the exercise of literary imagination. Conflicts between the individual and society, between lawlessness and law, between justice and mercy, rank at the forefront of literary subjects. Interest in legal issues has, if anything, increased among readers since the early twentieth century. Changes, such as those effected by the Civil Rights movement and various others rights movements of the 1960's, have created within the reading public an almost insatiable appetite for novels and films and television programs about the law, especially the law relating to crime and its prosecution.

Antecedents of Modern Crime Fiction

Crime and its attendant legal circumstances have a long history of attention from literature. Shylock's murderous envy in *The Merchant of Venice* (1597) by William Shakespeare is brought to justice by Portia. A murder trial anchors the final chapters of Fyodor Dostoevski's *The Brothers Karamazov* (1880). Herman Melville's posthumously published novella *Billy Budd, Foretopman* (1924) finds a morally innocent sailor tried for striking and killing a superior officer. Hetty Sorrell stands charged with killing her infant in George Eliot's 1859 novel *Adam Bede*. In fact, what is thought of as the first modern short story in the English language—Walter Scott's "The Two Drovers" (1827)—has as its central event the trial and execution of a Scotsman who kills a companion on English soil after a barroom fight.

The nineteenth and twentieth centuries witnessed a proliferation of both serious and popular literature about crime. Edgar Allen Poe, in such stories as "The Murder in the Rue Morgue" (1841), which he referred to as tales of "ratiocination" (reasoning) established influential models for future detective stories. Beginning with *A Study in Scarlet* (1887), Arthur Conan Doyle introduced Sherlock Holmes, perhaps the most famous fictional detective of all. Although Holmes was a professional, literature about crime has had plenty of room for talented amateurs, such as G. K. Chesterton's Father Brown, a Catholic priest with a knack for solving crimes, chronicled in *The Innocence of Father Brown* (1911) and *The Wisdom of Father Brown* (1914).

The most immediate forebears of modern literature about crime were the "hard-boiled" detective stories published between the twentieth century's two world wars. In these stories amateur detectives gave way to private investigators, who labored to solve puzzles created by criminal minds not out of mere intellectual curiosity but as a job, though one that did not pay very well. Instead of the pastoral scenes and manor houses that characterized British detective stories of the period, sometimes called "cozies," hard-boiled de-

Mystery writer Raymond Chandler. *(Library of Congress)*

tective stories planted their protagonists in the urban underworld spawned by the twentieth century.

Raymond Chandler and Dashiell Hammett, the best-known writers of hard-boiled detective fiction, created two of the most enduring fictional detectives: Philip Marlowe and Sam Spade. However, detective literature, while focused on the discovery of crime and its perpetrators, offered an incomplete view of the criminal justice system. In this system, the apprehension of an alleged wrongdoer stands at the beginning of the justice process, with crucial events yet to follow in its wake. Events such as trials, appeals, and incarcerations were not unknown to fiction writers, but these subjects took a decidedly secondary place to "whodunits," the colloquial name given to detective stories which focused on discovery of the criminals.

Crime and Its Aftermath

Modern literature about criminal justice is more realistic than its forebears at least in this regard—that the full breadth of the justice system is more regularly on display to readers. Nevertheless, the detection of criminal acts remains a recurring subject of crime fiction. However, modern readers have cause to be more informed than earlier generations about the criminal process at each stage because these various stages are regularly described, both in serious and popular literature. Serious works about crime, such as Truman Capote's "nonfiction" novel, *In Cold Blood* (1966), now routinely expose readers not only to investigations of crimes, but also to arrests of suspects, their arraignments, trials, appeals, and incarceration or execution. Popular or "pulp" fiction is, if anything, even more comprehensive in its treatment of the various stages in the investigation of crime and the arrest and punishment of its perpetrators.

Not only do readers have access to these stages of the criminal process, but they now have reason to be familiar with a host of subsidiary characters in that process: coroners, bail bondsmen, court reporters, and parole officers being only a few such examples. These characters themselves represent different aspects of the criminal justice system. The familiarity of modern readers with the functions of these various characters repre-

In the 1990 film adaptation of Tom Wolfe's *The Bonfire of the Vanities*, Sherman McCoy, played by Tom Hanks (center), is called to the bench by the judge (Morgan Freeman, right), as the prosecutor and defense attorney look on. *(Warner Bros., Inc.)*

sents a significant advance in the realism of crime fiction.

Despite this development, individual works of fiction still tend to focus attention on particular segments of the criminal process, especially on criminal investigation, arrests, and trials. Tom Wolfe's 1987 novel *The Bonfire of the Vanities* is typical in this regard, since its narrative emphasis is on stockbroker Sherman McCoy's arrest and trial for a hit-and-run accident. Patricia Cornwell's novels about Kay Scarpetta, Virginia's chief medical examiner, target attention chiefly on criminal investigations. Novels such as John Grisham's *The Chamber* (1994), on the other hand, spotlight the inevitable appeals that immediately precede applications of the death penalty. Viewed collectively, modern crime literature broadly canvasses the entire gamut of the criminal justice process.

Police and Private Investigators

Long part of the enduring furniture of crime fiction, descriptions of police took a fairly radical turn in the last decades of the twentieth century. Before that time, police characters populated the plots of crime fiction but seldom played major roles. Private detectives, both those whose services could be hired and those who were purely amateur investigators, assumed larger proportions than official law-enforcement officers. Thus, as between Arthur Conan Doyle's Sherlock Holmes and Inspector Lestrade of Scotland Yard, Holmes was the central figure, Lestrade nothing more than a foil.

In Edgar Allan Poe's "Murders in the Rue Morgue," the prefect of police takes a back seat to the independent detective, the Chevalier C. Auguste Dupin. Similarly, in Raymond Chandler's *The Big Sleep* (1939) and other hard-boiled detective stories by Chandler, Dashiell Hammett, and others, the criminal justice system is only a pale shadow behind the investigations of private detectives such as Philip Marlowe and Sam Spade.

Modern crime fiction has revised this hierarchy. After World War II, fictional crime seemed to mature and become less susceptible to solutions that involved only a single hero. Detection of crime depended increasingly on forensic scientific techniques and the ability to acquire and organize significant sums of information. Private investigators, whether of the professional or amateur variety, would not realistically have access to the products of forensic investigation or the information such as that contained in the voluminous records of the telephone company. Moreover, detection of crime, although still enormously important, found itself allied with arrest and enforcement issues. The police and police departments, accordingly, took on more importance in American public life and, consequently, more importance in fiction about late twentieth and early twenty-first century crime.

Beginning with *Cop Hater* in 1956, Ed McCain's police procedural novels focused less on individual police officers and more on teams of officers, specifically, the officers of the fictional 87th Precinct. As might be expected from narratives in

Edgar Allan Poe. *(Library of Congress)*

which an organization takes center stage, the bureaucratic forms of that organization find a place in McCain's novels. *Cop Hater* introduced readers to pistol permits, ballistics reports, and other standard law-enforcement forms. Even McCain could not resist the narrative attractions of paying special attention to the development of a central protagonist—Detective Steve Carella in his case. Nevertheless, his novels—and others in the police procedural genre—represented another genuine advance in realism insofar as they elevated the cooperative nature of law-enforcement work over its individual aspects.

Lone fictional heroes of criminal detection still exist. Notable examples are Agatha Christie's Belgian detective, the retired police official Hercule Poirot, or Walter Mosley's African American private eye Ezekiel "Easy" Rawlins. More often, however, even lone heroes are at least nominally attached to police organizations, such as Hollywood police detective Harry Bosch in *The Last Coyote* (1995), and other novels of the series by Michael Connelly. Lone detectives in the modern age must generally rely on webs of relationships among official law-enforcement agencies to have access to the information that only these agencies can acquire and compile—information that is often crucial to the solution of modern crimes.

Constitutional Rights and Criminal Processes

Reality infiltrated literature about crime nowhere more prominently than in the late twentieth century emphasis on constitutional criminal rights. Under U.S. chief justice Earl Warren, criminal procedure in the United States experienced a true rights revolution during the 1960's. Most famously in *Miranda v. Arizona* (1966), the Court expanded the constitutional protections available to those accused of crimes. *Miranda* instituted the now familiar requirement that suspects be advised of their rights, such as the right to counsel and the right to remain silent. Elsewhere the U.S. Supreme Court reaffirmed and expanded its allegiance to the exclusionary rule, which stipulates that evidence unlawfully obtained generally cannot be used in criminal prosecutions. Similarly, the Court developed doctrines such as the "fruit-of-the-poison-tree" rule, which limited the ability of the government to rely on evidence that is legally obtained but which is discovered as a result of other evidence that is obtained illegally.

These developments in constitutional law did not escape the notice of fiction writers. Crime fiction explored the initial—and in some ways continued—opposition in some quarters to these new protections and the means by which law-enforcement personnel sought to circumvent them. Often, as well, these protections were simply absorbed into the plots and vocabularies of crime fiction. Overall, the very titles of crime novels in the late twentieth century signaled a growing familiarity with constitutional developments on the part of fiction writers. Charles Brandt's *The Right to Remain Silent* (1988), Ridley Pearson's *Probable Cause* (1990), and Lisa Scottoline's *Final Appeal* (1994) capture in their titles the new focus on constitutional rights and procedures that began to infiltrate crime fiction in the last quarter of the twentieth century.

Writing from Experience

Writing fiction about the criminal justice system does not require authors to have had personal experience working within this system. Nevertheless, more than a few authors have precisely this kind of experience, or other personal connections to the justice system, that assists them in portraying the system with high degrees of accuracy. The father of the great nineteenth century British novelist Charles Dickens went to debtor's prison when Dickens was an adolescent and thus inadvertently gave the future author a firsthand perspective on the law's operation. Novelist Harper Lee's father practiced law in Monroeville, Alabama, and she herself studied law at the University of Alabama before writing one of the twentieth century's most famous novels about a criminal trial, *To Kill a Mockingbird* (1960). The mother of another contemporary author of crime fiction, James Elroy, was strangled to death when Elroy was ten years old, and this event partially inspired Elroy's career as a writer. In fact, Elroy's second novel, *Clandestine* (1982), offers a fictionalized portrayal of his mother's murder.

More often, however, writers of fiction about the criminal justice system have a past professional connection with this system themselves.

Former criminal justice professionals are fixtures among the authors of this genre. William F. Caunitz, a best-selling author of crime fiction is a retired lieutenant of the New York Police Department, and Joseph Wambaugh, author of such novels as *The Choirboys* (1975) and *The Black Marble* (1977), is a retired detective from the Los Angeles Police Department. Patricia Cornwell, the author of the best-selling series of novels about chief medical examiner Kay Scarpetta was a crime reporter for the *Charlotte Observer* and spent six years working for the Virginia chief medical examiner's office before writing *Postmortem* (1990), her award-winning first novel.

John Grisham practiced both civil and criminal law in Southaven, Mississippi, for nearly a decade and served as a Mississippi legislator before his second novel, *The Firm* (1991), catapulted him into the ranks of best-selling authors. He followed the success of another lawyer author, Scott Turow, who managed to pen several legal thrillers, beginning with *Presumed Innocent* (1987), while still practicing law, first as an assistant United States attorney in Chicago and later for a private law firm. Both these authors follow in the footsteps of Erle Stanley Gardner, the don of courtroom fiction in the United States. Gardner traded two decades of law practice for a writing career, which began with the publication of his first novel, *The Case of the Velvet Claws* (1933), which introduced Perry Mason, America's most famous fictional lawyer.

True Crime in Literature

Reliance by writers on accounts of actual criminal cases has often given an added measure of realism to literature about the criminal justice system. Sometimes, authors explicitly set out to portray actual cases, such as writer and prosecutor Vincent Bugliosi's portrayal of mass murderer Charles Manson in *Helter Skelter* (1974) or Joseph Wambaugh's *The Onion Field* (1973), which depicts the murder of a California policeman. Truman Capote, for example, famously depicted the real-life murders committed in the fall of 1959 by Perry Smith and Dick Hickock. His book *In Cold Blood*, which some critics have dubbed a "nonfiction novel," relied on extensive research about the case, including interviews with Smith and Hickock. Capote attended their trial as well

Scott Turow's Legal Thrillers

A veteran federal prosecutor, Scott Turow has been credited with launching the legal thriller genre of fiction with his best-selling novels *Presumed Innocent* (1987), *The Burden of Proof* (1990), *Pleading Guilty* (1993), *The Laws of Our Fathers* (1996), *Personal Injuries* (1999), and *Reversible Errors* (2002). Although his popularity as a novelist was eclipsed by that of John Grisham, Turow is also well known in legal circles for his nonfiction account of his first year of law school at Harvard, titled *One-L* (1977).

Presumed Innocent, Turow's first novel, is about an assistant district attorney, Rusty Sabich, who is assigned to investigate the murder of a female prosecutor, with whom he has just had an affair. Sabich is ultimately charged with the murder himself.

Turow's treatment of courtroom scenes in *Presumed Innocent* is generally accurate. However, virtually every character in the book bends or breaks the law at one time or another, and the novel thus downplays the legal profession's emphasis on ethical conduct. One might compare Turow's book, for example, with Norman Mailer's "nonfiction novel" *The Executioner's Song* (1979), which generally portrays the lawyers involved in the conviction and execution of Gary Gilmore as struggling to do right, whether they are the prosecution or the defense.

Timothy L. Hall

as their execution. In fact, he was apparently the last person to speak to the two men before their hanging, and he later paid for headstones for their graves.

Norman Mailer wrote another "nonfiction novel" in the tradition of Capote, called *The Executioner's Song* (1979), about Gary Gilmore. Gilmore was convicted of two murders in 1976, and on January 17, 1977, gained national notoriety by becoming the first person executed in the United States since the Supreme Court's declaration of a moratorium on the use of capital punishment until states rectified certain constitutional defects the Court found in the use of this punishment.

More commonly, however, authors use real cases as inspirations for their own fictional accounts of crime. For example, Theodore Dreiser's *An American Tragedy* (1925) is based on the real-life case of Chester Gillette, who was executed for murder in 1908. Like Dreiser's fictional Clyde Griffiths in the novel, Gillette had a sexual relationship with a victim who tried to persuade him

to marry her. In both the novel and the real case, the young man takes the woman out on a boat ride on a lake from which the woman does not return alive. Both women are ultimately discovered drowned; both men claim the boat accidentally capsized and they could not save the victim.

Another classic of American literature, *Native Son* (1940), by Richard Wright, demonstrates a similar pattern of borrowings from a real case. Wright, however, was half way through the first draft of his novel before he heard of the case of Robert Nixon, a young black man who—like his fictional protagonist Bigger Thomas—pleaded guilty to murder and received the death sentence. Both Dreiser and Wright achieve something more in their novels than the simple recreations of notorious crimes, but both were able to bring added verisimilitude to their writing by crafting fiction from fact.

Multiplied Professionalism

By the end of the twentieth century, crime detection and enforcement involved teams of professionals who brought different skills to their work. Standard figures such as police detectives, district attorneys, and judges remain, but they cooperate more with other professionals, such as medical examiners and crime lab technicians. Police departments, especially in urban contexts, divide law-enforcement tasks among specialized teams of officers: traffic, fraud, robbery/burglary, homicide, juvenile, internal affairs, and other divisions segregate the responsibilities of officers according to different types of crime. In addition, multiple law-enforcement agencies cooperate and sometimes compete. Highway patrol officers at the state level and federal agents of the Federal Bureau of Investigation (FBI), Bureau of Alcohol, Tobacco, Firearms and Explosives (ATF), Drug Enforcement Administration (DEA), and U.S. Secret Service, for example, all participate in the enforcement of criminal law.

One of the most helpful features of modern crime fiction is its revelation, to the reading public at least, of the multiple layers of law-enforcement personnel. Scarcely any significant actor within the criminal justice system lacks a novel these days. For example, Patricia Cornwell, beginning with *Postmortem*, has crafted a series of novels around a Virginia medical examiner named Kay Scarpetta. Dr. Alex Delaware, Jonathan Kellerman's serial character in novels such as *Therapy* (2004), is a police psychologist. Richard Quinn is the young judge featured in Philip Margolin's *The Undertaker's Widow* (1998).

Various agencies of the law-enforcement world also have their own protagonists in crime fiction. Some of them, such as Alex Cross in the novels of James Patterson, have careers that realistically involve moves between different law-enforcement positions, as Cross, for example, serves first as a homicide detective in the District of Columbia, and subsequently, beginning in *Big Bad Wolf* (2003) becomes an agent for the FBI. Even less familiar law-enforcement roles, such as that played by federal park ranger Anna Pidgeon in the novels of Nevada Barr, have become the subject of fiction series. Added to these multiple law-enforcement roles are descriptions of other collateral players in the criminal justice system, such as police reporter Jack McEvoy in Michael Connelly's novel, *The Poet*, or a forensic anthropologist Gideon Oliver in Aaron J. Elkins's *Old Bones* (1987).

Emancipation of the Criminal Law System

Among the many changes in American life produced by the Civil Rights movement was the emancipation of occupations formerly dominated by white men. Laws against employment discrimination, such as the federal Equal Employment Opportunity Act of 1972, contributed to the removal of obstructions that had previously limited access to certain occupations for women and minorities. As crime fiction of the last quarter of the twentieth century labored to picture the criminal justice system accurately, it inevitably recorded this new social development, and white men lost their monopoly on fictional law-enforcement positions. Women and minorities became cops and FBI agents and lawyers and any number of other kinds of actors in the justice system.

As late as the late part of the nineteenth century, in *Bradwell v. Illinois* (1873), the U.S. Supreme Court had found no constitutional difficulty with state laws that prohibited women from practicing law. However, by the last quarter of the twentieth century, the Court had reversed course and become increasingly skeptical of laws that discriminated between men and women. As a consequence of this and other social and legal developments, women flooded into the legal profession.

Fictional accounts of lawyers were swift to recognize the new role women played in the justice system, especially as lawyers. In the early twenty-first century, when roughly half the students in American law schools are women, female lawyer protagonists are well established in the genre of crime fiction. Barbara Parker, for example, has published a series of novels such as *Suspicion of Vengeance* (2001), featuring lawyer character Gail Connor. Perri O'Shaughnessy's character, Nina Reilly, is the protagonist in a series of novels including *Unlucky in Law* (2004).

Minority characters similarly populate modern crime fiction in a variety of professional roles. The novels of Tony Hillerman feature Native American Lieutenant Leaphorn and Detective Jim Chee. James Patterson's African American police detective (and now FBI agent) Alex Cross has inspired a series including *Kiss the Girls* (1995), which was made into a popular movie starring Morgan Freeman. Walter Mosley's character, Easy Rawlins, is a black private investigator in Los Angeles to whom the police come for help during the late 1950's in *White Butterfly* (1992).

The characters of both Patterson and Mosley were anticipated in the novels of Chester Himes, beginning with *A Rage in Harlem* (1959), which featured two black police officers who worked in Harlem—"Coffin" Ed Johnson and "Grave Digger" Jones. These and other fictional portrayals have helped to democratize crime literature in a manner parallel to the democratization of American society in the wake of the Civil Rights movement. Moreover, the introduction of women and minority characters in crime fiction has allowed authors to explore continuing legacies of discrimination in American life.

From the late 1930's through the early 1940's, actor Basil Rathbone played Sherlock Holmes in a series of films that are still regarded as the definitive film portrayals of Arthur Conan Doyle's immortal detective. *(Arkent Archives)*

Courtroom Fiction

Long before private investigators such as Sherlock Holmes began to appear in fiction about crime, courts and their officers had been a fixture of literature. Shakespeare had Dick the Butcher propose to "kill all the lawyers," in *Henry VI* (1592), thus reminding his audiences of the role lawyers play as bulwarks against anarchy. In *The Merchant of Venice*, Portia pretends to be an eminent male jurist and appears in court to foil the envious plans of Shylock.

In the main, however, lawyers receive far better treatment in literature than they do in modern lawyer jokes. In fact, the absence of defense lawyers in some literary courtroom scenes is a stark reminder of the value now placed on seeing criminal defendants represented by counsel. In George Eliot's *Adam Bede*, for example, Hetty Sorrell stands charged with murdering her newborn infant after allegedly abandoning it. Any lawyer reading the account of the trial in which she is found guilty imagines a brief that would be full of arguments that should acquit her. Similarly, in Herman Melville's *Billy Budd, Foretopman*, a young sailor stands charged with mutiny for striking and killing a superior officer.

Although Captain Vere, his chief accuser, views Budd as morally innocent, he presses for Budd's conviction and execution. No lawyer for Budd stands in his way, and Vere readily secures a conviction that would be hard to imagine in more realistic circumstances.

Modern fiction about criminal trials generally represents a significant improvement over that of earlier generations of writers. This improvement probably has a good deal to do with the large number of lawyers or former lawyers who are currently writing fiction. Following the tradition of Erle Stanley Gardner who practiced law before creating Perry Mason, writers such as John Grisham and Scott Turow have relied on their own legal experience to craft fiction about the work that lawyers do. Now readers are regularly exposed in crime fiction to virtually every stage of courtroom procedure, from arraignment to the final desperate appeals of a prisoner on death row. Moreover, in the best modern fiction, courtroom scenes are treated with great accuracy. Testimony is not simply summarized, but presented in question-and-answer form, as it occurs in real life. Authors can now be expected to understand such features of real courtroom practice as the difference between leading and nonleading questions—and when each form of question is permitted—and the general ineffectiveness of objections to evidence merely on the basis that it is "highly prejudicial."

Heroes and Villains of Criminal Justice

Modern fictional accounts of the criminal process portray law-enforcement officers and lawyers of varying moral hues, as one would expect in reality. Heroes are still to be found. Prominent examples include Atticus Finch, the lawyer who represents a black client accused of raping a white woman in *To Kill a Mockingbird*, and Perry Mason, Erle Stanley Gardner's fictional creation. The most prominent sins of Alex Cross, the FBI agent and former District of Columbia police detective in the novels of James Patterson such as

Along Came a Spider (1993), are that he works too hard and sometimes misses performances of his son's choir.

Villains also are to be found among both law-enforcement officers and lawyers in modern crime fiction. Peter Maas's *Serpico* (1973) chronicled the corruption rampant in the New York police department. This novel followed the release of the report of the Knapp Commission by New York City officials in 1972, that detailed widespread corruption among New York police. In a similar vein, the lawyers in the firm of Bendini, Lambert and Locke of John Grisham's *The Firm* (1991) are not adverse to killing young associates who try to reveal to the FBI the firm's close connection to the Chicago Mafia.

Although heroes and villains make for lively reading, actors within the real criminal justice system tend to be more complex. Crime fiction often captures this more nuanced understanding of human personality in which courage and ambition are frequently coupled together, selflessness and greed, compassion and occasional cruelty. Joseph Wambaugh's first novel, *The New Centurions* (1971), is a good example of a police novel that depicts the idealism of new police recruits gradually being corrupted by life on the streets. Sometimes, the dominant characteristics of characters in crime fiction are neither heroism nor villainy but simply competence. For example, the various lawyers chronicled by Norman Mailer in *The Executioner's Song*, about the execution of Gary Gilmore, are notable chiefly for the solid ability they bring to their different roles.

The Genealogy of Crime

Fiction about the criminal justice system has the capacity to explore the origins of criminal behavior. Richard Wright's *Native Son* famously used the account of Bigger Thomas to suggest that the racism of American society at the beginning of the twentieth century was an incubator for crime among black men. Bigger Thomas accidentally kills one woman, then deliberately kills another, but Wright attributes both crimes primarily to social sins, rather than to culpability on the part of Thomas.

Theodore Dreiser's *An American Tragedy* similarly traces criminal behavior to excesses embodied within the pursuit of the American Dream.

Crime by both accounts is not simply, or perhaps even mainly, the product of the individual, but of broader social conditions. Dreiser, in particular, suggests, moreover, that pursuit of the American Dream is shared not only by the criminal but by the participants in the justice system who stand in judgment of him.

Modern popular fiction tends to be less inquisitive about the origins of criminal behavior. Perhaps this is because the kinds of crimes committed in novels such as Wright's *Native Son* and Dreiser's *An American Tragedy* are crimes of outsiders and the dispossessed and are less frequent subjects than crimes of sociopaths. The serial killers and terrorists who dominate the pages of best-selling crime fiction of today may wish to accuse society for their crimes, but the authors who create them tend to spend little time exploring the origins of their sociopathic personalities. It may be that they were sexually abused as children or mocked by adolescent schoolmates. However, authors frequently tell their readers little more about the origins of criminal behavior. This reluctance to explore the social origins of crime has the effect of giving much modern crime fiction a conservative tenor and of disabling it from exploring ways in which the criminal justice system might respond not only to the crime and criminals, but to the origins and sources of crime.

Timothy L. Hall

Further Reading

Algeo, Ann M. *The Courtroom as Forum: Homicide Trials by Dreiser, Wright, Capote, and Mailer.* New York: Peter Lang, 1996. Analyses of four of the most famous works of twentieth century American literature involving the criminal process: Theodore Dreiser's *An American Tragedy*, Richard Wright's *Native Son*, Truman Capote's *In Cold Blood*, and Norman Mailer's *The Executioner's Song*.

Bertens, Hans, and Theo D'haen. *Contemporary American Crime Fiction.* New York: Palgrave, 2001. This book offers the perspective of two German scholars on American crime novels. It focuses on books from the last decades of the twentieth century and offers especially strong coverage of fiction by women and minority authors.

Bloom, Harold, ed. *Classic Crime and Suspense*

Writers. New York: Chelsea House, 1995. Edited by a noted literary critic, this volume includes biographies, commentaries, and references for further reading concerning thirteen of the most influential crime fiction writers of the first half of the twentieth century, including Raymond Chandler, Dashiell Hammett, Graham Greene, and Jim Thompson.

Breen, Jon L. *Novel Verdicts: A Guide to Courtroom Fiction*. 2d ed. Lanham, Maryland: Scarecrow Press, 1999. Annotated list of nearly eight hundred novels about trials, with plot descriptions and brief comments about the legal accuracy of various details. Covers books published through 1997.

Gorman, Ed, Martin H. Greenberg, and Larry Segriff, eds. *The Fine Art of Murder: The Mystery Reader's Indispensable Companion*. New York: Galahad Books, 1995. Useful collection of essays that is notable for the breadth of its coverage, discussing a great variety of different subgenres of crime fiction. Included are treatments of hard-boiled detective stories, police procedurals, true crime writing, as well as discussion of various regional settings for crime fiction, and the place of women and minority writers and characters in the world of crime fiction.

Herbert, Rosemary. *The Oxford Companion to Crime and Mystery Writing*. New York: Oxford University Press, 1999. One-volume encyclopedia containing entries about significant crime fiction authors, works, genres, and related issues.

Kelleghan, Fiona, ed. *One Hundred Masters of Mystery and Detective Fiction*. 2 vols. Pasadena, Calif.: Salem Press, 2001. Analytical essays on one hundred of the most important writers of detective and mystery fiction of all time. Each essay contains an exhaustive list of its subject's writings.

Messent, Peter, ed. *Criminal Proceedings: The Contemporary American Crime Novel*. Chicago: Pluto Press, 1997. This collection of essays about modern crime fiction covers both law-enforcement officers and lawyers. Thus, readers can find discussions of authors such as Elmore Leonard and Tony Hillerman, as well as John Grisham and Scott Turow.

Priestman, Martin, ed. *The Cambridge Companion to Crime Fiction*. Cambridge, England: Cambridge University Press, 2003. This collection of essays about the fiction of crime contains discussions of both nineteenth and twentieth century works. Subgenres of crime fiction, such thrillers and private eye novels are treated. The essay on "Post-War American Police Fiction" by Leroy L. Panek is especially helpful in understanding changes that occurred in the treatment of police in crime fiction during the late twentieth century.

Wingate, Anne. *Scene of the Crime: A Writer's Guide to Crime-Scene Investigations*. Cincinnati: Writer's Digest, 1992. Part of a series of practical guides for novelists who want to get facts and procedures right in their own writings, this book offers revealing insights into what goes into crime fiction. Its author is a veteran forensic detective who once headed the criminal identification section of a Texas police department.

See also Attorney ethics; Criminal justice system; Films and criminal justice; Miranda rights; Police detectives; Print media; Private detectives; Television courtroom programs; Television crime dramas.

Loitering

Definition: Act of lingering in public places without discernible reason

Criminal justice issues: Law codes; police powers

Significance: The difficulty of determining what constitutes loitering allows police to enforce antiloitering laws capriciously; loitering is consequently a controversial but rarely prosecuted offense.

Loitering laws have been passed in many localities at many times, primarily as a method of arresting or questioning persons who are under suspicion of other crimes. It is most often classified as a type of breach of the peace or disorderly conduct. A suspected prostitute, for example, may be ordered to move along under loitering statutes, even if no direct evidence exists that she is soliciting clients.

A central problem in enforcing loitering laws is that the U.S. Constitution guarantees citizens the right of assembly. Thus, unless criminal actions can be shown or property rights are infringed, laws that merely prohibit persons from staying in one place are unconstitutional. *(Brand-X Pictures)*

Loitering, in and of itself, is rarely prosecuted, because there have been many successful challenges to its constitutionality. It is, however, a valid cause for the police to stop and question persons, and if such persons seem to be engaged in or intending to engage in more serious crimes, an arrest can then be made.

The selective nature of enforcement is one reason that loitering laws are often challenged and rarely enforced. It is likely that a police officer will ignore the presence of a seemingly respectable person sitting or standing in a public place but may insist that a youth, a member of a minority group, or a possible vagrant move along.

The most crucial problem faced by those attempting to enforce loitering laws is that the First Amendment to the Constitution guarantees the "right of the people peaceably to assemble." This means that unless criminal content can be proven or private property rights are infringed, any law that merely prohibits a person from staying in one place is clearly unconstitutional.

This issue became a major source of controversy in the 1950's and 1960's, when mass political protests became common. An early example was sit-ins staged by African American customers in the white sections of restaurants and other businesses. While the laws allowing businesses to segregate their clientele had already been declared unconstitutional by the Supreme Court, localities still used loitering laws to remove protesters from their seats. Ultimately, such attempts at law enforcement could still be appealed on constitutional grounds, because the sit-in participants were there for a specific purpose and often tried to order goods or services. Somewhat later, the same principle was used to attempt to disperse peace demonstrations. A common tactic was to arrest large numbers of people for loitering and similar offenses, thereby disrupting the protests, and then quickly drop the charges before the constitutionality of the laws could be questioned.

Marc Goldstein

Further Reading

Brooks, George. "Let's Not Gang Up on Our Kids." *U.S. Catholic* 62, no. 3 (March 1, 1997).

Critcher, Chas, and David Waddington. *Policing Public Order: Theoretical and Practical Issues.* Vermont: Ashgate, 1996.

Schragger, Richard C. "The Limits of Localism: Gang Anti-loitering Law and Local Government." *Michigan Law Review* 100, no. 2 (November, 2001).

See also Commercialized vice; Disorderly conduct; Juvenile delinquency; Stop and frisk; Vandalism; Victimless crimes.

Lopez, United States v.

The Case: U.S. Supreme Court ruling on congressional powers

Date: Decided on April 26, 1995

Criminal justice issues: Constitutional protections; federal law; political issues

Significance: In this case, the Supreme Court ruled, for the first time since 1936, that a federal statute was unconstitutional because Congress had overstepped its authority to regulate interstate commerce.

Responding to crime in the schools, Congress in 1990 passed the Gun-Free School Zones Act, making it a federal crime to possess guns within one thousand feet of any school. More than forty states already had similar laws. After Alfonso Lopez, Jr., a high school student in San Antonio, Texas, was arrested for taking a .38-caliber handgun to school, he was tried under federal law because federal penalties were greater than they would have been under state law. The federal court of appeals, however, ruled that the 1990 statute was unconstitutional, referring to it as a "singular incursion by the federal government into territory long occupied by the states." The federal government appealed the case to the Supreme Court.

The issue of the case was the nature of federalism. Not since 1936, in *Carter v. Carter Coal Company*, had the Court overturned a statute because it exceeded federal prerogative to regulate commerce. In fact, in *Garcia v. San Antonio Metropolitan Transit Authority* (1985) the Court had ruled that the scope of the federal authority to regulate commerce was a question to be decided entirely by the political process rather than by the courts. The *Garcia* precedent was usually applauded by liberals and denounced by conservatives, but few on either side expected it to be soon overturned.

In *United States v. Lopez*, however, the Court ruled 5 to 4 that the 1990 statute did exceed Congress's authority under the commerce clause. Writing the majority opinion, Chief Justice William H. Rehnquist noted that possession of guns near a school had nothing to do with interstate commerce and that such an issue is traditionally a concern of local police power. As a principle, Rehnquist argued that Congress could regulate only "those activities that have a substantial relationship to interstate commerce." The four dissenters argued that guns in schools interfere with education and thus affect interstate commerce by damaging the national economy. Even more, they expressed deep concern that the deci-

sion would create "uncertainty" about the validity of many federal laws on the books.

The *Lopez* decision had many possible implications for the future relationship between the federal government and the states. In concluding that Congress had gone further than the commerce clause allowed, the Court opened the door for additional restrictions on the powers of the national government. Since such an important decision was based on a 5-4 vote, the significance of *Lopez* as a precedent largely depended on the future membership of the Court; therefore, the decision appeared to increase the stakes of the presidential election of 1996.

Thomas Tandy Lewis

Further Reading

Powell, H. Jefferson. "Enumerated Means and Unlimited Ends." *Michigan Law Review* 94, no. 3 (December, 1995): 651-673.

Regan, Donald H. "How to Think About the Federal Commerce Power and Incidentally Rewrite *United States v. Lopez*." *Michigan Law Review* 94, no. 3 (December, 1995): 554-614.

Smith, Richard W. "Interpreting the Constitution from Inside the Jury Box: Affecting Interstate Commerce as an Element of the Crime." *Washington and Lee Law Review* 55, no. 2 (Spring, 1998): 615-658.

Vile, John R. *A Companion to the United States Constitution and Its Amendments.* 3d ed. Westport, Conn.: Praeger, 2001.

See also Firearms; Gun laws; Justice Department, U.S.; School violence.

Lynching

Definition: Extralegal means of social control in which individuals—typically members of mobs—take the law into their own hands to inflict physical punishment or even death upon persons seen as violating local customs and mores

Criminal justice issues: Civil rights and liberties; hate crime; kidnapping

Significance: Through the late nineteenth century and much of the twentieth century, lynching was a primary means of intimidation and control of African Americans in the American South.

Lynching, the deadliest form of vigilantism, has a long history in America. At the time of the American Revolution, lynchings were used to punish Tories or British sympathizers. Until the 1850's, lynchings were associated with nonlethal forms of punishment such as beatings and tarring and feathering. In the years immediately before the Civil War, lynching took on its fatal connotation as it was used to suppress slave insurrections. Although lynching is often associated with hanging someone, lynching includes all sorts of violent acts, including flogging, dismemberment, torture, burning, and shooting.

History of Lynching

After the Civil War, lynching became more widespread as former slaves came to be viewed as a threat by their former slavemasters. Accurate numbers on lynching are hard to come by, and it was not until 1872 that there was a systematic effort to obtain reliable data. Records kept by the Tuskegee Institute indicate that there were 4,743 lynchings in the United States between 1882 and 1968. Of those lynched, 3,446 (73 percent) were African Americans and 1,297 (27 percent) were whites. Even these numbers underestimate what most scholars believe to be the actual number of lynchings. A more accurate estimate would be close to 6,000 lynchings.

Lynchings were most prevalent from the 1880's to the 1920's. During the last two decades of the nineteenth century, there was an average of 150 lynchings per year, with a high of 230 in 1892. Between 1901 and 1910 there was an average of 85 lynchings per year, and from 1911 to 1920 there was an average of 61 per year. Lynchings declined to an average of 28 per year during the 1920's, to 11 per year during the 1930's, and to only 3 per year during the 1940's. From 1951 to 1985 only 10 lynchings were reported in the United States. Although almost every state experienced lynchings, 82 percent occurred in the South. Mississippi ranks first with 581, followed by Georgia with 530 and Texas with 493.

Grounds for Lynching

Although lynching was often justified as a method of protecting white women from black

Do Not Look at The Victim His Earthly Problems Are Ended. Instead Look at The Seven Children Who Gaze at This Gruesome Spectacle

This Victim Suffered Physical Torture For A Few Short Hours. But What Psychological Havoc is Being Wrought in The Minds of The Children.?

Into What Kind of Citizens Will They Grow Up?

Poster prepared by the National Association for the Advancement of Colored People, which worked hard to persuade the U.S. Congress to enact antilynching legislation. *(Association for the Study of African-American Life and History)*

A Lynching Case That Will Not Go Away

In May, 2004, the U.S. Justice Department announced that it was reopening its investigation into the notorious murder of teenager Emmett Till, who was lynched in Mississippi in 1955 for allegedly flirting with a white woman. The two men tried for Till's murder decades earlier had been acquitted of all charges and had since died. However, evidence still remained that implicated other men in Till's lynching who were still alive in 2004. The five-year federal statute of limitations had long since lapsed, but persons charged with murder could still be tried in a state court. R. Alexander Acosta, the Justice Department assistant attorney general for civil rights leading the Till investigation, said, "We owe it to Emmett Till, we owe it to his mother and to his family, and we owe it to ourselves to see if, after all these years, any additional measure of justice is still possible."

On June 1, 2005, the Federal Bureau of Investigation (FBI) supervised the exhumation of Emmett Till's remains from a cemetery in Alsip, Illinois, near Chicago. No autopsy was performed on Till's body after his murder in 1955, and federal investigators hoped that an autopsy by a Cook County medical examiner would turn up new evidence. This picture shows the vault containing Till's coffin being loaded onto a truck. The exhumation was performed under a tent specially erected over the gravesite, where several members of Till's family held a brief service before the exhumation. *(AP/Wide World Photos)*

rapists, only 25 percent of lynching victims were suspected of rape or attempted rape. In most cases, lynching victims were summarily executed before receiving any trial. Their guilt was never established at all, let alone beyond a reasonable doubt. The justification for lynching in the cases of rape was to protect the white woman from the agony of testifying in court.

Approximately 40 percent of lynchings involved murder or attempted murder allegations. Nine percent involved assault or robbery charges, certainly not capital offenses, and 2 percent involved African Americans insulting whites, particularly white women. The most famous example of a black man who was lynched for flirting with a white woman was Emmett Till. Till, a fourteen-year-old Chicago native, was visiting relatives in Mississippi in 1955. Prodded by some friends, Till reportedly asked a white woman for a date. The woman immediately rejected him and

went to get a pistol. Till walked out of the store saying, "Bye, baby," and "wolf-whistled" at her.

Till's alleged actions violated one of the major cultural taboos in the South, and he would pay with his life. That same day, the woman's husband and her half-brother abducted Till from the home he was visiting. Three days later, Till's decomposing body was found floating in the Tallahatchie River. Till had been beaten and shot before his weighted-down body was thrown into the river. The two white men who abducted Till were charged with his murder, but it took an all-white jury less than one hour to acquit them.

The Campaign Against Lynching

Few individuals who participated in lynchings were ever prosecuted. Coroners' juries repeatedly concluded that the death had come "at the hands of parties unknown." Seldom was anything further from the truth. Oftentimes lynchings took on a festive air, and local newspapers provided complete coverage, sometimes including photographs. In the event someone was arrested for the crime, such as the two white men accused of murdering Emmett Till, they would be found not guilty by all-white juries.

Leading the effort to abolish lynchings were the Commission on Interracial Cooperation, headed by Will Alexander, and Southern Women for the Prevention of Lynching, led by Jessie Daniel Ames. Ames, one of the leading social reformers in the South, had forty thousand members in her organization within nine years of its establishment in 1930. When alerted about a possible lynching, Ames contacted women in the area who were members of her organization or sympathetic to its objectives.

One of the earliest objectives of the National Association for the Advancement of Colored People (NAACP), a civil rights organization established in 1909, was to pressure the U.S. Congress to pass a federal antilynching bill. On several occasions, the House of Representatives passed such legislation, but it was always filibustered by southern senators when it reached the Senate. During the late 1940's President Harry S. Truman appointed a President's Committee on Civil Rights (PCCR). The PCCR urged Congress to pass a federal antilynching law, but without success.

The NAACP met with greater success in attempting to mobilize public opinion against lynching. The NAACP investigated lynchings and often sent special investigators into areas where a lynching had occurred. The NAACP prepared written narratives of the lynchings, including photographs if available, and distributed them to any media outlet that would publicize the lynching. The effort was to try to shame the South into stopping this despicable practice.

Darryl Paulson

Further Reading

Baker, Ray Stannard. *Following the Color Line: American Negro Citizenship in the Progressive Era*. Introduction by Dewey W. Grantham, Jr.

1908. Reprint. New York: Harper & Row, 1964. Now classic work on race relations that was first published shortly before the NAACP was founded. Provides a vivid picture of the position of African Americans around the turn of the twentieth century.

Chadbourn, James. *Lynching and the Law*. Chapel Hill: University of North Carolina Press, 1933. Scholarly study of efforts to obtain antilynching legislation.

Raper, Arthur. *The Tragedy of Lynching*. 1933. Reprint. Mineola, N.Y.: Dover Publications, 2003. Modern reprint of a classic indictment of lynching that was originally published just as the annual rate of lynchings was starting to drop significantly.

Till-Mobley, Mamie, and Christopher Benson. *Death of Innocence: The Story of the Hate Crime That Changed America*. New York: Random House, 2003. The story of Emmett Till's lynching, as told by his mother nearly five decades later.

Wells-Barnett, Ida B. *On Lynchings*. Introduction by Patricia Hill Collins. Amherst, N.Y.: Humanity Books, 2002. Collection of three short works on lynching by Ida B. Wells (1862-1931), the most prominent female African American journalist of her era. After publishing an attack on lynching in a black Tennessee newspaper in 1892, she had to flee to the North for her own safety, and she spent the rest of her life campaigning against lynching.

White, Walter. *Rope and Faggot: A Biography of Judge Lynch*. 1929. Reprint. New York: Arno Press, 1969. Novel about lynching written by the director of the NAACP.

Zangrando, Robert. *The NAACP Crusade Against Lynching, 1909-1950*. Philadelphia: Temple University Press, 1980. History of the campaign of the NAACP to call national attention to the problem of lynching and to get the U.S. Congress to make lynching a federal crime.

See also Equal protection under the law; Gambling; Hate crime; Jim Crow laws; Ku Klux Klan; Murder and homicide; Terrorism; Vigilantism.

McCleskey v. Kemp

The Case: U.S. Supreme Court ruling on capital punishment

Date: Decided on April 22, 1987

Criminal justice issues: Capital punishment; civil rights and liberties

Significance: This Supreme Court ruling rejected a death-row inmate's claim that Georgia's system of sentencing people to death was unconstitutional because it discriminated on the basis of race.

In 1978, Warren McCleskey, a black man, was convicted of killing a white police officer during an armed robbery of a store in Atlanta, Georgia. McCleskey's jury—which consisted of eleven whites and one black—sentenced him to die in Georgia's electric chair. McCleskey sought a writ of *habeas corpus*, arguing, among other things, that the Georgia capital sentencing process was administered in a racially discriminatory manner and violated the U.S. Constitution. According to McCleskey, the jury's decision to execute him violated the Eighth Amendment because racial bias rendered the decision arbitrary and capricious. Also, the equal protection clause of the Fourteenth Amendment was violated because McCleskey, a black man, was treated differently than white defendants in the same position.

To support his claim of racial discrimination, McCleskey offered as evidence a careful statistical study performed by Professor David B. Baldus and his colleagues at the University of Iowa (the Baldus study). The Baldus study showed that race played a dual role in deciding whether convicted murderers in Georgia would be sentenced to death. First, the race of the murder victim played a large role in whether a defendant would be sentenced to die. According to the study, defendants charged with killing whites received the death penalty in 11 percent of the cases. Defendants charged with killing African Americans received the death penalty in only 1 percent of the cases. After taking account of thirty-nine variables that could have explained the disparities on nonracial grounds, the Baldus study concluded that, in Georgia, defendants charged with killing white victims were 4.3 times as likely to receive a death sentence as defendants charged with killing African Americans.

Second, the race of the defendant played an important role during capital sentencing. According to the Baldus study, black defendants were 1.1 times as likely to receive a death sentence as other defendants. Thus, the study showed that black defendants such as McCleskey who had killed white victims had the greatest likelihood of receiving the death penalty.

By a 5-4 vote, the Supreme Court ruled against McCleskey. The Supreme Court accepted the validity of the Baldus study but held that McCleskey failed to prove "that decision makers in his case acted with discriminatory purpose." In other words, McCleskey failed to show that his constitutional rights were violated because he did not prove that anyone involved in his particular case intentionally discriminated against him based on his race. Justice Lewis Powell's opinion for the majority expressed special concern that if the Court accepted McCleskey's argument—that racial bias impermissibly tainted capital sentencing proceedings—all criminal sentences would be subject to attack based on allegations of racial discrimination. The *McCleskey* decision is a landmark ruling in the modern era of capital punishment.

Warren McCleskey died in Georgia's electric chair on September 25, 1991. That same year Justice Powell, whose 5-4 majority opinion sealed Warren McCleskey's fate, told a biographer that he would change his vote in that case (thus sparing McCleskey's life) if he could. Also, although executions had resumed in the United States in 1977, 1991 marked the first time in the modern era of American capital punishment that a white defendant (Donald "Pee Wee" Gaskins) was actually executed for killing a black person.

Randall Coyne

Further Reading

Bohm, Robert M. *Deathquest: An Introduction to the Theory and Practice of Capital Punishment in the United States.* Cincinnati: Anderson Publishing, 2003.

Carter, Linda E., and Ellen Krietzberg. *Understanding Capital Punishment Law.* Newark, N.J.: LexisNexis, 2004.

Latzer, Barry, ed. *Death Penalty Cases: Leading Supreme Court Cases on Capital Punishment.* 2d ed. Burlington, Mass.: Butterworth Heinemann, 2002.

Sarat, Austin. *When the State Kills: Capital Punishment and the American Condition.* Princeton, N.J.: Princeton University Press, 2001.

See also Capital punishment; Equal protection under the law; Supreme Court, U.S.

McGruff the Crime Dog

Identification: Cartoon dog that serves as an advertising icon of the National Crime Prevention Council

Date: Introduced in 1980

Criminal justice issues: Crime prevention; media

Significance: McGruff may be the most recognized figure in community-based crime prevention in the United States. Introduced by the National Crime Prevention Council, McGruff reaches millions of citizens each year through various media.

In 2005, McGruff the Crime Dog celebrated his twenty-fifth year as the National Crime Prevention Council's (NCPC) advertising icon who urges citizens, especially children, to "Take a bite out of crime." In 1978, the Advertising Council was asked to educate the nation in crime prevention using public service advertising. The McGruff campaign, which was the collective brainchild of nineteen different volunteer advertising agencies, has been rated the most successful in American history. Research has shown that 99 percent of America children between the ages of six and twelve recognize McGruff and understand his

President Ronald Reagan meets McGruff during Crime Prevention Week in February, 1984. *(AP/Wide World Photos)*

messages, that 80 percent of adults can recall seeing McGruff public service announcements.

McGruff represents the belief, first echoed by Great Britain's early nineteenth century prime minister Sir Robert Peel and later by proponents of community-oriented policing, that the public has the power to take control of its streets and assist local law-enforcement officials in preventing crime and creating safer and healthier communities. McGruff can be seen on television, on the Internet, in printed materials, and on personal visits to local neighborhoods, where he provides helpful safety hints to people of all ages. The McGruff program provides video materials, booklets, and kits featuring McGruff in a host of crime-prevention activities.

The program has also introduced a second canine character, McGruff's nephew, Scruff, who is designed to relate more closely with children.

McGruff on the Web

McGruff-related materials and licensed products are available through the National Crime Prevention Council's Web site, at www.mcgruff .org. Designed to appeal to children, the colorful Web site itself is filled with interactive games and activities, solid information, and links to other sites.

Scruff's cartoon coloring books teach children about making correct choices in difficult and sometimes dangerous situations, such as situations involving drugs, bullies, and weapons.

The McGruff Truck program, which recruits and trains local utility workers to help children in distress, and the McGruff House program, which sets up havens in the community for children who are threatened or in trouble, are both invaluable resources in the fight to keep communities' most vulnerable members safe. The NCPC works closely with local law-enforcement offices to organize awareness events and to advocate citizen involvement in crime prevention.

T. Steuart Watson
Jennifer Ret

Further Reading

Hathcock, Jim. "Crime May Not Pay, but Crime Dog Pays Big for Local Puppet Producer." *San Diego Business Journal* 10, no. 3 (August, 1989).

Wagner, Arlo. "Metro Calls on Crime Dog: McGruff Warns About Stations." *Washington Times*, September 19, 1997.

See also Community-oriented policing; Juvenile justice; Law enforcement; Neighborhood watch programs; Police dogs; Television crime dramas.

Mafia

Identification: Elusive Italian American criminal organization

Criminal justice issues: Organized crime; robbery, theft, and burglary; violent crime

Significance: The Mafia has exerted a powerful influence on American society thanks to its wide-ranging criminal activity.

One of the most significant challenges faced by the U.S. criminal justice system is the organized, ongoing commission of multiple criminal acts. The Mafia represents such a challenge to law enforcement.

Mafia is sometimes used as a general term for any syndicated criminal unit defined by its own ethnicity, rituals, and rules (such as "the Russian mafia"). However, the word is more often associated with the powerful, tightly structured criminal organization whose members are of Italian Sicilian descent. Also known as the Cosa Nostra ("our thing"), the Italian American Mafia originated in Sicily. The early Sicilian Mafia was an assembly of extortionists, conflict resolvers, and local strongmen who maintained control of Sicilian villages through intimidation and violence as well as providing the services of social control and protection from bandits. When Sicilians and other Italians immigrated to the United States in the nineteenth century, elements of the Mafioso did as well. With the advent of Prohibition in 1920, the Mafia and other ethnic gangs expanded greatly in power and influence. That era saw a rise in the cooperation among various Cosa Nostra members as well as Jewish and Irish gangs. Gangster activities flourished in New York, Chicago, and other cities.

An American Mafia emerged, and the origins of what is understood today as the Mafia lie in the Castellemmerese war of 1931. This conflict pitted the entrepreneurial "young turks" against traditional Sicilian "Mustache Pete" bosses. The result of this conflict was a sharp departure from the feudal Sicilian organization and an expansion into national syndication, driven by profit and structured by a supposed code of conduct that has added to the mystique of the Mafia. This code, which includes omerta, or sworn silence about the Mafia's activities, is not always followed by its members. However, the structure of the Mafia that emerged from this event still presented a formidable wall of secrecy that challenges law-enforcement attempts to investigate Mafiosi.

Among the criminal activities that have been

attributed to the mafia are extortion, corruption, contract bid-rigging, operating prostitution and gambling rings, robbery, witness tampering, narcotics distribution, murder, and white-collar crimes such as insider trading and fraud. Almost any activity or scheme that will make money and identify a soldier as a "good earner" has been tried. The Mafia has represented challenges to the criminal justice system with its intimidation of witnesses, jury tampering, corruption of officials, and the refusal of members and citizens alike to cooperate with law-enforcement investigations.

Law-enforcement efforts that have relied upon infiltration, informants, electronic surveillance, and the powerful Racketeer Influenced and Corrupt Organizations (RICO) Act of 1970 have dented the Mafia's former power. Still, the American Mafia remains a formidable and troublesome challenge to U.S. society and the criminal justice system.

David R. Champion

Further Reading

Cressey, Donald R. *Theft of the Nation: The Structure and Operations of Organized Crime in America*. New York: Harper & Row, 1969.

Lyman, Michael D., and Gary W. Potter. *Organized Crime*. 3d ed. Upper Saddle River, N.J.: Prentice-Hall, 2000.

See also Blackmail and extortion; Commercialized vice; Electronic surveillance; Federal Bureau of Investigation; Films and criminal justice; Gambling; Organized crime; Organized Crime Control Act; Prohibition; Public-order offenses; Racketeer Influenced and Corrupt Organizations Act.

Magna Carta

The Law: Royal charter sealed by King John of England expressly granting certain feudal liberties to his vassals and the Church
Date: Signed in 1215
Criminal justice issues: Civil rights and liberties; constitutional protections; political issues

Significance: The first written recognition of obligations between a monarch and his subjects, the Magna Carta set legal precedents resulting in the weakening of monarchical power and expansion of individual rights, exerting a significant influence upon the British and American legal systems.

The Magna Carta, or Great Charter, was one of the first documents in the history of Western civilization to acknowledge individual liberties. Drafted by English nobility and sealed by King John under threat of revolt, the document gave credence to the notion of human rights and the obligation of a government to its citizens. Although initially concerned with relationships between the king, his lords, and clerics, the provisions of the charter took on greater significance as feudal rights were extended to all English citizens. Thus the article requiring new taxes to be approved by a council of nobles resulted in the creation of the English Parliament, and the clause prohibiting the punishment of a lord "except by the legal judgment of his peers or the law of the land" gave rise to the legal concepts of due process and trial by jury.

The legacy of the Magna Carta passed down through English common law to become an integral part of the legal system and governmental structure of the United States. The U.S. Congress was modeled on the bicameral British Parliament, and many of the provisions of the Bill of Rights and the Fourteenth amendment to the U.S. Constitution, such as the right to due process, trial by jury, and *habeas corpus* can be traced back to the Magna Carta.

Michael H. Burchett

Further Reading

Bowen, Frances, ed. *Documents of the Constitution of England and America: From Magna Charta to the Federal Constitution of 1789*. Buffalo, N.Y.: William S. Hein, 1993.

Daugherty, James. *Magna Charta*. Sandwich, Mass.: Beautiful Feet Books, 1998.

See also Bill of Rights, U.S.; Constitution, U.S.; Due process of law; *Habeas corpus*; Jury system; Probable cause.

Mail fraud

Definition: Use of government postal services to conduct fraudulent schemes

Criminal justice issues: Business and financial crime; federal law; fraud; white-collar crime

Significance: Since the creation of the first government postal services, the mails have been used for countless crimes and scams that have bilked unsuspecting citizens, businesses, and even governments. Mail fraud is a unique form of white-collar crime that can range from simple forms of deceptive mail schemes to elaborate scams involving numerous perpetrators in many different countries simultaneously.

Mail fraud dates back at least as far as the mid-seventeenth century, when King Charles II of England created postal inspectors to monitor corrupt carriers who were stealing revenue from his government's mail service. Since that time, the crime of mail fraud has flourished. Modern forms of mail fraud range from schemes as simple as distributing counterfeit currency by mail to more frauds as elaborate as the so-called Nigerian scam, which attempts to persuade victims to release information on their bank and other accounts.

Among the more elaborate mail fraud schemes are scams offering prizes in return for which victims are asked for credit card and bank account numbers for alleged verification purposes; mailings that appear to be from legitimate credit card companies asking for verifying account information, such as social security numbers; and bogus sweepstakes and lotteries that require victims to pay entry fees or purchase products. Regardless of their levels of ingenuity, however, all such crimes are considered serious felony offenses that are punished by both large monetary fines and, in some cases, prison sentences.

History

During the early colonial era in North America, the first postal inspector was Benjamin Franklin, who was appointed by the Crown in 1737. During the American Revolution, the Continental Congress appointed Franklin postmaster general of the new government that was forming, and Franklin set out to form the nation's first office of postal inspectors. The newly assigned inspectors became the nation's first and only line of defense against all forms of fraud, theft, and corruption that attempted to use the U.S. mails.

During the nineteenth century, mail fraud proliferated in both Great Britain and the United States. The most common types of mail fraud at that time was the so-called "sob story" scam. Prosperous and upper-class persons received let-

Boston volunteers working for the American Association of Retired Persons' (AARP) "Project Senior Sting" sort through junk mail in a project designed to raise the awareness of mail and telephone fraud among older persons. *(AP/Wide World Photos)*

ters describing the woes of poor families, sick children, and similar sad stories and felt obliged to send small amounts of money to help alleviate the alleged suffering. Similar schemes are still being practiced in the twenty-first century.

In 1872, the U.S. Congress enacted the first federal law designed to combat mail fraud. The Mail Fraud Act is also considered to be the oldest and most effective consumer protection law in the United States. The statute defined fraud as schemes and ploys that used the U.S. mails to obtain money or property through false and deceptive representations. Most mail fraud uses the mails to acquire money or other things of value from victims by offering products, services, or investment opportunities that fail to live up to their claims. The Mail Fraud Act has been amended numerous times and now includes stronger punishments for frauds against financial institutions; frauds committed against private mail carriers, such as Federal Express and United Parcel Service; and frauds associated with organized crime or terrorist activity.

Prevalence

Mail fraud is a white-collar crime, and few agencies are tasked to gauge the prevalence and scope of white-collar crimes. The Federal Bureau of Investigation's National Incident-Based Reporting System (NIBRS) collects data on mail fraud, but the statistics it compiles are mixed in with those of other types of fraud, making it impossible to determine exactly how many instances of mail fraud are being reported. The best source of information on mail fraud is the U.S. Postal Inspection Service.

Investigation

The U.S. Postal Inspection Service is the law-enforcement branch of the U.S. Postal Service empowered by Congress to enforce the more than two hundred federal statutes relating to the U.S. mails. In 2005, the Postal Inspection Service employed more than 1,900 inspectors to investigate mail fraud. Of the more than 1,900 inspectors who investigate crimes relating to the mail, 300 deal specifically with crimes of fraud. Also, the Postal Inspection Service has also created the Deceptive Mail Enforcement Team, which seeks to identify individuals and companies that dis-

seminate false promotions and sweepstakes offerings. Postal inspectors work closely with state and local law-enforcement organizations and other federal regulatory agencies. They base their case investigations primarily on complaints received from the general public.

Postal inspectors investigate well over 3,000 cases of mail fraud a year. In fiscal year 2003, the service investigated 3,150 cases and arrested 1,453 perpetrators. The numbers of mail fraud complaints, however, are far larger. In fiscal 2004, for example, the Postal Service answered roughly 80,000 complaints. With the skill and proficiency of the criminals becoming more refined coupled with technological advances, the numbers of mail fraud cases are increasing annually, making it necessary for the government to improve its own methods of investigation and analysis.

Prosecution and Punishment

When postal inspectors find evidence of postal-related crimes, they may either seek federal prosecution or request administrative actions against perpetrators. Inspectors work closely with federal prosecutors. To obtain convictions, they must establish two key points. First, they must show that defendants have used deceptive practices intentionally and willfully to defraud. Second, they must show that the defendants have attempted to the use the U.S. mails to carry out their fraudulent schemes.

Mail fraud brings varying types of sanctions to those who are found guilty. Based on the extent of the harm caused by the fraud, the penalties can range from fines, asset forfeiture, and probation to long periods of incarceration. In 2005, the maximum possible punishments for mail fraud were fines of one million dollars and prison terms of thirty years. The most severe punishments were awarded to frauds directly affecting financial institutions, such as banks, credit institutions, and mortgage companies.

Paul M. Klenowski

Further Reading
Baarslag, Karl. *Robbery by Mail: The Story of the U.S. Postal Inspectors.* New York: Farrar & Rinehart, 1938. Now classic account of the early history of postal inspectors.

Biegelman, Martin T. *Protecting with Distinction: A Postal Inspection History of the Mail Fraud Statute.* Washington, D.C.: U.S. Postal Inspection Service, 1999. Official Post Service history of the Mail Fraud Act of 1872.

Terrell, John Upton. *The United States Post Office Department: A Story of Letters, Postage, and Mail Fraud.* New York: Meredith Press, 1968. Brief popular history of mail fraud.

Thomas, John. *Law of Lotteries, Frauds, and Obscenity in the Mails.* Fred B. Rothman, 1980. General survey of the full range of crimes relating to misuse of the mails.

U.S. National Archives and Records Administration. *Deceptive Mail Prevention and Enforcement.* Washington D.C.: Government Printing Office, 1999. Government report on the Postal Service's ongoing battle against misuse of the mails.

See also Cybercrime; Embezzlement; Fraud; Identity theft; Money laundering; Political corruption; Telephone fraud; White-collar crime.

Mala in se and *mala prohibita*

Definition: Distinction between actions that are wrong in and of themselves and actions that are illegal because they are prohibited by statutory law

Criminal justice issues: Law codes; legal terms and principles; political issues

Significance: This legal principle recognizes the existence of an absolute moral law as distinguished from the relativism of pragmatic politics, which fluctuates from time to time and from society to society.

Mala in se is a Latin term referring to immoral acts that are wrong in and of themselves. Examples include murder, robbery, theft, burglary, and rape; these are actions that are universally condemned as evil. Historically they have been considered to be wrong in virtually every society, regardless of culture or historical period. As such they have a long history in the common law.

Mala prohibita (singular, *mala prohibitum*) refers to those things that are wrong because they have been prohibited by legislative law. Actions that are unlawful by statute are such actions as running a traffic light or failure to register one's car. These are wrong or illegal because they are prohibited by law, not because they are inherently and essentially evil.

Something that is inherently wrong can, of course, also be prohibited by law. For example, it is wrong to drive recklessly and endanger one's life and the lives of other people, but that is also legislatively illegal and a violation of motor vehicle codes. Similarly, contaminating a source of drinking water by dumping toxic materials is both immoral and illegal.

Most or all the offenses punishable under the common law are considered *mala in se*. A basic presupposition of the common law, time-honored through the centuries, is that law and morality cannot be separated. The strongest argument for something being wrong in the eyes of the law is that it is morally wrong. Ordinary citizens are much more ready to accept the inherent wrongness of an act than they are its mere prohibition by a body of elected legislators. This fact is what gives the "oughtness" and moral strength to lawful obedience.

The laws of evidence are different in the two types of cases. *Mala in se* offenses require a consideration of motivation. One's mental state, attitude, and intention may be weighed in assessing the degree of guilt or innocence. In *mala prohibita* cases, only the factuality of whether the accused actually committed the offense is at issue. For example, where it is illegal to sell alcoholic beverages to minors, the question is whether a person did, in fact, sell those drinks to a minor. It makes no difference in the eyes of the law that the person selling them sincerely believed the person was of the proper age or even that the minor lied to the seller.

William H. Burnside

Further Reading

Garner, Bryan A., ed. *Black's Law Dictionary.* 8th ed. St. Paul, Minn.: Thomson/West, 2004.

Wood, J. D., and Linda Picard, eds. *Dictionary of Law.* Springfield, Mass.: Merriam-Webster, 1996.

See also Common law; Criminal intent; Criminal law; Environmental crimes; Malice; Moral turpitude; Murder and homicide.

Malice

Definition: Intentional causing of harm to another, without justification or excuse
Criminal justice issues: Legal terms and principles; violent crime
Significance: Malice is an indication of the mind of the criminal and may determine with which crime a person is charged.

Malice is an indication of a person's mental state, a desire to cause specific or general harm with complete disregard of the possible consequences of the action and the possible resulting harm or hurt caused to others. Malice is deliberate, not accidental, and demonstrates a lack of social duty toward others.

There are several types of malice. Express malice is a deliberate, premeditated action intending harm; implied malice is inferred from the commission of an act. At its most serious, malice is malice aforethought, the specific intent to injure or kill another individual. Malice aforethought must be present prior to the commission of a murder and indicates an awareness of the outcome of the action. It is this intention prior to the action that separates murder from manslaughter. Under common law, when such a mental state exists, murder may be committed even if it was not originally intended. Universal malice, similar to malice aforethought, is marked by a desire to take the life of any person, not a specific individual.

Malice is associated not only with a physical act but also with the intention to do harm to another by slander or libel. Those who make statements that they know to be false, or that they doubt but make no attempts to verify, and who have the intention of causing harm to others by those statements, are guilty of malice. For example, a person who refers to another as an alcoholic in front of that person's employer, knowing or suspecting the statement to be false, is guilty of malice.

Elizabeth Algren Shaw

Further Reading
Brill, Stephen. *Trial by Jury*. New York: Simon & Schuster, 1990.
Garner, Bryan A., ed. *Black's Law Dictionary*. 8th ed. St. Paul, Minn.: Thomson/West, 2004.
Pellicciotti, Joseph M. *Handbook of Basic Trial Evidence: A College Introduction*. Bristol, Ind.: Wyndham Hall Press, 1992.

See also Competency to stand trial; Crime; Criminal intent; Insanity defense; *Mala in se* and *mala prohibita*; *Mens rea*.

Mandamus

Definition: A writ of *mandamus* is a court order requiring a lower court or government agency to carry out its lawfully mandated duties and functions
Criminal justice issues: Courts; federal law; legal terms and principles
Significance: Used only in unusual emergencies, writs of *mandamus* are most commonly issued by superior courts to correct abuses of power by lower courts.

The federal Judiciary Act of 1789 established the federal court system and gave the federal courts the power to issue writs of *mandamus*. These writs require that legally mandated acts be carried out by government or its agents. For example, Arkansas has one of the most liberal freedom of information acts of the fifty states. That Arkansas law requires that virtually all documents of government be open to public viewing during the normal operating hours of a public agency. The law requires that all criminal case files possessed by the police, excepting cases still under investigation, be made available to public viewing during the normal operating hours of the police agencies. If a police department were to refuse public access to those closed criminal case files, a citizen could petition a court to issue a writ of *mandamus* ordering the police department to open those files during normal operating hours.

Lawrence M. Salinger

Further Reading

Meyer, J. F., and D. R. Grant. *The Courts in Our Criminal Justice System*. Upper Saddle River, N.J.: Prentice-Hall, 2003.

Neubauer, D. W. *America's Courts and the Criminal Justice System*. 7th ed. Belmont, Calif.: Wadsworth, 2002.

Wood, Horace G. *A Treatise on the Legal Remedies of Mandamus and Prohibition: Habeas Corpus, Certiorari, and Quo Warranto*. 3d ed. Revised and enlarged by Charles F. Bridge. Littleton, Colo.: Fred B. Rothman, 1997.

See also *Certiorari*; *Habeas corpus*; Subpoena power; Summonses.

Mandatory sentencing

Definition: Laws requiring judges to impose predetermined penalties for certain specified crimes or third felony convictions

Criminal justice issues: Judges; prisons; punishment; sentencing

Significance: The adoption of mandatory sentencing guidelines during the 1980's and 1990's limited judicial discretion in sentencing offenders and contributed to sharp increases in prison populations.

Mandatory sentences for certain offenses have existed since the foundation of the United States. In the early days of the republic, specific sentences were imposed for certain crimes, including gossiping and murder. Early mandatory sentences reflected the forms of punishment used at the time and ranged from dunking stools for gossipers to hanging for convicted murderers.

Special habitual-offender laws that could impose life imprisonment for third felony convictions became common during the twentieth century. However, broader uses of mandatory minimum sentences did not develop until mid-century, when increasing public concern about drug abuse led to the creation of new sentences for drug offenses. For example, in 1951, the U.S. Congress passed the Boggs Act, which specified minimum sentences for federal narcotics offenses, with no possibility of parole or probation after first convictions. Many states then passed legislation modeled on the Boggs Act that specified mandatory minimum sentences for violations of their own drug laws.

During the 1960's, mandatory sentences were heavily criticized for eliminating judicial discretion, treating first-time offenders as harshly as hardened criminals and for the failure of the sentences to reduce drug violations. Such criticisms helped prompt Congress to pass the Comprehensive Drug Abuse Prevention and Control Act of 1970, which repealed most of the federal mandatory minimums for drug offenses. However, the 1970's saw a push for more uniform federal sentencing policies and the elimination of the indeterminate sentencing policies in favor of determinate sentences, without the possibility of parole. At the same time, some states were enacting mandatory minimum sentences for drug offenses on their own.

In 1973, New York passed a series of laws that required mandatory fifteen-year prison sentences for possession or sales of small quantities of narcotics. Michigan passed a similar law in 1978. Michigan's law was dubbed the "650 lifer law" because it required mandatory life imprisonment for the possession, sale, or conspiracy to sell or possess 650 grams of cocaine or heroin. By 1983, forty states had similar mandatory sentencing laws.

Sentencing Reform in the 1980's

The bulk of sentencing reform took place in the 1980's, due in large part to the Reagan administration's war on drugs. In 1984, Congress passed the Comprehensive Crime Control Act and the Sentencing Reform Act, which transformed the federal system of indeterminate sentencing to a system of determinate sentencing. Parole was eliminated and the United States Sentencing Commission was established to develop federal sentencing guidelines for judges. The Crime Control Act successfully limited judicial discretion on sentences for drug crimes, while adding new mandatory sentences for other crimes. The new requirements included adding five years to drug-offense sentences for using or carrying guns during drug crimes or crimes of violence. The law also mandated fifteen-year sentences for simple

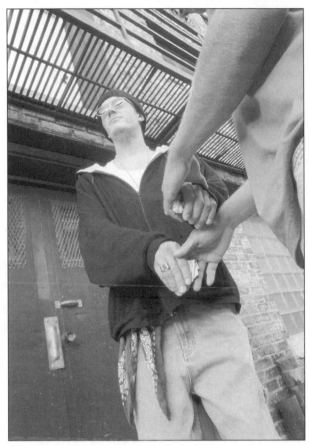

Much of the pressure for creating mandatory sentencing laws grew out of public concern about rising drug abuse during the mid-twentieth century. (Brand-X Pictures)

possession of firearms by persons with three previous convictions for burglary or robbery.

The Anti-Drug Abuse Act of 1988 established most of the drug-related mandatory minimums, including five- and ten-year sentences tied to quantities of illegal drugs. Further adding to the mandatory minimum sentences, the Omnibus Crime Control Act of 1988 mandated minimum sentences of five years for simple possession of crack cocaine; however, simple possession of other drugs remained a misdemeanor. The mandatory minimum for crack cocaine versus powder cocaine, often referred to as the 100:1 ratio, required five-year sentences for possession of 500 grams of powder cocaine or 5 grams of crack cocaine. The act made crack cocaine the only drug to carry a federally mandated sentence for simple possession. Another significant provision of the

1988 law was an increase in penalties for drug conspiracy, which could be applied equally to both major dealers and low-level participants in drug deals.

"Get Tough on Crime" Era

The punitive sentencing reforms adopted during the 1990's reflected the so-called "get tough on crime" attitudes of the public and the administration at the time. During that decade, additional federal mandatory sentencing laws were enacted, including some that did not apply to drugs. Many states also legislated mandatory sentences for felons possessing firearms or using firearms in the commission of crimes.

Washington (1993) and California (1994) both enacted mandatory life sentences for offenders receiving third felony convictions. Similar laws mandating sentences for habitual offenders were on the books in most states but were not widely used. However, they became an important issue in the 1990's after some highly publicized crimes, including the murder of a young girl in California by a repeat offender. California's new law, dubbed "three strikes and you're out," set mandatory twenty-five-year to life sentences for offenders convicted of third felonies. California's law became controversial because it applied to any third felony conviction. As a consequence, some highly publicized cases arose when nonviolent offenders were sentenced to exceptionally long prison terms for crimes as minor as shoplifting.

Mandatory sentencing laws were also heavily criticized for giving disproportionate punishment to nonviolent drug offenders by sentencing them to long prison terms. Appeals were made to Congress for relief, and in 1994 Congress enacted a so-called "safety valve" exception to the mandatory minimum sentences. The safety valve applied to nonviolent, low-level, and first-time drug offenders, but its eligibility criteria were so narrow that nonviolent drug offenders continued to be sentenced to long prison terms under the mandatory laws. The only way most defendants could avoid mandatory minimum sentences was to provide law enforcement with "substantial assistance" by disclosing information on other drug dealers or testifying against them in court.

Proponents of mandatory sentencing laws argue that these laws provide desirable sentencing uniformity. Critics argue that mandatory sentencing laws have placed unnecessary financial strains on the criminal justice system while failing to reduce the numbers of drug violations. Appeals have been made to Congress to address the large disparity in sentences awarded to crack cocaine and powder cocaine users. Congress has responded by introducing bills that would increase sentences for powder cocaine offenses while retaining the mandatory five-year minimum for simple possession of crack cocaine. Meanwhile, additional mandatory sentencing laws continue to be proposed in Congress.

Tammy L. Castle

Further Reading

Allen, Harry E., Clifford E. Simonsen, and Edward J. Latessa. *Corrections in America: An Introduction.* 10th ed. Upper Saddle River, N.J.: Pearson Education, 2004. Introductory discussion of the history of corrections, sentencing, incarceration, alternatives to confinement, types of offenders under correctional supervision, and reintegration.

Clark, J., J. Austin, and D. A. Henry. *Three Strikes and You're Out: A Review of State Legislation.* Washington, D.C.: National Institute of Justice, Government Printing Office, 1997. Report to the federal government outlining state three-strikes laws.

Demleitner, Nora V., Douglas A. Berman, Marc L. Miller, and Ronald F. Wright. *Sentencing Law and Policy: Cases, Statutes, and Guidelines.* New York: Aspen Publishers, 2003. Comprehensive text on all aspects of sentencing, with numerous case studies and texts of relevant laws and the actual federal guidelines.

Krantz, Sheldon, and Lynn Branham. *The Law of Sentencing, Corrections, and Prisoners' Rights.* St. Paul, Minn.: West Publishing, 1997. Excellent legal text that includes most of the important legal decisions related to sentencing and offers examples of state sentencing systems.

Stith, Kate, and Jose A. Cabranes. *Fear of Judging: Sentencing Guidelines in the Federal Courts.* Chicago: University of Chicago Press, 1998. Critical evaluation of the impact of federal sentencing guidelines on court decisions.

Tonry, Michael. *Reconsidering Indeterminate and Structured Sentencing.* Washington, D.C.: U.S. Department of Justice, Office of Justice Programs, National Institute of Justice, 1999. Federal government report on impact of sentencing guidelines on the entire U.S. justice system.

_____. *Sentencing Matters.* New York: Oxford University Press, 1996. Excellent history of sentencing with an analysis of contemporary reforms, such as sentencing guidelines, intermediate sanctions, and mandatory penalties.

Zimring, Franklin E., G. Hawkins, and S. Kamin. *Punishment and Democracy: Three Strikes and You're Out in California.* Oxford, England: Oxford University Press, 2001. Ambitious study of the impact and implications of California's controversial three-strikes law.

See also Comprehensive Crime Control Act; Comprehensive Drug Abuse Prevention and Control Act; Concurrent sentences; Discretion; Drug courts; Felonies; *Harmelin v. Michigan*; Incapacitation; Indeterminate sentencing; Just deserts; Prison overcrowding; Recidivism; *Rummel v. Estelle*; Sentencing; Sentencing guidelines, U.S.; United States Sentencing Commission.

Manhattan Bail Project

Identification: Government-sponsored study of pretrial release
Date: 1961
Place: New York, New York
Criminal justice issues: Arrest and arraignment; probation and pretrial release; trial procedures
Significance: The findings of the Manhattan Bail Project had a major influence on the federal Bail Reform Act of 1966.

Conducted by the Vera Institute of New York, the Manhattan Bail Project was undertaken to identify what kinds of defendants were the best risks for pretrial release. The project's report concluded that more than 90 percent of defendants released after promising to appear at future court proceedings actually appeared at those future hearings. The study also revealed that individuals who were released on bail were generally better able to assist in their own defenses. More-over, defendants released on bail were less likely to be convicted than those who were not, and those released on bail who were convicted were less likely to get prison time than defendants who were not released on bail.

The dollar figures that judges set for defendants' bail are generally based on two considerations: the flight risks of the defendants and the safety of the community. Factors such as the severity and types of crime are considered for the issue of community safety. Also considered are the numbers, strength, and types of ties that defendants have in the communities.

The Vera Institute's study is important for its impact on the issues of reasonable bail and equal rights under the law. The study revealed that defendants with adequate resources to pay for their bail typically spent little, if any time, in custody for minor offenses. By contrast, defendants charged with minor crimes who did not have the resources to post bail often spent their entire pretrial time in custody. Incarcerated defendants generally had difficulty assisting with their own defenses.

The Vera Institute developed a simple scoring system to help judges determine amounts of bail for defendants facing minor charges. Courts using the system reduced the numbers of defendants held in jails, helping save the expenses of incarceration. Many of the findings of the project were incorporated into the federal Bail Reform Act of 1966.

Gerald P. Fisher

Further Reading

Ares, Charles E., Anne Rankin, and Herbert Sturz. "The Manhattan Bail Project: An Interim Report on the Use of Pre-Trial Parole." *New York University Law Review* (January, 1963).

Shaughnessy, Edward J. *Bail and Preventive Detention in New York.* Washington, D.C.: University Press of America, 1982.

Singer, Richard G. *Criminal Procedure II: From Bail to Jail.* New York: Aspen, 2005.

See also Arraignment; Arrest; Bail system; Bounty hunters; Judicial system, U.S.; Marshals Service, U.S.; Probation, adult.

Mann Act

The Law: Federal law outlawing prostitution

Date: Enacted on June 25, 1910

Definition: The Mann Act, officially designated the White Slave Traffic Act, prohibits the interstate transportation of women for immoral purposes

Criminal justice issues: Federal law; sex offenses; women's issues

Significance: The Mann Act was the first national legislation specifically to outlaw sexually oriented activities considered immoral and detrimental to the public welfare.

Prostitution in the United States is as old as the country. Until the Mann Act, it was regulated by state statutes that generally prohibited the practice. Enforcement, however, was universally lax. The powerful men who controlled the syndicates that owned many of the brothels and controlled the women who worked in them had the political influence it took to protect their operations even though laws existed in virtually every state that specifically prohibited illicit sexual enterprises.

Vigorous enforcement of antiprostitution laws generally occurred only after vice commissions or outraged citizens' groups, often religiously oriented, raised a loud outcry against prostitution in their communities. Enforcement stepped up when such outcries arose, then died down quickly and continued to be sporadic. Many law-enforcement officials across the nation grew wealthy from the bribes they accepted from those who controlled prostitution.

Beginning in the reform era of the 1890's and continuing into the early twentieth century, however, sensational reports began to surface about the widespread existence of "white slavery," the name given to the transportation of women from depressed rural areas to large cities, where they were forced into prostitution.

Such reports alarmed a public that had already been shocked by Stephen Crane's *Maggie: A Girl of the Streets* (1896) and Theodore Dreiser's *Sister Carrie* (1900), two influential novels that drew widespread attention to prostitution and aroused strong public sentiment against it. Lincoln Steffens's *The Shame of the Cities* (1904), which focused attention on the corruption that pervaded most major American cities of that period, also aroused the public.

At this time, it must be remembered, the many women's suffrage groups actively crusading to gain the franchise for women were focusing considerable attention upon women's rights. Also active in the 1890's and early twentieth century were temperance groups, most of them dominated by women, who were calling for a constitutional amendment that would prohibit the sale of alcoholic beverages in the United States. Members of these groups, most notably members of the Anti-Saloon League, founded in 1893, were active in calling for strict enforcement of anti-prostitution statutes.

Responding to public sentiment and, assuredly, with an eye toward furthering his own political ambitions, James Robert Mann, U.S. Representative from Illinois, introduced legislation in 1910 that would ban the interstate transportation of women for immoral purposes. This legislation, which Congress passed on June 25, initially imposed a fine of up to five thousand dollars and a prison term of up to five years, or both, upon those who violated this law. These penalties were doubled if the victims were minors.

R. Baird Shuman

Further Reading

Chapkis, Wendy. *Live Sex Acts: Women Performing Erotic Labor*. New York: Routledge, 1997.

Critcher, Chas, and David Waddington. *Policing Public Order: Theoretical and Practical Issues*. Vermont: Ashgate, 1996.

Meier, Robert, and Gilbert Geis. *Victimless Crime? Prostitution, Drugs, Homosexuality, and Abortion*. Los Angeles: Roxbury, 1997.

See also Adultery; Commercialized vice; Comstock Law; Equal protection under the law; Federal Bureau of Investigation; Pandering; Victimless crimes.

Manslaughter

Definition: Unpremeditated killing of another human being

Criminal justice issue: Homicide

Significance: While manslaughter is considered a felony and a very serious offense involving the unlawful killing of a human being, it is a lesser included offense of murder and is thus punished less severely.

One of the most publicized manslaughter cases of the early twenty-first century was that of former professional basketball star Jayson Williams (seated), who was charged with aggravated manslaughter in the shooting death of his chauffeur in February, 2002. Williams apparently killed the chauffeur with a single shotgun blast in his own home while he was under the influence of alcohol. The central issue in his case was not whether the shooting was accidental but whether it constituted aggravated manslaughter—a criminal offense—or merely negligent manslaughter—a much lesser offense. Williams was also charged with other related offenses, including attempting to cover up the killing by trying to make it look like suicide. In April, 2004, a jury acquitted him on the aggravated manslaughter charge, but because of its mixed verdicts on the other charges, the judge later ordered that Williams be retried for reckless manslaughter. *(AP/Wide World Photos)*

Manslaughter generally is the unplanned or sudden killing of a person. In the United States, persons who commit manslaughter cannot be punished by death. Manslaughter is distinguishable from the more serious offenses of first and second-degree murder by the reduced degree of intent with which the killing is done. Manslaughter is a killing done suddenly, without planning or "premeditation," which is the hallmark of first-degree murder. It is often committed in a highly emotional state without calm or cool reflection, described in the law as "heat of passion." Although a person who commits manslaughter does not plan or premeditate the offense and does not coolly or calmly reflect or deliberate upon it, manslaughter is not an accidental killing. Thus, it is unlawful.

There are two types of manslaughter: voluntary and involuntary. Some states call these manslaughter in the first degree and manslaughter in the second degree. Voluntary (or first-degree) manslaughter is the more serious of the two offenses. Voluntary manslaughter is a homicide that occurs through impassioned actions, such as anger, jealousy, or fear. When these emotions are sufficiently heightened, a person is said to be unable to deliberate or reflect upon the act of killing. A voluntary manslaughter committed in a calm and thoughtful frame of mind would be a murder.

Involuntary manslaughter is a homicide that occurs through very reckless or dangerous actions, which may even be minor crimes such as careless driving. In some U.S. states involuntary manslaughter is called "negligent homicide." Involuntary manslaughter requires only a serious lack of care concerning a dangerous or possibly dangerous situation that causes a death. A typical example of involuntary manslaughter is an unintended death that occurs because someone committed a very risky or dangerous act, such as drag racing on a public street or leaving a vicious dog inadequately fenced in. Some states have defined a special type of manslaughter involving the reckless use of a motor vehicle that causes death. This offense is variously called "vehicular manslaughter," "vehicular homicide," or simply manslaughter. Penalties for manslaughter in the United States vary between states but generally can range from probation or short periods in jail for involuntary manslaughter to long terms of imprisonment of more than ten years for voluntary manslaughter.

David M. Siegel

Further Reading

Daly, Martin, and Margo Wilson. *Homicide*. New York: Aldine de Gruyter, 1988.

Geberth, Vernon J. *Practical Homicide Investigation*. 2d ed. New York: Elsevier, 1990.

Harries, Keith D. *Serious Violence: Patterns of Homicide and Assault in America*. 2d ed. Springfield, Ill.: Charles C Thomas, 1997.

See also Branch Davidian raid; Crimes of passion; Criminal intent; Hit-and-run accidents; Murder and homicide; Murders, mass and serial; Self-defense.

Mapp v. Ohio

The Case: U.S. Supreme Court ruling on illegally gathered evidence

Date: Decided on June 19, 1961

Criminal justice issues: Constitutional protections; evidence and forensics; privacy

Significance: This Supreme Court decision ruled that illegally obtained evidence must be excluded from criminal trials in state courts, a rule that previously had been applied to federal trials in 1914.

In 1957, Cleveland police officers went to the home of Dollree Mapp, acting on information that a suspect in a recent bombing and related paraphernalia were located in her home. After Mapp refused to admit them, the officers forcibly entered, conducted a widespread search of the house, and discovered some illegal pornography. Mapp was arrested and convicted of violating Ohio's antiobscenity statute. Unable to demonstrate that the officers had possessed a valid search warrant, the state of Ohio argued that even if the search had been illegal, precedents of the U.S. Supreme Court did not forbid the admission of the resulting evidence in a state trial.

For many years the Supreme Court had been debating the issue of the so-called exclusionary rule. Earlier in the century, in *Weeks v. United States* (1914), the Court had required that illegally obtained evidence be excluded from federal prosecutions. Thirty-five years later, in *Wolf v. Colorado* (1949), the Supreme Court applied the Fourth Amendment right of privacy to the states through the due process clause of the Fourteenth Amendment, but the Court decided against imposing the exclusionary rule as an essential element of that right. By 1961, nevertheless, about half the states had adopted the *Weeks* rule.

In *Mapp v. Ohio*, the Court ruled 5-3 to make the exclusionary rule binding on the states. In the majority opinion, Justice Tom Clark declared that the rule was "an essential part" of the constitutional rights of individuals, but he also pointed to the rule's deterrence as a justification for the decision. Experience demonstrated, he wrote, that other remedies were "worthless and futile" in preventing officials from disobeying the prohibition against unreasonable searches and seizures.

Three members of the Court were opposed to overruling the *Wolf* precedent. They objected that the briefs and oral arguments of the case had dealt more with the obscenity issue than with the exclusionary rule, but even more, they insisted that the principle of federalism should allow states to have flexibility in devising alternative remedies to deter unreasonable searches and seizures. Justice Potter Stewart wanted to decide the case on the basis of the First Amendment and refused to join with either the majority or the minority.

The *Mapp* decision, a landmark of the Warren court years, has been one of the most controversial opinions ever rendered by the Supreme Court. Since most criminal prosecutions take place in state courts, the decision's impact was much greater than that of *Weeks*. Many state officials resented *Mapp* as an intrusion into the traditional prerogatives of the states, and members of the public had difficulty understanding why there were not other means to enforce the right to privacy implicit in the Fourth Amendment. In later cases such as *Massachusetts v. Sheppard* (1984), the majority of justices of the Court have accepted the deterrent rationale for the exclusionary rule, and this has resulted in flexibility in its application.

Thomas Tandy Lewis

Further Reading

LaFave, W. R. *Search and Seizure: A Treatise on the Fourth Amendment*. 3d ed. St. Paul, Minn.: West Publishing, 1995.

Lynch, Timothy. "In Defense of the Exclusionary Rule." *Harvard Journal of Law and Public Policy* 23 (2000).

McWhirter, Darien A. *Search, Seizure, and Privacy*. Phoenix, Ariz.: Oryx Press, 1994.

Wetterer, Charles M. *The Fourth Amendment: Search and Seizure*. Springfield, N.J.: Enslow, 1998.

See also Bill of Rights, U.S.; *Escobedo v. Illinois*; Exclusionary rule; Incorporation doctrine; *Knowles v. Iowa*; *Leon, United States v.*; Perjury; Search and seizure; Search warrants; Supreme Court, U.S.

Marshals Service, U.S.

Identification: Oldest federal law-enforcement agency

Date: Created by the First Judiciary Act, September 24, 1789

Criminal justice issues: Federal law; law-enforcement organization

Significance: The Marshals Service has played a major role in the creation of law and order in the United States.

With the First Judiciary Act in 1789, Congress created the federal court system. As with most court systems, the enforcement arm associated with it provides security, serves court processes and generally enforces the orders issued by the court. To provide those services the First Judiciary Act also created the position of the United States marshal.

President George Washington appointed the first thirteen marshals within two days of the enactment of the act creating the position. By 1791, Washington had appointed the first sixteen marshals for the first sixteen federal judicial districts. The marshals played major roles in the growth and development of the United States. Their early duties included enforcing the Fugitive Slave Act, taking data for the national census, and helping create law and order in the American West.

Settling the West

The Marshals Service has a history of being a law-enforcement agency made up of generalists. This agency had the most broad law-enforcement powers and was used by the federal government and the courts to fill gaps that existed in the American federal judicial system. Prior to the Civil War and the creation of the Secret Service, marshals and their deputies were called upon to enforce laws against counterfeiting.

After the Civil War, famous Western lawmen served as deputy U.S. marshals. Among the most famous deputies were Bat Masterson and Wyatt Earp. The post-Civil War Oklahoma Territory was one of the deadliest places for deputy U.S. marshals to be assigned. It was in Oklahoma Territory that almost half of two hundred marshals and deputies were killed in the line of duty.

Beginnings of Modern Federal Law Enforcement

As the American justice system evolved, lawmakers created specialized federal law-enforcement agencies. By the mid-1920's, the Federal Bureau of Investigation (FBI), under the direction of J. Edgar Hoover, became what would be considered the premier federal law-enforcement agency. With the ascendancy of power and prestige for the FBI, and the quieting of the Wild West, the role of the United States marshal came to be reduced to one of bailiff for the federal courts. Marshals and their deputies called federal courts to order, maintained the peace in the courtroom, protected the judge, executed federal court orders, and transported federal prisoners.

After the passage of desegregation orders by the federal courts in the 1960's, U.S. marshals were called upon by then-attorney general of the United States, Robert Kennedy, to enforce the orders. With the passage of the Racketeer Influenced and Corrupt Organizations Act of 1970,

---

U.S. Marshals in the Movies

The 1993 film *The Fugitive*, directed by Andrew Davis, is about a distinguished surgeon (Harrison Ford) who is wrongly convicted of killing his wife. After escaping from incarceration, the surgeon attempts to find his wife's true killer. Meanwhile, a relentless U.S. marshal (Tommy Lee Jones) leads a team that tries to track him down. The marshall eventually comes to believe that his quarry is innocent, but that fact does not deter him from doing his duty.

Based on a long-running television series of the same title, *The Fugitive* highlights one of the roles played by a little-known branch of law enforcement: the U.S. Marshals Service. As the film reveals, marshals have responsibility for apprehending fugitives, as well as protecting witnesses and judges involved in federal cases. Other films about the U.S. Marshals include *U.S. Marshals* (1998), a sequel to *The Fugitive*, and *Out of Sight* (1998), in which Jennifer Lopez plays a marshal named Karen Sisco. The latter film also inspired the short-lived television series *Karen Sisco*.

Timothy L. Hall

---

there arose a need to protect witnesses who testified against organized crime figures. By 1971, witness security became a duty for the U.S. marshals.

In 1973, U.S. marshals were sent to Wounded Knee, South Dakota, to help quell violence on the Indian reservation there. During the 1970's, the marshals fulfilled a need for airport security created by a rash of skyjackings of commercial airliners. The marshals began profiling potential skyjackers and conducting weapons screening at airports. Eventually, the federal government created a permanent response to the threat of skyjacking by creating the "sky marshal" program within the Federal Aviation Administration. Although these agents are called "marshals," they are not associated with or part of the United States Marshals Service.

By the late 1970's, the marshals again began to establish themselves as the agency to track down and arrest fugitives. In 1984, the passage of the Comprehensive Crime Control Act permitted law-enforcement agencies at the federal, state, and municipal levels to use federal law to seize assets used in or gained through the trafficking in drugs. The U.S. marshals became the federal agency to seize, manage, and dispose of these assets according to the laws and the orders of the courts.

During the 1990's, the Marshals Service became the first federal law-enforcement agency to be accredited by the Commission on Accreditation for Law Enforcement Agencies (CALEA).

Twenty-first Century Roles

Among the duties of the modern United States Marshals Service are providing for the physical security of courtrooms, courthouses, and their occupants. Included in this charge is the personal protection of judges and prosecutors who may have been threatened in the course of their jobs. Marshals serve court orders, including restraining orders, writs of *habeas corpus*, summonses, subpoenas, warrants, and warrants in rem and writs of attachment for the court-ordered seizure of property. Marshals escort federal prisoners to and from court and also assist state and municipal agencies with international extradition and are involved in international prisoner exchanges.

U.S. marshals investigate fugitive cases for federal agencies without arrest authority—and for some agencies with arrest authority. The marshals have memoranda of understanding with both the U.S. Customs Service and the Drug Enforcement Administration to locate and arrest fugitives under their jurisdictions.

The Marshals Service helps the Department of State guard and protect foreign dignitaries while the General Assembly of the United Nations is in session in New York. Deputy marshals have been U.S. delegates to Interpol, the international police organization headquartered in France. It is through Interpol that the United States can share information on fugitives with other countries.

In 2004, U.S. marshals were appointed by and served at the pleasure of the president, and there were ninety-four United States marshals. Each federal judicial district has a marshal. The position of deputy U.S. marshal is a civil-service position which involves a competitive hiring process. In order to be deputized, individuals must compete for openings by taking a written test, undergoing an interview, and passing stringent physical exams as well as background investigations. The deputy select must then pass a rigorous training program at the Federal Law Enforcement Training Center in Brunswick, Georgia.

Gerald P. Fisher

Further Reading

Calhoun, Frederick S. *Hunters and Howlers: Threats and Violence Against Federal Judicial Officials in the United States, 1789-1993*. Arlington, Va.: U.S. Department of Justice, 1998. History of the U.S. Marshals Service by an agency historian.

Sabbag, Robert. *Too Tough to Die: Down and Dangerous with the U.S. Marshals*. New York: Simon & Schuster, 1992. Examination of the modern marshals that follows the exploits of some of the more colorful deputies.

Stroud, Carsten. *Deadly Force: In the Streets with the U.S. Marshals*. New York: Bantam Books, 1996. Exploits of modern federal fugitive hunters.

See also Attorney general of the United States; Bailiffs; Bench warrants; Justice Department, U.S.; Law enforcement; Parole; Prison escapes; Probation, adult; Ruby Ridge raid; September 11, 2001, attacks; Skyjacking; United States Parole Commission; Witness protection programs.

Martial law

Definition: Use of armed forces or National Guard units to help maintain public order during emergencies

Criminal justice issues: Jurisdictions; military justice; morality and public order

Significance: Martial law is a special condition during a state of emergency, not a body of laws and regulations as in civil law and military law, and the military's authority under martial law is never absolute.

Martial law is the temporary use of military personnel to enforce laws and judicial decisions domestically. In the United States the term usually refers to the declaration of martial law by the president of the United States, who may employ the federal armed forces, or by state governors, who may mobilize the National Guard of their respective states.

Whereas the constitutions of most states authorize the governors or legislatures to proclaim martial law and dispatch the National Guard to control insurrections, the U.S. Constitution is not so straightforward about the president's powers. Article IV, section 4, enables the federal government to help a state suppress domestic violence upon the request of the legislature or governor. Article I, section 8, empowers the U.S. Congress "To provide for calling forth the Militia to execute the Laws of the Union, suppress Insurrections and repel Invasions." Since the Constitution requires that the president ensure the faithful execution of the nation's laws (Article II, section 3) and makes him commander-in-chief of federal forces, he is considered to have the power to declare martial law, although Congress must approve the suspension of writs of *habeas corpus* (applications to a court to consider whether a person in custody is being held lawfully). Precedent suggests that only war or national emergency justifies the use of martial law, but neither the U.S. Constitution nor statutory law specifies such limits.

Throughout U.S. history, only two presidents have declared martial law. During the Civil War, Abraham Lincoln proclaimed martial law over Washington, D.C., and over areas of the Confederacy that were occupied by federal troops. He also suspended the privilege of writs of *habeas corpus*. Governor Joseph Poindexter instituted martial law for Hawaii on December 7, 1941, a move subsequently seconded by President Franklin D. Roosevelt. Roosevelt also authorized military commanders to exert direct authority over some areas of the United States; designated portions of the Western states were used to incarcerate Americans of Japanese descent. Other federal officials have occasionally declared limited martial law to quell or prevent riots. In some instances a president, without formally declaring martial law to enforce federal laws, has sent troops to a state, even over a governor's objection.

U.S. Supreme Court decisions have limited the power of the military during martial law. During the Civil War the Court ruled that trials of civilians by federal military tribunals were invalid when civilian courts were open. Only when civil administration completely breaks down may military tribunals try civilians (*Ex parte Milligan*, 1866). In 1946 the Supreme Court decided that the military did not have jurisdiction over civilian employees of a military installation (*Duncan*

v. Kahanamoku). However, the Court earlier appeared to approve some trials of civilians in state military courts by rejecting a suit for wrongful imprisonment resulting from one such trial (*Moyer v. Peabody*, 1909). The Court has also reserved the power to decide whether a governor's use of military forces is justified (*Sterling v. Constantin*, 1932).

Roger Smith

Further Reading

Schug, Willis E., ed. *United States Law and the Armed Forces: Cases and Materials on Constitutional Law, Courts-Martial, and the Rights of Servicemen*. New York: Praeger, 1972.
Whiting, William. *War Powers Under the Constitution of the United States*. 10th ed. Union, N.J.: Lawbook Exchange, 2002.

See also Courts-martial; *Habeas corpus*; Military justice; National Guard.

Maryland v. Buie

The Case: U.S. Supreme Court ruling on warrantless searches
Date: Decided on February 28, 1990
Criminal justice issues: Police powers; search and seizure
Significance: The Supreme Court's ruling in *Maryland v. Buie* expanded the power of police officers to conduct warrantless sweeps of premises while making in-house arrests, thereby increasing their opportunities to seize evidence found in plain view.

The Supreme Court's finding in *Maryland v. Buie* established two separate rules. First, following an in-house arrest, police may—without a search warrant—conduct a protective sweep of the entire premises if there is reasonable suspicion to believe that dangerous third parties are present. In addition to authorizing protective sweeps, the ruling also established that absent a search warrant or any suspicion, incident to an arrest, the police may automatically look into other spaces, including closets or rooms, in which a dangerous third person might be found, provided that such areas immediately adjoin the place of arrest. Under either rule, evidence found in plain view may be seized.

The *Maryland v. Buie* case originated in 1986. Following an armed robbery in Maryland by two men, one of whom was wearing a red running suit, police obtained arrest warrants for Buie and his suspected accomplice, Allen. Police in Prince George's County executed the warrant at Buie's house and arrested Buie when he emerged from his basement. After the arrest, the police performed a cursory check of Buie's basement for the purpose of locating dangerous persons and found a red running suit lying in plain view. A police officer seized the suit, which was later admitted as evidence at Buie's trial for armed robbery. Buie was convicted.

After Buie's conviction, Maryland's Court of Appeals reversed the lower trial court and appellate court decisions because those courts had accepted the running suit as evidence. The high court disallowed the suit because the police who had conducted the sweep that found it lacked probable cause to believe that a dangerous third party might be present in Buie's home.

Because a protective sweep is a search, it falls under the limitations of the Fourth Amendment, which requires that searches be reasonable. Under most circumstances, the U.S. Supreme Court has found that for searches to be considered reasonable, they require warrants and probable cause. However, the Court has dispensed with those two requirements in cases in which there has been risk of immediate physical danger to police officers performing their official duties. For example, the Court has held that in the interest of safety, "stop and frisk" searches on the street and roadside searches of automobile passenger compartments—equivalent to "frisking" a vehicle—are permissible under the Fourth Amendment.

In *Buie*, the Supreme Court drew on its earlier findings in *Terry v. Ohio* (1968) and *Michigan v. Long* (1983) to find analogous risks of immediate physical danger to police officers while making in-house arrests. Those risks justify protective sweeps with search warrants or probable cause. However, the fact that the Court's ruling permits officers to look in adjoining spaces allows police making in-house arrests *always* to presume that

dangerous third parties may be present. That aspect of the Court's ruling thus made it easier for police to collect evidence found in plain view.

LaVerne McQuiller Williams

Further Reading

Katz, Lewis R. *Questions and Answers: Criminal Procedure I and II*. Newark, N.J.: LexisNexis, 2003.

Loewy, Arnold H. *Criminal Procedure: Cases, Materials and Questions*. Cincinnati: Anderson Publishing, 2002.

See also Plain view doctrine; Probable cause; Reasonable suspicion; Search and seizure; Search warrants; Supreme Court, U.S.; *Terry v. Ohio*.

Maryland v. Craig

The Case: U.S. Supreme Court ruling on witnesses

Date: Decided on June 27, 1990

Criminal justice issues: Constitutional protections; witnesses

Significance: In this decision, which upheld a Maryland statute permitting a child to testify via one-way, closed-circuit television, the Supreme Court determined that the witness-confrontation rights of defendants guaranteed by the Sixth Amendment are neither absolute nor an indispensable part of criminal hearings.

In 1986, Sandra Ann Craig, an operator of a Maryland child-care center and kindergarten, was indicted for sexually abusing a six-year-old child in her care and was subsequently convicted. Under a state statute, the victim and other children were allowed to testify on a closed-circuit television without directly confronting the defendant. On the grounds that the law violated a defendant's right to face an accuser, guaranteed by the Sixth Amendment, Craig appealed the conviction. Although the Maryland Court of Special Appeals upheld the conviction, the next higher court, the Court of Appeals of Maryland, ordered a new trial, finding that the state prosecutors had not sufficiently justified their use of the closed-circuit television procedure. It also questioned the statute's constitutionality but did not determine it per se.

On *certiorari*, the U.S. Supreme Court vacated the lower court's order and remanded, holding that the confrontation clause of the Sixth Amendment did not invalidate the Maryland statute's procedure. Justice Sandra Day O'Connor, writing the 5-4 majority opinion, argued that under "narrow circumstances," when there are "competing interests," dispensing with witness-confrontation rights is warranted. Further, the Court stated that the term "confront" as used in the Sixth Amendment cannot be defined simply as "face-to-face." A state's concern for the psychological and physical well-being of a child-abuse victim, as reflected in the Maryland statute, was deemed important enough to supersede a defendant's right to face an accuser. The majority also argued that in previous cases other Sixth Amendment rights had been interpreted "in the context of the necessities of trial and the adversary process."

A vigorous dissenting opinion, presented by Justice Antonin Scalia, argued that "confront" as used in the Sixth Amendment clearly means "face-to-face," whatever else it may also mean. The majority was also chided for distorting explicit constitutional text to suit "currently favored public policy." Although granting that the procedure authorized by the Maryland statute may be fair, the dissenters maintained that it violated the constitutional protection afforded defendants in the confrontation clause of the Sixth Amendment.

A controversial case, *Maryland v. Craig* left in its wake the likelihood of additional problems of interpretation precisely because it held a constitutional guarantee to be less than absolute and incontrovertible. Determining which "narrow circumstances" will validate a suspension of a defendant's right to a face-to-face confrontation with an accuser will be an ongoing issue in jurisprudence, because it must be decided virtually on a case-by-case basis.

John W. Fiero

Further Reading

Best, J. *Threatened Children: Rhetoric and Concern About Child-Victims*. Chicago: University of Chicago Press, 1993.

Russell, Diana E. H. *Sexual Exploitation: Rape, Child Sexual Abuse, and Workplace Harassment*. Beverly Hills, Calif.: Sage, 1989.

Technical Working Group for Eyewitness Evidence. *Eyewitness Evidence: A Guide for Law Enforcement*. Washington, D.C.: U.S. Department of Justice, Office of Justice Programs, National Institute of Justice, 1999.

See also Bill of Rights, U.S.; Cross-examination; Due process of law; Juvenile justice system; Supreme Court, U.S.

Massachusetts v. Sheppard

The Case: U.S. Supreme Court ruling on searches

Date: Decided on July 5, 1984

Criminal justice issues: Police powers; search and seizure

Significance: The Court ruled that, the Fourth Amendment notwithstanding, a search authorized by a defective warrant was proper because the police had acted in good faith in executing what they thought was a valid warrant.

Osborne Sheppard was convicted in a Massachusetts state court of first-degree murder. Sheppard appealed his conviction to the Massachusetts Supreme Judicial Court on the basis that the police had knowingly searched his residence with a defective search warrant.

Boston police detective Peter O'Malley had drafted an affidavit to support an application for an arrest warrant and a search warrant authorizing the search of Sheppard's residence. The affidavit stated that the police wanted to search for such items as the victim's clothing and a blunt instrument that might have been used on the victim. The affidavit was reviewed and approved by the district attorney.

Unable to find a proper warrant application form, O'Malley found a previously used warrant form used in another district to search for controlled substances. After O'Malley made some changes on the form, it and the affidavit were presented to a judge at his residence. The judge was made aware of the defective warrant form, and he made further changes before he signed it. He did not change the substantive portion, however, which continued to authorize a search for controlled substances, nor did the judge alter the form to incorporate the affidavit.

The police believed that the warrant authorized the search, and they proceeded to act in good faith. The trial judge ruled that the exclusionary rule did not apply in this case because the conduct of the officers was objectively reasonable and largely error free. On appeal, Sheppard argued that the evidence obtained pursuant to the defective warrant should have been suppressed. The Supreme Judicial Court of Massachusetts agreed and reversed the lower court's conviction of Sheppard. The court held that it did not recognize a good-faith exception to the exclusionary rule.

Massachusetts filed a petition for writ of *certiorari*. Speaking for the U.S. Supreme Court, Justice Byron R. White stated that the police officers who conducted the search should not be punished. They acted in good faith in executing what they reasonably thought was a valid warrant— one that was subsequently determined invalid— issued by a detached and neutral magistrate (*United States v. Leon*, 1984). The exclusionary rule, White said, did not apply because it was adopted to deter unlawful searches by police, not to punish the errors of judges. He stated that an error of constitutional dimension may have been committed by the judge who did not make the necessary changes, but not the police. Judgment of the Supreme Judicial Court was therefore reversed and remanded for further proceedings consistent with the U.S. Supreme Court's opinion.

Bill Manikas

Further Reading

Bloom, Robert M. *Searches, Seizures, and Warrants*. Westport, Conn.: Praeger, 2003.

LaFave, W. R. *Search and Seizure: A Treatise on the Fourth Amendment*. 3d ed. St. Paul, Minn.: West Publishing, 1995.

McWhirter, Darien A. *Search, Seizure, and Privacy*. Phoenix, Ariz.: Oryx Press, 1994.

Wetterer, Charles M. *The Fourth Amendment: Search and Seizure*. Springfield, N.J.: Enslow, 1998.

See also Evidence, rules of; Exclusionary rule; Search and seizure; Supreme Court, U.S.

Massiah v. United States

The Case: U.S. Supreme Court ruling on the right to counsel

Date: Decided on May 18, 1964

Criminal justice issues: Attorneys; confessions; defendants; interrogation

Significance: This case expanded the exclusionary rule to disallow the prosecution from using any evidence that the police have deliberately elicited from an indicted defendant when not in the presence of a lawyer.

A federal grand jury indicted Winston Massiah and a codefendant on charges of illegally trafficking in cocaine. Massiah retained a lawyer and was released on bail. Unknown to Massiah, his codefendant agreed to cooperate with federal officers in exchange for a reduced sentence. In a private conversation with the codefendant, Massiah made incriminating statements that were overheard by an agent operating a transmitter.

At the subsequent trial, the judge allowed the agent to testify about Massiah's statements, which were tantamount to a confession. Based on this evidence, the jury quickly decided that Massiah was guilty. In appealing the conviction, defense lawyers pointed to the precedent of *Spano v. New York* (1959), in which the Supreme Court had held that the prosecution may not make use of a confession that police officers obtained by intimidating a defendant who had already been indicted. In getting Massiah to confess, however, the police had used only trickery, not threats or other forms of coercion.

The Supreme Court, by a 6-3 vote, overturned Massiah's conviction. Writing for the majority, Justice Potter Stewart held that once adversarial proceedings have been initiated, any statements deliberately elicited by government agents outside the presence of a defense lawyer must be excluded from a criminal trial, except if the defendant had explicitly waived his Sixth Amendment right to counsel. The justices in the majority made a linkage between this right and the Fifth Amendment privilege against self-incrimination, which they interpreted to mean that confessions not given voluntarily and intentionally are inadmissible as evidence. In this case, therefore, it was irrelevant that the police had not forcefully compelled Messiah to made incriminating statements to his colleague.

The *Massiah* holding applied only to statements obtained by law-enforcement officers after a person has been formally charged with a crime. Later that year, in *Escobedo v. Illinois*, the Court recognized that a suspect yet to be indicted has a right to counsel when in custody for the purpose of interrogation. The famous case of *Miranda v. Arizona* (1966) obligated the police to inform suspects of this right before interrogation. The Court further expanded the prohibition against using trickery to elicit information from detained suspects outside the presence of counsel in *Brewer v. Williams* (1977). In *Henry v. United States* (1980), the Court suppressed a conversation in which an incarcerated defendant made incriminating statements to a cellmate cooperating with the police, even though the cellmate had simply listened and had not encouraged the defendant to discuss the crime.

Thomas Tandy Lewis

Further Reading

Taylor, John B. *Right to Counsel and Privilege Against Self-Incrimination: Rights and Liberties Under the Law*. Santa Barbara, Calif.: ABC-Clio, 2004.

Whitebread, Charles, and Christopher Slobogin. *Criminal Procedures: An Analysis of Cases and Concepts*. 4th ed. New York: Foundation Press, 2000.

See also Confessions; Counsel, right to; Electronic surveillance; *Escobedo v. Illinois*; Exclusionary rule; Fifth Amendment; Police ethics; Supreme Court, U.S.

Medical examiners

Definition: Officers of state and local governments who investigate and certify homicides, suicides, accidental deaths, sudden deaths, and deaths with unknown causes

Criminal justice issues: Evidence and forensics; investigation; medical and health issues

Significance: Medical examiners are responsible for leading the investigations of all deaths that are sudden, unexpected, or violent, and they make determinations about the times, manners, and causes of the deaths.

The first government medical examiner was appointed in Boston in the late 1870's. Prior to that time, elected coroners handled death investigations. The coroner system has its roots in England, and dates back a millennium. However, because coroners were traditionally not required to have any medical training, dissatisfaction with the system arose, and medical examiner positions were created to provide an alternative. By the early twenty-first century, about one-half of the residents of the United States were living in jurisdictions with medical examiners. The jurisdictions still employing the coroner system were generally smaller and were predominantly rural areas in which sudden, unexpected, and violent deaths were uncommon. When deaths in those communities require autopsy services, medical examiners from nearby jurisdictions are often utilized.

Functions of Medical Examiners

Upon notification of a person's death, the medical examiner begins gathering facts relating to the deceased that help in making a determination as to time, manner, and cause of death. The initial call tells the medical examiner where and when the body was found and if there is any evidence of foul play. The body should not be moved until it has either been examined by a medical examiner, or a medical examiner has given permission to move the body.

Because the actual facts surrounding deaths may differ significantly from what they seem to

The Training of Medical Examiners

The only general requirement for becoming a medical examiner is graduation from an accredited medical school. However, many medical examiners also complete specialized training in pathology, the field of medicine that studies disease mechanisms and death, and forensic pathology, the study of how and why people die—which concentrates on sudden, unexpected, and violent deaths. Most medical examiners also have knowledge in other forensic areas, such as ballistics, serology, and DNA analysis. Medical examiners must continually update their training by attending professional conferences and taking specialized course work.

be at first glance, medical examiners gather as much information as they can from different sources before making their determinations. The decedents' medical records are considered, and their bodies are examined externally.

Time of death is usually not in question. However, when a body is found of a person whose death has not been witnessed, determining the time of death becomes important, regardless of the cause of death. Time of death is established first by looking at the interval between the time when a person was last seen alive and the time when the person's dead body was found. The larger this interval, the more difficult it is to pinpoint the time of death.

Medical examiners take into account many factors when determining time of death, including the air temperature surrounding a dead body, where a body is found (indoors, outdoors, in water), and if a body has already stiffened in rigor mortis, or if that stage has already passed. If a body is discovered more than a day after death, decomposition may already be apparent, or insects may have begun colonizing it. By analyzing such evidence, the medical examiner can use the physical condition of the body to estimate when death has occurred.

Manner of death is the way in which a person dies: through natural causes, such as disease; through accidents; by suicide; or by homicide. Everyone dies eventually, and many people— especially older people—die of natural causes

every day. However, medical examiners should not assume that merely because an individual dies while under a doctor's care or while in a hospital that the death results from natural causes. Similarly, medical examiners should not assume that merely because a death appears to be from an accident that the cause of death is accidental. Indeed, many apparent automobile accidents that involve only one vehicle are, in fact, suicides. Homicides also often appear to be accidents or suicides.

Medical examiners determine both the immediate and proximal causes of death. The immediate cause is the last event prior to a death, such as an acute myocardial infarction (heart attack), which may happen hours or days before death. The proximal cause is the first event leading up to a death, for example coronary vascular disease, which may have been evident in the decedent several years prior to death.

In homicide investigations, the victims' bodies are usually the single most important pieces of evidence that are processed. Moreover, the areas immediately surrounding the dead bodies generally contain most of the forensic evidence that is found in homicide cases.

Medical examiners also determine whether decedents have died at the scenes where they are found, or if their deaths have occurred elsewhere and their bodies have been moved. Livor mortis, the settling of blood in bodies after death and the accompanying purplish coloring (which resembles bruising), often indicates whether bodies have been moved.

Medical examiners may conduct autopsies, which include thorough interior physical examinations of the bodies and specialized laboratory tests, or forensic pathologists may do so. Medical examiners may also be called upon to testify in civil and criminal courtrooms regarding the findings from their completed investigation.

Ayn Embar-Seddon
Allan D. Pass

Further Reading

Baden, Michael M. *Unnatural Death: Confessions of a Medical Examiner*. New York: Random House, 1989. Discussions of cases handled by a veteran medical examiner who has worked in many high-profile cases.

Baden, Michael, M., and Marion Roach. *Dead Reckoning: The New Science of Catching Killers*. New York: Simon & Schuster, 2001. Detailed study of the use forensic autopsies in crime solving.

Bell, Suzanne. *Encyclopedia of Forensic Science*. New York: Facts On File, 2004. Comprehensive reference book on a wide variety of forensic science topics, including medical examiners.

Sachs, Jessica Snyder. *Corpse: Nature, Forensics, and the Struggle to Pinpoint Time of Death*. New York: Perseus Publishing, 2002. Detailed examination of the work that medical examiners perform, with special attention to recent technological advances in fields such as forensic entomology, forensic odontology, and forensic palynology.

See also Autopsies; Cold cases; Coroners; Crime scene investigation; Forensics; Toxicology; Trace evidence.

Mens rea

Definition: State of mind, or intent, behind criminal actions

Criminal justice issues: Defendants; legal terms and principles; prosecution

Significance: The concept of *mens rea* is central to the notion that people are legally responsible for committing crimes only when there is personal culpability for their acts. In other words, they have guilty minds.

The old Latin legal maxim, "*actus non est reus nisi mens sit rea*," literally means that an act is not bad unless the mind is bad. The maxim summarizes a real legal principle: the requirement that committing a crime consists of more than an overt act (*actus reus*); it must also include some type of fault that makes the perpetrator deserving of blame. A court once called this concept the most basic principle of criminal law.

Common-law definitions of crimes allude to such mental elements behind the crimes as "with malice aforethought" for homicide and "wilfully and corruptly" for perjury. The Model Penal

---

Mens Rea and the Crown Jewels

The 1967 British film *The Jokers*, is a big-heist story played mostly for laughs. However, its premise rests firmly on the serious legal principle of *mens rea*. Oliver Reed and Michael Crawford play brothers who enjoy pulling off clever stunts and set themselves the greatest challenge of all: stealing Britain's Crown Jewels from the Tower of London. In contrast to most thieves, they do not expect to get away with their loot. Indeed, even if they are not caught, they plan to return the jewels, taking their satisfaction in doing the impossible.

The brothers also expect to reap rewards from the publicity that a successful caper will generate. That raises the question of how they expect to stay out of prison if they succeed. The key to their scheme is their motive: By placing sealed confessions with lawyers, with instructions for their opening after the date of the planned heist, the brothers seek to establish in advance that they have no intention of permanently depriving the queen of her jewels; they wish merely to call public attention to the inadequacy of the security protecting the jewels. Under the principle of *mens rea*, therefore, they cannot be guilty of the crime. How their story actually unfolds, however, is another matter.

Code, issued by the American Law Institute in 1962, sought to simplify the classification of elements of crimes by reducing them to four categories, using the terms "intentionally or purposely," "knowingly," "recklessly," and "negligently." The appropriate mental state of a defendant depends on the type of crime with which the person is charged. For some crimes, "crimes of specific intent," there is a special *mens rea* element required. For example, burglary consists of breaking and entering the residence of another with the *intent* to commit a felony in the dwelling.

Critics of the *mens rea* doctrine have attacked its seeming reliance on proving what is in another person's mind. In reply to this point, it is noted that in practice the prosecution usually does not need to establish that a special mental state was present at the moment of the crime, but only that the defendant acted a particular way in some situation. From this, the *mens rea* element can be inferred. Some offenses have been added to criminal codes that serve as exceptions to the *mens rea* requirement, such as felony murder and so-called "strict liability" offenses. The latter include speeding and statutory rape.

Mario F. Morelli

Further Reading

Katz, Leo. *Bad Acts and Guilty Minds*. Chicago: University of Chicago Press, 1987.
Moore, Michael. *Act and Crime*. Oxford, England: Oxford University Press, 1993.

See also Criminal intent; Criminal law; Criminal liability; Criminals; Defenses to crime; Diminished capacity; Inchoate crimes; Insanity defense; Malice; Model Penal Code; Motives; Murder and homicide; Rape and sex offenses; Solicitation to commit a crime; Strict liability offenses; Vicarious liability.

Mental illness

Definition: Illness, disease, or condition that substantially impairs sufferers' thought processes, perceptions of reality, and sense of judgment, while grossly impairing their behavior and emotional well-being
Criminal justice issues: Medical and health issues; mental disorders
Significance: The importance of mental health issues in criminal justice can be measured, in part, by the fact that a significant portion of jail and prison inmates suffer from some type of mental illness.

Mental disorders are common. There are a variety of mental illnesses, and their severity ranges from mild to life-threatening. Many of these disorders are disabling and can profoundly affect the way a person thinks, behaves, and relates to other people. It has been estimated that one in five Americans suffers from one or more types of mental disorder during any given year. Most such afflictions are minor. However, the incidence of more serious mental health disorders among criminal offenders is much higher than that of the general population. About 16-20 per-

cent of jail and prison inmates suffer from such serious forms of mental illness such as schizophrenia, bipolar disorder, and major depression.

Affective disorders, also known as mood disorders, are mental disorders characterized by disturbance of mood. They include depression, mania, manic depression, and bipolar disorders. Mood disorders often affect sufferers' attitude and behavior. Depression causes sufferers to become withdrawn from their families, friends, and social activities and to lose interest in their work. Depression affects different people differently. Some sufferers become sad, others may become irritable or fatigued. Many lose their vitality and experience a sense of worthlessness and hopelessness. Often, their sense of judgment gets distorted or severely impaired.

Anxiety disorders are characterized by intense anxiety or by maladaptive behavior designed to relieve anxiety. These include generalized anxiety and panic disorders, phobic and obsessive-compulsive disorders, social anxiety, and post-traumatic stress disorder.

Psychotic disorders involve a loss of contact with reality. They have been grouped in three general classes: schizophrenia, manic depressive disorders, and paranoid states. The central feature of these disorders is loss of contact with reality, characterized by delusions; hallucinations; disorientation of time, place, and person; and general confusion.

Schizophrenia is the most chronic and disabling of all mental illnesses. Sufferers grow out of touch with reality and become unable to separate real from unreal experiences. Other symptoms may involve social isolation or withdrawal. In some cases, unusual speech, thinking, or behavior may precede or follow the psychotic symptoms. Persons suffering from auditory hallucinations hear voices and noises that are not heard by others.

Suicide

Suicide and suicidal behavior are not normal responses to the stresses experienced by most people. However, mental illnesses often alter brain chemistry in potentially dangerous ways so that some people suffering from such illness eventually take their own lives. Almost all people who kill themselves suffer from diagnosable mental disorders; a vast majority of them suffer from more than a single disorder.

Mental illness is a disease of mind and there are no objective tools to assess what actually goes on inside human minds. Psychiatry therefore defines and diagnoses mental disorders on the basis of subjective symptoms that are reported by the patients or observed by the doctors. Mental health professionals can only speculate about the causes of mental illness. Most emphasize biological causes, such as genetic inheritance or chemical imbalances in the brain. Others view mental illness as rooted primarily in environmental factors, such as family upbringing or social stressors. Relatively few attribute mental illness to individual culpability.

Almost all mental health professionals agree that mental illness is caused, or triggered, by complex interactions between genetic and environmental factors, such as troubled family upbringing. Recent advances in psychiatric research point out the role of neurotransmitters, or brain chemicals, in mental illness. According to the prevailing theory, depression and suicide are linked to low levels of the neurotransmitter serotonin, and the drugs known as SSRIs are expected to restore the chemical to healthy levels in the brain.

Serotonin theory is appealing to medical community because it makes the mind seem more knowable, less like a black box, and psychiatry seems more like a real science. If a patient is sick because of a deficiency in brain chemicals, drugs should restore the patient to normalcy and mental health. In actual practice, however, some drugs have triggered suicides and bipolar disorders in patients, so more extensive research is needed to ensure the drugs' safety across all patients.

Mental Illness in Prison Populations

On any given day, it is estimated that about 70,000 inmates in U.S. prisons are psychotic. As many as 200,000 to 300,000 male and female prison inmates suffer from mental disorders such as schizophrenia, bipolar disorder, and major depression. American prisons house three times as many people suffering from mental illness as psychiatric hospitals, Prisoners as a group have rates of mental illnesses that are up to four times greater than rates for the general population.

Prison environments are especially dangerous and debilitating for prisoners who have mental illness. Prisoners suffering from mental illness are more likely to be victimized by other inmates. Inmates with mental illness are often punished for such behavior as being disruptive and engaging in acts of self-mutation and attempted suicide. Moreover, their punishments often take the form of being placed in solitary confinement—restrictive isolation cells that exacerbate their mental health problems

The factors that contribute to prisoners landing in jail often related to their inadequate ac-

After spending forty years of his life in a Massachusetts prison—including stretches in solitary confinement, former convict Robert Dellelo joined the American Friends Service Committee to assist in its fight to improve conditions in maximum-security prisons that breed mental illness among inmates. Dellelo himself described life in solitary confinement as "maddening." (AP/Wide World Photos)

cess to high-quality mental health services. Without these services, people with mental illnesses are often fated to engage in behaviors that capture the attention of law enforcement and lead to their arrest. As a consequence, a large number of people are drawn into the criminal justice system because of their behavioral disorders.

Tulsi B. Saral

Further Reading

Diamond, P. M., et al. "The Prevalence of Mental Illness in Prison." *Administration and Policy in Mental Health* 29, no. 1 (2001): 21-40. Attempt to assess the full extent of mental health problems among U.S. prison populations.

Lamberti, J. S., et al. "The Mentally Ill in Jails and Prisons: Toward an Integrated Model of Prevention." *Psychiatric Quarterly* 72, no. 1 (2001): 63-77. Psychiatric perspective on the problem of mental illness in prison populations.

Lewis, Dorothy Otnow. *Guilty by Reason of Insanity: A Psychiatrist Explores the Minds of Killers*. New York: Ivy Books, 1999. Evaluation of research linking violent behavior to childhood trauma and brain damage.

Monahan, J. *Mental Illness and Violent Crime*. Washington, D.C.: U.S. Department of Justice, 1996. Federal government report on correlations between mental illness and criminal behavior.

Weiss, K. "Confessions and Expert Testimony." *Journal of the American Academy of Psychiatry and Law* 31 (2003): 451-458. Discussion of the problems in establishing mental illness through the inconsistencies of expert testimony.

Whitlock, Francis Antony. *Criminal Responsibility and Mental Illness*. London: Butterworths, 1963. An early attempt to determine the extent of culpability of individuals who commit crimes.

See also Competency to stand trial; Defendant self-representation; Defenses to crime; Diminished capacity; Excuses and justifications; Forensic psychology; Insanity defense; Prison health care; Psychological evaluation; Psychopathy; Solitary confinement; Supermax prisons.

Mexican justice system

Criminal justice issues: Constitutionally protected rights; International law; law-enforcement organization

Significance: Mexico has a criminal justice system that differs significantly from that of the United States in both its philosophy and practice. The most fundamental difference is the system's tendency to presume criminal defendants guilty before they are even tried and to make it almost impossible for defendants to be judged fairly on the basis of legally obtained evidence.

As in the United States, government in Mexico is organized at federal, state, and municipal levels, with each level divided into executive, legislative, and judicial branches. Mexico has thirty-one states, plus the Federal District (FD), and nearly 2,500 municipal governments. The nation's criminal justice system operates primarily on the federal and state levels, which have prosecution, police, and penal departments under executive branches and courts under their judicial branches. Also as in the United States, funding for the system is authorized by legislative actions on budgets that are prepared by the executive branches.

Mexico's legal system is based on Spanish civil law with some influence of Anglo-American common law. At all stages, the criminal justice system is heavily dominated by the executive branches— the presidents at the federal level and the state and FD governors at the state level. Through most of the twentieth century, one political party, the Institutional Revolutionary Party (known as "PRI," after Partido Revolucionario Institucional) dominated all branches and levels of government. Less visible but nonetheless apparent, has been the extent to which Mexico's criminal justice system has been politically suborned and manipulated.

The Pervasiveness of Crime

Since the mid-twentieth century, Mexico's justice system has been shaped and distorted by a vast increase in crime. Two factors especially have provoked this arching menace. The first has been the rapid growth of Mexico's population over the past half century. Agricultural and public health improvements have allowed the population to quadruple, but the national economy cannot provide sufficient employment or income for all Mexico's people, and the gap between the rich and the poor has grown larger. Amid this demography of inequality, there seethes another factor. Mexico has a long border with its northern neighbor, the United States, one of the largest consumers of illegal drugs in the world. With fertile tropical and subtropical lands, Mexico and its southern neighbors have become major producers and suppliers of drugs. Moreover, Mexico is a key regional transport nexus for shipping drugs into the United States.

The profits of producing and shipping for this illegal trade are as alluring as they are violent and deadly. It is impossible to understand the Mexican criminal justice system without first understanding both the structure of its operation and the dysfunctions it generates.

Structure of the System

Criminal cases in Mexico are prosecuted through the offices of federal, state, and FD attorney generals (*procurador general*). Through an implied interpretation of the Mexican constitution, attorney generals have come to hold almost exclusive right to this function. The attorney generals are members of the presidential and gubernatorial cabinets within the executive branches. The federal attorney general heads the Public Ministry (*Ministerio Público*). Its prosecutors have extraordinary power to pursue people as criminals. This authority is greatly, even definitively, augmented by their ability actually to produce and monitor the evidentiary material determining the outcomes of trials.

Public security for the investigation, apprehension, and detention of criminals is conducted by several types of police forces. The Public Ministry and the federal and state attorney generals command judicial police (*policía judicial*). At the federal level, the judicial police have been reorga-

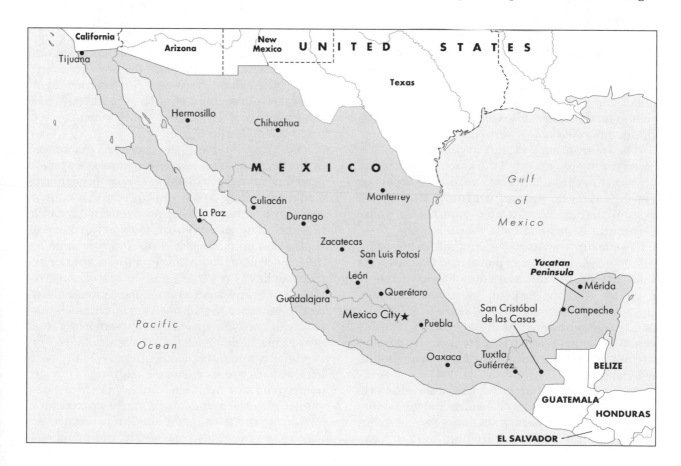

nized as the Federal Agency for Investigations (*Agencia Federal de Investigaciones*).

In further administrative response to Mexico's massive rise in crime, the federal Secretariat of Public Security was created. Commanding various types of federal police forces, it has also created the Federal Preventive Police (*Policía Federal Preventiva*). Made up mostly of soldiers from Mexico's regular army, the Federal Preventive Police are under mixed civilian-military command. Police affiliated with the national army who violate the rights of detainees do not face civil courts but military ones.

Police may apprehend individuals whom they suspect will commit crimes or whom they catch in the act of committing crimes. The capturing of individuals in flagrant criminal acts has a broad meaning in Mexican criminal terminology. "Flagrancy" has been defined to allow the police to apprehend suspects without arrest warrants for periods of up to forty-eight hours after crimes are committed (seventy-two hours in Mexico City). Thus, flagrancy may be interpreted to mean considerably "after" the act.

Arrested suspects are immersed in a police and prosecutorial processes that steadily accumulate evidence—by any means—that substantiates the suspects' responsibility for crimes. Mexico does not adhere to the American principle that defendants are to be considered innocent until proven guilty.

The international standard procedure whereby an individual arrested is assured a judicial review occurs through the issuance of a warrant or authorization for arrest by a court. The judicial system thereby records that someone is under prosecutorial custody for a possible trial.

By alleging that apprehending suspected criminals is "urgent," Mexican police may take suspects into custody without warrants. The principle of designating cases "urgent" case was originally conceived as an emergency measure to be invoked only rarely; however, it has become a routine practice—a convenient way for police to accelerate apprehensions and prosecutors to accelerate convictions.

Mexican law requires that apprehended persons should be brought before judges within forty-eight hours (ninety-six hours in cases of organized crime). However, this limit is not rigor-

ously followed, and prosecutors collaborate with police during the intervals to gather evidence to justify their arrests.

Prosecutors work hard to get confessions, and torture is commonly, even routinely, used to obtain them. Numerous Mexican and international agencies have collected evidence proving that the police routinely use torture to obtain evidence. By contrast, Mexicans make little use of American forensic and investigative techniques to collect evidence. Confessions can provide the bases for indictments that take suspects before judges. The judges, or magistrates review the evidence to determine whether it warrants keeping the accused in custody and proceeding to trial. Bail hearings are pursued by only the wealthiest suspects. Personal lawyers are also luxuries. Most accused are assigned *pro bono* public defenders.

Vulnerability of the Accused

For the average accused persons, the first moments before judges may have staggering consequences. The accused must reaffirm their confessions, effectively declaring themselves guilty. If, as is their right at that moment, they state that their confessions have been obtained through torture, the judges may call for new investigations. Meanwhile, however, the accused must also take into account that they are about to be remanded back to the same police who have tortured them.

The vulnerability of the accused is increased by the fact that before confessing to crimes before prosecutors and reaffirming the confessions before judges, they do not see lawyers. All interrogations up to this point are conducted without the presence of defense lawyers. Only at the moment that defendants appear before prosecutors or judges does Mexican legal practice allow the accused to have lawyers.

The public defenders assigned to most defendants look upon the accused not as clients but as poor charges. They see little personal or career advantage in defending such clients. Moreover, newly appointed public defenders typically have little experience or adequate training. They are poorly paid and may jeopardize their careers by challenging the actions of powerful prosecutors.

After they are remanded to the police, the accused are effectively confined in the penal system. Of the approximately 100,000 prisoners incarcerated in Mexico at any given moment, almost half are awaiting trials or sentencing.

Trials and Appeals

Trials are conducted in a variety of federal, state, and municipal courts. However, criminal cases are heard only in federal and state courts, depending on the severity, range, and types of crime committed. At the federal level, the twenty-one-member Supreme Court of Justice (*Suprema Corte de Justicia*) sits in Mexico City. It is divided into four five-member chambers, one of which is the Penal Affairs Chamber (*Sala Penal Civil*). In contrast to the U.S. Supreme Court, Mexico's Supreme Court does not act as a tribunal of constitutional review. It can only decide individual cases.

Below the Supreme Court are twenty-one collegiate and unitary circuit courts, located in the major state capitals of the country. Several magistrates sit on each court. These courts function as courts of appeal. There are also sixty-one single-magistrate district courts. The states also divide their own courts by function and level and have supreme courts and appeals courts. Among the more than two thousand separate municipal governments, there are several thousand local courts. Trial by jury in criminal cases is uncommon; verdicts and sentencing are decided by a trial magistrates or panels of magistrates.

Defendants who believe they have been unjustly sentenced and imprisoned have the right to *amparo*, which is similar to the American concept of *habeas corpus*). Through a procedure of judicial review, *amparo* cases can be judged for violations of civil or human rights. However, the legal costs of obtaining reviews place the process beyond the reach of the many poor defendants, who are also the ones who tend to be most abused.

Prisons

Prisons are administered at the federal, state, and municipal levels. The largest federally administered prison is in Mexico City. The Federal District concentrates the largest numbers of jails in the country, including one for women. Each state also has at least one penitentiary, and there are several thousand municipal jails.

Mexico's drug-related crime wave has spurred construction of new jails. Mexico's first maximum security facility, La Palma Prison, near Mexico City, accommodates several hundred of Mexico's most notorious felons and racketeers, who are monitored through closed-circuit televisions and other forms of electronic surveillance. Mexico has a prisoner transfer treaty with the United States that allows nationals of each country who are held in the other country's prisons to elect to serve their sentences in their home country.

As in the United States, prisons in Mexico remain seriously overcrowded and notoriously abusive. Prison guards and officials can be bribed (*mordida*, or "bite," is the Mexican term for bribery) by prisoners with financial resources. Prisoners live under a rigid system of social hierarchy and subordination. Those at the top of the hierarchy enforce compliance with forced labor (*fajina*) on those at the bottom. Prison gangs and their heads (*cabos*) enforce labor requirements; extort money from other prisoners; operate markets for small items such as cigarettes, special food, televisions, and even drugs; and extract sexual favors from the oldest and youngest inmates. However, Mexican prisons allow conjugal visits.

Dysfunctions and Reforms of System

Any adequately functioning criminal judicial system should have clearly demarcated stages through which people pass from the status of being detainees to being the accused, then trial defendants, sentenced convicts, and incarcerated prisoners. Such stages exist within legal systems that presume defendants are innocent until proven guilty. Under such systems, detained suspects are not required to say anything and when they do speak to police officers, prosecutors, or court officials, they have the right to counsel with a lawyer. When they go before judges, they have the right to continued legal counsel. No evidence forced from them is admissible in their trials. Moreover, while they are initially detained, they have the right to bail, or conditional release, based on court reviews of their prospects for flight or their danger to society. Once they are formally accused, they have the right to speedy trials that must prove their guilt on the basis of freely and competently obtained evidence. When they are found guilty, they have the right to

During a 2004 rally in Southern California, relatives and friends of a twelve-year-old boy who had been killed in a gang shooting while playing baseball in 1998 hold signs calling for the extradition of the boy's alleged killer, Alvaro Jara, who fled to Mexico to avoid prosecution. By that time, it was estimated that as many as three hundred persons who had committed murders in Los Angeles County alone were living in Mexico. (AP/Wide World Photos)

speedy sentencing and incarceration in conditions that guarantee respect for their basic human rights. They also have the right to appeal their guilty verdicts.

At all stages of this process, but most crucially at the earliest ones, the Mexican criminal justice system proves dysfunctional. Criminal suspects enter a system that does not presume their innocence but instead compels them to go through progressively more damaging stages of self-incrimination.

When suspects are detained, they initially confront only the police, who act for the prosecution, and they have no lawyers. They can be tortured to extract confessions of guilt. After they admit guilt and face the courts, their incarceration becomes almost inevitable because no adequate judicial or legal review process is in place

that considers how their confessions are obtained. Under such conditions, it is not surprising that half of those imprisoned in Mexico at any moment are awaiting trials and sentencing. There is little urgency for trials in a system in which verdicts are, in effective, already secured. For this reason, it may be said that Mexico's penal process actually begins before cases even reach the courts. For those who are eventually convicted, sentences are almost anticlimactic. Average sentences are less than ten years, but most convicts serve only half their terms.

The Roots of Injustice

Mexico's criminal justice system exists within a socio-economic system of extreme poverty. According to Mexican government statistics gathered during the 1990's—as crime was spiraling upward throughout the country—the majority of the people in one-half of the states were living in poverty, and most of the remaining states had significant populations living below the poverty line. Poverty was especially concentrated in the tropical states of southern Mexico, which are also the centers of illegal drug production. With soaring demand for illegal drugs from the United States and grinding poverty in the fertile lands of southern Mexico and Central America, supply responded to demand. The monitoring of this explosive illegal drug activity fell into the hands of Mexico's patently abusive criminal justice system.

Mexico's justice system exists not only within a desperate socio-economic system but also within a closed and manipulated political system. The most dysfunctional stages of the criminal justice system are its initial points, at the level of police apprehension and prosecution. These agents are controlled by the executive branch of government at all levels of Mexican government. Moreover, the judicial branches at every level are both subordinate to and dependent on the executive branches.

A dysfunctional criminal justice system can actually help to support a corrupt political system by providing the appearance of justice and legality, while suppressing social and political critics, marginalized minorities, and criminals competing with the established illegal activities and profits of political, military, and government officials. Throughout most of the twentieth century, the PRI controlled all levels and branches of government and directly benefited from the criminal justice system.

Pressures for Reform

Increasing socio-economic inequality, desperation to emigrate, and surging crime in Mexico have stirred a ferment of social criticism that during the 1990's began to erode the monolithic power of PRI. Increasing numbers of city and state elections have been won by candidates of opposition parties. Most significantly, in the year 2000, for the first time in seventy-one years, an opposition party candidate, Vicente Fox, won the presidency. With the erosion of PRI's political monopoly, there have been some modest reforms of the criminal justice system. An important,

though partial, step was the establishment in 1998 of the Institute for Public Defending. It endeavors to improve the training and independent status of public defenders, who constitute the majority of attorneys used by criminal defendants. President Fox has also attempted legislation, with halting effectiveness, that will improve the monitoring of prosecutors and police.

Despite the movements for reform, numerous Mexican and external organizations, including the Mexican Conference of Catholic Bishops, Amnesty International, the Organization of American States, and the United Nations High Commission for Human Rights, have continued to report on the appalling use of police and on the criminal operation of jails in Mexico. It is thus not surprising that a recent study, by Daniel Wilkinson, on the state criminal justice in Mexico is titled *Mexico—Justice in Jeopardy: Why Mexico's First Real Effort to Address Past Abuses Risks Becoming Its Latest Failure* (2003).

The abuses of the criminal justice system in Mexico are likely to endure so long as the majority of Mexico's people hold only phantom citizenship. Abuses can only end when citizenship solidifies into a reality of substantiated socio-economic participation.

Edward A. Riedinger

Further Reading

Aleman, José Vicente Aguinaco. *Nation's Supreme Court of Justice*. Mexico City: Nation's Supreme Court of Justice, 1997. Retrospective summary of the operations and organization of the supreme court of Mexico by its presiding magistrate, chief justice.

Avalos, Francisco. *The Mexican Legal System*. 2d ed. Littleton, Colo.: F. B. Rothman, 2000. Bibliographical research guide and index to all areas of current Mexican law including *amparo*, criminal justice, and judiciary law.

Buffington, Robert M. *Criminal and Citizen in Modern Mexico*. Lincoln: University of Nebraska Press, 2000. Analysis of the current state of criminal justice and citizen rights in Mexico that traces its historical development, from its colonial roots to the end of the twentieth century.

Vargas, Jorge. *Mexican Legal Dictionary and Desk Reference*. St. Paul, Minn.: Thomson/West,

2003. Explanation of terms used in the Mexican legal system and guide to their usage for Mexican federal codes, statutes, and international agreements.

Zamora, Stephen, José Ramón Cossío, and Leonel Pereznieto Castro. *Mexican Law*. New York: Oxford University Press, 2004. This volume contains a chapter on criminal law and procedure and provides a summary of Mexican criminal law and practices within the context of other types of law, legal history, and professional legal education.

See also *Alvarez-Machain, United States v.*; Border patrols; Canadian justice system; Deportation; Extradition; Illegal aliens; Immigration and Naturalization Service; International law.

Miami riots

The Event: Three-day race riot in which seventeen people were killed
Date: May 17-19, 1980
Place: Miami, Florida
Criminal justice issues: Civil rights and liberties; police powers; morality and public order
Significance: Miami's brutal race riots were triggered by indignation over the failure of the criminal justice system to convict police officers in the death of a black businessman.

Many of Dade County, Florida's poorest black residents live in Liberty City, a five-hundred-square-block unincorporated area created in the 1920's by a black realtor who wanted to establish a place for African Americans to live in "liberty." Conflicts between the police and Liberty City residents were common. Between 1970 and 1979, there were thirteen violent racial confrontations. During the five years preceding the Miami riot, more than 930 charges of police brutality were filed—an average of one charge every two days.

At 1:15 A.M. on December 17, 1979, Arthur McDuffie, an African American insurance agent, left his sister's house on his motorcycle. Almost immediately, police officers were in pursuit of McDuffie for traffic violations. After an eight-minute chase, McDuffie was stopped and beaten by at least six and perhaps as many as twelve officers. He lapsed into a coma and died four days later.

While McDuffie was being transported to the hospital, several officers demolished his motorcycle in an effort to make it appear that he had been in a traffic accident. The initial police report attributed McDuffie's death to injuries he had suffered in a motorcycle accident while fleeing police. Five police officers who were eventually charged with McDuffie's murder had been named in forty-seven citizen complaints, thirteen internal reviews, and fifty-five "use-of-force" incidents.

All five officers were tried at the same time, and the trial was shifted to Tampa, Florida. The defense used its challenges to remove all African Americans from the jury pool, and the case was heard by an all-white six-person jury. After deliberating for less than three hours, the jury found all defendants not guilty.

At 6:00 P.M. on May 17, 1980, approximately three hours after the verdict was read, riots began in Liberty City. After three days of rioting, the death toll stood at seventeen, with eight whites killed on the first day and nine African Americans killed on the second and third days. Some six hundred African Americans were arrested, and property damage amounted to $200 million.

Aftermath

In the aftermath of the riots, Dade County spent $100,000, and the Chamber of Commerce another $40,000, for studies on economic revitalization. No action was taken. On the state level, the response was minimal. Liberty City was designated as an enterprise zone, providing state and local tax credits to businesses that moved into the area. On the federal level, the administration of President Jimmy Carter provided financial assistance to damaged businesses through the Small Business Administration. The officers who were acquitted in the state courts of killing McDuffie were later tried in federal courts and convicted of violating McDuffie's civil rights. More than one-half of the damaged businesses closed or relocated, and the economic climate deteriorated further in the years following the riots.

Darryl Paulson

Further Reading

Dunn, Marvin. *Black Miami in the Twentieth Century*. Gainesville: University Press of Florida, 1997.

Porter, Bruce, and Marvin Dunn. *The Miami Riot of 1980: Crossing the Bounds*. Lexington, Mass.: Lexington Books, 1984.

"Riots, Unrest Plague Three Cities After Police Shootings, Allegations of Brutality." *Jet*, August 21, 1995.

See also Civilian review boards; Deadly force; Hate crime; King beating case; Police brutality; Race riots in the twentieth century; Reasonable force.

Military justice

Definition: System of justice designed to maintain order and discipline within the armed forces

Criminal justice issues: Courts; military justice

Significance: Military law is entirely penal, or disciplinary, in scope but is also analogous to civilian criminal law. The central purpose of having special military law is to give commanders strong tools to maintain the discipline and effectiveness of the military establishment.

American military law has developed in response to the special needs of the nation's military services. Some actions in the military services that may seem noncriminal to civilians have severe consequences due to the special needs of maintaining military discipline. For example, civilians who fail to appear at their jobs might simply be terminated. By contrast, service members who fail to appear for work may face criminal charges.

American military justice has its roots in the Articles of War legislated by the First Continental Congress in 1775. Modeled on the British Articles of War, the American code was deliberately designed to be harsh. Its primary function was to ensure discipline among troops, and it used courts martial as tools to promote obedience among service members. Until 1950, the U.S. Army did not even have a formal appeals process for court-martial convictions, and there was no sentencing uniformity throughout command units as well as the different service branches.

By the end of World War II, military courts had convened more than two million courts-martial and many former service members were proclaiming that grave injustices were being perpetrated in military courts. Among the most common complaints were lack of uniformity in the administration of justice and the capricious nature of some unit commanders. Public disenchantment over the military justice system eventually led toward reform. In 1950, the Uniform Code of Military Justice (UCMJ) was developed.

The first major overhaul of the military justice system since 1775, the UCMJ was designed to ensure that the administration of law would be uniform among all the armed services. The code created centralized review panels to hear appeals of defendants and the Court of Military Appeals, a three-member panel of civilian judges having jurisdiction to hear mandatory appeals involving the death penalty. Several other changes were implemented after 1950. Procedural changes to the Court of Military Appeals were addressed in the 1969 *Manual for Courts-Martial* (MCM).

The Military Justice Act of 1968 established a trial judiciary consisting of circuit judges in each service, and it also allowed accused persons to request trials by military judges alone, instead of having their cases heard by panels of court members. The Military Justice Act of 1983 provided for more procedural changes, including provisions for government appeals of some rulings by military judges. At the same time, however, the law did not allow the government to appeal findings of not guilty. The 1983 law also provided for defense and government appeals to the U.S. Supreme Court from the U.S. Court of Appeals for the Armed Forces.

Sources of Military Law

The primary source of military law for the U.S. armed services is the U.S. Constitution. Other sources include international law, congressional acts, individual service regulations, usages and customs of the armed forces, and decisions of the military court system.

Military law stems from two provisions in the

U.S. Constitution: those vesting certain powers in the legislative branch and those granting certain authority to the executive branch. The Fifth Amendment specifically recognizes that offenses in the armed services are to be handled in accordance with military law, thus recognizing that cases arising in military units must be handled separately from those occurring in similar circumstances in civilian society.

The Constitution also provides that the president serve as the commander in chief of the armed forces and is thus empowered to appoint all officers to ensure that the laws of the nation are faithfully served. The Constitution empowers Congress to make rules and regulations for the government and regulation of the land and naval forces, as well as to make all laws necessary to provide for the discipline of the armed services.

Apart from the Constitution, other sources have a great impact upon military law. Congressional legislation created the Uniform Code of Military Justice and the *Manual for Courts-Martial*, the procedural requirements for military justice. The MCM is implemented by presidential executive order. As the commander in chief, the president may promulgate other executive orders and service regulations, so long as they do not conflict with basic constitutional or statutory provisions.

Under international law, all American service members are subject to the Geneva Convention of 1949, as well as provisions outlined for international contingencies. Military personnel serving abroad are also required to abide by the laws of the host nations, as determined by arranged Status of Force Agreements (SOFA) between those nations and the United States.

The Uniform Code of Military Justice

The UCMJ was enacted in 1951 and implemented by the *Manual for Courts-Martial*. It established service courts of military review composed of appellate military judges. The code also provided for the U.S. Court of Military Appeals, which originally contained three civilian judges. In 1991, two more civilian judges were added to the appeals court, whose name was changed to the U.S. Court of Appeals for the Armed Forces.

The main purpose of the UCMJ, and in particular its punitive articles, is to ensure there is uniformity among all commands and across the branches of service in the punishments of crime. Under the code, soldiers in the Army who commit larceny face exactly the same charges and possible punishments as Marines and Navy sailors who commit the same offense.

The UCMJ is the basic source of military law. Persons subject to its provisions include members of all regular components of the armed forces, even those persons awaiting discharge, as well as volunteers from the time of their entry into the armed forces. Cadets, aviation cadets, and midshipmen in the military academies are subject to the UCMJ, as well as retired members of regular components of the armed forces who are still entitled to pay, and members of reserve components under certain circumstances. The important thing to note is that the jurisdiction of courts-martial depends solely on the accused person's status relative to the provisions of the code.

The core of the UCMJ can be found in the punitive articles that are numbered 77 through 134. All offenses listed in those articles are considered court-martial offenses. Each offense is listed, along with the elements of proof used to define it. The UCMJ also includes provisions for lesser-included offenses. For example, Article 119 defines manslaughter as a lesser-included offense for Article 118's murder. Military courts can convict defendants of less-included offenses when they are unable to find them guilty of the original charges. This procedure enables courts to make findings without having to amend the original charges. The code also lists maximum permissible punishments for each offense.

Nonjudicial Punishments

The UCMJ permits military punishments to be handled in either of two basic ways. The first, under Article 15, allows commanders to handle minor offenses with nonjudicial punishments. Minor offenses are generally considered to be those that might result in court-martial sentences of up to thirty days of confinement. However, the final decision to classify any offense as minor rests with the commanders of the accused persons.

Commanders using nonjudicial punishment must conduct prehearing inquiries to determine the truth of the matters. Once they are satisfied there is enough evidence to make possible conviction by court-martial, they may offer nonjudicial punishments when the accused elect not to go to trial by court-martial. The commanders must then advise the accused of their rights against self-incrimination and the charges that are being preferred against them. The accused are permitted to examine all evidence, present defenses, and have witnesses present for their nonjudicial hearings. They may then choose to accept nonjudicial punishments under Article 15 or to be tried by court-martial. However, service members who are attached to vessels that are about to embark or that have embarked, must accept punishments under Article 15.

Accepting punishment under Article 15 is not considered to constitute admission of guilt. Article 15

Courtroom artist's rendering of the interrogation of U.S. Army specialist Charles Graner, Jr. (left), who was convicted in his court-martial in January, 2005, for his role in the abuse of Iraqi prisoners held by U.S. troops in Iraq's Abu Ghraib prison. Under military justice, courts-martial are the equivalent of criminal trials in the civilian justice system (AP/Wide World Photos)

proceedings that are convened by field-grade officers (those in pay grades 0-4, such as majors), keep records of the proceedings that are permanently placed in the personnel files of the accused. Records of proceedings convened by junior officers are placed only in local files until the service members are either transferred from their duty stations or leave the service.

Field-grade officers may award punishments that are more severe than those that junior officers can award. Punishments under Article 15 can be appealed to higher authority, which may let the punishments stand, reduce them, or dismiss them. However, the higher authorities cannot increase the levels of punishment.

Courts-Martial

Offenses that cannot classified as minor are tried by court-martial, as are cases in which the accused refuse nonjudicial punishment. Article 32 of the UCMJ requires that before courts-martial convene, pretrial investigations must be conducted to inquire about the truth of the matters, determine the charges that can be preferred, and make recommendation about the disposition of those charges. When Article 32 investigations recommend that probable cause

exists to charge the accused, the charges are then forwarded to court-martial authorities by the commanding officers of the accused.

Convictions by courts-martial are considered federal felony convictions, and the courts may impose punishment as outlined by the UCMJ. For example, conviction for disobeying lawful orders of commissioned officers can result in the offenders being dishonorably discharged from the service and being sentencing to perform five years of hard labor in confinement. As in cases involving nonjudicial punishments, service members may appeal their court-martial convictions through the U.S. Court of Appeals for the Armed Services.

Military Justice Versus Civilian Justice

Although military justice differs substantially from civilian justice in many ways, accused service members are occasionally afforded more rights than civilians charged with the same crimes would be. Civilian and military law are based on the same Constitution, but differences in the makeup of military justice stem from the fact that the military has special needs regarding the status quo of military order and discipline.

A number of procedural differences separate military and civilian justice. For example, in civilian criminal justice, defendants accused of violating state laws are subject to the jurisdictions of the states in which the offenses occur. By contrast, military service members accused of similar crimes are subject to the UCMJ because of their status as service members, and the locations of the offenses are largely irrelevant.

When civilians are taken into custody, they are read their Miranda rights. When they elect to exercise those rights by requesting attorneys, they are escorted to holding cells to await arraignment. Service members, on the other hand, are advised of their rights under Article 31 of the UCMJ, which extends safeguards beyond Miranda in that they apply even to noncustodial questioning. When service members request attorneys, the investigators' interviews are concluded, and the service members are sent to their commanders, who decide whether to place them in pretrial confinement or other form of restriction.

All service members are entitled to representation by a military defense counsel free of charge. By contrast, civilians must show that they are indigent to qualify for free counsel. When charges against civilians are examined, grand juries meet in secret, without the presence of the accused. The military equivalent of grand juries are Article 32 hearings, which are not conducted in secret. During these hearings, accused service members and their attorneys are permitted to examine all evidence and witnesses and make statements and present evidence of their own.

Some states do not guarantee all defendants the right to appeal their convictions in noncapital cases. By contrast, the cases of service members who are sentenced to punitive discharges or confinement for periods of at least one year receive automatic appellate reviews.

D. Scott Canevit

Further Reading

Bishop, Joseph W., Jr. *Justice Under Fire: A Study of Military Law.* New York: Charterhouse, 1974. Critical study of military justice that argues that military law affords at least as many guarantees of due process as civilian criminal law and perhaps even more.

Borch, Frederick L. *Judge Advocates in Combat: Army Lawyers in Military Operations from Vietnam to Haiti.* Washington, D.C.: Office of the Judge Advocate General and Center of Military History, United States Army, 2001. Official government history of the performance of military attorneys in foreign actions from the Vietnam War of the 1960's-1970's to the U.S. incursion in Haiti in 1994.

Finn, James, ed. *Conscience and Command: Justice and Discipline in the Military.* New York: Random House, 1971. Collection of essays critical of military justice during the Vietnam War era. Most articles charge that the system was so outmoded that it was detrimental to military discipline.

Joint Service Committee on Military Justice. *The Manual for Courts-Martial.* Washington, D.C.: U.S. Department of Defense, 2002. Current edition of the U.S. military's official handbook for officers involved in conducting courts-martial. Contains details on questions relating to jurisdiction and sentencing.

Schug, Willis E., ed. *United States Law and the Armed Forces: Cases and Materials on Constitutional Law, Courts-Martial, and the Rights of Servicemen.* New York: Praeger, 1972. Broad discussion of military court procedures and celebrated cases from U.S. military history.

Ulmer, S. Sidney. *Military Justice and the Right to Counsel.* Lexington: University Press of Kentucky, 1970. Concise and lucidly written inquiry into individual rights under military law.

West, Luther. *They Call It Justice.* New York: Viking Press, 1977. Critical examination of the military justice system by a veteran military lawyer, who pays particular attention to cases arising during the Vietnam War.

See also Coast Guard, U.S.; Courts-martial; Due process of law; Fifth Amendment; International tribunals; Martial law; Punishment; United States Parole Commission; War crimes.

Minnick v. Mississippi

The Case: U.S. Supreme Court ruling on the right to counsel

Date: Decided on December 3, 1990

Criminal justice issues: Arrest and arraignment; confessions; defendants; interrogation

Significance: This Supreme Court decision found that a reinitiated interrogation of a murder suspect who had been advised of his Miranda rights and received counsel still violated the suspect's Fifth Amendment rights because it was conducted without counsel being present.

Robert S. Minnick, the petitioner, sought reversal of his conviction for murder in the circuit court of Lowndes County, Mississippi, on the grounds that his constitutional rights against self-incrimination had been violated when his confession was taken during an interrogation conducted without counsel present. Minnick, a fugitive from prison, had been arrested and held in a California jail, where two federal agents, after reading the Miranda warnings to him, began an interrogation on a Friday. He requested that they return on the following Monday, when he would have counsel present. The agents complied, breaking off their questioning. An appointed attorney then advised Minnick to speak to no one about the charges against him. After an interview with the agents on Monday, Minnick was questioned by a deputy sheriff from Mississippi. The deputy advised Minnick of his Miranda rights, and the accused, who refused to sign a waiver of those rights, confessed to the murder for which he was subsequently tried and sentenced to death.

At Minnick's murder trial in Mississippi, he filed a motion to suppress the confession, but his request was denied. The conviction was then upheld by the Supreme Court of Mississippi, which ruled that Minnick's right to counsel, as set forth in the Fifth Amendment, had been granted in accordance with the guidelines established in *Edwards v. Arizona* (1981), which stipulates that a defendant who requests counsel during questioning cannot be subjected to further interrogation until the counsel is "made available" to the defendant. According to the Mississippi Supreme Court, that condition had been met when Minnick consulted with his appointed attorney.

The U.S. Supreme Court, on *certiorari*, reversed and remanded in a 6-2 decision. In the majority opinion, written by Justice Anthony Kennedy, the justices ruled that in a custodial interrogation, once counsel is provided, questioning cannot be resumed without counsel being present. It stipulated that the *Edwards v. Arizona* ruling regarding protection against self-incrimination is not met, nor is that protection terminated or suspended, by the mere provision of counsel outside the interrogation process. The majority found that Minnick's confession to the Mississippi deputy sheriff should have been inadmissible at his murder trial. In a dissenting opinion, Justice Antonin Scalia argued the contrary, holding that the *Edwards v. Arizona* rule excluding self-incrimination without counsel was not applicable after Minnick's first interview with his appointed attorney.

The Court's relatively narrow interpretation of what constitutes right to counsel leaves a legacy of stringent procedural requirements on law-enforcement agencies, which must comply with a suspect's right to have counsel present during custodial interrogations that had been broken off and later resumed. From the point of view of such agencies, its practical effect is to inhibit an expeditious interrogation of suspects.

John W. Fiero

Further Reading

Dressler, Joshua. *Understanding Criminal Procedure*. 3d ed. New York: LexisNexis, 2002.

Taylor, John B. *Right to Counsel and Privilege Against Self-Incrimination: Rights and Liberties Under the Law*. Santa Barbara, Calif.: ABC-Clio, 2004.

Tomkovicz, James J. *The Right to the Assistance of Counsel: A Reference Guide to the United States Constitution*. Westport, Conn.: Greenwood Press, 2002.

See also Confessions; Counsel, right to; Self-incrimination, privilege against; Supreme Court, U.S.

Miranda rights

Definition: Rights afforded criminal suspects while being interrogated in police custody

Criminal justice issues: Arrest and arraignment; confessions; interrogation

Significance: Before suspects may be interrogated while in custody, they must be advised of their Miranda rights and accorded those rights requested. Failures to provide for suspects' Miranda rights result in confessions being inadmissible at trial.

Miranda rights consist of the right to refuse to answer questions that may incriminate oneself and the right to have an attorney present when being interrogated in a custodial situation. Additionally, a suspect's rights include the right to be advised of the aforementioned rights. Miranda rights are at issue only when a person is in law-enforcement custody and is being interrogated. A suspect who is arrested but not interrogated does not need to be advised of, nor afforded, Miranda rights. Similarly, a suspect being interrogated who is not in a custodial situation does not have any Miranda rights. Much litigation involving Miranda rights concerns whether the suspect was in police custody at the time a confession was obtained, or whether police conduct resulting in the obtainment of a confession constituted interrogation.

The primary purpose of the Miranda rights is to protect suspects' Fifth Amendment rights against self-incrimination. The U.S. Supreme Court recognized in *Miranda v. Arizona* (1966) that the safeguards provided by Fifth Amendment's due process clause and the Sixth Amendment's right to counsel clause had to be embodied in a specific procedure for police to use when questioning suspects.

To be admissible at criminal trials, confessions must be given voluntarily. The Court created the Miranda rights in response to police officers using psychological ploys to induce suspects to confess crimes. The Court recognized that police custodial situations create a coercive atmosphere, making suspects particularly susceptible to psychological ploys. In essence, confessions obtained under such circumstances are not truly volun-

tary in nature and thus may violate the provisions of the Fifth Amendment. To ensure that confessions obtained under such circumstances are voluntarily provided, the Court requires law-enforcement officers to advise suspects of their Miranda rights. If, after being advised of their Miranda rights, suspects indicate they do not wish to answer questions, then law-enforcement officers must terminate interrogations. Likewise, when suspects in custody indicate they wish to have an attorney present while being questioned, interrogations must desist until attorneys are present. While suspects may affirmatively waive their Miranda rights, absent such waivers, confessions obtained without affording suspects their Miranda rights will not be admissible at trial as evidence of their guilt.

Because Miranda rights are not constitutionally mandated, a violation of those rights will not taint subsequent confessions that are obtained in compliance with Miranda rights. In other words, if confessions are obtained in violation of Miranda rights, those confessions are not admissible at trial. However, if law-enforcement officers subsequently advise the suspects of their Miranda rights and those rights are waived, the officers may obtain confessions a second time, and the second confessions are admissible at trial.

Custody

Miranda rights are conditioned upon individuals being in police custody and the coercive atmosphere attendant with such custody. Clearly, people are in police custody when they are under arrest. However, for Miranda rights purposes, custody is broader than arrests and has generally been defined to include situations in which a reasonable person would not feel free to leave or terminate the encounter with law-enforcement officers. In determining whether a particular situation constitutes custody, the courts will view the totality of the circumstances.

Two particular law-enforcement situations frequently result in litigation with regard to whether suspects were in custody when interrogated: investigative stops and interrogations occurring at police stations. When law-enforcement officers have reasonable suspicion that a person has been involved in a crime, the officers may lawfully stop the person for questioning and thereby attempt to determine if there is probable cause to arrest the person. Supreme Court cases suggest that investigative stops will generally not constitute custodial situations triggering the application of Miranda rights. If the detention is too long or intrusive, however, investigative stops become what could be termed de facto arrests, constituting custodial situations.

Often suspects, not officially under arrest, are interrogated at police stations. In such cases, the suspects are not necessarily in custody for purposes of Miranda rights. In determining whether an interrogation at a police station constitutes a custodial interrogation, courts consider the events leading up to the suspect's presence at the police station (such as whether the suspect came voluntarily to the police station or was brought to the police station by officers), the actual interrogation process (was the suspect told he or she was not under arrest; was the suspect questioned as a suspect or as a witness), and the aftermath of the interrogation (whether the suspect was placed under arrest or allowed to leave the police station after questioning).

Interrogation

Interrogation encompasses more than the questioning of suspects. Miranda rights are intended to protect suspects from falling prey to psychological ploys employed to coerce confessions. Consequently, conduct known by the officer to likely elicit a confession is construed as interrogation. In concluding whether conduct was likely to elicit a confession, courts will consider whether officers knew of a particular sensitivity, or mental state, of a suspect that makes that person susceptible to the particular officer conduct. Thus when officers knew that a suspect had been in a mental institute and was very religious, the officers' conversation with the suspect about the victim's family needing to draw closure before the upcoming Christmas holidays was deemed to be interrogation and the officers' conduct a violation of the suspect's Miranda rights.

In contrast, a conversation between two law-enforcement officers in the presence of an arrested murder suspect was deemed not to be interrogation, even though the officers were discussing the danger the suspect's missing shotgun posed to children attending a nearby school for disabled kids. The suspect's volunteered disclosure of the location of the shotgun was determined to be admissible at trial, the Supreme Court noting that the suspect was not upset or displaying mental instability and that officers were not aware of any particular compassion the suspect held for disabled children.

David Blurton

Miranda Warnings

Minimal warning, as outlined in the *Miranda v Arizona* case:

> You have the right to remain silent. Anything you say can and will be used against you in a court of law. You have the right to speak to an attorney, and to have an attorney present during any questioning. If you cannot afford a lawyer, one will be provided for you at government expense.

Full warning:

> You have the right to remain silent and refuse to answer questions. Do you understand?
>
> Anything you do or say may be used against you in a court of law. Do you understand?
>
> You have the right to consult an attorney before speaking to the police and to have an attorney present during questioning now or in the future. Do you understand?
>
> If you cannot afford an attorney, one will be appointed for you before any questioning if you wish. Do you understand?
>
> If you decide to answer questions now without an attorney present you will still have the right to stop answering at any time until you talk to an attorney. Do you understand?
>
> Knowing and understanding your rights as I have explained them to you, are you willing to answer my questions without an attorney present?

Further Reading

Axtman, Kris. "The Tale Behind Cops' Most Famous Words." *Christian Science Monitor*, April 14, 2000. A review of the circumstances leading to the establishment of the Miranda rights.

"But Starting When?" *The Economist* (April 26, 2003). Discussion of Miranda rights in the context of a landmark case decided in 2000 and cases slated for discussion in 2004.

Cassell, P. G., and R. Fowles. "Handcuffing the Cops? A Thirty-Year Perspective on Miranda's Harmful Effects on Law Enforcement." *Stanford Law Review* 50 (1998). A discussion critical of the Miranda decision.

Richey, Warren. "Do Police Have the Right to Remain Silent?" *Christian Science Monitor*, November 4, 1999. Discusses the political and legal controversy regarding Miranda rights.

Savage, David G. "Speaking Up About Silence." *ABA Journal* (November, 2003). Discussion of unanswered questions about the nature of Miranda rights and upcoming U.S. Supreme Court cases that might answer the questions.

See also Arrest; Bill of Rights, U.S.; Booking; Confessions; Criminal procedure; Exclusionary rule; Federal Crimes Act; Fifth Amendment; *In forma pauperis*; Incorporation doctrine; Literature about criminal justice; *Miranda v. Arizona*; Self-incrimination, privilege against; Stop and frisk; *Terry v. Ohio*.

Miranda v. Arizona

The Case: U.S. Supreme Court ruling on custodial police interrogation

Date: Decided on July 13, 1966

Criminal justice issues: Arrest and arraignment; confessions; constitutional protections; interrogation

Significance: By requiring that police officers inform suspects of their right not to incriminate themselves, the Supreme Court's *Miranda* decision limited police interrogations and brought about a controversial revolution.

In 1963, an Arizona resident named Ernesto Miranda was arrested by the police eleven days after a woman had been kidnapped and raped. Miranda underwent a two-hour interrogation, without an attorney present, and then signed a statement confessing to the rape and kidnapping. At his ensuing trial, the prosecutor introduced as evidence against Miranda only the con-

fession he had made. The jury found him guilty, and the judge sentenced him to two years in prison. After Arizona's supreme court upheld Miranda's conviction, Miranda petitioned the U.S. Supreme Court to review his case, citing the prosecution's use of the confession he had signed without the benefit of legal representation. The Court agreed to hear the case, and since he had filed *in forma pauperis*, the Court appointed counsel to represent him.

Chief Justice Earl Warren's opinion for the Court found that the safeguards provided by Fifth Amendment's due process clause and the Sixth Amendment's right-to-counsel clause were not enough to prohibit the use of coerced confessions. He instead cited the Fifth Amendment's self-incrimination clause to craft a more substantial set of procedural safeguards.

The Court's ruling required arresting police officers to provide suspects with four specific warnings before any questioning could begin. Officers had to inform suspects that they had the right to remain silent; the right to know, if they chose to speak, that anything they said could be used against them in court; the right to the presence of attorneys; and the right to appointed attorneys, if they could not afford attorneys on their own. The ruling also forbade police from interrogating suspects if they invoked their right to remain silent. Moreover, any interrogations being conducted had to stop if suspects decided not to speak further or decided to consult with their attorneys. If interrogations continued and the suspects gave statements without attorneys present, such statements were to be presumed to have been coerced, and the government would have the burden of proving that the suspects' waivers of their rights were voluntary, knowing, and intelligent. Finally, if these warnings and waivers were not given, then any evidence acquired during custodial interrogation could not be used against the defendants at trial, and the prosecution would not be allowed to comment on a defendant's silence.

In separate dissents, Justices Tom Clark, John Marshall Harlan, Potter Stewart, and Byron White argued that the Court had exaggerated the evils of police interrogations and disregarded the noncoercive character of Miranda's interrogation. They found that the Court had not justified its finding that the due process clause was insufficient to deal with involuntary confessions, its extension of the privilege against self incrimination to police interrogations, and its creation of a Fifth Amendment right to counsel to protect the privilege against self incrimination. Finally, they believed that the court had undermined the legitimate value of police interrogations, impaired the apprehension of criminals, and undermined community security.

William Crawford Green

Further Reading

Berker, Liva. *Miranda: Crime, Law, and Politics.* New York: Atheneum, 1983.

Irons, Peter, and Stephanie Guitton, eds. *May It Please the Court.* New York: New Press, 1993.

O'Brien, David M. *Constitutional Law and Politics.* 6th ed. New York: W. W. Norton, 2005.

See also *Arizona v. Fulminante*; Booking; Confessions; Counsel, right to; *Escobedo v. Illinois*; Federal Crimes Act; Fifth Amendment; *In forma pauperis*; Incorporation doctrine; Miranda rights; Police; Police ethics; Public prosecutors; Self-incrimination, privilege against; Supreme Court, U.S.

Miscarriage of justice

Definition: Legal act, verdict, or punishment that is clearly unfair or unjust

Criminal justice issues: Government misconduct; trial procedures; verdicts

Significance: Whether a criminal justice outcome should be considered a miscarriage of justice is often difficult to determine and can be a source of controversy between groups with opposing viewpoints. Attention placed on an actual or perceived miscarriage of justice can result in political debate and sometimes government policy changes.

Miscarriages of justice fall into two basic groups: unfair acquittals of the guilty and unfair convictions of the innocent. Acquittals of defendants whom many people believe are guilty—such as former football star O. J. Simpson—often gener-

ate as much or more attention in the media as punishments of the guilty. Although acquittals of offenders who are perceived to be guilty can cause considerable heartache to the victims of crime and their families and can increase public skepticism about criminal justice, most people would consider convictions of innocent defendants to be the more serious of the two types of miscarriages of justice.

Miscarriages of justice occur not only in trial outcomes but also at other steps of the criminal justice process. For example, the wrongful arrest of an innocent person is as much a miscarriage of justice as a police officer's conscious decision not to arrest a guilty offender who has harmed another person.

Brion Sever

Further Reading

Dwyer, Jim, Peter Neufeld, and Barry Scheck. *Actual Innocence: Five Days to Execution and Other Dispatches from the Wrongly Convicted.* Garden City, N.Y.: Doubleday Books, 2000.

Gershman, Bennett. "Themes of Injustice: Wrongful Convictions, Racial Prejudice, and Lawyer Incompetence." In *Criminal Courts for the Twenty-first Century*, edited by Lisa Stolzenberg and Stewart D'Alessio. Upper Saddle River, N.J.: Prentice-Hall, 1998.

Westervelt, Saundra, and John Humphrey. *Wrongly Convicted: Perspectives on Failed Justice.* New Brunswick, N.J.: Rutgers University Press, 2001.

See also Appellate process; Cruel and unusual punishment; Exclusionary rule; False convictions; Harmless error; Jury nullification; Mistrials; Pardons; Perjury; Police corruption; Presumption of innocence; Scottsboro cases.

Misdemeanors

Definition: Criminal offenses that are more serious than infractions but less serious than felonies

Criminal justice issues: Convictions; law codes; punishment

Significance: Most crimes are misdemeanors

and are typically punishable by fines, not more than one year of incarceration, or both.

The origin of the American classification of criminal activity, with the distinction between felonies and misdemeanors, can be traced to the history of criminal law in Europe. The word misdemeanor is French, meaning to "conduct oneself ill." During the Middle Ages, throughout Europe there was little effort to classify criminal acts for purposes of prosecution or punishment. No uniform criminal code existed, and all acts were considered private matters between individuals to be settled by those individuals. Little effort was made to uniformly mete out punishments for criminal acts. Over time, however, uniform criminal codes developed as the concept of crime against the state emerged.

In England, the term misdemeanor originally referred to any criminal act that was not considered treason or a felony. Eventually, criminal acts punishable in England by forfeiture of property, physical mutilation, or execution were considered felonies. Crimes not classified as a felony were called misdemeanors. The English system of criminal classification, with the distinction between felonies and misdemeanors, continued until 1967, when it was replaced by "arrestable" and "nonarrestable" classifications.

In the United States the felony and misdemeanor classifications introduced by English settlers in the New World are still widely used. A misdemeanor is most often defined as a crime punishable by a fine of not more than $1,000 and/or not more than one year of incarceration. Some jurisdictions classify crimes based on the place of possible confinement. Other factors include the severity of the criminal act in question. For example, theft or shoplifting can be classified as a felony if the value of the goods stolen is above a set value or a misdemeanor if the value of the goods stolen is below that amount.

Most misdemeanors committed in the United States are not serious in nature. In fact, most Americans plead guilty to misdemeanors at least once during their lifetimes. Petty theft, speeding, possession of illegal drugs, public drunkenness, and trespassing are a few examples of the more common offenses.

Several states and jurisdictions have added a third category of criminal activity known as infractions, also sometimes referred to as violations. The category of infractions, or violations, evolved out of the redefinition of certain offenses as less serious than misdemeanors. In the state of New York, for example, a violation is an offense for which the punishment may not exceed fifteen days of incarceration. Examples of violations and infractions include disorderly conduct, loitering, illegal parking, and jaywalking. In contrast to committing felonies, being convicted of misdemeanors or infractions does not necessarily exclude persons from potential employment, military service, or educational opportunities.

Donald C. Simmons, Jr.

Further Reading

Del Carmen, Rolando V. *Criminal Procedure: Law and Practice*. 6th ed. Belmont, Calif.: Thomson/Wadsworth, 2004.

Garner, Bryan A., ed. *Black's Law Dictionary*. 8th ed. St. Paul, Minn.: Thomson/West, 2004.

Wood, J. D., and Linda Picard, eds. *Dictionary of Law*. Springfield, Mass.: Merriam-Webster, 1996.

See also Arraignment; Arrest; Breach of the peace; Citations; Common law; Criminal records; Felonies; Indecent exposure; Indictment; Lesser-included offenses; Pandering; Principals (criminal); Traffic courts; Traffic fines; Trespass; Vandalism.

Missing persons

Definition: Persons who are abducted or inexplicably leave home or remain away from home

Criminal justice issues: Investigation; kidnapping; victims

Significance: Because missing persons cases take so many different forms, law enforcement has no standardized procedures for dealing with missing-person cases. However, determining the types of cases that come to hand is a crucial component in guiding police responses to incidents.

Missing-person poster circulated after Laci Peterson disappeared from her Modesto, California, home in December, 2002. She was eventually discovered to have been murdered, and her husband, Scott Peterson, was later convicted of killing her and her unborn child. *(AP/Wide World Photos)*

Little is known about the actual number of missing persons in the United States in any given year. A 1997 estimate indicated that as many as one million people had been reported missing in 1994. The vast majority of cases involve children and adolescents. It is thus not surprising that there is a lack of research on adult missing-persons cases. Because adults are far more able than children to live independently, the label of "missing" may not be assigned to cases of individuals who are not seen or heard from over short periods of time. By contrast, children and adolescents who do not report home for brief periods are more likely to be regarded as missing. Furthermore, it is difficult to assess the real numbers of adult missing persons when those individuals do not have consistent contact with family, friends, or coworkers.

The overwhelming majority of missing-persons cases involve individuals who voluntarily leave

their homes for brief periods. This runs contrary to popularly held images of a traditional stranger kidnapping or the extraordinary disappearance cases portrayed in the media. Most missing persons are found by police or return on their own within a few days and have histories of previous voluntary absences. Research has found trends that separate missing-child cases from missing-adult cases. Missing children are most often white girls from middle-class backgrounds who leave home because of dysfunctional or harmful home environments or for fun. Missing adults tend to come from lower socioeconomic backgrounds; they often have substance-abuse or psychological problems and are unemployed.

Police Response to Missing-persons Cases

Police departments tend to respond differently to adult and juvenile missing-person cases. Historically, police imposed waiting periods before filing missing-person reports. Waiting periods were employed because the vast majority of missing persons returned on their own, making the time invested in creating missing-person files a wasteful burden on police departments. However, since passage of the federal National Child Search Assistance Act of 1990, police may no longer impose waiting periods in cases involving missing children.

Most police departments do not have standard procedures for dealing with missing-persons cases. In the early twenty-first century, individual states and jurisdictions began assembling task forces to correct that shortcoming.

Categories of Missing Children

Five categories of missing children have been defined by the National Center for Missing and Exploited Children: stranger, or nonfamily, abductions; parental abductions; runaways; thrownaways; and otherwise lost or missing children. Police responses generally vary with the perceived levels of threats to the children in the different types of cases.

Stranger abductions occur when persons other than family members coerce or take children a distance of at least twenty feet from their original locations, when children are lured away for the purposes of such criminal acts as molestation and murder, and when children are detained for more than one hour. Police typically respond rapidly and aggressively to stranger abductions, in which perceived threats to the children's safety are high.

Popular stereotypes of child kidnapping associate the crime with demands for ransom. Such kidnappings constitute one major subcategory of stranger abductions. The other subcategory comprises cases in which children are abducted for reasons other than money. This second subcategory includes cases of people who abduct children because they simply want children of their own and abductions undertaken as a means to commit other crimes.

Parental abduction occurs when noncustodial parents take their own children away from legal custodial parents. Resolutions of these cases are sometimes complicated when both parents have apparently valid copies of custody orders. Such situations occasionally occur when the abducting parents obtain custody orders in different states or countries. Such circumstances make it difficult for police to determine the most appropriate actions to take.

Runaways are youths who voluntarily leave or stay away from their homes. Typical runaways leave home because of unpleasant situations, such as abuse. The vast majority of research on missing persons has been done on runaways. Runaway cases are also often difficult for law enforcement to handle because of lack of resources, the recurring nature of the offenses, and the occasional unwillingness of parents to divulge information on their children.

"Thrownaways" may be considered a subset of runaways. Although no universal definition exists for this type of missing child, such children are generally kicked out of their homes or abandoned by their parents or other caregivers. Lost or otherwise missing children is a miscellaneous category that encompassed all children whose whereabouts are unknown and whose reasons for disappearance are not ascertainable. Homeless children may fit in this category.

Elizabeth Quinn DeValve

Further Reading

Fass, Paula S. *Kidnapped: Child Abduction in America.* Cambridge, Mass.: Harvard University Press, 1999. Comprehensive history of kidnapping in the United States, with particular attention to the role of the media in kidnapping cases during the twentieth century.

Finkelhor, D., G. Hotaling, and A. Sedlak. *Missing, Abducted, Runaway, and Thrownaway Children in America: First Report, Numbers, and Characteristics, National Incidence Studies.* Washington, D.C.: U.S. Department of Justice, Office of Justice Program, Office of Juvenile Justice and Delinquency Prevention, 1990. Federal government report summarizing data collected on missing children during the 1980's.

Forst, M. *Missing Children: The Law Enforcement Response.* Springfield, Ill.: C. C. Thomas, 1990. Examination of the diverse procedures employed by different police departments in responding to missing-children cases before Congress passed the National Child Search Assistance Act.

Hutchinson, Anne-Marie, and Henry Setright. *International Parental Child Abduction.* 2d ed. Bristol : Family Law, 2003. Study of the international dimensions of child abduction—a problem that elevates child-abduction cases to subjects of international law.

See also Child abduction by parents; Forensic anthropology; Forensic odontology; Kidnapping; Lindbergh law.

Mistrials

Definition: Trials that are terminated before they reach their normal conclusions

Criminal justice issues: Judges; trial procedures; verdicts

Significance: Mistrials end judicial proceedings without final decisions or judgments. Their ultimate impact on criminal cases may vary with the reasons for the mistrials.

Mistrials typically involve serious errors, mistakes, or extraordinary events that cannot be corrected within the trials themselves while still allowing the trials to maintain the interest of justice. In declaring a mistrial, a judge nullifies all trial proceedings completed up to that point. No judgment or final order is entered in the case, and in most instances the parties are put back to the positions they held immediately prior to the beginning of the trial.

Mistrials may be declared for a number of reasons, but one of the most common is known as a hung jury—a jury that cannot reach a verdict under the law applicable to the case. To reach a guilty verdict in a criminal case, the jurors must unanimously decide that the government has proven a defendant's guilt beyond a reasonable doubt. If a single juror disagrees with the other jurors, or if the jurors as a group simply cannot agree, then the judge may declare a mistrial after all reasonable efforts to reach a verdict are exhausted.

Mistrials may also be declared for procedural or substantive legal reasons, such as lack of jurisdiction. If a court determines that it lacks authority over the parties or the subject matter, then an order of mistrial is entered in place of a judgment. Likewise, a mistrial may be declared when some prejudicial error occurs. Such an error would occur if a court were to allow irrelevant evidence to be admitted to trial; when such evidence is found to have a prejudicial effect on the outcome of the trial, then calling a mistrial is proper.

In some criminal cases, mistrials may prevent defendants from facing second trials for the same offenses under the doctrine of double jeopardy. An exception would occur in a situation in which the mistrial arises under the concept of manifest necessity, that is, a sudden and overwhelming emergency beyond the court's control. For example, manifest necessity might arise when a severe storm or other natural event prevents litigants from reasonably continuing the trial. In such a situation, a mistrial might be declared so that a new trial can be held at a later time, when conditions are more favorable.

In limited instances, the conduct of the parties, or their attorneys, may be grounds for declaring mistrials. One example would be a situation in which a prosecutor makes inappropriate comments during the closing argument. For instance, if the prosecutor were to comment on the race of a defendant when race has no bearing on the crime in question, such comments might create an undue prejudice that would not be cured by the judge's subsequent instructions to the jury to ignore the remarks. In such an instance, the interest of justice would demand that the court declare a mistrial in order to correct the egregious conditions caused by the inappropriate remarks.

Carl J. Franklin

Further Reading

Acker, J. R., and D. C. Brody. *Criminal Procedure: A Contemporary Perspective.* 2d ed. Sudbury, Mass.: Jones and Bartlett, 2004.

Bodenhamer, David J. *Fair Trial: Rights of the Accused in American History.* New York: Oxford University Press, 1997.

LaFave, Wayne R., Jerold H. Israel, and Nancy J. King. *Criminal Procedure.* 4th ed. St. Paul, Minn.: Thomson/West, 2004.

See also Change of venue; Dismissals; Harmless error; Hung juries; Trials; Verdicts; *Voir dire.*

Mitigating circumstances

Definition: Circumstances relating to violations of law that may cause decreases in the sentences

Criminal justice issues: Convictions; defendants; legal terms and principles; sentencing

Significance: Special circumstances surrounding commission of crimes can influence the severity of the penalties given to convicted defendants. Whereas aggravating circumstances can increase the penalties, mitigating circumstances can reduce them.

All crimes are surrounded by facts that must be proven before defendants can be found guilty of them. These are called attendant circumstances. When the attendant circumstances are reasons for regarding the crimes as less severe, they are known as mitigating. When judges are allowed discretion in setting penalties, they usually take the mitigating circumstances into account and lessen the penalties. However, the discretionary powers of judges vary among the states, so the effect of mitigating circumstances on sentences for similar crimes is not the same in all states.

When judicial discretion is allowed, defense attorneys call attention to all the factual circumstances that may persuade judges to award lesser sentences to their clients than they would otherwise. Such circumstances are not in themselves justifications or defenses for the crimes, but they may be considered as reasons for lessening punishments.

When it can be proven that mitigating circumstances have occurred, sentences may be decreased. Some states permit judges limited discretion and have developed their punishment options into mandatory models that specify lengths of sentences. In addition to deciding placements of offenders—prison, probation, or other sentences—these charts also include sentencing ranges based on presumptive, aggravating, and mitigating circumstances.

Janice G. Rienerth

Further Reading

Garner, Bryan A., ed. *Black's Law Dictionary*. 8th ed. St. Paul, Minn.: Thomson/West, 2004.

Wood, J. D., and Linda Picard, eds. *Dictionary of Law*. Springfield, Mass.: Merriam-Webster, 1996.

See also Aggravating circumstances; Bifurcated trials; Convictions; Cultural defense; Defendants; Defenses to crime; Diminished capacity; Excuses and justifications; Ignorance of the law; Jury duty; Self-defense; Sentencing.

Examples of Mitigating Circumstances

✓ defendant has a limited history of past criminal conduct

✓ defendant was an accessory to the crime and not the principal actor

✓ crime was committed when the defendant was under great personal stress, such as after having lost a job

✓ no one was hurt during the commission of the crime

Model Penal Code

Identification: Concise statement of modern criminal law written by the American Law Institute

Date: Published in 1962

Criminal justice issue: Law codes

Significance: Although the Model Penal Code has no official legal standing, it has served as a guide for legislators and judges to reform and unify criminal law in the United States.

The Model Penal Code was promulgated in 1962 by the American Law Institute, a nongovernmental organization of judges, lawyers, and law professors. The institute crafted the code for the state legislatures to use as a model in drafting new criminal codes, because the common law of crimes was too chaotic to merit mere restatements of the law.

The code's substantive criminal law provisions include a general section that contains the principles for imposing criminal liability, defenses to liability, inchoate offenses, and definitions of common terms. This part of the code adopts a system of offenses defined in terms of offenses against persons, property, and the public order. The code eliminated the common law's confusion about the mental state (*mens rea*) of offenses and based each offense on one of four mental states: purpose, knowledge, recklessness, and negligence. The code also adopted a milder version of the so-called M'Naghten right-wrong test with one that recognized advances in psychiatry.

Since its creation, the Model Penal Code has been a major force in state American criminal law reform. Court opinions frequently cite the code as persuasive authority, and the code itself has been the focus of substantial criminal law scholarship. However, the most recent scholarship has focused on the need to revise the code, because it does not address changes in social norms regarding sexual relations and new statutory crimes, such as hate crime, and it says nothing about drug offenses, computers, and the Internet.

William Crawford Green

Further Reading

American Law Institute. *Model Penal Code and Commentaries*. Philadelphia: ALI, 1985.

Dubber, Markus Dirk. *Criminal Law: Model Penal Code*. New York: Foundation Press, 2002.

Fletcher, George P. "Dogmas of the Model Penal Code." *Buffalo Criminal Law Review* 3 (1998).

See also Annotated codes; Arson; Bureau of Prisons; Burglary; Common law; Criminal intent; Criminal law; Defenses to crime; Discretion; Excuses and justifications; Insanity defense; *Mens rea*; Self-defense; United States Statutes at Large; Vagrancy laws.

Money laundering

Definition: Methods of concealing the source of illegally obtained money

Criminal justice issues: Business and financial crime; organized crime; terrorism

Significance: Money laundering provides the means to fund criminal enterprises, including drug trafficking and terrorism.

Money laundering enterprises are inventive and widespread. The participants vary from small-time gangsters to drug traffickers and international terrorists. In 2002, for example, three clerks were convicted of laundering more than $300,000 at the race track in Saratoga Springs, New York. The same year, executives of a large offshore trust program in Costa Rica were indicted for conspiring to launder $370,000 though a complex network of foreign and domestic accounts. The Internal Revenue Service Web site lists numerous examples of money laundering investigations from Fargo, North Dakota, to Miami, Florida.

Money laundering schemes process criminal finances in order to make the funds appear to have originated from a legitimate source. Money laundering allows the true source of funds to remain hidden while converting the money into assets that appear to have a legal basis. In simple terms, money laundering is cleaning dirty money.

Criminal activity often requires considerable capital and generates substantial profits. Money laundering operations need to control and change the form of the funds while concealing the principal activities and people involved. This usually consists of three stages: placement, layering, and integration.

In the placement stage, the illegal funds enter the financial system. Criminals might attempt to break up large amounts of money into smaller, less conspicuous amounts by employing the services of casinos, banks, and other financial institutions. Money may be moved or placed through a variety of measures: smuggling cash; wire or electronic transfers; purchasing cashier's checks, money orders, traveler's checks, or securities; or cashing third-party checks. During this stage, the funds are most vulnerable to detection and seizure by law enforcement.

Once the money has been placed in the financial system, a series of secondary transactions take place that obscure the trail by moving the funds from location to location. This is called the layering stage. The funds are channeled through the purchase and sale of assets in order to distance them from the original source.

In the final stage, or integration stage, the funds are reintroduced into the economy as legitimate money. This money is used to pay employees, fund business ventures, or purchase luxury items and properties.

Because money laundering is a necessary process in any profit-generating crime, it can occur anywhere in the world. Generally, illegal organizations will use countries that have weak or ineffective anti-money-laundering laws. After the terrorist attacks of September 11, 2001, Congress passed the Patriot Act. The act was passed in order to prevent and detect money laundering and funding of terrorist activities. Under it, financial institutions report suspicious activity, such as large monetary transfers and withdrawals.

According to the U.S. Securities and Exchange Commission, banks develop "watch lists" of clients who have exhibited suspicious behavior and monitor these clients' accounts, screen wire transfers and client backgrounds, and review new account documentation. As of July, 2004, Swiss banks and securities dealers were required to have electronic monitoring systems to identify high-risk transactions and accounts.

Alison S. Burke

Further Reading

Block, Alan A. *All Is Clouded by Desire: Global Banking, Money Laundering, and International Organized Crime*. Westport, Conn.: Praeger, 2004.

Lyman, M. D., and G. W. Potter. *Organized Crime*. 3d ed. Englewood Cliffs, N.J.: Prentice-Hall, 2001.

See also Corporate scandals; Counterfeiting; Embezzlement; Forgery; Fraud; Insurance fraud; Interpol; Mail fraud; Organized crime; Patriot Act; Secret Service, U.S.; Tax evasion; White-collar crime.

Moral turpitude

Definition: Personal condition of depravity, baseness, or shameful behavior

Criminal justice issues: Law codes; morality and public order; victimless crime

Significance: Many statutes and legal documents used the phrase "moral turpitude"—a sometimes ambiguous concept that is judged by the moral standards of individual communities and their times. Historically, the concept has been used by the U.S. State Department as a basis for excluding foreign visitors and immigrants.

The term "moral turpitude" derives from a Middle English phrase with Latin roots that means "shame" and connotes immoral behavior. In legal language, moral turpitude is understood to mean behavior that is evil in and of itself, and not evil merely because it is prohibited. In this context, the criminal act itself, not the statute defining the crime, determines the presence of moral turpitude. The term often appears in legal decisions to indicate the intent of crimes. Professional sports contracts sometimes include clauses voiding the contracts if the athletes are found guilty of moral turpitude. Sometimes homeowner and condo associa-

Crimes Involving Moral Turpitude in the U.S. State Department Foreign Affairs Manual

✓ alcohol and drug violations	✓ mail fraud
✓ arson	✓ malicious destruction of property
✓ assault with dangerous weapons	✓ mayhem
✓ bigamy	✓ misrepresentation of office
✓ blackmail	✓ murder
✓ bribery	✓ pandering
✓ counterfeiting	✓ perjury
✓ desertion from the military	✓ prison escape
✓ extortion	✓ prostitution
✓ forgery	✓ robbery
✓ gambling violations	✓ smuggling
✓ incest	✓ tax evasion
✓ kidnapping	✓ theft and related crimes
✓ larceny	✓ vagrancy
✓ loan sharking	

tions have rules to exclude residents guilty of moral turpitude.

The term "moral turpitude" also permeates federal and state statutes and case law. During the twentieth century, moral turpitude was a basis for denying aliens visas to enter the United States. Notable cases in which moral turpitude was invoked include the U.S. attorney general's warning to British film star Charles Chaplin in 1952 that his entry into the United States might be blocked on the basis of his moral turpitude. In 1968, the U.S. government invoked moral turpitude in its threat to deport singer John Lennon, who had been convicted of drug possession in Great Britain.

David Struckhoff

Candy Lightner, the founder of MADD, in 1981, holding a picture of her daughter who was killed by a drunk driver. *(AP/Wide World Photos)*

Further Reading

Feinberg, Joel. *Harmless Wrongdoing: The Moral Limits of the Criminal Law.* New York: Oxford University Press, 1988.

Greenawalt, Kent. *Conflicts of Law and Morality.* New York: Oxford University Press, 1987.

See also Attorney ethics; Background checks; Deportation; *Mala in se* and *mala prohibita*; Pandering.

Mothers Against Drunk Driving

Identification: Now known as MADD, lobbying organization established to raise awareness of the perils of drunk driving and advocate enactment of stronger laws against it

Date: Established in 1980

Criminal justice issues: Substance abuse; traffic law; women's issues

Significance: Pressure exerted by MADD during the late twentieth century resulted in significant changes in traffic law and public regulation of alcohol in the United States.

Mothers Against Drunk Driving (MADD) was founded in 1980 by a group of California women led by Candace (Candy) Lightner, whose thirteen-year-old daughter was killed in a car crash involving a drunk driver with multiple prior convictions. The stated purpose of the organization was to inform the public of the dangers of driving while intoxicated and to lobby federal and state governments to pass legislation to toughen drunk driving laws and deter potential drunk drivers.

MADD's lobbying efforts produced significant results during the early 1980's, as states began to institute tougher penalties for intoxicated drivers, such as mandatory jail terms, automatic license suspensions for drivers who refuse blood-alcohol testing, and confiscation of repeat offenders' vehicles. Statistics showed that a disproportionate number of fatal alcohol-related crashes involved drivers under twenty-one years of age. Citing these data, MADD successfully lobbied the federal government to pass the National Minimum Drinking Age Act of 1984, which mandated that states raise their minimum drinking ages to twenty-one or lose federal highway funds. This increased focus upon drunk driving and regulation of alcohol sales, combined with public awareness campaigns by MADD and other groups, appeared to exert an impact upon highway safety.

According to the Department of Transportation, alcohol-related fatalities declined 26 percent between 1982 and 1997.

As the campaign against drunk driving begun by MADD evolved into a national crusade during the mid-1980's, the profile of the organization and its founder, Lightner, increased dramatically. Internal tensions, however, had begun to disrupt the organization. In 1985, the executive board of MADD fired Lightner from the organization she had founded, citing financial and philosophical disagreements. Lightner subsequently criticized the organization, accusing its leadership of shifting focus away from drunk driving toward the advocacy of alcohol prohibition.

In 1998, MADD revised its mission statement to reflect an emphasis upon combating underage alcohol use, lending credence to the assertions of Lightner and a growing number of critics who accused the organization of deviating from its original emphasis upon highway safety. MADD remained an active and powerful force in shaping U.S. alcohol policy at the outset of the twenty-first century but drew increasing criticism for its successful efforts to force states to lower their blood-alcohol level at which drivers were presumed to be intoxicated to 0.08. Critics believed such measures were ineffective in reducing drunk driving fatalities and excessively punitive toward social drinkers.

Michael H. Burchett

Further Reading

Frantzich, Stephen E. *Citizen Democracy: Political Activists in a Cynical Age*. Totowa, N.J.: Rowman & Littlefield, 2004.

Jacobs, J. B. *Drunk Driving: An American Dilemma*. Chicago: University of Chicago Press, 1989.

Lightner, Candy, et al. *Giving Sorrow Words: How to Cope with Grief and Get On with Your Life*. New York: Time Warner, 1990.

Robin, Gerald D. *Waging the Battle Against Drunk Driving: Issues, Countermeasures and Effectiveness*. Westport, Conn.: Greenwood Press, 1991.

Spinoza, Charles, et al. *Disclosing New Worlds: Entrepreneurship, Democratic Action, and the Cultivation of Solidarity*. Cambridge, Mass.: MIT Press, 1997.

See also Alcohol use and abuse; Drunk driving; Highway patrols; Hit-and-run accidents; Sobriety testing; Traffic law; Vehicle checkpoints; Victimology.

Motives

Definition: Reasons behind the commission of crimes

Criminal justice issue: Defendants

Significance: Most criminal behavior is considered to have *mens rea*, or criminal intent. When no criminal intent is present, there is usually no crime. Behavioral scientists tie intent closely to motivation, so identifying offenders' motives is a key element of establishing their criminal intent. However, while establishing motives can help prosecutors win convictions, it is not an essential part of the process.

Theorists who study motivation have come to think of it as part of all learned responses. Motivation thus activates learned responses. The importance of motivation is still being studied as behavioral scientists try to learn if it is a primary force in behavior or is merely a contributor. Motivation is not considered generally to be an emotion. Emotion does not have an inherent directedness, but motivation does have directedness, that is, it is the reason for or force behind behaviors.

Motivation arises from many sources of human existence. Sources include external behavioral stimuli. The most basic external stimuli are pleasure and avoidance of pain. Social sources include the satisfaction of imitating role models or being integral parts of social activities.

When police seek motives for criminal actions, they usually try to identify the precipitating reasons for specific crimes or series of crimes. As a type of explanation of criminal behavior, motivation requires that the behavior in question is being held up for assessment (as in police investigation). Second, the underlying reasons or ends toward which the behavior is directed are sought. Third, a motivation must, in police cases, explain this particular behavior, not all behavior.

David Struckhoff

Further Reading

Abrahamsen, David. *Crime and the Human Mind*. 1944. Reprint. Montclair, N.J.: Patterson-Smith, 1969.

Franken, R. *Human Motivation*. Pacific Grove, Calif.: Brooks/Cole, 1994.

Hickey, Eric W. *Serial Murderers and Their Victims*. Belmont, Calif.: Wadsworth, 1997.

Lillyquist, Michael J. *Understanding and Changing Criminal Behavior*. Englewood Cliffs, N.J.: Prentice-Hall, 1980.

See also Crimes of passion; Criminal intent; Defenses to crime; Excuses and justifications; Forensic psychology; *Mens rea*; Proximate cause; Psychological evaluation.

Motor vehicle theft

Definition: Unlawful taking of motor vehicles that belong to others for one's own use or for profit

Criminal justice issues: Crime prevention; robbery, theft, and burglary; technology

Significance: The numbers of automobile thefts began increasing greatly during the last decades of the twentieth century, as both the numbers and values of vehicles on American roads were rapidly rising. In response, both police and vehicle owners have adopted new tactics to prevent theft and to track down stolen vehicles.

The proclivity of Americans to travel has placed great importance on the forms of transportation they choose. Before the mass production of automobiles during the early twentieth century, most Americans who traveled on their own used horses and wagons. Horse theft was considered such a serious crime that in some parts of the West, it was treated as a capital offense during the nineteenth century. During the following century, as Americans switched from horses to automobiles, the criminals who earlier would have stolen horses became car thieves, and laws were updated to make motor vehicle theft a serious crime. However, there was a considerable difference between horse and car theft. The mass production of cars made more of them available for purchase, and the rise of the automobile insurance industry allowed vehicle owners to protect themselves financially from thefts of their automobiles.

States and local jurisdictions had been primarily responsible for capturing and punishing horse thieves. Car theft took on a new federal dimension. In 1919, the federal government became more involved in catching car thieves beginning with Congress's passage of the Dyer Act. This law made it a federal crime for thieves to move stolen cars across state lines. The law was designed to reduce car thefts by increasing the penalties for selling stolen cars for profit, but it proved unable to handle the increasing number of car thefts.

Motives Behind Car Theft

Automobile thieves practice their trade for a variety of reasons, ranging from stealing cars for fun, to stealing them for personal use, and to stealing them for profit. Many thefts are committed by adolescents who want the thrill of taking "joyrides" in expensive and high-profile cars. Such thefts are generally short lived, with the thieves abandoning the stolen vehicles after their joyrides. In most joyride-theft cases, the stolen vehicles are recovered by police after suffering minimal damage. However, on occasion, joyriding leads to serious accidents, especially when the car thieves are inexperienced drivers who lack the skill to handle the stolen cars safely in high-speed and off-road conditions.

Because joyriding is usually done by juveniles, its prosecution is weaker than for other types of car theft. However, as joyriding reached epidemic proportions in some states, new laws were passed that mandated jail time for juvenile offenders. A film, *New Jersey Drive* (1995), celebrates joyriding by depicting youths stealing cars to impress their friends.

Joyriding may provide thrills to some car thieves, but others who steal cars do so to fill their transportation demands. Such thieves typically steal vehicles, use them to drive certain distances, or until the vehicles run out of fuel, and then steal other vehicles to continue their journeys. Stolen cars are also used as getaway vehicles for other crimes, notably bank robbery, kidnapping, rape, and murder. Thieves who use stolen cars are less likely to be traced, and the stolen cars can be easily discarded without leaving incriminating evidence. Cars stolen for getaway purposes are usually taken immediately before or during commission of the other crimes. Getaway cars often suffer damage, particularly when they become involved in high-speed chases.

The intrinsic values of cars make them tempting targets for thieves seeking quick profits. Moreover, many cars contain expensive accessories, such as audio equipment and even televisions, that can be removed from stolen cars and sold for quick cash on the street. Thefts of that nature are usually known as "smash-and-grab" operations, in which thieves break vehicle windows, remove the accessories, and flee without taking the vehicles.

The used auto part business is a multi-billion-dollar industry, and many cars are stolen simply for their parts. Some stolen cars pass through "chop shops," which dismember them for parts ranging from fenders to wheels, engines, seats, brakes, and other parts. The shops generally pay the thieves who supply the stolen cars fixed prices for specific types of cars and then sell the parts themselves.

Although the profits obtained from selling sto-len cars intact may be less than those obtained from selling dismembered parts, many stolen cars are nevertheless sold whole. Selling stolen automobiles is also riskier because whole cars are easier for law enforcement to trace than individual parts. Because of the various checks placed on sales of used automobiles in the United States, it can be difficult and risky to sell stolen cars within the country, so many stolen cars—especially expensive models—are taken to other countries, which generally require less documentation of ownership than U.S. jurisdictions. Transporting stolen cars to foreign countries can be costly and time consuming, so organized crime groups sell most of the stolen autos that go overseas.

Most owners of stolen cars are true victims of theft, but growing numbers of owners arrange for the theft of their own cars in order to collect insurance settlements. Some owners dispose of their cars on their own—by burning them or abandoning them in isolated spots. Alternatively, they may sell their cars to chop shops for small sums and then report the vehicles stolen and collect full insurance settlements.

Carjacking

Most car thefts are nonviolent crimes, but as antitheft technologies have become more effec-

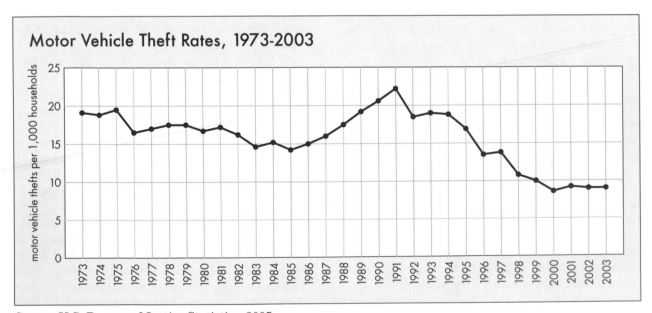

Source: U.S. Bureau of Justice Statistics, 2005.

tive, increasingly numbers of car thieves are turning to carjacking. Carjackings seemed to reach epidemic proportions during the late 1980's and early 1990's as antitheft technology made stealing cars more difficult. Nevertheless, the numbers of carjackings during that time remained low when compared to the number of total automobile thefts.

Although carjacking spares thieves the problem of defeating antitheft security devices, it often involves them in violent crimes because it involves stealing vehicles whose drivers are in or near them. Most carjacking is done on streets and parking lots of urban and suburban areas. Carjackers watch for motorists who are in vulnerable situations—such as when they are idling their cars while waiting for traffic lights to change. The carjackers then take advantage of open windows or unlocked doors to assault the drivers and take their cars. Drivers are typically forced out of their cars before the thieves drive off, but in many instances, drivers are pushed out of moving vehicles and suffer serious injuries.

Some carjackings are well planned and involve accomplices. For example, a tactic called "bumping" uses accomplices who are driving separate vehicles. The accomplices bump target vehicles from behind, creating what appear to be minor rear-end collision accidents. When the drivers of the target vehicles get out to check the damage, the thieves jump into their cars—after snatching keys from the drivers when necessary—and then both vehicles take off, leaving their dumbfounded victims alone in the street.

Some carjackings are impulse crimes tied to other crimes. For example, fugitives fleeing police on foot occasionally carjack vehicles to complete their getaways. Although that type of carjacking is rare, such crimes are widely reported by the media when they do occur. Carjackings make for dramatic television news stories, particularly when the carjacked vehicles are caught by television cameras in helicopters flying overhead.

Passenger automobiles are the most frequently stolen vehicles, but some thieves target other kinds of vehicles. Motorcycles are favorites of some thieves because of the ease with which they can be carried away. Locking motorcycles securely is difficult, and hot-wiring motorcycles

to start them does not require breaking into doors or windows. Large semitrailer freight trucks are usually hijacked for their cargoes. Such vehicles require special driving skills, so only thieves who know how to handle them are likely to be successful at stealing them.

Vehicles with the lowest theft rates include motor homes, trailers, and airplanes. Only thieves with special knowledge of or special needs for such vehicles are likely to steal them.

Prevalence

Improving antitheft technologies are actually reducing the numbers of vehicle thefts. The National Highway Traffic Safety Administration (NHTSA) maintains statistics on car theft that include data on the models most and least likely to be stolen. For example, the NHTSA has found that passengers cars are more likely to be stolen than trucks or vans. Of the thirty-eight different models of vehicles most frequently stolen in 2002, thirty-four were cars, the rest trucks and vans. Cars produced by foreign manufacturers tend to be stolen more frequently than domestic cars, probably because there are more Toyotas, Nissans, Mitsubishis, and Hondas than American cars on the roads. The more time cars spend on the road, the more likely they are to be stolen. Car thieves also tend to focus on cars of later model years. However, while new cars are frequently stolen, older cars are also attractive to thieves because their parts are needed more than those of newer models.

In 2003, the total number of vehicles stolen in the United States declined to just over 1.25 million—the lowest figure since the mid-1980's. Part of the decline may be attributable to new federal laws increasing penalties for car theft and giving federal law enforcement greater authority to find and prosecute car thieves. During the 1990's, the Federal Bureau of Investigation (FBI) began collecting statistics on incidents of carjacking. These statistics shiowed that carjackings tend to be more violent than other types of car theft, more than 90 percent of carjackings involving the use of guns, knives, and other weapons against vehicle owners. Carjackers using weapons succeeded in only one-half of their attempts, but in one-fourth of the crimes, victims were seriously injured.

Prevention

With the large numbers of privately owned automobiles on American roads, combatting car theft requires vehicle owners and police to work together. Owners must take steps to prevent their vehicles from being stolen, while the police focus on finding stolen cars and apprehending those who steal them or buy them.

Federal law enforcement relies on two central tools to arrest and prosecute car thieves. In 1984, Congress responded to the growing problem of car theft by passing the Motor Vehicle Theft Law Enforcement Act, which required automobile manufacturers to place vehicle identification numbers (VIN) inside cars, on places such as engines, bumpers, and seats. VINs enhance the likelihood of finding stolen car parts and connecting them to specific vehicles. Other identifying numbers are voluntarily placed on car parts by manufacturers. The federal law also made it a crime to remove or change VIN numbers. The 1984 act also took particular aim at car-theft rings, many of which were connected with organized crime. The law extended the Racketeer Influenced and Corrupt Organizations Act (RICO) of 1970 to include car theft. RICO provides for extensive jail terms for violations of the law.

In 1992, Congress added the terms of the Anti-Car Theft Act onto those of the 1984 law. The act extended the VIN number requirement to include vans and SUVs. It was also the first federal law to take aim at chop shops by making operating such shops a federal crime, with severe penalties for anyone who owned one.

While VINs assist police to find parts of stolen cars, car owners themselves have a variety of options for reducing the chances of having their cars stolen. The simplest tactic is to remove keys from vehicles and lock doors. A surprising number of car thefts are of vehicles that are left running by owners who get out of them to run quick errands. Parked cars are also targets. Parking cars in busy areas and under lights can reduce the chances of theft. Thieves are less likely to try stealing cars when they might be seen breaking in.

Many car owners have alarm systems installed in their vehicles by the cars' manufacturers. Car alarms are designed to emit loud warning signals when thieves attempt to break into cars; the signals serve to attract attention to thieves and to scare the thieves away. Less technologically advanced are antitheft devices attached to steering wheels that are designed to inhibit the steering of stolen vehicles. None of these devices is foolproof. Car alarms, for example, are often triggered by wind or harmless contacts made by passersby, and the blaring sounds of car alarms have become so common in many urban areas that they are often ignored, except when their owners are fined for disturbing the peace. Antitheft devices attached to steering wheels are strong and secure; however, the steering wheels themselves are not. The devices can be easily defeated by simply breaking or cutting the steering wheels.

A 1994 federal law provided another tool for law enforcement and car owners. The law gave grants to local police to run programs in which car owners sign agreements allowing police to pull over their cars during early morning hours, times when they are normally unlikely to be driving their cars. Car owners place stickers on their cars that can easily be seen. When police see vehicles with the stickers late at night, they automatically become suspicious and can stop and check the vehicles. Because many car thefts occur late at night or early in the morning, the program allows police to target cars at a time they are more likely being used by a thief.

Investigation and Prosecution

Local, state, and federal law enforcement are all involved in the investigation and prosecution of car thieves. State laws against property theft and unauthorized used of motor vehicles are the main tools used to prosecute car thieves. Local police handle most calls about car theft. In joyriding cases, police often find the stolen cars while they are still being driven by the thieves. In cases in which cars are stolen by professional thieves for resale or consignment to chop shops, local police are unlikely to be able to recover them. Their main responsibility, then, is to file reports used in insurance claims.

Police investigating stolen vehicle reports generally begin their searches for stolen cars on the streets. Cars stolen for joyrides are much more likely to be found than vehicles stolen for their parts. While watching for stolen vehicles on the road, police pay special attention to cars being driven too fast or too slow and cars that stop suddenly—all signs that the drivers are unfamiliar with the vehicles. Altered license plates are another sign, as thieves sometimes change plates to prevent the cars from being traced. Marks on vehicle bodies left by physical break-ins, including jimmied door and trunk locks, also attract law-enforcement attention.

Many stolen cars are abandoned on streets, and such vehicles are frequently stripped of all their valuable removable parts including their tires, batteries, doors, seats, and other internal parts. Abandoned cars are also recognizable because they generally remain parked in the same places for extended periods. Parked cars containing the kinds of items used in thefts may also signal that they have been stolen. Such evidence might include coat hangers used to unlock doors from outside, lock picks, and hot-wiring devices.

Abandoned cars also often provide evidence that can be used to track thieves. Tools used to steal cars can sometimes be matched to the marks they leave in the stolen vehicles. For example, forensic experts may be able to match a screwdriver belonging to a suspect with marks left on a picked ignition switch. In addition, many thieves leave fingerprints, shoe prints, and hair samples that can be collected and used for identification in subsequent prosecutions.

Some police, particularly in urban areas, actively search for chop shops. However, because many car-theft rings operate in different localities and states, state and federal law enforcement are usually involved in investigating such operations. At the federal level, the FBI is the main investigator of car-theft rings. Under the 1992 Anti-Car Theft Act, federal penalties for car theft were strengthened and the U.S. Customs Service was given the task of actively seeking out stolen cars being shipped from the United States for resale overseas. The federal government itself can become involved only when stolen cars or

An officer of the Arizona Vehicle Theft Task Force attempting to open a vehicle that had been reported stolen in July, 2004. The vehicle was parked outside a shabby motel in Phoenix—the type of place where inordinate numbers of expensive stolen vehicles are parked, according to police. (AP/Wide World Photos)

their parts are shipped or driven across state or national borders.

Catching car thieves in the act is difficult. Professional thieves can break into cars within seconds, and with the huge numbers of cars on the road and in parking areas, law enforcement does not have the personnel to protect them. For this reason, many police departments focus on car-theft rings that target specific models and specific neighborhoods. Police occasionally conduct sting operations in which they plant cars in neighborhoods with frequent robberies. The cars are equipped with tracking devices that the police can follow when thieves steal them. The devices often lead police directly to the headquarters of car-theft operations, which they then shut down. Some departments mount sting operations with specially designed cars that contain hidden television cameras and automatic shutdown systems that can be used to stop the vehicles with the thieves inside, allowing for easy capture.

Government investigations are aided by private industry—both car manufacturers and insurance companies. Because most stolen cars are insured against theft, the insurance companies lose large sums to car theft. The companies are also alert to fraud when car owners report thefts. With the combination of private owners, the insurance industry and all levels of law enforcement, car theft declined in the 1990's and car thieves found that stealing cars was becoming much more difficult.

Douglas Clouatre

Further Reading

Brown, A. L. *Vehicle Security Systems*. New York: Newnes Publishing, 1999. Describes various electronic and manual methods that car owners can use to protect their cars from thieves

Cole, Lee. *Claims, Costs and Crime: A Study of Insurance Frauds from Invention to Prevention*. New York: Lee Books, 1995. Discusses insurance fraud in several areas including the theft or destruction of cars.

Cole, Lee, and Gerald Boyer. *Investigation of Vehicle Thefts*. New York: Lee Books, 1991. Now a little dated, but still a useful guide to the steps through which police go when investigating car theft.

Klaus, Patsy. *Carjackings in the United States. 1992-1996*. Washington, D.C.: U.S. Department of Justice, 1999. Brief examination of carjacking statistics in the United States after the passage of federal law intended to combat carjackings.

Maxfield, Michael, and Ronald Clark. *Understanding and Preventing Car Theft*. Chicago: Criminal Justice Press, 2004. Practical guide to simple steps that car owners can take to reduce the chances of their vehicles being broken into or stolen.

Plate, Thomas Gordon. *Crime Pays*. New York: Simon & Schuster, 1995. Fascinating exploration of how professional criminals—including car thieves—live and work.

Rapp, B. *Vehicle Theft Investigation*. Chicago: Loompanics Unlimited, 1999. Primer on the types of evidence police look for when searching for stolen vehicles.

See also Carjacking; Federal Bureau of Investigation; Felonies; Juvenile delinquency; Motor vehicle theft; Theft; United States Code.

MOVE bombing

The Event: Attempt to evict illegal squatters that killed eleven people and destroyed sixty-one homes

Date: May 13, 1985

Place: Philadelphia, Pennsylvania

Criminal justice issues: Government misconduct; police powers

Significance: One of the most controversial government actions of modern times, the Philadelphia city government's use of a bomb to evict squatters was widely condemned and raised questions about the limits of government power.

MOVE, founded in 1972 by Vincent Leaphart, who adopted the name "John Africa," was a group of "back-to-nature" activists with an unusual and inconsistent philosophy. Although they advocated going back to nature, they were an urban movement. They shunned modern technology but used an elaborate loudspeaker system to bombard neighbors with their views. They decried pollution but littered property with their garbage and human waste.

The origin of the name "MOVE" is unclear. Not an acronym, it is generally believed to be merely a shortened form for the term "movement." MOVE first received media attention in 1978, when Philadelphia police clashed with members when police tried to evict them from an illegally occupied house. One police officer was killed, and eight officers and firefighters were wounded. Nine MOVE members were convicted of murder.

After failing to win the release of their imprisoned colleagues, MOVE members barricaded their new residence in a middle-class neighborhood, hooked up an elaborate sound system, and bombarded their neighbors for twelve hours per day with their profanity-laced speeches. This continued for more than two years, despite repeated appeals to the city by neighborhood residents. Philadelphia Mayor Wilson Goode, that city's first African American mayor, chose to ignore the appeals of local residents. At one point, Mayor Goode announced that he preferred "to have dirt and some smell than to have death." The denouement, however, included dirt, smell, and death.

After local residents held a press conference on May 1, 1985, criticizing the city's inaction, city officials decided to take aggressive action. On May 13, 1995, Police Commissioner Gregore Sambor told MOVE members to vacate their two-story row house. Tear gas was fired into the house, and a gun battle commenced. Twelve hours later, MOVE members still occupied the house. Police officials requested and received Goode's permission to drop a satchel filled with explosives onto the roof of MOVE's house. The goal was to dislodge a rooftop bunker; the result, however, was a fire that quickly got out of control. By the time the fires were controlled, eleven MOVE members, including four children, were dead. Only one thirty-year-old woman and one thirteen-year-old boy escaped alive. In addition to the deaths, two city blocks were destroyed, and sixty-one homes were reduced to embers.

Aftermath

Newspapers across the nation and throughout the world condemned the mayor's decision to drop the bomb, but a majority of local residents, both black and white, supported Goode and the police department. By the mid-1990's, the MOVE bombing had cost Philadelphia $30 million, and legal action was still pending. The city rebuilt the sixty-one destroyed homes, paid settlements to residents for lost belongings, and paid damages to the families of slain MOVE members. A 1986 citizens' commission concluded that Goode and the police and fire commissioners had "exhibited a reckless disregard for life and property." Goode was reelected to another four-year term in 1987.

Darryl Paulson

Further Reading

Anderson, John, and Hilary Hevenor. *Burning Down the House: Move and the Tragedy of*

Philadelphia row houses burning after city authorities dropped a bomb on the MOVE headquarters on May 13, 1985. *(AP/Wide World Photos)*

Philadelphia. New York: John Wiley & Sons, 1990.

Assefa, Hizkias, and Paul Wahrhaftig. *The MOVE Crisis in Philadelphia: Extremist Groups and Conflict Resolution*. Pittsburgh, Pa.: University of Pittsburgh Press, 1990.

"MOVE Plaintiffs Awarded $1.5 Million in 1985 Bombing." *Jet*, July 15, 1996.

Wagner-Pacifici, Robin. *Discourse and Destruction: The City of Philadelphia Versus MOVE*. Chicago: University of Chicago Press, 1994.

See also Bombs and explosives; Deadly force; King beating case; Police powers.

Multiple jurisdiction offenses

Definition: Criminal offenses that are subject to prosecution in more than one jurisdiction

Criminal justice issues: Jurisdictions; law-enforcement organization; legal terms and principles

Significance: State and federal statutes grant dual, or multiple, jurisdiction for offenses involving several jurisdictions.

Law enforcement was originally a local activity. Increasingly, criminal activity crosses state lines. A growing number of federal statutes take into account multiple jurisdiction offenses. The National Computer Crime Squad of the Federal Bureau of Investigation (FBI), for example, investigates violations of the Federal Computer Fraud and Abuse Act of 1986. Computer crimes are classic examples of offenses that frequently take place across state and national boundaries. The multiple jurisdiction offense permits a computer crime to be prosecuted in a number of states.

Gambling, drug trafficking, and other multiple jurisdiction criminal activities frequently involve individuals and conduct that cut across national and international boundaries. Drug activity, for example, may involve a regional or national illegal distribution network. Congress has enacted a number of statutes against multiple jurisdiction offenses to prosecute illicit activities that occur across state lines. Prior to multiple jurisdiction offenses, criminal justice officials were unable to prosecute activities involving more than one state.

Many drug statutes provide for the prosecution of offenses in multiple jurisdictions. An example of a state dealing with a multiple jurisdiction offense is the federal statute against the distribution of controlled substances. When a drug offense or any element of a drug offense is committed in an aircraft, vehicle, train, or other mode of transportation, criminal activity may occur in several jurisdictions. The federal criminal code permits the offense to be tried in any jurisdiction through which the defendant or the illicit drugs passed. Statutes against multiple jurisdiction offenses are useful in prosecuting defendants who transport stolen property across state lines. When the offense involves the unlawful taking or receiving of property, the offender may be tried in any jurisdiction in which the property was taken or received. Similarly, when the offense is a conspiracy, the offender may be tried in any jurisdiction in which the conspiracy or any of its elements occurred.

In recent years the U.S. Congress has passed many statutes that provide for continuing jurisdiction without regard to state boundaries. For example, the U.S. Code defines criminal offenses involving the use of the mails as a continuing offense. A federal crime involving the use of the mails may be prosecuted in any district from which mail was transported or imported. Many states set out rules granting multiple jurisdiction in cases involving marriage and family relationships. An example of a multiple jurisdiction offense is the abandonment or nonsupport of children.

Michael L. Rustad

Further Reading

Gaines, Larry K., and Peter B. Kraska, eds. *Drugs, Crime, and Justice*. Prospect Heights, Ill.: Waveland Press, 2003.

Meyer, J. F., and D. R. Grant. *The Courts in Our Criminal Justice System*. Upper Saddle River, N.J.: Prentice-Hall, 2003.

Neubauer, D. W. *America's Courts and the Criminal Justice System*. 7th ed. Belmont, Calif.: Wadsworth, 2002.

See also Conspiracy; Criminal law; Jurisdiction of courts; National Crime Information Center; Skyjacking.

Murder and homicide

Definition: Killing of other human beings under circumstances that may be either criminal, justifiable, or excusable

Criminal justice issues: Capital punishment; homicide; violent crime

Significance: It is generally accepted that no other human act is as serious as homicide—the taking of another person's life. In its criminal form, homicide challenges the criminal justice system to perform at its maximum efficiency, as such crimes cause intense fear and anxiety throughout society. Moreover, the standards that must be met to execute persons convicted of criminal homicide, or murder, are the highest in the American criminal justice system.

There has never been a period in recorded history when homicide was not considered the most serious and troubling of human behaviors. The killing of one person by another has consistently been regarded as an example of the ancient principle of *mala in se*, a behavior that is always considered wrong, in contrast to a behavior that may or may not be wrong, depending upon circumstances.

The greatest numbers of intentional killings have occurred in military combat and are not legally defined as criminal. It is the clearly illegal killings about which the American criminal justice system is most concerned. Moreover, no other crime is as frequently—or inaccurately—portrayed in novels, television shows, and films as criminal homicide.

Varieties of Homicide

"Homicide" is a general term for the causing of one person's death by another. Not all homicides are considered criminal. However, the term is often inaccurately used to describe specific types of illegal killings, such as murder. Homicides are generally classified under two broad categories: nonfelonious and felonious.

Most state criminal codes consider nonfelonious homicides to be either excusable or justifiable in nature. Excusable killings generally involve elements of fault, but the actions are not sufficient to be judged as criminal. Examples of excusable homicides include accidental shootings and car accidents that do not involve gross negligence or the intent to harm.

Justifiable homicides differ from excusable homicides in involving intent, while also being considered legal by society. Examples include state-ordered executions, shooting of criminal suspects who pose clear and immediate threats to life, and the killing of enemy soldiers in wars.

By contrast, felonious homicides are always considered illegal and are often generically referred to as criminal homicides. Many states broadly subdivide criminal homicides into murder and manslaughter, but some jurisdictions prefer to classify illegal killings by numerical degrees, such as murder in the first or second degree. Contrary to what may be popular belief, most criminal homicides are not, by definition, "murders." Most definitions of murder in legal codes require the element of premeditation, which is often termed a design to kill or malice aforethought.

Criminal homicides that lack premeditation are commonly known as manslaughter. Like murder, manslaughter is always illegal. It differs in lacking premeditated intent. Most criminal homicides committed in the United States fall under the classification of manslaughter, not premeditated murder.

History of Homicide

Descriptions of criminal homicide can be found in the earliest records of human societies. Early Greek verse and Roman theater often selected murder as a central dramatic theme. Most sacred religious foundation sources also contain many examples of homicide, as evidenced by numerous accounts of murder in the Bible and the Qurʾān. Modern laws defining criminal homicide are the products of many hundreds of years of legal evolution. In some parts of the world—such as the Muslim world—legal systems incorporate religious sources to define and punish those who kill. Most modern legal systems have separated religion from their homicide codes.

Within the United States, most states and the federal government have modeled their homicide statutes on early English common law. In 1500, English law defined murder as the sole form of criminal homicide; the crime of manslaughter emerged nearly fifty years later.

The first reported murder in England's North American colonies occurred in 1630. John Billington, a member of the original band of Pilgrims who arrived on the *Mayflower* a decade earlier, was tried and executed for the firearm death of a neighbor. However, many believe the first American murder case to attract national attention was committed in 1849 by John Webster, a Harvard University professor of chemistry. Convicted of killing a local physician within his campus laboratory, Webster became the first subject of a long line of celebrity murder cases to draw intense media coverage. The Webster case also was one of the earliest murder investigations to utilize forensic science identification, as the murder victim's false teeth were found in the ashes of his killer's furnace and identified by a dentist.

Other historic American criminal homicides include John Wilkes Booth's assassination of President Abraham Lincoln in 1865 and the Lizzie Borden case. Lincoln's killing was the first successful assassination attempt on an American president. His murder was part of a conspiracy that also unsuccessfully targeted Lincoln's vice president and secretary of state.

The 1892 murder trial of Lizzie Borden ranks as one of the most sensational criminal cases of the nineteenth century. The defendant's father and stepmother were killed in their Fall River, Massachusetts, home by repeated axe blows. Despite considerable circumstantial evidence against her, Borden was acquitted in a jury trial.

Criminal homicide by mob action, known as lynching, became frequent during the late 1880's and continued into the first decades of the twentieth century. The so-called lynching era produced an estimated three thousand to four thousand mob homicides—mostly African American men murdered by white mobs.

While the vast majority of early twentieth century criminal homicides were not sensational, that era is notable for a wave of killings linked to organized crime. The gangster decade, which extended from the mid-1920's through the 1930's, saw hundreds of homicides, many of which were linked to territorial rivalries among the gangs. The illegal sale of alcohol during Prohibition, and

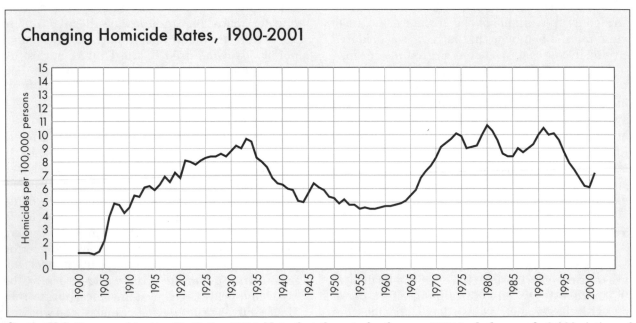

Changing Homicide Rates, 1900-2001

Source: U.S. Bureau of Justice Statistics, 2004. Note that the rate for the year 2001 includes nearly 3,000 victims of the September 11 terrorist attacks.

the emergence of organized narcotics trafficking often fueled gangster homicides.

Among the most sensational murder cases of that era that were not linked to organized crime was that of Richard Loeb and Nathan Leopold, who murdered a Chicago newspaper delivery boy during the early 1920's simply to demonstrate their intellectual superiority by committing a perfect crime. Their case generated exceptional media interest because of their wealthy backgrounds, their youth, and because they were defended by the country's most famous attorney, Clarence Darrow.

Another celebrated murder case grew out of the 1932 kidnapping of the twenty-month-old son of the famous aviator Charles Lindbergh. The kidnaped baby was eventually found murdered, and the later trial and conviction of Bruno Hauptmann for the crime generated so much public interest that his case was dubbed the "trial of the century."

The later part of the twentieth century produced several unique trends in criminal homicide. Killings linked to youth gangs and drug dealing peaked in the 1980's, and the phenomena of serial and mass murder became a subject of public fascination.

The late twentieth century saw a number of new sensational murder cases, whose notoriety was magnified by the new medium of television broadcasting. In 1954, for example, the Ohio physician Sam Sheppard was convicted of killing his wife in a suburb of Cleveland. His case fulfilled all the requisite elements of a celebrity homicide trial: a wealthy couple, sex scandal, and vicious violence.

During the mid-1990's, the entire nation was transfixed by the prosecution of former football star O. J. Simpson, who was tried for the murders of his former wife and one of her friends. Simpson's case was the first televised example of a sensational double murder trial of national interest. Watched by millions of viewers over several

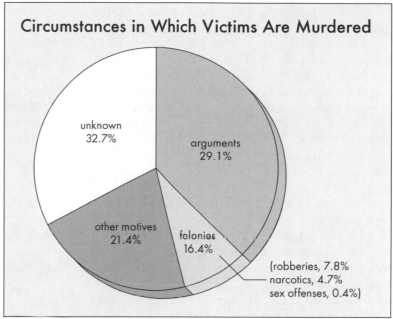

Circumstances in Which Victims Are Murdered

unknown 32.7%

arguments 29.1%

other motives 21.4%

felonies 16.4%

(robberies, 7.8%
narcotics, 4.7%
sex offenses, 0.4%)

Source: Federal Bureau of Investigation, *Crime in the United States.* Figures reflect a total of 14,274 murders in the United States in 2002. Due to rounding of figures for unseen subcategories, percentages do not total 100.

months, the case set a new benchmark in the expanding trend of televising criminal homicides. Although Simpson was found not guilty of the murder of his former wife and her friend, he was found liable for their deaths in a civil trial two years later.

Prevalence

Within the United States, approximately 14,000 criminal homicides occurred during each of the first years of the twenty-first century. This figure is much lower than past rates. For example, criminal homicides were especially frequent during the 1930's and early 1980's.

Contrary to popular opinion, the United States does not have the highest criminal homicide rate in the world. A number of other countries have more illegal killings in proportion to their populations than the United States. These include Brazil, Jamaica, Russia, and Kuwait. Interpol and the United Nations track international homicide rates, but the rates of some countries may be significantly underreported as a result of fragmented justice systems and other data collection problems.

The frequency of a specific crime can be determined in any of three basic ways: reported rates, victimization surveys, and self-report surveys. Of the various felonies known to police, criminal homicide is considered to be the one that is most accurately reported. Few criminal homicides go undiscovered or unreported. This conclusion is confirmed by victimization and self-report surveys. Moreover, it is believed that nearly all victims of attempted murders report the attempts to authorities.

Homicide trends documented by annual Federal Bureau of Investigation (FBI) reports point to the South as having the highest regional rate of criminal homicide. Criminal homicide primarily involves adults, as juvenile homicides rarely exceed 8 to 10 percent of the annual totals. Homicides are most common in large metropolitan areas and tend to peak during the summer months. Increased rates are also observed during holiday periods and on weekends—possible indications of the influence of alcohol and leisure time upon violent behavior.

The overwhelming majority of both victims and perpetrators of criminal homicide are male. Killers and their victims are also overwhelmingly likely to be members of the same racial groups. Homicides are particularly high in both Hispanic and African American communities. Indeed, criminal homicide is the leading cause of death among African American men between the ages twenty-five and thirty-four. Homicide ranks as the nineteenth-most frequent cause of death among white Americans but is the sixth-most common cause of death among black Americans.

The majority of homicide victims know their killers, with an estimated 70 percent to 80 percent of all victims having had at least some acquaintance with their killers. However, the rate of stranger-to-stranger killings has steadily risen since the mid-1970's. Firearms are not a necessary component of criminal homicide, but most such crimes involve their use. Handguns are used particularly often.

Special Aspects of Criminal Homicide

Serial criminal homicide—the killing of multiple victims at different locations over a period of time—is a popular subject in fictional media but is statistically rare in real life. The FBI has esti-

mated that only about thirty serial killers may be operating in the United States at any given time. Mass murder is another rare form of criminal homicide. This form of criminal homicide involves the killing of two or more victims, usually at the same place during a short time frame.

Studies have found residential kitchens and bedrooms to be particularly common sites of homicide, possibly due to the frequency of arguments in those rooms and the ready availability of lethal weapons. Although the majority of illegal killings occur in residences, criminal homicides in workplaces are increasing. Every year, approximately 1,000 people are victims of criminal homicide in their workplaces. Among people who die at their workplaces from any cause, criminal homicide is the third-leading cause of death.

While many factors can cause a criminal homicide, most occur as a consequence of emotional disputes or heated arguments among acquaintances or family members. Individuals who kill their relatives often have records of domestic violence against their victims that have required past police contact. Outside families, many emotional disputes leading to homicide develop in bars and similar social gathering places. More than 50 percent of criminal homicide cases are connected with alcohol use.

Although not as common as deaths resulting from disputes, homicides occurring during the commission of other crimes are growing in frequency. Such killings presently constitute about 22 percent of all criminal homicides. The greatest number of related-crime killings are linked to robberies,. Links with narcotics transactions and sexual assaults are also common.

Investigation

Because of the universally recognized seriousness of criminal homicide, standard comprehensive methods of investigating such crimes are routinely followed by police. It is estimated that American police now successfully clear, by arrest, slightly more than 60 percent of all reported criminal homicides. This clearance rate is the highest of all serious felony occurrences known to the authorities. However, the rate has actually steadily dropped since it approached 80 percent in 1979.

Ideally, homicide investigations are completed in the shortest possible time to avoid possible

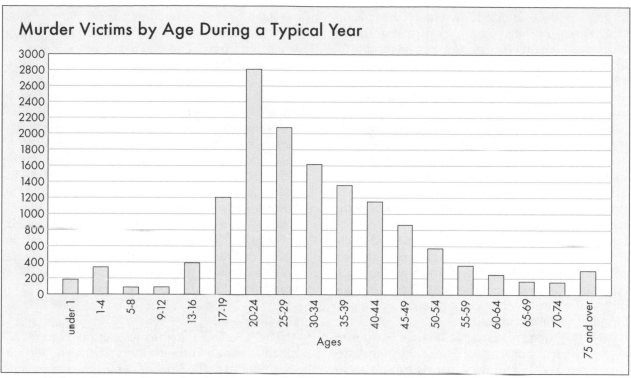

Murder Victims by Age During a Typical Year

Source: Federal Bureau of Investigation, *Crime in the United States*. Figures total 14,274 victims, 10,932 of whom were male, in the year 2002.

problems with witnesses or alteration of evidence. However, cases often drag on for indefinite periods. Because of the obvious importance of homicide, criminal homicide is one of the few crimes exempted from state and federal statute of limitation rules. Such rules normally prohibit the arrest or prosecution of suspects after specified periods of time have passed—usually three to five years after crimes are reported to police.

When criminal homicides are discovered or reported to police, a comprehensive series of investigative procedures are immediately set into motion. Homicide investigations and judicial prosecution are often lengthy and expensive and have the potential to cause strains between communities and their police. When homicide investigations fail to produce arrests and when suspects are unsuccessfully prosecuted, public concern over the effectiveness of the police and courts rises.

Every year, almost 2.5 million Americans die from a variety of causes. While most die as a result of illnesses or accidents, about 14,000 meet

their deaths through criminal causation. Most criminal homicides are of the manslaughter variety—killings that lack premeditation. The remaining criminal homicides are generally termed murders because they possess elements that indicate planning, or premeditation, to kill that can be demonstrated by the criminal justice system through investigation. Since nearly 80 percent of all Americans die outside established care institutions, such as hospitals, the first step in all homicide investigative processes is to determine whether police involvement is necessary.

Deaths may be grouped under four general classifications: natural, accidental, suicidal, and homicidal. Police investigators may be involved initially at the scenes of all four types of death, extended investigations generally center upon only homicide cases. Moreover, police investigators deal mainly with illegal killings generically termed criminal homicides.

Virtually all types of police officers—whether uniformed officers or plainclothes detectives—can be involved in homicide investigations. In large and medium-sized law-enforcement agencies, cases are often initially investigated by uniformed patrol officers, who are generally the first to arrive at crime scenes. After these officers determine that the scenes involve suspicious deaths, they generally summon specialized homicide detectives.

Because the majority of illegal killings occur in large metropolitan areas served by large police departments, most criminal homicides are investigated by specially trained police detectives. In contrast, criminal homicides in small towns and rural areas are often investigated by local police with the assistance of state police. Medical and forensic assistance is routinely requested in the course of the homicide investigations. Such expertise is required to help establish various facts regarding the nature of the death and painstakingly to process physical evidence commonly found at violent crime scenes.

Investigations of criminal homicide are retroactive discovery processes: They take place after the criminal acts and work backward in time in their attempts to reconstruct relevant facts. As in all major criminal investigations, homicide in-

vestigators seek to answer the six classic questions of criminal events: who, what, where, why, when, and how. Three general areas of inquiry are particularly significant to the homicide investigations: motive, opportunity, and means.

Homicide cases fall into two broad categories; known and unknown investigations. Known cases involve identified suspects, and their investigative efforts focus on gathering evidence to confirm the primary assumptions, while building evidence for prosecution of the suspects. Unknown cases provide the classic challenge to the homicide investigator; their perpetrators' identities are not immediately known and must be discovered and linked to the homicides. Investigations involve three primary areas of inquiry: the deceased, the crime scenes, and the results of medical and forensic examinations.

The Deceased

The bodies of homicide victims can reveal much to trained investigators, including the victims' identity, the time of death, the nature and extent of wounds, the victims' occupations, the possible motives for the killings, and a host of other information.

When police encounter an apparently deceased victim at a crime scene, they must never assume the victim is necessarily dead. Many medical conditions and accidents can simulate death, such as shock, immersion in frigid water, drugs, and electric shock. Accordingly, only trained medical and emergency-care personnel are qualified formally to pronounce death.

After the fact of death is legally confirmed, every effort is made to identify the deceased. This task is easily accomplished in many cases because of the presence of identifying documents and statements of witnesses. However, the task can present formidable investigative challenges when nothing can be found at a scene to identify a victim. Persons who cannot be easily identified are often victims of stranger-to-stranger homicides. In such cases, missing-person reports are reviewed, fingerprints and dental impressions are compared, and DNA samples are obtained for possible matches in state and national databases. In cases in which the remains are in advanced states of decomposition, anthropological techniques can be used to create identifiable like-

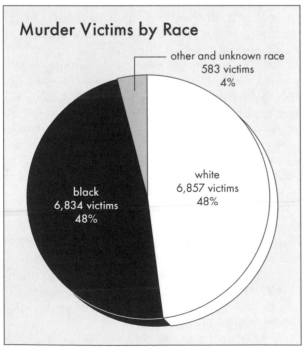

Murder Victims by Race

other and unknown race
583 victims
4%

white
6,857 victims
48%

black
6,834 victims
48%

Source: Federal Bureau of Investigation, *Crime in the United States.* Figures total 14,274 victims in 2002.

nesses through skull analysis, and skeletal remains are analyzed to yield information about the victims' age, race, gender, past injures, and other identifying features.

Time-of-death determinations are routinely attempted in most criminal homicide investigations. Such findings may later prove significant in corroborating or disputing alibis or reveal details of the victims' movements immediately prior to death. In contrast to media portrayals, however, determining how long a person has been dead is far from an exact science. In most cases, expert medical opinion can estimate death only within time frames of from five to ten hours.

Many methods are used to approximate time of death, including assessments of the extent of rigor mortis and postmortem lividity. Rigor mortis is an after-death chemical change within the muscles that causes a stiffening process that develops at a known rate. Postmortem lividity involves the settling of blood due to gravity after cessation of cardiac activity. As the blood settles, distinct skin color patterns are noted as time passes. Although these methods are useful, neither is particularly accurate. Cooling rates are far more useful. Because the temperatures of dead bodies adjust to the temperatures of their surroundings at known rates, measurement of body temperatures can be used to calculate rates of heat loss, which can be used to produce comparatively accurate estimates of the moments of death. However, after bodies reach the temperatures of their surrounding, this technique cannot be used.

Accurate knowledge of the causes of homicides is of great investigative value. Establishment of the true cause of a death can justify a criminal investigation, alert society to an accident or suicide pattern, reveal leads to the identity of a perpetrator who uses a recognizable method of killing, and affect insurance claims and will settlements.

The first task of investigations is to rule out natural, accidental, or suicidal causes of death. Such determinations are often made by establishing causes of death through detailed examinations of wounds. Although it rarely happens in real life, killers and even their victims sometimes attempt to stage scenes to make the causes of death appear to be other than what they really are. For example, persons who commit suicide may stage their deaths so they will appear to be

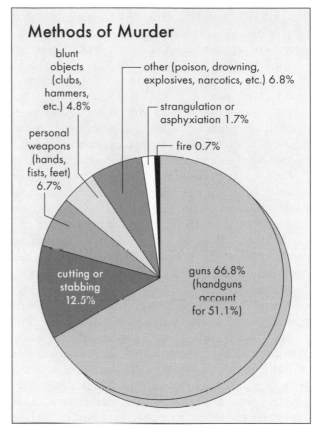

Source: Federal Bureau of Investigation, *Crime in the United States.* Figures are based on 14,274 murders in the United States in 2002.

accidental. Conversely, a killer may try to alter a scene to make a murder appear to be a suicide.

Other facts that can assist police in determining causes of death may include evidence of other persons who have been present at the death scenes, the numbers and locations of wounds, the presence or absence of physical struggles, the psychological and criminal backgrounds of the victims, and analyses of motives, opportunities, and means. Since most suicides and criminal homicides are perpetrated with firearms, edged weapons, and various forms of asphyxia, homicide investigators must be knowledgeable in all these areas.

Crime Scenes

Most homicides contain large quantities of evidence. Because such scenes generally involve physical struggles, obvious and trace evidence is likely to be present. Since it is probable that physiological evidence linked to victims and perpetrators is present, great care must be taken not to contaminate such evidence. Most illegal killings are not planned and premeditated murders but the results of arguments that escalate to someone's death. Killers who do not plan murders in advance are almost certain to leave behind such trace evidence as fingerprints or body tissues or fluids containing DNA evidence.

Processing of homicide scenes is conducted in three major phases: recording, searching, and packaging evidence. After a death is confirmed and a scene is protected from contamination and alteration, all possible relevant information about it must be recorded. This is generally accomplished through still photography and video recording. Later analyses of visual recordings can assist judges and juries and may also provide investigative leads not apparent at the time when the scenes were first processed.

After recording is completed, thorough searches of the immediate and external areas follow. Although a homicide may occur entirely within a single room, the entire surrounding structure and area should be searched, as criminals often discard evidence as they enter and exit the scenes of their crimes. Extensive neighborhood canvasses are then conducted to locate witnesses who may provide leads to suspects, vehicle descriptions, and insights into times of death based on what they may have seen or heard. They may also provide background data on victims that can assist in establishing motives. As evidence is located, it is recovered, marked, and packaged for subsequent examination by police and specially trained crime scene investigators.

Finally, evidence is transported to local, state, or federal crime labs for analysis. Generally the police investigators determine which specific tests should be performed at the labs on specified items. For this reason, investigators must be knowledgeable about the forensic tests that are available and the particular results that can be obtained from them, even though they do not actually perform the laboratory tests themselves.

Medical Expertise

Homicide investigations nearly always utilize medical expertise. Physicians who specialize in

the examination of suspicious deaths and who frequently perform postmortem autopsies are properly termed forensic pathologists. Approximately five hundred doctors in the United States are trained in this field. Many of them hold government positions as coroners and medical examiners. The medical examiner system was originated in Massachusetts in 1877 and is the more recent of the two systems. Medical examiners are almost always forensic pathologists. Some coroners are physicians, but many are simply elected county officials who lack medical backgrounds.

Medical expertise assists the homicide investigator in specifying cause of death and determining if the cause was due to criminal means. They can determine the number and severity of wounds, estimate time of death, and provide investigative leads relating to motive and means. Forensic pathologists also assist in cases when it is necessary to disinter a body previously buried; known as exhumation.

Prosecution

The crime of murder is one over which the states usually have jurisdiction, and it is typically prosecuted by states unless the crime has occurred on federal territory or against a federal officer or agent. Federal prosecutions for murder typically derive from violation of specific congressional legislation protecting federal interests or involving matters of interstate concern. Each state adopts its own statutes proscribing criminal conduct and establishes its own rules of criminal procedure, subject only to the limitation that such law must meet constitutional standards. Thus the definitions of murder and manslaughter, the punishments imposed on those convicted, and the procedural steps from arrest to conviction, sentencing, and imprisonment differ somewhat among the various states.

The decision whether to prosecute a suspect for murder rests with the local prosecutor within the jurisdiction in which the crime occurred. The prosecutor has the discretion to reject cases when available evidence to prove guilt is weak, and the prosecutor may decline to file a case even when police have recommended that charges be brought. When this discretion is abused by local prosecutors, state authorities may intervene. However, when both the local and state prosecutors decline to go forward for improper reasons or when a jury fails to convict a defendant in a murder case under suspicious circumstances, federal prosecutors may seek to file charges under federal statutes such as those making it unlawful to deprive a person of civil rights guaranteed by the Constitution. This type of intervention has been employed when local authorities have declined to prosecute or juries have failed to convict white persons accused of murdering African Americans.

Murder prosecutions are conducted procedurally like other felony prosecutions, and the same constitutional safeguards apply. Nevertheless, the consequences to society and to the defendant—especially in murder cases in which capital punishment is a sentencing option—are so great that exceptional efforts are typically expended by both sides to contest all legal and factual issues. Usually, the most experienced prosecutors and defense attorneys try murder cases.

All criminal cases have a *corpus delicti*, which literally means the "body of a crime." In a murder prosecution, it is a reference to more than the deceased victim's corpse. It is evidence of the components of the crime: evidence that the victim is actually dead, that the death was caused by the criminal act of another, and, in some jurisdictions, that the defendant is that criminal. The importance of the *corpus delicti* rule, which is of practical significance primarily in murder cases, is that a conviction cannot rely upon the uncorroborated out-of-court statement or admission of the accused. The prosecution must offer additional evidence to establish the *corpus delicti* in order to obtain a conviction. Of course, a plea of guilt or other confession made in court is ordinarily sufficient to prove the *corpus delicti* and to support a conviction in a murder prosecution.

Punishment

Murder is punished by imprisonment, sometimes for life without possibility of parole, and by death. Criminal sentencing is usually left up to the discretion of the judge, within guidelines set by statute, even in cases tried before a jury. Some states, however, require that the jury determine or participate in the determination of whether capital punishment should be imposed. Many state statutes declare that the death penalty is proper only when certain aggravating factors occur during the crime. Those who oppose capital punishment contend that it is imposed arbitrarily, has little deterrent effect, and constitutes cruel and unusual punishment in violation of the Eighth Amendment to the Constitution. Nevertheless, most polls indicate that the majority of Americans support the use of the death penalty, and the Supreme Court has upheld the validity of properly drafted death-penalty legislation against constitutional challenges.

James N. Gilbert and the Editors

Further Reading

Corwin, Miles. *Homicide Special: On the Streets with the LAPD's Elite Detective Unit*. New York: Henry Holt, 2003. Dramatic look at modern detective work as an elite homicide unit investigates challenging murder cases.

Fox, James F., and Jack Levine. *The Will to Kill*. Boston: Allyn & Bacon, 2001. Board examination of criminal homicide as to prevalence and motive.

Gilbert, James N. *Criminal Investigation*. New York: Prentice Hall, 2004. Comprehensive college text that explains investigative processes through field and forensic fundamentals. Explores the origins of the detective, how specific types of crimes are investigated, and develops an appreciation for crime laboratory capabilities.

Graham, Hugh D., and Ted Gurr. *Violence in America: Historical and Comparative Perspectives*. New York: Sage, 1979. Historical discussion of violence and homicide trends within the United States.

Harries, Keith D. *Serious Violence: Patterns of Homicide and Assault in America*. 2d ed. Springfield, Ill.: Charles C Thomas, 1997. Comprehensive study of violent crime in the United States, addressing the subject from a variety of perspectives.

Hickey, Eric W. *Serial Murderers and Their Victims*. 3d ed. Belmont, Calif.: Wadsworth, 2002. Broad scholarly examination of serial killers, their victims, and their apprehension.

Levin, Jack, and James F. Fox. *Dead Lines: Essays in Murder and Mayhem*. Boston: Allyn & Bacon, 2001. Collection of newspaper editorials detailing murder trends.

Pinkerton, Alan. *Criminal Reminiscences and Detective Sketches*. New York: Fredonia Books, 2002. Autobiography of the famous nineteenth century private detective whose pioneering private investigative agency solved numerous criminal homicides.

Simons, David. *Homicide: A Year on the Killing Streets*. New York: Houghton Mifflin, 1991. Details the frequency of murder in urban America through the investigative efforts of Baltimore's homicide unit.

See also Abortion; Capital punishment; Cold cases; Common law; Crimes of passion; Criminal law; Drive-by shootings; Lynching; *Mala in se* and *mala prohibita*; Manslaughter; *Mens rea*; Murders, mass and serial; Self-defense; Suicide and euthanasia; *Tison v. Arizona*; Victimology.

Murders, mass and serial

Definition: Killing of multiple victims in a short period of time (mass murder) or over a longer period of time (serial murder)

Criminal justice issues: Deviancy; homicide; media

Significance: Although mass and serial murders are rare occurrences, they have an impact on American culture that far outweighs their statistical significance. These crimes, and the people who commit them, have made indelible marks upon folklore, the criminal justice system, and popular culture.

No single definition fully covers both mass murder and serial murder. Both crimes are types of multiple murders in that they involve the killing of multiple victims by the same offenders. What has been called "mass murder" involves the killing of at least three to five people within a brief period of a time by a single perpetrator. "Serial murder" also involves the killing of at least three to five people by a single perpetrator but is differentiated from mass murder in that it is carried out over a longer period of time—at least one week but usually months or even years.

The terms serial and mass murder are usually applied only to certain types of multiple homicides—generally those perpetrated by private individuals. War crimes, political murders, and most gang-related killings might technically be considered mass or serial murders, but they usually are not so classified. Although both kinds of crimes result in the deaths of multiple people, most serial killers are quite different from most mass murderers in profile, history, and motive.

History of the Crimes

Multiple murders of all kinds have occurred for untold centuries. It is impossible to get accurate numbers on such crimes in the remote past because of the meager law-enforcement resources that were long available to societies. Many mass and serial murderers doubtless went unpunished because of scanty investigative capabilities, or because of the offenders' personal, political, or financial influence on government. Nevertheless, some multiple murderers of the past are known to history. They include Gilles de Rais, a fifteenth century Frenchman who killed dozens of children; Elizabeth Bathory, a sixteenth century Hungarian countess; and the infamous Vlad III Dracula, or the "Impaler," the fifteenth century Transylvanian ruler who inspired the title character of Bram Stoker's novel about a vampire, *Dracula* (1897).

However, it was not until the end of the nineteenth century that serial killings began to be reported with any frequency at all. Perhaps improved investigative techniques or more crowded urban conditions made it less likely that these killings would go undetected. Perhaps the often-squalid living conditions in large cities and the increasing mobility of the population inspired more motives or opportunities for serial killings. In any case, the newly developed popular press made the public more aware of multiple murders. The late nineteenth century was a period in which members of the public in Western countries began to read sensationalized accounts of murderers such as London's Jack the Ripper, Chicago's H. H. Holmes, and France's Henri Landru.

Throughout the twentieth century, occasional serial or mass murders would capture the public's attention. For example, Howard Unruh killed thirteen people in Camden, New Jersey, during a

Multiple Murders in the Media

During the late twentieth century, both the news media and the entertainment industry were fascinated by multiple murders. Serial and mass murderers made frequent appearances on both television crime dramas and in mass-market paperbacks. They were also popular in films. According to a study of serial killers by Eric W. Hickey, during the 1950's, only four feature films had serial-killer themes. By contrast, twenty-three such films were made during the 1980's, and 117 during the 1990's.

Like gangsters and outlaws, serial killers and mass murderers are often portrayed in fiction as sympathetic antiheroes. A classic example is novelist Thomas Harris's psychopathic Hannibal Lecter of *The Silence of the Lambs* (1988). Despite his loathsome crimes, Lecter not only escapes punishment but also ultimately "gets the girl" in that novel's sequel, *Hannibal* (1999). Lecter is a prime example of a fictional serial killer who is portrayed as nearly superhuman in his intellectual abilities.

single afternoon in 1949. Charles Whitman shot and killed fifteen people from the tower on the University of Texas campus in 1966. During that same year, Richard Speck murdered eight student nurses. However, it was not until the end of the twentieth century that mass and serial murder truly captured the public imagination.

Popularizing Multiple Murders

By the late 1970's, multiple murderers, especially serial killers, suddenly seemed to be proliferating, and names such as Edmund Kemper, Charles Manson, John Wayne Gacy, Wayne Williams, Kenneth Bianchi, and James Huberty were constantly in the news. A charismatic serial killer named Ted Bundy attracted unprecedented media and public attention and helped to promote interest in serial killers generally. Meanwhile, law-enforcement authorities focused increasing attention on serial killers. New methods were developed for law-enforcement agencies to share information with one another—which was important because serial killers typically move about from place to place.

During the mid-1980's, the Federal Bureau of Investigation (FBI) began developing a criminal profiling system to assist in apprehending serious violent offenders. After the U.S. Congress held hearings, in which the frequency of serial killing was much exaggerated, it approved special funding for this program.

As the twentieth century drew to a close, attention to multiple murder was far from waning. New incidents received extensive media attention, such as a mass shooting of students and staff at Colorado's Columbine High School in 1999; the necrophilic and cannibalistic Jeffrey Dahmer, who killed more than fifteen people during the 1980's; the manifesto-writing "Unabomber," Ted Kaczynski; and murders committed by Aileen Wuornos, a woman who was widely—and falsely—proclaimed America's first female serial killer.

Frequency of Multiple Murders

Despite the attention that they receive, multiple murders are rare. Around the turn of the twenty-first century, it was estimated that twenty to one hundred serial killers were active in the United States at any given time. Serial killers appear to be even less common in other countries.

Although some observers claimed that serial killing was on the rise at that time, it was unclear whether this was true. It is probable that improved forensic and information-sharing capabilities have allowed law enforcement to link related murders that would previously have gone unconnected. Overall, violent crime rates (including murder) began decreasing nationwide beginning in the mid-1990's and continued going down through the middle of the following decade. However, there were some indications that the proportion of homicides committed against strangers—who are the most typical victims of serial killers—was increasing. There were also some data that suggested that mass murders were occurring with increasing frequency by the late 1990's.

Although multiple-murder crimes are rare, they do exact a serious toll on society. Not only do their victims lose their lives, but the victims' families are often left to grieve over the senselessness of the relations' deaths. Furthermore, the public at large suffers from increased anxiety as people tend to overestimate the chances of being killed by serial or mass murderers themselves. Serial killings also often carry exceptionally high monetary costs, as it is particularly difficult and expensive to investigate and prosecute these crimes. For example, it was estimated that it cost the state of California more than fourteen million dollars in 1999 to convict Charles Ng of murdering eleven people.

Why the Killers Kill

From the growing body of research on the underlying motives behind multiple murders, it appears that serial killers and mass murderers are driven by very different motivations. A number of theories have been developed to explain typologies of serial killers, as well as what inspires their behavior. Although a small number of these killers are motivated by financial gain (such as by collecting on insurance payments), most of them are driven by the desire physically or sexually to dominate and terrorize others. Some kill simply to silence their victims, while others enjoy the killing itself. Many killers enjoy media and law-enforcement attention, and when apprehended, not only confess to their crimes but sometimes even exaggerate how many murders they have committed.

Although most serial killers can be classified as having Antisocial Personality Disorder, most are not psychotic. Many, but not all, have suffered from horrific abuse as children. Some theorists believe that these people truly are "natural born killers" who literally have genes that predispose them to murderous behavior. Other theorists focus on other biological or biochemical factors, such as brain damage. Still others focus on psychological and social causes. Despite all the studies of serial killers, the puzzle of what creates them remains unsolved.

From a behavioral and psychological standpoint, most mass murderers differ greatly from serial killers. Mass murderers typically suffer from serious mental problems, including depression and psychosis. Many have experienced recent personal misfortunes, such as divorces or losses of their jobs. Compared to the behavior of serial killers, the behavior of mass murderers is less calculated. Many seem to "snap" and may view their violence as a last attempt to gain control over those who they believe are responsible for their woes. Unlike serial killers, mass murderers usually make little or no attempt to escape apprehension, and they frequently either kill themselves or are killed by police. They are generally not interested in winning media attention or notoriety.

Director Oliver Stone's 1994 film *Natural Born Killers* is an ultraviolent satire about a young couple, played by Juliette Lewis and Woody Harrelson, who go on a senseless killing spree. The film takes its title from the popular notion that some criminal behavior can be explained by the fact that some people are simply "natural-born killers." *(Museum of Modern Art, Film Stills Archive)*

Mass Murders

From the perspectives of law-enforcement officials and prosecutors, mass murders are very different from serial killings. With mass murders, there is rarely any question of who the perpetrators are, so identifying suspects does not become an issue. Moreover, apprehending mass murderers is also usually not a major issue. If they do not kill themselves or get killed by police, they are generally arrested at or near the scenes of their crimes.

In cases involving mass murder, police rarely need to use investigative techniques to identify, track down, or apprehend offenders. Moreover, because mass murders usually occur in one confined location, law-enforcement officers rarely have to coordinate their investigative work with agencies in other jurisdictions. Instead, law-enforcement action in these cases generally focuses on protecting potential victims, arresting—or killing or incapacitating—the offenders, and collecting evidence after the crimes end.

Because approximately one-half of mass murderers kill themselves or are killed by others, prosecutions for these crimes are uncommon. When these crimes are prosecuted, it is usually not difficult to prove that the offenders have committed the acts in question, as mass murderers generally make little attempt to hide their crimes or identities. The more difficult prosecutorial task often lies in proving the defendants' legal responsibility for their murders. Mass murderers frequently suffer from mental illness and may plead not guilty by reason of insanity. However, insanity defenses are not necessarily successful. For example, after a woman named Andrea Yates drowned her five children in Texas in 2001, she claimed to have been suffering from postpartum depression—a believable claim, considering the horrific nature of her crime. Nevertheless, the jury rejected her insanity defense, and she was convicted. However, the jury may have been influenced by testimony about her mental state when it sentenced her to life in prison rather than execution. (In early 2005, a Texas appeals court reversed Yates's capital murder conviction be-

cause testimony from an expert witness had been flawed. However, she remained in prison, where she was receiving psychiatric care.)

Like Andrea Yates, most convicted mass murderers receive severe sentences, usually either life in prison—often without possibility of pa-

---

Profiling Serial and Mass Murderers

Every serial and mass murderer is unique. It can be dangerous to generalize about "typical" offenders, but multiple-murder offenders have many characteristics in common.

Trait	Patterns
Gender	Most offenders are male. Female serial killers occur but are much less common than male killers. Female mass murderers are extremely rare.
Race	Most offenders are white, but there are exceptions to this rule. For example, Wayne Williams, the Atlanta child killer of 1979-1981, was African American.
Age	Serial killers usually begin killing when they are in their twenties; mass murderers are typically ten to twenty years older when they begin.
Intelligence	Serial killers are typically intelligent but often have experienced severe failures in their careers and personal lives. Mass murderers are often unemployed, sometimes only recently.
Personal histories	Serial killers often display patterns of sociopathic behavior and may have histories of deviant sexual or violent behavior, including animal abuse; mass murderers usually do not.
Fantasy lives	Serial killers often fantasize about their crimes.
Alcohol and drugs	Serial killers sometimes use drugs or alcohol before or while committing their crimes; mass murderers rarely do.
Childhoods	Serial killers often have had miserable childhoods and have suffered physical or mental abuse. They may also have histories of serious head trauma and neurological disorders.
Military	Mass murderers often have served in the military.

role—or death. Because of legal complications involving capital punishment, the notorious mass murderers Charles Manson and Richard Speck had their death sentences changed to life in prison while they were facing execution during the early 1970's.

Serial Killers

In comparison to investigating mass murders, investigating serial killings is difficult. Many serial killers are mobile, so investigating their crimes requires that law-enforcement agents in several jurisdictions share information. Moreover, it may not even be clear that serial murders are linked. In addition, many victims of serial killers are not found until long after they are killed, by which time evidence relating to their murders may have become lost or degraded. To

Aileen Wuornos, one of the few female serial killers known in U.S. history, was convicted of killing at least six middle-aged men along the highways of central Florida in 1989-1990. This 2001 photograph was taken when she was about to ask a court to drop her appeals so she could be executed. On October 9, 2002, she was executed by lethal injection. *(AP/Wide World Photos)*

make investigation even more difficult, serial killers typically have no prior connections with their victims and nearly always take careful, even elaborate, steps to avoid detection.

By the end of the twentieth century, a number of advances were helping law-enforcement identify and apprehend serial killers. These included computerized databases that are shared across jurisdictions and, when a serial killing is recognized, the creation of special task forces. Because serial killers often cross state lines, the FBI may become involved. Since the 1980's, police have made use of a variety of kinds of profiling, including offender and crime scene profiling. Advances in forensic science have also proved invaluable, such as new DNA analysis techniques.

Prosecution of serial killers is usually time-consuming and can be expensive. It is more difficult to tie accused serial killers to their crimes than to link mass murderers to theirs. Prosecution of serial killers also usually requires cooperation among law-enforcement jurisdictions and agencies. When killings occur in more than one state, the defendant may need to be tried multiple times. Once serial killers are caught, some of them readily confess, and may cooperate with authorities, which makes prosecution easier. However, they may also make exaggerated or false claims about their own misdeeds. Some may also enjoy manipulating the criminal justice system, deliberately drawing out trial processes as long as possible. Although some serial killers do attempt to use the insanity defense, as in the case of Jeffrey Dahmer, they are rarely successful.

When serial killers are convicted, they are nearly always sentenced to death or, if they are in a state that does not have capital punishment, life imprisonment. As in most capital cases, appeals typically go on for years, which adds to the already high costs associated with serial killings.

Spree Killers

A third type of multiple murderer, distinct from both mass and serial killers, is the spree killer. Spree killers murder several people in several locations over a period of a few days or weeks. One of the earliest and best-known spree killers was Charles Starkweather, who, together with his fourteen-year-old girlfriend, Caril Ann Fugate, killed eleven people in Nebraska in 1958.

Unlike serial killers, spree killers make little effort to hide their crimes and allow no cooling-off periods between their crimes. The people they kill are often victims of circumstance, not people they seek out for any specific reasons. Spree killers often commit their murders simply as a means toward other ends, such as stealing their victims' cars.

Spree killings often appear to be sparked by single events, such as botched robberies or prison escapes that kill associates and leave the survivors feeling desperate. Some spree killers are driven by a need to carry out a particular mission. For example, Andrew Cunanan went on a cross-country killing spree in 1997, seeking revenge on people he thought responsible for his having contracted AIDS. Similarly, a white supremacist named Benjamin Nathan Smith went on a spree shooting members of minority groups over a period of three days in 1999. Most spree killers—like Cunanan and Smith—end up dying by their own hands or those of the police.

Phyllis B. Gerstenfeld

Further Reading

Hickey, Eric W. *Serial Murderers and Their Victims*. 3d ed. Belmont, Calif.: Wadsworth, 2002. Broad scholarly examination of serial killers, their victims, and their apprehension.

Jenkins, Philip. *Using Murder: The Social Construction of Serial Homicide*. New York: Aldine de Gruyter, 1994. An examination of the sensationalism and mythology surrounding serial murder.

Kelleher, Michael D. *Flash Point: The American Mass Murderer*. Westport, Conn.: Praeger, 1997. Examines the causes of mass murder.

Lewis, Dorothy Otnow. *Guilty by Reason of Insanity: A Psychiatrist Explores the Minds of Killers*. New York: Ivy Books, 1999. Psychiatrist Lewis discusses her research linking violent behavior to childhood trauma and brain damage.

Morrison, Helen, and Harold Goldberg. *My Life Among the Serial Killers: Inside the Minds of the World's Most Notorious Murders*. New York: William Morrow, 2004. Memoir of a psychiatrist who has worked with more than eighty serial killers.

Ressler, Robert K., and Thomas Schachtman. *Whoever Fights Monsters: My Twenty Years Tracking Serial Killers for the FBI*. New York: St. Martin's Press, 1993. Memoirs of the man who created the FBI's criminal personality profiling system.

Rule, Ann. *The Stranger Beside Me*. New York: Signet, 2001. Rule writes about her one-time friend, Ted Bundy.

Schechter, Harold. *The Serial Killer Files: The Who, What, Where, How, and Why of the World's Most Terrifying Murderers*. New York: Ballantine, 2003. A broad and comprehensive overview of issues related to serial killers.

See also Animal abuse; Capital punishment; Cold cases; Criminals; Manslaughter; Murder and homicide; Psychological profiling; Violent Criminal Apprehension Program.

N

National Commission on the Causes and Prevention of Violence

Identification: Federal body appointed by President Lyndon B. Johnson to examine the causes, consequences, and prevention of violence in American society

Date: 1968-1969

Criminal justice issues: Morality and public order; political issues; violent crime

Significance: The commission was created in response to recent political assassinations and a wave of urban rioting growing out of racial disorders and protests against U.S. involvement in the Vietnam War.

President Lyndon B. Johnson created the National Commission on the Causes and Prevention of Violence shortly after civil rights leader Martin Luther King, Jr., and Senator Robert F. Kennedy were gunned down in early 1968. The mission of the government body was to examine the broad nature, causes, and consequences of individual and collective violence in the United States.

The commission was chaired by Milton S. Eisenhower, the brother of former president Dwight D. Eisenhower. On December 10, 1969, the commission issued its final report titled *To Establish Justice, to Insure Domestic Tranquility*. That report had been preceded by several volumes of task-force reports broadly covering the causes, processes, and consequences of violence as well as recommendations for research and prevention.

During its investigations, the commission examined specific forms of violence including assassinations and political violence, individual and group acts of violence, firearm offenses, confrontations of demonstrators and police, and histori-cal perspectives of violence in America. One of the commission's task-force reports examined the sociological and psychological effects of media portrayals of violence—particularly those on television—on audiences. The commission noted its concerns about the powerful influence television had on what children learned. Television, it noted, "is never too busy to talk to them, and it never has to brush them aside while it does household chores."

Another commission report considered law and order in America, discussing the role of law enforcement, including issues of accountability, training, staffing, and finances, in light of governmental reaction to public disorders in Chicago and Washington, D.C., in 1968. In its final report, the commission suggested a reordering of national priorities and recommended specific steps to accelerate research initiatives that would address the causes and prevention of violence in American society.

Anthony J. Luongo III

Further Reading

Curtis, Lynn A., ed. *American Violence and Public Policy: An Update of the National Commission on the Causes and Prevention of Violence*. New Haven, Conn.: Yale University Press, 1985.

Lange, David L., Robert K. Baker, and Sandra J. Ball. *Mass Media and Violence: A Report to the National Commission on the Causes and Prevention of Violence*. Washington, D.C.: Government Printing Office, 1969.

National Commission on the Causes and Prevention of Violence. *To Establish Justice, to Insure Domestic Tranquility*. Washington, D.C.: Government Printing Office, 1969.

See also Criminal justice system; Domestic violence; National Institute of Justice; Neighborhood watch programs; President, U.S.; Prison violence.

National Crime Information Center

Identification: Federal agency with computerized index consisting of individuals and records

Date: Established in 1971

Criminal justice issues: Crime statistics; federal law; law-enforcement organization

Significance: The National Crime Information Center (NCIC), a powerful computer database maintained by the Federal Bureau of Investigation (FBI), provides law-enforcement agencies with access to recorded criminal justice information through its computerized records and library collection. The NCIC allows agencies to gather cross-boundary criminal justice information efficiently.

Since its creation during the early 1970's, the National Crime Information Center has amassed a substantial collection of criminal justice databases. Topics covered in the databases include missing persons, wanted persons, stolen and recovered guns, stolen securities, stolen and recovered motor vehicles, stolen license plates, and other stolen articles. NCIC users are able to access these data when they need them. Users have expressed satisfaction with NCIC and have requested enhancements over time.

To enhance the NCIC, the FBI has established NCIC-2000, which allows full on-line computer search and retrieval of crime incidents nationwide. Police officials can use it to check liens, images (such as photographs and fingerprints), license plates, and other routine items instantly. It is believed that this increased functionality helps reduce false arrests.

The FBI has merged NCIC with the National Incident-Based Reporting System (NIBRS) and Automated Fingerprint Identification System (AFIS) to create the Criminal Justice Information Services division (CJIS).

The CJIS serves as a single source for state, local, and private law-enforcement officials seeking crime analysis data, incident information, and criminal imaging data. In addition, the division provides information services for the FBI and its direct enforcement divisions. Among the stated goals of the CJIS are to develop consistent crime information collection and recording standards and to develop and implement a strategy for assisting state and other users in creating linkages to the FBI's computer systems. The CJIS also offers training and support services for federal, state, and local CJIS users.

Dale K. Nesbary

Further Reading

The National Crime Information Center and You. Washington, D.C.: U.S. Department of Justice, Federal Bureau of Investigation, 1976.

National Crime Information Center: The Investigative Tool: A Guide to the Use and Benefits of NCIC. Washington, D.C.: U.S. Department of Justice, Federal Bureau of Investigation, National Crime Information Center, 1984.

See also Booking; Computer information systems; Law enforcement; Multiple jurisdiction offenses; National Stolen Property Act; Neighborhood watch programs; Uniform Crime Reports.

National Crime Victimization Survey

Definition: Biannual collection of data on crime conducted by the U.S. Bureau of Justice Statistics

Date: Established in 1973

Criminal justice issues: Crime statistics; victims

Significance: The statistics collected by the National Crime Victimization Survey are considered an outstanding source for understanding crime in the United States.

The National Crime Victimization Survey (NCVS) program was originally published as the National Crime Survey (NCS) in 1973. The federal program collects data through surveys of approximately 100,000 individuals, aged 12 and older, from about 50,000 households. The survey methodology attempts to offer a sample that represents nearly all sociodemographic and geographical categories in the United States. The large sample size allows the NCVS to offer comprehensive pictures of reported and unreported crimes.

The Bureau of the Census collects the data under the direction of the Bureau of Justice Statistics. This bureau's work allows researchers to address the primary flaw in the Federal Bureau of Investigation's Uniform Crime Reports (UCR). Because data from the UCR include only crimes that are reported to police, many crimes go unrecorded. Recent reports suggest that more than two million violent crimes go unreported every year in the United States.

Because the survey is performed every six months, respondents' recollections of details are considered reasonably fresh in their minds. Also, publishing data from each year allows for an understanding of crime trends. The survey was updated and redesigned in 1992, but continued to measure specific annual crime rates in a consistent and reliable manner.

Data from this survey make it possible to study characteristics of crime victims and offenders and relationships among them and the consequences they face, as well as actual crime incidence rates, whether or not reported to the police. The data also make possible clearer understanding of crime trends by providing consistent crime definitions and measures over time and location.

Some professionals in the field of criminal justice have questioned the validity of the NCVS because self-reported data may be inaccurate and not subject to detailed scrutiny of respondents' reported validity. However, the survey methodology itself is widely respected as a legitimate source of understanding the nature of crime in the United States.

John C. Kilburn, Jr.

Further Reading

Doerner, William G. *Victimology*. Cincinnati: Anderson Publishing, 2002.

Mosher, Clayton J., Terance D. Miethe, and Dretha Phillips. *The Mismeasure of Crime*. Thousand Oaks, Calif.: Sage, 2002.

Crime Statistics on the Web

The findings of the National Crime Victimization Survey can be quickly found on the Web site of the U.S. Department of Justice's Bureau of Justice Statistics at www.ojp.usdoj.gov/bjs/cvict.htm. To reach the site quickly, simply type "BJS home page" in a search engine such as Google. This well-organized site offers textual summaries, tables, and graphs of crime statistics. The site also offers links to other sites with crime statistics.

SEARCH, The National Consortium for Justice Information and Statistics. *Public Attitudes Toward Uses of Criminal History Information*. Washington, D.C.: Bureau of Justice Statistics, 2001.

See also Bureau of Justice Statistics; Crime Index; Domestic violence; National Organization for Victim Assistance; Uniform Crime Reports; Victim and Witness Protection Act; Victim assistance programs; Victimology; Victims of Crime Act.

National District Attorneys Association

Identification: National professional organization of government prosecutors

Date: Established in 1950

Criminal justice issues: Prosecution; law-enforcement organization

Significance: The National District Attorneys Association (NDAA) offers training to state prosecutors, assists with networking, and conducts research on prosecutors to assist prosecutors with maintaining community safety.

Founded in 1950 to help communities, victims, and prosecutors, the NDAA is based in Alexandria, Virginia, and has the mission of supporting prosecutors throughout the United States to ensure that prosecutors protect the rights and safety of citizens. The organization comprises approximately seven thousand members, who voice the concerns of prosecutors to policymakers to improve legislation. The NDAA publishes National Prosecution Standards, which summarize the best information and the ideal practices available to prosecutors that have been adopted by many district attorney offices. The NDAA also publishes *The Prosecutor*, a newsletter designed to aid prosecutors in their daily work. Perhaps the most beneficial tool offered to prosecutors by the NDAA may be its networking services. Through the NDAA, local prosecutors can connect with other prosecutors across the United States for assistance with cases. The NDAA also connects prosecutors with experts and pertinent information about which practices are most successful.

The NDAA promotes education and skills of prosecutors through three satellite organizations. In 1984, it founded the American Prosecutors Research Institute (APRI) to conduct research on prosecutors, organize prosecutor training, and provide technical assistance to the NDAA. The APRI offers training on a variety of specialized topics, including antiterrorism, child abuse, community prosecution, use of DNA, drug crimes, gun violence prosecution, hate crimes, juvenile justice, violent crimes against women, and white-collar crime.

The NDAA also sponsors the National College of District Attorneys (NCDA), which was founded in South Carolina in 1970. That body provides training and continuing legal education to prosecutors. Finally, the NDAA collaborates with the U.S. Department of Justice to offer prosecutor training through the National Advocacy Center (NAC).

Jennifer C. Gibbs

Further Reading

ABA Standards for Criminal Justice: Prosecution and Defense Function. 3d ed. Washington, D.C.: American Bar Association, 1993.

Forst, Brian. "Prosecution's Coming of Age." *Justice Research and Policy* 2, no. 1 (Spring, 2000): 21-46.

Gershman, Bennett L. *Prosecutorial Misconduct.* New York: Clark Boardman Callaghan, 1999.

Stewart, James B. *The Prosecutors.* New York: Simon & Schuster, 1987.

See also Attorney ethics; Criminal prosecution; District attorneys; Public prosecutors.

National Guard

Identification: Federal military force with the dual mission of being on call to serve as state militia units and acting as a reserve force of the U.S. Army and Air Force during war time and in federally declared emergencies

Date: Authorized under the Uniform Militia Law of 1792; established as the National Guard Association in 1878

Criminal justice issues: Federal law; law-enforcement organization; military justice

Significance: Although organized, equipped, and trained for combat as part of the federal military, the National Guard is on call to state government to serve as militia units during state emergencies such as riots and natural disasters.

In the late nineteenth and early twentieth centuries, the National Guard replaced the old organized militia as well as the regiments that the individual states had raised for federal service during wartime. The National Guard became the vehicle for continued state participation in federal war efforts. However when the National Guard is not performing its federal military missions, its units are available to state governments for local law-enforcement and disaster relief missions.

State and Federal Origins

The modern National Guard originated during widespread labor strikes in the coal industry in 1877. State militia units then in existence were either unable or unwilling to confront the strikers. As a result, state and business leaders supported the idea of increased federal support for militia in the form of the National Guard. The National Guard's first complete mobilization occurred during World War I, when the entire National Guard entered the Army of the United States, thus leaving the states without organized militias.

A need for militia arose during the two years following the war, when new labor and racial unrest often overwhelmed police forces. When the Boston police went on strike in 1919, Massachusetts mobilized its own state guard, which it had formed to replace the National Guard as the state militia to maintain order during the war. However, most states did not have replacements for their National Guard forces and could only petition the federal War Department to reconstitute the National Guard.

Posse Comitatus

Federal military forces are limited in their authority to perform civil law-enforcement duties by the Posse Comitatus Act of 1878. That federal law limits the ability of sheriffs to compel federal soldiers to enforce civil law. Although the National Guard is primarily a federal military force, its units are not inhibited by the Posse Comitatus Act while it is under state authority. State governors can therefore employ their National Guard units for law enforcement without the restrictions that would be placed on federal soldiers.

Prior to the creation of state police forces between the world wars, the National Guard pro-vided many of the services later provided by state police. However, the National Guard as well as the federal government has always seen state missions as secondary to the guard's federal warfighting mission. As a consequence, National Guard units are organized, trained, and equipped primarily for military combat. National Guard leaders encouraged the development of state police, allowing guard units to distance themselves from controversial civilian disturbances, such as strike breaking, which had cost the guard the support of organized labor.

The Civil Rights and Antiwar Movements

The late 1950's and 1960's saw new civil disorders with the rise of the Civil Rights movement and widespread opposition to the Vietnam War, and the guard again became involved with civil law enforcement. For political and global strategic reasons, few National Guard units were sent to Vietnam. In Tennessee and Kentucky, the

National Guard troops acting under federal orders to clear a safe pathway for African American students to enter Little Rock's Central High School during the 1957 integration crisis. *(Library of Congress)*

guard provided credible service in protecting black students entering what had been white-only public high schools. The attempt by Arkansas governor Orville Faubus to use the National Guard units to prevent black students from attending Central High School in Little Rock in 1957 moved President Dwight D. Eisenhower to federalize Arkansas's National Guard troops and order most of its members to stay home while federal soldiers and a small number of guardsmen kept order and ensured that the black students were allowed to enter the school safely. Similar uses of the National Guard continued into the 1970's, when the Massachusetts National Guard was called to maintain order at several Boston schools during the busing unrest.

The National Guard was also called up during episodes of urban voting. In 1965, for example, California's National Guard responded to rioting in the Watts section of Los Angeles. Two years later Michigan called out its National Guard to restore civil order in Detroit. As a result of the evident shortcomings in the guard's performance during the Detroit riots, guardsmen received additional training and equipment to deal with civilian law-enforcement missions. In 1968, the National Guard responded to riots in twenty-seven states and the District of Columbia. Many of these disturbances followed the assassination of civil rights leader Martin Luther King, Jr., in April of that year.

Opposition to the Vietnam War also brought increased use of the guard in domestic police actions during the 1960's and early 1970's. The most infamous incident occurred on Kent State University in Ohio. On May 4, 1970, a clash between protesters and a company of the National Guard ended when guardsmen opened fire on the protesters. Four civilians were killed and another nine were injured, after almost sixty guardsmen had been injured by rocks and bottles thrown at them. After the Kent State incident, guardsmen received more training in riot control; however, governors became increasingly hesitant to use the guard for similar missions.

Barry M. Stentiford

Further Reading

Brown, Roger Allen, William Fedorochko, Jr., and John F. Schank. *Assessing the State and Federal Missions of the National Guard*. Santa Monica, Calif.: Rand National Defense Research Institute, 1995. Study of the problems faced by the National Guard during the 1990's, as it shrank following the Cold War. Assesses the ability of the National Guard to perform both its state missions and federal military combat missions within a more limited structure.

Doubler, Michael D. *I Am the Guard: A History of the Army National Guard, 1636-2000*. Washington, D.C.: Army National Guard, 2001. Official history of the Army National Guard, with emphasis on the period since World War II.

Higham, Robin, ed. *Bayonets in the Streets: The Use of Troops in Civil Disturbances*. Lawrence: University of Kansas Press, 1969. History of the use of both federal and state soldiers during riots and other periods of civil unrest.

Mahon, John K. *History of the Militia and the National Guard*. New York: Macmillan, 1983. Part of the Macmillan Wars of the United States series. Especially valuable for its coverage of the nineteenth century militia.

Stentiford, Barry M. *The American Home Guard: The State Militia in the Twentieth Century*. College Station: Texas A&M Press, 2002. Study of state militia units not part of the National Guard. Emphasizes the inability of the National Guard to perform state functions during full federal mobilizations.

See also Boston police strike; Coast Guard, U.S.; Homeland Security Department; Martial law; Military justice; Race riots in the twentieth century; Right to bear arms; State police.

National Institute of Justice

Identification: Federal research agency charged with investigating certain criminological program areas

Date: Established in 1968

Criminal justice issues: Crime statistics; federal law; professional standards

Significance: Since its founding, the National Institute of Justice has been a major na-

National Institute of Justice Program Areas

✓ Crime control and prevention, including policing
✓ Drugs and crime
✓ Justice systems and offender behavior, including corrections
✓ Violence and victimization
✓ Communications and information technologies
✓ Critical incident response
✓ Investigative and forensic sciences, including DNA
✓ Nonlethal weapon technologies
✓ Law-enforcement officer protection
✓ Education and training technologies
✓ Testing and standards
✓ Technology assistance to law enforcement and corrections agencies
✓ Field testing of promising programs
✓ International crime control

Further Reading

Adams, K., et al. *Use of Force by Police: Overview of National and Local Data*. Washington, D.C.: U.S. Department of Justice, National Institute of Justice and Bureau of Justice Statistics, 1999.

Brady, T. V. *Measuring What Matters, Part One: Measures of Crime, Fear, and Disorder*. Washington, D.C.: National Institute of Justice, 1996.

National Institute of Justice. *Evaluation Plan*. Washington, D.C.: National Institute of Justice, 1991.

_____. *National Institute of Justice Journal*. Washington, D.C.: National Institute of Justice, 1992.

_____. *National Institute of Justice/ NCJRS: Meeting Your Needs for Criminal Justice Information*. Washington, D.C.: National Institute of Justice, 1984.

tional and international center for criminal justice research, policy experimentation aimed at professionalizing law enforcement, and more effective ways of controlling crime.

Following recommendations from President Lyndon B. Johnson's 1967 Committee on Law Enforcement and Administration of Justice, Congress enacted the Omnibus Crime Control and Safe Streets Act of 1968. The law created, within the Department of Justice, the Law Enforcement Assistance Administration (LEAA), which in turn established the National Institute of Justice (NIJ).

The NIJ has multiple research responsibilities aimed at revising extant criminal justice policies and practices, producing new crime-control programs, encouraging the professionalization of law enforcement, sponsoring experimental training programs, and assessing law enforcement and criminal justice standards and performance. It also collects and disseminates relevant data and information. During its first decades of operations, the NIJ provided important resources for the study of violent crime, career criminals, sentencing, rehabilitation, the use of police resources, community crime prevention, and pretrial processes.

Clifton K. Yearley

See also Attorney general of the United States; Justice Department, U.S.; National Commission on the Causes and Prevention of Violence; Omnibus Crime Control and Safe Streets Act of 1968; President's Commission on Law Enforcement and Administration of Justice.

National Narcotics Act

The Law: Federal legislation that established a high-level government board to coordinate law-enforcement efforts in the federal war on drugs

Date: Signed into law on October 12, 1984

Criminal justice issues: Federal law; substance abuse

Significance: Passage of the National Narcotics Act centralized federal drug-control efforts for the first time by creating the National Drug Enforcement Policy Board, which later evolved into the current Office of National Drug Control Policy.

The National Narcotics Act represented an effort by the U.S. Congress to improve the effectiveness and efficiency of federal drug-law enforcement. The act established the National Drug Enforcement Policy Board (NDEPB), whose mission was to develop a national drug-control policy, implement that policy, and coordinate the efforts of multiple federal law-enforcement agencies.

Before passage of the National Narcotics Act, federal agencies responsible for drug-law enforcement operated without the direction or coordination of a central agency or official. At its inception, the NDEPB was chaired by Attorney General Edwin Meese and comprised additional members of President Ronald Reagan's cabinet. The board represented a compromise between Congress, which had favored creation of a new cabinet-level drug control official, and President Reagan, who believed a new cabinet member would create additional bureaucracy that would disrupt existing law-enforcement efforts.

In November, 1988, the NDEPB was formally dissolved with the repeal of the National Narcotics Act, which was superseded by passage of the National Narcotics Leadership Act. This new legislation created the Office of National Drug Control Policy (ONDCP) and fulfilled Congress's original intention to establish a cabinet-level drug-control official. The head of ONDCP, commonly referred to as the "drug czar," is responsible for developing national drug-control strategy and coordinating federal law-enforcement efforts.

Damon Mitchell

Further Reading

Gray, James. *Why Our Drug Laws Have Failed and What We Can Do About It: A Judicial Indictment of the War on Drugs*. Philadelphia: Temple University Press, 2001.

Maccoun, Robert J. *Drug War Heresies: Learning from Other Vices, Times, and Places*. New York: Cambridge University Press, 2001.

Musto, David F. *The American Disease: Origins of Narcotic Control*. New York: Oxford University Press, 1999.

President's Commission on Organized Crime. *America's Habit: Drug Abuse, Drug Trafficking, and Organized Crime*. Washington, D.C.: Government Printing Office, 1986.

See also Comprehensive Crime Control Act; Comprehensive Drug Abuse Prevention and Control Act; "Drug czar"; Drug Enforcement Administration; Drug legalization debate; Drug testing; Drugs and law enforcement; Organized crime.

National Organization for Victim Assistance

Identification: Oldest victim-assistance organization in existence, a private, nonprofit organization made up of practitioners, academics, criminal justice agents, victims, and survivors

Date: Founded in 1975

Criminal justice issues: Medical and health issues; victims

Significance: In addition to advocating for victims' rights, the National Organization for Victim Assistance (NOVA) helps crime, trauma, and disaster victims by providing direct services and education.

The mission of the National Organization for Victim Assistance is to bring attention to victims' rights and services. NOVA has four main purposes: national advocacy for the purpose of implementing or promoting victims' rights; direct services to victims, including training staff, volunteers, and others to meet the needs of victims; assistance to professional colleagues, including aiding victim advocates and others through training and publications and identifying imminent issues; and services to member organizations and individuals, including monthly bulletins and up-to-date programs concerned with victim assistance.

NOVA's Web Site

More information about involvement opportunities and services offered by the National Organization for Victim Assistance can be found on the World Wide Wed at www.trynova.org.

As explained on the site, the organization promotes rights and services for victims of crime and crisis everywhere.

Significant contributions to victim assistance by NOVA include crime victim compensation programs in every state, the District of Columbia, and the U.S. Virgin Islands; establishing the practice of reading victim impact statements at sentencing and parole in most states; enactment of victims' bills of rights in almost every state; providing support to victims through personal contact; improvement of agency response to major incidents; providing training to all manner of personnel who work with victims, including criminal justice, mental health, clergy, and medical personnel; and identifying key issues in victim assistance that need attention.

Elizabeth Quinn DeValve

Further Reading

Office for Victims of Crime. *New Directions from the Field: Victims' Rights and Services for the Twenty-first Century*. Washington, D.C.: U.S. Department of Justice, 1998.

Young, Marlene A. *Victim Assistance: Frontiers and Fundamentals*. Dubuque, Iowa: Kendall/ Hunt, 1993.

See also National Crime Victimization Survey; Victim and Witness Protection Act; Victim assistance programs; Victimology; Victims of Crime Act.

National Stolen Property Act

The Law: Federal legislation that makes trading and transporting many categories of stolen goods across state lines a federal crime

Criminal justice issues: Federal law; fraud; robbery, theft, and burglary

Date: Became law on May 22, 1934

Significance: The National Stolen Property Act—and its many revisions—is a crucial federal law-enforcement tool that has been used to prosecute offenders in a wide range of criminal activities.

Since it was first passed in 1934, the National Stolen Property Act has been revised numerous times. The law was originally enacted to broaden the provisions of the National Motor Vehicle Theft Act of 1919 to include stolen goods other than automobiles. The new law increased regulations on interstate commerce and trade shipments worth at least five thousand dollars that were fraudulently obtained or stolen. The law was also broadened to cover persons who knowingly accepted pilfered goods or securities. However, the act does not apply to fraudulent securities connected to the U.S. or foreign governments.

Punishments for offenders convicted under the original National Stolen Property Act included maximum fines of ten thousand dollars and prison sentences not to exceed ten years. Revisions to the law have left the maximum prison sentences unchanged, but maximum fines are now left open to judicial discretion. Other amendments to the law have added other categories of stolen goods, such as fraudulent state tax stamps and counterfeiting materials. The law has been used to prosecute criminals in a wide variety of criminal fields, ranging from art and antiquity theft, to espionage and cybercrime.

Kathryn Vincent

Further Reading

Friedman, Lawrence M. *American Law in the Twentieth Century*. New Haven, Conn.: Yale University Press, 2002.

Gonzalez, Jorge C. "Punishing the Causer as the Principal: *Mens Rea* and the Interstate Transportation Element of the National Stolen Property Act." *San Diego Law Review* 38, no. 2 (2001): 629.

See also Burglary; Computer crime; Forgery; Fraud; Motor vehicle theft; National Crime Information Center; Robbery; Theft.

Neighborhood watch programs

Definition: Community programs designed to reduce local crime and fear of crime and help restore a sense of community

Criminal justice issue: Crime prevention

Significance: Since the 1970's, citizen involvement in crime prevention has increased, but

A regular feature of formal neighborhood watch programs is the posting of signs to help deter possible offenders from attempting to commit crimes. *(AP/Wide World Photos)*

questions about the effectiveness of citizen participation in reducing crime remain unanswered.

The modern movement of community crime prevention grew out of the realization that government institutions represented by the police and courts were failing in their efforts to reduce crime and restore social order. During the late 1960's and early 1970's, the neighborhood watch movement began as a grassroots effort to reduce residential burglaries,. It quickly became linked with other urban police programs.

Neighborhood watch programs are grounded in two theoretical crime prevention models: informal social control and opportunity reduction. Informal social control assumes that maintaining public peace is not the primary responsibility of the police. Order should be maintained by unconscious networks of voluntary controls and standards among members of communities and en-

forced by the people themselves. The opportunity reduction model emphasizes the value of deterrence through modifying physical environments to improve security and maintain an informed group of citizens who adapt certain techniques to reduce criminal victimization.

Neighborhood watch programs involve small groups of people connected by their neighborhoods who share information provided by local law-enforcement agencies on local crime problems. Block meetings are organized by police officers who are trained in crime prevention techniques. The meetings offer training in crime strategies, surveillance, home security surveys, internal communications, and property markings or signage.

Neighborhood residents help provide surveillance by becoming the "eyes and ears" of the police, to whom they report suspicious activities. They also establish communication networks by setting up telephone trees with which to disseminate information quickly, utilizing computer communications, and holding periodic meetings. Individual residents improve their own home security by creating written, photographic, and electronic records of their assets. Residents participating in the programs post permanent signs in their yards advertising the fact that neighborhood watch programs are at work.

Effectiveness of the Programs

Citizen involvement in crime prevention began increasing rapidly during the mid-1990's. Neighborhood watch programs have forged partnerships between the police and communities and helped to reduce the isolation and fear that criminal activity fosters within communities. However, questions remain whether the programs are effective tools in reducing crime. Two types of empirical studies have been used to support the concept of neighborhood watch; neighborhood surveys on citizen participation, and reactions to crime and the evaluation of crime prevention programs.

Neighborhood watch studies have garnered varied responses. Some studies have confirmed that citizen participation and informal social control mechanisms such as neighborhood watch can be implanted in communities where they do not already exist. However, some researchers find that citizen participation is a middle-class phenomenon and that neighborhood watch programs do not work in poor neighborhoods.

Tracie L. Keesee

Further Reading

Garofalo, James, and Maureen McLeod. *Improving the Use and Effectiveness of Neighborhood Watch Programs*. Washington, D.C.: National Institute of Justice, 1988.

Mann, Stephanie, and M. C. Blakeman. *Safe Homes, Safe Neighborhoods: Stopping Crime Where You Live*. Berkeley, Calif.: Nolo Press, 1993.

Monson, Thomas N., et al. *Community Watch Administration Manual*. 3d ed. Medford, Oreg.: Crime Prevention Resources, 2003.

Tonry, Michael, and David P. Farrington. *Building a Safer Society: Strategic Approaches to Crime Prevention*. Chicago: University of Chicago Press, 1995.

See also Citizen arrests; Community-based corrections; Community-oriented policing; Community service; Law enforcement; McGruff the Crime Dog; National Crime Information Center; National Institute of Justice; "Not-in-my-backyard" attitudes; Police; Strategic policing; Youth gangs.

New Jersey v. T.L.O.

The Case: U.S. Supreme Court ruling on search and seizure

Date: Decided on January 15, 1985

Criminal justice issues: Juvenile justice; privacy; search and seizure

Significance: This decision established the standards by which the protections of the Fourth Amendment apply to searches of students by school officials.

A teacher at Piscataway High School in New Jersey found two students smoking cigarettes in a school restroom in violation of the school's rules. After being sent to the school office, one of the students, "T.L.O.," a fourteen-year-old freshman, denied smoking. Based on the report he had received from the teacher, the assistant vice principal searched T.L.O.'s purse and discovered a pack of cigarettes. As he reached for the cigarette pack, he then noticed other items, including cigarette rolling papers, which he associated with marijuana use. He then searched the purse more thoroughly and discovered marijuana, a pipe, plastic bags, a large sum of money in single dollar bills, a list of students who owed T.L.O. money, and two letters which suggested T.L.O. was involved in marijuana sales. School officials notified T.L.O.'s mother and the police.

On the basis of this evidence and a later confession, the state brought delinquency charges against T.L.O. The student appealed the charges, arguing that because the search of her purse was improper under the Fourth Amendment, the evidence was inadmissible. The U.S. Supreme Court, however, ruled that the search was conducted within the constitutional standards of the Fourth Amendment. In its opinion, the Court established standards to be used by school officials in searches of students' pockets, purses, and other items associated with the student's person. The Court did not specifically address searches of school lockers.

Until this case, public school officials had typically relied on the doctrine of *in loco parentis*, whereby school officials had broad search powers akin to those of a student's parents. The U.S. Supreme Court rejected this argument and held that when public school officials conduct a search of a student, they may be held to the same Fourth Amendment standards as government officials. In its analysis, the Court recognized that public school students maintain an expectation of privacy in their personal effects even on a public school campus, but the Court did not go so far as to hold school officials to exactly the same standards as police officers in conducting searches.

Although police officers are usually required to show they have probable cause to believe that a person has violated the law, the Court allowed that school officials may need to show only that they have a reasonable suspicion that a search would produce evidence that a student has violated a school code. The Court justified this relaxed standard for school officials by citing the major social problems evident in schools nationwide and a school's need to maintain an educational environment.

Paul Albert Bateman

Further Reading

Bloom, Robert M. *Searches, Seizures, and Warrants*. Westport, Conn.: Praeger, 2003.

LaFave, W. R. *Search and Seizure: A Treatise on the Fourth Amendment*. 3d ed. St. Paul, Minn.: West Publishing, 1995.

McWhirter, Darien A. *Search, Seizure, and Privacy*. Phoenix, Ariz.: Oryx Press, 1994.

Wetterer, Charles M. *The Fourth Amendment: Search and Seizure*. Springfield, N.J.: Enslow, 1998.

See also Juvenile justice system; Probable cause; Search and seizure; Supreme Court, U.S.

New Mexico state penitentiary riot

The Event: Inmates enraged over conditions in their prison seized control of the prison for thirty-six hours, killing thirty-three inmates and taking twelve guards hostage before surrendering to authorities
Date: February 2-3, 1980
Place: Santa Fe, New Mexico
Criminal justice issues: Prisons; violent crime
Significance: Regarded by many as the most brutal and destructive prison riot in U.S. history, it is also noteworthy for the fragmentation among the inmates. The riot and lack of action by officials led to changes in the New Mexico prison system.

The New Mexico State Prison riot was years in the making. The prison had been plagued by abuse, corruption, inefficiency, and overcrowding. By the spring of 1980 the prison was operating at 150 percent of its rated capacity. Several inmates were involved in a federal class-action suit against the state of New Mexico over these conditions.

Officials had been warned that the inmates were angry over their living conditions but these warnings were ignored. At 1:40 A.M. on February 2, inmate frustrations exploded into a riot when four guards were overpowered in Dormitory E-2. The riot quickly spread throughout the prison, as openings had been left by renovations being made to the facility. The renovation crew had also left behind blow torches, which were used by inmates to open doors and murder and mutilate other inmates. The inmates gained access to the entire prison when they took over the control center.

Over the next thirty-six hours, more than two hundred inmates were injured, and thirty-three inmates were killed, most of whom were being held in protective custody. Twelve guards were taken hostage, several of whom were brutalized and sodomized. The riot exhausted itself, and when prison guards, state police, and National Guardsmen stormed the facility, they were met with no resistance.

The riot brought poor conditions to the attention of the public, conditions that did not change after the riot. Change came only through the actions of federal district court that oversaw the operations of all New Mexican medium- and maximum-security facilities.

Mark Anthony Cubillos

Further Reading

Carlson, Peter, and Judith Simon Garrett. *Prison and Jail Administration: Practice and Theory*. Boston: Jones & Bartlett, 2000.

Morris, Roger. *The Devil's Butchershop: The New Mexico Prison Uprising*. Albuquerque: University of New Mexico Press, 1988.

Rolland, Mike. *Descent into Madness: An Inmate's Experience of the New Mexico Prison Riot*. Cincinnati: Anderson Publishing, 1997.

Useem, Bert, and Peter Kimball. *States of Siege: U.S. Prison Riots, 1971-1986*. Reprint. New York: Oxford University Press, 1991.

Wicker, Tom. *A Time to Die: The Attica Prison Revolt*. Reprint. Lincoln: University of Nebraska Press, 1994.

See also Attica prison riot; Bureau of Prisons; Prison and jail systems; Prison escapes; Prison guards; Prison health care; Prison overcrowding; Prison violence; Solitary confinement; Supermax prisons.

News source protection

Definition: Shielding of the identities of confidential news sources by professional journalists

Criminal justice issues: Government misconduct; media; privacy; testimony

Significance: Journalists and the courts are engaged in an ongoing struggle over permissible uses of the information that journalists gather from confidential sources. The news media seek protection of their sources under the principle of freedom of the press guaranteed by the First Amendment, but court rulings and state shield laws do not always protect them from having to violate their pledges of confidentiality to their sources.

In September, 2004, eighteen newsgroups, including the Associated Press, banned together to seek greater protection for journalists from having to reveal their confidential news sources in court. The issue is an old one but one that in 2004 had been highlighted by attention given to reporters ordered to testify before a grand jury about the identity of a covert Central Intelligence Agency officer through confidential sources. The news organizations insist that this protection is essential if the media are to continue to meet their mission of providing the fullest possible information to a free society.

Political insiders often leak information to the media that reveals matters such as government corruption and other problems. From Washington, D.C., to the local police stations, leaking information to the new media in return for promises of confidentiality has long been considered a routine way of getting vital information to the public. After the September 11, 2001, terrorist attacks on New York and Washington, D.C., President George W. Bush's administration attempted to crack down on this practice by arguing that national security and safety were at risk.

Protection of news sources is not limited to government information leaks or corporate whistle-blowers. It may also involve shielding the identities of juvenile offenders, victims of sex crimes and child abuse, and criminal suspects before formal charges are filed. Balancing the public's right to know with fair and ethical reporting is a continuous legal challenge in the journalism profession.

The First Amendment

Journalists claim protection under the First Amendment of the U.S. Constitution, which supports the free flow of information and an independent press. This special allowance is based on the idea that journalists are not acting as ordinary citizens but as watchdogs for the community. Nevertheless, their right to protect their sources has been repeatedly challenged. In 1972, the U.S. Supreme Court examined the question of forced disclosure of confidential sources based on four separate cases, later known as *Branzburg v. Hayes*. In that ruling, the Court established that journalists did not have a constitutional right to avoid subpoenas. In 1998, the U.S. Court of Appeals for the Fifth Circuit found that the *Branz-*

burg ruling created First Amendment protection for journalists when subpoenas were intended to harass them. Because judicial interpretations are inconsistent, laws in lower courts have been established to protect the media and information sources.

State Shield Laws

By 2003, thirty-one U.S. states had adopted shield laws as a First Amendment safeguard. Although the protection these laws provided varies among the states, lower courts considering challenges to journalists generally consider whether the cases are public or private, whether the protected information is likely to bear directly on the cases at hand, and whether the information can be obtained through other means. The various states differ on such matters as protecting sources versus protecting the information itself and the professional status of the journalists who are protecting their sources. However, because the protections that the shield laws provide tend to be minimal, many journalists are still subpoenaed to court.

Although the subpoena process, guaranteed by the Sixth Amendment of the Constitution, protects the right of defendants to obtain witnesses and information needed for fair trials, journalists argue that the free flow of information in a free society is compromised when they are required to identify their sources and turn over to courts their notes, photographs, videotapes, and taped recordings of interviews. Sources often confide in journalists in confidence, in return for promises that their identities will be protected. Without such promises, the information sources—particularly political and legal sources—may end. Moreover, newspapers, broadcasting media, and other news outlets may also be less willing to invest resources into investigative reporting if the possibility exists that their salaried journalists may spend time testifying in court and possibly even serving time in jail, instead of fulfilling their job duties.

Members of the news media often ignore subpoenas and face the risk of being charged with contempt of court and being penalized by fines, jail sentences, or both. There are two basic kinds of contempt citations: criminal and civil. Criminal citations, which often result from disruptive behavior during court proceedings, may carry fines and prison time. Civil citations, which are generally issued to persons who refuse to supply information that is deemed important to trials, are punishable by daily fines and incarceration until the offending journalists comply with the courts' requests.

When subpoenas fail to produce compliance, the courts may issue police search warrants to obtain information from the journalist. In an attempt to protect the media from the searches in 1980, the U.S. Congress passed the Privacy Protection Act, which requires law enforcement to use subpoenas before resorting to searches and seizures. Exceptions include situations when the information sought is connected with pursuits of criminal suspects, when it may prevent death or injury, or when there is a danger that it may be hidden or destroyed.

Ethics Versus Legal Protection of Sources

Journalists often offer protection to their sources, promising anonymity to those who give them vital information. Most journalists believe that breaking such promises violates their ethical standards. However, the nature of the anonymity they offer to sources can be misleading, particularly as they must often reveal their sources to their editors before their stories are published. When journalists break their promises, they may be sued for breech of promise. Sources have been known to seek legal damages against journalists and their employers, who are also protected by the First Amendment. Media lawyers generally recommend that news organizations adopt specific guidelines for using anonymous sources and that clear limitations be set on the promises of confidentiality that their employees make.

Betty Attaway-Fink

Further Reading

Brooks, Brian S., George Kennedy, Daryl R. Moen, and Don Ranly. *News Reporting and Writing.* 8th ed. Boston: Bedford Books, 2004. Comprehensive textbook on journalism that covers all aspects of working with news sources.

Day, Lois A. *Ethics in Media Communication: Cases and Controversies.* 4th ed. Belmont, Calif.: Thomson/Wadsworth, 2003. Legal textbook on the special needs of journalism and communications. Accessible to general readers and well supported by numerous case studies.

Goldstein, Norm. *Associated Press Stylebook and Briefing on Media Law*. Cambridge, Mass.: Perseus Publishing, 2004. Best-selling handbook on journalistic writing. Most of the book deals with matters of terminology and writing style, but the book also contains useful chapters on copyright, libel law, and other legal issues.

Knowlton, Steven R. *Moral Reasoning for Journalists: Cases and Commentary*. Westport, Conn.: Praeger Publishers, 1997. Detailed analyses of more than two dozen legal cases relating to issues of journalistic ethics, including some cases on the protection of news sources.

Pember, Don R., and Clay Calvert. *Mass Media Law*. 14th ed. New York: McGraw-Hill, 2004. One of the most widely used works on media legal issues, this textbook is known for its clarity and well-organized use of case studies. Each edition adds new material on changing issues, such as military censorship in the U.S. war in Iraq.

See also Constitution, U.S.; Gag orders; Print media; Privileged communications; Radio broadcasting; Television news; Trial publicity.

Night courts

Definition: Courts holding their sessions during evening hours

Criminal justice issues: Courts; jurisdictions

Significance: Court proceedings conducted at times other than those considered normal working hours are becoming an increasingly common part of the modern criminal justice system.

Almost entirely criminal courts, night courts have become a necessity as a result of several federal court rulings. Due process requirements, mandated by state and federal courts, and state statutes require that individuals arrested or detained by the police must be brought before a magistrate and given formal notice of charges against them within twenty-four to forty-eight hours in an ef-

fort to minimize the time a presumably innocent individual spends in jail.

Jurisdictions unable to handle staggering caseloads during regular working hours have been forced to operate courts twenty-four hours a day, seven days a week as a result. The Criminal Court of New York City, for example, the largest and busiest court in the United States, handled approximately 40 percent of its 1997 arraignments during the night and early morning hours. Many other court systems, especially those in densely populated areas, have been forced to establish similar courts or risk being forced to release criminals who might be denied their due process rights.

Donald C. Simmons, Jr.

Further Reading

Meyer, J. F., and D. R. Grant. *The Courts in Our Criminal Justice System*. Upper Saddle River, N.J.: Prentice-Hall, 2003.

Neubauer, D. W. *America's Courts and the Criminal Justice System*. 7th ed. Belmont, Calif.: Wadsworth, 2002.

Warner, Ralph. *Everybody's Guide to Small Claims Court, National Edition*. Berkeley, Calif.: Nolo Press, 2004.

See also Court types; Criminal law; Judges; Misdemeanors; Traffic courts; Traffic fines; Traffic law.

No-knock warrants

Definition: Written orders allowing police to enter structures without first announcing their presence

Criminal justice issues: Constitutional protections; search and seizure

Significance: The U.S. Supreme Court has stated that the Fourth Amendment usually requires police to knock and announce their intention to enter a structure. However, certain special orders allow the police to circumvent this requirement.

During the colonial period of American history, British authorities utilized search warrants as a tool to search and seize the property of the colonists. The warrants were written and came in two forms: the general warrant and the writ of assistance. General warrants gave British officers the ability to enter shops and homes without warning, while writs of assistance compelled bystanders to help officers carry out searches. These orders authorized their holders to conduct searches for the lifetime of the monarch who issued them.

After the American Revolution, the Fourth Amendment to the U.S. Constitution required that searches and seizures be conducted with warrants based on evidence legally collected and that they be reasonable under the circumstances. The U.S. Supreme Court has held that part of that requirement included the admonition that police should announce their arrival and that they obtain a search warrant before breaking into a home. In other words, the police had to know what they were looking for, had to have evidence that they would find it, and had an obligation to let the occupants know that they were coming in.

Naturally, police have encountered situations where, if they identified themselves prior to entry, their investigation might be derailed. Under these circumstances, the police may obtain special permission to enter a structure without having to announce their presence. This type of special order is called a no-knock warrant, and the Supreme Court has held that such warrants are legal. However, the Court has also ruled that such warrants can be issued only in an emergency. Legitimate exceptions to the knock-and-announce rule are: the possible destruction of evidence, escape of the suspect, or the likelihood that serious injury could take place if the presence of the officers was made known.

These types of warrants are unique in that they are only rarely given and only when the police can show that they have a reasonable belief that one of the above mentioned exigencies is likely to occur. Not only are these types of warrants rare, but they are also difficult to obtain. The Court has further ruled that no-knock warrants must be applied for, so that a judge can determine if such an entry would meet the requirements of the Constitution. Basically, police cannot just enter a home without announcing

themselves simply because they think an emergency situation might exist; their evidence for that belief must be reviewed by a judge, and only then can a no-knock warrant be issued.

Michael A. Cretacci

Further Reading

Del Carmen, Rolando V., and Jeffrey T. Walker, eds. *Briefs of Leading Cases in Law Enforcement.* 5th ed. Cincinnati: Anderson, 2004.

Zalman, Marvin. *Criminal Procedure: Constitution and Society.* 3d ed. Upper Saddle River, N.J.: Prentice-Hall, 2002.

See also Arrest warrants; Criminal procedure; Fourth Amendment; Probable cause; Search and seizure; Search warrants; Special weapons and tactics teams (SWAT); Supreme Court, U.S.; *Wilson v. Arkansas.*

Nolle prosequi

Definition: Announcement made into a court record that a plaintiff or prosecutor will not proceed forward with a lawsuit or indictment

Criminal justice issues: Legal terms and principles; prosecution; trial procedures

Significance: In criminal law, prosecutors enter *nolle prosequi* motions to terminate their cases early; however, such motions are rare and usually require the approval of judges.

From a Latin phrase meaning "we shall no longer prosecute," *nolle prosequi* is a type of defendant disposition occurring after the filing of a case, but before judgment, in court. Such a filing means that the plaintiff in a civil case, or prosecutor in a criminal case, wishes to drop prosecution of all or part of a suit or indictment.

In civil cases, a *nolle prosequi* is considered an agreement by the plaintiff to not proceed, either against some of the defendants, or to part of the suit. It may be entered for one of several counts, or for one of several defendants. In criminal cases, *nolle prosequi* is an entry made on records by prosecutors stating that they will no longer pursue prosecution. Common reasons for *nolle prosequi* include insufficient evidence, reluctance of witnesses to testify, and police errors. Such motions are extremely rare, however, and prosecutors who wish to file them generally need the permission of judges to do so.

The awarding of a *nolle prosequi* is not a bar to future action for the same cause, as it does not prevent the charge from being brought up at a later date. Conversely, in some jurisdictions, a *nolle prosequi* of a charge enables the defendant later to file a petition requesting expungement of police records and court records relating to the charge.

Pati K. Hendrickson

Further Reading

Champion, Dean John. *The American Dictionary of Criminal Justice.* 2d ed. Los Angeles: Roxbury Publishing, 2001.

Territo, Leonard, James B. Halsted, and Max L. Bromley. *Crime and Justice in America: A Human Perspective.* 6th ed. Upper Saddle River, N.J.: Pearson Prentice-Hall, 2004.

See also Acquittal; Criminal procedure; Discretion; District attorneys; Mistrials; Public prosecutors; Trials.

A case of *nolo contendere* that helped save a career occurred in 1995, after British film star Hugh Grant was arrested in Hollywood, California, charged with lewd conduct involving a prostitute. Many media observers thought that the sordid incident might ruin Grant's promising career. However, instead of avoiding the media and making excuses for his behavior, Grant pleaded no contest in court and took every opportunity publicly to admit he had made a mistake and apologize. The public embraced him for his honesty, and his career was actually boosted by the incident. *(AP/Wide World Photos)*

Nolo contendere

Definition: Plea that refuses to contest charges brought against a defendant

Criminal justice issues: Defendants; legal terms and principles; pleas; trial procedures

Significance: *Nolo contendere* pleas are most commonly made when civil cases against defendants are possible. Although this form of plea has been criticized for lacking logical and theoretical purpose, some authorities argue that the passage of time has shown *nolo contendere* to perform a useful and practical function in the court process.

Defendants in criminal court are provided the option to plead guilty, not guilty, and, sometimes, *nolo contendere.* Latin for "no contest," the term *nolo contendere* indicates that defendants are not contesting the charges against them. Instead, the defendants are essentially accepting penalties without admitting guilt. Defendants who plead no contest are thus subject to the same penalties they would receive if they instead simply pleaded guilty to the charges. *Nolo contendere* pleas are also similar to guilty pleas in that they must be made voluntarily and without force or threats. However, *nolo contendere* pleas differ from guilty pleas in not acknowledging wrongdoing. For that reason, they cannot be used against defendants in later civil proceedings resulting from the same offenses.

While the right to plead guilty or not guilty is a fundamental right in the American justice sys-

A *Nolo Contendere* Plea That Created a President

In 1973, Spiro Agnew became the first U.S. vice president to resign his office while under criminal investigation. After having served under President Richard M. Nixon since 1969, Agnew was investigated on charges that during his earlier years as a Baltimore County executive and governor of Maryland, he had taken bribes from contractors in return for helping them get government contracts. Agnew repeatedly denied any wrongdoing then suddenly resigned the vice presidency on October 10, 1973. In an agreement with the federal Department of Justice, he then pleaded *nolo contendere* to a single charge of federal income tax cheating for the year 1967. A federal judge pronounced Agnew's plea to be equivalent to a plea of guilty, fined him ten thousand dollars, and sentenced him to three years of unsupervised probation.

After Agnew's resignation, Nixon appointed Congressman Gerald R. Ford vice president. A year later, Ford became president himself, when Nixon resigned from office under pressure from the Watergate scandal. Meanwhile, Maryland disbarred Agnew, a licensed attorney, from practicing law because of his *nolo contendere* plea. Another state court later ordered Agnew to pay Maryland the bribe money, plus interest, that it ruled he had accepted while in office. In 1983, Agnew paid Maryland $268,482.

tem, defendants do not have an unqualified right to plead *nolo contendere*. *Nolo contendere* pleas are allowed in federal courts and in the majority of states but are mainly used for misdemeanor offenses. In cases that qualify for *nolo contendere* pleas, defendants usually have to acquire permission from either the prosecution, the court, or both.

Brion Sever

Further Reading

ABA Standards for Criminal Justice: Pleas of Guilty. Chicago: American Bar Association, 1999.

Burnett, C. "*Nolo Contendere*: Efficient or Effective Administration of Justice?" *Criminal Law Bulletin* 23 (1987): 117-134.

See also Arraignment; Convictions; Criminal procedure; Plea bargaining; Pleas; Self-incrimination, privilege against.

Nonlethal weapons

Definition: Weapons that are unlikely to kill or cause serious bodily injuries to living persons and animals when used properly

Criminal justice issues: Police powers; technology; violent crime

Significance: Nonlethal weapons hold out the promise of providing adequate protection to law-enforcement and corrections personnel who need to bring violent offenders under control, while minimizing the chances of killing or seriously injuring the offenders.

Technological advances of the late twentieth and early twenty-first centuries have improved the possibility of stabilizing violent incidents through the employment of nonlethal weapons by law-enforcement personnel. However, even weapons classified as "nonlethal" may have the potential to cause death if used inappropriately. In acknowledgment of that risk, some people in law enforcement prefer to describe such weapons as "less-lethal" or "less-than-lethal."

Examples of nonlethal weapons are batons, including "billy sticks" and "night stick"; water cannons; beanbag shotguns; plastic and rubber bullets; tear gas and pepper spray dispensers; and stun and laser guns. Batons, pepper spray, and stun and laser guns are most effective in one-on-one and small-scale confrontations. Water cannons, beanbag shotguns, and plastic and rubber bullets can be used in small-scale confrontations and are also effective in controlling crowds. A key to using any of these weapons properly is avoiding directing them against sensitive body parts, especially when using them at close range. A rubber bullet fired into a human chest from a dis-

Ohio police officer holding a stun gun. In late 2003, Cincinnati's mayor proposed arming police with nonlethal stun guns after the accidental killing of a police suspect in the city. *(AP/Wide World Photos)*

tance of one hundred feet is likely to cause a painful bruise; the same bullet fired into a face at fifty feet might be lethal

A typical scenario in which law-enforcement personnel might employ a nonlethal weapon is stabilizing a domestic dispute involving a knife-wielding man. If the man refuses to surrender his weapon to the police, he would be quickly disarmed by a pepper spray projectile fired into his chest. The pepper spray would cause him such facial irritation that he would instinctively drop his knife to grab his face, allowing police officers to take him into custody safely.

Civil litigation and public pressure have caused criminal justice professionals to seek less dangerous and less intrusive methods to subdue suspects, arrestees, and prison inmates who present potentially dangerous threats. Nonlethal weap-

ons are one answer to the problem. They have the potential of protecting officers and guards, while reducing the changes of killing or causing serious injuries to the offenders.

Jay Zumbrun

Further Reading

Adams, K., et al. *Use of Force by Police: Overview of National and Local Data*. Washington, D.C.: U.S. Department of Justice, National Institute of Justice and Bureau of Justice Statistics, 1999.

Gillespie, T. T., D. G. Hart, and J. D. Boren. *Police Use of Force: A Line Officer's Guide*. Kansas City, Mo.: Varro Press, 1998.

Pate, Anthony, and Lorie A. Fridell. *Police Use of Force*. 2 vols. Washington, D.C., 1993.

See also Assault and battery; Deadly force; Domestic violence; Firearms; Gun laws; Murder and homicide; Police brutality; Police civil liability; Police powers.

Nonviolent resistance

Definition: Any deliberate refusal to comply with laws and government policies in a nonviolent manner
Criminal justice issues: Civil rights and liberties; police powers; political issues
Significance: Nonviolent resistance has long been a central component of efforts to express political dissent and marshal the power necessary to bring about political change in the United States.

Although the term "nonviolent resistance" is a twentieth century concept based on analysis of the strategies and conditions necessary for successful nonviolent action, its practice is deeply rooted in United States history. Religious groups from Europe such as the Amish and the Society of Friends (Quakers), who practiced a literal understanding of Jesus' teachings forbidding the use of violence, fled to North America to escape persecution. Their continued witness to principles of pacifism has influenced a tradition and philosophy of nonviolent protest. Additionally, the early colonists engaged in nonviolent resistance against British rule. In 1766, Great Britain legislated an import tax called the Stamp Act. American merchants organized a boycott of goods, causing the repeal of the act. This action marked the first organized resistance to British rule and led to the establishment of the First Continental Congress in 1774. The legal basis for nonviolent action was established in the First Amendment to the Constitution, which protects the rights of persons to "freedom of speech," peaceful assembly, and petitioning the government "for a redress of grievances." The United States has a long history of expression of such rights.

Nineteenth and Twentieth Centuries

In 1845, Henry David Thoreau was jailed for refusing to pay a poll tax in protest of the Mexican-American War. In his essay "Civil Disobedience," Thoreau proclaimed the moral necessity of resistance in the face of immoral government action. Nonviolent protest has accompanied every war in which the United States has engaged, and it was so widespread during the Vietnam War that it became a central reason for U.S. withdrawal from Vietnam in 1974. Nonviolent protest has also been central to various movements seeking to ban and limit nuclear weapons and in wartime tax resistance movements, in which members refuse to pay taxes to support the military budget. Strategies of nonviolent resistance were also employed by the women's rights movement, which culminated in the right to vote (1920) and in greater social and economic equality for women. The labor movement has used nonviolent tactics in the form of strikes, labor slowdowns, and boycotts to force improvement of working conditions and income.

Despite strong, often violent responses by corporate owners, the Wagner Act, passed by Congress in 1935, recognized the legal right of workers to organize and use such methods. California farmworker leader César Chávez effectively used consumer boycotts in the 1970's and 1980's to win better conditions for farmworkers. Nonviolent strategies have been used by environmental groups to block construction of nuclear power plants, stop the cutting of forests, or alter policies considered to be ecologically hazardous. They have also been employed since the 1980's by antiabortion groups attempting to close abortion clinics.

The most prolonged, successful use of nonviolent resistance, however, came in the Civil Rights movement led by Martin Luther King, Jr., in the 1950's and 1960's. Drawing on the work of Mohandas K. Gandhi, the movement used marches, sit-ins, and boycotts to force an end to legal racial segregation in the South and informal (*de facto*) segregation in the North. This campaign demonstrated the ambiguity of governmental response to such tactics. Often participants were arrested and convicted under local statutes, only to have such laws ruled invalid by higher courts; this occurred during the Montgomery bus boycott. On the other hand, King and his followers were under constant surveillance by the Federal Bureau of Investigation and were considered threats to political stability by many government officials.

The debate has also focused on what constitutes "freedom of expression" and "peaceful assembly." The "plowshares eight," in 1980, protesting nuclear weapons, entered a General Electric plant in Pennsylvania and dented the nose cone of a warhead. They were sentenced to prison on grounds of trespass and destruction of private property.

Theory and Strategy

Nonviolent resistance has two distinct traditions. The religious tradition centers on the moral claim that it is always wrong to harm another and that only love of the "enemy" can transform persons and societies. Violence and hatred cannot solve social problems or end social conflict, for each act of violence generates new resentments. This spiral of violence can be ended only if some group absorbs the violence and returns only nonviolence and love. Central to this vision is a commitment to justice that requires adherents to engage injustice actively wherever they find it. The political tradition focuses on strategies for organizing political and social power to force another, usually a political authority, to change policies. As Gene Sharp, a leading analyst, notes, government requires the consent of its citizens. In nonviolent resistance, dissenters organize forms of power including economic power, labor power, and the power of public opinion in order to undermine consent and force authorities to change policies.

The use of these theories and techniques remains important in stable, democratic societies as a way of resolving conflict, generating social change, and challenging power structures, especially on behalf of the powerless, whose rights are often ignored. Without the legal sanctions that permit such protest, the only recourse becomes open societal violence and conflict, even to the point of civil war.

Charles L. Kammer

Further Reading

Ackerman, Peter, and Christopher Kruegler. *Strategic Nonviolent Conflict: The Dynamics of People Power in the Twentieth Century.* Westport, Conn.: Praeger, 1994. Broad discussion of the use of nonviolence in the twentieth century Civil Rights and antiwar movements.

Holmes, Robert L., ed. *Nonviolence in Theory and Practice.* Belmont, Calif.: Wadsworth, 1990. Extended essay on the difficulty of putting into practice the theory of nonviolence.

King, Martin Luther, Jr. *A Testament of Hope: The Essential Writings and Speeches of Martin Luther King, Jr.* Edited by James M. Washington. San Francisco: Harper & Row, 1991. Personal perspectives on nonviolence by the most outstanding American advocate of nonviolent direct action.

Moses, Greg. *Revolution of Conscience: Martin Luther King, Jr., and the Philosophy of Nonviolence.* Forward by Leonard Harris. New York: Guilford Press, 1997. Examination of the influences behind King's adoption of a policy of nonviolence in the Civil Rights movement and its implementation in practice.

Steger, Manfred B. *Judging Nonviolence: The Dispute Between Realists and Idealists.* New York: Routledge, 2003. Balanced treatment of the arguments for and against nonviolence, written in the aftermath of the September 11, 2001, terrorist attacks on the United States, with discussions of major social political movements that employed nonviolence.

See also Arrest; Civil disobedience; Hit-and-run accidents; Jaywalking; Resisting arrest.

"Not-in-my-backyard" attitudes

Definition: Supporting socially and environmentally valuable policies and projects while opposing the location of facilities to provide those policies or projects in the local neighborhoods of the supporters

Criminal justice issues: Medical and health issues; morality and public order; prisons; substance abuse

Significance: Not-in-my-backyard (NIMBY) attitudes may lead to social injustice, prevent the construction of facilities in the most effective and efficient locations, and limit the availability of needed services to client populations.

The NIMBY syndrome develops when members of a community say they support a policy or project so long as it is located where others bear the social and economic costs of the project. They claim their neighborhood is not suited for the proposed project because of the size of the facility, the clients to be served, or some other issue.

The earliest reference to the term "NIMBY" appeared in a 1980 article referring to citizen opposition to locating landfills anywhere nearby. The term was originally associated with opposition to environmentally sensitive facilities but has been expanded to include the location of power lines, rental housing, public housing, homeless shelters, halfway houses for troubled teens or drug abusers, medical facilities for diseased patients, housing for parolees, and any other facilities deemed undesirable. Opposition may be directed toward the nature of the facility, the administration and procedures of the facility, or the nature of the clients being served, including race, criminal background, or income status. The term "LULU" refers to all locally unwanted land uses.

Typical NIMBY Projects

✓ Airports
✓ Day-care facilities
✓ Drug rehab centers
✓ Garbage dumps and landfills
✓ Group homes for troubled youths
✓ Halfway houses for alcoholics
✓ Low-income housing
✓ Mental hospitals
✓ Nursing homes
✓ Oil refineries
✓ Power plants
✓ Prisons and jails
✓ Recycling centers
✓ Schools
✓ Sports arenas and other venues that draw crowds
✓ Windmill farms

Three major concerns expressed by potential neighbors of unwanted facilities are reduction in local property values, decreased personal and neighborhood security, and increased social fragmentation and community disorganization. Related concerns include the appearance and size of the facility, parking and traffic patterns, noise and odor, and lax operating procedures and supervision. Tactics used by neighborhood residents include creating petitions, letter writing and media campaigns, lobbying public officials, staging demonstrations, forming opposition groups, and packing zoning hearings with opponents. These residents are generally supporters of no- or slow-growth policies, dwellers in rural or pleasant neighborhoods, and earners of middle or high income who are educated and professionally employed. They often show a strong social concern but are also motivated to protect what is theirs.

Social Justice and Inefficiency Issues

The NIMBY attitude, when successfully integrated into law or government decisions, forces people and communities without political or economic clout, or without the persistence and stamina to last the course of the battle, to bear the costs of social goods desired by those with political and economic clout. Social justice requires that all those who play a part in creating the problem or need, and in deciding the policy, must share in the subsequent burden. This includes paying the taxes, suffering the economic or commercial loss, and sharing in the siting of the facilities.

While Benjamin Chavis was executive director of the United Church of Christ Commission for Racism and Justice, he created the term "environmental racism" to describe a 1970's and 1980's correlation that he saw between the racial composition of neighborhoods and the siting of unwanted facilities, especially hazardous waste facilities. Subsequent studies proved that 76 percent of landfills were located in predominantly nonwhite neighborhoods. Social and environmental facilities were located in areas where the geology, geography, low land values, zoning laws, and political climate allowed the siting. These factors were also correlated with low incomes, depressed communities, and only coincidentally with the homes and businesses of racial and ethnic minorities.

NIMBY attitudes lead to siting social facilities where they are less efficient than they could be in meeting needs. For example, new, environmentally sound landfills are often sited on preexisting, already contaminated sites in depressed neighborhoods where their use is grandfathered into zoning, but the facility is bound to suffer the effects of the earlier abuse of the land. Some facilities are located in geographically remote locations where they cause problems related to traffic, fuel, and trucking or make access difficult for less mobile citizens.

Because the NIMBY attitude makes siting facilities so difficult, construction of needed facilities is delayed and sometimes abandoned. Communities go without hospitals, prisons, waste disposal facilities, or services for the most needy citizens.

Implications for Criminal Justice

Delayed or abandoned construction has meant a continuation of prison crowding and early release of unrehabilitated offenders, denial of rehabilitation and education services to incarcerated youth and adults, delay in the introduction of new incarceration and alternative sentencing methods, and the continued housing of mentally ill, substance-addicted, or homeless persons in facilities intended for criminals. Perceptions of social injustice that are a consequence of the NIMBY syndrome lead to social dissatisfaction, racial and social class animosities, and subsequent criminal behavior. The concentration of social facilities in already depressed areas leads to further economic and social depression of the neighborhood and to other social problems. On the positive side, some depressed communities have benefited from increased employment and the development of secondary service industries as a consequence of siting large-scale social projects like penitentiaries, secure hazardous or nuclear waste facilities, power plants, and mental hospitals.

Gordon Neal Diem

Further Reading

Davy, Benjamin. *Essential Injustice: When Legal Institutions Cannot Resolve Environmental and Land Use Disputes*. Wien, N.Y.: Springer, 1997. Explores justice issues; provides case studies.

Dear, M. J. "Understanding and Overcoming the NIMBY Syndrome." *Journal of the American Planning Association* 59, no. 3 (1992): 288-300. Concise overview of NIMBY syndrome.

Horah, Jan. *NIMBYs and LULUs*. Chicago: Council of Planning Librarians, 1993. Brief handbook for community leaders and professionals.

Inhaber, Herbert. *Slaying the NIMBY Dragon*. New Brunswick, N.J.: Transaction, 1998. Proposes incentives, including "reverse Dutch Auction" to encourage communities to accept LULUs.

McAvoy, Gregory. *Controlling Technocracy: Citizen Rationality and the NIMBY Syndrome*. Washington, D.C.: Georgetown University Press, 1999. Covers citizen participation in land use decisions.

Munton, Don, ed. *Hazardous Waste Siting and Democratic Choice*. Washington, D.C.: Georgetown University Press, 1996. Proposes democratic negotiations between facility developers and host communities.

O'Looney, John. *Economic Development and Environmental Control: Balancing Business and Community in an Age of NIMBYs and LULUs*. Westport, Conn.: Quorum Books, 1995. History and evolution of LULU problems, property law, and land use controls.

Piller, Charles. *The Fail-safe Society: Community Defiance and the End of American Technological Optimism*. New York: Basic Books, 1991. Explores public concerns about new science technologies, NIMBY, and democratic decision making.

See also Community-based corrections; Environmental crimes; Halfway houses; Neighborhood watch programs; Prison and jail systems; Prison escapes; Regulatory crime; Work camps.

O

Objections

Definition: Expression of disagreement with a statement or procedure during a trial by an attorney involved in a case

Criminal justice issues: Attorneys; courts; trial procedures

Significance: The ability to object during trials gives attorneys a means to alert judges that they believe statements or procedures should not be permitted.

During the trial process, attorneys can verbally object to the admission of evidence into the proceedings. That evidence may include oral testimony, physical evidence, or the types of questions being asked by opposing attorneys. If the latter, attorneys may raise their objections after questions are asked but before they are answered. They may object on the grounds that the questions are irrelevant, immaterial, prejudicial, or call for witnesses to speak on subjects about which they have no direct knowledge.

Once an objection is made, the judge rules on it. The judge may decide to sustain the objection or overrule it. A judge who sustains an objection is stating that the objection itself has merit. In such a case, the offending attorney may be instructed to rephrase a question or discontinue a behavior, such as being rude or harsh to a witness. A judge who decides that an objection lacks merit will overrule it and allow the other attorney to continue as before. Occasionally, there are instances in which a judge does not make an immediate ruling on an objection. In some instances, the judge may require the attorneys to argue the legal point outside the presence of the jury, in what is known as a side-bar conference.

Jenifer A. Lee

Further Reading

Neubauer, David W. *America's Courts and the Criminal Justice System.* 8th ed. Belmont, Calif.: Wadsworth/Thomson Learning, 2005.

Rabe, Gary A., and Dean John Champion. *Criminal Courts: Structure, Process, and Issues.* Upper Saddle River, N.J.: Prentice-Hall, 2002.

See also Judges; Subpoena power; Testimony; Trials; Witnesses.

Obstruction of justice

Definition: Efforts to interfere with the operations of court or their officials

Criminal justice issues: Courts; trial procedures

Significance: Obstructing justice may deny a party the right to due process or justice.

Obstruction of justice is an attempt to impede justice by any means. It may include physical disruption of trial courts in session; attempts to interfere with judges, court officials, or jurors; and attempts to bribe or create doubt regarding the integrity of those involved in court proceedings. Concealing or falsifying evidence obstructs justice, as does resisting a court-appointed process server.

Obstructing Justice in the Movies

The 1996 film *Before and After* is about parents (Meryl Streep and Liam Neeson) struggling to cope with their son's investigation and eventual arrest on charges of murdering his girlfriend. The father destroys evidence that he believes will implicate his son and later refuses to testify against him. In real life, the father's destruction of evidence would subject him to liability for the serious charge of obstruction of justice. In fact, in real life, criminal defendants who might otherwise be acquitted of the substantive crimes of which they are charged often find themselves convicted of obstruction of justice for attempts to conceal evidence.

Timothy L. Hall

Because police are officers of the court, intentional interference with their duties may be considered an obstruction of justice. In federal practice, obstruction extends to agencies, departments, and committees conducting their work. A witness concealing evidence from an investigation by a congressional committee is as guilty of obstruction as a person concealing evidence in a trial court.

Elizabeth Algren Shaw

Further Reading

Del Carmen, Rolando V. *Criminal Procedure: Law and Practice*. 6th ed. Belmont, Calif.: Thomson/Wadsworth, 2004.

Garner, Bryan A., ed. *Black's Law Dictionary*. 8th ed. St. Paul, Minn.: Thomson/West, 2004.

Wood, J. D., and Linda Picard, eds. *Dictionary of Law*. Springfield, Mass.: Merriam-Webster, 1996.

See also Contempt of court; Corporate scandals; Evidence, rules of; Films and criminal justice; Perjury; Subpoena power; Watergate scandal.

Olmstead v. United States

The Case: U.S. Supreme Court ruling on wiretaps

Date: Decided on June 4, 1928

Criminal justice issues: Privacy; search and seizure; technology

Significance: Although a majority of justices rejected the argument that government wiretaps on telephones constituted illegal searches and compelled self-incrimination, Justice Louis D. Brandeis's famous dissenting opinion laid the groundwork for the later development of a constitutional right to privacy.

During the Prohibition era, Roy Olmstead was convicted of being the general manager of a significant illegal smuggling operation that brought liquor to the United States from Canada in violation of federal law. Olmstead's illegal business had fifty employees and reportedly earned more than two million dollars each year. The evidence that produced the convictions of Olmstead and his associates was gathered through the use of wiretaps. Law-enforcement officials had attached wires to the telephone lines leading from Olmstead's residence and office. Officials had listened to and had stenographers take notes on the conversations secretly overheard through the telephone lines.

Olmstead and his codefendants challenged the use of such investigative techniques and evidence. They claimed that the wiretaps constituted an illegal search and seizure in violation of the Fourth Amendment and that the use of private conversations as evidence violated the Fifth Amendment's prohibition on compelled self-incrimination.

In an opinion by Chief Justice William Howard Taft, the Supreme Court rejected Olmstead's arguments. Taft concluded that the Fourth Amendment protected only against unreasonable searches of material things and that telephone lines running between two people's property could not be considered protected against intrusion by the government. Taft also declared that the defendants' conversations were voluntary and therefore could not be regarded as compelled self-incrimination.

In a famous dissenting opinion, Justice Louis D. Brandeis made an eloquent plea for the recognition of a constitutional right to privacy. According to Brandeis, the authors of the Constitution "sought to protect Americans in their beliefs, their thoughts, their emotions, and their sensations. They conferred, as against the government, the right to be let alone—the most comprehensive of rights and the right most valued by civilized men."

Brandeis was not the lone dissenter in the case; Justices Oliver Wendell Holmes, Jr., Pierce Butler, and Harlan F. Stone also found fault with Taft's conclusions. Brandeis, however, was the lone justice to place great emphasis on a general right of privacy. The other justices were also concerned about the definition of a search under the Fourth Amendment or the legality of police methods.

Brandeis could not manage to gain majority support for his ideas during his lifetime. Instead, his eloquent defense of a right to privacy stood for more than thirty years as the primary argument against government intrusions into citizens' private lives. Beginning in the 1960's, when the Supreme Court's composition had changed significantly, Brandeis's words were used by a generation of justices who followed his ideals and established the existence of a constitutional right to privacy in *Griswold v. Connecticut* (1965).

Christopher E. Smith

See also Electronic surveillance; Evidence, rules of; Fourth Amendment; Gangsters of the Prohibition era; Privacy rights; Stakeouts; Supreme Court, U.S.; Wiretaps.

Omnibus Crime Control and Safe Streets Act of 1968

The Law: Federal legislation designed to provide grants to help state and local governments recruit and train law-enforcement officers and to evaluate community crime-prevention initiatives
Criminal justice issues: Crime prevention; federal law; law-enforcement organization
Date: Enacted in June, 1968
Significance: The Omnibus Crime Control and Safe Streets Act established the Law Enforcement Assistance Administration to help expand and improve state and local law-enforcement personnel, equipment, and crime-prevention strategies.

The Omnibus Crime Control and Safe Streets Act of 1968 was passed by the U.S. Congress less than one year after President Lyndon B. Johnson's Commission on Law Enforcement and the Administration of Justice issued its final report, *The Challenge of Crime in a Free Society*. Following the presidential commission's suggestion that crime is a national, as well as a state and local problem, Congress authorized the establishment of the Law Enforcement Assistance Administration (LEAA), a new federal agency described in Title I of the Omnibus Act.

The LEAA was authorized to make grants available to state and local governments to recruit, educate, and train law-enforcement offi-

cers. Title II of the act addressed the admissibility and reviewability of confessions, eyewitness testimony, and other criminal-law procedures. Title III concerned wiretaps and the interception of oral communications. Issues of state firearms control assistance by the federal government were addressed in Title IV.

Under the Omnibus Act, the Department of Justice significantly expanded federal government support for the prevention and reduction of local crime. Between 1968 and 1982, the federal government disbursed approximately $7.5 billion in grant money to state and municipal law-enforcement agencies. Some of the grants were awarded for the formation of specialized law-enforcement units to prevent riots and other civil disturbances and to combat organized crime. Funding for officer education was channeled through the Law Enforcement Education Program (LEEP). Police officers who enrolled in college classes received tuition subsidies and book stipends. The program thus prompted many colleges and universities to form academic programs in criminal justice to accommodate increasing enrollments and interest in the field. Finally, the act established the Bureau of Justice Assistance (BJA) to provide extensive assistance in establishing evaluation programs to state and local community crime prevention initiatives.

Anthony J. Luongo III

Further Reading

Brekke, Jerald. *An Assessment of the Bloc Grant Provisions of the Omnibus Crime Control and Safe Streets Act of 1968: The Missouri Experience*. Washington, D.C.: University Press of America, 1977.

Index to the Legislative History of the Omnibus Crime Control and Safe Streets Act of 1968. Washington, D.C.: Office of General Counsel, Law Enforcement Assistance Administration, 1973.

See also Comprehensive Crime Control Act; Criminal justice education; Justice Department, U.S.; Law Enforcement Assistance Administration; National Institute of Justice; Organized crime; President, U.S.; President's Commission on Law Enforcement and Administration of Justice; Wiretaps.

Opinions

Definition: Written explanations by judges of the reasons for their rulings

Criminal justice issues: Appeals; judges; trial procedures

Significance: The judicial system generally expects judges who decide cases to explain their decisions in written opinions. The collected opinions of relatively important courts—state appellate courts and federal courts—form the bases for subsequent judicial decisions. Later courts strive to adhere to the results of previously published opinions in keeping with the judicial principle of *stare decisis*, which means, "let the decision stand."

To facilitate the legal system's reliance on previous opinions to guide subsequent ones, legal publishers have traditionally collected judicial opinions into bound volumes referred to generically as "reporters." Reporters may collect all the opinions of a specific court, such as the *United States Reports*, which includes the opinions of the U.S. Supreme Court. Other reporters contain the opinions of courts in a particular geographic region, such as the *Pacific Reporter*, which includes opinions from the courts of California and other western states. Computerized databases and Internet sites now make most, if not all, reported opinions available to those without access to bound volumes of reporters.

In the U.S. system appellate judges write most opinions. Appellate courts generally have three or more members, a majority of whom determine the outcome in particular cases. One member of this majority then typically writes the opinion explaining the result, or holding, of the case. This opinion is called the majority opinion. Sometimes a judge who agrees with the majority's result in a case may nevertheless not agree with the reasoning offered by the majority opinion or may wish to explain the decision in some fashion other than that adopted by the majority. This judge may write what is referred to as a concurring opinion. A judge who disagrees not only with the reasoning of a case but with the result reached by the majority might write a dissenting opinion to express this disagreement. Finally, in a few cases judges may agree about a decision and publish a *per curiam* opinion, which bears the name of no particular author. Courts publish *per curiam* opinions most frequently to express decisions in minor or noncontroversial cases.

Timothy L. Hall

Further Reading

Amar, Akhil Reed. *The Constitution and Criminal Procedure: First Principles*. New Haven, Conn.: Yale University Press, 1997.

Lewis, Thomas T., and Richard L. Wilson, eds. *Encyclopedia of the U.S. Supreme Court*. 3 vols. Pasadena, Calif.: Salem Press, 2001.

Rehnquist, William. *The Supreme Court*. New York: Alfred A. Knopf, 2001.

See also Appellate process; Case law; Court types; Precedent; Supreme Court, U.S.

Opium Exclusion Act

The Law: Federal law banning the importation of opium and opium compounds, except those used expressly for medicinal purposes

Date: Became law on April 1, 1909

Criminal justice issues: Federal law; substance abuse

Significance: Designed to prevent the importation of mass quantities of opium into the United States, this law was one of the first attempts by the U.S. government to limit the importation of a specific substance.

The Opium Exclusion Act targeted one of the social ills of its era. Opium-based commerce became a highly visible issue during the mid-nineteenth century, and the dangers of opium abuse were further highlighted by the elevated rate of opium addiction in Great Britain, whose government actually fostered opium production in its Asian colonies. Restricting access to opium became an important component of American foreign policy as the United States called for the global outlawing of opium at the inaugural Shanghai Opium Commission meetings in January, 1909. Eager to prove that the nation was willing to enforce this policy at the domestic level, the U.S. Congress drafted and passed the Opium Exclusion Act in the spring of 1909.

The act itself called for the banning of the importation of opium or any opium containing compound beginning on April 1, 1909, with an exception made for opium used for medicinal purposes. This importation also included derivatives of opium such as morphine, codeine and heroin— various narcotics that were gaining in popularity in the early twentieth century. The regulation of the sale of opium, and other narcotics, was further restricted in the Harrison Narcotic Act of 1914.

Robert D. Mitchell

Further Reading

Berridge, Virginia, and Griffith Edwards. *Opium and the People: Opiate Use in Nineteenth-Century England*. New York: St. Martin's Press, 1981.

Maccoun, Robert J. *Drug War Heresies: Learning from Other Vices, Times, and Places*. New York: Cambridge University Press, 2001.

Walker, William O. *Opium and Foreign Policy: The Anglo-American Search for Order in Asia, 1912-1954*. Chapel Hill: University of North Carolina Press, 1991.

See also Commercialized vice; Comprehensive Drug Abuse Prevention and Control Act; Drug Enforcement Administration; Drug legalization debate; Drugs and law enforcement; Organized crime.

Organized crime

Definition: Syndicated enterprises characterized by pyramidal structures, specialization of functions, and unity of command that engage in ongoing criminal activities

Criminal justice issues: Business and financial crime; fraud; organized crime

Significance: Organized crime threatens the safety and peace of the entire United States and its citizens by supplying illicit goods and services through complex structures of criminal conspiracies and corruption.

While definitions of organized crime vary from agency to agency and country to country, there is a consensus that organized crime constitutes systematic and planned criminal activities for profit by means of conspiracies. Organized crime groups are generally criminal enterprises built around ethnic or business relationships or both, that monopolize certain products or services. Organized crime groups rely on violence, corruption, and intimidation to protect their enterprises from rival crime groups and government interference.

A common myth about organized crime is that it is synonymous with the so-called Mafia, or La Cosa Nostra. There are actually many crime organizations, such as the Russian Mafia, the Japanese Yakuza, the Colombian and Mexican drug cartels, Chinese Triads, outlaw motorcycle gangs, and common street gangs. Although there are many similarities among these groups, their backgrounds vary. For example, the Russian Mafia imports its culture to America, while the motorcycle gangs are an entirely American phenomenon.

No single theory explains why organized crime exists. Organized crime is a dynamic phenomenon that responds opportunistically to markets that are constantly changing. As social and economic conditions affect demand by the public, organized groups adjust to the changes and remain powerful enterprises. Indeed, enterprise theory itself is often used to explain the existence of organized crime. This theory maintains that when legitimate markets do not provide the goods and services demanded by the public, criminal syndicates form to meet those demands.

The impetus behind the growth of most organized crime groups centers on market opportunities to provide illicit services and goods demanded by the public. These have included alcohol during the Prohibition era, loan sharking, illegal drugs, gambling, and prostitution. Another myth about organized crime is that it is a "big city" problem. Indeed much of the market demand for illicit services, such as illegal sports betting and contraband drugs emanates from rural America.

Characteristics of Organized Crime

Organized crime groups may be separated into traditional organizations, such as La Cosa Nostra and Yakuza and their allies; groups that specialize in drug trafficking, such as the Mexican and South American cartels; and groups that are broadly entrepreneurial, such as Russian, Nigerian, and Ukrainian organizations. Other groups include the so-called Italian criminal enterprises (ICE), which are close allies of the Mafia: the Ndrangheta; Sacred Crown; Sicilian Mafia; and the Camorra.

While there are many differences among organized crime groups, many of them share certain characteristics. Among the most pronounced common traits are these:

✓ nonideological motives
✓ monopolization of products and services
✓ permanent structures
✓ organized hierarchies
✓ use of force and intimidation
✓ restricted memberships
✓ provision of illicit goods and services
✓ profits based on criminal activities
✓ use of strategic planning to obtain goals
✓ reliance on government and law-enforcement corruption for immunity and control
✓ internal job specialization
✓ use of money laundering
✓ investments in legal businesses
✓ opportunistic adaptation to changing markets
✓ diversification of legal and illicit operations
✓ use of legal business as fronts for criminal activity

In addition, many modern organized crime groups operate nationally, transnationally, or internationally. The twenty-first century has also seen a growing trend among crime groups to form alliances with one another to increase their power and spheres of influence.

Economic Impact

The impact of organized crime on the United States is both economic and social. The economic impact can be measured in the indirect costs of unpaid tax revenues on the illicit goods and services offered by organized crime, and in billions of dollars in direct losses of companies and individuals to fraud, theft, hijacking, robbery, and other crimes.

Organized crime has also profited from labor racketeering when crime groups have taken control of large labor unions. In addition to controlling the membership dues of union members, corrupted unions can control the prices of goods by withholding labor, threatening strikes, and stopping deliveries of material, equipment, or goods. Unions that have been compromised by organized crime include the truckers' International Brotherhood of Teamsters, the International Longshoremen's Association, and the Laborers International Union of North America. By controlling these unions, organized crime has manipulated the construction, trucking, and shipping industries—all of which play central roles in the national economy. Through puppet unions, organized crime has had a powerful influence on the prices and quality of goods and services. Other industries whose unions have been infiltrated by organized crime include real estate, banking, hotels, bars, entertainment, legal gambling, meat and fish markets, and the garment industry.

Another major concern in the United States is the increase of environmental crime. Organized crime is heavily involved in the transporting and disposing of waste products, including hazardous wastes. The ability of organized crime to infiltrate legitimate businesses through intimidation and threats has contributed to unlawful dumping of wastes.

Social Impact

The social impact of organized crime is more difficult to measure than its economic impact but is clearly great. For example, organized crime's most profitable enterprise is drug trafficking—a multibillion dollar business. By making contraband drugs more available to the public, organized crime makes a huge contribution to problems resulting from addiction and misuse of the drugs. The costs of drug treatment and prevention, the enforcement of drug laws, and losses of productivity due to drug use are difficult to estimate but are clearly substantial.

Both La Cosa Nostra and ICE groups are heavily involved in drug trafficking, but Colombian and Mexican drug cartels now play the major role in supplying to the United States cocaine, heroin, methamphetamines, and marijuana. There is also a substantial Asian-controlled traffic in drugs, particularly heroin. Many other groups, including urban street gangs and outlaw motor-cycle gangs also traffic in illegal drugs.

Another, less-publicized, organized crime activity is trafficking in human beings. In addition to what amounts to a trade in female sex-slaves, there is also well-organized traffic in illegal immigrants, children offered for adoption, and low-wage workers for industry and agriculture. Another disturbing activity in which some organized crime groups reportedly engage is trafficking in human body parts. There have been reports of involuntary "donors" being murdered for their organs and other people who have been intimidated to sell their organs and sometimes even those of their children.

When the profits and impact of drug trafficking, trafficking in people, and financial crime are combined, it is clear that organized crime enterprises demand serious attention from governments and law enforcement. However, a long and ongoing tradition of corruption has rendered ineffective most efforts by law enforcement to combat organized crime. Presidential commissions and scholars who have examined organized crime have consistently concluded that organized crime cannot exist without the corruption of officers in the criminal justice system, elected and appointed government officials, and union and legitimate business leaders.

Organized Crime Structures

Every organized crime group has some form of structure. The forms those structures take range from well-defined hierarchical organizations such as La Cosa Nostra and Yakuza to loosely structured groups such as ethnic street gangs. Many criminal organizations have rules and codes of conduct that combine with their well-organized structures to make them as efficient as legitimate businesses. In fact, criminal organizations sometimes take over legitimate businesses and run them very effectively, while using them as fronts for criminal activities, vehicles for paying taxes to avoid being prosecuted for tax evasion, and money laundering operations.

The structures of different crime groups vary considerably. For example, the structure of La Cosa Nostra fits the patron-client model, which connects families with clients through tradition and emotional bonds. In this model, reciprocal relationships exist between the family patrons, or bosses, and their clients. The patrons provide resources, services, and goods, and the clients respond with shows of loyalty and respect and other, more tangible, forms of support.

The bureaucratic model of crime organizations is exemplified by the Colombian drug cartels and the outlaw motorcycle gangs. The Colombian cartels have bureaucratic structures with defined leadership positions and special functions such as distribution, transportation, production, security, financial management, and administration. Cartels resemble the structures of legitimate businesses, from the latters' chief executive officers down to their workers.

Law-Enforcement Response

Combating organized crime requires enormous resources and team approaches that involve both national and international cooperation. Federal agencies such as the Drug Enforcement Administration, Federal Bureau of Investigation, Internal Revenue Service, and others, are involved in the investigation and prosecution of organized crime. However, it is a long-term problem that requires long-term solutions.

Seizing the assets of criminal organizations and putting their members in prison has proved possible through the use of modern investigative techniques and technology. The creation of task forces to target major groups has allowed for the sharing of both information and resources among law enforcement agencies. The task force concept with federal, state, local, and international participation is perhaps the most effective tool against organized crime.

Despite the arrest and convictions of almost all La Cosa Nostra bosses, that organization remains a major player in the twenty-first century. Likewise, outlaw motorcycle gangs still exist after many of their members have been arrested and convicted. The success of law enforcement comes with substantial expenditures of personnel, time, and money. The gathering, analysis, and dissemination of timely and accurate intelligence is a key to building successful cases against these complex and powerful groups. Intelligence provides information for both tactical and strategic planning. After the structures, methods of operation, geographic locations of activity, and

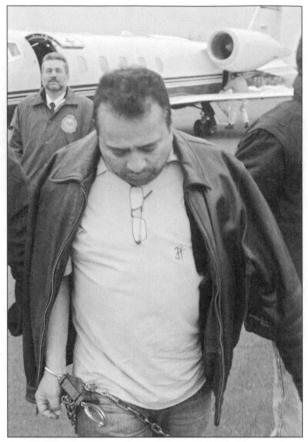

Agents of the federal Bureau of Immigration and Customs Enforcement accompany Jesus Henao Montoya to a waiting car after arresting him in January, 2004. A top official in Colombia's Norte Valle drug cartel, Montoya represented a major arrest for the agency. *(AP/Wide World Photos)*

identities of leaders are known, law-enforcement strategies can be developed.

The most effective tools of law enforcement against organized crime have been physical and electronic surveillance, combined with networks of informants. The best informants are members of the criminal organizations who are willing to gather evidence against other members. Another successful law-enforcement strategy involves financial investigations that follow the cash flow emanating from illegal activities until the money is in the possession of the criminal organizations themselves.

Investigative grand juries are also effective tools against organized crime. They have the power to subpoena documents and grant immunity from prosecution to force members of organized crime to testify. The law most frequently used against organized crime is the federal Racketeer Influenced and Corrupt Organizations Act (RICO) of 1970 and its amendments. Other useful laws include federal and state conspiracy statutes and tax and antidrug laws.

Twenty-first Century Trends

Alliances among such groups as the Russian Mafia, La Cosa Nostra, the Colombian cartels, and others are producing a new transnational crime trend through their operations in many countries. Some alliances have even been forged among terrorist groups, Russian gangs that sell weapons, and Colombian cartels that sell drugs for profits to support terrorism. The unholy alliance between drug traffickers and terrorists has given rise to the term "narco-terrorism."

Organized crime is expected to remain strong in the United States, especially as new groups, such as the Russian Mafia, Triads, Tongs, and Latin American drug cartels of Mexico and Colombia become more powerful. Meanwhile, groups such as La Cosa Nostra continue to work themselves into the fabric of American social, political, and business structures, ensuring that they will remain powerful and influential.

To combat organized crime, law enforcement must develop dynamic strategies to match the evolving complexity and globalization of organized crime groups. This will require extraordinary national and international cooperation, innovative strategies and laws, and a public will to control and prevent criminal groups from threatening the nation and the world.

Stephen L. Mallory

Further Reading

Abadinsky, Howard. *Organized Crime*. 7th ed. Belmont, Calif.: Wadsworth, 2003. Survey of all aspects of organized crime by a scholar who also has more than twenty years experience in the criminal justice system. Abadinsky covers both national and international dimensions of the subject.

Albanese, Jay S., and Robert D. Pursley. *Organized Crime in America: Some Existing and Emerging Issues*. Englewood Cliffs, N.J.: Prentice-Hall, 1992. Survey of organized crime issues that emphasizes the most current concerns, including drug trafficking and youth gangs. Makes extensive use of case studies.

Block, Alan A. *All Is Clouded by Desire: Global Banking, Money Laundering, and International Organized Crime*. Westport, Conn.: Praeger, 2004. Study of a major money laundering scandal involving the Bank of New York's Eastern European division that presents a revealing case study of the global dimensions of organized crime.

Clinard, Marshall B., Richard Quinney, and John Wildeman. *Criminal Behavior Systems: A Typology*. 3d ed. Cincinnati, Ohio: Anderson Publishing, 1994. Classic work on criminals that classifies offenders by the types of crimes they commit and provides some insights into people involved in organized crime.

Cressey, Donald R. *Theft of the Nation: The Structure and Operations of Organized Crime in America*. New York: Harper & Row, 1969. Somewhat dated study that provides a comprehensive overview of the nature of organized crime during the mid-twentieth century.

Einstein, Stanley, and Menachem Amir, eds. *Organized Crime: Uncertainties and Dilemmas*. Chicago: University of Illinois at Chicago, Office of International Criminal Justice, 1999. Collection of essays and articles represents a comprehensive compendium of issues related to international organized crime.

Hill, Henry, with Gus Russo. *Gangsters and Goodfellas: The Mob, Witness Protection, and Life on the Run*. New York: M. Evans, 2004. First-hand account of a former criminal living under the witness protection program by the man whose criminal life was dramatized in the film *Goodfellas* (1990).

Kenny, Dennis J., and James O. Finckenauer. *Organized Crime in America*. Belmont, Calif.: Wadsworth, 1995. Survey of various theories about organized crime, with discussions of the major forms of organized crime, and the strategies used to combat it. Covers both historical and modern crime organizations.

Lyman, Michael D., and Gary W. Potter. *Organized Crime*. 3d ed. Upper Saddle River, N.J.: Prentice-Hall, 2003. Up-to-date textbook on organized crime that addresses the most current issues, such as arms trafficking, counterfeiting, environmental crime, high-tech crime, and trafficking in women and children.

Philcox, Norman W. *An Introduction to Organized Crime*. Springfield, Ill.: C. C. Thomas, 1978. General study of organized crime in the United States that includes an overview of RICO and its application.

Reppetto, Thomas. *American Mafia: A History of Its Rise to Power*. New York: Henry Holt, 2004. Critical history of La Cosa Nostra in the United States, from its origins until the U.S. Senate hearings on organized crime of the early 1950's. Pays particular attention to the connections between organized crime and politicians.

See also Anti-Racketeering Act of 1934; Asset forfeiture; Conspiracy; Criminals; Drugs and law enforcement; Federal Bureau of Investigation; Gangsters of the Prohibition era; Mafia; Money laundering; Omnibus Crime Control and Safe Streets Act of 1968; Organized Crime Control Act; Prohibition; Racketeer Influenced and Corrupt Organizations Act.

Organized Crime Control Act

The Law: Federal law designed to make it easier to prosecute offenders involved in organized crime

Date: Became law on October 15, 1970

Criminal justice issues: Federal law; organized crime

Significance: The Organized Crime Control Act includes the Racketeer Influenced and Corrupt Organizations (RICO) statute, the law under which the majority of organized criminals are indicted in the federal justice system.

The Organized Crime Control Act defines organized crime as "unlawful activities of . . . a highly organized, disciplined association." In 1970, President Richard M. Nixon signed the act into law to combat organized crime groups, along with certain illegal gambling operations. In addition, the law gave new power to grand juries, allowed detention of uncooperative witnesses, authorized indicting witnesses for perjury when they give contradictory testimony, and authorized the U.S. attorney general to create a witness protection program.

Title IX of the Organized Crime Control Act is the Racketeer Influenced and Corrupt Organizations Act, which is best known simply as RICO. RICO was devised to prevent organized crime and racketeering from permeating legitimate organizations. However, the statute is expansive enough to include most illegal activity that affects interstate and foreign commerce. RICO also authorizes harsher penalties for illegal activity that stems from an ongoing criminal organization.

Kathryn Vincent

Further Reading

Bourgeois, Richard L., Jr., et al. "Racketeer Influenced and Corrupt Organizations." *American Criminal Law Review* 37, no. 2 (2000): 879-940.

Dash, Samuel. "The American Bar Association's Impact on the Organized Crime Control Act of 1970." *American Criminal Law Quarterly* 9, no. 1 (1970): 2-162.

See also Anti-Racketeering Act of 1934; Attorney general of the United States; Comprehensive Crime Control Act; Hobbs Act; Mafia; Organized crime; Racketeer Influenced and Corrupt Organizations Act; Victim and Witness Protection Act; Wiretaps.

Outlaws of the Old West

The Event: Classic era of Western outlaws
Date: c. 1850-1890
Criminal justice issues: Law-enforcement organization; media; robbery, theft, and burglary
Significance: Lack of efficient law enforcement in pioneering communities and the promise of easy wealth fostered lawlessness and vigilante justice on America's last frontier.

The classic era of the Wild West—roughly the latter half of the nineteenth century—has captured the imaginations of Americans since the very years in which it unfolded. Bandits such as Jesse James and Billy the Kid and female criminals such as Belle Starr and Pearl Hart have become American icons who have inspired countless novels, plays, and films that have transformed their criminal careers into romantic folklore.

The last major American frontier was opened to eastern settlers and European immigrants in 1862, when the federal government made land available through the Homestead Act. California's gold rush of the late 1840's and 1850's had already attracted a flood of get-rich-quick hopefuls into California and the Oregon Territory. After 1856, new mining camps sprang up in response to major silver strikes in southern Arizona. In Texas and New Mexico, cattle ranchers were kings; cowboys drove herds of thousands of cattle to shipping towns such as Dodge City, Kansas, which relayed beef to eastern markets. In 1889, the federal government opened up much of the Indian Territory—later known as Oklahoma—to settlers. By 1890, most of the land in the West was owned by settlers, Indian nations, or the federal government, and the frontier was effectively closed.

Frontier Law Enforcement

While the Western frontier remained open, criminality flourished. The area was vast, law-enforcement officials were both few and poorly trained, and the few court systems lacked resources. Municipal constables, sheriffs, and federal marshals commonly had no training other than what they learned on their own; many even had to provide their own weapons and horses. Basic tools for lawyers and magistrates, such as law books containing statutes and codes for the nascent Western states and territories were hard to find.

Courts were administered by justices of the peace, many of whom were untrained magistrates elected from pools of local townspeople. One such magistrate who won fame was Texas's Judge Roy Bean, who was notorious for making rulings in his saloon that were supported by his single law book and pistol.

Politics also often played a part in the frontier's lack of justice. Since sheriffs and marshals were often appointed or elected, they generally avoided doing things that might upset voters—including those who were not law-abiding citizens. Cattle rustlers, horse thieves, cardsharps, highwaymen, and bank and train robbers often escaped conviction in the sparsely inhabited frontier.

Frustrated by lawless conditions, settlers and prospectors sometimes took the law into their own hands, forming vigilante groups that captured and summarily executed larcenous bandits. Lawmen were rarely able to charge the vigilante groups with crimes because their members scattered or kept silent. By contrast, citizens often deemed desperadoes heroes, especially if their targets were unpopular rich ranchers or companies such as Wells Fargo or the Union Pacific Railroad. Legends grew around these ostensible Robin Hoods, who purportedly stole from the rich and gave to the poor.

The James-Younger Gang

One of the most celebrated criminal gangs of the Old West was the James-Younger gang, which was led by Jesse James and his brother, Frank James, of Missouri. After the Civil War broke out in 1861, Frank joined a band of Confederate guerrillas who terrorized Union sympathizers in Missouri, a southern state that never declared for the Confederacy. Sixteen-year-old Jesse also signed up after a band of Union militia tortured him and his parents on their farm. The war taught him the power of brutality.

After the war ended in 1865, making the transition from military raiding to criminal raiding and robbery was easy for the James brothers and their partners, Cole Younger and three of his brothers. The gang's first recorded robbery took place at a Gallatin, Missouri, bank in December, 1869. They stole seven hundred dollars and killed a clerk. Although one of the gang's horses was traced back to Jesse James's home, Jesse and Frank managed to escape. It began a pattern that would continue through the next decade: Jesse and his gang outsmarted the authorities and eluded capture by coercing guides or circling behind posses. They robbed banks and trains—both seen by locals as reprehensible symbols of Yankee domination—in six states and found refuge

within a support network that stretched from the James family's farm to Indian Territory. Not even the Pinkerton Detective Agency, whose men had captured train robbers in the past, could foil the James-Younger gang.

Even though the James-Younger gang often shot unarmed bank clerks and train engineers, the public hailed its members as bandit heroes above the law. In July, 1876, the gang's unraveling began with a bloody failed bank robbery in Northfield, Minnesota, that left a bank employee and an innocent bystander dead. Three members of the gang were killed and the Youngers were captured. Only the James brothers got away. In 1881, the brothers had a new gang, with which they robbed a Kansas City train. In the process, they shot a conductor in the back and killed an elderly railroad man—both crimes that turned the public against them. Nevertheless, the James brothers may have continued to elude the law, had not Bob Ford, a member of their own gang, assassinated Jesse James in 1882 after being promised clemency.

Billy the Kid

Born Henry McCarty in 1859, Billy the Kid was a legend during a lifetime that lasted not quite twenty-two years. In New Mexico, he fell in with a group of petty thieves and was caught stealing a Chinese man's clothes. After escaping from jail by climbing up through a chimney, he fled to Arizona. In mining camps there, he gambled and dealt cards, but it was stealing horses at which he excelled.

Horse thieves were particularly reviled criminals on the frontier because horses were always in short supply and needed by farmers, ranchers, lawmen, and others alike. Private citizens thought it their right to capture, try, and hang horse thieves without involving the law. Billy the Kid soon left horse thieving for cowboy work and became involved in a deadly feud between ranchers. When his boss was assassinated in 1878, Billy vowed revenge. After he was deputized, he and his companions, known as the "Regulators," hunted down and killed two of the alleged assassins. Two months later, they gunned down the county sheriff.

Billy then fled and returned to horse and cattle rustling. However, he grew tired of being a fugitive and asked New Mexico's governor for a pardon in exchange for his testimony about the sheriff's murder. Thinking that he and the governor had struck a deal, he eventually testified; however, he was jailed and tried in a federal district court. He was convicted of murder and scheduled to hang, but he killed the deputies guarding him and escaped. After the government issued a five-hundred-dollar reward for Billy's capture, the new sheriff, Patrick Garrett, caught up with him and shot him to death. Like Jesse James, Billy the Kid was seen more as a folk hero than as a criminal.

Olivia Boler

Further Reading

Butler, Anne M. *Gendered Justice in the American West: Women Prisoners in Men's Penitentiaries*. Chicago: University of Illinois Press, 2000. Examination of the treatment of female prisoners in nineteenth century male-inmate dominated prisons.

Hough, Emerson. *The Story of the Outlaw: A Study of the Western Desperado*. Lanham, Md.: Cooper Square Publishers, 2001. Reissue of a collection of unembellished profiles of outlaws and lawmen by a writer who lived in the Old West.

Metz, Leon Claire. *The Encyclopedia of Lawmen, Outlaws, and Gunfighters*. New York: Facts On File, 2002. Collection of more than four hundred brief biographies of Western outlaws and lawmen.

Nash, Jay Robert. *Encyclopedia of Western Lawmen and Outlaws*. New York: Da Capo Press, 1994. More than one thousand entries on criminals and lawmen, with bibliographies and illustrations.

Tuska, Jon. *Billy the Kid: His Life and Legend*. Albuquerque: University of New Mexico Press, 1994. Thorough account of the celebrated outlaw with a discussion of his popularity in fiction and film.

See also Bank robbery; Criminal justice in U.S. history; Criminals; Marshals Service, U.S.; Prison escapes; Robbery; Sheriffs; Theft; Vigilantism.

Palko v. Connecticut

The Case: U.S. Supreme Court ruling on double jeopardy

Date: Decided on December 6, 1937

Criminal justice issues: Constitutional protections; defendants

Significance: In this case, while refusing to apply the Fifth Amendment right against double jeopardy to the states, the Supreme Court established an influential test for determining which fundamental rights contained within the Bill of Rights are incorporated into the Fourteenth Amendment's due process clause.

On the night of September 29, 1935, Bridgeport, Connecticut, police officers Wilfred Walker and Thomas J. Kearney were shot and killed. Frank Palko was charged with first-degree murder, a charge which carried a death sentence. On January 24, 1936, a trial jury found Palko guilty of only second-degree murder because the killings were not sufficiently premeditated. Palko received a sentence of life imprisonment. On July 30, 1936, the Supreme Court of Errors of Connecticut ordered a new trial by finding that the trial judge gave improper instructions to the jury. On October 15, 1936, a second jury found Palko guilty of first-degree murder, and he was sentenced to death. Palko's case came to the U.S. Supreme Court with the claim that the second trial violated his Fifth Amendment right to not "be subject for the same offense to be twice put in jeopardy of life or limb." At the time, however, the Supreme Court had applied the Fifth Amendment right against double jeopardy only to criminal cases in federal, rather than state, courts.

For most of American history, the provisions of the Bill of Rights protected individuals only against actions by the federal government. The ratification of the Fourteenth Amendment in 1868 applied constitutional rights to protection against the states, but those rights were vaguely worded protections involving "due process" and "equal protection." People repeatedly brought cases to the Supreme Court asserting that the provisions of the Bill of Rights should apply against state as well as federal government officials. Beginning in 1925, the Supreme Court gradually incorporated a few rights—speech, press, and religion—into the Fourteenth Amendment's due process clause and thereby made those rights applicable to the states.

Unfortunately for Palko, the Court was unwilling to incorporate the Fifth Amendment's protection against double jeopardy in 1937. Thus Palko's conviction was affirmed, and he was subsequently executed for the murders. Justice Benjamin Cardozo's majority opinion, however, established a test for determining which rights to incorporate by declaring that only rights which are "fundamental" and "essential" to liberty are contained in the right to due process in the Fourteenth Amendment. In analyzing Palko's case, Cardozo decided that many criminal justice rights contained in the Bill of Rights, such as trial by jury and protection against double jeopardy and self-incrimination, are not fundamental and essential because it is possible to have fair trials without them.

The importance of *Palko v. Connecticut* is that Cardozo's test established an influential standard for determining which provisions of the Bill of Rights apply against the states. Although justices in later decades disagreed with Cardozo's specific conclusions and subsequently incorporated double jeopardy and other rights for criminal defendants, most justices continued to use Cardozo's basic approach of evaluating whether each specific right was fundamental and essential to liberty.

Christopher E. Smith

Further Reading

Garcia, Alfredo. *The Fifth Amendment: A Comprehensive Approach*. Westport, Conn.: Greenwood Press, 2002.

Holmes, Burnham. *The Fifth Amendment*. Englewood Cliffs, N.J.: Silver Burdett Press, 1991.

Rudstein, David S. *Double Jeopardy: A Reference Guide to the United States Constitution*. Westport, Conn.: Praeger, 2004.

See also Bill of Rights, U.S.; Double jeopardy; Due process of law; Incorporation doctrine; Supreme Court, U.S.

Palmer raids

The Event: Federal government sweep through dozens of American cities to arrest alien residents suspected of being radicals

Date: January, 1920

Place: Throughout the United States

Criminal justice issues: Espionage and sedition; government misconduct; political issues

Significance: The Palmer raids represented one of numerous aspects of post-World War I hysteria that resulted in the infringement of the civil liberties of both foreign residents and American citizens and helped to give rise to a period known as the "Red Scare."

After the United States entered World War I, a strong desire to eliminate political dissent arose throughout the country. That desire was intensified by the Bolshevik overthrow of the Russian government in 1917 and what was perceived as a developing communist threat to American institutions. Anticommunist fear continued into the post-World War I years. In 1918, Congress passed a Sedition Act that authorized the secretary of labor to deport aliens belonging to revolutionary organizations.

After that law was enacted, U.S. attorney general A. Mitchell Palmer became concerned that it was not being applied as rigorously as necessary. Without the knowledge of Secretary of Labor William Wilson, Palmer obtained arrest warrants from a Labor Department official with which he could deport aliens. On the evening of January 2, 1920, Palmer initiated a series of raids that led to arrest of more than three thousand suspected radicals in thirty-three cities. The raids continued on January 5 and rounded up many people who were only remotely connected with revolutionary

---

The Man Behind the Palmer Raids

Attorney General A. Mitchell Palmer was born in 1872 in Pennsylvania, where he was raised a Quaker. After training as a lawyer, he was active in Democratic Party politics and became a prominent supporter of Woodrow Wilson. After serving three terms in the House of Representatives, he lost a bid for the U.S. Senate and took a job as the federal government's alien property custodian during World War I. In 1919, President Wilson appointed him attorney general. Palmer used his two years in that office to wage vigorous campaigns against political radicals of all stripes. He is best known for deporting anarchist Emma Goldman and for his notorious "raids" in 1920. His blatant disregard for due process and civil liberties during those raids probably ruined his bid for the Democratic presidential nomination that same year. However, he remained an active supporter of Democratic leaders until his death in 1936.

---

organizations, including many innocent people visiting relatives in jails. Many of those arrested were held for long periods without being charged.

Outraged by Palmer's abuse of government power, Secretary Wilson took charge of the deportation hearings. Eventually, 556 of the arrested aliens were deported. The remainder were released.

Richard Adler

Further Reading

Feuerlicht, Roberta Strauss. *America's Reign of Terror: World War I, the Red Scare, and the Palmer Raids*. Foreword by Norman Dorsen. New York: Random House, 1971.

Hoyt, Edwin Palmer. *The Palmer Raids, 1919-1920: An Attempt to Suppress Dissent*. New York: Seabury Press, 1969.

Pfannestiel, Todd J. *Rethinking the Red Scare: The Lusk Committee and New York's Crusade Against Radicalism, 1919-1923*. New York: Routledge, 2003.

See also Federal Bureau of Investigation; Illegal aliens; Presumption of innocence; Rosenberg espionage case; Smith Act.

Pandering

Definition: Act of promoting the business of prostitution by soliciting customers, maintaining houses of prostitution, deriving support from prostitution, or transporting persons for the purpose of prostitution

Criminal justice issues: Sex offenses; women's issues

Significance: The acts of intermediaries who exploit prostitutes or who act as agents for prostitutes are prohibited in all states. Such conduct is variously known as pandering, pimping, procuring, promoting prostitution, and deriving support from prostitution. Laws against such behavior are directed against those who act as agents for prostitutes or who derive support from prostitutes, not against prostitutes themselves.

Under most circumstances these offenses are characterized as misdemeanors, but some states provide harsher punishments for pandering offenses than for prostitution itself. Some statutes provide higher penalties for those who compel others to enter into prostitution by force or threat of force, for those who promote the prostitution of a minor, or for those who promote the prostitution of a spouse, child, or ward. The Model Penal Code, for example, makes such offenses felonies as opposed to misdemeanors.

Commonly, persons who engage in pandering are called either pimps or madams. Pimps are usually men who obtain customers for prostitutes, who induce other people to enter into prostitution, or who receive all or part of the earnings of a prostitute. The relationship between a pimp and the prostitutes who work for him is frequently characterized by violence and exploitation. Pimps are notorious for supplying drugs to prostitutes in order to keep them in a state of dependence and generally induce prostitutes to work for them either by promises of protection and money or by force or threat of force. Prosecutions against pimps can be difficult to maintain, since the testimony of the prostitutes they exploit is often necessary to support a conviction and prostitutes may be reluctant to testify.

Madams are usually women who operate houses of prostitution. They procure customers for prostitutes, provide a place for prostitution to be performed, and take a percentage of prostitutes' earnings. Maintaining a house of prostitution is illegal in almost every state. Laws against this offense generally require that prostitution be regularly engaged in on the premises and that the person maintaining or having control of the property have knowledge of the activity.

In some jurisdictions it is also illegal to transport a person for the purpose of prostitution. In order for state laws of this nature to be valid, they must encompass transportation only within that particular state. Any state laws which presume to prohibit interstate transportation of persons for the purpose of prostitution will be held invalid as being in conflict with the federal White Slave Traffic Act of 1910, also known as the Mann Act, which prohibits such interstate transportation under the principle that federal legislation regarding any form of interstate commerce always supersedes state legislation on the subject.

Michele Leavitt

Further Reading

Chapkis, Wendy. *Live Sex Acts: Women Performing Erotic Labor*. New York: Routledge, 1997.

Fleiss, Heidi. *Pandering*. Los Angeles: One Hour Entertainment, 2002.

Meier, Robert, and Gilbert Geis. *Victimless Crime? Prostitution, Drugs, Homosexuality, and Abortion*. Los Angeles: Roxbury, 1997.

See also Commercialized vice; Criminal justice system; Criminal law; Criminal prosecution; Disorderly conduct; Mann Act; Misdemeanors; Moral turpitude.

Paralegals

Definition: Law office employees with limited legal training who perform certain legal functions under the supervision of accredited attorneys

Criminal justice issue: Attorneys

Significance: Although paralegals are not authorized to practice law, they play an important role in the justice system by assisting lawyers and clients in law-related matters.

The paralegal profession was developed in order to increase access to legal services at a reduced cost. Paralegals work among attorneys in private law firms, corporations, government offices and agencies, banks, and insurance and real estate organizations. Paralegals may not give legal advice requiring the exercise of independent legal judgment, represent clients in litigation, or fail to disclose that they are not attorneys. Some of their general duties include the compilation of legal documentation and pretrial materials, the search for court dockets and files, and the preparation of law memorandums, leases, mortgages, deeds, citations, summonses, depositions, and subpoenas. They also assist attorneys in areas of litigation, divorce law, domestic relations, probate and estate law, and corporate law.

Paralegals in private law firms conduct research, interview clients, gather information, and prepare agendas for meetings and complex transactions. In the public sector, paralegals assist clients in filling out forms, negotiate with agencies, represent clients before certain administrative authorities, and disseminate materials on legal concerns affecting the local community. Paralegals are in particular demand by the federal government for handling many of the functions traditionally provided by more highly paid lawyers. For example, agencies involved in Social Security administration have programs that employ paralegals to conduct some prehearing conferences, research issues, and write decisions.

Training

Formal training in paralegal services started during the late 1960's. In the United States, paralegal programs exist at many colleges, universities, and law schools, as well as at private training institutions, government agencies, and bar associations. In 1995 there were 500 paralegal programs in the United States, but only 185 were approved by the American Bar Association (ABA). Paralegal students do not need prior legal experience, and most have never been inside a law office. Prospective paralegal students will ask, prior to selecting a program, whether a program in which they are interested is a two- or four-year program, what the program's educational objectives are, whether the program is ABA approved, what the reputation of the institution and program is, what the quality of the faculty is, and whether the program provides assistance with career development. Some of the courses a paralegal student might take include legal research, legal writing, legal ethics, interviewing, litigation, estates and trusts, real estate law, business law, criminal law, family law, and computer skills.

Thousands of paralegals were employed by law firms and agencies in the United States in 1998, and the paralegal field was the eighth fastest growing profession in the United States. In some states, after paralegals have successfully completed their academic work and their on-the-job training, they are allowed to take bar examinations to become accredited attorneys.

Alvin K. Benson

Further Reading

Larbalestrier, Deborah E. *Paralegal Practice and Procedure: A Practical Guide for the Legal Assistant*. 3d ed. Englewood Cliffs, N.J.: Prentice-Hall, 1994.

Mauet, Thomas, and Marlene Maerowitz. *Fundamentals of Litigation for Paralegals*. 3d ed. Boston: Little, Brown, 1998.

See also Attorney ethics; Defense attorneys; Effective counsel.

Pardons

Definition: Legal release from the punishment for a crime

Criminal justice issues: Government misconduct; pardons and parole; political issues

Significance: The power of government to pardon criminals is an essential part of the checks and balances of the American constitutional system, as it allows executive branches to check the fairness of rulings from the judicial branches.

Modern government's power to pardon has its origin in ancient Hebrew law. It also existed within

The Text of Ford's Pardon of Nixon

Richard Nixon became the thirty-seventh President of the United States on January 20, 1969 and was re-elected in 1972 for a second term by the electors of forty-nine of the fifty states. His term in office continued until his resignation on August 9, 1974. . . .

As a result of certain acts or omissions occurring before his resignation from the Office of President, Richard Nixon has become liable to possible indictment and trial for offenses against the United States. . . .

It is believed that a trial of Richard Nixon, if it became necessary, could not fairly begin until a year or more has elapsed. In the meantime, the tranquility to which this nation has been restored by the events of recent weeks could be irreparably lost by the prospects of bringing to trial a former President of the United States. The prospects of such a trial will cause prolonged and divisive debate over the propriety of exposing to further punishment and degradation a man who has already paid the unprecedented penalty of relinquishing the highest elective office of the United States.

NOW, THEREFORE, I, Gerald R. Ford, President of the United States, pursuant to the pardon power conferred upon me by Article II, Section 2, of the Constitution, have granted and by these presents do grant a full, free, and absolute pardon unto Richard Nixon for all offenses against the United States which he, Richard Nixon, has committed or may have committed or taken part in during the period from January 20, 1969 through August 9, 1974. . . .

President Gerald Ford. *(Library of Congress)*

European churches and monarchies that had the power of clemency during medieval times. Centuries later, in England, the pardon power was recognized as the "royal prerogative of mercy." In the United States, pardons are viewed as a way for the executive branches of state and federal government to check the judiciary.

Many scholars view the pardon power as antidemocratic because it permits one person to subvert the rulings of the criminal justice system. However, the Framers of the U.S. Constitution supported the idea of a pardon power because it allowed executive leaders to use well-timed pardons during times of crisis to quell rebellion among dissatisfied segments of the population.

The chief executive officers at the national and the state levels may issue pardons in particular cases. In each of the fifty states, a board of pardons makes recommendations—often in consultation with the state boards of parole—on persons who should be given pardons. Three main goals are served through the use of the pardon

power: remedying injustice, removing the disgrace of conviction, and mitigating the punishment stage of the criminal justice system. It is rare for pardons to be issued for injustices, but many convicted persons are released from prison after they are found to have been wrongfully convicted. Pardons are more commonly employed in cases in which young offenders seek to expunge their criminal records in order to pursue careers that are not open to convicted felons. Pardons allow all former convicts to find employment more easily and generally remove the disgrace of criminal records.

Presidential Pardons

The U.S. Constitution provides U.S. presidents with the power to pardon individuals for offenses against the United States, except in cases of impeachment. President pardons generally receive little attention, but they have been exercised frequently throughout history. In *Ex parte Garland* (1866), the U.S. Supreme Court ruled that Congress cannot limit the president's pardon power through legislation. Hence, the power to pardon at the federal level is potentially unlimited. Moreover, presidents can issue pardons at any time during judicial proceedings and for any offense. In fact, offenses do not even have to be specified, and a person need not be convicted of a crime to be issued a pardon.

By contrast, a large majority of states have placed limitations on their governors' power to pardon. For example, many states have imposed postconviction requirements upon governors, requiring that a person must first be convicted of a crime to be eligible for a pardon.

The Pardon of Richard M. Nixon

The most controversial pardon in American history was issued on September 8, 1974, when President Gerald R. Ford pardoned former president Richard M. Nixon one month after succeeding Nixon as president. At that moment, Nixon had not even been charged with any crime; however, he was under investigation for his involvement in a burglary at the Democratic headquarters at the Watergate hotel in Washington, D.C. Nevertheless, Ford's proclamation pardoned Nixon for all offenses against the United States that he may have committed during his presidency.

Many Americans believed that Ford's pardon of Nixon was motivated by partisan interests and contradicted the assumption of the Framers of the Constitution that presidents would not break the law. In fact, some speculated that Ford promised to pardon Nixon even before Nixon named him vice president on Spiro Agnew's resignation, thus putting him in line for the presidency. Nevertheless, in *Murphy v. Ford* (1975), a federal district court judge upheld the constitutionality of Ford's pardon of Nixon. Citing *Ex parte Garland* as precedent, the judge reaffirmed that the president's power to pardon is not subject to any limitations.

Bush's Pardons of Iran-Contra Figures

In December of 1992, President George Bush pardoned six key figures in the Iran-Contra scandal, which involved members of President Ronald Reagan's administration illegally selling weapons to Iran during the 1980's in exchange for funds to support the Contras who were fighting against Nicaragua's Sandinista government. Congress had specifically addressed the issue of the Contras by passing legislation to keep the U.S. government out of the Nicaraguan civil war. In December, 1992, Reagan's former vice president, George Bush, was himself a lame-duck president, after losing his bid for reelection in November. Bush pardoned former defense secretary Caspar Weinberger, three Central Intelligence Agency officials, and two former advisers to Reagan. By pardoning these people, Bush halted the criminal justice process and prevented more information from surfacing about the scandal. His action was troubling because many people speculated that Bush was acting in his own self-interest, as criminal trials might have produced information about his own involvement in the scandal during his time as vice president.

The pardon power is a significant grant of authority bestowed upon U.S. presidents. The pardons issued by Ford and Bush demonstrate that the power might be used for political purposes and, more important, might pose risks to democratic government. The pardon power has the potential of being used by governors and presidents to conceal criminal and other government misconduct. Therefore, some politicians, such as former senator Walter Mondale of Minnesota, have proposed constitutional amendments to place a postconviction limitation on the president's power to pardon individuals for federal crimes. Until such an amendment is ratified, however, the U.S. Supreme Court's interpretation of the pardon power prohibits restrictions upon presidents.

Scott P. Johnson

Further Reading

Chabot, Steve. *Presidential Pardon Power: Hearing Before the Committee on the Judiciary, U.S. House of Representatives.* Collingdale, Pa.: Diane Publishing, 2003. Report on the deliberations conducted in the House of Representatives regarding the president's power to pardon.

Genovese, Michael. *The Power of the American Presidency, 1789-2000.* New York: Oxford University Press, 2000. Overview of presidential power, including the power to pardon.

Johnson, Scott P., and Christopher E. Smith. "White House Scandals and the Presidential Pardon Power: Persistent Risks and Prospects for Reform." *New England Law Review* (1999). Exploration of the dangers of the pardon power with suggestions on how to limit the power of the pardon in order to hold executives accountable within the democratic system.

Macgill, Hugh C. "The Nixon Pardon: Limits on the Benign Prerogative." *Connecticut Law Review* (1974). Legal case for limiting the pardon power of U.S. presidents written in the wake of Gerald Ford's pardon of Richard M. Nixon.

Mollenhoff, Clark R. *The Man Who Pardoned Nixon*. New York: St. Martin's Press, 1976. Analysis of Gerald Ford's presidency focusing on his pardon of Richard Nixon.

See also Amnesty; Clemency; Constitution, U.S.; Criminal justice system; False convictions; Good time; Miscarriage of justice; Parole; Parole officers; Political corruption; President, U.S.; Probation, adult; United States Parole Commission.

Parens patriae

Definition: Legal doctrine granting authority to the government to take responsibility for the welfare of children

Criminal justice issues: Juvenile justice; legal terms and principles; mental disorders

Significance: The principle of *parens patriae* provides the legal basis for courts to supervise and treat minors and legally incompetent adults whose families are not available or able to provide them with proper care and guidance.

During the early nineteenth century, increasing attention was given in urban areas to rapid population growth, social problems, and the placement of juvenile delinquents in adult jails and prisons. Concerns over these issues eventually led to the first house of refuge being opened in New York in 1825. This facility was established to house poor children and delinquents who were in need of care and guidance that was not being provided by their families. Additional houses of

"Parent of the Country"

Parens patriae is a Latin phrase that means, literally, "parent of the country." One of the many Latin terms that has found its way into legal language, the phrase is etymologically similar to *amor patriae*, which means "love of one's country." In legal parlance, *parens patriae* alludes to the principle that minor children and helpless adults who have no one else to take care of them are, in effect, the children of the state. In other words, the government is their parent.

refuge soon opened in other major cities. In 1838, the Pennsylvania case of *Ex parte Crouse* established the doctrine of *parens patriae* as the legal basis for the government to supervise and treat children when their parents were either unable or unwilling to do so.

The term *parens patriae* was first used in English chancery courts to assist juveniles with their legal inheritances. In the United States, the concept was applied to dependent, neglected, and delinquent children who were deemed in need of assistance. In Illinois, after the 1870 case of *People v. Turner* threatened the use of *parens patriae* by criminal courts, a child-saving movement in Chicago resulted in the establishment of the first juvenile court in 1899. *Parens patriae* has since been used as the legal doctrine allowing juvenile courts to adjudicate, supervise, and treat children and youth who are determined to be in need of governmental intervention.

David L. Myers

Further Reading

Champion, Dean John. *The Juvenile Justice System: Delinquency, Processing, and the Law.* 4th ed. Upper Saddle River, N.J.: Prentice-Hall, 2003.

Cox, Steven M., John J. Conrad, and Jennifer M. Allen. *Juvenile Justice: A Guide to Theory and Practice.* 5th ed. New York: McGraw-Hill, 2003.

Hess, Karen M., and Robert W. Drowns. *Juvenile Justice.* 4th ed. Belmont, Calif.: Wadsworth/Thomson Learning, 2004. Comprehensive overview of the juvenile justice system that connects theory and practice.

Williams, Frank P., and Marilyn D. McShane, eds. *Encyclopedia of Juvenile Justice*. Thousand Oaks, Calif.: Sage, 2003.

See also Criminal justice system; Due process of law; *Gault, In re*; Juvenile courts; Juvenile delinquency; Juvenile justice system; Parole; Probation, juvenile; Rehabilitation; Status offenses; Uniform Juvenile Court Act.

Parole

Definition: Conditional release of prisoners before the completion of their full sentences

Criminal justice issues: Convictions; pardons and parole; punishment; rehabilitation

Significance: In order to rehabilitate criminals and manage overcrowding in prisons, the state releases, or paroles, prisoners before the end of their sentences on the promise that they will not break the law again or violate the conditions of parole.

The word "parole" comes from the French word *parol*, which means "word of honor." Originally, it referred to the practice of releasing prisoners of war who promised not to resume fighting. Modern parole is the conditional release of prisoners by a parole board before the expiration of their sentences. Parole does not mean that a felony offender is free from the legal custody and supervision of the state. Parole is a privilege granted by the state, which could just as easily keep the prisoner in jail.

Purpose of Parole

The mission of parole is to prepare, select, and assist offenders who, after a reasonable period of incarceration, could benefit from early release. At the same time, the state protects the public through the conditions of release and supervision. The state and the prisoner sign a contract under which the prisoner promises to abide by certain conditions in exchange for conditional freedom. The state justifies parole on the grounds that prisoners need supervision and help if they are to readjust to freedom successfully. Most parole failures occur relatively soon after release. In fact, approximately one-quarter of parole failures occur within the first six months.

Incarceration ensures the protection of society, acts as a deterrent to criminal activity, and functions as punishment for criminal acts. However, it is limited in its ability to prepare offenders for return to the free world. Parole is based on the belief that the majority of offenders can benefit from a period of transition back into the community. Conditional release affords a continuing measure of protection to the public while supporting parolees in their effort to become productive, law-abiding citizens. If parolees violate the conditions of their parole or commit crimes, parole can be revoked and the offenders returned to jail.

Not all offenders have the same potential and motivation to earn or to benefit from conditional release. Offenders must be judged on their own merits and in the light of their offenses, sentence lengths, and personal backgrounds. Parole authorities use risk assessment tools to evaluate the potential success of offenders if paroled. These studies help determine whether prisoners should be released and the conditions of parole.

Society benefits from a successful parole program. Most incarcerated offenders eventually complete their sentences and return to the community. Parole is viewed as a positive means of promoting successful reintegration. It also helps reduce unnecessary expenses at correctional institutions while, at the same time, maintaining an appropriate degree of supervision and control to ensure the protection of society. Parole also mitigates the harshness of criminal law, equalizes disparities in sentencing, and helps prison authorities maintain order and reduce crowding.

The purpose of parole is to improve public safety by reducing the incidence and impact of crime committed by parolees. Parole is not leniency or clemency but a logical extension of the sentence to provide the opportunity to return offenders to society after a reasonable period of incarceration and when they are assessed to have the capability and desire to succeed and live up to the responsibilities of their release.

Offenders who comply with the conditions of their parole and do not violate the law receive an absolute discharge at the end of their sentences. The parolee may be required to abstain from alcohol, keep away from undesirable associates, maintain good work habits, and not leave the community without permission. The revocation of parole occurs when the parolee commits a new crime or violates the conditions of parole. Half of all convicted felons are released on parole. Parole boards release approximately 99 percent of prisoners from prison to serve the remainder of their sentences outside prison walls. An estimated 35 to 40 percent of all parolees have their paroles revoked and are sent back to prison.

Legal Issues

The U.S. Constitution does not require states to maintain a parole system. There is no constitutionally protected right to parole or to due process in release hearings unless state statutes or regulations create a liberty interest in parole release. The parole board can do just about anything it pleases with respect to a prisoner's parole release. Whatever the board decides and does prevails, because it enjoys immense discretion in the parole decision process. Although parole boards are not constitutionally required to provide reasons for denying release, the use of state-mandated parole guidelines provides prisoners with such information.

Prisoners' federal constitutional rights with respect to parole are limited. For example, the U.S. Constitution places few limits on parole boards. Boards may rely on allegations of conduct of which the prisoner was found innocent or may even consider information from charges of which the prisoner was not convicted. The board can deny parole because of the severity of a prisoner's crime. The parole board may not consider race or inaccurate information to make its decision. To obtain judicial relief, prisoners must show that their files contain errors and that the board relied on false information in denying or revoking parole or time off for good behavior. Prisoners must also show that they requested prison authorities to correct their files but that the latter refused to do so. Often state law and regulations provide prisoners with greater rights. Even when an offender has a federal constitutional claim, a prisoner must exhaust remedies available in state courts before a federal court will intervene.

History of Parole

America's parole system originated during the late 1870's. Well-behaved prisoners in the reformatory in Elmira, New York, had their prison sentences shortened. This system was based on programs developed in England and Ireland. The concept of parole was created by Alexander Maconochie, who was superintendent of the British penal colony on Norfolk Island, off the coast of Sydney, Australia, during the mid-nineteenth century. Sir Walter Crofton, director of the Irish prison system during the late nineteenth century, was influenced by Maconochie's work. A modified version of the Irish system, under which a prisoner could earn early release from prison, was adopted in England and then at Elmira. Other American prisons copied the Elmira system.

A feature of the Elmira system was the indeterminate sentence. Under this system a judge

Inmates of the Mississippi Department of Corrections (MDOC) attending a class on basic life skills in preparation for their release. Development of inmates' employment and life skills is a central part of all parole systems. *(AP/Wide World Photos)*

imposed a prison sentence with a minimum and a maximum length. The parole board determined the prisoner's release date. In most states inmates who followed prison rules were entitled to good time off—time deducted from a prisoner's maximum sentence. A prisoner could shorten his sentence by one-third under the good-time-off system. A side effect of indeterminate sentencing was that persons convicted of the same crime could receive different sentences.

Under determinate sentencing systems, a judge imposes a sentence of a specific length. This sentencing system provides for early release because of good behavior—often one day off a sentence for every day served. In theory, this system promotes prison discipline. Violation of prison rules could result in jail time being added to the sentence.

The idea of parole release spread slowly throughout the United States until the Great Depression of the 1930's. Pressing economic conditions—notably the cost of incarceration, not the press of prison reform—led to the rapid spread of parole release systems. Conditional release is the term used to describe prisoners released on good time.

Many efforts to abolish or change the parole system have been tried. For example, the Sentencing Reform Act of 1984 abolished parole eligibility for federal offenders who committed offenses after November 1, 1987. It also provided for the abolition of the U.S. Parole Commission on November 1, 1992. However, the Judicial Improvements Act of 1990, the Parole Commission Phaseout Act of 1996, and the Twenty-first Century Department of Justice Appropriations Authorization Act of 2002 extended the commission in five-year increments through November 1, 2005.

The history of prisons and parole in the United States shows that parole release has been used, and possibly misused, to maintain prison discipline and to reduce prison overcrowding. Parole boards evolved out of the power of governors to issue pardons to selected prisoners. Before the creation of parole boards, governors often used their pardoning powers to relieve overcrowding in state prisons. For example, during the mid-nineteenth century, pardons accounted for over 40 percent of prisoner releases.

The Parole Decision

The goal of all parole decisions is the protection of society. In the short term, the parole board examines whether there is a high degree of risk to society if it releases the prisoner. To meet the longer-term goal, the board considers whether parole would help the offender return to the community.

Parole may be discretionary or mandatory. Discretionary parole occurs when the parole board voluntarily grants parole before the offender completes a sentence. Mandatory parole is the automatic release of an offender upon completion of the sentence (less any good time credit). Under many state parole systems, the department of corrections determines when an offender is eligible for parole. The corrections department uses a formula that includes, but is not limited to, length of sentence, institutional adjustment, treatment or educational program involvement, and prior prison experience.

To guide its decision, the board conducts a risk assessment. The assessment has two parts—a preliminary risk assessment and a special factor evaluation. The first part includes gathering information about the offender. The information includes details of the offense, criminal history, social problems such as alcohol or drug use and family violence, mental status (especially if it affects the likelihood of future crime), performance on earlier releases, information about family relationships, and employment prospects. The board then consults statistical guidelines that assess the probability that the offender will commit another crime. The guidelines indicate how often a group of offenders with characteristics and histories similar to those of the prisoner under review commits new offenses. The second step focuses on a review of reports from psychologists, police, victims, and prison authorities.

After considering the evidence and holding a hearing with the prisoner, the board decides whether to grant parole. If denied, another parole review date may be set. The offender usually has the option to appeal the board's decision when errors in fact, unknowingly considered during the review process, are identified later. The board reconsiders cases when significant new information is presented that was unavailable when the case was originally examined. If parole is

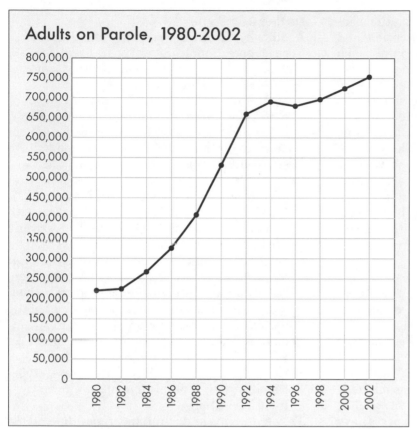

Adults on Parole, 1980-2002

Source: U.S. Bureau of Justice Statistics.

granted, the board determines the conditions of release. A parole board may be independent of the prison system or a division of the organization that administers correctional institutions. In most states, parole board members are appointed by the governor.

The core services of parole boards are to help offenders develop release plans and to supervise persons released on parole. Parole authorities may also provide employment and life skills counseling, halfway house accommodations, counseling, community work programs, and family services. Parole board members usually hold release hearings in the state prison. Prisoners usually do not have legal representation at such hearings.

During the 1990's, many states permitted victims or their next of kin to appear before the parole board. Some states permitted victims to introduce written statements at parole hearings. Such statements could include information concerning the crime, the extent and severity of the

personal or family injury and economic loss, and the victim's attitude toward the offender's potential parole release. All parole boards consider opposition to an inmate's parole from the police and news media. The parole board determines the actual amount of time to be served based on the prisoner's institutional adjustments as measured by the prisoner's accomplishments, vocational education, academic achievement, work assignments, therapy, and interpersonal relationships with other inmates and prison authorities. Other factors include the prisoner's prospects for outside employment, education, training, eligibility for community services such as halfway house placements, and help with personal problems.

Overcrowded and underfinanced prisons pressure parole boards into accelerating the release of inmates. Unfortunately, there are too few parole officers to cope adequately with all the parolees.

During most of the twentieth century, parole boards decided when most prisoners would be released. With the advent of determinate sentencing and parole guidelines, releasing power has essentially been taken away from the parole boards in many states.

Parole Violations

If after a reasonable length of time parolees continue to show that they can obey all the rules of parole, they may be discharged from parole supervision. At that time, they receive a certificate stating that the current sentence and parole obligations have been met and discharged.

Every paroled prisoner signs an agreement to abide by certain regulations, including obeying the law and not possessing or using narcotics or carrying weapons. Parole violations are either technical violations or new offense violations. Technical violations occur when the conditions of parole are violated. New offense violations involve an arrest and criminal prosecution and conviction. Parolees alleged to have committed a violation are given a preliminary hearing to determine whether there is probable cause to believe the conditions of parole were violated. If probable cause is determined, the offender is held in custody pending a hearing to determine whether parole should be revoked. The purpose of the revocation hearing is to determine whether the violation is serious enough to revoke parole and return the parolee to prison. If probable cause is not determined, the prisoner is released. Prisoners are entitled to due process at parole revocation hearings.

Reinventing Parole

Parole boards are often criticized when a parolee commits a high-profile crime. Studies of intensive-supervision programs for high-risk parolees have found that the programs cut neither recidivism nor costs. Critics have favored some types of "three strikes and you're out" laws or a no-parole policy after three convictions for some categories of violent and repeat felons. In an effort to reinvent the parole system, some experts have advocated use of a voucher system. For a specific period, parolees can use the voucher to seek an education, job training, drug treatment, or other services from state-selected providers. If parolees want to help themselves, they can. If not, they are on their own. Parolees who commit new crimes are sent back to prison to do their time and are given additional time for the new violation.

Some experts have advocated privatizing the parole system and would have bail bond agencies manage the parole system. With their own money at risk, bondsmen would supervise their parolees closely. Privatizing the parole system would save taxpayers money. Prisoners eligible for parole would be required to post a financial bond against specified violations such as reporting regularly to their bail bond agents or submitting to drug testing. Persons violating parole would forfeit their bond, generating revenue for the state and victim compensation. Bond would be set by the courts or parole boards based on the criminal's history and prospects for a productive, law-abiding life.

Fred Buchstein

Further Reading

Abadinsky, Howard. *Probation and Parole*. 7th ed. Upper Saddle River, N.J.: Prentice-Hall, 2000. Detailed description of probation and parole in the United States.

Boston, John, and Daniel E. Manville. *Prisoners' Self-Help Litigation Manual*. Dobbs Ferry, N.Y.: Oceana, 1995. Self-help guide for prisoners seeking parole. Offers other readers insights into prisoners' perspectives on parole.

Clear, Todd R., and George F. Cole. *American Corrections*. Belmont, Calif.: Wadsworth, 1997. Excellent overview of correctional system with a thorough discussion of how parole works and fits in the correctional system.

Glaze, Lauren, and Seri Pella. *Probation and Parole in the United States, 2003*. Washington, D.C.: Bureau of Justice Statistics, 2004. Federal government report on the workings of the parole system over the previous year.

Petersilia, Joan, ed. *Community Corrections: Probation, Parole, and Intermediate Sanctions*. New York: Oxford University Press, 1998. Broad survey of parole and other alternatives to incarceration.

Travis, Jeremy, and Sarah Lawrence. *Beyond the Prison Gates: The State of Parole in America*. Washington, D.C.: Urban Institute, 2002. Evaluation of the workings of the parole system at the turn of the twenty-first century.

See also Clemency; Community-based corrections; Discretion; Marshals Service, U.S.; Pardons; *Parens patriae*; Parole officers; Prison and jail systems; Probation, adult; Probation, juvenile; Suspended sentences; United States Parole Commission; Work-release programs.

Parole officers

Definition: Government employees charged with supervising parolees, convicted criminals who have been released, or exempted, from incarceration

Criminal justice issues: Pardons and parole; probation and pretrial release; punishment

Significance: Parole officers, or parole agents as they are called in some states, are responsible for ensuring that parolees, or criminals who have been allowed to serve the remainder of their sentences outside prison, abide by the conditions stipulated at the time of their release.

It is the duty of the parole officer to ensure that the parolee abide by the conditions of parole, as dictated by the parole board, until final discharge is granted. The requirements for employment as a parole officer vary considerably. Some states require that parole officers have graduate degrees in appropriate fields. Others expect that parole officers have only a high school diploma or a general equivalency diploma (GED) and limited training. Persons interested in becoming parole officers often study law enforcement, social work, or counseling. Parole officers must acquire expertise in all these areas of study, because they are responsible for supervising, assisting, and monitoring the persons assigned to them. In their role as counselors, parole officers assist convicted felons under their supervision who try to reenter society.

Parole officers offer counseling and help parolees find employment and job training, if needed. Many persons released from prison, as well as their families, find the transition very difficult. Persons are often reluctant to accept ex-convicts into the community, and many employers will not hire convicted felons. The transition is sometimes made more difficult in some states by legislation requiring that communities be notified when a parolee moves into the area. Some states have special units and programs that focus on specific problem areas complicating the transition, such as alcoholism, drug addiction, and unemployment. Mentally ill and developmentally challenged offenders often require special programs as well.

It is the goal of the parole officer to smooth a former convict's transition from being a prisoner to being a productive member of society. Although assisting with the transition to life outside prison is a primary concern, parole officers are also required to police the activities of those under their supervision. Parole officers are recognized as armed law-enforcement officers in many states and are required to undergo the same training as other law-enforcement personnel. Such training is often necessary, as parolees tend to be dangerous offenders who have been imprisoned for long periods of time. In Delaware and South Carolina the responsibilities of the parole officer and probation officer are performed by the same individual. Other states, however, make a clear distinction between these two law-enforcement functions.

Donald C. Simmons, Jr.

Further Reading

Abadinsky, Howard. *Probation and Parole*. 7th ed. Upper Saddle River, N.J.: Prentice-Hall, 2000. Detailed description of probation and parole in the United States.

Glaze, Lauren, and Seri Pella. *Probation and Parole in the United States, 2003*. Washington, D.C.: Bureau of Justice Statistics, 2004. Federal government report on the workings of the parole system over the previous year.

Petersilia, Joan, ed. *Community Corrections: Probation, Parole, and Intermediate Sanctions*. New York: Oxford University Press, 1998. Broad survey of parole and other alternatives to incarceration.

Travis, Jeremy, and Sarah Lawrence. *Beyond the Prison Gates: The State of Parole in America*. Washington, D.C.: Urban Institute, 2002. Evaluation of the workngs of the parole system at the turn of the twenty-first century.

See also Community-based corrections; Criminal law; Pardons; *Parens patriae*; Parole; Probation, adult; Probation, juvenile; United States Parole Commission; Work-release programs.

Patriot Act

The Law: Revision of federal laws governing warrants, electronic surveillance, access to private records, custody, and definitions of terrorism

Date: Became law on October 26, 2001

Criminal justice issues: Federal law; police powers; terrorism

Significance: A rapid response to the terrorist attacks of September 11, 2001, the Patriot Act was designed to protect the United

States by making it easier to uncover and defeat foreign and domestic terrorism.

On October 26, 2001, only forty-five days after terrorists crashed skyjacked jetliners into the World Trade Center and Pentagon, President George W. Bush signed Public Law 107-56. Formally titled the Uniting and Strengthening America by Providing Appropriate Tools Required to Intercept and Obstruct Terrorism Act, the law is better known by its acronym, USA PATRIOT Act, or simply Patriot Act. The new law altered more than fifteen existing federal statutes, some in major ways, primarily to equip law-enforcement and intelligence personnel with legal tools for fighting international and domestic terrorism.

Tracking Terrorists and Their Money

The act streamlines the legal processes for obtaining authorization to perform surveillance on suspects persons and for seizing money that may be used to support terrorism. Among its measures, it requires financial institutions to report suspicious activity, identify new customers effectively, cut ties to fraudulent shell banks in foreign countries, and maintain anti-money-laundering programs. Financial institutions are encouraged to share information with law-enforcement agencies, and the federal government is empowered to confiscate the property of any person or organization that performs terrorist acts or plans to do so. The act also expanded the kinds of money-laundering and fraudulent activities—such as those involving American credit cards—that fall under the definition of supporting terrorism.

In order to catch terrorists, the act changed requirements for issuing search warrants and reduced judicial oversight. Previously, local judges—or the eleven-member Foreign Intelligence Surveillance Court in the case of suspected foreign spying—issued warrants to authorize electronic surveillance, such as wiretaps, for specific instruments or facilities. The Patriot Act permits any federal judge to issue a nationwide warrant to tap phones and electronic mail in any instruments that suspects may conceivably use. It also allows "sneak and peek" search warrants; permits delays in serving some warrants until one week after the surveillance authorized by

the warrants; and requires libraries, bookstores, and Internet service providers to supply information about client use. In the case of foreign suspects, antiterrorism agents can request authorization for warrantless searches when gathering foreign intelligence is a significant reason for the searches. Before the Patriot Act was passed, foreign intelligence gathering had to be the sole reason.

Expanded Scope of Antiterrorism Efforts

The Patriot Act is designed to stop terrorists from staying in the United States. When there are reasonable grounds to believe that foreign visitors pose a threat to national security, they can be arrested and held for seven days without being charged, pending investigation or their deportation. There is no judicial review except for *habeas corpus*, and the U.S. attorney general may order aliens held indefinitely if no countries agree to accept them upon deportation.

The act makes even unknowingly associating with terrorists or terrorist organizations a deportable offense. To track and identify suspects, the act further increases rewards for information about terrorism, expands the exemptions to the Posse Comitatus Act of 1878, and permits the U.S. attorney general to collect samples of deoxyribonucleic acid (DNA) from convicted federal prisoners. It also adds a new category, domestic terrorism, applicable to any U.S. citizen who commits acts intended negatively to influence government policy or to coerce civilians by intimidation. Such acts, whether by citizens or foreigners, include attacking mass transportation, releasing biological agents, using weapons or explosives, spreading false information about terrorist attacks, or conspiring with terrorists.

The Patriot Act warns citizens not to mistreat Muslims and Arabs, and it penalizes government officials and law-enforcement agents who misuse it. The act "sunsets" many of its provisions on December 31, 2005—that is, it requires congressional reapproval by that date.

Despite its various safeguards, the act received extensive criticism from both conservative and liberal commentators. The act essentially requires citizens and legal aliens to accept reductions in civil liberties in exchange for increased security. However, critics charge that the act's infringements on civil liberties are unnecessary or excessive. Philosopher Cornel West captured the basic objection when he said that the fundamental fear is "that the present American obsession with safety may undermine freedom, that security could trump liberty, that democracy might be lost in the name of declaring war on terrorism."

Critics specifically decry the act's reduction of judicial oversight of surveillance procedures and detention of aliens, fearing that such measures give the executive branch excessive freedom and upset the balance of power in government. Although Attorney General John Ashcroft insisted in April, 2004, that neither Congress nor the courts found a single instance of abuse under the act, critics were not mollified. By then, more than two hundred local communities and four states had passed resolutions asking that the scope of the Patriot Act be narrowed. At the same time the act's supporters, including some members of Congress, argued to expand it and eliminate the sunset provision.

Roger Smith

Further Reading

Chang, Nancy. *Silencing Political Dissent*. New York: Seven Stories Press, 2002. Argues that antiterrorism policies, including the Patriot Act, threaten civil liberties and may lead to excessive executive power.

Goldberg, Daniel, Victor Goldberg, and Robert Greenwald, eds. *It's a Free Country: Personal Freedom in America After September 11*. New York: Nation Books, 2003. Forty-one articles and cartoons emphasizing civil liberties issues arising from antiterrorism efforts.

Reams, Bernard D., Jr., and Christopher T. Anglim, comps. *USA PATRIOT Act: A Legislative History of the Uniting and Strengthening of America by Providing Appropriate Tools Required to Intercept and Obstruct Terrorism Act, Public Law No. 107-56*. 5 vols. Buffalo, N.Y.: William S. Hein, 2002. Exhaustive compilation of documents and records intended as a legal resource on the Patriot Act.

Smith, Norris, and Lynn M. Messina, eds. *Homeland Security*. New York: H. W. Wilson, 2004. Twenty-eight articles reprinted from newspapers and magazines about aspects of national security, terrorism, and civil liberties.

Uniting and Strengthening America by Providing Appropriate Tools Required to Intercept and Obstruct Terrorism Act of 2001. Washington, D.C.: Government Printing Office, 2001. The complete text of the Patriot Act. The text of the law can also be found on the Government Printing Office's Web site, at purl.access .gpo.gov.

See also Attorney general of the United States; Bill of Rights, U.S.; Drugs and law enforcement; Electronic surveillance; Espionage; Homeland Security Department; Illegal aliens; Money laundering; Search warrants; September 11, 2001, attacks; Skyjacking; Terrorism; Treason; Wiretaps.

Payne v. Tennessee

The Case: U.S. Supreme Court ruling on evidence

Date: Decided on June 27, 1991

Criminal justice issues: Evidence and forensics; victims

Significance: In a dramatic departure from *stare decisis* (the practice of basing decisions on precedents of previous cases), the Supreme Court overruled two cases it had decided within the past four years and held that victim-impact evidence would be permitted in capital sentencing hearings.

In 1987, the Supreme Court in *Booth v. Maryland* had held that prosecutors in capital cases would not be permitted to use victim-impact evidence to persuade the jury that the defendant deserved to be executed. The five members of the *Booth* majority held that evidence about the personal characteristics of the murdered person and evidence about the impact of the crime on surviving family members was irrelevant to the jury's decision whether the character of the defendant and the circumstances of the crime called for the death penalty or for some lesser punishment. Because victim-impact evidence focused the jury's attention on the victim and surviving family members, it diverted the jury's attention from the defendant. Most important, it created a risk that a death sentence might be based on arbitrary and capricious reasons, such as the willingness and ability of surviving family members to articulate their grief, or the relative worth of the murder victim to the community.

Four justices had sharply dissented. In their view, victim-impact evidence was relevant to the defendant's moral blameworthiness because it gave the jury important information about the extent of the harm caused by the defendant.

The *Booth* decision was reaffirmed two years later in *South Carolina v. Gathers*, when another bare majority of the Court held that prosecutors could not present victim-impact evidence to the jury during closing arguments in death-penalty cases. By 1991, however, two members of the *Booth* majority had retired from the Court and had been replaced by more conservative justices. That same year, the Court agreed to reconsider its recent decisions and granted *certiorari* in *Payne v. Tennessee*.

Pervis Tyrone Payne had stabbed to death twenty-eight-year-old Charisse Christopher and her two-year-old daughter, Lacie. Payne also stabbed and left for dead Charisse's three-year-old son, Nicholas. Nicholas survived his stab wounds, several of which passed completely through his body. During Payne's trial, Nicholas's grandmother testified emotionally as to the effect of the murders on Nicholas. In addition, during closing arguments to the jury, the prosecutor strongly implied that returning a death sentence would somehow help Nicholas. The jury sentenced Payne to die.

In the Supreme Court, Payne argued that the grandmother's testimony and the prosecutor's argument to the jury constituted victim-impact evidence and thereby violated *Booth* and *Gathers*. In a radical departure from past practice, the Supreme Court discarded those recent decisions and announced a new rule: Victim-impact evidence would be permitted in capital sentencing proceedings. According to the majority, victim impact evidence gave the jury important information about the extent of the harm caused by the defendant.

Justice Thurgood Marshall, who voted with the majority in *Booth* and *Gathers*, was enraged and disheartened. Breaking tradition, Justice Marshall read his dissent from the bench on the last day of the Court's 1991 term. He said: "Neither the law nor the facts supporting *Booth* and *Gathers* underwent any change in the last four years. Only the personnel of this Court did." Within two hours of reading his dissent, Justice Marshall announced his resignation from the Court.

Randall Coyne

Further Reading

Doerner, William G. *Victimology*. Cincinnati: Anderson Publishing, 2002.

Karmen, Andrew. *Crime Victims: An Introduction to Victimology*. 5th ed. Belmont, Calif.: Wadsworth, 2004.

Office for Victims of Crime. *New Directions from the Field: Victims' Rights and Services for the Twenty-first Century*. Washington, D.C.: U.S. Department of Justice, 1998.

See also Capital punishment; Sentencing; *Stare decisis*; Supreme Court, U.S.

Peace Officers Standards and Training

Identification: State programs establishing training and performance standards for law-enforcement officers

Date: First programs begun in 1959

Criminal justice issues: Police powers; professional standards

Significance: Professional training and standards play a critical role in the quality and quantity of services delivered by the police, who are a major component of the American criminal justice system.

One criterion of any profession is that it defines minimum standards of performance and minimum amounts of training or preparation for its practitioners. Peace officers, or police or law-enforcement officers as they are more frequently called, throughout the American criminal justice system all now claim professional status.

Development

By the middle of the nineteenth century, most large northeastern cities in the United States had some type of police, but there were no recognized standards or professional training for them. The idea that the police should have training and display the best of ethics had originated in 1829 in Great Britain's capital, London, where Sir Robert Peel created the Metropolitan Police Service. In 1893, the International Association of Chiefs of Police was formed in the United States, and it began advocating the training of police officers. However, it was not until 1960 that this association was to develop minimum training standards and promote them to the fifty states.

In 1929, President Herbert Hoover created The National Commission on Law Observance and Enforcement, which became known as the Wickersham Commission. It was the first major body to look into the workings of what would later become known as the American criminal justice system; it was also the first federal assessment of law enforcement throughout the United States. The commission's final reports on the police were highly critical, highlighting the lack of training and standards. The commission's official report made many recommendations, but as they were only recommendations, police around the nation were slow to change and adopt new ways.

Mid-Twentieth Century Progress

In 1953, the American Bar Association drafted a *Model Police Training Act* that sought to provide a model for those involved in or monitoring police training. During the mid-1960's, for the first time in the history of public-opinion polling, crime became the leading concern of Americans. President Lyndon Johnson created the President's Commission on Law Enforcement and Administration of Justice, and numerous blue-ribbon panels were appointed to study the problem. In 1968, the presidential commission published *The Police*, which made many recommendations for improving police training and education. *The Police* also recommended that each state establish a police officers standards and training body.

In 1959, California and New York became the first states to establish peace officers standards and training agencies. Over the next twenty-five years, the remaining states established their own agencies. Some states use different names for their offices, which makes for some confusion; however, California was the first with the name "Police Officers Standards and Training," and most police forces now simply use the term POST.

POST personnel serve as liaisons between government policy- and lawmakers and law-enforcement agencies. They work with law-enforcement and police officers in general and with the heads of police academies and police training divisions, in particular.

Functions and Benefits

POST agencies work to increase the efficiency and effectiveness of the police by improving the quality and increasing the quantity of their training. Since police officers perform as they are trained, improved training helps to improve their performance. Systematic training also helps to make police work more uniform and more predictable within the state offering the training and lends an air of enhanced professionalism to the police.

Studies of police departments have found an inverse correlation between the numbers of hours of training that officers receive and the numbers of lawsuits that are brought against the departments. Training is perhaps the best insurance a law-enforcement agency can have against litigation. POST bodies closely monitor lawsuits against police departments because they point to areas in which additional training is needed. POST agencies function to assist police departments in reducing their liabilities.

If training appears not to affect how police and the public interact, then the POST agency must question whether the training being given is relevant to the work of the police. POST must take account of what the public expects and the nature of problems the police are facing. POST agencies function to keep training and standards current by ensuring that policing meets the needs and expectations of current conditions, in contrast to the desires of the police clique. As POST agencies work to improve the quantity and quality of training, society enjoys the benefits of more effective delivery of police services and increased public safety.

The beginning of the twenty-first century saw police standards and training being taken to higher levels. British and American police have long been the two models of modern policing for the rest of the world. During the 1990's, the U.S. State Department begin work that led to the creation of four international law-enforcement academies. They are located in Roswell, New Mexico; Budapest, Hungary; Gaborone, Botswana; and Bangkok, Thailand. The concept of peace officers standards and training now serves to promote democracy and represent U.S. foreign policy worldwide.

Vic Sims

Further Reading

Charles, Michael. *Police Training: Breaking All the Rules*. Springfield, Ill.: Charles C Thomas, 2000. Study of the application of adult education models to police training.

Guthrie, Edward. "Higher Learning and Police Training." *Law and Order* (December, 2000): 124. Brief study of the benefits of college education in police training.

Kenny, Dennis J., and Robert P. McNamara, eds. *Police and Policing: Contemporary Issues*. 2d ed. Westport, Conn.: Praeger Publishing, 1999. Discusses challenges faced by those concerned with standards and training of law-enforcement officers.

Morash, Merry. *The Move to Community Policing: Making Change Happen*. Thousand Oaks, Calif.: Sage Publications, 2002. Broad study of the trend toward community-oriented policing, with some attention to its relevance to police training.

Office of the United Nations High Commissioner for Human Rights. *Human Rights Standards and Practice for the Police*. New York: United Nations, 2004. United Nations report on basic standards for police work that should be followed in all nations.

See also Community-oriented policing; DARE programs; International Association of Chiefs of Police; International Brotherhood of Police Officers; Law enforcement; Police; Police academies; Police Activities League; Police ethics; Wickersham Commission.

Pedophilia

Definition: Adult sexual disorder that makes children sex objects
Criminal justice issues: Deviancy; juvenile justice; sex offenses
Significance: Psychiatric disorders create many difficult problems for the criminal justice system. Pedophilia is a psychiatric disorder that has entered the legal system as a major public safety issue and is being dealt with accordingly.

The term pedophilia has its roots in Greek words for child (*paido*) and love (*philos*), and the term's basic definition is childlove. The word was introduced into the English language in 1886 in a distinguished work on the psychopathology of human sexuality by psychiatrist Richard von Krafft-Ebing. In the modern medical profession, pedophilia has long been viewed as a mental disability. Psychiatry has viewed pedophilia in a similar way—as a diagnosable disorder that should be treated medically, either through medication or psychiatric treatment, such as cognitive-behavior therapy. The American Psychiatric Association classifies pedophilia as a form of paraphilia, the general term for conditions in which one becomes sexually aroused by objects, situations, or other persons in unusual or socially unacceptable ways.

Persons diagnosed as pedophiles must be over the age of sixteen and be experiencing chronic intense sexual fantasies, urges, or behavior toward prepubescent children—those under the age of about thirteen. Moreover, the symptoms must last for at least six months and either disturb the sufferer greatly or impair the person's day-to-day functioning. Sexual attraction toward children is not related to sexual orientation and is not defined by the sex of the objects of pedophilia. Male pedophiles may be primarily attracted to prepubescent boys and at the same time be married to women and have children of their own. The prevalence rate of pedophilia is unknown, especially because many pedophiles do not seek help or acknowledge their disorder because of its taboo nature.

Pedophilic Associations

Many organizations promote the idea of sexual relations between adults and children. Such organizations are often monitored by law enforcement because of their possible links to pedophilia and sex offenses. In encouraging sexual relationships between adults and children, members of such associations advocate lowering the age of consent or legalizing all sexual acts between children and adults.

To true pedophiles, having sexual desire for children is not something to be ashamed of. They often see it as a beautiful expression of their love for a child. Pedophiles are known for surrounding themselves with children by working closely with them. Many coach sports or work as camp counselors or teachers and do not understand why society considers their sexual feelings and behaviors abnormal and wrong. Moreover, these organizations generally believe that the rights of the children themselves are being violated by not allowing them to choose to engage in sexual relationships with adults. Pedophiles who are asked about the devastating physical and emotional effects that sexual abuse has on children are apt to reply that they personally do not condone abuse and that the relationships with children they seek are purely consensual. However, the rebuttal to this assertion is that children, because of their immaturity, are incapable of consenting to such relationships. Therefore, all sexual contact between adults and children is abusive and may cause irreparable harm to children.

Pedophilia and the Criminal Justice System

Pedophilia itself is neither a crime nor a recognized legal term. The term is often applied by people in the criminal justice system to adults who commit sexual acts that involve children, but such usage may be incorrect. It is important to recognize that pedophiles are not necessarily sex offenders and that not all child sexual abusers and child molesters are pedophiles. Many pedophiles never attempt to have sexual contact with children, and not all offenders have recurrent intense feelings toward children, as diagnoses of the condition require.

Pedophiles do, however, enter the criminal justice system when they act on their sexual fantasies and urges by engaging in sexual acts with children, by intentionally exposing themselves to children for the purpose of sexual arousal, or by knowingly possessing child pornography—sexual images of children. By doing any of those things, pedophiles become sex offenders and are subject to monitoring and punishment within the criminal justice system. Although the level of monitoring varies by state, convicted sex offenders are required to register with state agencies, such as law enforcement, and may become the subjects of community notification when they are convicted.

In many states, child pornography laws are used to prosecute pedophile sex offenders. In the United States, it is illegal to produce, promote, distribute, advertise, or knowingly possess child pornography. Lawmakers and many researchers believe that handling child pornography may increase the existing propensity of pedophiles to act on their urges and fantasies. In addition, pornography is often used by pedophiles who engage in child molestation as a tool to lower the inhibitions of their young victims.

Pedophilia and the Court System

The U.S. court system has accepted psychiatric diagnoses of pedophilia as a serious mental disorder. In the case of *Kansas v. Hendricks* (1997), the U.S. Supreme Court upheld Kansas's Sexually Violent Predator Act. The Kansas law permitted persons deemed to be sexually violent predators to be committed to psychiatric hospitals for control, care, and treatment until they are judged no longer to pose dangers to themselves or society.

The Kansas case arose when the defendant, Leroy Hendricks, was due for release from prison. He had a long history of sexually molesting children, and the state judged him a sexually violent predator and civilly committed him to a state hospital. Hendricks challenged his commitment, even though at trial he had agreed not only with a state physician's diagnosis of his pedophilia but also that he continued to have sexual fantasies and urges involving children that he could not control. Finding that pedophilia qualifies as a mental disorder under the act, the Supreme Court upheld Hendricks's commitment.

In some states incarcerated offenders diagnosed as pedophiles must accept treatment as a condition of their release from prison. An example of this is California's mandatory chemical castration laws. California requires that some male sexual offenders take the drug medroxyprogesterone, which is more commonly known as Depo-Provera, to lower their testosterone levels to reduce their sexual drives. Mandatory use of this drug is being employed by other states as well.

Lisa A. Williams

Further Reading

Briere, J., and American Professional Society on the Abuse of Children. *The APSAC Handbook on Child Maltreatment*. Thousand Oaks, Calif.: Sage, 1996. Handbook of the American Professional Society on the Abuse of Children that discusses major types of child abuse, their treatment, and legal issues.

Browne, Angela, and David Finkelhor. "Impact of Child Sexual Abuse: A Review of the Research." *Psychological Bulletin* 99 (January, 1986): 66-77. Psychological study of research through the mid-1980's on sexual abuse of children.

Crosson-Tower, Cynthia. *Understanding Child Abuse and Neglect*. 5th ed. Boston: Allyn & Bacon, 2001. Textbook covering all aspects of child maltreatment, including sexual abuse, from symptoms and signs to parental motivations, and the role of the social service system.

Jenkins, Philip. *Pedophiles and Priests: Anatomy of a Contemporary Crisis*. New York: Oxford University Press, 2001. One of many studies of the widespread sexual abuse of children by priests that rocked the Roman Catholic Church during the late 1990's and early years of the twenty-first century.

McCabe, Kimberly A. *Child Abuse and the Criminal Justice System*. New York: Peter Lang, 2003. Broad study of the many forms of child abuse, including sexual abuse, and the responses of the criminal justice system to them.

Russell, Diana E. H. *Sexual Exploitation: Rape, Child Sexual Abuse, and Workplace Harassment*. Beverly Hills, Calif.: Sage, 1989. Sociological study of different forms of sex offenses, including sexual abuse of children.

See also Child abuse and molestation; Police psychologists; Pornography, child; Roman Catholic priests scandal; Sex offender registries.

Perjury

Definition: Lying under oath

Criminal justice issues: Trial procedures; witnesses

Significance: Perjury undercuts the constitutional rights and due process of defendants, denies juries access to facts, and undermines respect for and faith in the criminal justice system.

Perjury is willfully swearing as true any material matter the witness does not believe to be true. Attorney and law professor Alan M. Dershowitz claims that the most frequently committed felonies are perjury and false statements, and that false-statement crimes are the most underprosecuted crimes in the United States. Police officer, witness, and defendant perjury is so com-

The oaths to which witnesses swear before giving evidence make the witnesses liable to criminal prosecution for perjury if they knowingly give false testimony. *(Brand-X Pictures)*

monplace that pundits say cases are often decided on a preponderance of perjury. Perjuries, in addition to trial perjury, include filing false tax returns, making false statements to government authorities, and lies, including lies by omission, in testimony or on official documents.

Perjury represents less than 1 percent of prosecutions, and sentences are often lenient. Perjury enforcement is often for revenge, some political end, legal strategic advantage, or to punish a suspected criminal who is difficult to convict. Suborning perjury is procuring or inciting another to commit perjury, even if no perjury is committed, and is a crime that is rarely prosecuted.

If witnesses believe their claims are true, even if they are not, or do not know that their claims are false, there has been no perjury. This perjury defense encourages police and prosecutors to investigate crimes only to the point where they can attest to enough facts for conviction but not so far as to find contradictory information that negates the facts which police and prosecutors believe to be true. Rather than seeking full and complete truth, police and prosecutors seek only enough attestable facts for conviction.

The 1994 Milton Mollen Commission in New York, the 1992 Myron Orfield study in Chicago, and other investigations found rampant falsifying of arrest papers, courtroom perjury by police, and the tolerance by prosecutors and judges of perjury by prosecution witnesses. Police coined the term "testilying" to describe their perjury.

Proving Perjury

Prosecuting perjury requires the government to prove the person was under oath, that the statement attested to was false, and that the person knew at the time that the testimony was false. The government must have multiple proofs for perjury, such as testimony from more than one witness or other evidence, such as written statements, to support the falsity. Withholding, destroying, or merely failing to collect evidence is a tactic to prevent prosecution for perjury.

Gordon Neal Diem

Further Reading

Christianson, Scott. *Innocent: Inside Wrongful Conviction Cases*. New York: New York University Press, 2004.

Klockers, Carl, Sanja Ivkovic, and Maria Haberfield, eds. *The Contours of Police Integrity*. Thousand Oaks, Calif.: Sage Publications, 2004.

Lersch, Kim, ed. *Policing and Misconduct*. Upper Saddle River, N.J.: Prentice-Hall, 2002.

United States Congress. *The Consequences of Perjury and Related Crimes: Hearing Before the (House) Committee on the Judiciary*. Washington, D.C.: United States Government Printing Office, 1998.

See also Color of law; Cross-examination; Due process of law; Evidence, rules of; Eyewitness testimony; False convictions; Federal Crimes Act; *Leon, United States v.*; *Mapp v. Ohio*; Miscarriage of justice; Obstruction of justice; Police corruption; Police ethics; Testimony; Witnesses.

Pickpocketing

Definition: Form of larceny that involves the sudden or stealthy stealing of property directly from persons, usually in public places

Criminal justice issue: Robbery, theft, and burglary

Significance: As a form of larceny that involves stealing things directly from the persons of victims, pickpocketing is treated as a distinct offense in some jurisdictions because it carries the additional possibility of physically endangering its victims.

A longstanding issue concerning pickpocketing cases is the question of whether pickpocketing offenses should constitute larceny from a person, or simple robbery, because the offender takes property by force. Both larceny and robbery are theft crimes that involve the taking and carrying away of property of others with the intent permanently to deprive the rightful owners of their property. However, larceny differs from robbery in that the former does not involve the use of force or intimidation.

In most pickpocketing cases, offenders are considered guilty of larceny from the person, rather than robbery, because picking pockets requires only enough force to lift and remove the pockets'

A crime closely related to pickpocketing is purse-snatching. As with pickpocketing, when more force is used than is necessary for the mere snatching of a purse, the theft can be prosecuted as strong-arm robbery. *(Brand-X Pictures)*

contents, with only minimal physical handling of the victims, such as a shove. Acts of pickpocketing that are not resisted are considered larceny. However, when victims become aware of the attempts on their property and offer resistance, or when pickpockets employ violence or intimidation, pickpocketing offenses are considered robbery because violence or the threat of violence is used.

For an act of pickpocketing to be considered a crime, property must be taken from the victim. Most jurisdictions also require that the property must be carried away from the scene of the crime—an aspect called asporation. In pickpocket cases, a question that frequently arises is whether there has been sufficient asporation. However, courts have consistently held that any asporation, however slight, is sufficient. Thus, it is not necessary for a pickpocket actually to remove an item from a pocket. Rather, it is sufficient for the pickpocket to have com-

plete control of the item, even for only an instant. Therefore, a pickpocket who moves a victim's wallet only three inches before being caught satisfies the asporation requirement. On the other hand, pickpockets who are detected before their hands actually seize items can be convicted only of attempted pickpocketing.

LaVerne McQuiller Williams

Further Reading

Samaha, J. *Criminal Law*. 8th ed. Belmont, Calif.: Thomson/Wadsworth, 2004.

Yeager, Wayne B. *Techniques of the Professional Pickpocket*. Port Townsend, Wash.: Loompanics Unlimited, 1990.

See also Attempt to commit a crime; Robbery; Theft.

Plain view doctrine

Definition: Exception to the search warrant requirement that allows law-enforcement officers to seize evidence that is in plain sight when they have probable cause to believe that the evidence is connected to crimes

Criminal justice issues: Police powers; search and seizure

Significance: The U.S. Supreme Court has extended the plain view doctrine to include other senses such as "plain touch."

The Fourth Amendment requires law-enforcement officers to obtain search warrants to search for and seize evidence. The plain view doctrine is one

---

Exceptions to the Plain View Doctrine

The plain view doctrine does not apply when certain sense-enhancing technology is used in protected areas. For example, most courts do not permit thermal imaging and high-powered telescopes to qualify as "plain view." Use of basic items, such as flashlights and eyeglasses, is acceptable for the plain view doctrine to apply. Viewing evidence from aircraft is also acceptable, so long as the aircraft are flying in legal airspace.

of the exceptions to the search warrant requirement established by the Supreme Court. Three main elements must be satisfied for the plain view doctrine to apply. First, law-enforcement officers must be legally present in the places where they are making their observations. Second, the law-enforcement officers must believe that the items they are viewing are "immediately apparent" to be evidence of a crime. Finally, the officers must have lawful access to the items in order to seize them without warrants.

Law-enforcement officers often invoke the plain view doctrine during car stops and searches of houses. For example, if officers serving a valid search warrant on a home for drugs and happen to find evidence of child pornography in plain view, they may seize it without obtaining an additional warrant. Conversely, if the officers do not have warrants and see evidence of crimes while entering homes unlawfully, they cannot seize it to be used at trial. Moreover, if police officers were lawfully to stop a motorist for speeding and plainly see a dead body in the back seat of the motorist's vehicle, they may seize the body without obtaining a search warrant.

The Supreme Court has extended the plain view doctrine to include "plain touch." This is most commonly applied when police officers are conducting lawful pat-downs of suspects and touch the suspects' pockets or clothing. If the officers can identify—without tactile manipulation—that items they feel are probable evidence of crimes and they have lawful access to the items, they can seize those items without search warrants.

Daria T. LaTorre

Further Reading

Del Carmen, Rolando V., and Jeffery T. Walker. *Briefs of Leading Cases in Law Enforcement.* 5th ed. Cincinnati: Anderson, 2004.

Hall, John Wesley. *Search and Seizure.* 3d ed. Charlottesville, Va.: LEXIS Law Publishing, 2000.

LaFave, Wayne R. *Search and Seizure: A Treatise on the Fourth Amendment.* 3d ed. St. Paul, Minn.: West Publishing, 1996.

See also Automobile searches; Bill of Rights, U.S.; *California v. Greenwood;* Citations; Drugs and law enforcement; Exclusionary rule; *Maryland v. Buie;* Search and seizure; Search warrants; Stop and frisk; Vehicle checkpoints; *Whren v. United States.*

Plea bargaining

Definition: Negotiations between prosecuting and defense attorneys designed to reduce criminal charges against defendants in return for guilty pleas

Criminal justice issues: Convictions; defendants; pleas; trial procedures

Significance: Plea bargaining is an increasingly frequent practice, and both sides in cases see advantages for themselves by striking successful bargains. Defendants seek reduced sentences and perhaps less

Hustler magazine publisher Larry Flynt (right) and his brother, Jimmy Flynt, waiting for a Cincinnati judge to pass sentence after a plea bargaining agreement reduced the charges against them in a 1999 obscenity case. As is common in plea bargaining agreements, the settlement was reached before jury selection was completed. Had Larry Flynt been convicted on the original charges, he could have faced twenty-four years in prison. *(AP/Wide World Photos)*

Plea Bargaining in the Movies

Jodie Foster won her first Academy Award for her performance as Sarah Tobias in the 1988 film *The Accused*. Tobias is the victim of a brutal gang rape in a public bar. Based on a real-life case, the film portrays the difficult choices that prosecutors sometimes make in relying on plea bargains to dispose of the vast majority of cases. In the film, the three perpetrators of the crime accept a plea bargain from the prosecutor (Kelly McGillis); by pleading guilty to the lesser crime of reckless endangerment, the rapists receive less severe sentences than they would receive if they were convicted of rape.

Outraged by the comparatively lenient sentences that her attackers receive, Tobias goes after three other men who cheered on her attackers during her rape. The prosecutor eventually charges the three men with the crime of criminal solicitation, alleging that they encouraged the rape. At trial, the three men are convicted, chiefly on the basis of the testimony of another bar patron, who feels personally guilty about not having tried to stop the rape. The conviction of the bystanders also owes something to the fact that their defense counsel—quite unrealistically—fails to challenge an essential point of the prosecution's case: that a rape, rather than consensual sex, has occurred.

Timothy L. Hall

damning criminal records; prosecutors seek to reduce the costs and time consumed by trials while assuring convictions.

Plea bargains might be initiated by either side in criminal cases. One study indicates that one reason for plea bargaining is to save the cost, time, and reputation of the defense attorney. That person must deal with the same judge, prosecutor, and police officers in other cases and does not want to get a bad reputation. Furthermore, the defense attorney must make a living and does not want to get bogged down in difficult cases for little money. However, the plea bargain might be initiated by a more self-sacrificing defense attorney or by the state.

The plea bargain typically involves reducing the seriousness of charges against a defendant. Instead of battery, for example, the charge might be changed to assault or to disturbing the peace. Instead of murder, the accusation might be changed to manslaughter. Another type of plea bargain involves dropping some charges against the defendant and keeping others. For example, encouraging the prosecution to drop a charge of

selling cocaine and retain a charge of possessing marijuana might be the goal of plea bargaining. Still another objective of plea bargaining involves a defendant's pleading guilty to a charge with the understanding that the sentence will be lighter instead of heavier.

The judge is officially not in on the bargain, and whether the judge has been consulted is a matter that only the judge and the attorney know. Some judges refuse to be consulted, and all or almost all conduct themselves as if they had not been consulted. It is typical, for example, for judges to tell defendants in court that they cannot, and have not been asked to, reduce the defendants' sentences in return for pleas of guilty. The defendants must act on faith and on the advice of their defense attorneys. That faith is not likely to be violated. An attorney who finds that the prosecution (and the judge, if consulted) will not abide by the bargain is unlikely to bargain again, and that can be harmful to the offending attorney.

Some defendants plead guilty to charges even though they consider themselves to be innocent in order to be spared the expenses of trials or the ordeals of long sentences. It is difficult to say how often that happens, because many defendants contend after sentencing that they are innocent. Plea bargaining is frequently condemned by the public and by politicians, but unless the time, help, and budget of the prosecutor is unlimited, it is likely to continue.

Dwight Jensen

Further Reading

Fisher, George. *Plea Bargaining's Triumph: A History of Plea Bargaining in America*. Stanford, Calif.: Stanford University Press, 2003.

Rosett, Arthur I. *Justice by Consent: Plea Bargains in the American Courthouse*. New York: Lippincott Williams & Wilkins, 1976.

Vogel, Mary E. *Coercion to Compromise: Social*

Conflict and the Emergence of Plea Bargaining, 1830-1920. Rev. ed. New York: Oxford University Press, 2005.

See also Arraignment; *Brady v. United States*; Convictions; Criminal prosecution; Defendants; Discretion; District attorneys; *Nolo contendere*; Pleas; Public prosecutors; *Rummel v. Estelle*; *Santobello v. New York*; Sentencing; Trials; Unabomber.

Pleas

Definition: Formal statements of guilt or otherwise by defendants in response to formal charges or indictments
Criminal justice issues: Arrest and arraignment; defendants; pleas; verdicts
Significance: Pleas are crucial components in the arraignment phase of the criminal process.

During the arraignment the judge presents the criminal charges, advises defendants of the right to court-appointed counsel, schedules hearings, determines the trial date, and resolves issues with regard to bail. At the arraignment defendants respond with a plea of not guilty, guilty, or *nolo contendere*. The defendants' choice of pleas is critical, as the disposition of the case rests on the plea.

Not Guilty and Guilty Pleas

The first option, and the one most often selected, is not guilty. The not guilty plea allows defendants time to consider the strength of their cases and to determine the chances of a favorable outcome in court. Therefore, the plea does not necessarily mean that defendants are innocent; it means that they wish to have their cases heard in court and want a judge or jury to determine whether there is enough evidence to return a guilty verdict. If defendants do not enter a plea, the court automatically enters a not guilty plea based on the precept that one is innocent until proven guilty. Persons who plead not guilty have a right to have a judge or jury trial. At trial the decision makers listen to the evidence. In order for a judge or jury to return a guilty verdict in a crimi-

nal proceeding, the prosecutor must demonstrate guilt beyond a reasonable doubt.

Defendants may also choose to plead guilty. The implications of this decision are serious. Defendants waive their right to a trial and to prepare a defense, the right against self-incrimination, the right to confront witnesses, and the right to appeal the decision. Thus, when defendants relinquish such fundamental rights, the judge must question them to determine whether they understand the implications of the guilty plea. The judge must determine whether the plea is voluntarily made or whether threats or promises were made to force a guilty plea. The judge also must ensure that defendants understand the charges against them and the corresponding sentences or fines.

Last, the judge must ascertain the factual basis of the plea to make sure that there is proof that defendants have actually engaged in the conduct with which they are charged. If defendants choose this plea and the judge has determined that they understand the ramifications of pleading guilty, the court may immediately convict as if a judge or jury returned a guilty verdict in a trial. Defendants may be sentenced at the arraignment or the judge may order a presentencing report and schedule a sentencing hearing.

Nolo Contendere

The last plea option allows defendants to plead *nolo contendere*, which means no contest, or "I do not wish to contend." Typically, defendants use this plea in order to avoid an admission of wrongdoing in the event of a subsequent civil suit regarding the same matter. If defendants are sued for monetary damages, a guilty verdict would provide evidence of wrongdoing, whereas a plea of *nolo contendere* would not. When defendants plead *nolo contendere*, a conviction is handed down, just as a guilty plea is adjudicated. The defendants relinquish their rights just as persons who plead guilty and are subject to the same sentences or fines as persons who plead guilty and are convicted. The judge must take the same precautions to ensure that defendants are aware of the relinquishment of rights involved in the plea of *nolo contendere* and that the decision is voluntary.

Ann Burnett

Further Reading

ABA Standards for Criminal Justice: Pleas of Guilty. Chicago: American Bar Association, 1999.

Bergman, Paul, and Sara J. Berman-Barrett. *The Criminal Law Handbook*. Berkeley, Calif.: Nolo Press, 1997.

Farnsworth, E. Allan. *An Introduction to the Legal System of the United States*. 3d ed. New York: Oceana, 1996.

See also Arraignment; Convictions; Criminal prosecution; Defendants; Fifth Amendment; Insanity defense; *Nolo contendere*; Plea bargaining; Presumption of innocence; Reasonable doubt; Trials.

Police

Definition: Officers of municipal law-enforcement agencies whose primary mission is to protect their communities from crime and other threats to public safety and well-being

Criminal justice issues: Law-enforcement organization; police powers

Significance: Municipal police are the only segment of government that normally has the authority to use coercive force. As such, they represent the coercive power of government. They have many responsibilities but because it is they who decide whom to arrest and take into custody, they may be considered the gatekeepers of the criminal justice system. During an average twenty-four-hour period, police make about forty thousand arrests—a fact that contributes to the United States having the highest incarceration rate in the world.

After the turn of the twenty-first century, almost one-half million uniformed and armed municipal police officers were employed by about 13,000 separate police departments to provide a variety of services to citizens. Before the terrorist attacks on the United States of September 11, 2001, municipal police were in the process of rapidly changing their philosophies to adopt more of a service orientation. This movement has contin-

ued; however, the threat of terrorism has renewed emphasis on law enforcement.

Police in a Changing Society

Police forces never find an easy fit in a democracy. Balancing the rights of individuals against the needs of society is always difficult but especially so in democracies. Municipal police do much more than enforce the law. The fact that most of them are armed and uniformed makes them the most visible representatives of government, and this, in turn, makes them lightning rods for individual and public woes.

Modern police have come to realize that their tasks are far more difficult and sometimes even impossible to accomplish without the cooperation and assistance of the public and individuals who make up the public. As public ideas of what the police should do evolve, and as other variables come into play, the only obvious conclusion appears to be that the police are changing and changing at an unprecedented rate. In the early twenty-first century, some police watchers even suggested that American police had changed more in the previous ten years than they had in the previous century. Several things have contributed to the changes that define modern municipal police.

Some of the changes have been driven by the recognition of a vast gulf between what police officers actually do and what the public thinks they do. For example, while the public long believed that municipal police spent most of their time investigating and solving crimes, arresting suspects, and generally enforcing laws, research has shown that most officers now spend 20 percent or less of their time in such efforts. Most of their time is spent responding to calls for other types of service.

In contrast to the manner in which working police distribute their time, basic police training in police academies has historically devoted at least 80 percent of training on crime and law-enforcement functions and the remainder of the time to miscellaneous services. Modern police training is changing to reflect the tasks that police actually do, but task-analysis research focusing on the police is woefully lacking.

The federal Violent Crime Control and Law Enforcement Act of 1994 was the most far-reaching piece of anticrime legislation in U.S. history. Among other things, it provided for the hiring of 100,000 new police officers—an approximately 25 percent increase nationwide. Many of the new officers were hired under the Police Corps program that was funded by the 1994 law and were four-year college graduates.

Changing Face of Police

The 1994 federal law changed the face of modern policing in several ways but perhaps none more profound than its injection of college-educated people into police roles. Research has repeatedly suggested that more highly educated people make better officers than those without college education. By 2003, about 25 percent of all adult Americans were college graduates—roughly the same percentage that was found among municipal police officers. At the same time, a higher percentage of American police chiefs had four-year college degrees. The relatively rapid influx of leaders with a college education into a profession as traditionally conservative and static as policing has helped to make municipal police more sensitive and responsive to society's changing needs.

A rapid increase in the number of women in policing has also contributed to changing the face of modern policing. Although only about 13 percent of police officers nationwide are women, it appears that a critical mass has been reached and that the numbers of women police will continue to rise. Research and replicated studies point to several attributes women bring to policing.

Although both men and women enter policing wishing to help people, they seem to be attracted to the profession for different reasons. Men tend to be attracted by the potential for excitement and action, while women tend to have more of a service orientation. Women officers are far less likely than men to be involved in cases involving police brutality or police violence. At the same time, female officers initiate far more non-police contacts than male officers. This alone seems to cause increased interaction between the police and individuals members of the community. Male officers are far quicker to employ force than female officers, but research has shown that fe-

As the only representatives of municipal government authorized to use deadly force, police represent the coercive power of government to enforce its laws and apprehend wrongdoers. *(Brand-X Pictures)*

male officers do not hesitate to use force when it is clearly necessary. Women are also better than men at handling certain types of cases, such as sexual assaults and problems involving female victims or complainants in lower-income housing. Overall, women have contributed positively to policing, and this effect will only increase as more women enter the occupation.

It appears that the effectiveness of police increases as the composition of police forces more closely reflects that of the communities in which they serve. For example, African Americans constitute about 12 percent of the total national population. The fact that African American police officers also now constitute about 12 percent of all police officers in the nation has contributed to making police forces more effective. Likewise, it is expected that as the percentage of women in policing grows, police effectiveness will continue to improve.

Standards and Training

The training of municipal police has improved significantly in both quantity and quality since the mid-1990's, and this development has improved delivery of police services. Some of this improvement can be quantified. Municipal governments have had to pay out millions of dollars in settlements with plaintiffs who have sued their police departments, and police now realize that improved training of officers is the best defense against future litigation. The availability of government funding has always been a powerful incentive. The move to community policing and the endless desire on the part of the police to improve and professionalize also played roles in increasing the hours and quality of training for municipal police officers. The increasing complexity of police work contributed to the necessity of additional training.

Every state has a Police Officers Standards and Training, or POST, office that oversees municipal police departments and offers guidelines for training officers. The states now mandate minimum numbers of training hours for new officers; these requirements range from a low of 320 hours to a high of more than 1,200 hours—the equivalent of thirty forty-hour weeks of training. After officers complete the their initial training, they must spend several additional months working under the supervision of field training officers. Only after both phases of their training are complete are the new officers allowed to work without supervision, and even then, most new officers remain on probationary status for several

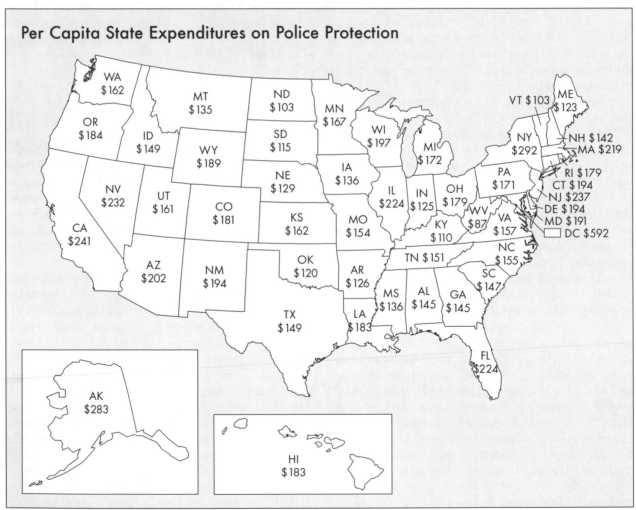

Per Capita State Expenditures on Police Protection

Source: U.S. Bureau of Justice Statistics, 2002. Figures represent average per capita state expenditures for all police protection in 1999. Figures are rounded to nearest dollar.

months more. Finally, many states now require all officers to continue their training with minimum numbers of in-service hours.

Municipal police have profited greatly from advances in technology. While automobiles remain the most common type of police patrol vehicle, several other methods are used by police across the nation to complement and improve police effectiveness and efficiency. For example, more than three-fourths of U.S. residents are served by police departments that regularly use bicycle patrols, and more than two-thirds are served by departments that regularly employ foot patrols.

The refinement and sophistication of small portable radios and cell phones have freed field officers from dependence on patrol cars, while permitting them to remain in constant communication with their departments as they become far more accessible to the public. Virtually all municipal police departments now make extensive use of computers, and all large-city police departments enjoy the benefits of geographic information systems, which are used for crime mapping. Geographic information systems enable community policing to change the focus from the individual criminal to the areas where the crimes are committed, thus striking more closely at the roots of problems. Three-fourths of municipal police officers have access to in-field computers, and more than one-half have Internet access. Such technology greatly increases information sharing among different agencies.

Scholarly research on policing did not begin in earnest until the 1970's, and it was another two or three decades until replication studies were used to implement and institutionalize scholarly research findings into police practice and policy in the field. Through those years, research-based policing gradually replaced policing driven by emotions and tradition. Fewer police officers overlooked the law and proper procedures for the sake of expediency or custom. The quality of police services improved noticeably because research-based policing proved far more effective than traditional policing.

Community-Oriented Policing

Of all the changes in municipal policing around the turn of the twenty-first century, none was as well known or had an impact as great as the adoption of the new philosophy of community-oriented policing. Community policing has been defined in many ways, but as is the case with many complex subjects, it seems to defy precise definition. In general, community policing attempts to move municipal police ever closer to the ideal of the early nineteenth century founder of London's metropolitan police, Sir Robert Peel, that the people are the police, and the police are the people.

The most successful community policing efforts and programs have been those that have resulted in closer permanent working relationships between police and individual citizens. The idea that the police are the experts and always know what is best for a city quickly has given way to the understanding that more can be accomplished when everyone works together to solve serious problems with long-range solutions, rather than applying quick fixes to the symptoms of the problems. Community-oriented policing involves community leaders who are often better equipped than police to engage fresh challenges and transform problems into opportunities.

During the 1990's, community policing reached a point of critical mass when the U.S. Congress passed the Violent Crime Control and Law Enforcement Act, which made billions of federal dollars available to municipal police departments to adopt community policing. Much of the funding was used to recruit a new breed of police officers, who quickly made their presence felt. At the same time, a new generation of college-educated police chiefs provided leadership that helped municipal policing to reach an unprecedented level of effectiveness.

The United States has always been an energized, dynamic society, and the terrorist attacks of September 11, 2001, served to renew the country's commitment to improve and strengthen itself. As society changes, so do the police. In 2002, the International Association of Chiefs of Police adopted a resolution that recognized that the country's most powerful intelligence source is its citizenry and that community policing is the best means of tapping into that intelligence.

Meanwhile, American society continues to change. Among the new challenges that police face are growing numbers of legal and illegal immigrants, an increasingly aging population, and the end of white domination. Because municipal police have risen to overcome hurdles in the past, there is good reason to believe that they will meet the challenges of the future.

Vic Sims

Further Reading

Dunham, Roger G., and Geoffrey P. Alpert. *Critical Issues in Policing*. 4th ed. Prospect Heights, Ill.: Waveland Press, 2001. Assessment of the state of American policing at the turn of the twenty-first century and the nature of the most pressing challenges to police work.

Gaines, Larry, and Victor Kappeler. *Policing in America*. 4th ed. Cincinnati: Anderson, 2002. Explanation of the functions, culture, and discretionary authority of police officers, with a useful discussion on uses of force and racial profiling.

Langworthy, Robert H., and Lawrence F. Travis III. *Policing in America: A Balance of Forces*. 3d ed. Upper Saddle River, N.J.: Prentice Hall, 2003. Textbook covering broad issues relating to municipal police, including the historical developments that have created modern police forces. The authors provide detailed descriptions of police work and examine the challenges that police face within their communities.

Lardner, James, and Thomas A. Reppetto. *NYPD: A City and Its Police: The Inside Story of New York's Legendary Police Department*. New York: Henry Holt, 2000. Inside look at the day-to-day operations of the largest municipal police department in the United States.

Lesce, Tony. *Cops! Media vs. Reality*. Port Townsend, Wash.: Loompanics, 2001. There are many differences between the ways in which police are depicted in the media and what they are really like. This book explores the reasons for these discrepancies and explains how law enforcement really operates.

Morash, Merry, and Kevin J. Ford. *The Move to Community Policing*. Thousand Oaks, Calif.: Sage Publications, 2002. Community policing continues to be of great interest to policymakers, scholars, and, of course, local police agencies. Successfully achieving the transformation from a traditional policing model to community policing can be difficult. This book aims to illuminate the path to make that change as easy as possible.

Peak, Kenneth. *Policing in America: Methods, Issues, Challenges*. Upper Saddle River, N.J.: Prentice-Hall, 1997. Discussion of general issues facing police officers, including civil liability.

Stevens, Dennis J. *Policing and Community Partnerships*. Upper Saddle River, N.J.: Prentice Hall, 2002. Textbook that could serve as a manual for police and community leaders interested in improving community-oriented policing.

Walker, Samuel, and Charles M. Katz. *The Police in America: An Introduction*. 5th ed. New York: McGraw-Hill, 2005. Standard source on all aspects of American police by one of the leading authorities in the field.

See also Campus police; Community-oriented policing; Highway patrols; Police academies; Police brutality; Police chiefs; Police civil liability; Police corruption; Police ethics; Police powers; Sheriffs; Special weapons and tactics teams (SWAT); State police; Women in law enforcement and corrections.

Police academies

Definition: Training schools for police recruits

Criminal justice issues: Law-enforcement organization; professional standards

Significance: For almost all new police recruits, police academies provide the only formal training they receive before they begin their initial police assignments.

Before the establishment of the first state-accredited police training academies, local police departments had little assistance in the training of their recruits. Many recruits were simply handed badges and guns and then expected to learn all they needed to know in the course of their work. Now, however, training for new officers is both intense and nearly universal in the United States. Most police officers must undergo from 400 to 800 hours of training before they take up their duties. Instructors at police academies are mostly police officers, either retired or active. Experts in their fields, instructors often bring to bear many real-life examples from their own field experience.

The atmosphere in police academies has traditionally been paramilitary and autocratic. Since the 1980's, however, increasing numbers of academies are emphasizing educational training, while relaxing some of their paramilitary traits, such as rigid dress codes. A traditional emphasis on weapons training, handling of suspects, and physical aspects of police work has not greatly changed, but it has been supplemented by training in other areas. For example, modern police academies' curricula may include courses on the American criminal justice system and the role of police within it; constitutional law, particularly due process issues and police civil liability; ethics; cultural diversity issues; and interaction with such "special needs" groups as persons with mental disabilities, the elderly, and victims of rape and domestic violence.

In addition to their formal curricula, police academies help recruits adjust to the culture of police service. As trainees hear the firsthand experiences of veterans, they come to think of themselves as part of a brotherhood whose members must band together and constantly be on guard against unforeseen perils. Such perils may come from civilians they encounter in their work, regardless of age or sex. An element of professionalism is another by-product of academy training, as recruits learn about proper dress and appearance, acceptable behaviors in public, and the importance of having a network of respectable friends.

Negative Aspects of Academies

Along with their positive characteristics, police academies sometimes foster, directly or indirectly, questionable views and behaviors among recruits. For example, careful studies of academies have documented sexist attitudes and comments among both recruits and instructors that reflect a lack of confidence among male police officers that female officers are capable of meeting the physical demands of police work, such as handling weapons and violent suspects. In its grossest manifestations, antifemale bias takes

the form of sexual harassment during academy training and later in the field.

Although police academies do not officially sanction such bias, researchers have documented "hidden" curricula that may actually encourage it. Examples include the use of exclusively male pronouns by instructors in references to law-enforcement personnel, including the recruits themselves; uses of exclusively male examples when discussing matters related to police work methods and dress; and established male "zones" of casual conversation and activities that female recruits are discouraged from entering. Instructors occasionally perpetuate assumptions that women are less able than men to fight and handle weapons and that it is dangerous for officers to have female partners in physically challenging situations.

In the guise of "protecting" women by treating them more gently, academy instructors and recruits sometimes reinforce stereotypes about feminine fragility. It has also been charged that the images of women used in academy training materials sometimes portray women as weak sex objects. This in turn sometimes leads male recruits to pay less serious attention to aspects of their training relating to domestic violence and rape intervention. There is also some evidence indicating that female academy instructors are treated with less respect than their male counterparts.

Another dark side in the development of a police culture in academy training is drinking behavior. Some research indicates that the amount of time that recruits spend drinking with their relatives and friends decreases significantly after they have spent six months in academies, while the amount of time they spend drinking with other recruits increases significantly. There are also increases in the overall frequency and quantity of drinking.

A survey of Australian police recruits on this problem found that nearly one-half of the recruits felt some pressure to drink more during their training. Moreover, the increased drinking that began during their training did not decrease during their first six months as officers in the field. These patterns develop despite the fact that more than 90 percent of the recruits reported receiving some alcohol education during their academy training.

While clearly there are areas for improvement in academy policies and procedures, one aspect of their rapid growth has been the incorporation of new forms of technology in training curricula. Grants have enabled police departments to develop advanced simulation labs, with exercises on such matters as defensive driving, handling suspects, and searching buildings. Moreover, academy coursework has made increasing use of computers and the Internet. Future technological vistas include academies "without walls"— a distance-learning approach that may in turn pave the way for internationalization of police training. In an era of increased globalization of types of crime, including terrorism, international training should assist law enforcement to develop new and more effective crime-fighting approaches.

Eric W. Metchik

Further Reading

Baker, Thomas. "Computer Technology in Police Academy Training." *Law and Order* (August, 2002): 107-110. Brief survey of innovative uses of computers in police training.

Charles, Michael. *Police Training: Breaking All the Rules*. Springfield, Ill.: Charles C Thomas, 2000. Proposals for using adult-education models in police training.

Guthrie, Edward. "Higher Learning and Police Training." *Law and Order* (December, 2000). Evaluation of the benefits of college education to police recruits.

Ness, J. J. "The Relevance of Basic Law Enforcement Training: Does the Curriculum Prepare Recruits for Police Work—A Survey Study." *Journal of Criminal Justice* 19, no. 2 (1991): 181-193. Evaluation of the appropriateness of modern police training to the most basic responsibilities of police officers.

Prokos, Anastasia, and Irene Padavic. "'There Oughtta be a Law Against Bitches': Masculinity Lessons in Police Academy Training." *Gender, Work and Organization* 9, no. 4 (2002): 439-459. Critical study of the prevalence and impact of sexism in police academies.

See also Community-oriented policing; Criminal justice education; International Association of Chiefs of Police; Law enforcement; Peace Officers Standards and Training; Police; Police chiefs; Police civil liability; Police ethics; Special weapons and tactics teams (SWAT); Women in law enforcement and corrections.

Police Activities League

Identification: Police-sponsored and community-based organization that offers youths sports and other productive activities as alternatives to criminal behavior

Date: Established in 1915

Place: New York, New York

Criminal justice issues: Crime prevention; juvenile justice

Significance: Using sports and a variety of other positive social activities, the Police Activities League draws on volunteers from state and local law-enforcement agencies to work as role models for children and adolescents to prevent crime.

In 1915, Captain John Sweeney of the New York City Police Department founded the Police Activities League on the premise that young people need positive recreational outlets. He recognized that by interacting with youth in sports and social activities, the police can more effectively prevent crime and drug abuse, improve the health and mental well-being of young people, strengthen family and community ties, and reduce tensions between police officers and young people.

Nearly a century after its founding, branches of the Police Activities League serve more than 1.5 million young people between the ages of five and eighteen in seven hundred cities throughout Canada, the United States, and U.S. dependencies. The league operates out of 1,700 facilities and employs the assistance of more than three hundred law-enforcement agencies. The Police Activities League remains a volunteer-based organization that is largely dependent on private-sector support for funding, and the league works closely with many community-based policing programs.

James J. Nolan III

Further Reading

Goetz, Barry, and Roger Mitchell. "Community-Building and Reintegrative Approaches to Community Policing: The Case of Drug Control." *Social Justice* 30, no. 1 (2003).

Susser, Ida Edward. *Norman Street: Poverty and Politics in an Urban Neighborhood.* New York: Oxford University Press, 1982.

See also Community-oriented policing; International Brotherhood of Police Officers; Peace Officers Standards and Training; Police.

Police brutality

Definition: Abuses of authority that amount to serious and divisive human rights violations involving the excessive use of force that may occur in the apprehension or retention of civilians

Criminal justice issues: Government misconduct; police powers; professional standards

Significance: Persistent and pervasive patterns of abuse and the enduring obstacles to justice in American policing have contributed to increasing international scrutiny since 1999, when the United States was placed on the Human Rights Watch list of major human rights abusers, along with such countries as Rwanda, Cambodia, and Zimbabwe. Although the impact of cases of police brutality and the disparities in criminal justice in the United States represent substantial threats to institutional legitimacy, it is important to note that the incidence of police use of force is in fact quite rare given the large numbers of contacts between police and members of the large and diverse American public.

Article 3 of the United Nations (U.N.) Code of Conduct for Law-Enforcement Officials states that the legitimate use of force is only that which is "strictly necessary" to subdue persons under the circumstances confronting officers. The U.N. Basic Principles on the Use of Force and Firearms by Law Enforcement Officials restricts the use of force and firearms to situations in which the "use of force and firearms is unavoidable." Meanwhile, law-enforcement officials are expected to "exercise restraint in such use and act in proportion to the seriousness of the offense and the legitimate objective to be achieved." Definitions and justifications for "reasonable" and "necessary" force provided by U.S. law have varied throughout history. The proper use of force by the police maintains the substance of the U.S. Constitution and is fundamental to legitimacy because the police hold a virtual monopoly over the power to exercise lethal force against citizens.

Background

Excessive and lethal force have always been major sources of conflict between members of minority groups and the police in the United States. Despite substantial improvements in race relations, race remains central to police brutality in the United States. A vast body of multidisciplinary literature on the use of force by the police has revealed that members of minorities face a significantly higher risk than other citizens of becoming victims of police violence, and that members of racial and ethnic minorities are more likely to be incorrectly fired at by police, regardless of the race or ethnicity of the officer.

Incidents of police violence against members of ethnic and religious minorities and immigrants have reinforced the public perception that some citizens are subjected to harsher treatment and greater bias than others. Incidents in which real or perceived abuses are made public often spark civil unrest that results in costly and violent uprisings and reinforces public distrust. In 1968, the National Advisory Commission on Civil Disorders, also known as the Kerner Commission, concluded that abusive policing tactics had contributed significantly to the widespread civil disorder of the 1960's.

Later investigatory commissions came to the same conclusions. These include the Christopher Commission, which was appointed to investigation the Los Angeles riots that had followed the acquittal of police officers who had beaten Rodney King; the 1992 St. Clair Commission on excessive force in Boston; and the Mollen Commission on police misconduct in New York. The reports of all these commissions revealed the same patterns that were evident in the Kerner

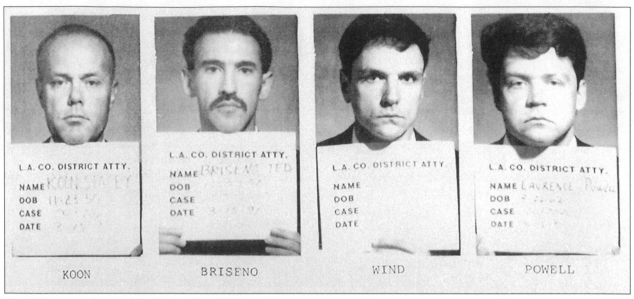

After the four Los Angeles police officers indicted for beating motorist Rodney King in 1991 were tried on criminal charges in a state court, their surprising acquittal touched off the most destructive rioting in the history of Los Angeles. Afterward, all four officers were indicted by a federal grand jury on the charge of violating King's civil rights. Stacey Koon and Laurence Powell were found guilty and served prison time, and all four officers lost their police careers. *(AP/Wide World Photos)*

Commission report and reached essentially the same conclusions. Nevertheless, the recommendations made by these commissions remain unrealized.

Law-enforcement institutions implement their charges through the complex signaling relationships among the various branches of government. Police must try to balance responsiveness to the law, responsiveness to electoral institutions, and responsiveness to the public with the demands of keeping the peace. The impact of "law and order" candidates on both the law and the executive direction of bureaucratic agencies, such as police departments, has been tremendously influential on the history of police brutality. For example, President Richard M. Nixon's White House chief of staff H. R. Haldeman once noted that "President Nixon emphasized that you have to face the fact that the whole problem is really the blacks. The key is to devise a system that recognizes this without appearing to." Given the rampant criminality of the Nixon administration itself, political leadership lacking credible commitments to the public perpetuate institutional legacies that define classes of people who are deemed unworthy of protection by the police.

In addition, the "tough on crime" attitude that pervades public opinion is another element that makes it such that those deemed unworthy of constitutional protections are further disadvantaged, as they are perceived to fail to contribute in valuable ways to society. Citizens who are targets of policy are more likely to be victims of police brutality because they are likely to have more interactions with the police. Moreover, they are less likely to have access to avenues of recourse when they are victimized, and they are not likely to be supported by institutions of justice or the public. Consequently, whether the police respond to the law, politics, or the public, police brutality can be understood at least in part as a reflection of the intolerance of American society.

Prevalence

Although incidents of improper use of force by officers are actually statistically rare, individual cases have tremendous implications for social cohesion. A nationwide study conducted by the National Institute of Justice (NIJ) in 1999 found that officers used force in slightly less than 1 percent of their encounters with the adult public. There are obviously a number of methodological issues related to this study. First, there is no universal definition of what constitutes "reasonable" and "necessary" force in a given situation. Second, the NIJ study did not address police interactions with juveniles, and there is no indication as to what amounts to excessive force against a child. Third, compliance and discretion in reporting vary considerably.

Rates of the use of force by the police vary widely and are significantly impacted by both departmental policies and state laws as well as the compliance of statutes and policies with U.S. Supreme Court guidelines. By 2004, approximately thirty states had laws on their books allowing police officers to use all means necessary to effect arrests, including arrests of unarmed citizens suspected of nonviolent crimes. The Supreme Court's 1985 ruling in *Tennessee v. Garner* outlined the boundaries of the police use of force such that permissive statutes, such as the fleeing felon rule, are considered unconstitutional. *Garner* has been shown to have reduced fatal shootings by the police by an estimated 60 percent. However, between that 1985 ruling and 1990, only four states had changed their laws to bring them into compliance with the constitutional rule.

Ultimately, the elemental task of law enforcement, the application of lawful force to protect society, creates a dilemma in which social cohesion is both preserved through and threatened by force. The prevalence of police brutality is profoundly affected by expectations in ways that are self-reinforcing. Given the history of police brutality in the United States and the self-perpetuating nature of reputations, distrust between members of minority communities and the police are not likely to change without affecting expectations.

The dilemma of forced peace makes it such that society cannot expect to eliminate all cases of brutality against the public. Therefore, implementing effective analysis of what is reasonable and necessary force and what are credible commitments by the police to all members of society is essential to affecting the prevailing patterns of police brutality. In addition, credibility must be earned and commitments are likely to be tested.

Responsible leadership committed to reducing the prevalence of police brutality requires at least the following conditions:

✓ establishing and using a reputation that reinforces the notion that police protect all members of society
✓ making it costly to the careers of individual officers to violate their commitments to the public
✓ investing in incremental changes
✓ employing mandatory negotiating agents such as external complaint collection and automatic civilian review

The principal of "rule of law" should protect citizens from arbitrary power, and the legitimacy of democratic policing is integrally linked to police compliance with legal standards. The exercise of discretion by the police is fundamental to the duty of police to protect and facilitates their ability to serve the public. Excessive use of force is a federal crime that makes it criminal for an individual acting under the color of law, including private and contracted security personnel, to deprive any citizens of their civil rights. Concerns about arbitrary police power and racial bias represent a significant threat to the principles of the U.S. Constitution. Therefore, transparency and accountability are essential to the fair and effective pursuit of justice.

Investigation

Addressing brutality is a matter of political will. In many cases, organizations are in place to counter such behavior effectively, but the parties responsible for oversight operate in hostile environments or are themselves unwilling to engage in preventive or retributive actions. Limits on effective oversight and organizational leadership that is designed to protect officers, rather than the public, magnify shortcomings and contribute to a climate wherein officers are aware that punitive actions are unlikely.

There are three primary obstacles to effective oversight: lack of public accountability and transparency, failure to investigate and prosecute incidences of brutality, and obstructionism. The first of the three, lack of accountability and transparency, enables the others. One approach to monitoring police accountability is through internal review, which is a formal bureaucratic process that is often referred to as internal affairs (IA).

Most internal mechanisms designed to investigate incidences of abuse operate with secrecy and often allow officials to refuse to furnish the public with relevant information regarding investigation. This institutional secrecy manifests itself even in cases in which such information is supposed to be publicly available. The provision and availability of data and systematic analysis of the use of force by the police at the local, state, and federal levels rely on voluntary compliance and are inconsistent at best. Furthermore, the data collected by the Federal Bureau of Investigation and held by the Department of Justice do not include injuries that fall short of death and also are known to be inaccurate.

One of the inherent difficulties in internal monitoring is that the police do not always recognize their own violations. Although departments are required to train their officers to deal with citizen claims regarding brutal treatment, myriad problems pervade the process of compiling information from the public regarding interactions with the police. The vast majority of citizens who feel they have been mistreated by the police do not attempt to address the issue formally, primarily out of fear of retribution. Police efforts to dissuade members of the public from making complaints are widespread and persistent.

Citizens who express interest in filing complaints against police may be threatened with the notorious "trilogy" of disorderly conduct, resisting arrest, and assaulting an officer. Scholar James J. Fyfe has dubbed this phenomenon "contempt of cop," citing a small percentage of officers who repeatedly file such charges because they are offended by citizens' demeanor without a legitimate law-enforcement purpose. Complainants may face civil countercharges as well. Since the 1990's, there has been a trend in which police officers have filed suits against plaintiffs and attorneys after unsuccessful litigation, alleging defamation, malicious prosecution, or abuse of process. It should also be kept in mind that police deal regularly with people motivated to make claims against police that might diminish their own culpability.

Civilian review is another approach to oversight that constitutes independent, external review of police activities. Citizen oversight bodies are often created in response to demands for external accountability and take a number of different forms. Because demands for citizen oversight tend to occur in communities in which police use of excessive force is consistently a divisive issue between the police and public, and because of the political bargaining that takes place in the formation of civilian review boards, evidence on the effectiveness of citizen participation in this form is limited. Public participation in this form does, however, afford the

The Abner Louima Case

In one of the most infamous cases of police brutality on public record, Haitian immigrant Abner Louima was brutally beaten and sodomized by officers of the New York Police Department (NYPD) while under arrest in 1997 for a scuffle outside a nightclub. Louima suffered severe internal injuries requiring several surgeries to repair. He also claimed that while he was in custody, he was walked past several officers in the NYPD's 70th Precinct building while his pants were down around his ankles before he was tortured in the bathroom.

NYPD officer Charles Schwartz was convicted of holding down the handcuffed Louima, as fellow officer Justin Volpe rammed a wooden stick into Louima's rectum and then forced it into Louima's mouth, breaking his teeth. Volpe was sentenced to thirty years in prison for violating Louima's civil rights, but the convictions of Charles Schwartz, Thomas Wiese, and Thomas Bruder were overturned by the Second Circuit Court of Appeals in 2002. Michael Bellomo, charged with lying to cover up the incident, did not agree to testify until two years after the incident.

After the brutality incident was publicly exposed, the disorderly conduct charges against Louima were dropped, and the city of New York settled a civil suit that paid him $8.7 million. The involvement of five white officers using racial epithets during the beating and engaging in obstruction of justice during the criminal investigation of the assault on Louima provoked widespread protest regarding police practices and accountability. The Louima case continues to be a source of mistrust and undermines police-community relations.

police some relief from the occupational demands that characterize police work, in that civilian review can inform police departments and share the responsibility that comes with broadly defined objectives and authority.

The increased relative risk to minorities and the relative inability of personnel diversity to affect police killings make external institutional checks on authority an investment rather than a cost. A considerable amount of scandal that can undermine legitimacy arises from incidents in which police officers kill suspects. Departments spend a substantial amount of time and resources dealing with situations in which lethal force is used. Additionally, officers involved in killings often experience trauma that necessitates counseling services to deal with situations in which they have used lethal force, they may have their careers interrupted, and their reputations can be damaged by such incidents. Instituting structural mechanisms that influence the likelihood of excessive or deadly force also means that officers will not have to experience this form of violence either.

Prosecution

There are essentially two paths to exacting justice for unlawful use of force by the police: criminal and civil prosecution. Criminal prosecution may occur at the local, state, and federal levels. At the local level, prosecutors can bring criminal charges against officers under state laws regarding such violent offenses as assault, battery, murder, and rape. A few states have laws that specifically address excessive police force. Federal prosecutors also have the authority to bring charges against officers under relevant federal laws, and federal and state grand juries also have the power to investigate and indict officers for the alleged criminal use of force. However, less than 1 percent of cases reported to the U.S. Department of Justice actually lead to prosecution.

Criminal prosecution is an extremely limited mechanism of accountability. Judges and juries tend to afford considerable deference to police testimony, making conviction incredibly difficult and ultimately making successful prosecution less likely. In addition, criminal prosecution does not address the systematic organizational, lead-ership, political, and policy problems that contribute to the abuse of power by officers.

Most states do not compile data on rates of prosecution, conviction, and sentencing, but there is substantial evidence for concluding that criminal prosecution for police use of excessive force is extremely rare. The lack of support by public officials, the need for good working relationships between police and prosecutors, and the low probability of conviction contribute to a reluctance to bring charges against officers. There are also few referrals from internal affairs. Moreover, the standard of proof that requires prosecutors to demonstrate that officers had "specific intent" to deprive citizens of their civil rights represents a significant obstacle to convictions.

Civil liability is another potential vehicle for achieving justice in cases of police brutality. The necessary elements of proof and legal standards vary widely from state to state. Although the law permits plaintiffs to recover both monetary damages and equitable relief, civil suits alleging excessive force are exceedingly difficult to win. On the other hand, the amounts awarded in civil cases of excessive force have risen steadily since the 1970's, and large settlements for police brutality have strained the resources of some city governments. Nevertheless, potential financial burdens have not served as effective deterrents to excessive force, primarily because civil suits provide little incentive for individual officers to cease using excessive force. Civil suits also fail to influence systemic change in organizational culture, departmental policies, unfair institutional structures, and patterns of political bias.

Punishment

The avenues for addressing police brutality include, but are not necessarily limited to, criminal conviction, civil litigation leading to job loss, early warning systems that expect supervisors to impose penalties for misuse of power, exacting additional education and training requirements for officers exhibiting contempt, and victim-offender mediation. The reality, however, is that none of these avenues is regularly or consistently utilized.

Institutional bias within police departments often favors officers and can include such protections as police officer bills of rights. Although most bureaucrats are required to give up some of their individual civil liberties for the privilege of government work, strong police unions and professional associations afford exceptions for the police. Exceptions for officers allow for the purging of instances of abuse from officers' personnel files and negotiated contracts that can prevent the disciplining and dismissal of officers when appropriate. Moreover, because police officers rely on one another for their own personal physical safety, the use of lethal force to protect fellow officers is central to cohesion among officers. Finally, the high degree of isolation inherent in police work contributes further to the organizational culture known as the "blue wall of silence." All these factors insulate the police from both necessary and unnecessary punitive measures.

Addressing police brutality requires an understanding of the character of the law, the history of disparities in criminal justice in the United States, and the fundamentally paradoxical nature of police work. Justice is an abstract idea that is never perfectly actualized from all possible perspectives. Punitive measures are not only extremely unlikely, but also are often unsatisfactory and insufficient means for restorative justice. Punitive measures do not prevent police brutality in the future, nor do they provide any means for re-establishing the trust that underlies the authority of the state, the legitimacy of police power, and mutually beneficial community relations.

Holona L. Ochs
Kuroki M. Gonzalzles

Further Reading

Greenwald, Anthony G., Mark A. Oakes, and Hunter G. Hoffman. "Targets of Discrimination: Effects of Race on Responses to Weapons Holders." *Journal of Experimental Social Psychology* 39 (2003): 399-405. Findings of tests that reveal both perceptual sensitivity and response biases that increase the risks of members of minorities being shot by police, regardless of the race of the shooting officers.

Human Rights Watch. *Shielded from Justice: Police Brutality and Accountability in the United States*. New York: Human Rights Watch, 1998. Systematic investigation of police brutality in the United States by one of the world's most respected human rights advocacy organizations.

Mauer, Marc. "Race, Class, and the Development of Criminal Justice Policy." *Review of Policy Research* 21, no. 1 (2002): 79-91. Extensive review of the research on the historical development of criminal justice policy and disparities in the application of criminal justice in the United States.

National Research Council. *Fairness and Effectiveness in Policing: The Evidence*. Washington, D.C.: National Academies Press, 2003. Comprehensive review of the research on police policy and practices.

Ostrom, Elinor, R. Parks, and Gordon Whitaker. *Patterns of Metropolitan Policing*. New York: Praeger, 1978. Broad multidisciplinary study of police practices, utilizing various data sources and both quantitative and qualitative methods of analysis.

Prosecuting Police Misconduct: Reflections on the Role of the U.S. Civil Rights Division. New York: Vera Institute of Justice, 1998. Organizational analysis of the systematic problems that contribute to police misconduct.

Skolnick, Jerome H., and James J. Fyfe. *Above the Law: Police and Excessive Use of Force*. New York: Free Press, 1993. Comprehensive examination of the effect that departmental rules, administrative policies, and legal standards have on the use of force by the police.

Smith, Rogers. *Civic Ideals: Conflicting Visions of Citizenship in U.S. History*. New Haven, Conn.: Yale University Press, 1997. Explores the nativist, racist, and sexist traditions in the historical struggles over the political, civil, and social rights that define citizenship in the United States.

Tennenbaum, A. N. "The Influence of the *Garner* Decision on Police Use of Lethal Force." *Journal of Criminal Law and Criminology* 85 (1994): 241-260. Analysis of compliance with constitutional standards and the impact of Supreme Court guidelines on police use of force.

Walker, Samuel. *Police Accountability: The Role of Citizen Oversight*. Belmont, Calif.: Wadsworth, 2001. Study of the effectiveness of citizen oversight on controlling police misconduct by one of the leading American authorities on police.

See also Assault and battery; Civilian review boards; Confessions; Deadly force; Internal affairs; King beating case; Miami riots; Police; Police corruption; Police ethics; Reasonable force; Special weapons and tactics teams (SWAT); *Tennessee v. Garner*; Wickersham Commission.

Police chiefs

Definition: Top officers in urban police departments

Criminal justice issues: Law-enforcement organization; police powers; professional standards

Significance: Establishment of the office of chief of police is crucial to enabling the successful operation and underpinnings of a police department.

The history of police chiefs can be traced to the mid-nineteenth century, when the highest-ranking police officers in American cities were called "superintendents." The duties of modern police chiefs, like those of their predecessors, are varied and are functions of the composition of the departments in which the chiefs work. For example, a small-town chief of police may be the town's only salaried law-enforcement officer, assisted by numerous volunteers. By contrast, a police chief in a large metropolitan area may command thousands of sworn officers, along with thousands of civilian employees. In direct contrast to sheriffs, who are usually elected county officials, police chiefs are commonly appointed by mayors or police commissions. In some jurisdictions, police commissioners also serve as police chiefs.

The main function of any chief of police is to perform administrative and managerial functions directly related to supervising the activities of the police department. In addition, the chief also acts as the main facilitator in the enforcement of all city statutes and state laws for which the police department is held accountable.

In 1893, the International Association of Chiefs of Police (IACP) was formed as a professional organization designed to facilitate exchanges of information and experiences among police administrators throughout the world. One of the most influential chiefs of police was August Vollmer, who became the first police chief of the newly created police department of Berkeley, California, in 1909. Vollmer pioneered the use of automobiles in patrols, established the first police training school, served as president of the IACP in the 1920's, and created the first academic criminology curriculum in the United States in 1939. Vollmer has been dubbed by many as the founder of modern professional policing because of his countless innovations in the establishment of police professionalism.

Lisa Landis Murphy

Los Angeles chief of police Daryl Gates posing in 1992 with copies of his memoir about his police career. As the top officers of city police departments, police chiefs are accountable for the success of their agencies. Gates was chief of Los Angeles's police at the time of the police beating of motorist Rodney King and during the riots that followed the acquittal of the officers who beat him; Gates was blamed for many of his department's failures and was forced out of office. *(AP/Wide World Photos)*

Multifaceted Duties of Police Chiefs

Typical responsibilities of police chiefs include but are not limited to

✓ planning, coordinating, and directing all department operations

✓ supervising and evaluating all police department personnel

✓ administering the enforcement of laws/ordinances

✓ developing training programs for new/existing employees

✓ developing and implementing the departmental budget and controlling expenditures

✓ formulating, enacting, and evaluating policies and procedures

✓ coordinating law-enforcement work with county, state, and federal officers involving police activities

✓ maintaining public relations efforts with news media and local civic groups

✓ acting on all matters relating to disciplinary issues and recommending awards for exemplary conduct among employees

✓ participating in general officer duties

✓ disseminating critical information to the general public

Further Reading

Bennet, W., and Karen Hess. *Management and Supervision in Law Enforcement*. 4th ed. Belmont, Calif.: Wadsworth, 2004.

Miller, L., and Karen Hess. *Police in the Community: Strategies for the Twenty-first Century*. 3d ed. Belmont, Calif.: Wadsworth, 2002.

Schmalleger, Frank. *Criminal Justice Today: An Introductory Text for the Twenty-first Century*. 8th ed. Upper Saddle River, N.J.: Pearson/Prentice-Hall, 2005.

See also Civilian review boards; International Association of Chiefs of Police; Law enforcement; Police; Police academies; Police ethics; Sheriffs.

Police civil liability

Definition: Police officers' obligations to refrain from acts within the course of duty that may cause undue harm to another

Criminal justice issues: Government misconduct; immunity; police powers

Significance: Police officers may be held financially responsible in civil court for on-duty conduct that harms a civilian. Lawsuits against officers have increased markedly, making it necessary for police departments to consider ways to reduce the threat of potential liability.

Police officers come into contact with the public in a variety of difficult situations, some of which give rise to civil liability cases. Lawsuits against the police had sharply increased by the end of the twentieth century. Considering the tendencies of juries to award large monetary settlements in police civil liability cases, government officials took notice of public concern and began exploring ways to minimize the prevalence of lawsuits against their departments.

In response to the need to develop better methods of protecting the public, many police departments have realized that the threat of civil liability cannot be eradicated but can be reduced. Attempts to do so include implementation of better policies regarding hiring, retention, and supervision of officers. These policies include tougher screening processes for police recruits, better education, and stricter disciplinary measures for misconduct.

Tort Claims

Many lawsuits against police officers involve intentional torts, or private wrongs against a person or property. Wrongful-death lawsuits arise when officers directly cause a person's death or fail to prevent the death of a person. These suits often involve pursuits, shootings, or handling of prisoners. Police officers are also subject to lawsuits for battery if they use unlawful force to effect an arrest or perform an improper search of a suspect. Officers may also incur liability for false arrest if they detain someone without probable cause or other legal justification.

Police officers are also sometimes sued for negligence. In order to be found liable for negligence, an officer must have had a duty to act which went unfulfilled or was performed without reasonable care. Claims in this area of law are most often made for failure to operate a vehicle safely or for failure to protect persons who need assistance, such as a motorist on the side of the road or a suspect in the rear of a patrol car. Police supervisors can be held liable for the acts of their subordinates if they fail to supervise adequately or to investigate claims of misconduct.

Federal Claims

A type of lawsuit that may be brought against police officers involves a violation of a person's civil rights, under Title 42 of the United States Code, Section 1983. Such claims are federal and must involve the deprivation of a right provided by the U.S. Constitution. For a Section 1983 claim to be sustained, officers must have been acting in their official capacity, which is referred to as "acting under color of law."

Lawsuits brought against the police for First Amendment violations involve some action by the officers that prevent people from exercising their freedom of speech, religion, or peaceful assembly. This issue most often arises when police break up protests. Fourth Amendment claims arise when officers effect an unreasonable search or seizure that is not based on probable cause. Police officers may also be held liable for depriving suspects of their Fifth Amendment rights, such as failing to recite Miranda warnings prior to custodial interrogation, if a statement made by the suspect is later used at trial.

Many lawsuits are brought against the police for excessive force, under several different legal theories. Lawsuits based on the Fourth Amendment require showing that the force used was unreasonable. Lawsuits based on the Eighth Amendment by convicted offenders require showing that the force used inflicted "cruel and unusual punishment." Lawsuits based on the Fourteenth Amendment require showing that the force used "shocks the conscience." Although each amendment requires a different level of proof, claims of excessive force often include combinations of these amendments.

Defenses

Because police officers must continue to protect the public regardless of the threat of civil liability, the criminal justice system has built-in controls to make sure that only cases that appear to have merit will be allowed to proceed. Otherwise, police officers would not be able to do their jobs out of fear of being sued. The defense avail-

---

The High-Speed Chase in *The French Connection*

In director William Friedkin's 1971 thriller, *The French Connection*, New York City cops played by Gene Hackman and Roy Scheider discover that an urbane French drug lord (Fernando Rey) is planning to smuggle a huge shipment of heroin to the United States. When the drug lord reaches New York City and learns that the officers are watching him, he orders a henchman to kill them. After the would-be assassin's attempt to shoot one of the cops fails, the hit man becomes the hunted, as the officer (Hackman) takes off after him. The ensuing chase reaches its climax when the hit man hijacks an elevated train, and the cop pursues him from the street below, driving a car that he commandeers from a civilian. The tense high-speed pursuit that follows is one of the most famous chase scenes in film history.

Although high-speed pursuits by police are common occurrences in both real life and the cinema, filmmakers rarely convey to audiences the legal reality that such chases may expose police officers and police departments to liability if the chases recklessly disregard public safety, as does the chase in *The French Connection*. As the cop's car races after the elevated train, it narrowly misses pedestrians and slams into several other vehicles, doing considerable damage to both the commandeered car and the other vehicles. However, the film gives no hint that the officer suffers any consequences afterward. Further evidence of the officer's disregard for public safety comes in the climactic confrontation between law-enforcement officers and the drug dealers, when the officer accidentally kills a federal agent.

Timothy L. Hall

able to an officer depends upon the type of lawsuit involved.

Police officers facing a lawsuit involving an intentional tort can attempt to show that their acts were unintentional or, alternatively, that no actual harm was suffered. An officer facing a negligence suit can attempt to show that the action taken was not unreasonable or that any damage resulting from the alleged act was brought about by something other than the officer's conduct.

In federal lawsuits, an officer may seek qualified immunity from the court. Qualified immunity is an affirmative defense that will completely bar a plaintiff from recovery. To establish qualified immunity, an officer must have been performing a discretionary act, one which requires judgment. The court will then determine whether there was a clearly established constitutional right involved. If the law was not clearly established, or if it was clearly established but the officer's conduct was objectively reasonable, qualified immunity applies, and the lawsuit will be dismissed.

Kimberly J. Belvedere

Further Reading

Gaines, Larry, and Victor Kappeler. *Policing in America*. 4th ed. Cincinnati: Anderson, 2002. Explanation of the function, culture, and discretionary authority of police officers, with a useful discussion on uses of force and racial profiling.

Kappeler, Victor. *Critical Issues in Police Civil Liability*. 3d ed. Prospect Heights, Ill.: Waveland, 2001. Comprehensive account of issues and trends in police civil liability.

Peak, Kenneth. *Policing in America: Methods, Issues, Challenges*. Upper Saddle River, N.J.: Prentice-Hall, 1997. Discussion of general issues facing police officers, including civil liability.

Ross, Darrell. *Civil Liability in Criminal Justice*. 3d ed. Cincinnati: Anderson, 2003. Addresses problems confronting criminal justice practitioners because of the rising number of civil lawsuits against them.

Worrall, John. "Administrative Determinants of Civil Liability Lawsuits Against Municipal Police Departments: An Exploratory Analysis." *Crime and Delinquency* 44, no. 2 (1998): 295-313. Explores the effects of administrative decisions and practices on police civil liability.

See also Color of law; Community-oriented policing; Immunity from prosecution; Internal affairs; International Brotherhood of Police Officers; Nonlethal weapons; Police; Police academies; Police corruption; Police ethics; Reasonable force; Vicarious liability.

Police corruption

Definition: Unethical, dishonest, and other criminal conduct or deviant behaviors by police officers that involve abuses of their authority for personal gain

Criminal justice issues: Government misconduct; police powers; professional standards

Significance: Police corruption, which may take the form of soliciting, taking, or offering bribes; selling favors; accepting gifts; abusing authority; and aiding and abetting criminal behavior, is anathema to the repository of public trust in institutions that are entrusted with protecting citizens from crime and bringing criminals to justice. In a nation that regards democracy and justice as cardinal values, the investigation, prosecution, and punishment of corrupt police officers are crucial for preservation and advancement of social order, as well as efficacy of the criminal justice system itself.

Police corruption poses a dilemma for the criminal justice system because of the unique trust that the public has in police to stamp out crime and bring criminals to justice. Police corruption puts courts at odds with their supposed primary ally in the pursuit of justice. Although corrupt officers constitute a minuscule percentage of sworn officers, corruption is a serious matter that needs to be addressed to maintain police morale and retain public confidence in the police.

History

Corruption among police is as old as the profession of policing. In fact, prevention of crime and elimination of bribery were two of the major reasons why the first police force was established in London in 1829. In colonial America, corrupt practices and official recklessness punctuated the history and development of law enforcement. Citizen groups exercised responsibility for law and order in their small and homogeneous communities through the watch, or vigilante, system. Over time, new immigration and industrialization transformed small settlements into large communities until many of them became true towns and cities.

Although the watch system persisted into the twentieth century in many communities, it became obvious that it could no longer effectively police crime in heterogeneous societies. In frontier communities, especially in the Far West, corrupt and dishonest bounty hunters, similar to private police agents called thief takers in eighteenth century England, were often hired by private citizens for debt collection and the apprehension of felons. Vigilantism and bounty hunting were riddled with corruption, particularly as they were sometimes used to extract money from both honest citizens and criminals at the same time.

County sheriffs were officially the most important law officers. They were charged with keeping the peace, crime fighting, tax collection, and election supervision. For their services, they were paid by the fee system, an outdated practice in which peace officers kept percentages of the taxes they collected and received fixed amounts for every arrest they made. With time, it became obvious to many that tax collection and graft were more lucrative than crime fighting, so those pursuits consumed much of the time of early law officers. Meanwhile, burgeoning cities looked toward the successful London type of policing to deal with their own spiraling crime problems.

In 1838, the first formal police department in the United States was created in Boston. New York followed in 1844 and Philadelphia in 1854. Between the 1840's and the 1890's, corruption spurred by political patronage permeated the newly established police departments. Some officers had to pay bribes for promotions or assignments in areas offering opportunities for graft. The roles and functions of early police departments were ill defined; they were utilized primarily as enforcement arms of the reigning political powers and concentrated on controlling Euro-

pean immigrants and protecting private property. Later, many of the corrupt practices of this early system carried over into the more professional police departments of the twentieth century, and some have remained fixtures of city police departments into the twenty-first century.

Types of Corruption

The most prevalent forms of police corruption are accepting gratuities, selective enforcement of laws, outright theft and burglary, bribery and extortion, and internal corruption. Other forms include aiding and abetting criminal behavior, abuse of authority, perjury, favoritism, and brutality.

A gratuity is any type of payment received by the police in the form of gifts made with the expectation of later receiving favors in return. Some police departments have strict guidelines prohibiting acceptance of any form of gift from citizens.

Selective enforcement occurs when officers exercise legitimate discretion in deciding what action to take but for improper reasons. An example would be letting a criminal act go unpunished in exchange for something of value.

Theft and burglary involve active criminality by sworn officers. Examples include an officer keeping part of the money seized during a drug bust or taking money from suspects arrested for public drunkenness who are unlikely to remember how much cash they should have. A petty form of police theft, called "shopping," is the police taking small items, such as gum, candy, and cigarettes, from stores that are left unlocked after business hours. Some police also actively engage in premeditated and outright burglary that involves forced entry into business places for the sole purpose of robbery. Police burglary rings have been uncovered in such major American cities as Atlanta, Chicago, Cleveland, Nashville, and Reno.

Other categories of police theft include shakedowns and stealing money, drugs, and other property from department evidence rooms and unguarded business premises. "Shakedown" is a corrupt police practice of extorting expensive items for personal use while responding to emergency calls for break-ins or burglaries and attributing the resulting losses to the burglars.

Bribery is the voluntary offer of something of value to a police officer aimed at influencing the officer's duty performance. For an offense to qualify as bribery, citizens must initiate the offer, such as by offering officers money in return for not being arrested. Extortion differs from bribery in being initiated by officers who use their power to demand money, services, or goods from criminal suspects in return for favors. A typical example is an officer who refrains from arresting a drug dealer in return for cash payments.

Bribery and extortion take a variety of forms. For example, the "pad" is a regular weekly, biweekly, or monthly payoff by a criminal enterprise to police, usually in exchange for protection against arrest and interference. A "score" is a one-time payment solicited by an officer from a violator to avoid ticketing or arrest. "Mooching" involves the acceptance of gifts such as liquor or even donuts from retail establishments in exchange for such favors as ignoring city code violations by the establishments. "Chiseling" is a demand made by an officer for price discounts or free admission to events not connected to police duty.

Police who commit perjury intentionally lie while under oath in court, usually for the purpose ensuring the conviction of a defendant or to cover up for a fellow officer caught in unlawful activity. Favoritism is the selective favoring of one citizen or group at the expense of another. An example is giving immunity to friends or relatives from citations for traffic violations.

Police officers who aid criminal behavior are present at the scenes of crimes and render assistance to the perpetrators without personally taking part in the crimes. By contrast, abetting involves constructive presence during the commission of crimes or assisting or encouraging others to commit crimes without directly participating in their commission.

Police brutality encompasses the use of abusive language, unnecessary use of force or coercion, threats, and harassing searches while dealing with suspects. Police brutality is considered a form corruption because it entails abuse of authority.

Internal corruption involves corruption at the departmental level. For example, in some police departments, promotions and favorable assignments are sold to the highest bidders. The Knapp Commission that investigated the New York City Police Department during the early 1970's noted that systematic payoffs permeated the entire departmental apparatus. Investigators even found a chart listing the selling prices of every police rank.

Departmental corruption can be classified in three categories: rotten apples and rotten pockets, pervasive unorganized corruption, and pervasive organized corruption. A "rotten apples and rotten pockets" department is one in which a minority of officers use their positions for personal gain. When there is no organized effort by other members of the force to institutionalize such behavior, the culpable officers can usually be identified and flushed out. Pervasive unorganized corruption develops in departments in which the corruption of a few officers goes unchecked, and other officers join them. The main difference between this and the previous form of department corruption is the numbers of officers involved. Pervasive organized corruption is found in departments in which large numbers of officers practice organized corruption with the cooperation of their administrators, as was found in New York City by the Knapp Commission.

Prevalence

Police corruption is still a serious problem in the twenty-first century, and the police departments of the largest cities tend to be most prone to the problem. As the largest and one of the oldest American police departments, the New York City Police Department has a long history of pervasive corruption, but New York is not the only American city that has faced the problem. Most big cities have had similar cases of official corruption.

During the early years of the twenty-first century, an investigation into the Los Angeles Police Department found that officers in its Rampart Division had persistently engaged in such active criminal pursuits as bank robbery, false imprisonment, theft of drugs, planting evidence on victims, and outright brutalizing of arrestees. The investigation led to the indictment of several officers on charges ranging from drug dealing and framing of innocent people to using torture to force confessions and murder.

In Cleveland, forty-nine police officers and jail guards were convicted of accepting bribes to protect drug shipments. In Detroit, the city's first black police chief was convicted of diverting nearly $1.3 million of departmental money to his own personal use. In Miami, Florida, police officers were convicted of active burglary of private homes and the theft of two million dollars worth of cocaine. In an unrelated case, four Miami officers were convicted of stealing thirteen million dollars worth of cocaine from a drug-smuggling boat. Two separate suspicious deaths have also been linked to two Miami police officers. Other cases include the disappearance of $150,000 from a police department safe.

A much different kind of case of police corruption occurred in Tulia, Texas. There it was found that the convictions of forty-three persons on drug charges in 1999 had been based on the uncorroborated evidence of one corrupt undercover officer who framed all of them. That same officer had earlier fled from his previous law-enforcement job to avoid theft charges. These and other examples of corrupt practices in different states suggest that police corruption is a pervasive problem.

Investigation

Three major ways of controlling police corruption and brutality include establishing rules and regulations, initiating civil liability lawsuits, and prompting investigative processes. Rules and regulations are written departmental policies that inform all officers of expected standards of behavior, thereby establishing clear grounds for easy supervision and discipline of erring officers. Such rules also communicate to the community what standards to expect from their officers. Civil liability lawsuits are tort actions designed to make erring officers and their departments pay compensatory damages to litigants for personal harm resulting from the officers' unreasonable actions.

The third method of controlling corruption is through investigative processes. In directed efforts to restore public trust and confidence in the police, most big cities have instituted police administrative and civilian review boards to reduce police control by special interests and stem corruption. These boards are assigned the responsi-bility of appointing police administrators and overseeing police affairs, including investigations of all allegations of corruption. Additionally, most large city departments have established internal affairs units.

Internal affairs units are committees made up of officers within departments that investigate allegations of corruption and brutality by members of their departments. These bodies generally involve high-ranking officers in their investigations. After they complete fair and impartial evaluations of complaints, they can take any of four actions: unfound the allegations, exonerate the accused, declare the allegations not sustained, or declare the allegation as sustained. "Unfounded" rulings are issued when the evidence is insufficient to be sure the alleged incidents have actually taken place. Exonerations are issued when investigations find the accused officers' conduct to have been both lawful and justified. "Not sustained" rulings are issued when investigations lack sufficient evidence to proceed with the cases. Allegations are "sustained" when there is sufficient evidence to prove them and thereby justify disciplinary actions against the accused officers.

Civilian review boards are independent tribunals made up of leading members of the civilian community. These boards review internal affairs recommendations on grievances leveled against the police, especially in brutality and corruption cases. Civilian review boards serve as independent oversight agencies and tend to be most popular in jurisdictions that practice community policing. In such communities, police departments generally go out of their way to accommodate diverse interests and maintain cordial relations with members of the community to clear all doubts about their officers' conduct.

Special commissions have frequently been created to investigate charges of police corruption. One of the most famous was created in May, 1970, by New York City's Mayor John V. Lindsay, in response to an article in *The New York Times* charging widespread corruption in the city's police department. To investigate the allegations, Lindsay appointed the Knapp Commission, which issued its report in August, 1972. The document was a massive indictment of the New York City Police department. New York is generally regarded as having the highest levels of police corruption of any American city. Since the 1880's, its police have been investigated by special commissions an average of once every twenty years. The Knapp Commission itself was preceded by the Gross Commission of 1954 and followed by the Mollen Commission of 1994.

By the turn of the twenty-first century, the focus of police corruption investigations was shifting to drug-related offenses and publicized cases of police involvement in illegal drug trafficking, especially in New York, Miami, Chicago, and Philadelphia. During the 1990's, for example, the Mollen Commission found serious incidents of drug trafficking and related corruption in the New York City Police Department. Officers in some precincts were caught selling drugs and beating suspects. The Mollen Commission found the worst examples of police corruption and brutality in neighborhoods with large minority populations. The commission also found that vigilante justice and power were additional factors influencing drug-related police corruption.

Prosecution

During the 1990's, police corruption remained sufficiently pervasive to cause serious concern in political circles and government. Corruption in this sense also encompasses police brutality because it involves police abuse of its legitimate authority. Persistent incidents, especially drug-related corruption, attracted so much media attention that the U.S. House of Representatives, through the U.S. General Accounting Office (GAO), commissioned an investigation into drug-related police corruption. The commission's 1998 report found wide-scale police involvement in drug-related corruption, particularly in eleven major cities.

In 1995, six Atlanta police officers were convicted on drug-related crimes, and another five were suspended though not charged. During the following year, seven Chicago police officers were indicted for robbery and extortion of money and narcotics from known drug dealers, and another three officers were arrested in 1997 for conspiracy to commit robbery and sale of illegally confiscated narcotics. In 1998, forty-four officers from local police, sheriff, and corrections departments were charged with taking money to protect co-

caine traffickers. In another incident in 1991, nine Detroit police officers were prosecuted on charges of conspiracy to aid and abet the distribution of cocaine, attempted money laundering, and other crimes.

Other prosecutions have included twenty-seven Los Angeles County sheriff's deputies and one officer of the city of Los Angeles's elite narcotics unit being convicted in 1994 for hiding drug money. During that same year, eleven New Orleans police officers were convicted for receiving more than $100,000 from Federal Bureau of Investigation (FBI) undercover agents posing as cocaine suppliers. Similarly, more than one hundred Miami police officers were convicted and punished for drug-related offenses during the 1980's.

The results of FBI-led investigations into police corruption and convictions between 1993 and 1997 indicate that indictments and convictions for police corruption were on an upward trend. In 1993, there were 129 convictions of law-enforcement officers for corruption throughout the United States; 59 of the convictions were for drug-related offenses. In 1994, 1995, and 1997 the numbers of convictions exceeded 135 each year, and the proportions of drug-related convictions were similar to the 1993 figures.

Punishment

Two major methods of punishment have been used to discipline officers convicted of corruption: administrative and judicial processing. Possible forms of administrative punishments for convicted officers include departmental warnings, suspensions of pay and from duty, relief of command especially for commanders, demotions in rank, referrals for criminal prosecution, and outright dismissals from departments. Typical judicial outcomes are warnings, fines, and incarceration.

Emmanuel C. Onyeozili

Further Reading

Gaines, Larry, and Victor Kappeler. *Policing in America*. 4th ed. Cincinnati: Anderson, 2002. Survey of the functions, culture, and discretionary powers of police officers that includes some discussion police misuse of force and related matters.

Katz, Charles M. *The Police in America: An Introduction*. 5th ed. New York: McGraw-Hill, 2005. General textbook on police work that covers the history of American police forces, their organization and functions, and issues such as corruption.

The Knapp Commission Report on Police Corruption. New York: George Braziller, 1972. Official report of the commission that investigated corruption among New York City's police.

Langworthy, Robert H., and Lawrence F. Travis III. *Policing in America: A Balance of Forces*. 3d ed. Upper Saddle River, N.J.: Prentice Hall, 2003. Textbook covering broad issues relating to municipal police, including the historical developments that have created modern police forces. The authors provide detailed descriptions of police work and examine the challenges that police face within their communities.

Lardner, James, and Thomas A. Reppetto. *NYPD: A City and Its Police—The Inside Story of New York's Legendary Police Department*. New York: Henry Holt, 2000. Inside look at the day-to-day operations of the largest municipal police department in the United States and the one that has earned the most notoriety for corruption.

Palmiotto, Michael J. *Community Policing: A Policing Strategy for the Twenty-first Century*. Gaithersburg, Md.: Aspen Publishers, 2000. Comprehensive and up-to-date survey of all aspects of community-oriented policing by an expert in the field.

Sherman, Lawrence W. ed. *Police Corruption: A Sociological Perspective*. Garden City, N.Y.: Anchor Books, 1974. Sociological examination of police corruption that first came out shortly after the revelations of New York City's Knapp Commission.

Siegel, Larry J., and Joseph J. Senna. *Essentials of Criminal Justice*. 4th ed. Belmont, Calif.: Wadsworth/Thomson Learning, 2004. General textbook introduction to criminal justice that places subjects such as police corruption within the perspective of the entire justice system.

Walker, Samuel, and Charles M. Katz. *The Police in America: An Introduction*. 5th ed. New York: McGraw-Hill, 2005. Standard source on all aspects of American police by one of the leading authorities in the field.

See also Bounty hunters; Civilian review boards; Discretion; False convictions; Knapp Commission; Miscarriage of justice; Perjury; Police; Police brutality; Police civil liability; Police ethics; Police powers; Political corruption; September 11, 2001, attacks; Wickersham Commission.

Police detectives

Definition: Police officers who specialize in criminal investigations

Criminal justice issues: Evidence and forensics; investigation; police powers

Significance: Trained detectives increase the effectiveness of police efforts to solve crimes. As specialists in the art and science of criminal investigation, they help to ensure professional and thorough responses to serious crimes.

Glorified in fiction and essential in fact, detectives are both common and crucial figures in American law enforcement. Although full-time police detectives are not nearly as numerous as uniformed patrol officers, they can be found in almost all large and medium-sized police departments. Although the popular image of police detectives is of plainclothes officers assigned full time to criminal investigative work, almost all police officers perform at least some detective work in the course of their routine duties.

History

The development of professional police detectives is closely linked to crimes that could not be prevented or deterred by uniformed patrol officers. When the first American police departments began forming in the early nineteenth century, they consisted only of uniformed patrol officers. Over time, it became obvious that crimes were continuing to occur despite the work of routine police patrols and that methods of investigating crimes after they occurred was necessary.

In England and France, criminals known as "thief catchers" were used by police forces to help catch other criminals, as it was believed that only criminals themselves could know enough about the habits of criminals to solve crimes. However, that method of crime detection failed—primarily because of the dishonesty of the thief catchers themselves—so agencies began experiments using sworn police officers as investigators of crimes. The London Metropolitan Police pioneered the use of plainclothes detectives in the mid-nineteenth century. These detectives were stationed in a London building that had been formerly used by Scottish royalty, and their work was closely followed by the press and by the novelist Charles Dickens, who wrote positive articles about the detectives who came to be known as "Scotland Yard," or "the Yard," after their headquarters. In addition to writing about the detectives' heroic work, Dickens coined the term "detective" in his 1853 novel *Bleak House*.

In the United States, detectives began appearing in police departments during the 1840's, most notably in Boston, Chicago, and New York City. By the end of the Civil War, in 1865, nearly all large American cities had detective units. Many of them were kept busy by a postwar crime wave and problems of urban overcrowding brought on by new waves of European immigration. Some detectives became well known as newspapers closely followed their exploits.

New York City's Inspector Thomas Byrnes promoted the theory of modus operandi (MO), which was based on the principle that individual criminals tend to use the same methods of operation in their crimes and that recognizing those distinctive methods can help identify the perpetrators of crimes. In 1886, Byrnes published a book detailing the methods of hundreds of felons then active along the East Coast.

In contrast to those in Europe, American private detectives rivaled public detectives in popularity and effectiveness. Allan Pinkerton emerged as the country's foremost private detective, setting an example that was copied by many police investigators. In addition to establishing a series of highly profitable private detective branch offices across the country, Pinkerton also served as Chicago's first public detective and headed the United States Secret Service during the Civil War.

During the twentieth century, the develop-

ment of motor vehicle transportation and the rise of statewide crime rings promoted the creation of state police and highway patrols with detective units of their own. Meanwhile, a number of specialized federal offices of criminal investigation arose during the late nineteenth and early twentieth centuries. In addition to the Secret Service, these included the U.S. Customs Service, the Bureau of Investigation—which later became Federal Bureau of Investigation—and the Internal Revenue Service.

Types of Detectives

The largest numbers of full-time, plainclothes detectives are found in local law-enforcement agencies. In 2004, approximately 10 percent of all sworn police officers were detectives, almost 60,000 of whom were working in city and county agencies. An additional 30,000 to 40,000 worked at the state and federal levels. The New York City Police Department had the largest number of detectives of any single agency, with nearly 4,000; the FBI had the most federal investigators, with nearly 12,000.

Most city, county, and state detectives are selected from among officers already working in regular patrol divisions. Unlike many European police departments that allow college graduates to begin their police careers as investigators, most American agencies regard patrol work to be an invaluable part of the maturing and learning process that officers should have before becoming detectives. Although some federal criminal investigators have prior patrol experience, it is not required for federal special agent positions.

In addition to sworn police officers, thousands of other government investigators and private detectives also do detective work in the United States. Investigators who assist public defenders' offices and coroners, and other government employees who perform state and federal background applicant checks, are also numerous. The numbers of private detectives vary considerably from state to state, with fewer than 90 in Nebraska and about 9,000 in California.

Police Detective Duties

Crime cases come to the attention of police agencies through three channels: victim and witness reporting, patrol observation, and initiatives undertaken by investigators. The majority of cases are reported by the general public. After they are reported, cases are assigned to individual detectives either through systems of rotation or because of the detectives' investigative specialties. Although most detectives are able to investigate all types of crime, individual detectives tend to specialize. Some concentrate on violent crimes, others on serial crimes, high-loss property offenses, or cases involving unidentified perpetrators.

Criminal investigations are typically divided into three phases: preliminary investigations; continuing, or follow-up, investigations; and concluding investigations. Preliminary investigations focus on processing crime scenes and the initial interviewing of victims and witnesses. Often completed by regular patrol officers, the preliminary investigations serve as case foundations.

In larger police agencies, continuing and concluding investigations are undertaken exclusively by detectives. Continuing investigations seek to establish the identities of suspects, find new victims and witnesses, and coordinate evidence processing with crime laboratories. During the concluding phase, decisions must be made whether to suspend the cases or prepare them for prosecution.

Success rates of detective work vary with the types of crimes. The general arrest rate for all reported serious crimes is about 20 percent. However, the rates for criminal homicide are much higher and those for larceny are lower.

Traits of the Detective

Certain personality traits appear to be important to successful detective work. For example, an ability to reason logically and objectively is essential. Deductive and inductive reasoning are both commonly employed in detective work. Detectives employing the deductive method form their general conclusions before all facts are explained and then use additional facts to modify or verify those conclusions. Detectives using the inductive method wait for all relevant facts and information to emerge before drawing any conclusions. The inductive method is most commonly

used in complex white-collar crimes and drug cases involving many suspects.

Other traits essential to proper detective work include strong organizational ability, heightened observational skills, ability to communicate with a wide variety of people, advanced search and seizure legal knowledge, and a thorough understanding of forensic science capabilities.

James N. Gilbert

Further Reading

Corwin, Miles. *Homicide Special: On the Streets with the LAPD's Elite Detective Unit.* New York: Henry Holt, 2003. Dramatic look at modern detective work that follows Los Angeles's elite homicide unit as it investigates challenging murder cases.

Douglas, John. *The Anatomy of Motive: The FBI's Legendary Mindhunter Explores the Key to Understanding and Catching Violent Criminals.* New York: Pocket Books, 2000. A former criminal profiler for the FBI explores how understanding motive is essential for successful detective work.

Gilbert, James N. *Criminal Investigation.* New York: Prentice Hall, 2004. Comprehensive college text that explains investigative processes through field and forensic fundamentals. Explores the origins of detectives and how specific types of crimes are investigated and develops an appreciation for crime laboratory capabilities.

Micheels, Peter. *The Detectives: Their Toughest Cases in Their Own Words.* New York: Pocket Books, 2003. Experienced criminal investigators recount difficult cases and how they successfully apprehended perpetrators.

Sanders, William. *Detective Work.* New York: Free Press, 1980. A foundation participant-observation study of criminal investigators within a major California county sheriff's office. Provides a unique look at detective discretion and the policies of an investigative unit.

See also Cold cases; Crime labs; Crime scene investigation; Literature and criminal justice; Private detectives; Television crime dramas.

Police dogs

Definition: Dogs used by law-enforcement professionals to help find missing persons and criminal suspects and to sniff out controlled substances

Criminal justice issues: Investigation; police powers

Significance: Police dogs are now trained in more varied and diverse missions than ever before.

Dogs' work in law enforcement began in Belgium in 1899, with the deployment of Belgian sheepdogs, and quickly spread through the law-enforcement agencies around the world. Police dogs were first used in the United States by the New York City Police Department in 1907. The growth in the police dog service has been explosive; in 2004 there were more than fourteen thousand police dogs serving law-enforcement agencies in the United States. These dogs are referred to as K-9 officers.

Different breeds of dogs have been trained for police work. Trainers find that a dog needs to have a distinct set of characteristics for police work. These traits include intelligence, loyalty, an excellent sense of smell, and natural aggression. The breeds most often chosen are Belgian sheepdogs, German shepherds, Doberman pinschers, and a variety of hounds and beagles. The last two groups are used primarily for tracking and smell detection. Non-neutered males are used for their natural aggression.

During the early twenty-first century's climate of terrorism awareness, the role of police dogs and their companion officers expanded dra-

One of the many specialized uses to which police dogs are put is sniffing for explosives and other hazardous materials. *(AP/Wide World Photos)*

matically. A dog's sense of smell is fifty times more acute than that of its human companion. Dogs can smell substances present in trace amounts of less than 1 gram and are 70 percent more effective than odor detection machines. These olfactory skills are put to use searching for explosives, drugs, and people.

The use of police dogs has seen challenges to its legality. When a large, well-trained dog attacks and bites a suspect, the question of reasonable force can arise. The U.S. Supreme Court has heard two cases that address the deadly force issue. In 1985, *Tennessee v. Garner* reviewed the Fourth Amendment and the use of deadly force. In 1989, *Graham v. Connor* discussed the "reasonableness" of the use of force by a police dog. At the appellate court level, almost all circuits have heard cases discussing the deployment of police dogs, their training, and what constitutes reasonable force. Virtually all cases found police dogs to be a "reasonable force" when used correctly.

Robert Stewart

Further Reading

Albrecht, Kathy. *Lost Pet Chronicles: Adventures of a K-9 Cop-Turned-Pet Detective*. New York: Bloomsbury, 2004.

Johnson, Glen R. *Tracking Dog: Theory and Methods*. 4th ed. Mechanicsville, Pa.: Barkleigh Productions, 1999.

Schillenberg, Dietmar. *Top Working Dogs: A Training Manual—Tracking, Obedience, Protection*. Rev. ed. Oslo: I.D.I., 1994.

See also Bombs and explosives; Deadly force; McGruff the Crime Dog; Nonlethal weapons; Police civil liability; Reasonable force; Trespass.

Police ethics

Definition: Written and unwritten rules of acceptable conduct by law-enforcement personnel within their agencies, in their dealings with other agencies, and in their dealings with the public

Criminal justice issues: Civil rights and liberties; confessions; interrogation; professional standards

Significance: The conceptualization of what constitutes "proper" behavior in a wide variety of law-enforcement situations has heavily influenced both public attitudes toward police and the legal system's response to allegations of unethical police conduct.

The parameters defining acceptable and unacceptable police behavior are as old as law enforcement itself and have evolved continuously. Police ethics touch on many issues, such as intentional deception in investigations and court proceedings, the use of deadly force, corruption, and selective law enforcement.

The development of formalized codes of police ethics in the United States can be traced back to O. W. Wilson's work with the Wichita, Kansas, police during the late 1920's. However, the first statewide ethics code was developed in California in 1955. Two years later, the International Association of Chiefs of Police adopted it as the Law Enforcement Code of Ethics. With minor modifications in 1991, that code has served as the model for many police departments. Central elements of the code include a statement of the officer's basic service mission, the obligation to uphold constitutional rights, and a charge that one's private life and public actions exemplify honesty and integrity. The code also enjoins officers to enforce the law without bias, to avoid unnecessary force, and to reject bribes and other forms of corruption.

Police ethics codes serve multiple purposes. They assure the public that officers who are granted unique powers to further their investigative work are nonetheless required to behave in ways that meet at least minimal acceptable standards. Having such codes can improve the public image of police and serve as an alternative to external review and regulation. Codes may seen as providing a "moral compass" that guides officers' decision making in uncertain situations, while contributing to the development of a police culture and a cohesive work environment.

Interrogations

While ethics codes provide laudable blueprints for police behavior, the actual everyday work experiences of officers present many stressful ethical challenges. One broad category that invites unethical behavior is the use of deception during police interrogations with suspects. The courts have clearly outlawed physical abuse of suspects and mandated that police give them their Miranda warnings; however, deceptive behaviors are handled on a case-by-case basis.

Police may employ a variety of deceptive tactics during interrogations. For example, some officers try to convince suspects that they are not really being held in custody and that their interrogations are merely "interviews." Adoption of that tactic may officially relieve the officers from having to issue Miranda warnings to the suspects, even though the officers' actual agendas may be to elicit confessions so that they can commence arrest procedures.

Sometimes police read the Miranda warnings to suspects in such a perfunctory manner that the suspects mistakenly conclude that they can waive their rights without serious consequences. Another tactic is for police to attempt to lessen the actual severity of offenses in murder suspects' eyes by leading them to believe that one or more murder victims are still alive and able to testify. At other times, police may try to increase the perceived severity of offenses so that suspects will admit to lesser offenses. Yet another tactic is for officers to pretend to be investigating one crime while actually gathering information about another. Officers also sometimes express sympathy toward suspects, while trying to convince them that confessing is the best way for them to resolve matters. Promises of more lenient judicial treatment after confessions cannot be guaranteed, but they often produce confessions.

Confronting suspects with falsified evidence pointing toward their guilt is another frequently used tactic for eliciting confessions during interrogations. Confessions resulting from deceptive interrogation techniques are a major ethical concern and must be balanced against their usefulness in finding and convicting guilty suspects. Deceptive tactics may also undermine police credibility.

Prospects for the Future

During the early years of the twenty-first century, it was expected that the movement toward community-oriented policing and the escalating fight against terrorism were likely to influence the development of police ethics. For example, a central tenet of community policing is the empowerment of foot-patrol officers by assigning them to "quality of life" community projects. However, their increased power may cause them to lose some of their sensitivity to civil liberties in police-citizen interactions. Similarly, a national concern with preventing future terrorist acts in the United States has already led to a reduction in civil liberties, exemplified most prominently by the U.S. Patriot Act that was enacted shortly after the terrorist acts of September 11, 2001.

While the ends in both cases may be noble, they cannot be used to justify the reduction of individual liberties. Community policing poses new moral challenges that will need attention. For example, closer interactions with members of the community may lead police to discover law violations committed by their new "citizen partners." The police will then have to decide whether such violations should be vigorously prosecuted and thus imperil police-citizen collaboration. On the other hand, as citizens become more involved in law-enforcement practices, should they have a greater voice regarding police responses to violators? Will citizens want to take justice more in their own hands, through vigilante-type actions? Finally, what is the proper police reaction if their associated citizen groups adapt racist or otherwise unacceptable agendas? Twenty-first century law-enforcement personnel must take specialized intensive training programs to best confront all types of traditional and new ethical dilemmas.

Eric W. Metchik

Further Reading

Braswell, Michael C., Belinda R. McCarthy, and Bernard J. McCarthy. *Justice, Crime and Ethics*. Cincinnati: Anderson Publishing, 2002. Contains a section on "Ethical Issues in Policing" that includes key terms, discussions of issues, and applied exercises.

Close, Daryl, and Nicholas Meier. *Morality in Criminal Justice*. Belmont, Calif.: Wadsworth Publishing, 1995. Scholarly examination of whistle-blowing, the use of force, deception, and corruption in law enforcement and corrections contexts.

Goodman, Debbie J. *Enforcing Ethics*. Upper Saddle River, N.J.: Pearson/Prentice-Hall, 2004.

Scenario-based approach to teaching police ethics.

Pollock, Joycelyn M. *Ethics in Crime and Justice*. Belmont, Calif.: Thomson/Wadsworth, 2004. Includes a comprehensive review of law-enforcement ethics in the context of broader analyses of morality, justice, and social control.

Souryal, Sam S. *Ethics in Criminal Justice*. Cincinnati: Anderson Publishing, 2003. Discusses police ethics in terms of moral theory and criminal justice management.

See also Civilian review boards; Community-oriented policing; Internal affairs; International Association of Chiefs of Police; International Brotherhood of Police Officers; Miranda rights; Peace Officers Standards and Training; Perjury; Police; Police brutality; Police civil liability; Police corruption; Police powers; Racial profiling.

Police lineups

Definition: An investigative tool used by police to identify possible suspects of a crime

Criminal justice issues: Evidence and forensics; investigation; witnesses

Significance: Police lineups may be useful tools in police investigations, but if performed improperly they violate suspects' rights and lead to false identifications by witnesses.

Police investigators use lineups as an analytical tool based on the premise that eyewitness testimony is the strongest evidence to use in the investigation of crime. The purpose of police lineups is to check the veracity of eyewitness statements for the purpose of identifying a suspect.

There are essentially three forms of police lineups. The photographic lineup can be done exclusively with the use of photographs (or "mug shots") in which a photograph of the suspect can be placed within an array of other photographs. A more common form of lineup is to have a suspect stand in a room with other people, known as foils, who look similar. Sometimes a lineup consists only of foils. Police may also make use of show-

ups, in which one suspect appears before a victim or witness. Some investigators prefer to use a combination of these techniques, such as first requesting a photographic lineup and then later a regular police lineup or showup.

Investigators are bound by constitutional requirements concerning the use of lineups. As in all other investigative procedures, police cannot violate the suspect's due process rights; thus, in some cases the accused must be provided with counsel during the lineup procedure. The U.S. Supreme Court ruled in *Kirby v. Illinois* (1972) that a person at a lineup or showup is entitled to counsel if the investigative procedure is held at or after the time that criminal proceedings have begun. However, if the lineup is conducted before the beginning of criminal proceedings, a suspect is not entitled to counsel. Counsel is also not required for photographic lineups. A defendant may request a waiver of rights to have counsel at a lineup or showup provided that the defendant is made aware of the procedure and the fact that the purpose of the procedure is for the identification of a criminal suspect.

The Problem of Misidentification

The issue of the possibility of misidentifications in police lineup procedures has been debated both by the Court and by scholars. In *Neil v. Biggers* (1972), the Court opined that five factors should be used to detect misidentification. The factors include the opportunity of the witness to view the criminal at the time of the crime, the witness's degree of attention, the accuracy of the witness's prior description of the criminal, the level of certainty demonstrated by the witness at the confrontation, and the length of time between the crime and the confrontation.

Further, scholars suggest that misidentification could be reduced by using either double-blind police lineups or sequential lineups. The double-blind procedure is based on a premise posited by several scholars that police officers who know the identity of the suspect may influence the decision of the eyewitness. The double-blind procedure thus prevents this by having the supervising police officer of a lineup unaware of who the possible suspect is. Sequential lineups require that eyewitnesses view potential suspects one at a time, rather than all at once. The sequential lineup procedure is based on the belief that eyewitnesses may be prone to make relative judgments and thus choose a suspect who looks most like the perpetrator when all of the suspects are viewed at once. Many police departments have begun utilizing both of these procedures in recent years.

D. Scott Canevit

Further Reading

Loftus, Elizabeth F. *Eyewitness Testimony*. Cambridge, Mass.: Harvard University Press, 1979.

Technical Working Group for Eyewitness Evidence. *Eyewitness Evidence: A Guide for Law Enforcement*. Washington, D.C.: U.S. Department of Justice, Office of Justice Programs, National Institute of Justice, 1999.

See also Booking; Counsel, right to; Due process of law; Eyewitness testimony; False convictions; Police; Police ethics; Suspects.

Police powers

Definition: Authority conferred on law-enforcement officers to enforce the law

Criminal justice issues: Police powers; professional standards

Significance: Police officers are in a precarious situation since they must balance their right to enforce the law and the discretion inherent in their profession with the judgments of their peers, supervisors, and members of the community.

Although American police officers gained both new respect and expanded powers after the terrorist attacks of September 11, 2001, there remain those who judge them as too often overzealous, biased, or even corrupt in the exercise of their powers. Over the years, there have been many investigations into the behavior of police officers, especially in the light of what has been labeled "profiling" of suspects—a potentially effective but controversial tool for identifying possible suspects.

Police power is generally understood as the lawful exercise of the sovereign right of govern-ment to promote order, safety, and security. It has also been referred to as a right of the government itself to regulate personal conduct. However, the state may limit this activity for the good of all the people. In general, the authority to preserve order and peace is subject to constraints by the U.S. Constitution. In fact, the concept of police power became important after ratification of the Fourteenth Amendment in 1868. One clause in that amendment states that "No State shall make or enforce any law which shall abridge the privileges or immunities of citizens of the United States; nor shall any State deprive any person of life, liberty, or property, without due process of law; nor deny to any person within its jurisdiction the equal protection of the laws."

In the past, the U.S. Supreme Court has justified police power to intrude into citizens' lives. For example, officers have been allowed to question persons who fit the "profile" of drug couriers by entering or exiting areas known for drug activity and carrying one-way airplane tickets and no luggage. In *Florida v. Royer* in 1983, the Supreme Court ruled that police could approach and ask questions of such individuals on the street or in any public places without violating the Fourth Amendment. Although this type of profiling appears logical and may contribute to apprehending drug couriers, it can also be viewed as racially or ethnically motivated and therefore biased.

Racial Profiling

Over the years, the term "profiling" has taken on a taboo-like character. State police have been criticized for stopping disproportionate percentages of drivers who are members of racial and ethnic minorities. The practice has given rise to two slang terms: "driving while black" and "racial profiling." Studies have shown that police often do target members of minorities in traffic stops, and that race does influence the likelihood of officers using force in encounters with suspects. Notions such as the assumption that typical drug-law offenders are young male African Americans who drive rundown cars reflect racial stereotypes and are discriminatory. Although that type of profiling can be useful to pick out actual offenders, it also stigmatizes all young, black males.

Since the terrorist attacks of 2001, police officers have been trained to look for the typical

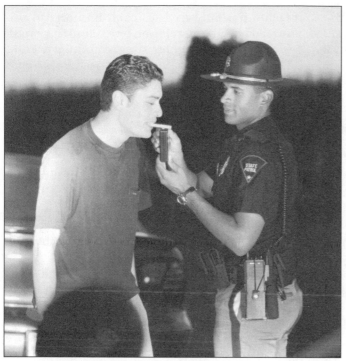

Highway patrol officer administering a field sobriety test on a motorist with a breath analyzer. Whenever police officers detain citizens and intrude on their privacy, they must balance their right to enforce the law with the citizens' constitutional rights. *(Brand-X Pictures)*

characteristics of foreign terrorists in order to help in the protection of the United States. The result has been a renewed emphasis on profiling that focused on people of Middle Eastern origin or descent. Although erring on the side of caution may enhance public safety, such profiling has the result of unfairly treating an entire group of people. The news media published many accounts of embarrassing mistakes made by police attempting to profile suspects that have led to unjustifiable detentions and arrests, as well unnecessary delays at airports, airplane rerouting, and forced landings.

Crime Control Versus Due Process

Although many citizens may support police power to act in ways deemed appropriate, there are others who are more concerned with the due process rights of the accused. Those who believe that the rights of the accused should outweigh the investigative work of police are naturally anxious about the processes used to gather evidence against suspects. They may find the powers of the police to be too vast and argue for restrictions on them.

Decisions made in the exercise of police power are rarely "cut and dried." Often, the lowest-ranking police officers have the most discretion because they are often alone on the street—sometimes with potentially dangerous suspects—and have much power to act as they see fit. Additionally, members of communities often regard officers on patrol as their enemies and distrust their motives.

On the other side of the spectrum are those who support all police efforts to get criminals off the street. These individuals focus on crime control, and they tend to expect police to use their power to intrude despite legal restrictions. They are more focused on outcomes than on the rights of offenders. However, it can be difficult to please both sides. Officers who use their power to enforce the law based on their experience and on-the-job training may not find support from the more conservative observers; officers who use their power to enforce the law based on the letter of the law may not find support from more liberal observers. Consequently, police may feel vast pressures on them and believe that their powers are limited by politics, precedents, and various interpretations of the law.

Reasonable Suspicion

What gives an officer the power to intrude? Case law has set precedent for proper police behavior on the streets. Regardless of the amount of discretion police have, they are bound by the law. There are different levels of intrusiveness possible by the police. They can range from encounters as serious as a search and seizure based on probable cause, to a stop and frisk initiated on reasonable suspicion, to encounters in which police and citizens are simply engaging in verbal interaction.

Under the Fourth Amendment to the Constitution, police may arrest and take suspects into custody with probable cause. Probable cause means that arresting officers believe—based on the circumstances and facts at hand—that crimes have been or are about to be committed. In *Terry v. Ohio* (1968), however, the U.S. Supreme Court ruled that police could act on less than probable cause, or what is called reasonable suspicion. This case set a precedent that justified police action without probable cause. Instead, a lower standard of proof could be used to justify a stop and detention if officers reasonably believe that suspects are committing or are about to commit crimes. Previous, officers could not act unless they believe their own lives were in danger.

Reasonable suspicion allows police to make the initial "stop." However, frisking, or patting down, is allowed after a stop only when the evidence discovered elevates an officer's level of suspicion. Thus, if officer who obeys the legal ruling in what is now called a "Terry" stop can please both liberal and conservatives alike. One group will appreciate the legality of the approach, and the other will appreciate the lower burden of proof needed to justify the stop in the first place.

Citizen Perceptions and Police Ethics

Modern police and police administrators have increasingly incorporated public perceptions into their decision making. Community-oriented policing and civilian police academy programs are among the new efforts being made to coordinate community views into the roles police should play.

Policing research has been focused upon educating laypersons about the role of police while determining the role citizens want police to play. The difficult next step has been to train police to place themselves in the citizens' place to determine how the power they use may be interpreted by the public. Balancing their legal rights against the strict scrutiny of others is a challenging task. However, to take away police power or to limit their discretion could have disastrous consequences. The main reason police have so much discretion is that often no clear-cut responses to street encounters are known.

Part of the problem with entrusting police with so much power is that individual officers handle their power differently. Discretion may work well in the hands of fair, ethical, and moral officers. However, some officers do not adhere to the same standard and thus exercise their power in unfair, prejudicial, and inequitable ways. It may be that only time will tell if efforts to improve police-citizen relations will close the gap in perceptions of legitimate uses of police power.

Gina M. Robertiello

Further Reading

Barnett, R. "The Proper Scope of Police Power." *Notre Dame Law Review* 79 (2002): 429-495. Legal treatise on the proper limits of police power.

_____. *Restoring the Lost Constitution: The Presumption of Liberty*. Princeton, N.J.: Princeton University Press, 2004. Broad essay on the erosion of civil liberties in the United States after the terrorist attacks of September 11, 2001.

Dunham, Roger G., and Geoffrey P. Alpert. *Critical Issues in Policing*. 4th ed. Prospect Heights, Ill.: Waveland Press, 2001. Assessment of the state of American policing at the turn of the twenty-first century and the nature of the most pressing challenges to police work.

Gaines, Larry, and Victor Kappeler. *Policing in America*. 4th ed. Cincinnati: Anderson, 2002. Explanation of the functions, culture, and discretionary authority of police officers, with a useful discussion on uses of force and racial profiling.

Langworthy, Robert H., and Lawrence F. Travis III. *Policing in America: A Balance of Forces*. 3d ed. Upper Saddle River, N.J.: Prentice Hall, 2003. Textbook covering broad issues relating to municipal police, including the historical developments that have created modern police forces.

Morash, Merry, and Kevin J. Ford. *The Move to Community Policing*. Thousand Oaks, Calif.: Sage Publications, 2002. Detailed study of the impact on police work of the modern move toward community-oriented policing.

Robertiello, G. M. *Police and Citizen Perceptions of Police Power*. Lewiston, N.Y.: Edwin Mellen Press, 2004. Broad study of the changing relationships between police and the communities they serve, and the consequent changes in both police and community views of the proper limits on police power.

Stevens, Dennis J. *Policing and Community Partnerships*. Upper Saddle River, N.J.: Prentice Hall, 2002. Textbook that could serve as a manual for police and community leaders interested in improving community-oriented policing.

See also Color of law; Community-oriented policing; Knapp Commission; Nonlethal weapons; Police; Police corruption; Police ethics; Racial profiling; Reasonable suspicion; Search and seizure; Search warrants; Special weapons and tactics teams (SWAT); Stop and frisk; *Terry v. Ohio.*

Police psychologists

Definition: Professionally trained psychologists who work in law enforcement
Criminal justice issues: Interrogation; law-enforcement organization; medical and health issues
Significance: Police psychologists play a significant role in many aspects of law enforcement.

The social science discipline of psychology is utilized by law enforcement in a variety of different ways. For example, police psychologists are involved in the interviewing and testing processes relating to the hiring of new police officers. Virtually all candidates for police officer vacancies undergo psychological testing to determine if they are emotionally stable and free of mental illness.

Police psychologists are also used in the interviewing of both witnesses and victims of crimes, as well as the interrogation of suspects. Psychologists' skills assist law enforcement in the calming of victims and the accurate representation of the facts from witnesses of a crime.

Police psychologists also perform the critically important function of offering psychological therapy to police officers and their families. The daily stress of law enforcement can influence the emotional health of officers and their families. Psychologists play an especially important role in providing counseling intervention to officers following traumatic and dangerous duty experiences, such as the horrific events of September 11, 2001.

Police psychologists are also utilized in criminal investigations. Perpetrators of violent crimes

A Human Side of Police Officers

Veteran Los Angeles police officer Joseph Wambaugh is known for the gritty realism of his novels about aspects of police work that generally receive little attention in fiction. One of these novels, *The Choirboys* (1975), explores one of the unusual ways in which police officers cope with the stresses of their work.

The novel's ten police officer characters meet after hours in Los Angeles's MacArthur Park to engage in "choir practice"—police slang for alcohol-fueled recaps of the day's events. Using this organizing structure, the novel explores events in the day-to-day lives of cops, both on the job and during "choir practice." Wambaugh excels at depicting the human side of law enforcement and the stresses it inflicts upon police; however, his novel does not attempt to investigate the personal lives of the officers, beyond their after-hours wrap-up meetings. Wambaugh also has a dark view of human nature, which leaves little room for descriptions of police professionalism.

Timothy L. Hall

against other persons often provide psychological clues in the commission of their crimes. For example, those who commit sexual assault and lust homicide typically do so to fulfill their intrinsic psychological needs, which reflect mental health or personality disorders. Police psychologists analyze the specific characteristics of victims and the specific manners in which the crimes are performed. The information they collect provides them with psychological profiles of the offenders that aid the officers investigating the crimes.

A hypothetical case provides an example of how a police psychologist works. If a prepubescent girl were to be found sexually assaulted and suffocated, a police psychologist in the case would probably suggest that the unknown perpetrator is afflicted with the sexual paraphilia known as pedophilia. The suspect would thus be likely to experience recurrent and intense episodes of sexual arousal around prepubescent children, in this case, preadolescent girls. The police psychologist would advise investigating officers that the perpetrator is likely to be found loitering around locations frequented by young girls. This knowledge helps to delineate the suspect group and orients the criminal investigation. This process is commonly referred to as "profiling."

Duane L. Dobbert

Further Reading

American Psychiatric Association. *The Diagnostic and Statistical Manual of Mental Disorders* (4th ed, text revision). Washington, D.C.: Author, 2000.

Dobbert, Duane L. *Halting the Sexual Predators Among Us: Preventing Attack, Rape, and Lust Homicide*. Westport, Conn.: Praeger, 2004.

See also Forensic psychology; Pedophilia; Police ethics; Polygraph testing; Psychological evaluation; Psychological profiling; Psychopathy; Victimology.

Political corruption

Definition: Misuse of public office for personal gain

Criminal justice issues: Fraud; government misconduct; political issues

Significance: Political corruption encompasses a wide variety of criminal behaviors by elected and appointed government officials including bribery, extortion, embezzlement, illegal kickbacks, influence peddling, voting fraud, and conflicts of interest. A common denominator among all these offenses is the illicit procurement of political influence with wealth. Unscrupulous wrongdoing by public officials erodes the foundations of a liberal democracy, undermines the healthy functioning of a market economy, and hampers the development of a vibrant civic society.

Although political corruption is often a consensual and ostensibly victimless crime in its appearance, it is one of the most socially harmful activities in a society, especially a democracy. It contributes to alienating citizens from political processes that are hijacked by well-connected interests. Arbitrariness and cronyism weaken the rule of law and ultimately diminish the legitimacy of the state through perversion of the democratic ideals of inclusion, equality, and participation.

Economically, political corruption contributes to the squandering of taxpayer money and generates economic inefficiencies. It causes businesses to waste time with government bureaucrats negotiating licenses, permits, and signatures. It can cause governments to engage in the wrong kinds of projects and contracts and to overspend on projects that are basically sound. It fosters a lack of openness and competition that leads to misallocations of resources to the general detriment of the citizenry. All the while, it fosters public cynicism and mutual distrust between government officials and the public, deepens socioeconomic inequalities, and facilitates the emergence of organized crime.

Political Corruption in History

Corruption has been an integral part of American political life since at least the end of the Civil War in the mid-1860's. The rapid postwar growth of New York City and the massive influx of new immigrants fostered political corruption in the nation's largest city on an unprecedented scale. Leaders of the city's Tammany Hall—the political machine of the Democratic Party—won elections by soliciting bribes from real state developers, placing political cronies on the city's payroll, and using dishonest judges to speed the naturalization of immigrants in return for the promise of their votes. Tammany Hall's leader, "Boss" William Macy Tweed, was expelled after *The New York Times* exposed the graft dealings of the ring based on the information provided by a county bookkeeper. However, although quick and effective legal action convicted Tweed of embezzlement and sentenced him to twelve years of incarceration, urban corruption survived.

Around the turn of the twentieth century, the journalist Lincoln Steffens published a series of sensational exposés of corruption in major American cities and revealed that instead of new immigrants and the poor, the business establishment was the real source of political corruption. Steffens initiated a new era of so-called "muckraking" investigative journalism that raised civic consciousness and motivated public reform.

In response to the public outcry that responded to Steffens's exposés, changes were implemented at all levels of government to ensure greater accountability and transparency. Many local governments replaced corrupt urban political machines with professional city managers, commissioners, and more efficient system of municipal administration that were accountable to city councils. State laws mandating elections by secret ballot, popular initiatives, referendum, recall votes, and direct primary elections were enacted to weaken the influence of party bosses. At the federal level, the Seventeenth (1913) and Nineteenth (1920) Amendments to the Constitution institutionalized the direct election of U.S. senators and granted suffrage to women in national elections—both changes that allowed the people to play more direct roles in political processes.

However important those Progressive reforms were, they made only a minor dent in corrupt machine politics. The survival of urban corruption through the 1920's and 1930's was in part reinforced by the Eighteenth Amendment's (1919) national prohibition of alcoholic beverages. Prohibition encouraged organized crime and political corruption to flourish, as public demand for illegal liquor soared. Pernicious crime syndicates corrupted local law-enforcement agencies, government officials, and judges. Eventually, public disgust, aroused by the Wickersham Commission report of 1931, as well as municipal investigations led to a fierce crackdown on urban corruption. After the repeal of Prohibition in 1933, surviving organized crime leaders turned to labor racketeering, gambling, and drug dealings for profits.

After World War II, congressional committees began to investigate the extent to which criminal organizations and labor rackets had penetrated into local governments. The preferred method of government infiltration was to support friendly politicians through campaign contributions. Organized crime groups utilized their political capital to influence land-use decisions, purchase kickbacks, exploit social benefit programs, and embezzle government funds. The cozy relations between the underworld and political clans in local politics would later be replicated at the national level, between corporate interests and political parties. Without radical reforms, the American democracy was in danger of being shaped by private wealth rather than by ordinary people.

Public repugnance for political corruption reached a new height during the second presidency of Richard M. Nixon. In 1971, Nixon commuted the sentence for racketeering of the notorious union figure Jimmy Hoffa. Later, he was rewarded by becoming the first Republican presidential candidate to be endorsed by a major union, Hoffa's own mob-ridden Teamsters Union. In June, 1972, the police arrested burglars from Nixon's re-election campaign as they attempted to wire the offices of the Democratic National Committee in Washington's Watergate Hotel. During the congressional investigation of the ensuing Watergate scandal, Vice President Spiro Agnew resigned because of unrelated criminal charges of tax evasion and bribery during his earlier tenure as governor of Maryland. Nixon himself resigned in 1974 for his role in the Watergate scandal and its cover-up.

By the mid-1970's, as America celebrated its bicentennial, it was evident that democratic elections were not a sufficient or necessary cure for political corruption. Electoral systems are extremely vulnerable to special interest influence. The right to contribute to electoral campaigns, although protected by the First Amendment of the Constitution, has since become a key agenda-setting mechanism for powerful entities with vested interests in local, national, and international issues, including gun control, energy, telecommunications, banking regulation, and the Israeli-Palestinian conflicts, among others.

Although the Bipartisan Campaign Reform Act of 2002 implemented the most sweeping changes of the campaign finance system in recent history, political elections remained infested with attempts to conceal the origins of campaign contributions and to evade contribution and spending limits that incorporate a variety of money-laundering techniques. These techniques include the use of shell companies, straw donors, and the funneling of money through political action committees, unions, and nonprofit organizations. The blatant sale of political access, such as the infusion of foreign money into the Republican and Democratic National Committees and the Clinton-Gore re-election campaign in 1996, de-

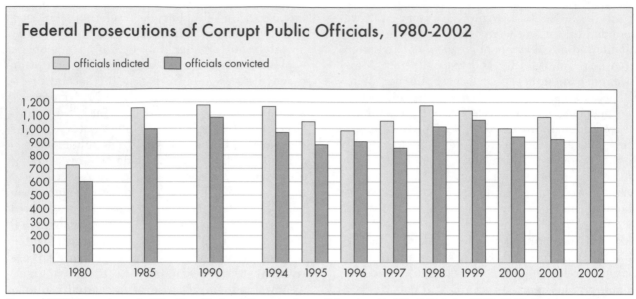

Federal Prosecutions of Corrupt Public Officials, 1980-2002

officials indicted   officials convicted

Source: U.S. Department of Justice, *Federal Prosecutions of Corrupt Public Officials, 1970-1980; Report to Congress on the Activities and Operations of the Public Integrity Section,* annual.

mands more creativity and resolve in the stamping out of complex networks of patron-client relationships in American politics.

Prevalence and Causes

The most complete statistics on political corruption in the United States are collected by the Public Integrity Section of the U.S. Department of Justice, which investigates and prosecutes elected and appointed officials at all levels of government who are accused of public corruption, ballot fraud, campaign-financing offenses, and criminal conflicts of interest. The Justice Department reports only federal actions, but up to 80 percent of corruption prosecutions are brought against federal officials.

In 2002, a total of 1,136 U.S. public officials were indicted and 1,011 officials were convicted of public corruption. Of the convicted offenders, 42 percent were federal officials, 13 percent were state officials, and 26 percent were local officials. The remaining 19 percent were private citizens involved in corruption offenses. Annual rates of indictment and conviction between 1983 and 2002 were comparatively stable. During that period, a total of 23,246 officials were indicted and 20,497 were convicted on corruption charges.

Judging by conviction rates (the numbers of

convictions per 100,000 people between 1993 and 2002), the five most corrupt states in the nation are Mississippi, North Dakota, Louisiana, Alaska, and Illinois, in that order. The five least corrupt states are Nebraska, Oregon, New Hampshire, Iowa, and Colorado. When the District of Columbia is included, it tops the list as the most corrupt jurisdiction.

In 2002, the Better Government Association (BGA) completed an independent report on government integrity using criteria based on the relative strengths of anticorruption laws, including freedom of information, whistle-blower protection, campaign finance, gifts, trips, and honoraria, and conflict of interest disclosure. The worst five states in the BGA Integrity Index were Louisiana, Alabama, New Mexico, Vermont, and South Dakota. The five top five states were Wisconsin, Rhode Island, Kentucky, Hawaii, and California.

Another way of evaluating the problem of political corruption is to ask how members of the public experience corruption in their daily lives. Every year, Transparency International (TI), a nongovernment organization at the forefront of combating global corruption, surveys corporate executives and business analysts around the world about their perceptions of government corruption and ranks countries according to the obtained indices. In the 2003 TI rating, the United States ranked seventeenth among the thirty member countries of the Organization for Economic Co-operation and Development. There is clearly plenty of room for improvement.

Political corruption is a behavior motivated by rational calculations of expected utility. Opportunities for corruption emerge when high payoffs are expected and little risk of being physically detected, socially stigmatized, or legally punished exists. Opportunities are structured by the convergence of three key determinants:

✓ motivated offenders, such as low-paid public officials, businesses seeking lucrative contracts, and politicians building larger power bases
✓ risky governmental policies or practices, such as non-bid contracts, excessive

bureaucratic red tape, and nonsecret balloting
✓ absence of effective institutional guardians to monitor and punish offenders, such as intra-agency audits, independent judiciaries, and courageous investigative journalists

Investigation, Prosecution, and Punishment

Legal proscriptions against corruption fall into two main categories: those that specify that anyone engaging in corruption meet with some sort of penal sanction, and those that provide for impeachment, removal from office, and permanent exclusion from holding elective offices.

Investigations of allegations of political corruption can be initiated by independent anticorruption agencies, administrative audit bodies, or judicial-prosecutorial authorities. An example of standing anticorruption agencies is the New Jer-

Citizens of Providence, Rhode Island, awaiting the verdict in one of the most publicized trials for political corruption of the early twenty-first century. The so-called "Operation Plunder Dome" case revolved around Vincent "Buddy" Cianci, Jr., the mayor of Providence, who was found guilty in a federal court on racketeering conspiracy charges in June, 2002. Cianci and two other city officials were convicted of soliciting bribes in exchange for city jobs, contracts, and tax breaks. *(AP/Wide World Photos)*

sey State Commission of Investigation, which is a fact-finding agency required by law to identify and investigate organized crime, corruption and waste, fraud, and abuse of taxpayers' money. Findings from its inquiries are made public through written reports and public hearings.

Sometimes, independent investigation can be initiated in response to particular scandals, such as the administration of special counsel by the Justice Department. Many government agencies have established their own offices of inspector general for financial, compliance, performance, and ethical audits. The success of either independent anticorruption commissions or offices of inspector general hinges on adequate funding, operational independence, and the ability to trigger formal investigation by judicial-prosecutorial authorities.

Political corruption has often been immune from prosecution because of the offenders have power and connections. In cases of successful prosecution, investigators have relied on investigative techniques usually used for white-collar and organized crime, including undercover operations (where fictitious companies are set up and agents pose as crooked businessmen), informants, surveillance, immunity against prosecution for cooperation, and witness protection programs.

The first step in grand jury investigation of unlawfully derived wealth is to examine defendants' income tax returns and banking information. Financial evidence is critical in securing convictions and may include failure to disclose a specific item of income, net worth, expenditures, bank deposits, lack of loans or checks to cash, unusual use of cash, lack of credit charges, safe deposit box activity, or use of third parties in financial transactions.

An instructive and controversial example of effective investigation and prosecution of corruption is the Abscam scandal resulting from a sting operation begun in 1978 by the Federal Bureau of Investigation. The FBI created a front organized called "Abdul Enterprises, Ltd." (hence, Abscam). Its undercover agents posed as associates of a Middle Eastern sheik and offered selected members of Congress money in exchange for helping the sheik to obtain asylum in the United States, participating in an investment venture, and as-

sisting the ring to transfer money out of its home country. Videotaped meetings of the FBI agents and the congressmen involved in the scheme led to the indictments and convictions of one senator and four congressmen on charges of bribery and conspiracy in separate trials. Another congressman was convicted on lesser charges. All but one of the politicians resigned from office to avoid impeachment and expulsion. The FBI's actions raised questions about entrapment and prompted the establishment of two congressional committees to investigate the allegations. Although no wrongdoing by the FBI was found, the conviction of Florida congressman Richard Kelly was later overturned.

The punishment of persons convicted of political corruption is not harsh compared to that of traditional street offenders in the United States. In 2000, 379 convicted federal bribery offenders were under community supervision, and 53 were incarcerated. The average length of prison time served by incarcerated federal bribery offenders was only twelve months.

Hung-En Sung

Further Reading

The BGA Integrity Index. Chicago: Better Government Association, 2002. Analysis and ranking of the fifty states according to the relative strengths of their laws promoting integrity and preventing corruption.

Grossman, Mark. *Political Corruption in America: An Encyclopedia of Scandals, Power, and Greed*. Santa Barbara, Calif.: ABC-Clio, 2003. Encyclopedic reference work that includes 250 entries on people, laws, scandals, and basic concepts associated with political corruption in the United States.

Prosecution of Public Corruption Cases. Washington, D.C.: U.S. Department of Justice, 1988. Now slightly dated but still valuable compendium that describes patterns of judicial, law-enforcement, regulatory agency, legislative, and narcotics-related corruption at all levels of government. Election and conflicts of interest crimes also are considered. Contributors also discuss tactics and strategies of investigation and prosecution, methods to counter common defenses in public corruption cases, and principles of media relations.

Report to Congress on the Activities and Operations of the Public Integrity Section for 2002. Washington, D.C.: U.S. Department of Justice, 2003. Annual Department of Justice report documenting the prosecutions and convictions of individuals nabbed in federal corruption investigations. It also provides a summary description for every corruption case processed by the department's Public Integrity Section.

Rose-Ackerman, Susan. *Corruption and Government: Causes, Consequences, and Reform.* New York: Cambridge University Press, 1999. Comprehensive treatise on the causation, prevention, and control of corruption. Drawing illustrations and insights from around the world, it is one of the richest discussions available on issues of political corruption.

See also Anti-Racketeering Act of 1934; Blackmail and extortion; Gangsters of the Prohibition era; Organized crime; Pardons; Police corruption; Racketeer Influenced and Corrupt Organizations Act; Teapot Dome scandal; Voting fraud; Watergate scandal; White-collar crime; Wickersham Commission.

Polygraph testing

Definition: Method of measuring physiological responses to questioning in order to detect lies

Criminal justice issues: Evidence and forensics; interrogation; technology

Significance: Although polygraph testing has been used since the 1920's, it has failed to gain widespread acceptance as a reliable tool in criminal justice.

Also known as "lie detectors," polygraphs are instruments that record the physiological responses of persons being asked questions for the purpose of ascertaining the truthfulness of their answers. Questions are assembled in a testing format commonly called a psycho-physiological detection of deception (PDD) examination.

The word "polygraph" has Greek roots that mean "many writings." In polygraph testing, each "writing," or pen marking, on a chart paper represents a unique physiological response, such as blood pressure, upper body movement, or galvanic skin response (perspiration). Any increases in these measurements indicate that the subject of the test is being discomforted by the questions being posed. Through careful questioning, monitoring of the tests, and evaluation of the overall results, testers can generally determine the truthfulness of the subjects' responses to individual questions.

History

The Italian criminologist Cesare Lombroso is credited with developing the principles behind polygraph testing during the 1890's. A pioneer of modern scientific criminology methods, he sought to explain criminal behavior through human biology. He discovered that human blood pressure increases following deceptive responses. Later, William Marston and John Larson separately came to the conclusion that blood pressure and respiration were correlated. Larson constructed the actual recording device in 1921, but Leonarde Keeler and Walter Summers refined the direct predecessor of the modern polygraph testing device around 1924. Following their advances, investigators and employers began to use the polygraph as a matter of practice.

Legal controversies over the use of polygraph testing began around the same time. In 1923, a convicted murderer name Frye took his appeal to the U.S. Supreme Court, arguing that he had been wrongly convicted because the trial court had refused to admit evidence in his favor that was based upon the findings of a crude precursor to the modern polygraph that involved periodic readings from a blood-pressure cuff. Because the scientific community did not accept that method, the Court found it to be unreliable and therefore ordered the evidence to be excluded in *Frye v. United States* (1923).

Although polygraph technology has advanced greatly since Frye's time, by the turn of the twenty-first century, only the state of New Mexico admitted polygraph tests into evidence at the trial level. However, in 1998, the U.S. Supreme Court declared that individual courts have the discretion to admit such tests as evidence if they so choose.

Examination Type and Format

Polygraph examinations are most commonly used in two settings: pre-employment screening and criminal investigations. Pre-employment testing involves series of exploratory questions about job candidates' possible histories of job trouble, substance abuse, and criminal behavior. Until the practice was outlawed in 1988, private employers could require applicants to submit to polygraph examinations for purposes of job suitability and, after they were hired, could require them to take additional examinations at any time. However, passage of the federal Employee Polygraph Protection Act prohibited such testing, exempting only law-enforcement agencies, nuclear power facilities, and pharmaceutical companies.

Polygraph examinations conducted on behalf of law-enforcement agencies or defense attorneys usually focus on specific criminal issues. Depending upon the information available to them,

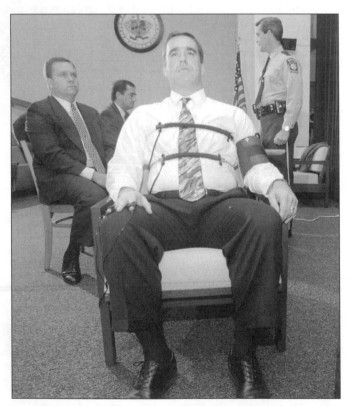

Pennsylvania police officer demonstrating a new polygraph device that was believed to produce results that are more accurate than those of earlier models. *(AP/Wide World Photos)*

examiners utilize one of many specific-issue question formats. One of the most commonly used is the Control Question Technique (CQT) developed by John Reid. Tests using that format begin by asking subjects "control" questions designed to elicit deceptive, or untruthful, responses from ordinarily truthful subjects. The questions that follow concern the relevant or specific issues at hand. For example, if the polygraph examination concerns the theft of money from a corporation, a control question might be, "Have you ever taken something from someone who trusted you?" The following, specific-issue question would be, "Are you the person who took the money from Company X on the date and time in question?"

Subjects "pass" the tests when their physiological responses to control questions are stronger than those to the specific-issue questions. Conversely, they "fail" the tests when the results are the opposite. However, contrary to the ways in which lie detectors are depicted in the popular media, there is much more to polygraph testing than simply asking questions.

The classic polygraph testing format begins with pre-test interviews that establish rapport between subjects and examiners and allows the examiners to create psychological sets—the focus of attention. Examiners formulate their questions based upon the information they gather during the interviews. After they attach the polygraph to the subjects, "stimulus tests" are conducted that require subjects to lie to certain questions. These trial tests indicate to examiners whether the subjects are testable. Next, the examiners conduct the actual examinations regarding the specific issues at hand. When the subjects are judged to have failed their tests, the examiners begin the post-interview stage and attempt to elicit admissions or confessions.

Technology, Profession, and Industry

For many years, polygraph instruments recorded responses with several ink pens moving across continuously flowing paper charts. Modern polygraph instruments are now computerized. The physiological responses of subjects received by the instruments are digitized and displayed on computer screens. Polygraph software and equipment are now commercially available to both public and private examiners.

Regulation of the polygraph industry varies throughout the United States. Some states have stringent licensing requirements regarding examiner training, test formats, and examinee fitness. Other states simply require examiner registration; many states have no licensing requirements whatsoever. In states requiring licensing, prospective polygraph examiners must attend ten-week polygraph schools, in which they receive training in psychology, physiology, interviewing and interrogation, and chart interpretation. Following their coursework, they must satisfactorily pass several examinations and, in some instances, complete academic research projects.

The American Polygraph Association (APA), the largest professional group of the trade, has attempted to standardize the industry by offering accreditation status to polygraph schools that follow standards approved in its bylaws. In addition to attending regional training sessions, APA members gather once each year to review recent research and practices.

Douglas A. Orr

Further Reading

Clifton, Charles. *Deception Detection: Winning the Polygraph Game*. New York: Paladin Press, 1991. How-to manual that offers tips on beating polygraph tests. Although the advice offered may or may not be useful, the book provides valid insights into the nature of polygraph testing.

Kleiner, Murray, ed. *Handbook of Polygraph Testing*. San Diego, Calif.: Academic Press, 2001. Collection of up-to-date articles assessing the scientific bases of polygraph testing and its modern applications. Designed as a handbook for professionals who administer the tests and interpret their results.

Matte, James A. *Forensic Psychophysiology Using the Polygraph: Scientific Truth Verification, Lie Detection*. Williamsville, N.Y.: J. A. M. Publications, 1996. Most comprehensive work on the use of polygraph testing in psychophysiology. Provides details on the theory and operation of polygraph equipment and assesses the validity of its applications. A supplement to this work was published in 2002.

Moore, Mark H., Carol V. Petrie, and Anthony A. Braga, eds. *The Polygraph and Lie Detection*. Washington, D.C.: National Academies Press, 2003. Collection of critical analyses of polygraph testing and its impact on law enforcement; also discusses alternative methods of testing truthfulness of subjects.

Segrave, Kerry. *Lie Detectors: A Social History*. Jefferson, N.C.: McFarland, 2003. History of lie-detecting techniques used from the 1860's to the present day for general readers.

U.S. Congress, Office of Technology Assessment. *Scientific Validity of Polygraph Testing: A Research Review and Evaluation*. Stockton, Calif.: University Press of the Pacific, 2004. First published in 1983. Government report that focuses narrowly on the scientific validity of the ability of polygraph testing to measure truthfulness.

See also Confessions; Embezzlement; Private police and guards; Suspects.

Pornography, child

Definition: Visual depictions of minors in sexually explicit poses

Criminal justice issues: Deviancy; juvenile justice; sex offenses

Significance: Although adult pornography has been a tolerated, if not fully accepted, part of human culture throughout recorded history, child pornography is another matter—one that evokes nearly universal disgust across all social boundaries. However, Internet technology has added a new dimension to child pornography that presents unprecedented challenges to the criminal justice system's efforts to combat the spread of child pornography and its associated exploitation of children.

The roots of child pornography date back to ancient Greece, and it flourished in England during the nineteenth century. However, the true birth of child pornography occurred during the mid-

A police detective in Mt. Vernon, Illinois, monitors homemade child pornography videotapes seized in a raid in an operation working to break up a child pornography and prostitution ring that was believed to be connected with a private boarding school, a junior high school basketball coach, and others in early 2004. *(AP/Wide World Photos)*

1960's, with an explosion in the production of sexually graphic photographs of children in Europe, Asia, Australia, and North Africa. By the late 1960's and early 1970's, child pornography was the basis of a major worldwide market. This development was partly the result of relaxation of laws against magazines containing child pornography in many countries.

The U.S. government began to take action against the widespread availability of child pornography with the Supreme Court's 1982 *New York v. Ferber* ruling. That case came to the Court in a challenge to a New York anti-child pornography law, which the Court upheld. The case brought child pornography to the attention of the American public. In response to a subsequent public outcry, a series of campaigns was waged against this burgeoning problem. By the mid-1980's, child pornography was virtually abolished in the United States. Its production was laborious and costly, and purchasing it was

difficult and subject to severe criminal penalties.

Since then, however, technological advances, particularly in the Internet, have altered the situation by making pornographic materials convenient and inexpensive to distribute in volume. This has allowed for the almost instantaneous and anonymous dissemination of child pornography through sites on the World Wide Web, electronic mail, instant messaging, bulletin boards, and chat rooms. Indeed, the advent of the Internet has acted as the impetus for the resurgence of a nearly extinct subculture that has become part of a global network devoid of boundaries.

While the trafficking of child pornography literature was once limited by geography, the Internet has served as a hunting ground for sexual predators. The fact that child pornography has now found an electronic safe haven has made it one of the most controversial issues of modern law enforcement and has provoked enormous social concern. It has been estimated that nearly one-half of computer crime cases involve the electronic sexual exploitation of children.

Defining Child Pornography

Because of conflicting laws in various countries, there is considerable disagreement over definitions of child pornography. Most laws prohibit depictions of sexual activities involving children below specified ages, but the ages vary from country to country. Some countries disallow all illustrations of nude minors, some forbid written works describing sexual activities of minors, and others even prohibit simulated pornography—cartoons, paintings, drawings, and computer generated images.

The United States Criminal Code now defines child pornography to include all photographs, films, videos, and other visual representations, regardless of how they are made, showing persons who are, or who are depicted as, being under the age of eighteen years, engaged in explicit sexual activity. The second part of the code's definition includes written materials and visual representations that promote sexual activity with persons under the age of eighteen.

Prevalence of Child Pornography

The incidence and prevalence rates of child pornography are difficult to ascertain given the plethora of unsubstantiated statistics and the dearth of available resources that have been allocated to measure the problem. Child pornography is an industry of high profitability that was estimated to generate two to three billion dollars in annual revenue in 2004. By that time, more than 100,000 sites were offering child pornography on the World Wide Web. Moreover, it appears that millions of youths receive sexual propositions from adults over the Internet every year.

Another dimension of the problem of online pornography is its accessibility to youths. It has been estimated that more than 90 percent of American children between the ages of ten and sixteen have viewed some form of pornography online. As many as 80 percent reported having multiple exposures to online pornography.

Another Internet feature through which pornography is disseminated is the so-called virtual chat room. The spread of Internet chat rooms has created a virtually dangerous playing field for pedophiles because of the anonymity they permit. Approximately 70 percent of convicted sex offenders use the Internet. When children enter Internet chat rooms, they have an extremely high chance of coming into contact with sexual predators. Children are especially vulnerable because of their capacity for trust. Surprisingly, nearly 30 percent of teenagers who use chat rooms freely release their home addresses. To further widen this problem, the National Center for Missing and Exploited Children conducted a survey revealing that 20 percent of parents had no knowledge of their children's Internet passwords, instant-message names, or e-mail addresses.

Prosecution and Punishment

The possible prison terms for violating federal laws against child pornography and related crimes laws are severe:

✓ possession, distribution, or receipt of child pornography: 5-20 years
✓ importation of child pornography: maximum of 10 years
✓ producing child pornography: 15-30 years
✓ selling or buying of children for sexual exploitation: 30 years-life

Several initiatives aimed at reducing the problem were launched in 1998 in response to the public demand to end child pornography. Congress enacted the Child Online Protection Act to require online commercial pornographers to verify ages of Internet users before allowing them to view pornography. During that same year, Congress also passed the Sexual Predators Act, which required Internet service providers, such as AOL, to notify law enforcement when they discover child pornography on their Web spaces.

Cybertipline was also established in 1998 by the National Center for Missing and Exploited Children. This is a congressionally mandated system for reporting child sexual exploitation and is a joint venture with federal agencies, including the Federal Bureau of Investigation, U.S. Immigration and Customs, the U.S. Secret Service, the U.S. Postal Inspection Service, and state and local law-enforcement agencies.

Lisa Landis Murphy

Further Reading

Barnitz, L. A. *Commercial Sexual Exploitation of Children: Youth Involved in Prostitution, Pornography, and Sex Trafficking*. Washington, D.C.: Youth Advocate Program International, 1998. Explores the extent to which children are used for commercial sexual exploitation.

Ferraro, M., and E. Casey. *Investigating Child Exploitation and Pornography: The Internet, Law and Forensic Science*. Burlington, Mass.: Academic Press, 2004. Provides case histories of child exploitation and pornography and discusses legal issues associated with the detection and prosecution of cases of the use of child pornography on the Internet.

Jenkins, P. *Beyond Tolerance: Child Pornography Online*. New York: New York University Press, 2001. Detailed examination of the prevalence of online child pornography as it continues to challenge the criminal justice system.

Svedin, C. G., K. Back, and R. Barnen. *Children Who Don't Speak Out: About Children Being Abused in Child Pornography*. Sweden: Radda Barren, 1997. Study of the effectiveness of the early detection system used by Swedish law enforcement to solve child pornography cases.

Taylor, M., and E. Quayle. *Child Pornography: An Internet Crime*. New York: Brunner-Routledge, 2003. Survey of the wide availability of child pornography on the Internet.

See also Battered child and battered wife syndromes; Child abduction by parents; Child abuse and molestation; Commercialized vice; Comstock Law; Pedophilia; Pornography and obscenity; Roman Catholic priests scandal; Sex offender registries.

Pornography and obscenity

Definition: Depiction of erotic behavior that is intended to arouse sexual excitement

Criminal justice issues: Constitutional protections; morality and public order; sex offenses; women's issues

Significance: Pornography occupies an equivocal place in the American criminal justice system. While it has been outlawed in many states and communities, it has never been clearly defined, and U.S. Supreme Court rulings have tended to treat it as protected expression under the First Amendment.

Pornography is a concept closely associated with obscenity, but although pornography and obscenity have never been clearly defined by law, it is generally recognized that they are not the same thing. The key to the place of pornography in American criminal justice is the Supreme Court's long and complex history of rulings on the subject.

Obscenity is one of several categories of speech deemed unprotected by the First Amendment in the U.S. Supreme Court's 1942 ruling in *Chaplinsky v. New Hampshire*. In that case, the Court argued that obscenity and lewdness are analogous to libel—knowingly false speech that injures a person's reputation—and fighting words—speech that may incite the persons to whom it is addressed to attack the speaker. The Court reasoned that such speech is not essential to the rational exchange of ideas cherished by the First Amendment and is of little value to society. Any harm arising from suppression is outweighed by society's interest in maintaining order and morality.

Defining Obscenity

The Supreme Court did not directly address the question of obscenity's constitutional status until *Roth v. United States* and *Alberts v. California* (1957). Writing for a 6-3 majority, Justice William Joseph Brennan, Jr., held that obscenity is unprotected by the First Amendment because it is "utterly without redeeming social importance." Brennan stressed that "sex and obscenity are not synonymous" and distinguished between them by explaining that obscene material deals with sex in a manner appealing to "the prurient interest." Brennan defined prurient as "having a tendency to excite lustful thoughts" or appealing to a "shameful and morbid interest in sex." What became known as the Roth-Alberts test for obscenity was formulated by Brennan in this way: Material was obscene if "to the average person, applying contemporary community standards, the dominant theme of the material taken as a whole appeals to the prurient interest."

In later years, the Supreme Court found it difficult to define more precisely each element of the Roth-Alberts test. In *Jacobellis v. Ohio* (1964), Justice Potter Stewart questioned whether he could "intelligibly" define obscene material, though he said, "I know it when I see it" and went on to find that the material involved was not obscene. Three years later, in *Redrup v. New York* (1967), the Court overturned an obscenity conviction in a *per curiam* decision (an opinion "by the court" that briefly expresses the decision but identifies no author), and for the next six years in more than thirty obscenity cases, the Court decided each *per curiam*, the individual justices applying their own understanding of the definition of obscenity.

These Warren court decisions were criticized for failing to provide clear guidelines to law-enforcement officials charged with applying federal, state, and local antiobscenity statutes. There was also concern that nonobscene sexually explicit speech might be stifled if speakers feared that speech they thought protected might later be found punishable. However, others found the Warren court's standards too permissive, and these decisions, among others, were issues in the 1968 presidential election.

In *Miller v. California* and *Paris Adult Theatre v. Slaton* (1973), the Burger court reaffirmed *Roth*'s finding that obscenity is not protected by the First Amendment and expounded the current test for obscenity. Writing for a 5-4 majority, Chief Justice Warren E. Burger held that three requirements must be met to find material obscene. First, the average person, applying contemporary community standards, must find the material appealing to his or her prurient interest. Second, the material must depict sexual conduct in a patently offensive way. Third, material is obscene if, taken as a whole—not simply focusing on isolated passages or pictures in, for example, a book or magazine—it "lacks serious literary, artistic, political, or scientific value." In short, obscenity is "hard core" pornography.

In *Paris Adult Theatre v. Slaton*, decided the same day as *Miller*, Justice Brennan, who wrote the majority opinion in *Roth*, questioned whether this new approach would bring stability to the law of obscenity and suggested that fundamental First Amendment values were jeopardized. He

In his majority decision in the Supreme Court's 1973 rulings on obscenity, Chief Justice Warren E. Burger laid down three criteria for finding material obscene. *(Robert Oakes/Collection of the Supreme Court of the United States)*

argued that government's interest in regulating sexually explicit materials was confined to distribution to minors or unwilling adults and that regulation of the distribution of such materials to consenting adults was inconsistent with the First Amendment. Obscenity opponents praised the Court for achieving a majority opinion defining obscenity and rejecting an earlier approach—used by the Court in the 1966 *Fanny Hill* case (*A Book Named "John Cleland's Memoirs of a Woman of Pleasure" v. Attorney General of Massachusetts*)—that a work is obscene if it is "utterly without redeeming social value." This minimal social value test placed a heavy burden on prosecutors, in essence requiring them to prove a negative. Under *Miller*, prosecutors merely have to show that a work lacks "serious" literary, artistic, political, or scientific value.

In *New York v. Ferber* (1982), the Court created an important exception to the principle that nonobscene sexually explicit material is entitled to First Amendment protection. The *Ferber* case involved a New York State law prohibiting the knowing production, exhibition, or distribution of any material depicting a "sexual performance" by a child under sixteen. Ferber was convicted for selling two films showing young boys masturbating. The Court upheld the conviction, even though this material did not meet the *Miller* test for obscenity. The Court reasoned that the state had a "compelling interest" in protecting the physiological, emotional, and mental health of children, citing the close relationship between child pornography and child abuse.

In *Osborne v. Ohio* (1990), the Court held that the government may regulate private possession of child pornography. The Court reasoned that an earlier case, *Stanley v. Georgia* (1969), was not applicable here. In *Stanley*, the Court overturned a conviction for possession of obscenity. Justice Thurgood Marshall's opinion for the Court stressed the freedom of individuals to read or watch what they choose in the privacy of their own homes. (*Stanley* has never been overruled, but neither has it been extended. In *United States v. Reidel* [1971], for example, the justices rejected the argument that a right to possess obscene materials entails a right to receive them despite a governmental ban on shipment of such materials.) In *Osborne*, over a dissent by Justice Brennan in which he argued that the controlling precedent was *Stanley*, the Court reasoned that the privacy interest was outweighed by the state's need to protect children by attacking the "market for the exploitative use of children."

Sexually Oriented Nonobscene Speech

Some types of sexual speech, while not meeting the definition of obscenity, are treated by the Court as low-value speech. The government has more room to regulate such speech than it would if it were targeting a political speech or a newspaper editorial. The Court has used the metaphor of a ladder. Obscenity, libel, or fighting words are at the bottom of the ladder, while a speech at a political rally or a newspaper editorial are at the top. Sexually oriented nonobscene speech is somewhere in between and, in the eyes of some justices, closer to the bottom.

The Court has never given a detailed definition of this category, but it is clear that sexually explicit nonobscene material is included. One example involves movie theaters specializing in "adult" entertainment—material involving "specified sexual activities" or "specified anatomical areas." In *Young v. American Mini Theaters* (1976), the Court said cities could limit how many adult theaters could be on any block and exclude them from residential neighborhoods. The Court stressed that attempts to place complete bans on such establishments would raise First Amendment problems. Subsequently in *City of Renton v. Playtime Theaters* (1986), the Court approved a zoning ordinance that banned adult theaters located within one thousand feet of any residential zone, church, park, or school. The practical effect of Renton's law was to exclude such establishments from 95 percent of the land in the city. The remaining 5 percent was unsuitable for such establishments, but the Court, relying on *Young*, upheld the ordinance.

Also near the bottom of the ladder is nude dancing. In *Barnes v. Glen Theatre* (1991), the Court held that the government may completely ban nude dancing. At issue in *Barnes* was an Indiana statute prohibiting public nudity. The Court split five to four, and there was no majority opinion. The plurality opinion by Chief Justice William H. Rehnquist described nude dancing as "within the outer perimeters of the First Amendment, though . . . only marginally so." Rehnquist argued that the ban on nude dancing was needed to protect "societal order and morality." In the chief justice's view, Indiana was not proscribing erotic dancing but rather targeting public nudity. Justice Byron R. White's dissenting opinion argued that nudity is an expressive component of the dance rather than "merely incidental 'conduct.'"

Whatever the exact definition of sexually oriented nonobscene speech, the Court has indicated that nudity per se is not enough to place the communication near the bottom of the ladder. In *Erznoznik v. Jacksonville* (1975), the Court overturned a Jacksonville, Florida, ordinance prohibiting a drive-in movie theater from showing films including nude scenes if the screen was visible from a public street or any other public place. The Court stressed that nudity alone is not obscene and not enough to curtail First Amendment protections.

Profane and Indecent Language

Profane and indecent language, the familiar Anglo-Saxon four-letter word being the prototypical example, does not meet the *Miller* definition of obscenity, and the Court has found such language protected by the First Amendment. The notion that the government may not punish speech simply because some find it offensive, a bedrock principle of First Amendment interpretation, found classic expression in *Cohen v. California* (1971). In *Cohen*, the Court overturned the conviction of an anti-Vietnam War protester charged with disturbing the peace by wearing, in the corridor of a courthouse, a jacket with the words "F— the Draft" emblazoned on its back. Justice John M. Harlan II's majority opinion rejected the notion that the state can prohibit offensive language. Harlan was concerned that, under the guise of prohibiting particular words, the government might seek to ban the expression of unpopular views. Additionally, Harlan endorsed Cohen's argument that words are often used as much for their emotive as their cognitive impact. Cohen could not have conveyed the intensity of his feeling if the jacket said "I Don't Like the Draft." In *Sable Communications v. Federal Communications Commission* (1989), the Court reiterated that government may prohibit obscene but not indecent speech.

However, the Court has also recognized situations in which the government can ban profane or indecent language. One such situation is broadcasting. In *Federal Communications Commission v. Pacifica Foundation* (1978), the Court allowed the Federal Communications Commission (FCC) to punish indecent language broadcast over an FM radio station. The station aired a portion of a monologue on "seven dirty words" by comedian George Carlin. Chief Justice Burger's opinion emphasized that broadcast media are unique in their pervasiveness and in their ability to intrude into the home. Burger also expressed

The so-called "adult bookstore" industry arose in response to increasingly permissive Supreme Court rulings in pornography cases. During earlier eras, purveyors of pornographic materials would have been subjected to criminal prosecution. *(McCrea Adams)*

concern about the accessibility of such broadcasts to children.

In 1996, applying *Pacifica* to another pervasive and intrusive medium, cable television, the Court considered several provisions of a federal law regulating the broadcast of "patently offensive" sexually oriented material on cable. The Court held in *Denver Area Educational Consortium v. Federal Communications Commission* that cable operators could refuse to carry sexually explicit broadcasting. The Court again stressed the need to protect children. At the same time, the Court found unconstitutional a requirement that sexually oriented programs be confined to a single channel that could not be viewed unless the cable subscriber requested access in writing. Although concerned about the availability of such material to children, the Court felt the law could have chosen less restrictive alternatives, such as facilitating parental blockage of such channels.

In *Reno v. American Civil Liberties Union* (1996), the Court overturned a 1996 federal law, the Communications Decency Act, which attempted to protect minors by criminalizing "indecency" on the Internet. Justice John Paul Stevens's 7-2 majority opinion found that the act placed too heavy a burden on protected speech and threatened "to torch a large segment of the Internet community." The Court said the Internet is analogous to the print rather than broadcast media and therefore entitled to full First Amendment protections. The Court voiced concern that the law would threaten legitimate discussion of sexual topics posted online by the plaintiffs, for example, groups such as Stop Prisoner Rape or Critical Path AIDS Project.

Another exception to the Court's protection of profane and indecent language arises in the context of schools. The Court upheld the right of public school officials to punish a student for indecent speech. In *Bethel School District No. 403 v. Fraser* (1986), the Court found that Fraser's school assembly speech, containing no profanity but numerous sexual innuendoes, was "wholly inconsistent with the 'fundamental value' of public school education." *Bethel* exemplifies the Court's tendency to defer to school authorities and to emphasize an orderly educational process over student free speech rights.

Philip A. Dynia

Further Reading

Abraham, Henry J., and Barbara A. Perry. *Freedom and the Court*. 7th ed. New York: Oxford University Press, 1998. Comprehensive overview of the Supreme Court's approach to civil rights and liberties issues. The book's fifth chapter offers an excellent introduction to the Court's First Amendment jurisprudence and includes a thorough and balanced discussion of pornography and obscenity.

Baird, Robert M., and Stuart E. Rosenbaum. *Pornography: Private Right or Public Menace?* Buffalo, N.Y.: Prometheus Books, 1991. Collection of essays presenting a balanced overview of issues pertaining to pornography.

Clor, Harry M. *Obscenity and Public Morality*. Chicago: University of Chicago Press, 1969. Conservative treatise on the role of pornography and obscenity in modern American society.

MacKinnon, Catharine. *Only Words*. Cambridge, Mass.: Harvard University Press, 1993. Radical feminist approach to pornography by the leading advocate of the view that pornography should be regulated because it is a form of discrimination against women.

Procida, Richard, and Rita James Simon. *Global Perspectives on Social Issues: Pornography*. Boston: Lexington Books, 2003. Provides international perspective on pornography by surveying research on public opinion, pornography laws, and the production of pornography in Europe, North America, Asia, Australia, and elsewhere.

Stack, Steven, Ira Wasserman, and Roger Kern. "Adult Social Bonds and Use of Internet Pornography." *Social Science Quarterly* 85, no. 1 (2004): 75-88. Application of mainline criminological theories to issues of cyberporn.

Strossen, Nadine. *Defending Pornography*. New York: Scribner, 1995. Rebuttal to Catharine MacKinnon's argument against pornography.

See also Child abuse and molestation; Commercialized vice; Comstock Law; Cybercrime; Date rape; Pornography, child; Psychopathy; Rape and sex offenses; Sex offender registries; Sexual harassment; Victimless crimes.

Posse comitatus

Definition: Group of people pressed into service to help civilian officials enforce the law

Criminal justice issues: Law-enforcement organization; morality and public order; police powers

Significance: The *posse comitatus* concept requires able-bodied adults to assist civilian law-enforcement officials when requested to do so; under federal law, the principle specifically exempts military involvement.

Posse comitatus means "the entire power of the county" from which the sheriff can draw able-bodied adults to help quell civil disturbances. The name derives from ancient Roman times, when traveling government officials were accompanied by their retainers, a practice known as *comitatus*. The *posse comitatus* can be traced to the *jurata ad arma* of the feudal kings of England, whereby all freemen over fifteen years of age were required to own weapons and to be available for the king's defense. Eventually this civilian force became known as the *posse comitatus*, or simply posse.

The issue of who should be allowed to be in a posse has long been scrutinized. Except in extreme circumstances, the *posse comitatus* is composed of civilians under civilian authority. In English tradition, this separation of civil from military law enforcement can be traced to King John's signing of the Magna Carta in 1215. In the United States, the Posse Comitatus Act of 1878 stated that military personnel were not to be included in posses.

Passed in response to post-Civil War complaints of southerners that federal troops were being used to enforce civilian laws during Reconstruction, the Posse Comitatus Act instituted the separation between civilian forces under a civil control from martial forces under military control and proscribed the use of the military to quell civilian disturbances. Although the Navy and Marines are not specifically governed by the act, those branches of the military adhere to the act's prohibitions as a matter of policy. The Air Force was included in later amendments to the act.

The 1981 amendments to the act eroded its stand against the involvement of the military in law enforcement. These amendments, enacted in response to the increased power of drug smugglers, whose organizations and equipment rivaled those of some countries' military forces, delineated the military's role in civil law enforcement. In theory, the separation between civil and military law enforcement is still intact, but the 1981 amendments allow the military to supply civilian law-enforcement authorities with equipment, information, and facilities. They do not allow direct involvement of military personnel in civilian law enforcement.

The familiar posse of the American frontier was used to apprehend felons. Members of the community were deputized by sheriffs and federal marshals to chase rustlers and others who breached the peace. Sometimes the formation of posses led to abuses and vigilantism under the color of law, including abuses by groups such as the Ku Klux Klan. In modern times, the name "Posse Comitatus" was taken by an antitax vigilante group. This Posse Comitatus, a militant, armed survivalist group founded in the 1960's, believes in a reading of the U.S. Constitution that excludes all amendments beyond the first ten.

Paul Albert Bateman

Further Reading

Abrahams, Ray. *Vigilant Citizens: Vigilantism and the State.* Cambridge, England: Polity Press, 1998.

Neely, Richard. *Take Back Your Neighborhood: A Case for Modern-Day "Vigilantism."* New York: Penguin USA, 1990.

See also Criminal justice in U.S. history; National Guard; Outlaws of the Old West; Patriot Act; Police powers; September 11, 2001, attacks; Sheriffs; Terrorism; Vigilantism.

Powell v. Alabama

The Case: U.S. Supreme Court ruling on effective counsel

Date: Decided on November 7, 1932

Criminal justice issues: Capital punishment; defendants; juries

Significance: The Court ruled that the concept of due process requires states to provide effective counsel in capital cases when indigent defendants are unable to represent themselves.

In 1931, Ozie Powell and eight other black youths whose ages ranged from twelve to nineteen, known as the "Scottsboro boys," were tried and convicted before an all-white jury in Scottsboro, Alabama, charged with having raped two white women while traveling on a freight train. Although the Alabama constitution required the appointment of counsel for indigent defendants accused of capital crimes, no lawyer was definitely appointed to represent the defendants until the day of their trial. An atmosphere of racial hostility influenced the proceedings, and after a trial lasting one day, seven of the youths were sentenced to death, while the two youngest were transferred to the juvenile authorities. The trial attracted considerable attention, so that procommunist lawyers of the International Labor Defense volunteered to represent the young men on appeal. After the majority of the Alabama Supreme Court affirmed the convictions, the U.S. Supreme Court granted review.

The Court voted 7 to 2 to reverse the conviction and to remand the case to Alabama for a new trial. Writing for the majority, Justice George Sutherland did not speak of the Sixth Amendment, which had not yet been made applicable to the states, but rather asked whether the defendants had been denied the right of counsel, contrary to the due process clause of the Fourteenth Amendment. Sutherland noted that from the time of arraignment to the time of the trial, the defendants had not had "the aid of counsel in any real sense." The right to be heard implied the right to be heard with the assistance of counsel, for even most educated and intelligent persons would not have the training or experience to represent themselves in a criminal trial. Sutherland was impressed with "the ignorance and illiteracy of the defendants" and with the "circumstances of public hostility." In this particular case, therefore, the failure of the trial court to make "an effective appointment of counsel" was a denial of due process within the meaning of the Fourteenth Amendment.

The "Scottsboro boys case" represented transi-

tional steps in three important directions. First, the decision came very close to incorporating the right to counsel into the meaning of the Fourteenth Amendment, so that this portion of the Sixth Amendment would apply to the states. Second, it recognized that at least in capital cases, the state must provide counsel for indigents unable to defend themselves. Third, it included the provocative suggestion that the state had the obligation to provide "effective" assistance of counsel. These three issues would become increasingly important in subsequent cases.

Thomas Tandy Lewis

Further Reading

Carter, Dan T. *Scottsboro: A Tragedy of the American South*. Rev. ed. Baton Rouge: Louisiana State University Press, 1979.

Goodman, James E. *Stories of Scottsboro*. New York: Pantheon Books, 1994.

Horne, Gerald. *"Powell v. Alabama": The Scottsboro Boys and American Justice*. New York: Franklin Watts, 1997.

National Association for the Advancement of Colored People. *Guide to the Papers of the NAACP, Part 6: The Scottsboro Case, 1931-1950*. Frederick, Md.: University Publications of America, 1986.

See also *Argersinger v. Hamlin*; Counsel, right to; Death-row attorneys; Due process of law; Equal protection under the law; Incorporation doctrine; Scottsboro cases; Supreme Court, U.S.

Precedent

Definition: Court rulings that guide later court interpretations of the law

Criminal justice issues: Courts; judges; law codes

Significance: When judges see factual similarities between current cases and earlier cases, they look for rules of law on which the earlier cases were based and apply them to their present cases.

Much law is written in terms that do not lend themselves to a single, unequivocal interpreta-

Harlan Fiske Stone, chief justice of the United States from 1941 to 1946. (Collection of the Supreme Court of the United States)

tion. For example, the First Amendment to the U.S. Constitution states that "Congress shall make no law . . . abridging the freedom of speech." However, because the authors of the Bill of Rights did not anticipate the invention of radio and television, contemporary judges must decide whether electronic communications broadcasts over the airwaves are a form of "speech."

When judges confront such ambiguous situations for the first time, they apply the written Constitution according to what they consider just principles. In doing so they effectively fill in the blank spaces in the document. In that sense they are actually making constitutional law. Because judges are bound to follow established law when they make decisions, all judges in similar cases in the future must follow the precedent established in the earlier case.

Law made by legislatures—called "statutory law"—is often characterized by the same ambiguity. When the U.S. Congress passed the Sherman Anti-Trust Act of 1890, the Supreme Court had to decide whether the law's prohibition of "every contract, combination . . . or conspiracy in

restraint of trade or commerce" made union-organized strikes illegal. In *Loewe v. Lawlor* (1908) the Court said that a union strike was such an illegal restraint of trade. This decision prompted Congress to amend the antitrust law six years later to exempt union activity from its coverage.

U.S. legislators do not write laws to cover every conceivable circumstance. If judges find that there simply is no applicable statute, they must make a decision in the case on the basis of their understanding of justice. Such judge-made law is called common law and is found in judges' written decisions. Once a judge has made a common-law decision, the decision carries the force of law, and other judges must apply the principle in deciding future cases.

A precedent is binding only in the jurisdiction in which it has been decided. Thus, if a Maine court decides that an optometrist's failure to test for glaucoma constitutes negligence, that decision does not bind a Mississippi judge. When it comes to federal constitutional and statutory law, the U.S. Supreme Court's interpretations govern the entire country.

It is possible to overturn a precedent. Common law can be overruled by a statute. A court's interpretation of a statute may be overruled by a subsequent statute. A court may overrule itself but rarely does so. A precedent may or may not be a good law, but as former U.S. Supreme Court Justice Harlan Fiske Stone said, "It is often more important that a rule of law be settled than that it be settled right."

William H. Coogan

Further Reading

Amar, Akhil Reed. *The Constitution and Criminal Procedure: First Principles*. New Haven, Conn.: Yale University Press, 1997.

Meyer, J. F., and D. R. Grant. *The Courts in Our Criminal Justice System*. Upper Saddle River, N.J.: Prentice-Hall, 2003.

Neubauer, D. W. *America's Courts and the Criminal Justice System*. 7th ed. Belmont, Calif.: Wadsworth, 2002.

See also Annotated codes; Case law; Common law; Constitution, U.S.; Jurisdiction of courts; Opinions; *Stare decisis*; Statutes.

Preliminary hearings

Definition: Proceedings held to determine whether a crime has been committed and whether the accused should be tried

Criminal justice issues: Arrest and arraignment; trial procedures

Significance: In this phase of the judicial process, the prosecutor attempts to present enough evidence to demonstrate the accused's probable guilt. The judge must then decide whether to proceed toward trial.

In the judicial process, if there is enough evidence to prove that the accused has committed a felony, the next step is the preliminary hearing. At the hearing, the prosecutor must determine whether there is sufficient evidence, known as probable cause, that a crime has occurred and that the accused has committed that crime. A preliminary hearing is scheduled after the prosecutor has filed a criminal complaint. The preliminary hearing is sometimes known as an evidentiary hearing.

Preliminary hearings must take place within a specified amount of time, usually within a few days after charges are placed and an arraignment is held. Defendants can waive the preliminary hearing and are sometimes advised to do so by their counsel.

During the preliminary hearing, the prosecutor presents only the amount of evidence necessary to demonstrate probable guilt. If the presiding judge determines that there is probable cause, the case will proceed to the next phase. In some states, this next phase may be a grand jury hearing, and in others it may be the trial. If the presiding judge determines that there is insufficient evidence to indict the accused, the charges are dropped. The prosecution may next choose to take the evidence to the grand jury.

Kimberley M. Holloway

Further Reading

Garner, Bryan A., ed. *Black's Law Dictionary*. 8th ed. St. Paul, Minn.: Thomson/West, 2004.

Glannon, Joseph W. *Civil Procedure: Examples and Explanations*. 4th ed. Aspen: Aspen Law and Business, 2001.

See also Arraignment; Criminal procedure; District attorneys; Due process of law; Grand juries; Hearings; Indictment; Information; Inquests; Presumption of innocence; Testimony.

Presentence investigations

Definition: Reports drafted by probation officer or court officials that detail significant information that may be used in sentencing a defendant

Criminal justice issues: Investigation; probation and pretrial release; sentencing

Significance: Presentence investigation reports are essential to ensuring that all circumstances are taken into account in the formulation of just sentences.

Before defendants are sentenced for crimes in most criminal courts, judicial officers—most frequently probation officers—are asked to complete presentence investigations. These written reports offer information about the defendants that may assist the court in determining appropriate sentences. Factors such as the defendants' criminal histories, their educational and employment backgrounds, and their medical and psychological histories are all taken into account. These reports are not intended as entire life histories; it is important that reports be succinct and not burden courts with extraneous information.

In addition to the reports, statements of the defendants, which may show either mitigating circumstances in the commission of the offenses or remorse on the part of the defendants, may play a role. The rights of victims are also addressed to some extent by the inclusion of statements assessing the impact of the crimes on the victims and the possibilities of restitution.

Numerous options are available for sentencing, and specific recommendations are frequently made by the judicial officers. For example, probation may be granted if offenders demonstrate the capability of living crime-free lives and have not broken laws that mandate incarceration or other punishments. Alternatively, fines may be imposed. If incarceration occurs, presentence investigations may influence the classification of the correctional settings for the defendants. Options such as community release may be affected by the defendants' histories in particular settings. Also, some individuals may have had previous experiences in certain programs that had either positive or negative effects on their behavior.

Although characteristics of offenders play a role in the sentencing process, some offenses do not offer substantial flexibility in the actual sentences conveyed. Mandatory sentencing guidelines sometimes take precedence over mitigating circumstances or offender characteristics.

John C. Kilburn, Jr.

Further Reading

The Presentence Investigation. Washington, D.C.: Division of Probation, Administrative Office of U.S. Courts, 1984.

Stith, Kate, and Jose A. Cabranes. *Fear of Judging: Sentencing Guidelines in the Federal Courts.* Chicago: University of Chicago Press, 1998.

Tonry, Michael. *Reconsidering Indeterminate and Structured Sentencing.* Washington, D.C.: U.S. Department of Justice, Office of Justice Programs, National Institute of Justice, 1999.

See also Convictions; Discretion; Judges; Pleas; Punishment; Sentencing; Verdicts; Victim and Witness Prosecution Act of 1982.

President, U.S.

Definition: Chief of state of the federal government

Criminal justice issue: Political issues

Significance: As the top elected government official in the United States, the president of the country is the commander in chief of all U.S. armed forces and plays a pivotal role in criminal justice, from the appointment of Justice Department officers and federal judges to signing congressional legislation.

As the chief of state and commander in chief of the United States, the president has many responsibilities that relate to criminal justice. For example, as the leader of the executive branch of the government, the president appoints the secretary of justice and other top Justice Department officials and is ultimately responsible for the enforcement of federal law. The president also appoints federal judges, including the justices of the U.S. Supreme Court. The president shares responsibility with Congress for the federal prison population.

Under the American system of checks and balances, the president must work closely with the legislative branch, whose Senate confirms presidential appointments. The president, in turn, endorses congressional legislation by signing laws and has the power of veto over new legislation. The president may also send legislative initiatives to Congress for consideration. A major part of the president's role in criminal justice is symbolic; the legislation that a president proposes and a president's responses to congressional initiatives can influence public attitudes toward criminal justice and help or hinder public support of law enforcement and other parts of the criminal justice system.

A major example of the role a president can play in criminal justice occurred in 1965, when President Lyndon B. Johnson appointed the first President's Commission on Law Enforcement and Administration of Justice. The commission was charged with undertaking a comprehensive review of the criminal justice system and proposing strategies for its betterment. The commission issued recommendations for reform in structure, selection, training, coordination of services, and overall management practices. That commission's finding led to the creation of the Law Enforcement Assistance Administration and the Safe Streets and Crime Control Act of 1968, which provided funding for state and local efforts aimed at the control of criminal activity. Federal support of local law enforcement rose to an even higher level in 1994, when President Bill Clinton signed the Violent Crime Control and Law Enforcement Act, which provided billions of dollars in funding for crime prevention strategies, building prisons, and hiring of police officers and prison guards.

Among the many roles that presidents play in the U.S. criminal justice system is approving congressional legislation and signing it into law. Here, President Bill Clinton signs the Child Abuse Protection and Enforcement Act in the White House on March 10, 2000, as people who were involved in the bill's creation look on. *(AP/Wide World Photos)*

The September 11, 2001, terrorist attacks on the United States prompted the most extensive restructuring of the federal government in more than fifty years. Under the direction of President George W. Bush, the Department of Homeland Security was created to consolidate twenty-two separate agencies into one cabinet-level department to improve protection against future terrorist attacks. For the first time in history, the investigation of terrorist activity became the main priority of all law-enforcement entities. Bush also signed the Patriot Act to furnish law enforcement with the necessary tools to combat terrorism while affording judges heightened levels of power to impose more stringent sentences.

Lisa Landis Murphy

Further Reading

Andrew, C. *For the President's Eyes Only: Secret Intelligence and the American Presidency from Washington to Bush*. New York: Perennial, 1996.

Genovese, Michael. *The Power of the American Presidency, 1789-2000*. New York: Oxford University Press, 2000.

Smith, Norris, and Lynn M. Messina. *Homeland Security*. New York: H. W. Wilson, 2004.

See also Homeland Security Department; National Commission on the Causes and Prevention of Violence; Omnibus Crime Control and Safe Streets Act of 1968; Pardons; President's Commission on Law Enforcement and Administration of Justice; Secret Service, U.S.; Teapot Dome scandal; Warren Commission; Watergate scandal.

President's Commission on Law Enforcement and Administration of Justice

Identification: Federal commission established to study sequences of events in the criminal justice system

Date: Established on July 23, 1965

Criminal justice issues: Law-enforcement organization; professional standards; trial procedures

Significance: The president's commission examined the apparatus of the American system of justice from the perspective of balancing crime reduction against protection of constitutional rights.

On July 23, 1965, President Lyndon B. Johnson established the Commission on Law Enforcement and Administration of Justice through Executive Order 11236. The body was charged with examining the nature of crime and juvenile delinquency in the United States. In 1967, the commission issued its official report, *The Challenge of Crime in a Free Society*. The report detailed the commission's findings and offered a criminal justice system diagram tracing the sequence of events through the apparatus of the criminal justice system: from prosecution, and the courts, to corrections.

To understand the breadth and depth of the American system of justice, commission members worked closely with the Federal Bureau of Investigation; the U.S. Bureau of Prisons; the Department of Health, Education, and Welfare; and state, local, and private entities involved in criminal justice.

While undertaking its work, the commission documented hundreds of recommendations. Among these were recommendations for organizing and expanding research of criminal justice agencies, advancing science and technology in the administration of justice, increasing the education and standards of criminal justice personnel, exploring community-based correctional alternatives for offenders, and developing a coordinated and cooperative crime prevention strategy on federal, state, and local levels. The commission's recommendations also extended to family life quality, housing and economic conditions, alcohol and narcotic addictions treatment, school system standards, and neighborhood cohesiveness and efficacy.

In its summary conclusions, the commission regarded crime as a social problem, requiring more than specialists literate in the criminal justice process for its solution. The commission suggested that the foundation for effective crime control is the "business of every American" and every American institution—religious, community, professional, business, and collegiate.

Anthony J. Luongo III

Further Reading

Federal Bureau of Investigation. Crime in the United States (1960-2003 annual reports). Washington, D.C.: U.S. Department of Justice.

U.S. Department of Justice. *The Challenge of Crime in a Free Society: Looking Back Looking Forward*. Washington, D.C.: Office of Justice Programs, 1998.

See also Bureau of Justice Statistics; Criminal justice system; Federal Bureau of Investigation; Judicial system, U.S.; Law enforcement; National Institute of Justice; Omnibus Crime Control and Safe Streets Act of 1968; President, U.S.; Uniform Crime Reports; Wickersham Commission; Wiretaps.

Presumption of innocence

Definition: Principle of justice holding that a person is innocent until proven guilty

Criminal justice issues: Defendants; pleas; probation and pretrial release

Significance: A fundamental tenet of the American system of justice, the presumption of innocence places the burden of proof in criminal trials upon the prosecution.

It is a violation of basic law for people to be punished unless they have been convicted of crimes in courts of law. The greatest restraint that can

---

A Film About the Presumption of Guilt

Director Steven Spielberg's *Minority Report* (2002) is a futuristic film set in the year 2054, when Washington, D.C., boasts a pilot "pre-crime" program that may soon be launched on a national basis. In this program, three individuals with precognitive abilities help the police identify perpetrators of violent crimes before they actually commit the crimes. The not-yet-offenders are then sentenced—without the benefit of trials—to incarceration in states of suspended animation. As might be expected, the supposedly foolproof system turns out to be not so foolproof at all: The innocent are judged for crimes they will not commit, and the guilty, at least those with the know-how, can get away with murder. The film makes an important contribution to the understanding of criminal justice by reminding viewers that even the best-intended law-enforcement schemes make mistakes. This is why trials are important.

Timothy L. Hall

---

be placed on an accused individual before conviction is the restraint considered necessary to ensure that the person shows up for trial. A judge sets bail based on the probability that the person will appear for trial. If the judge believes that the accused person will attend the trial, there is often no bail or bail is set at a reasonable level. If the judge concludes that an accused person is likely to flee if released on bail, regardless of the amount, that accused person might be held without bail.

The accused person must be indicted by a grand jury, held for trial as a result of a preliminary hearing, or sometimes both. The grand jury is always a secret proceeding, while the preliminary hearing may be secret. The purpose of secrecy is to prevent the state from publicly claiming that a person has committed a crime unless a panel of citizens or a judge first declares that this is possible.

Preferably at the time of arrest, accused persons must be informed of the exact charges against them. The proceeding at which charges are specified is known as an arraignment. Arraignments serve four purposes: to notify the accused persons of the exact charges against them, to notify the accused persons of their rights, to set bail, and to accept pleas. If a case goes to trial, accused persons are entitled to have trials before

juries or judges, whichever the accused prefer.

The judicial body must begin the trial by making the case against the accused, or defendant. The accused is entitled to know all or most of the evidence before the trial begins. If the prosecution fails during trial to make any important point required by law, the defendant cannot be convicted of the crime to which the point is relevant. Only when and if the prosecution has established a case must the accused respond to that case.

If the accused in a criminal trial raises a reasonable doubt in the mind of the judge or jury hearing the case, the judge or jury must find the accused innocent. The criterion is not beyond a shadow of a doubt but beyond a reasonable doubt—a doubt based on the sound thinking of the judge or jury.

It is against the law to arrest a person and hold that person for trial unless the arresting agency genuinely believes that the person committed the crime in question. One should not be surprised that the police or prosecutors behave as if accused persons are guilty—it would be against the law for them to arrest persons if they do not believe in their guilt. However, unless there is a conviction, the defendant is supposed to be considered innocent and is not supposed to be punished.

Dwight Jensen

Further Reading
Pellicciotti, Joseph M. *Handbook of Basic Trial Evidence: A College Introduction*. Bristol, Ind.: Wyndham Hall Press, 1992.
Stopp, Margaret T. *Evidence Law in the Trial Process*. Albany, N.Y.: West/Delmar, 1999.

See also Arrest; Bail system; Convictions; Criminal law; Criminal prosecution; Defendants; Jury system; Miscarriage of justice; Pleas; Preventive detention; Reasonable doubt; Standards of proof.

Preventive detention

Definition: Confinement of a criminal defendant before final conviction and sentencing

Criminal justice issues: Defendants; probation and pretrial release; sentencing

Significance: Federal and state statutes permit preconviction detention upon finding that the accused is likely to flee or is a threat to the safety of the community.

Under the English system at the time of the American Revolution, some criminal defendants were released on bail while those accused of the most serious felony offenses, especially crimes subject to capital punishment, were detained pending trial. Although some legal writers suggest that this pretrial detention was to protect the community from the dangerous propensities of the accused, case law indicates that detention was to make sure the defendant was present at trial. Current American practice, which evolved from English law, allows defendants to remain free on bail or on personal recognizance except in capital offenses with abundant evidence of guilt, when the defendant is likely to flee, or when the accused poses a danger to the community or to witnesses.

Preventive detention statutes call into question three important principles of American law: the presumption of innocence, the right to due process, and the prohibition against excessive bail. Indispensable to the American criminal justice system is the proposition that one who is accused of a crime is presumed innocent until proven guilty. Opponents of preventive detention contend that an accused person has no less of a right to freedom than any other member of society and that the only proper basis for preconviction confinement is the risk of flight. Nevertheless, other grounds for detention are recognized by federal and state law.

The Fifth Amendment prohibits the deprivation "of life, liberty, or property, without due process of law." However, due process is satisfied by a hearing before a judicial officer in which the person to be detained has the right to be present and to contest the evidence favoring detention. The mandate of the Eighth Amendment, that "excessive bail shall not be required," is also frequently cited by those who condemn preventive detention. They argue that this implies a right to be released on bail in all cases, except perhaps capital cases for which bail was not available under English common law. The courts, however, have consistently held that this amendment only limits the discretion of judges to set high bail in cases for which Congress or a state legislative body has authorized that bail be granted. The right to bail is fundamental but not absolute. It is not a constitutional violation to provide bail in some cases and deny it in others. The requirement is only that courts must act reasonably and conform to the Constitution and statutes.

The Bail Reform Act gives judicial officers the discretion to detain defendants in federal criminal cases upon finding that no condition or combination of conditions will reasonably assure the appearance of the accused to stand trial or protect the safety of others in the community. Preventive detention may be ordered for those accused of crimes of violence, of offenses which may be punishable by life imprisonment or death, or of certain drug-related offenses. It also may be ordered for defendants with two or more previous felony convictions, for those who pose a serious risk of flight, and for those whom the court finds will obstruct justice or intimidate witnesses or jurors.

State courts also have the power to deny bail in order to assure the presence of the accused at trial and to protect the community unless such powers are limited by the Constitution or by statute. Typical statutes permit criminal defendants to be released on bail except in capital cases where the facts are evident or the presumption of guilt is great. Some statutes also allow preventive detention for felony offenses involving acts of violence in which guilt is obvious or when the defendant would be likely to harm another if released.

Scot Clifford

Further Reading

Flemming, Roy B. *Punishment Before Trial: An Organizational Perspective of Felony Bail Processes*. New York: Longman, 1982.

Garcia, Alfredo. *The Fifth Amendment: A Comprehensive Approach*. Westport, Conn.: Greenwood Press, 2002.

Shaughnessy, Edward J. *Bail and Preventive Detention in New York*. Washington, D.C.: University Press of America, 1982.

Singer, Richard G. *Criminal Procedure II: From Bail to Jail*. New York: Aspen, 2005.

See also Arrest; Bail system; Criminal justice system; Criminal procedure; Discretion; Due process of law; Mexican criminal justice system; Presumption of innocence; Prison and jail systems; *Schall v. Martin*.

Principals (criminal)

Definition: Primary perpetrators of crimes in criminal cases

Criminal justice issues: Defendants; legal terms and principles

Significance: The practical distinction between principals and accomplices and accessories to crimes has minimal significance in the modern U.S. justice system.

Under the common law, people who acted together to commit a crime were distinguished as either principals or accessories. Principals were the main actors who participated in an actual offense while accessories were people who aided the principal either before or after the commission of the offense. An example of this would be a principal who plans to rob a bank but who needs a vehicle and firearms to effectuate the robbery.

A person who supplies the principal with the firearms and the vehicle, knowing of and agreeing to the criminal purpose, would be an accessory before the fact under the common law. A person who met with the principal after the robbery in order to assist in the concealment of money and evidence would be an accessory after the fact. The principal is the person who actually commits the robbery or anyone who is actually or constructively present who aids in the commission of the robbery.

These distinctions have for the most part been rendered moot by modern statutes which generally provide that all persons who participate in a criminal venture may be prosecuted as principals. Thus, a person who advises or encourages another in the commission of an offense may be found guilty as a principal even if that person is too far away from the actual scene of the crime to aid in its actual commission. An example of this would be a person who sets up a sale of narcotics by introducing a seller and a buyer by way of a telephone call. Even if not present at the actual exchange, that person could be prosecuted as a principal under a statue prohibiting the distribution of narcotics. In some states, these secondary actors are prosecuted and punished as principals under conspiracy statutes.

Most modern statutes that abolish the practical distinctions between principals and accessories do so by stating that people are guilty of criminal offenses that they commit themselves or that are committed by the conduct of other persons for whom they are legally accountable. Such statutes define accomplices as a class of persons who are legally accountable for the conduct of others—that is, principals. Under such statutes, accomplices may be held liable as principals even if the primary actor has not been prosecuted or convicted. An accomplice may be charged as a principal if there is proof that the crime was committed and that the accomplice acted in furtherance of the crime. This is true even if the person who is claimed to have actually committed the offense is acquitted. Similarly, accomplices may be prosecuted as principals even if they would ordinarily be considered legally incapable of committing the offense.

Michele Leavitt

See also Accomplices and accessories; Acquittal; Common law; Conspiracy; Criminal intent; Criminal law; Criminal prosecution; Misdemeanors.

Print media

Definition: Coverage of criminal justice in newspapers and news magazines

Criminal justice issue: Media

Significance: Because the print media are responsible for conveying much of the information on crime and criminal justice that the public receives, they play a significant role in helping to form public opinion on criminal justice issues. Understanding the reasons for media distortions can provide greater understanding of the relationship between media and public perception of crime.

In the twentieth century world of proliferating electronic communication, the American print media remain a booming industry. The advent of the Internet has actually increased public access to print media resources, and the print media and local and national network news sources remain important sources of information for the general public. However, the public draws on the print media's heavy coverage of crime and criminals to form its opinions, and these media often present biased views. Scholars have presented a variety of perspectives and theories concerning the processes that are at work that lead to such media distortion.

Distortions in the News

One aspect of print media coverage that has garnered attention from researchers is the issue of prevalence of crime that appears in print. To examine this issue, researchers generally use a research method known as content analysis to examine how much coverage of crime actually appears in newspapers. Studies of media content have reported that crime news represents between 4 and 28 percent of all newspaper news coverage. Some studies have placed the figure as high as 50 percent.

While it is generally well known that issues of crime and justice are popular topics in media coverage, it is not as well known how accurate this coverage is. Researchers have found that in many ways, the images of crime presented by the mass media in general, and the print media in particular, tend to distort the realities of crime, particularly in the disproportionate attention they pay to violent crime. For example, an analysis of New Orleans newspapers found that murder and robbery cases accounted for 45 percent of news items while only accounting for 12 percent of actual crimes in the region covered. Another study found that 55 percent of the stories in Canadian newspapers concerned violent offenses, whereas violent offenses represented only 6 percent of actual crimes. Another study, in 1991, found that

for every two studies in the media on property crime, there were eight stories about violent crime, although property crimes outnumbered violent crimes nine to one.

Research has also suggested that changes in print media crime coverage do not necessarily reflect changes in actual local crime rates. A study made as early as 1951 found no correlations between newspaper coverage of crime and local crime rates. A study found that imbalanced crime coverage still persisted. Moreover, even as violent crime rates were declining in society, television and newspaper coverage of crime was increasing by more than 400 percent.

The Impact of Distortions on Society

There are also other, and more subtle, ways in which the print media can distort the realities of crime, such as by giving disproportionate coverage to certain types of victims, offenders, or social circumstances. For example, the print media tend to focus more attention and resources on crimes involving female victims, young victims, elderly victims, white victims, and affluent victims. At the same time, the print media emphasize cases involving offenders who are members of minority groups.

An example of skewed attention to social circumstances and contexts is the print media's emphasis on crimes involving offenses committed by strangers on local victims, while simultaneously downplaying offenses that committed by acquaintances and relatives of victims. Crimes involving multiple offenders consistently receive intensive coverage. The media also foster distorted notions about causes behind crimes by focusing on individual explanations and emphasizing crimes with unusual motives that do not match the typical patterns of the same offenses.

Media distortion of crime images potentially affects public opinion of crime and criminal justice issues. Researchers have found that people who pay the attention to entertainment and news media depictions of crime tend to hold more negative views of society. Similarly, people who consume more media news coverage are more likely to hold exaggerated views of the amount and seriousness of crime in society. They also are more likely to fear crime and support the idea of retribution. Moreover, people who consume the most media news are more likely to have negative attitudes toward African Americans and other minorities.

It is clear that news media coverage of crime can have a negative impact on social policy. This can be seen in the tendency of politicians and legislative bodies to justify "get tough" stances on criminal justice issues by citing public opinion, much of which is formed by distorted news coverage of crime.

Theories of Mass Media Behavior

Media scholar Gregg Barak has developed a theory of mass media coverage of crime that acknowledges the importance of power and interests in determining media behavior but sees power as broadly distributed. Instead of arguing for the existence of a monolithic source of power—such as the elites who own mass media outlets—as Marxist and radical media theories do, Barak sees power as more evenly dispersed among competing sources. Barak calls this "newsmaking criminology." His view holds that diverse social institutions, including the media, special inter-

est groups, politicians, government officials, and private interests, all have power in society and all compete for the ability to shape public perception about a particular issue, such as crime. Therefore, the mass media behavior can be influenced by outside sources competing to shape public perceptions about crime. This view sees the media as conduits of information that act as middlemen to convey information to the public. Media treatment of crime is thus governed by the daily activities of the politicians, government officials, and interest groups on which the mass media subsequently report. The activities of these interest groups serve as constraints on the daily activities of journalists as they convey and report crime information to the public.

Barak's newsmaking criminology perspective also suggests that mass media reporting practices are governed by the interests of news organizations—and one overriding interest of such organizations is producing news that sells. Decisions of editors and journalists therefore reflect their interpretations of what the public wants to know about. The general assumption is that the public wants to know a great deal about crime, particularly violent crime. This view has given rise to a journalistic adage, "If it bleeds, it leads," in media coverage. The print media achieve success by selling more newspapers and magazines and increasing their advertising revenue. The broadcast media succeed by boosting their audience ratings and increasing their advertising ratings.

Another issue that news organizations consider in decisions about their news coverage is the degree to which readers can identify with stories. There is evidence suggesting that news editors and journalists make these judgments about the news items that they produce. Milwaukee journalists who were the subject of a 1997 research study confirmed this view by openly acknowledging that when they wrote stories they considered the types of people who were most likely to read

Headlines trumpeting sensational crime stories help to sell newspapers, and the print media are always quick to respond to developing events. Here, several women hold copies of a special edition of a Northern California newspaper reporting the conviction of Scott Peterson in November, 2004. Peterson's trial for the murder of his pregnant wife was one of the most closely watched criminal trials of 2004. *(AP/Wide World Photos)* them. One reporter explained, "If the reader could say 'that could have been me that was killed,' then that has more news value."

The Use of News Themes by Media

News organizations occasionally pursue interests that influence their news decisions that may have little or nothing to do with the type of information presented. These other interests typically have more to do with the gathering and synthesizing of information for presentation to the public. For example, a 1978 study found that a "crime wave" of offenses against elderly New York City residents reported in the media had nothing to do with actual increases in such crimes. The apparent "crime wave" perceived by citizens and politicians was nothing more than the continued and heavy coverage of numerous occurrences of crime that were being covered by the media as a single topic. The manner in which the media organized the news gave the public the false impression that a crime wave against the elderly was developing.

From that New York incident, a sociologist developed a theory of how media distortions can result from the ways that the media organize their news. The research coined the term "news theme" for methods of organizing and unifying massive amounts of potential news items into a single thematic framework to give them structure and reduce confusion. The practical implication of that study was that media news emphases are sometimes determined by decisions to link individual items thematically to other events occurring around the same times.

To illustrate how the generation of news themes work, the 1978 study summarized an actual package of news stories that included these segments:

✓ Police apprehend juveniles who mugged an elderly couple in Queens
✓ Police and citizens in Queens meet to discuss crimes against the elderly
✓ Feature segment on Senior Citizens Robbery Unit
✓ Police seize guns and drugs that intended for warring gangs
✓ Two members of a youth gang are arrested for robbery at knifepoint

✓ An ROTC cadet is arrested in the stabbing death of another cadet
✓ A city audit finds that police have been mishandling funds
✓ The city and the police union are working on a contract at the same time that laid-off firemen and subway cops are being rehired

This package of news items is strongly suggestive of a broader news theme of crime in general, as every item in the list covers an aspect of crime or criminal justice. However, within this broader theme, subthemes are evident as well. For example, the lists highlights crimes against the elderly, crimes committed by juveniles, and issues concerning the city police department. It seems unlikely that stories about the senior citizens robbery unit and the meeting to discuss crime against the elderly would normally be deemed newsworthy, if not for the more dramatic story about the mugging of an elderly citizen. By presenting the three stories together, the media conveyed the appearance that crime against the elderly was a serious problem that was receiving much attention by the police, even though the stories were about unrelated events.

Informational Constraints

An additional aspect of news processing that can influence print media behavior is information limitations. News media organizations rely heavily on information that is obtained and filtered by official agencies, including the police and the courts. The amount of coverage that the media can give to stories is often limited by the amount of information they receive from those agencies. Furthermore, official agencies have different types of motives that can determine the amount of information that is released to the media. These motives can include case-management objectives, attempts to prevent organizational liability, and police attempts to legitimize their work to the public.

Mass media behavior, including the behavior of print media organizations in generating news, therefore, can be explained by considering both cultural influences and organizational influences. Cultural influences affect news organizations by providing the organization with an implicit script to follow outlining the types of news items that are considered culturally interesting, stimulating, and acceptable for news coverage. Organizational factors regarding media process in the generation of news also place considerable limitations on news organizations both in terms of how information is thematically presented, and in terms of the availability of information.

Kevin G. Buckler

Further Reading

Barak, Greg. *Media, Process, and the Social Construction of Crime: Studies in Newsmaking Criminology*. New York: Garland Publishing, 1994. Collection of eleven essays that examine various aspects of the newsmaking criminology framework. The collection includes two separate content analyses of crime appearing in newspaper coverage, as well as essays that examine the meaning and usefulness of the newsmaking criminology framework.

Chermak, Steven M. *Victims in the News: Crime and the American News Media*. Boulder, Colo.: Westview Press, 1995. Examination of the role of victims in the coverage of crime news. The central contention of the work is that victim characteristics determine how the media cover crime in the United States.

Lipschultz, Jeremy H., and Michael L. Hilt. *Crime and Local TV News: Dramatic, Breaking, and Live from the Scene*. Mahwah, N.J.: Lawrence Erlbaum Associates, 2002. Although not specifically addressing the print media, this analysis of local television news emphasizes theories of market-driven journalism and lack of interest in public affairs coverage as factors explaining media emphasis on crime.

Potter, Gary W., and Victor E. Kappeler, eds. *Constructing Crime: Perspectives on Making News and Social Problems*. Prospect Heights, Ill.: Waveland Press, 1998. Collection of fifteen essays examining media and crime. The essays examine how popular images of crime are generated, the effects of these images, and who benefits from the images that are constructed.

Prichard, D., and K. D. Hughes. "Patterns of Deviance in Crime News." *Journal of Communication* 47, no. 3 (1997): 49-67. Examination of media coverage of homicide in Milwaukee, Wisconsin, that considers four forms of deviance: statistical deviance, cultural deviance, normative deviance, and status deviance. This study provides an exceptional demonstration of how crime-related and media-related variables are measured in media research.

Surette, Ray. *Media, Crime, and Criminal Justice*. 2d ed. Pacific Grove, Calif.: Brooks/Cole Publishing, 1998. Arguably the definitive work on media and criminal justice issues, this book explores media treatments of crime and offers extensive discussions of relevant Supreme Court decisions and summaries of research on media and crime issues.

Wykes, Maggie. *News, Crime, and Culture*. Sterling, Va.: Pluto Press, 2001. Explores the links between culture, crime, and the social control of crime by emphasizing perspectives concerning how and why crime is defined. Special attention is given to how news reporting reinforces popular notions about class, race, gender, and poverty.

See also Criminals; Films and criminal justice; Gag orders; Literature about criminal justice; News source protection; Radio broadcasting; Television crime dramas; Television news; Television police reality shows; Trial publicity.

Prison and jail systems

Definition: Government facilities that hold individuals suspected of, or convicted of, committing crimes

Criminal justice issues: Prisons; punishment; rehabilitation

Significance: Prison and jail systems make up the corrections arm of the criminal justice system. For many offenders, arrival in these systems signals the last step in the criminal justice process.

In American society, confinement is used for punishing individuals who have broken the law. Corporal punishment (flogging, stocks and pillory, and so on) was replaced by confinement, or incarceration, because the latter was considered to be more humane. It is not exactly known when the use of confinement for punishment began, but this method became dominant in the United States near the end of the eighteenth century. There are two types of systems that incarcerate offenders: prison and jail systems. Although there are many differences, prison and jail systems often are distinguished based on the offenders' length of sentences. Prisons, also known as correctional facilities or penitentiaries, are institutions that house offenders serving a sentence longer than one year. Jails are systems for temporary confinement and house individuals at different stages in the criminal justice process, including offenders serving sentences of less than one year.

History of the Modern Prison

In ancient times, confinement was used to hold offenders until trial or until a sentence (some form of corporal punishment) was delivered. The beginning of the modern prison can be found in sixteenth century Britain. Although corporal punishment or banishment was the preferred method of punishment, houses of correction were built in which offenders charged with minor crimes lived and had to work under guard supervision to repay the debt. Workhouses were similar but were used to house the poor, who also had to work under guard supervision. In addition, jails were developed to detain suspects until trial.

Criminal justice reformers in Britain incited the movement toward the use of prisons for punishment as alternatives to the brutality of corporal punishment. These reformers argued that the punishment should be proportional to the offense, or in other words, the punishment must fit the crime. Also, the reformers protested the appalling conditions in the jails, workhouses, and ships, where prisoners awaiting banishment to Australia were forced to live in the hulks of ships that never left the dock. The demise of the use of corporal punishment was set in motion by the reformers, and prisons were built. However, the conditions in the early prisons were deplorable because of rampant disease, filth, and overcrowding.

Prisons did not exist in Britain's American colonies originally. Jails primarily were used to hold debtors or confine offenders until the trial or sentence of punishment. The early jails in the colonies were similar to their British counterparts as overcrowded depositories for disease. Replacing corporal punishment with confinement was an idea first postulated by William Penn, a Quaker. The founder of Pennsylvania argued that offenders should be punished by using confinement. Penn passed the Great Law of 1692, which abolished corporal punishment, except in the case of murder, and mandated the building of prisons. A visionary, Penn established prisons nearly a century earlier than Britain and the other U.S. colonies. However, the Great Law was repealed one day after his death in 1718.

After the American Revolution

Corporal punishment continued to be the primary method of punishment through the American Revolution. The Constitution and the Bill of Rights, developed as a guide for the newly independent states, included many protections for individuals suspected of crimes. The emphasis on protection from the abuses of government was influenced by the abuses the colonists had suffered under Britain's rule. The concept of the penitentiary, based on the work of William Penn, was developed and implemented by the Quakers in Pennsylvania. These penitentiaries would allow the offenders the time and solitude to repent for the crimes, to pay penance through manual labor, and to reform. The first prison under this new system was the Walnut Street Jail, opened in Philadelphia in 1790. The Walnut Street Jail served as a model for the prisons built in Pennsylvania in the 1820's.

By 1830, Western Penitentiary was opened in Pittsburgh and Eastern Penitentiary in Philadelphia. These prisons followed the philosophy of the Quakers' penitentiary and were referred to as the Pennsylvania system or the separate system. A similar system, minus the complete isolation of the inmates, was employed in the Auburn prison opened in New York in 1817. The slightly different system became known as the Auburn system, the New York system, or the congregate system. Both types of systems operated under the assumption that crime was a result of problems in the external environment.

Eventually, the Pennsylvania system was abandoned because of multiple factors, including the financial burden of operating a prison in which inmates were individually celled. The Auburn system became the model for the American penitentiary until after the Civil War. A large prison reform movement protesting the squalid prison conditions gained momentum after the war. In part because of the prison reform movement, a prison emphasizing rehabilitation was opened in Elmira, New York, during the late 1870's. The Elmira Reformatory adopted indeterminate sentencing practices whereby prison officials could determine how much of a sentence the inmate served by using reward systems for good behavior and work or educational achievements.

The Elmira model, or reformatory model, gained popularity, and by the 1920's nearly every state had adopted the system. The focus on rehabilitation continued, and new treatment programs continued to be implemented in American prisons until after World War II. By the 1950's, the number of prisoners was increasing, and the prison system experienced a wave of riots, thought to be caused by deplorable prison condi-

tions. During the 1960's and 1970's, several landmark Supreme Court and federal court cases passed legislation that allowed certain prisoner rights and mandated improved prison conditions.

The 1970's sparked a shift in penal philosophy from an emphasis on rehabilitation to one on deterrence and incapacitation. Indeterminate sentencing was replaced with determinate sentencing systems in which the parole boards could no longer release an inmate before the sentence expired. The shift in philosophy was influenced by published research studies claiming that not one of the rehabilitation programs in place in U.S. prisons actually reduced recidivism or crime rates.

The shift from rehabilitation to deterrence and incapacitation marked the "get tough on crime" era that began during the 1970's and continued through the end of the twentieth century. The in-

California governor Arnold Schwarzenegger (right) inspecting his state's Mule Creek State Prison in August, 2004. Afterward, Schwarzenegger called for massive reforms of the state's correctional system, the nation's largest. (AP/Wide World Photos)

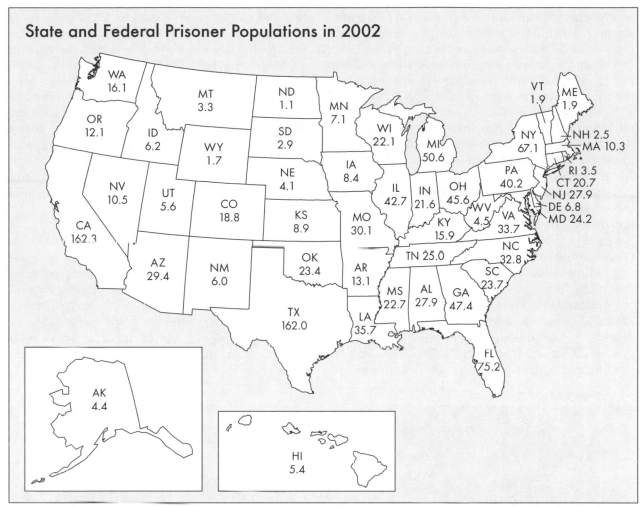

State and Federal Prisoner Populations in 2002

State	Value
WA	16.1
MT	3.3
ND	1.1
MN	7.1
VT	1.9
ME	1.9
OR	12.1
ID	6.2
WY	1.7
SD	2.9
WI	22.1
MI	50.6
NY	67.1
NH	2.5
MA	10.3
NV	10.5
UT	5.6
NE	4.1
IA	8.4
IL	42.7
IN	21.6
OH	45.6
PA	40.2
RI	3.5
CT	20.7
NJ	27.9
CA	162.3
CO	18.8
KS	8.9
MO	30.1
WV	4.5
KY	15.9
VA	33.7
DE	6.8
MD	24.2
AZ	29.4
NM	6.0
OK	23.4
AR	13.1
TN	25.0
NC	32.8
SC	23.7
MS	22.7
AL	27.9
GA	47.4
TX	162.0
LA	35.7
FL	75.2
AK	4.4
HI	5.4

Source: U.S. Bureau of Justice Statistics, *Prisoners in 2002.* Figures represent total state and federal prison population for each state. Numbers are 1000's.

crease in availability of crack cocaine in the 1980's ensured that a continual supply of drug offenders filtered into the prison system through sentencing reforms resulting from the so-called war on drugs. These reforms included mandatory minimums for possession of certain amounts of drugs, "truth-in-sentencing" laws that forced offenders to serve the full sentence, and "three-strikes" laws that gave life sentences to inmates receiving convictions for a third felony. The impact on the prison system was profound, resulting in overcrowded conditions and millions of dollars toward new prison construction as more prisoners were incarcerated and for longer periods of time.

State Prison Systems

Currently, all fifty states operate prison systems. Operation and oversight of the state prisons falls under the state Department of Corrections. The two goals of prison systems are custody and treatment. The custody function serves to keep the inmate incarcerated so that inmates, staff, and society are safe. Vocational training, educational programs, and counseling and drug abuse programs fall under the treatment function and serve to help the inmate rehabilitate, thereby preventing future crimes. As a result of the "get tough on crime" era, custody is now the primary focus of the prison and is the prison guard's primary responsibility.

The custody function is emphasized when designing a facility. Facility designs vary across states, with factors such as financial considerations and upkeep taken into consideration during the planning. The popular prison designs of the last two hundred years offer advantages and disadvantages depending upon the style. For example, the radial-design prison, similar to the Auburn prison in New York, contains cells and areas that radiate out from a central control hub. An advantage of this type of design is that it restricts the inmates' movements, because all of the inmates must pass through the hub to travel to any other part of the facility. On the other hand, if inmates get control of the hub during a riot, then they have control of the entire facility.

In addition to prison design, the physical layout of the living units is important for administrators and staff. The linear cell design is the oldest, and many prisons still operate facilities marked by long hallways containing cells or dormitories. The cells are controlled from the end of the hallway, and officers must walk the length of the hallway to observe the insides of the cells directly. A modified version of this design was implemented in some prisons and includes clusters of individual cells that share a common living area. The more modern, "podular" design most closely resembles the modified linear design. Cells also are situated around a central living area, but the defining characteristic of the podular design is direct supervision. The prison guard works inside the pod and has direct contact with the inmates and can observe them at all times. This design has most recently been implemented in jails, known as "new generation" jails.

Inmate and Prison Classification

Upon entering prison, inmates are assessed for classification as a tool in the custody and control of inmates. The tests used for classification purposes determine the proper security level for the inmate. Classifications are made based on characteristics of inmates that may prove problematic (gang affiliation, status, race, and so on) or predictions of inmate behavior. Based on the

Inmates in the Southern Nevada Correctional Center learning computer skills designed to help them find jobs after their release. *(AP/Wide World Photos)*

classification, the inmate will be assigned to a maximum-, medium-, or minimum-security facility.

The maximum-security facility, also known as the "Big House," is a colossal structure with many physical security features, including towers manned by guards, high walls, and searchlights. Facilities such as this are reserved for the inmates considered to be the most dangerous or violent in the prison system. Some programming is available to inmates in maximum-security facilities; however, the main function is custodial. One of the most famous maximum-security prisons is the San Quentin prison in California.

A medium-security facility typically houses property offenders and other inmates considered less dangerous than those housed in maximum-security facilities. In some states, the maximum- and medium-security facilities are combined. Medium-security facilities lack most of the physical security measures present in the maximum-security facilities, and guarded towers are replaced with barbed-wire fences. In some medium-security facilities, inmates reside in dormitories that are similar to military barracks.

A minimum-security facility houses property and drug offenders who are considered the least dangerous offenders and are serving the shortest sentences. Also, inmates from higher-level facilities who are close to release may serve out the end of their sentences in minimum security to ease the transition from incarceration to freedom. Minimum-security facilities rely on electronic monitoring and locked doors to prevent escape, rather than barbed-wire fences. Inmates in minimum security have access to more programs and services and are allowed greater freedom of movement.

Due to the surge in incarceration rates, some prisons and jails have undergone privatization, which involves private companies in the building or operation of prisons and jails. Arguments for and against the privatization of prisons and jails abound, and although some private prisons have been closed down, private prisons are still being used by some states to house the overflow of inmates in the state system. In addition to private prisons and jails, supermax (or maxi-max) prisons and boot camps gained popularity and continue to operate in the United States.

Federal Prison Systems

The first federal prison opened in Atlanta in 1902. Until then, federal prisoners had been housed in local jails or state prisons. The federal Bureau of Prisons was established by President Herbert Hoover in 1930 to oversee the federal prison system. The federal prison system has seen a surge in incarceration rates since the 1970's, mainly resulting from mandatory sentencing and federal antidrug policies. The federal system operates mostly minimum-security facilities because most violent crimes fall under state jurisdiction.

Unlike state prisons, the federal system operates four different types of facilities that are related to the five security levels in the federal system: high, medium, low, minimum, and administrative. The United States penitentiaries (USP) are classified as high-security level but are comparable to maximum-security prisons in the state system. The Metropolitan Correctional/Detention Centers (MCC/MDC) are all at the administrative level. The administrative-level prisons are the jails of the federal system and house offenders at every stage in the legal process. The security level varies based one's location in the center. The federal prison camps (FPC) and satellite camps are all minimum security and house the prisoners who represent the lowest risk, including white-collar criminals or other nonviolent offenders. Finally, the federal correctional institutions (FCI), ranging from low to high security, are similar to the state correctional facilities.

Women's Prisons

Until the reformatory era of the 1870's, prisons were not segregated by gender, and abuses were common. During the late nineteenth century, three states (Indiana, New York, and Massachusetts) opened separate prison facilities for women, which were also staffed by women. By 1975, thirty-four states had opened separate facilities for women. In the states that did not have a separate facility, women and men were segregated, or the state contracted with private companies or other states to house its women inmates. In 1925, the first federal prison for women opened in Alderson, West Virginia.

The early prisons for women followed the cottage system design, which embodied the rehabilitation philosophy of the late nineteenth century. The facilities were operated by women staff, and the inmates' time of incarceration was spent learning domestic skills. When the popularity of reformatory prisons waned, a college campus design replaced the cottage system. Although these prisons offered vocational training programs, the programs were gender-specific. For example, the inmates learned job skills that would translate into secretarial positions upon release.

In 2004, women made up a small percentage of the incarcerated population. However, this number continues to rise. Many states have only one facility for women, which houses inmates from every classification. In the modern prison, the vocational skill training now includes training considered to be traditionally male-oriented, such as firefighting. An administrative and medical issue in prisons for women is that of inmate pregnancies. Some women enter prison pregnant, and the institution must provide specialized care for these inmates. Some prisons have allowed infants to remain with the incarcerated mother for a brief period of time after the delivery.

Jail Systems

Jails are different from prisons in a number of ways. Typically, jails are operated by cities and counties, whereas prisons are run by the state Department of Corrections or the federal Bureau of Prisons. Jails house offenders at different stages of the criminal justice system, including pretrial detention, those serving misdemeanor sentences of less than one year, felony offenders awaiting sentencing or transfer to a state or federal facility, offenders with mental illness awaiting transfer to an institution, felony offenders serving more than one year when no beds are available in the state prisons, offenders awaiting release back into the community after serving the sentence, and individuals held for other reasons such as contempt of court.

Jails also differ in design. Most jails fall into one of the following categories: traditional, second generation, or new generation. Traditional jails are similar to the linear-design prisons, with the cells situated along hallways and intermittent supervision of inmates. Second-generation jails have cells situated around a central "day room," where staff supervise inmates from a con-

trol booth. New-generation jails have a podular design and contain a separate living area, where staff supervise and interact with the inmates directly. New-generation jails have risen in popularity with a philosophy that direct supervision of the inmates allows for more control.

Tammy L. Castle

Further Reading

Allen, H. E., C. E. Simonsen, and E. J. Latessa. *Corrections in America*. 10th ed. Upper Saddle River, N.J.: Pearson/Prentice-Hall, 2004. An introductory textbook for undergraduate courses in corrections. In addition to detailed descriptions of correctional systems, this book covers related topics, such as alternatives to imprisonment and rights of inmates.

Gido, R. L., and T. Alleman, eds. *Turnstile Justice: Issues in American Corrections*. 2d ed. Upper Saddle River, N.J.: Pearson/Prentice-Hall, 2002. A collection of critical readings on issues facing corrections. Each chapter covers a major topic or policy that is generating debate. Good supplemental reading to an introductory text.

Herivel, T., and P. Wright, eds. *Prison Nation: The Warehousing of America's Poor*. New York: Routledge, 2003. A collection of critical readings on current issues in corrections. A good supplemental text that includes essays on prison labor, medicine, violence, litigation, and private prisons.

Johnson, Robert. *Hard Time: Understanding and Reforming the Prison*. 3d ed. Belmont, Calif.: Wadsworth, 2002. This book includes in-depth personal accounts of living in prison by the inmates. Also includes essays on the issues that develop from working in a prison. A good supplemental text because it focuses less on the history of corrections and more on modern issues.

Mays, L. G., and T. L. Winfree. *Contemporary Corrections*. 2d ed. Belmont, Calif.: Wadsworth, 2002. This text is an alternative to the broad introductory corrections book. Fewer topics are covered in more detail; focus is on the role corrections plays in society. Includes a variety of discussions ranging from the history of corrections to new advances in community corrections.

Owen, B. *In the Mix: Struggle and Survival in a Women's Prison*. Albany: State University of New York Press, 1998. This book reports the findings of a study conducted by the author, which describes the subculture in a women's prison in detail. Includes discussions about the paths to imprisonment and the inmates' relationships inside the prison and with family outside the prison.

Santos, M. G. *About Prison*. Belmont, Calif.: Wadsworth, 2004. Discusses the prison subculture and living in prison from an inmate's point of view. Includes profiles of other inmates as well as a discussion of the tremendous growth in the prison population and the effect of the increase on the inmates' lives in prison.

See also Attica prison riot; Auburn system; Boot camps; Bureau of Prisons; Chain gangs; Elderly prisoners; New Mexico state penitentiary riot; Preventive detention; Prison escapes; Prison guards; Prison industries; Prison overcrowding; Prison violence; Supermax prisons; Walnut Street Jail.

Prison escapes

Definition: Unauthorized departures by lawfully incarcerated inmates from state and federal corrections facilities

Criminal justice issues: Pardons and parole; prisons

Significance: Completion of criminal sentences is an important measure of the success of the criminal justice system, so preventing prison escapes is an important goal in corrections.

Different prisons have several levels of security that vary with the size of the facilities and the types of criminals they house. The lowest level of security starts with community treatment centers, or as they are sometimes called, halfway houses. Such facilities are considered halfway between jails and prisons and full release into society. The next level up includes institutions such as prison camps, which are often located in rural

In 1970, radical philosopher Angela Davis made the Federal Bureau of Investigation's most-wanted list for her alleged involvement in the attempted escape of Jonathan and George Jackson, radical African American prisoners known as the "Soledad Brothers," after the name of their California prison. While the brothers were involved in a courtroom trial in Marin County, Jonathan Jackson got hold of guns and took hostages. However, in the confrontation with police that followed, both he and the judge were killed. Afterward, it was discovered that the guns he used had been purchased by Davis. Seen as Jackson's accomplice, Davis was charged with murder, kidnapping, and conspiracy, but when her case went to trial in 1972, she was acquitted of all charges. *(Library of Congress)*

areas. They typically do not have fences, and their inmates work with minimal supervision.

Escapes from halfway houses and prison camps occasionally occur; however, efficient prisoner classification systems tend to minimize such escapes by identifying the prisoners who are the greatest escape risks and sending them to facilities with higher levels of security. Prisons at the medium and maximum levels have security procedures and physical equipment designed to prevent escapes. The highest, or maximum, level of security is maintained in facilities known as supermax prisons. Designed with the goal of making escape physically impossible, these prisons house prisoners who are consider the "worst of the worst."

Prisons differ from "jails" in being designed to house criminals who are sentenced to at least a full year of incarceration. Both state and federal governments run prisons. State prisons house inmates convicted of felony violations. Federal prisons hold inmates who violate federal laws. Most federal prisoners commit felony offenses, but because the federal government does not have the equivalent of county jails, the federal prison population includes inmates convicted of misdemeanor offenses.

Security Levels and Possibilities of Escape

At the state level, departments of corrections usually determine the security levels of the institutions in which convicted prisoners serve their sentences. At the federal level, the Bureau of Prisons makes this determination. Although it is the prerogative of prison system officials to determine what types of institutions in which inmates are to serve their sentences, the recommendations of judges and prosecutors may carry some weight.

Decisions concerning the security levels of the institutions in which offenders serve their sentences take into account such factors as severity of the offenses, prior criminal histories of the offenders, and the extent and strength of the offenders' ties with their communities. The decisions are typically made while the offenders are held in classification centers. Prison officials weigh these factors with the offenders' risk of flight and the dangers they might pose to the communities if they escape back into society. The higher the levels of risk that offenders pose, the greater the levels of security that are required in the institutions in which they are to be housed.

Prisoners can and do escape from every type of prison facility. The attention that prisoner escapes attract is in proportion to the security levels of the institutions from which they flee. When a prisoner escapes from a maximum-security prison's death row, news of the escape makes national news. In December, 2000, for example, seven prisoners escaped from a maximum-security Texas prison. Several of them were awaiting death sentences. Their escapes and subsequent trail of terror led law-enforcement officers from numerous state and federal agencies on a multistate chase that ended with the death of one escapee and the arrest of the others in a rural Colorado community.

Prisoners also occasionally escape while on authorized furlough releases or while they are in transit. Any furloughed prisoner who fails to return to the designated facility at the end of the furlough is considered to have escaped. Although strict security measures are usually the practice for transporting prisoners, the levels of security cannot be as strict as they are when prisoners are inside prison facilities. To escape while in transit, prisoners may use smuggled handcuff keys or makeshift weapons or have outside assistance to attack the guards escorting them.

Consequences of Escape

Recaptured escapees face felony charges for their escapes. If they are convicted, their prison sentences are extended, and they are likely to be housed in more secure facilities. Should recaptured escapees not be prosecuted for the offense of escape, they will probably lose whatever good time they have accumulated for past good behavior. The only generally accepted excuse for escape is to evade a death threat. For that defense to be successful, the escapee must not hurt anyone during or after the escape and surrender to authorities as soon as possible after escaping.

Gerald P. Fisher

Further Reading

Burns, Robert E. *I Am a Fugitive from a Georgia Chain Gang*. New York: Vanguard Press, 1932. Memoir of a famous prison escapee whose story prompted calls for prison reform during the 1930's.

De Simone, Donald. *I Rob Banks, That's Where the Money Is*. New York: SPI Books, 1992. Memoir of a professional bank robber who made several successful escapes from prisons.

Elsner, Alan. *Gates of Injustice: The Crisis in America's Prisons*. Upper Saddle River, N.J.: Financial Times/Prentice-Hall, 2004. Critical analysis of the many problems faced by federal and state prisons, including the deterioration of facilities and failings in security.

See also Bureau of Prisons; Marshals Service, U.S.; New Mexico state penitentiary riot; "Not-in-my-backyard" attitudes; Prison and jail systems; Prison guards; Prison violence; Solitary confinement; Supermax prisons; Surveillance cameras; Ten-most-wanted lists.

Prison guards

Definition: Government employees responsible for custody and control of inmates

Criminal justice issue: Prisons

Significance: The role of prison guards has changed since the 1970's as a result of problems in U.S. prisons and an increase in incarceration rates.

Prison guards, more commonly known today as correctional officers, are primarily concerned with keeping prison inmates in custody and maintaining control of the facilities. These are the two most important prison guard functions. Guards are also responsible for ensuring the safety of all staff and inmates in the prison.

Guards follow procedures in order to guarantee security in the facilities. In addition to the standard security features (such as cameras, locks, and so on), other procedures are implemented to maintain safety and control. For example, one of the primary safety concerns is the existence of contraband, which may include drugs, weapons, or other items banned within the facility. Guards attempt to control the distribution and circulation of contraband by conducting unannounced body and cell searches. Some guards, however, actually participate in the underground prison economy by bringing contraband into the facility and profiting by its sales.

Along with security and order maintenance functions, the role of guard involves a great degree of human service work. Guards are responsible for tending to the daily needs of the inmates living in their cell block, which includes everything from letting the inmates out to go to work and scheduling medical appointments to helping them solve institutional problems. Sometimes prison guards are not prepared for the amount of human service work their

job entails, as training can focus heavily on security measures. The illusion that guards control the prison quickly vanishes for new guards as they learn that control is maintained not only through force but primarily through inmate cooperation. As there are more inmates than guards in every prison, guards may grant small privileges to inmates in exchange for good behavior.

In the past, the job of prison guard held low status and pay. Little formal education was required, and the job carried few opportunities for advancement or promotion. However, the need for a more professional guard became necessary after years of problems in the nation's prisons, the dramatic increase in incarceration rates since the 1970's, and the system's inability to retain officers. The move to professionalize the prison guard incorporated more training, psychological screenings, the replacement of the title prison guard with that of correctional officer, and an attempt to recruit minorities and women.

Overall, the role of prison guard can be very stressful and alienating. Organizational factors

The professionalization of prison guards—who are now generally known as correctional officers—is a relatively late development that was prompted by rapidly growing prison populations during the 1970's. *(Brand-X Pictures)*

853

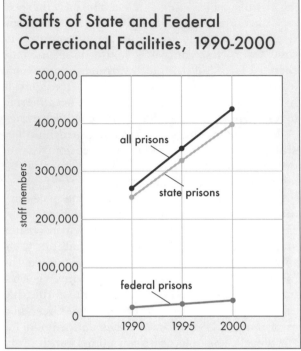

Staffs of State and Federal Correctional Facilities, 1990-2000

Source: U.S. Bureau of Justice Statistics, *Census of State and Federal Correctional Facilities, 2000.* Figures include all prisons, prison farms, boot camps, halfway houses, and work-release centers and exclude local jails, military facilities, and certain other federal detention centers.

contribute to low job satisfaction and job stress, including a lack of supervisory support, a lack of participation in decision making, low pay, and little opportunity for advancement or promotion. Also, role conflict may contribute to stress because the officer must perform the human service functions in addition to those of custody and control. These roles often conflict, and the "people work" aspect of working with the inmates may lead to chronic stress or burnout.

Tammy L. Castle

Further Reading

Conover, T. *Newjack: Guarding Sing Sing*. New York: Random House, 2000.

Herman, P. G., ed. *The American Prison System*. New York: H. W. Wilson, 2001.

Steinberg, E. *Correction Officer*. New York: Macmillan, 1997.

See also Attica prison riot; Chain gangs; New Mexico State Penitentiary riot; Prison and jail systems; Prison escapes; Prison overcrowding; Prison violence; Solitary confinement; Women in law enforcement and corrections.

Prison health care

Definition: Preventive care, medical treatment, and other health services offered in correctional facilities

Criminal justice issues: Medical and health issues; prisons and jails

Significance: Prison health care has become an increasing concern as correctional institutions across the United States have experienced significant growth in the numbers of inmates, especially those who have physical disabilities or are aging or are chronically or terminally ill.

Prison health care presents unique challenges to the medical professionals responsible for the care and treatment of inmates. Prison health care resources are limited, and inmates are more likely than members of the general population to have serious illnesses, such as cancer, diabetes, heart disease, and HIV/AIDS. The treatments for such diseases are costly, and the financial resources of many prisons are limited. Moreover, prison health care systems are often significantly understaffed. Despite these obstacles, however, correctional facilities are constitutionally required to provide adequate medical care to their inmates. In an effort to assist prisons with constitutional compliance, professional health care organizations have developed standards of care and ethical codes.

Legal Standards of Care

Prior to the 1960's, the judicial system practiced a judicial restraint or "hands-off" policy with regard to administration of prisons. During that period, judicial officials were reluctant to get involved in correctional issues. Many judges claimed they not only lacked the authority and expertise to intervene in correctional matters, but that court intervention might result in undermining the work of correctional administrators.

The lack of judicial intervention and court deference to prison administrators resulted in a number of abuses, especially in inmate health care. In many facilities, prisoners were routinely denied the most basic standards of medical care and treatment. However, in the landmark 1976 case of *Estelle v. Gamble*, the U.S. Supreme Court affirmed federal jurisdiction over correctional health care systems and ruled that when constitutional rights are at risk, the courts have not the right but the duty to intervene. In addition, the Supreme Court ruled that "deliberate indifference to the serious medical needs of inmates" was a violation of the Eighth Amendment's ban on cruel and unusual punishment. The Court reasoned that because prisoners are wholly dependent on the state for their needs, the state is obligated to provide for their serious medical needs. Therefore, correctional administrators or authorities can be held civilly liable under Section 1983 of the U.S. Code for failing to provide adequate medical care to prisoners.

Accreditation and Professional Standards of Care

During the early 1970's, the American Medical Association (AMA) surveyed the nation's jails and found that medical services were lacking in three primary areas: adequacy, access, and availability. The AMA then developed a set of standards for the delivery of health cares services in jails and prisons and initiated a voluntary accreditation program for correctional facilities that met these standards.

Accreditation is a process in which an independent outside agency certifies that correctional institutions have met acceptable national standards for health care services. In 2004, three national bodies offered accreditation to correctional facilities: the American Correctional Association (ACA), which accredits the entire operation of institutions, including health care services; the Joint Commission on Accreditation of Health Organizations (JCAHO),

which oversees the accreditation of a variety of health care organizations, including correctional facilities; and the National Commission on Correctional Health Care (NCCHC), which sets standards of health care for jails, prisons, and juvenile facilities. Of these organizations, the NCCHC is considered the leading authority on correctional health care. NCCHC standards are wide ranging and include administrative and personnel issues, environmental and preventive health care, routine and emergency health services, and medical-legal issues.

The courts have not ruled that correctional facilities are constitutionally required to undergo accreditation. An increasing number of prisons have sought voluntary accreditation in the hope of reducing inmate litigation, but the implementation of these standards does not guarantee that result. In *Bell v. Wolfish* (1980), for example, the Supreme Court ruled that standards developed by professional associations, such as the NCCHC, are at best only advisory and do not necessarily define what is minimally required by the Consti-

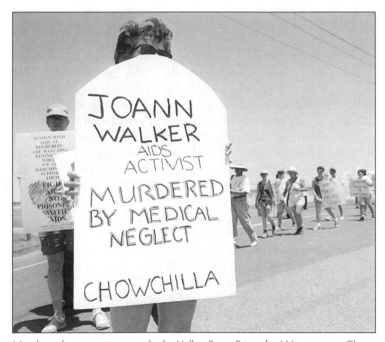

Marchers demonstrating outside the Valley State Prison for Women near Chowchilla, California, to call attention to the need for better health care for women in the state's prisons in 1996. The sign in the foreground alludes to a prisoner in another facility who died from fungal meningitis, allegedly because of medical neglect. *(AP/Wide World Photos)*

tution. Nevertheless, correctional institutions frequently set health care guidelines in accordance with NCCHC standards.

Ethical Considerations

In addition to developing standards of health care and accreditation, many professional organizations have stressed the need for prison health care providers to develop and adopt a code of professional ethics to guide the conduct of professionals and establish moral duties and obligations in relation to their clients, institutions, and society. Although a number of correctional health care organizations have adopted such codes, correctional institutions are neither constitutionally nor professionally required to do the same. However, as with accreditation, prison officials who adopt ethical standards of care and treatment of prisoners reduce the chances of inmate litigation.

Many of the ethical issues that arise for prison health care providers are similar to those encountered by health care providers practicing in the larger society. However, in contrast to the issues faced by their outside world counterparts, the ethical challenges that correctional health care providers face may be complicated by the settings in which they administer care and the clients whom they serve. For example, health care providers must disregard the criminal records of their prison patients. Providers are often aware of their patients' crimes and may have difficulty administering care because of what may be disturbing knowledge. Moreover, all patients also have a right to make autonomous decisions about their own medical care, regardless of the settings in which they receive care. Their rights includes the right to be fully informed about all medical treatments they receive and the right to refuse medical care. Finally, as in the outside world, doctor-patient confidentiality is essential, and medical staff should never discuss the medical diagnoses or treatments of prison patients with anyone other than the patients themselves.

Kimberly D. Dodson

Further Reading

Altice, Frederick, Peter Selwyn, and Rita Watson, eds. *Reaching In, Reaching Out: Treating HIV/AIDS in the Correctional Community.* Washington, D.C.: National Commission on Correction Health Care, 2002. Volume offering a model for the care of prison inmates suffering from AIDS and HIV; also offers a model for dealing with end-of-life issues for prisoners with terminal conditions.

Faiver, K. L. *Health Care Management Issues in Corrections.* Lanham, Md.: American Correctional Association, 1998. General survey of prison health care issues that affect the administration of correctional facilities.

Puisis, Michael, ed. *Clinical Practice in Correctional Medicine.* St. Louis, Mo.: Mosby, 1998. Collection of articles by clinicians in the penal system experienced in prison health care. Contributors address the often harsh realities of prison health care and how it differs from outside health care. The book opens with a chapter on the history of the subject.

See also AIDS; Attica prison riot; Bureau of Prisons; Cruel and unusual punishment; Elderly prisoners; Mental illness; Preventive detention; Prison guards; Prison industries; Prison overcrowding; Prison violence; Supermax prisons.

Prison industries

Definition: Government-operated enterprises that employ and provide job training to state and federal prisoners

Criminal justice issues: Prisons; rehabilitation

Significance: Proponents of prison industries cite reduced rates of recidivism among participants; critics, however, say the programs do not adequately compensate prisoners for their labor.

Prison industries provide work opportunities, directly or indirectly, for inmates. Some observers view these as helpful for prisoners, while others believe that they either exploit prisoners or harm private-sector businesses.

The federal government and forty states operate government-owned corporations that provide goods and services to consumers, although there are generally limitations on who can purchase those goods and services.

The government established the Federal Prison Industries (FPI) in 1934, by an act of Congress. Prisoners had previously provided goods and services through the auspices of the U.S. Treasury Department. The new law permitted the FPI, using a trade name of Unicor, to keep surplus revenue as operating capital.

The aims of FPI are to teach employable skills to as many inmates as possible, to promote better environments at federal prisons by providing constructive opportunities for prisoners, and to produce and market high-quality goods for use by federal agencies while having minimal effects on the private sector.

The state prison industries organizations usually restrict purchases of their products to their state government or to qualified nonprofit organizations within their state. In most states, prison industries compete with private-sector business, although California requires that government organizations purchase needed materials from its Prison Industry Authority.

Inmate of Ohio's Dayton Correctional Institution with a puppy he is training to be a guide dog for the blind. During the late 1990's, Ohio developed guide-dog training programs at eight of its prisons in one of the more innovative and socially useful prison industries in the United States. *(AP/Wide World Photos)*

Prison Industries Products

Prison industries produce a wide range of products and services—not just license plates, as is popularly thought. Prison goods and services range from furniture, such as desks and other office equipment, to agricultural products to clothing. In Oregon, prisoners produce "Prison Blues" blue jeans, which have proved to be very popular. The California prison industries had sales of more than $150 million in 1998, according to a University of California at Berkeley study.

The FPI markets about 150 goods and services to federal agencies. Products include furniture, textiles, and electronic components. Services include data entry, engine repair, furniture refinishing, recycling, bulk mailing, and laundry services. In 2003, the FPI's revenues exceeded $700 million.

Only a small percentage of prisoners are able to participate in prison industries. For example, the Texas program employs less than 10,000,

even though the state has approximately 100,000 inmates. About 16 percent of federal prisoners participate in the programs.

Studies have suggested a lower rate of recidivism among participants in these programs, compared with inmates who have not been thus employed. Proponents of prison industries argue that prison industries are not just about earning money; rather, they are a means of promoting public safety. Supporters assert that participants in prison industries are not just the prisoners deemed most likely to do well outside prison; the participants are a broad cross section of the prison population. Prisoners who participate in this programs are also said to gain skills and work experience.

Criticisms of Prison Industries

Some observers argue that the goods produced are of limited quality and thus that prison industries furnish inferior goods to government agencies. A Government Accounting Office report in 1998 described some problems with the goods produced and the inability of the FPI to meet its published deadlines. The study clearly indicated problems but stated that some improvements had already been made.

Other critics argue that prison industries interfere with the business activities of law-abiding citizens. Some in Congress have sought to require government agencies to use competitive bidding rather than purchasing from the FPI. A measure that would have enacted this change was passed by the House of Representatives in 2004, but it did not pass in the Senate.

Prisoners' net wages are typically less than $1 per hour because money is taken from their gross earnings to pay for administration of the prison industry program and for some of the expenses that the prisoners incur in confinement. In California, prisoners receive only 20 percent of the wages that they earn; the other 80 percent is divided among an antidrug campaign, victims' rights organizations, a state compensation fund, and an inmate trust fund. Some critics of prison industries argue that this is tantamount to exploitation of prisoners. Others assert that working conditions in prisons are usually inadequate or dangerous. Still others argue that such government corporations are inefficient because of their bureaucratic structures. For example, after its creation in 1983, the California Prison Industry Authority lost money in five of its first thirteen years of operation. Despite these criticisms, it is unlikely the politicians will change the system of prison industries because they are viewed by many as cost-effective and fair to prisoners.

Michael Coulter

Further Reading

Burton-Rose, Daniel, Dan Pen, and Paul Wright, eds. *The Celling of America: An Inside Look at the U.S. Prison Industry*. Monroe, Maine: Common Courage Press, 1998. Essay from *Prison Legal News* in which inmates describe their experiences in prison, including that of working for prison industries.

Christie, Nils. *Crime Control as Industry: Towards Gulags, Western Style*. New York: Routledge, 2000. This book describes the operation of prisons within the United States and examines the means by which incarceration can prevent crime.

Goldman, George. *The Economic Impact of Production in California's Prison Industries*. Berkeley: Department of Agriculture and Resource Economics, University of California at Berkeley, 1998. Discusses California's Prison Industry Authority and its activities' effects on the state economy.

See also Auburn system; Bureau of Prisons; Elderly prisoners; Halfway houses; Prison and jail systems; Rehabilitation; Walnut Street Jail; Work camps.

Prison overcrowding

Definition: Incarceration of more prisoners than the prisons are designed to house

Criminal justice issues: Prisons; punishment; sentencing

Significance: In 2000, the number of persons incarcerated in the United States was nearly six times greater than it had been in 1970. Although the numbers of both state and federal prisons had also increased, the total numbers of prisoners greatly exceeded their intended maximum capacities.

From the mid-nineteenth century through around 1980, the rate of incarceration in the United States remained fairly stable. During the early 1980's, however, the rates of incarceration rose exponentially. The largest period of growth occurred between 1980 and 1995, when the rate of imprisonment grew four times larger than the rate that had been relatively stable for more than a century. Although the numbers of prisons increased, the number of inmates was too great a burden for the correctional system to bear. The result was many badly overcrowded prisons.

Although incarceration rates appear have leveled off since the mid-1990's, state and federal prisons still struggle to keep up with the impact of the population surge. The numbers of state and federal prisons increased by 14 percent between 1995 and 2000, expanding the total rated capacities of all prisons by 31 percent. Nevertheless, the average state prison was still operating 1 percent above its rated capacity and federal prisons were operating at a rate 34 percent over their capacities.

Causes of Overcrowding

The simplest explanation for the prevalence of prison overcrowding is that there are too many inmates for the available prison beds. Accordingly, more substantive explanations account for what societal or criminal justice system factors led to the growth in imprisonment. From the mid-1970's through the mid-1980's, the prison population expanded as courts began sentencing unprecedented numbers people convicted of less serious offenses to prison. However, the courts were merely responding to rising crime rates and public disenchantment with the criminal justice system that had begun in the 1960's and continued into the 1980's.

Rising crime rates supported the long-standing conservative argument that individualized rehabilitative treatment of offenders does not deter criminals from reoffending. While liberals had previously countered this claim, it was during that period that they argued for increasing rights and treating offenders alike, and abandoning the individualized approach. As a result, a "get-tough" movement developed in which prison terms became the foremost sentencing option for the courts.

A second reason for the population increase followed from the first: the so-called "war on drugs," which prompted renewed public calls for tougher punishments. In the past, most minor drug offenders had been sentenced merely to probation and community treatment. However, from the mid-1980's through the early 1990's, increases in incarceration of drug offenders accounted for one-third of prison population growth. Although the proportion later decreased, drug offenders accounted for nearly 20 percent of the total prison population growth during the 1990's.

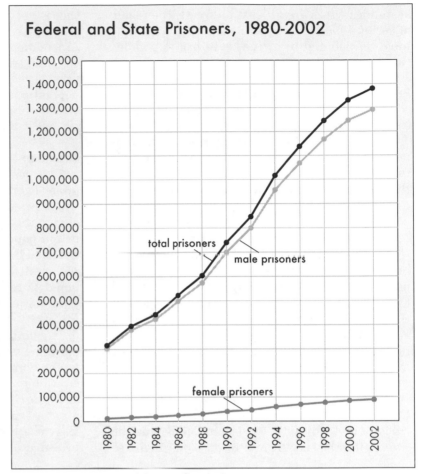

Source: U.S. Bureau of Justice Statistics.

During the 1990's, the major cause of prison population growth shifted from the rate of admissions to longer sentences for those who were incarcerated. Lengths of sentences were increased for all major crimes, such as murder, rape, drug law violations, and burglary. These longer sentences were the result not only of the courts becoming more punitive, but also the get-tough movement in criminal justice policy.

Criminologists have found evidence suggesting that criminal justice system factors such as structured sentencing guidelines and mandatory minimums, which force judges to impose sentences with fixed minimums for specific offenses, have contributed to prison overcrowding. In addition, many states have abolished their parole systems or limited the discretion of parole boards to decide when to release offenders. Although these systemic factors are at least indirectly the result of societal factors, they are specific policies that have contributed to increases in prison populations.

Prison Overcrowding and the Courts

Prison overcrowding has been examined in the courts as a challenge to the Eighth Amendment's cruel and unusual punishment clause. The majority of the courts have held that the total conditions of an institution must be examined before the collective effects of overcrowding on inmates can be understood.

The U.S. Supreme Court has heard several cases pertaining to prison overcrowding. In *Rhodes v. Chapman* (1981) the Court allowed the housing of two inmates in cells designed for one person. In *Wilson v. Seiter* (1991) the Court found that for crowding to be considered a violation of the Eighth Amendment, plaintiffs must demonstrate deliberate indifference to basic inmate needs by prison staff that does not include the mere fact of an institution's operating above its rated capacity.

Finally, in *Farmer v. Brennan* (1994) the Court defined deliberate indifference more specifically by holding that prison officials must be aware that the specific indifference may increase the risk of substantial harm to inmates. Despite making it more difficult to prove that Eighth Amendment violations result from prison overcrowding, nearly 9 percent of all state and federal prisons were under court orders to limit their populations in 2000. However, that figure was considerably less than the nearly 21 percent of prisons rated as overcrowded in 1990.

Effects of Prison Overcrowding

The most significant and far-reaching effect of prison overcrowding is cost. The cost of housing a single prisoner may range between twenty and eighty thousand dollars per year. The rise in prison populations between 1982 and 1992 was reflected in a rise in annual spending in U.S. corrections from roughly nine billion to nearly 32 billion dollars—the largest increase in any area of criminal justice expenditures over that time period.

In addition to increasing costs, prison overcrowding affects both staff and inmates negatively. Some evidence suggests that prison overcrowding has increased staff and inmate tension and contributed to more assaults on staff and greater staff turnover. The effects on inmates are less clear. Some empirical studies have suggested prison crowding is associated with increased levels of prisoner stress, anxiety, and tension. Accordingly, crowded prisons have been associated with poor inmate adaptation, higher levels of inmate assaults, and collective actions, such as rioting. On the other hand, an equal number of empirical studies have suggested that overcrowding has little or no negative effect on inmates, and that inmate misconduct and increases in anxiety are caused by other factors. Nonetheless, no matter which of these viewpoints is indeed the case, overcrowding, which is still prevalent in many prisons, does not have positive effects and thus must be considered a significant issue in criminal justice.

Two inmates share a cramped cell at the Maine Correctional Center. *(AP/Wide World Photos)*

Benjamin Steiner

Further Reading

Alarid, Leanne, and Paul Cromwell, eds. *Correctional Perspectives: Views from Academics, Practitioners, and Prisoners*. Los Angeles, Calif.: Roxbury, 2002. Collection of articles on prisons encompassing views of scholars, correctional professionals, and even prisoners.

Call, Jack. "Prison Overcrowding Cases in the Aftermath of *Wilson vs. Seiter.*" *The Prison Journal* 75 (1995): 390-406. Analysis of the impact of the Supreme Court's 1991 ruling that prison overcrowding by itself is not necessarily a violation of the Eighth Amendment.

Gaes, G. "Prison Crowding Research Reexamined." *The Prison Journal* 74 (1994): 329-363. Review of studies conducted on the surge in U.S. prison populations between the mid-1980's and early 1990's.

Irwin, John, and James Austin. *It's About Time: America's Imprisonment Binge*. 3d ed. Belmont, Calif.: Wadsworth, 2001. Incisive and very readable examination of the impact on prisons of the movement toward using incarceration as the primary solution to crime. This book incorporates a wide variety of views on the prison system, including those of inmates, and one of its authors is a former prison inmate who has become a noted criminologist.

Stephan, James, and Jennifer Karberg. *Census of State and Federal Correctional Facilities, 2000*. Washington D.C.: Bureau of Justice, 2003. Federal government summary of statistics on prison populations across the country.

Tonry, Michael, ed. *The Future of Imprisonment*. New York: Oxford University Press, 2004. Broad overview of the current state and future prospects of American prisons by one of the leading authorities on corrections.

See also AIDS; Attica prison riot; Auburn system; Community-based corrections; Cruel and unusual punishment; Halfway houses; Mandatory sentencing; Prison and jail systems; Prison guards; Prison violence; Recidivism; Three-strikes laws.

Prison violence

Definition: Forms of violence and sexual assault committed on and by prison inmates

Criminal justice issues: Prisons; sex offenses; violent crime

Significance: Government studies have shown that assaults on staff and inmates of correctional facilities are rising across the United States, even though many assaults—especially sexual assaults—are underreported by prison officials. Trends toward making convicted offenders serve longer sentences and lose more privileges make it seem likely that prison violence will continue to increase.

Prison violence and sexual abuse may be an inevitable consequence of being locked up. Television dramas such as Home Box Office's *Oz* and popular films such as *The Shawshank Redemption* (1994) have highlighted the dangers and brutality that inmates often face from guards and fellow prisoners. Many people can visualize the lasting images from films in which inmates are beaten, raped, and abused for a variety of reasons. In some cases, the victims may be seen as easy targets for others; in others, violence may be a manifestation of gang activity, and some inmates resort to violence simply in order to protect themselves from others.

Many dramatic productions treat prison violence and sexual abuse as normal aspects of prison life. These productions contribute to the public expectation that violence is a natural by-product of housing criminals together under one roof. At the same time, some people charge that state and government agencies too often turn a blind eye to the abuses suffered by inmates.

Prison violence and sexual abuse are potential problems faced by all prisoners; however, many prisons are reluctant to provide adequate information about the abuse taking place within their facilities. For this reason, statistics on prison violence and abuse must be examined with caution. Statistics on violence and sexual abuse tend to underestimate incidence rates. Solid and unbiased research on prison violence is difficult to find and even more difficult to conduct because of the inherently taboo nature of the subject.

Reasons for Violent Behavior

Two long-standing and competing theories have been advanced to explain prison violence. Developed during the 1950's and 1960's, the deprivation theory suggests that inmates act violently because of the "pains" they experience while incarcerated. From this perspective, prison is a harsh, degrading place that controls inmates totally. Inmates are told when to eat and when to sleep. Stripped of their identities, they become mere bodies with numbers. Under the harsher conditions imposed by many modern prisons, inmates' pains take on new forms. Many inmates spend twenty or more hours in their cells every day with few or no recreational or educational programs. Research indicates that variables such as lack of programs, higher security levels, gang activity, and overcrowding may all increase violent behavior.

The second major explanation for prison violence is the importation theory. It holds that inmates engage in violence because they are violent people to begin with. In fact, inmates merely carry into prisons the same violent attitudes and behaviors they have outside prisons. This theory points to variables such as age, race, gender, and aggressive personality as causes of increased violent behavior during incarceration. The most recent research on prison violence combines elements of both theories. It looks at how inmates with such traits as aggressive personalities react in particular prison environments.

Individual and Collective Violence

Prison violence takes several different forms. It can be individual, when it occurs between fellow inmates or between inmates and staff members. It has been estimated that inmates of U.S. prisoners kill about one hundred fellow inmates every year. Research has shown that male inmates are much more likely to be sexually and physically violent than female inmates. However, the most influential and important predic-

---

The Shawshank Redemption

One of the most gripping Hollywood films about prison life is *The Shawshank Redemption*, a 1994 film adapted from a novella by Stephen King. In the film, a falsely convicted inmate (Tim Robbins), who is befriended by another inmate (Morgan Freeman), survives the brutality of prison life.

Much credible evidence has established that brutality is a fact of life in American prisons. However, *The Shawshank Redemption* does not accurately convey the presence of law within prisons. Many films have portrayed prisons as closed societies in which wardens wield absolute control. In real life, however, prison administrations are regularly the objects of litigation brought by their inmates. Litigation is also often brought against prisons by outside public-interest groups that support prisoner rights for the very reason that under the American system of criminal justice, prisoners are not thought to be outside the superintendence of law.

Timothy L. Hall

---

tor of violent behavior is age. All research on the subject has indicated that inmates under the age of twenty-five are the most likely to behave violently. Moreover, as inmates age, they tend to commit fewer acts of violence. Other individual characteristics, such as race, education, prior criminal history, marital status, and personality, showed mixed results when predicting violent behavior.

Prior to the prisoner rights movement of the late 1960's and 1970's, physical beatings, extended solitary confinement, strip searches, torture, and other forms of inhumane treatment by prison guards were commonplace in American prisons. Interestingly, research has indicated that staff abuse of inmates tends to occur most often in maximum-security facilities. In general, however, individual acts of staff violence against inmates were more common before the 1980's, but sporadic incidents still occur. Data on staff violence is especially difficult to find and should be looked at with an especially cautious eye.

Collective violence typically involves large groups of inmates acting out together. The most common form of collective violence is rioting. More than three hundred prison riots have occurred in U.S. history. The most notable occurred at New York's Attica prison in 1971 and at New Mexico's state penitentiary in 1980. Both of those riots resulted in the deaths of both inmates and guards and millions of dollars in property damage. Studies of both riots emphasize issues relating to overcrowding, poor food, lack of medical facilities, guard brutality, and other forms of inhumane treatment. Most important, however, those incidents attracted public attention to the mistreatment of inmates in U.S. prisons and helped bring about sweeping prison reforms.

Sexual Abuse

Government reports have estimated that 13 percent of all prison inmates in the United States are sexually assaulted at least once. Other studies claimed that as many as 20 percent of inmates suffer some form of sexual abuse while incarcerated. For a variety of reasons, the exact numbers of inmates who suffer from this form of abuse may never be known precisely. Some inmates are reluctant to report such abuse, and some prison officials are inclined to ignore it. Moreover, many staff members may not be adequately trained to respond to incidents of sexual abuse.

Compounding the problem of quantifying sexual abuse in prisons is the fact that definitions of sexual abuse vary greatly from institution to institution. For example, some prisons classify rape, sexual harassment, and sexual abuse as the same offenses, while others classify them as separate offenses. Nevertheless, research studies do indicate which inmates are most at risk of becoming victims of sexual abuse.

The most likely to be victimized are young first-time offenders and physically weak older inmates. Also at increased risk are inmates who fit the stereotype of educated middle-class members

Police and National Guard troops mass outside the Southern Ohio Correctional Facility in April, 1993, on the tenth day of a riot that began spontaneously during a fight among prisoners in the maximum-security prison and developed into the longest siege in U.S. prison history. The uprising ended the next day, when SWAT teams and National Guard troops stormed the facility. By then, nine prisoners and one guard had been killed, and an entire cellblock was destroyed. One of the main legacies of the riot was a move toward even tighter prison security and the development of supermax prisons in Ohio and other states. *(AP/Wide World Photos)*

of outside society who lack "street smarts." At the same time, inmates with mental disabilities are also likely targets of sexual violence.

Sexual abuse among inmates is of even greater importance now than in the past because of the increased threat of HIV/AIDS and other sexually transmitted diseases. In 2004, at least 25,000 inmates in the United States were believed to be infected with HIV/AIDS. As more inmates enter prisons than ever before, these numbers are expected to rise.

To address the overlooked issue of prison violence, the U.S. Congress passed the Prison Rape Elimination Act in 2003. This law was designed to collect more accurate and reliable data on prison violence, to protect inmates from violence, and to increase the accountability of prison staff and inmates to report these actions.

Karen F. Lahm

Further Reading

Braswell, Michael C., Reid H. Montgomery, and Lucien X. Lombardo. *Prison Violence in America*. 2d ed. Cincinnati: Anderson Publishing, 1994. Broad and thorough overview of issues related to prison violence, both individual and collective.

Edgar, Kimmett, Ian O'Donnell, and Carol Martin. *Prison Violence: The Dynamics of Conflict, Fear and Power*. Cullompton, Devon, England: Willan, 2003. Comprehensive examination of violence in British prisons.

Ross, Jeffrey Ian, and Stephen C. Richards. *Behind Bars: Surviving Prison*. Indianapolis: Alpha Books, 2002. Book written by and for inmates about surviving the criminal justice system, particularly life in prison. It examines a number of different prisons across the United States and offers specific advice on how to survive in each of them.

Toch, Hans. *Living in Prison*. New York: Free Press, 1977. This book is one of the earliest and most comprehensive examinations of prison life and the prison subculture from both psychological and sociological perspectives.

Williams, Stanley "Tookie," and Barbara Cottman Becnel. *Life in Prison*. Minneapolis: Sagebrush Education Resources, 2001. Memoir of a death-row inmate describing his long experiences in prison.

See also AIDS; Attica prison riot; Cruel and unusual punishment; Elderly prisoners; New Mexico state penitentiary riot; Prison and jail systems; Prison escapes; Prison guards; Prison overcrowding; Solitary confinement; Supermax prisons

Privacy rights

Definition: Constitutional protection against unlawful government intrusions on citizens' privacy

Criminal justice issues: Civil rights and liberties; constitutional protections; police powers; search and seizure

Significance: The increasing dependency of modern police forces and investigative agencies on electronic surveillance and search techniques presents new challenges to constitutionally protected privacy rights.

Privacy rights involve the protection of citizens against government intrusion into their personal affairs. In the criminal justice system, privacy issues arise when the police engage in surveillance of individuals and search and seizure of people and their personal effects. Nowhere in the U.S. Constitution is privacy expressly mentioned as a protected right. However, most legal scholars conclude that the Framers of the Constitution intended citizens to have fundamental privacy rights, whose scope has been left to interpretations by the courts. This issue is an important one, as modern police often become involved in surveillance and search and seizure activities, during which they may violate the privacy of citizens.

References in several amendments to the Constitution, court decisions, and legal writings have instilled the privacy concept in American law. One famous legal commentary declared that citizens have a right to be left alone by government. In its landmark *Griswold v. Connecticut* decision in 1965, the U.S. Supreme Court stated that citizens have a constitutional right to a certain "zone of privacy" which is free from government intrusion. In fact, during the very next year, in *Schmerber v. California* (1966), the Court added that the "overriding function" of the Fourth Amendment is to protect personal privacy and dignity against unwarranted intrusion by the State.

In 1967, in *Katz v. United States*, the Supreme Court established the "expectation of privacy" doctrine. This principle stated that citizens are entitled to a reasonable expectation of privacy as long as they demonstrate that expectation through words or actions. In the *Katz* case, federal police electronically eavesdropped on Katz's public telephone booth conversation, even after he had purposefully closed the door behind him. The Court ruled that Katz's actions established a reasonable expectation of privacy, thus protecting him from government surveillance, and therefore the police in his case acted illegally.

Following the creation of the expectation of privacy rule, the courts established a "balancing of competing interests" test to weigh the needs of police to gather evidence for criminal prosecution against the right of citizens to be protected from government agents who may violate their personal privacy. Privacy protection took on a new dimension when the courts established additional exceptions to the warrant requirement of the Fourth Amendment. In 1985, the Supreme Court expanded the scope of the "special needs" exception by allowing school officials to search students and their personal effects on school premises. Any illegal contraband discovered, such as drugs or weapons, could be given to the police for possible prosecution.

Privacy in the Criminal Justice Process

Persons entering the criminal justice system forfeit some privacy protection, but courts have declared that arrested, convicted, and incarcerated persons do have a limited expectation of privacy within the system. Many courts use electronic monitoring of pretrial detainees who have been released from custody awaiting their criminal trials. These individuals consent to have electronic devices (bracelets or anklets) attached to them during their release to ensure that they comply with the court requirements restricting their movement. Also, the courts allow probation and parole officers to search, without a warrant, the homes and personal effects of individuals who are subject to community supervision. Al-

though probationers and parolees must consent to specific conditions of their release, many requirements include drug urinalysis, warrantless searches, and electronic monitoring of their movements. Persons found through monitoring or testing to have violated their conditions of release may have their privileges revoked.

Incarcerated persons can be subject to more extensive search and confiscation of personal property in jails and prisons. One personal identification method in use within correctional institutions is obtaining and cataloging individual DNA samples from inmates. Obtaining body fluids and tissue specimens for DNA purposes is more intrusive than traditional fingerprinting because officials remove specimens directly from bodies. Correctional institutions may also monitor inmate telephone conversations and use surveillance cameras for safety purposes.

Electronic Surveillance and Privacy

Police increasingly rely on electronic technology to combat crime. As such practices become more common, they raise privacy issues. Technological applications in criminal justice cover a broad spectrum of activities. The use of surveillance cameras is increasing in an effort to identify known offenders, prevent crime, and gather information in public places. These devices have been used to monitor traffic and to cite drivers running red lights. Courts have ruled that the police can electronically monitor citizen activities in public places but cannot intrude into homes without a warrant or other legal justification.

Other devices such as pen registers, which record dialed telephone numbers, and "trap and trace" devices, which document the electronic signatures of computer transmissions, can be used by police to gather information without a warrant. However, federal law governs much of the interception of electronic telephone transmissions. These laws require the police to obtain either a warrant or consent from the one of the parties to intercept telephone wire communications. Although users of cordless telephones have a lesser expectation of privacy and transmissions may be intercepted, federal laws require the police to obtain a warrant and follow guidelines in acquiring information from cellular phone service providers.

In 2001, Congress passed the Patriot Act to give law enforcement greater counterterrorism powers. The law is extensive and redefines several traditional police search procedures. It allows police to search homes and businesses without the notice typically required in conventional search warrants. It also allows the use of computer and telephone tracking devices as well as roving wiretap warrants if the investigation at hand involves counterterrorism or foreign intelligence investigations.

William P. Bloss

Further Reading

Del Carmen, Rolando V. *Criminal Procedure: Law and Practice*. 6th ed. Belmont, Calif.: Thomson/Wadsworth, 2004. Comprehensive and readable review of criminal procedure that includes discussions of privacy rights.

Etzioni, Amitai. *The Limits of Privacy*. New York: Basic Books, 1999. Critical consideration of the acceptable limits on constitutional protections of individual privacy rights.

Hall, John Wesley. *Search and Seizure*. 3d ed. Charlottesville, Va.: LEXIS Law Publishing, 2000. Textbook focusing on issues surrounding search and seizure, which often raises privacy rights issues.

Long, Robert. *Rights to Privacy*. New York: H. W. Wilson, 1997. Broad treatise on constitutional and legal issues relating to privacy rights.

McWhirter, Darien A. *Search, Seizure, and Privacy*. Phoenix, Ariz.: Oryx Press, 1994. Book written to make subjects such as search and seizure, the exclusionary rule, and privacy rights interesting for high school and undergraduate college students.

Monmonier, M. S. *Spying with Maps: Surveillance Technologies and the Future of Privacy*. Chicago: University of Chicago Press, 2002. Examination of the privacy rights issues arising from modern high-tech police surveillance of suspects.

See also Abortion; Bill of Rights, U.S.; *Bowers v. Hardwick*; Computer crime; Electronic surveillance; Fourth Amendment; *Illinois v. McArthur*; *Olmstead v. United States*; Search and seizure; Surveillance cameras; Trespass; Wiretaps.

Private detectives

Definition: Nongovernment investigators who hire out to attorneys, companies, and private citizens

Criminal justice issues: Evidence and forensics; fraud; investigation

Significance: Although the role of private detectives in crime investigation is highly romanticized in fiction, modern private detectives often play important roles in helping to track down criminals.

When people think of private detectives, or private investigators, many of them think of classic detective characters such as Raymond Chandler's Philip Marlowe and Dashiell Hammett's Sam Spade—hard-drinking characters who drink too much, act mysteriously, and frequently get into trouble with the law. The truth is that real-life private investigators are often the opposite of their fictional counterparts. Modern-day private detectives do much of their work from offices and spend much of their time not chasing dangerous murderers, but investigating embezzlement, forgery, cybercrime, insurance fraud, workman's compensation claims, missing persons, and do-

Slang and Underworld Terms for Private Detectives

The real and fictional worlds of crime have coined many colorful terms for detectives. This list is a collection of some of the best-known terms.

✓ dick (from "detective")
✓ gumshoe
✓ house dick (hotel detective)
✓ op (operative)
✓ peeper
✓ P.I. (private investigator)
✓ private dick
✓ private eye (from Pinkerton's company logo)
✓ shamus (various spellings; possibly from a Yiddish word)
✓ sleuth (from Middle English *sleuth hund*, a type of bloodhound)
✓ snoop, snooper

mestic problems, such as cheating spouses.

Like their fictional counterparts, some private detectives and investigators work alone, but that is more unusual than it once was. Private detectives often work for investigating firms that specialize in specific types of cases, such as forgery. Private investigators also work for attorneys, banks, and others who may need their skills. Special investigators include retail detectives, who work undercover for retail stores to prevent theft; financial investigators, who help companies locate the assets they win in court cases; legal detectives, who are hired by law firms; and corporate investigators, who deal with matters such as theft and employee drug use.

Private detectives are now licensed by almost all fifty U.S. states for their profession, but this was not always the case. Until the late 1960's and early 1970's, anyone who wanted to be a detective could take up investigating work merely by doing it. The absence of professional standards caused police and other law-enforcement professionals to look down upon the private-investigating profession.

The first well-known private detective agency was Pinkerton's National Detective Agency. Founded in Chicago by the Scottish-born Allan J. Pinkerton in 1850, the agency was commended for the way it handled various problems, and its agents became known for their cleverness in solving their cases. The term "private eye" (which became synonymous with a private detective) came from Pinkerton's agency logo, which was a picture of a human eye surrounded by the motto "We Never Sleep."

The licensing of private detectives by states during the late twentieth century controlled who could work in the field. This change made relations between law enforcement and private detectives much easier. By the time the twenty-first century arrived, private detectives were using state-of-the-art equipment to do their work and

Lawyers Turned Investigators in Fiction

Private investigators are such a staple of fiction, films, and television dramas that it is not surprising that fictional characters in other professions take up similar work. Steve Martini's *The Arraignment* (2003) is an example of a novel in which an attorney seems to morph into private investigator. The novel's attorney Paul Madriani becomes involved in the investigation of the murder of his friend, Nick Rush, a criminal defense attorney in San Diego. Rush and a client are gunned down in front of Madriani, whose later search for clues to his friend's death ultimately leads him to Cancún, Mexico.

Although Madriani, a recurring character in Martini's novels, is a trial attorney himself, he spends little time in court in this book. That fact alone is not unrealistic, because most cases handled by trial lawyers never make it to trial. Less realistic, but common among novels in the thriller genre that have lawyers as their protagonists, is a plot that turns Madriani into the equivalent of a private investigator. Modern legal thrillers are partially descended from the "hard-boiled" detective stories of the early twentieth century, but they generally place lawyers in the roles once occupied by private detectives. In real life, lawyers tend to rely on real detectives or paralegals (persons with some legal training or experience who are nevertheless not licensed to practice law) for the kind of fact-finding in which Madriani engages.

Timothy L. Hall

were frequently used by attorneys and other businesses—as well as by members of the public—to solve problems that were personal, financial, and legal. Private detectives do not have to have any previous experience, but most come from the military, law enforcement, or the insurance industry.

Kelly Rothenberg

Further Reading
Croce, Nicholas. *Detectives: Life Investigating Crime*. New York: Rosen, 2003.
Horan, James D. *The Pinkertons*. New York: Bonanza Books, 1967.
Meltzer, Milton. *Case Closed: The Real Scoop on Detective Work Life*. New York: Orchard Books, 2001.

See also Cybercrime; Embezzlement; Identity theft; Literature about criminal justice; Police detectives; Private police and guards; Television crime dramas.

Private police and guards

Definition: Nongovernment security personnel who provide protective services that supplement law-enforcement protection

Criminal justice issues: Crime prevention; law-enforcement organization

Significance: Private security personnel make a valuable contributions to the criminal justice mission of safeguarding lives and property by supplementing the work of government law enforcement; however, their contributions are limited by restrictions on their enforcement powers and by the lack of training that many of them receive.

As American society has developed and the challenges of crime have become more formidable, private policing and security services have increased. Public or governmental policing has the primary responsibility to ensure that lives are protected and property is safeguarded, but individual corporations, private persons, and residential communities have turned to private security agencies to supplement the governmental services provided by government police. Since the mid-nineteenth century, the growth of private security agencies and private police has been tremendous. In early 2005, it was estimated that approximately 1.8 million private security personnel were working in the United States. That figure was more than double the number of public law-enforcement officers.

History

The earliest significant private security services in the United States were offered by the Pinkerton National Detective Agency that began in Chicago in 1850. Allan Pinkerton, the founder of the agency, contributed the term "private eye" to the English language by creating a logo that placed the company's slogan, "We never sleep," under a picture of a human eye that came to symbolize private detective work. The development of the Pinkertons, as they were called, and other private detective and security agencies was directly related to railroad security, counterfeiting investigations, and other property-related crimes. Eventually, the private security business took on investigations of violent crimes.

Growth of the Private Security Industry

The growth of private security and loss prevention agencies has been fueled by a number of factors, such as the limited budgets of government police agencies. As governmental law-enforcement agencies have had to do more with less, pressure has grown on corporations and residential communities to look to the private security industry to provide needed protective services such as building security, armored car guards, asset protection, personnel protection, and general increased security presence.

Another factor has been the increasing specialization of security services. As society becomes more complicated with improved technology and special needs, public police resources are more strained. This trend has prompted the need for the employment of specialized private security services that can be employed quickly and efficiently. For example, a corporation detecting signs of internal theft can quickly respond by employing the services of a private security company that specializes in such problems. If the corporation opted to seek the services of local police, it would be competing with the many other priorities and budget constraints of the police. The alternative, private security arrangements, might serve as an ongoing initiative to reduce long-term corporation losses.

Another example of a special problem focus might be threats against a top corporation official by a terrorist group. By employing the protective services of a private security agency, the targeted official would receive around-the-clock protection that few public law-enforcement agencies would be able to provide.

Private police and guards sometimes offer the additional advantage of being able to act without the same legal restraints placed on government agencies. The U.S. Constitution holds public law-enforcement officials to high standards of accountability, particularly in matters of search and seizure and interrogation of suspects. Private security officials are not held to the same standards and may engage in some actions that are not allowed to police. For example, corporations may require their employees to submit to polygraph (lie detector) testing conducted by private security officials and use negative results as justification for terminating employees. Public police officials cannot become involved in such matters, except in cases in which they are specifically targeting suspects in investigations and the suspects consent to be tested.

Challenges to the Private Security Industry

The growth of private policing brings with it a wide variety of challenges and issues. These challenges will increase as public police budgets come under closer scrutiny and public demands for private services increase. One major challenge is finding and training qualified personnel. Demands for private security personnel are increasing in a world in which crime is becoming increasingly high tech, and in which domestic and international terrorism are growing threats. Attracting, training, and retaining qualified personnel is an ever-present concern in the private security industry. Whereas public police have defined standards of training and certification to meet government mandates, the private security industry is lagging in this regard.

The global dimensions of crime require public and private security professionals to engage in ongoing dialogues and cooperative partnerships in their efforts to prevent, detect, and investigate crime. For example, local public police may reach out to their private security counterparts to gain information concerning investigations that only the private security personnel may have. Conversely, private security personnel may seek the assistance of the public police in complicated criminal investigations, particularly in situations in which eventual criminal prosecution is likely.

One of the personnel trends in private security is the hiring of off-duty public police officers. Although this practice allows private security firms to benefit from the services of well-trained and experience law-enforcement officers, it also has the potential of creating problems relating to identifying who is liable for the actions of such personnel.

Jay Zumbrun

Further Reading

Cunningham, William, John Strauchs, and Clifford Van Meter. *The Hallcrest Report II: Private Security Trends, 1970-2000*. McLean, Va.: Hallcrest Systems, 1990. Private security industry assessment of trends in the industry over the last decades of the twentieth century.

Holder, Philip, and Donna Lea Hawley. *The Executive Protection Professional's Manual*. Boston: Butterworth-Heinemann, 1997. Detailed guide to all aspects of corporate security for both professionals in the field and corporations that use their services.

Horan, James D. *The Pinkertons*. New York: Bonanza Books, 1967. Popular history of the famous Pinkerton Detective Agency founded in the mid-nineteenth century.

June, Dale L. *Introduction to Executive Protection*. Boca Raton, Fla.: CRC Press, 1998. How-to guide for persons interested in becoming executive security guards. Written by a veteran in the security field, the book offers many insights into the nature of private security work.

Nemeth, Charles P. *Private Security and the Law*. 2d ed. Cincinnati: Anderson Publishing, 1995. Comprehensive textbook on all the legal issues relating to private police and guards.

See also Campus police; Citizen arrests; Law enforcement; Police; Polygraph testing; Private detectives; Women in law enforcement and corrections.

Privileged communications

Definition: Statements made by individuals within protected relationships—such as attorney-client, husband-wife, physician-patient, cleric-penitent, and journalist-source—that state laws protect from compelled disclosure at trial or deposition

Criminal justice issues: Attorneys; professional standards

Significance: Privileged communication laws encourage full and free disclosure between certain classes of individuals when the speaker needs to be able to make confidential statements, including statements about the person's own misdeeds, with the assurance that the recipient of this information cannot be compelled to reveal it at a later date.

Legal scholars, such as John Henry Wigmore, have observed that there are four fundamental conditions necessary to the establishment of a privilege against the disclosure of communications. First, the communications must originate in a confidence that they will not be disclosed. Second, the element of confidentiality must be essential to the maintenance of the relation between the parties. Third, the relationship must be one that, in the opinion of the community, ought to be diligently fostered. Finally, any injury that would occur to the relationship by disclosure of the communication must be greater than the benefit that would be gained by requiring it to be revealed.

The concept of privileged communications goes against the fundamental judicial principle that the courts have a right to require anyone who may have relevant information to testify. Therefore, the courts strictly construe such privileges and accept them "only to the very limited extent that permitting a refusal to testify or excluding relevant evidence has a public good transcending the normally predominant principle of utilizing all rational means for ascertaining the truth" (*Elkins v. United States*, 1960).

Attorneys and Clients

Clients have a privilege to refuse to disclose, and to prevent their attorneys from disclosing, confidential communications made for the purpose of facilitating the rendition of professional legal services to them. The attorney-client privilege has been justified by the theory that disputes which could result in litigation can be handled most expeditiously by attorneys who have been candidly and completely informed of the facts by their clients. Such full disclosure will best be promoted if clients know that their disclosures cannot, over their objections, be repeated by their attorneys in court. In the criminal context, the attorney-client privilege is necessary to protect the accused's Fifth and Sixth Amendment rights to the effective assistance of counsel.

Privileged attorney-client communications can be waived only by the client. Further, if the client is called to testify during trial, the client can assert the privilege when asked by the opposing counsel what he told his own attorney. In most states, the death of the client will not relieve the attorney from the privilege that existed while the client was alive.

The privilege is not recognized if the client's purpose is the furtherance of an intended future crime or fraud. The privileged communications may be a shield of defense as to crimes already committed, but it cannot be used as a sword or weapon of offense to enable persons to carry out contemplated crimes against society (*Gebhart v. United Railways Company*, 1920).

Husbands and Wives

This privilege is considered necessary for the encouragement of marital confidences, which promote harmony between husband and wife. It is most commonly asserted in criminal proceedings, in which accused persons can prevent their spouses from testifying against them. Either spouse may assert the privilege.

In some states, the privilege extends past the death of one of the spouses. Communications between the husband and wife before marriage or after divorce are not privileged, however, and the privilege does not extend to proceedings in which one spouse is charged with a crime against the person or property of the other or against a child of either.

Physicians and Patients

The American physician-patient privilege originated in a New York testimonial provision of 1828 which reads:

> No person authorized to practice physic or surgery shall be allowed to disclose any information which he may have acquired in attending any patient, in any professional character, and which information was necessary to enable him to prescribe for such patient as a physician, or to do any act for him as a surgeon.

This statute set forth the general scope and purpose of the privilege. In some states it has been extended to communications between a patient and nurse, psychologist, psychotherapist, or social worker. The policy behind the privilege is that the physician must know all that a patient can articulate in order to identify and treat disease; barriers to full disclosure would impair diagnosis and treatment.

Attorney-Client Confidentiality in Fiction and Movies

In the 1988 film *Criminal Law*, directed by Martin Campbell, a defense attorney played by Gary Oldman wins an acquittal for his client (Kevin Bacon) from the charge of committing a brutal murder. However, after the lawyer becomes convinced that his client is, in fact, a serial killer, he continues to represent him—but now with the intention of proving that he is a killer so he can stop him from committing more crimes.

In real life, lawyers are severely constrained in their ability to reveal confidential information about their clients. Most jurisdictions allow lawyers to reveal information about clients to authorities if they reasonably believe that such revelations are necessary to prevent imminent crimes that might lead to serious bodily injury or death. However, the criminal defense lawyer in *Criminal Law* probably never has this kind of reasonable belief. His only options, therefore, are to represent his client diligently or to withdraw from the representation.

A more realistic treatment of attorney-client confidentiality can be found in the 1994 novel *The Advocate's Devil* by Harvard Law School professor Alan Dershowitz. In this novel, prominent defense attorney Abe Ringel represents a professional basketball player accused of rape. One of the most important issues raised in the novel is that of attorney-client confidentiality. Lawyers, with only few exceptions, are absolutely prohibited from revealing information relating to the representation of clients. Dershowitz wrestles with issues relating to attorney-client confidentiality in ways that are realistic and adroitly explained.

Timothy L. Hall

For the privilege to apply, the patient must have consulted the physician for treatment or diagnosis. Only that information which is necessary to enable the doctor to prescribe or act for the patient is privileged. The privilege is not recognized where the patient sees the physician at the request of another, such as a public officer. It does not apply in an examination by a court-appointed doctor or prosecutor or in an examination requested by the patient's own attorney for personal injury litigation purposes. The privilege is not recognized when patients have unlawful purposes in the consultations, such as securing illegal abortions, obtaining narcotics in violation of the law, or having their appearance disguised by plastic surgery when they are fugitives from justice.

In most jurisdictions, an implicit waiver of the privilege occurs when a plaintiff files a civil suit for personal injury damages. Plaintiffs are not permitted to sue for personal injuries while preventing their doctors, pursuant to the physician-client privilege, from disclosing pertinent treatment information. The privilege is also often statutorily waived in actions for workers' compensation, prosecutions for homicide, assault with a deadly weapon, commitment proceedings, and will contests.

Clerics and Penitents

The cleric-penitent privilege recognizes the need to disclose confidentially to a spiritual or religious counselor what are believed to be flawed acts or thoughts and to receive guidance in return. This privilege also recognizes that members of the clergy often assume roles as counselors, doing much work that overlaps with psychiatrists and psychologists, both of whom have the benefit of privileged physician-patient communications in most states.

David R. Sobel

Further Reading

Green, Eric D. *Problems, Cases, and Materials on Evidence*. Boston: Little, Brown, 1993. Textbook on the use of evidence that includes a discussion of privileged communications.

McCormick, Charles Tilford. *McCormick on Evidence*. 4th ed. St. Paul, Minn.: West Publishing, 1992. General work on evidence with a useful discussion of privileged communications.

Vickery, Alan B. "Breach of Confidence: An Emerging Tort." *Columbia Law Review* 82 (November, 1982). Discussion of the trend toward punishing persons who violate privileged communications.

Wigmore, John Henry. *Evidence in Trials at Common Law*. 2d ed. Boston: Little, Brown, 1961. A classic work on the subject.

See also Diplomatic immunity; News source protection; Public defenders; Witnesses.

Probable cause

Definition: Standard of proof necessary for government representatives to make arrests or search and seize suspects' belongings

Criminal justice issues: Arrest and arraignment; legal terms and principles; police powers; search and seizure

Significance: Probable cause is the standard of proof necessary for law-enforcement officers to make arrests or to search and seize the belongings of suspects.

The Fourth Amendment to the U.S. Constitution laid down the principle protecting people from unreasonable searches and seizures that forbids arresting officers from conducting these procedures without probable cause. The Framers of the Bill of Rights were concerned about government intrusions into the lives of citizens, and through the Fourth Amendment they sought to ensure that individual privacy would be respected.

The question as to what constitutes probable cause has been considered a number of times by the U.S. Supreme Court. In 1949, in deciding the case of *Brinegar v. United States*, the Court stated, "probable cause is the facts and circumstances within the officers' knowledge and of which they had reasonably trustworthy information and are sufficient in themselves to warrant a man of reasonable caution in the belief that an offense has been or is being committed." This requires that the officer or agent of the government be fairly certain (to have some tangible proof, even if it is not admissible in court) before making an arrest or search or before making application for a warrant.

Probable cause, as a standard of proof, may best be considered as lying on a continuum with

The Fourth Amendment

The right of the people to be secure in their persons, houses, papers, and effects, against unreasonable searches and seizures, shall not be violated, and no Warrants shall issue, but upon probable cause, supported by Oath or affirmation, and particularly describing the place to be searched, and the persons or things to be seized.

mere suspicion at one end and absolute certainty at the other end. Courts have held that reasonable suspicion, a level of proof somewhat lower than probable cause, is needed to stop and frisk suspects. On the scale somewhat higher than probable cause is preponderance of evidence, which is the standard of proof necessary to determine liability in civil cases.

Observational and Informational Probable Cause

There are two basic ways probable cause can be developed: through observation and information. Observational probable cause is formulated by police officers by using their five senses. If they can see, hear, smell, taste, or touch evidence that a crime has been or is being committed, an arrest or a search may be made. When determining the sufficiency of observational probable cause, courts take into consideration police officers' training and experience. Thus, a police officer trained to detect the scent of marijuana is recognized as being able to distinguish that odor to develop probable cause, even if an ordinary citizen may not make that distinction. With observational probable cause the "totality of circumstances" standard is often used by the courts. With this standard, surveillance and other observations over time are compounded to determine whether probable cause exists. Informational probable cause is usually developed through investigations that yield certain facts about suspects. Included here are statements given by witnesses to crimes, victims' statements, and statements given by other police officers and informants. Although probable cause is always required to arrest or search, warrants are not always necessary.

Warrantless Searches

It is clear from the language of the Fourth Amendment that the Founding Fathers intended for agents of the state to produce warrants prior to searching or arresting citizens. However, the courts have recognized the impracticality of that requirement in modern society. As early as 1925 a challenge to the need for officers to actually produce a physical document (warrant) was made by a man named Carroll whose car was searched during Prohibition. After government agents seized illegal liquor from his vehicle, Carroll appealed his conviction, alleging that the search was unconstitutional because the agents had no warrant. The U.S. Supreme Court, in deciding for the government in *Carroll v. United States*, reasoned that automobiles can be moved before a warrant can be obtained and that the police need flexibility when probable cause exists.

A lesser standard of proof, reasonable suspicion, is needed by police officers before officers may stop a car. Once the car is stopped, probable cause for a full search may be developed by the circumstances. For example, a police officer may stop a car because it is weaving and, while talking to the driver, may smell marijuana. Although the weaving was not probable cause to search the car (it was reasonable suspicion to stop the car), the smell of marijuana provides the officer with probable cause to search. The U.S. Supreme Court has ruled in *Ross v. United States* (1982) that once probable cause to search a vehicle has been established, the police have the right to search the entire vehicle, including all containers therein.

The probable cause requirement for police to conduct a valid search can be waived if the party consents to the search. The consent must be voluntary and intelligently given. Evidence seized without consent or probable cause is subject to exclusion from criminal proceedings pursuant to the exclusionary rule.

Reasonable Expectation of Privacy

Although the Fourth Amendment protects people and not places, not every location is protected by the language of the Fourth Amendment. The U.S. Supreme Court has determined that the requirement for probable cause is restricted to areas in which there is a reasonable expectation of privacy. Evidence or contraband that is in plain view of a police officer is subject to seizure without probable cause. Likewise, if marijuana is grown in an open field behind one's home, no reasonable expectation of privacy exists. The courts have held that persons have a reasonable expectation of privacy in a closed public phone booth but that they do not have a reasonable expectation of privacy while being detained in the rear seat of a police car. Issues related to the expectation of privacy have often generated controversy as increasingly advanced surveillance techniques have been developed.

Although police officers are the most likely criminal justice practitioners to develop probable cause, an independent tribunal (a judge or magistrate) must verify probable cause prior to the issuance of a search or arrest warrant. The police officer applying for a search or arrest warrant must outline the probable cause in an affidavit, and the judge or magistrate must decide if the evidence is sufficient to support the warrant. As a systemic check, a probable cause hearing is held during the pretrial stage after an arrest so that a judge can ensure that probable cause exists. If it does not exist, the defendant must be released.

C. Randall Eastep

Further Reading

Del Carmen, Rolando V. *Criminal Procedure: Law and Practice.* 6th ed. Belmont, Calif.: Thomson/Wadsworth, 2004. Comprehensive and readable review of criminal procedure that contains an extended discussion of the application of the principle of probable cause.

Hall, Daniel. *Survey of Criminal Law.* 2d ed. Albany, N.Y.: Delmar, 1997. Excellent overview of criminal law with clear discussion of probable cause.

Hall, John Wesley. *Search and Seizure.* 3d ed. Charlottesville, Va.: LEXIS Law Publishing, 2000. Textbook focusing on issues surrounding search and seizure.

Wallace, Harvey, and Cliff Robertson. *Principles of Criminal Law.* White Plains, N.Y.: Longman, 1996. Another excellent textbook with a good discussion of probable cause.

See also Arrest; Automobile searches; Bill of Rights, U.S.; *Bivens v. Six Unknown Named Agents*; Consent searches; *Illinois v. Gates*; Illinois v. McArthur; Illinois v. Wardlow; Kyllo v. United States; Maryland v. Buie; New Jersey v. T.L.O.; No-knock warrants; Police powers; Racial profiling; Reasonable suspicion; Search and seizure; Search warrants; Stop and frisk; Suspects.

Probation, adult

Definition: Sentencing procedure through which adults convicted of crimes are released by the court and stay out of prison, so long as they adhere to conditions set by the judges

Criminal justice issues: Convictions; probation and pretrial release; sentencing

Significance: By the end of the twentieth century, probation was the most commonly used punishment in the U.S. criminal justice system.

During the 1990's, approximately 3,600,000 people were on probation in the United States, compared with approximately 1,500,000 persons in prisons and jails. The number of people on probation amounts to one out of every thirty-eight adults and one out of every twenty-one males. Most people on probation have committed relatively minor crimes, such as driving with a suspended license, committing petty theft or larceny, or possessing small amounts of drugs or other controlled substances. The offenders have typically been released to the community under the supervision of a probation officer and are usually required to meet briefly with the officer once a week or perhaps only once a month for counseling.

Probationers must usually meet a series of requirements. Sometimes probationers must stay away from certain persons, such as wives or children they may have harassed or threatened, or from particular places, such as street corners at which drugs are sold. Judges may also order that probationers stay free of drugs or alcohol or that they find and hold a job. Employers generally do not need to be told that a job applicant is on probation. Breaking any of these conditions can lead to imprisonment for violating probation procedures.

The average cost of probation nationwide is about $850 a year per offender, which compares favorably with the average $22,000 a year it costs to keep someone in prison. In many states some of the costs of probation are recovered by requiring probationers to pay part of the cost of their supervision. This cost-effectiveness is one reason that the number of persons on probation has increased dramatically in recent years.

History and Goals of Probation

Probation comes from the Latin *probatus*, which means "tested" or "proved." In the early United States, persons convicted of crimes were eligible for a suspended sentence if they promised to behave well and offered proof that they could observe the laws. The modern system began in Boston in 1841, when John Augustus, a businessman and advocate of rehabilitation, began bailing out convicted offenders, found them jobs, and gave the court monthly reports on their progress toward a better life. Augustus gained the release of more than two thousand prisoners using this method, most of whom were effectively rehabilitated. In 1878 Massachusetts became the first state to allow judges to choose probation as an alternative to a prison sentence.

By 1940 all American states allowed probation for juvenile offenders and all but six permitted adult probation. Not until the 1980's, however, did all states and the federal government provide for adult probation. The first statistics on probation were collected in 1976, when it was reported that nearly 1,000,000 adults were found to be on probation and 457,528 persons were in prison in the United States.

Probation began as an alternative to imprisonment and was justified as a method of rehabilitation that would save many people, especially nonviolent criminals, from the horrors and potential violence of prison life. Because prisons did not seem to do a very good job of reforming convicts and always seemed to be terribly overcrowded, judges would have an alternative to sending people to the penitentiary. The goal was to reduce crime by allowing offenders an opportunity to prove their goodness in society. The principal goal was rehabilitation, reforming the guilty party, rather than simply punishment, retribution, or revenge.

Central to probation is the notion that persons found to be "good risks" can be placed on probation and that they will not commit more crimes if they are given supervision and counseling. The philosophy of probation is that convicted persons can become law-abiding again. All they need is to be provided with treatment programs, employment, and other services. The focus is not on the harm done by the criminal but on the future reduction of criminal behavior, which can be achieved through proper treatment and supervision.

Violations of probation can be controlled by the ever-present threat that violators will be sent to prison if they break the rules. The idea of probation challenges the "just deserts" school of criminal justice, which proclaims that the purpose of the system is to make those convicted of crimes pay for the damage they have done by undergoing imprisonment. The goal of this method of criminal justice is to punish offenders, not to rehabilitate them.

Probation Decisions

The decision to place a convicted person on probation is one alternative available at a sentencing hearing. The judge is usually informed of the details of the offense in each case and makes the decision to place a person on probation after considering a variety of factors. These include the defendant's prior criminal record, social history, and family and employment record. This information is usually provided by a probation officer assigned to investigate the case. Normally, probation is given only in felony cases, not in misdemeanor cases.

Probation is granted by the judge in most cases if the probation officer recommends it. Two key factors are involved in this decision: the seriousness of the crime and the report on the person's prior criminal record. In most cases the seriousness of

the crime is the single most important factor. Generally, persons convicted of having committed nonviolent crimes are much more likely to receive probation than those who have committed violent or drug-related criminal acts. The judge's decision is also influenced by the likelihood of rehabilitation. Persons considered "good risks" are very likely to receive probation, especially if their crimes did not involve violence.

Only a few studies have been done on the revocation of parole. Decisions to end probation and send people to prison follow no particular pattern or set of rules. There seems to be no consistent standard in revocation hearings. Judges are often inconsistent in arriving at these decisions. Generally, however, revocation depends on the nature of the probation violation. Failure to appear at meetings with parole officers is considered particularly grave. Revocation also depends on the probationer's age, prior record, and employment history. For example, the failure to find

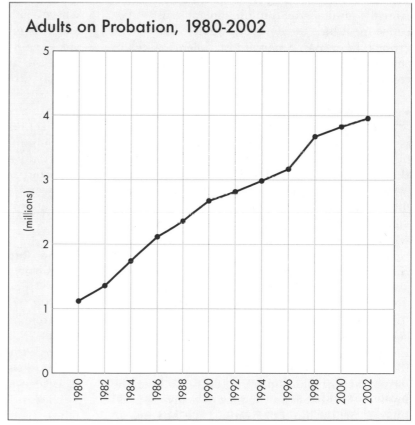

Source: U.S. Bureau of Justice Statistics.

or retain a job can lead to revocation. However, any decision to revoke probation must be made by a judge, not simply by a probation officer.

Intensive Probation

One alternative to sending a violator to prison for violating probation is to order more intensive probation. This method can also be applied in cases in which a convicted person has committed a serious or violent crime. Intensive probation provides much closer supervision of offenders and is more than three times more expensive than regular probation. Offenders in intensive programs are required to contact parole officers very frequently, sometimes as often as once a day or at least once a week.

Georgia, a state with a large investment in intensive probation, requires that serious nonviolent offenders have five face-to-face contacts with probation officers every week. The failure rate in this program is about 16 percent, or about one-half the failure rate for regular probationers. Prisoners on either type of probation are extremely unlikely to commit violent crimes, because most have never been convicted of violent crimes. Less than 1 percent of violent crimes in the United States (0.8 percent to be exact) are committed by probationers.

Probation Officers

The major problem with the probation system is the huge caseloads carried by most probation officers. Experts consider thirty cases per officer the best possible situation. However, the average officer in the United States has at least two hundred cases each month. Such huge caseloads prevent many officers from getting actively involved with their clients. Instead, all probationers receive the same treatment, regardless of whether they have been convicted of income tax evasion or armed robbery. Few probationers can get the individual attention they need to remain successfully employed and motivated. The problem seems not to be the idea of probation but the way the system works. There is too little money and too few probation officers to do an effective job.

Another problem since the 1980's has been the fundamental belief on the part of many criminal justice practitioners, from police officers to judges, that probation does not reduce crime. A majority of the U.S. public seems to accept this view. This has led to a major shift in how judges determine sentences. During the 1960's and 1970's, probation officers and judges believed that their mission was to reform and rehabilitate persons under their supervision and authority. Probation was supposed to help people convicted of crimes work their way back into society through employment opportunities and counseling. Probation officers saw their job as helping their clients overcome drug or alcohol dependency while meeting their family obligations.

During the 1980's, however, a much harsher form of criminal justice was instituted, with "just deserts" being the most prominent philosophy. In this view, punishment rather than rehabilitation was the goal, and parole officers responded by focusing their attention on catching probation violators and reporting them to the courts for confinement. New technologies and monitoring devices have made this practice more common. Electronic monitoring devices attached to probationers' legs or ankles enable officers to know where a subject is every minute of the day. House arrest is much more possible with such new devices, many of which have been available only since the mid-1990's. Nevertheless, probation is primarily reserved for people convicted of nonviolent crimes. The costs of normal, nonintensive probation are still about one-twentieth the cost of imprisonment, and a majority of probationers do not commit additional crimes. Probation is a system that works well to reduce future criminal activity by providing rehabilitation for offenders. It has been shown to be the best sentencing alternative to imprisonment.

Leslie V. Tischauser

Further Reading

Abadinsky, Howard. *Probation and Parole*. 7th ed. Upper Saddle River, N.J.: Prentice-Hall, 2000. Detailed description of probation and parole in the United States.

Carter, Robert M., and Leslie T. Wilkins, eds. *Probation, Parole, and Community Corrections*. New York: John Wiley & Sons, 1976. Discussions of the procedures and guidelines used in considering probation.

Glaze, Lauren, and Seri Pella. *Probation and Parole in the United States, 2003*. Washington,

D.C.: Bureau of Justice Statistics, 2004. U.S. Department of Justice report on the workings of probation programs throughout the United States.

Hussey, Frederick A., and David E. Duffee. *Probation, Parole, and Community Field Services: Policy, Structure, and Process*. New York: Harper & Row, 1980.

Lipton, Douglas, Robert Martinson, and Judith Wilks. *The Effectiveness of Correctional Treatment: A Survey of Treatment Evaluation Studies*. New York: Praeger, 1975. Evaluation of the effectiveness of probation versus incarceration.

Petersilia, Joan, ed. *Community Corrections: Probation, Parole, and Intermediate Sanctions*. New York: Oxford University Press, 1998. Examination of the use of probation and parole in community-based corrections programs.

See also Clemency; Community-based corrections; Drug testing; Marshals Service, U.S.; Pardons; Parole; Parole officers; Presentence investigations; Probation, juvenile; Sentencing; Suspended sentences.

Probation, juvenile

Definition: Sentencing procedure through which juveniles convicted of crimes are released by the court and stay out of prison, so long as they adhere to conditions set by the judges

Criminal justice issues: Convictions; probation and pretrial release; sentencing

Significance: As an alternative to or in addition to time spent in correctional institutions, probation is often imposed on persons who have been convicted of crimes, especially juveniles.

Probation is a general term for alternative sentencing, allowing convicted criminals to live outside prison, either in the community or in supervised residential programs. The emphasis is on rehabilitation. By the use of education, training, and counseling, it is hoped that the convict will be able to lead a useful life and not continue criminal activities. Because youthful offenders are often perceived as more likely than older ones to change their outlooks and because prison is often viewed as a "school for criminal activities," juveniles are very often sentenced to probation.

Probation has its roots in the harsh laws of the Middle Ages in Europe, where corporal or even capital punishment was imposed for crimes that would be considered minor by modern standards. Judges sometimes suspended sentences or imposed lesser punishments than those ordinarily called for, especially when children were involved.

The modern American system of probation began in the nineteenth century, especially in Massachusetts, where the first paid probation officer was hired in Boston in 1878. In the latter half of the twentieth century, as Americans became more interested in social problems and the welfare of underprivileged citizens, probation, especially of inner-city youth, became widespread.

The Rationale Behind Probation

There have long been a variety of responses to antisocial activities in society. The biblical method of "an eye for an eye," combined with Christian concepts of good and evil, led to a general attitude that those who harm others must suffer pain in retribution. By the nineteenth century and the onset of the Industrial Revolution, this attitude began to change, at least in part thanks to the writings of reformers, notably Charles Dickens, whose novels emphasized the difficult conditions among which members of the working class were forced to live.

In the wake of the Industrial Revolution and the sudden increase of immigration to the United States by people who had few skills, little education, and little knowledge of the English language, an underclass developed, and crime became the only solution for many persons. The problem became more intense in the twentieth century, as American cities became increasingly populated by minority groups, often living in desperate conditions. Reformers became interested in improving the conditions under which such people lived rather than sending them to prison. In more recent times, there has been a great deal of concern that U.S. prisons are overcrowded and that people convicted of relatively minor offenses should be given alternative sentences.

The result of these changes in attitude was a system of alternatives to actual jail sentences, especially for young offenders. Particularly in the latter part of the twentieth century, young criminals began to be viewed as victims of society as much as villains, and new methods were proposed.

The Mechanics and Types of Probation

In modern times the process of sentencing begins with an arraignment, at which time accused persons are brought before a judge and their alleged crimes are stated. At this stage, a probation officer may file a petition with the court if it is felt that an alternative to incarceration is advisable. The decision is based on the seriousness of the crimes, the likelihood of reform, and the environment to which the accused will be returning.

If probation is imposed, it is always conditional. Criminals are assigned probation officers, who monitor their activities. Conditions are generally imposed; persons on probation must refrain from criminal activities, attend school or training programs, and often confine themselves to a particular geographic area. Probationers are kept under regular surveillance, sometimes by electronic means. If they violate the conditions of probation, they may be resentenced to prison. After the probational period has expired, they may be released into society as free citizens.

Juvenile probation is an attempt to give youthful offenders a second chance at leading useful lives in society. There are a great many opinions as to what sort of environment is most likely to allow and encourage youth to take such a course. The first consideration is the environment in which they lived before being arrested. If they came from reasonably sound homes, they would probably be returned to the custody of their parents and be supervised by a probation officer. They would be required to attend school on a regular basis and might also be assigned to community projects. This method was common in the 1960's but was perceived as less desirable in later decades.

Intensive supervised probation, begun in the 1960's for adults and expanded to include juve-

niles in the 1980's, is a more structured version of community probation. Probationers are often monitored electronically and may be required to pay restitution to their victims. Intensive counseling is also involved.

At the end of the twentieth century, residential programs for juvenile probationers became far more common. Such programs had their origins in the reform schools of the nineteenth and early twentieth centuries, but many varieties were developed. At one extreme is the boot camp system, modeled on military training methods. Probationers are given intensive physical and educational training, and their lives are very highly structured. It is hoped that such harsh discipline will be effective in teaching the youths to abide by the rules of society.

Somewhat less restrictive are group homes, in which the juveniles live together in the community, under the supervision of adults, who either live on the premises or work in shifts. The probationers may be entirely restricted to the home, may be taken on supervised outings, or may even be given limited privileges in the outside environment, depending on their behavior. The rationale behind this system is to allow offenders to gradually work their way back into the community.

Another system, which became increasingly popular in the 1980's, was to involve youths with the natural environment. This might involve something very much like a year-round summer camp, involving sports, swimming, hiking, arts and crafts, and educational programs. It may be an intensive wilderness survival program. In either case, useful work for the Forestry Service or other government agencies may be involved, including the improvement of trails and the cleanup of wilderness areas. The wilderness approach is often considered especially appropriate for juveniles from inner-city areas. It is suggested that an extreme change of environment may change youths' outlook and priorities.

If the court has determined that probationers have broken the law primarily because of an unfortunate home environment, the probationers may be placed in foster care. It is hoped that given a more supportive environment, they will change their ways. Parental visitation may or may not be granted. Along with these methods, a tactic called "shock probation" was introduced late in the twentieth century. Youths are taken to prisons, where they are shown the conditions in the hope that they will change their behavior in order to avoid going to prison themselves.

The Effectiveness of Probation

There is a great deal of controversy surrounding the effectiveness of assorted types of juvenile probation and the effectiveness of actual time in prison. Many statistical and individual studies have been conducted, but they have produced mixed results.

It is necessary to balance the welfare of juvenile offenders with the safety of the communities in which they live. At one extreme are those who believe that prisons are a bad influence in themselves. Young people who may be arrested for relatively minor offenses, such as vandalism or petty theft, will associate with hardened criminals and learn to adopt their lifestyle. Also to be considered is that there is a great deal of violence within the prisons, including sexual abuse of young inmates, both male and female.

On the other hand, there are those who cite an apparent increase in crime among youths and stress that lawful members of the community must be protected. These people often point out that a disproportionate number of juvenile offenders come from inner-city environments, in which crime and drug use is rampant, and that if they return to these communities, they are likely to return to crime.

The increasing use of alcohol and illegal drugs among youths confuses the situation further. The use of alcohol by someone under the legal age or the use of relatively benign drugs such as marijuana is a highly significant factor in the statistics involving youthful crime. As opinions on the law involving such offenses vary widely, the statistics are very often biased according to the viewpoints of those doing the studies.

Generally, it has been found that residential programs involving community involvement and useful training have at least some effect, although accurate figures are difficult to come by. Releasing offenders into the community is generally ineffective, especially if the community involved is an area in which both adult and juvenile crime is common.

Conclusions

The prevalence of criminal activities among young people in modern times has led to various attempts to control this problem. Beginning during the late twentieth century there was an increasing call for youths who commit serious crimes, especially violent crimes, to be tried and punished as if they were adults, even including subjecting them to capital punishment. At the same time, there were many attempts to consider alternative punishments in order to prevent young offenders from becoming lifetime criminals.

The problem is not easy to solve. On one hand, there is a natural tendency to want to treat children as gently as possible in the hope that they can overcome unfortunate environmental conditions and become useful members of society. On the other hand, the increasing presence of street gangs and juvenile criminal activity causes great fear among the adult population.

Marc Goldstein

Further Reading

Carter, Robert M., Daniel Gluer, and Leslie T. Wilkins. *Probation, Parole, and Community Corrections.* 3d ed. New York: John Wiley & Sons, 1984. Statistical analysis of assorted probation methods.

Champion, Dean John. *Criminal Justice in the United States.* 2d ed. Chicago: Nelson Hall, 1997. General survey of the modern legal system of the United States, with an extensive treatment of juvenile crime and alternatives to incarceration.

_____. *The Juvenile Justice System: Delinquency, Processing, and the Law.* 4th ed. Upper Saddle River, N.J.: Prentice-Hall, 2003. Broad overview of delinquency and the juvenile justice system response, including police, prosecutorial, and judicial decision making. It examines juvenile legal rights and the courts' decisions regarding adjudication, disposition, and sanctions.

Coffey, Alan R. *Juvenile Corrections: Treatment and Rehabilitation.* Englewood Cliffs, N.J.: Prentice-Hall, 1975. General discussion of juvenile crime, with an emphasis on alternatives to actual imprisonment.

Cox, Steven M., John J. Conrad, and Jennifer M.

Allen. *Juvenile Justice: A Guide to Theory and Practice*. 5th ed. New York: McGraw-Hill, 2003. Comprehensive examination of the juvenile justice system that connects theory and practice.

Currie, Elliott. *Crime and Punishment in America*. New York: Metropolitan Books, 1998. General discussion of sentencing alternatives, including probation, based on the premise that traditional prisons are not effective.

McCord, Joan, Cathy Spatz Widom, and Nancy A. Crowell, eds. *Juvenile Crime, Juvenile Justice*. Washington, D.C.: National Academy Press, 2001. In addition to a historical perspective, this book describes how cases move through juvenile courts and how recent legislation has affected court procedures, including transfers to criminal court, sentencing, and probation.

See also Juvenile courts; Juvenile delinquency; Office of Juvenile Justice and Delinquency Prevention; Juvenile justice system; Juvenile waivers to adult courts; *Parens patriae*; Parole; Probation, adult; Sentencing; Youth authorities.

Prohibition

The Event: Period during which a constitutional amendment banned the production, sale, and distribution of alcoholic beverages throughout the United States

Date: January 17, 1920-December 5, 1933

Criminal justice issues: Morality and public order; organized crime; substance abuse

Significance: Called a "noble experiment" by President Herbert Hoover, Prohibition was the most prominent attempt to legislate morality in the twentieth century; its failure brought an end to a major reform effort.

The prohibitionist movement existed as early as the colonial period, but most historians date the modern form to the 1850's. The movement met with local and state successes during the late nineteenth century. By 1900 a quarter of the U.S. population was living in "dry" areas (areas where the sale of alcohol was illegal); by 1917, twenty-nine states were dry.

The Eighteenth Amendment

Congress first enacted a temporary prohibition of the sale of alcohol in 1917 as a war measure. Then, in December, 1917, a proposed amendment to the U.S. Constitution stating that the "manufacture, sale, or transportation of intoxicating liquors within, the importation thereof into, or the exportation thereof from the United States and all territory subject to the jurisdiction thereof for beverage purposes is hereby prohibited" was introduced into Congress. It speeded its way through the Senate and the House of Representatives and was sent to the states for ratification. Mississippi was the first state to ratify (on January 8, 1918), and a little more than a year later, Nebraska became the thirty-sixth, the last required. Passage of the Volstead Act, a measure designed both to continue the wartime prohibition and to provide enforcement of Prohibition as mandated by the Eighteenth Amendment, followed on October 28, 1919. The Volstead Act defined alcoholic beverages as those containing at least 0.5 percent alcohol.

The Prohibition Era

Almost from the first, Prohibition appeared to be largely unenforceable. Those who wanted to drink had little trouble locating bootleggers, and speakeasies (clubs that served alcohol illegally) abounded. The Prohibition Bureau's budget was small, and all the presidents of the period—Warren G. Harding, Calvin Coolidge, and Herbert Hoover—expressed doubts about the government's ability to enforce Prohibition.

One of the side effects of Prohibition was the rise of organized crime. Until the 1920's gangs had been local, but that soon changed. Although there were bootleggers and illicit distillers and brewers in all parts of the country, Al Capone, who operated out of Chicago, became the symbol of them all. By 1927 the Capone gang was grossing an estimated $60 million a year on beer alone, and by 1929 the figure approximated $100 million. Capone's beer earnings were said to be larger than the profits of Standard Oil of Indiana, Ford, or General Electric. Without Prohibition, this situation would have been impossible. That Prohibition was considered the most divisive American political question of the 1920's is generally conceded by historians who study the period.

A popular cause among women during the late nineteenth century, prohibition became national law when the Eighteenth Amendment to the U.S. Constitution was ratified in 1920. *(Library of Congress)*

The matter was addressed directly in the 1928 presidential election, when the country was presented with a choice between Republican Herbert Hoover, who supported Prohibition, and Democrat Al Smith, who opposed it. The election resulted in a Hoover landslide, although it was attributable more to the fact that the nation was basking in prosperity than to other issues. Despite his support of Prohibition, Hoover indicated his conviction that the Volstead Act was unenforceable. On May 29, 1929, he appointed a group to study Prohibition and make recommendations. The National Commission on Law Observation and Enforcement, headed by former attorney general George Wickersham, released its findings in 1931. The Wickersham Report concluded that a more serious attempt at enforcement would be required if the federal government expected the public to take the Volstead Act seriously.

Prohibition was a major issue in the 1932 presidential race. The Republicans renominated Hoover and at his insistence adopted a conciliatory position on Prohibition, calling for the Eighteenth Amendment to be resubmitted to the states for ratification. The Democrats, led by Franklin D. Roosevelt, supported outright repeal.

Repeal of Prohibition

Roosevelt's election spelled the end of Prohibition. On December 7, 1932, the House Ways and Means Committee held hearings on the matter of modifying the Volstead Act. Shortly thereafter, Representative James Collier introduced a measure to legalize beer with a 2.75 percent alcohol content. It won approval in the House and was sent on to the Senate. There it became the Collier-Blaine Bill, which in its new form upped the alcoholic content to 3.05 percent—another sign that Prohibition was a fading crusade.

On February 20, 1933, Congress passed what would become the Twenty-first Amendment, repealing the Eighteenth. It was sent to the states for ratification. Roosevelt did not have to wait until ratification to ask for changes in the Volstead Act, however; legislation based on the Collier-Blaine Bill, now known as the Cullen-Harrison Bill, which legalized 3.2 percent beer, was passed by Congress. On March 22, during the midst of his famous "hundred days," in which a rush of legislation was passed to fight the Great Depression, Roosevelt signed into law the Beer and Wine Revenue Act—the title was significant—which legalized beer and wine with an alcohol content of 3.2 percent, effective April 7, 1933, in those states and areas without local laws to the contrary.

At the same time, the proposed amendment made its way through the states. Utah ratified it on December 5, whereupon it became part of the Constitution. Prohibition at the federal level died.

Most historians agree that Prohibition marked a major step in the development of a federal presence in law enforcement. The modern Federal Bureau of Investigation had its origins in the enforcement of Prohibition statutes. Prohibition also made possible the growth of organized crime. Defenders of the "war against drugs" observe that liquor consumption fell in the 1920's; opponents point to the experience of Prohibition as an indication that criminalization of such behavior does not work. Both sides agree, however, that the way in which the laws were enforced (or not enforced) prompted a disrespect for law in general.

Robert Sobel

Further Reading

Behr, Edward. *Prohibition: Thirteen Years That Changed America*. New York: Arcade, 1996. History of the Prohibition era that examines the social consequences of the law, the rise of organized crime, and the corruption of government.

Chidsey, Donald Barr. *On and Off the Wagon: A Sober Analysis of the Temperance Movement from the Pilgrims Through Prohibition*. New York: Cowles, 1969, Fascinating study of the historical forces that led up to Prohibition.

Kerr, K. Austin. *Organized for Prohibition*. New Haven, Conn.: Yale University Press, 1985. Scholarly study of the political legal processes that created Prohibition.

Kobler, John. *Capone: The Life and World of Al Capone*. New York: Da Capo Press, 2003. Up-to-date biography of the most notorious organized crime leader of the Prohibition era.

See also Blue laws; Capone, Al; Commercialized vice; Drug legalization debate; *Ex post facto* laws; Gangsters of the Prohibition era; Mafia; Organized crime; Victimless crimes.

Proximate cause

Definition: Action that results in an event, particularly an injury or damage even, due to negligence or intentionally wrongful behavior

Criminal justice issues: Government misconduct; legal terms and principles; traffic law

Significance: Litigation, particularly that relating to police actions, raises important questions pertaining to the causes of injuries or damage that involve claims of negligence or liability.

Proximate cause is established by determining if any injuries or damage that occur would also have occurred in the absence of an individual's conduct or negligence. In instances of law-enforcement litigation, for example, courts are required to ask whether injuries or damage that are sustained would have occurred regardless of a law-enforcement officer's conduct. If the courts conclude that the injuries or damage would *not* have occurred without the actions of the officer or other individual, then proximate cause is established.

On the other hand, if courts find that police officers or other individuals have not acted in a negligent fashion, then their conduct would not be considered the proximate cause of the injuries, and there would be no subsequent liability on their part. Even in cases in which officers are found to act in unreasonable manners and breaches of duty have been established, litigants would still be required to demonstrate that the officers' conduct was the proximate cause of the subsequent injury or damage.

Police vehicular pursuits have been notoriously rich in litigation because of the many accidents occurring during high-speed chases. Courts have adopted two strategies in dealing with high-speed pursuit litigation. Some courts have been reluctant to rule in favor of plaintiffs on issues of proximate cause in cases concerning pursuits if the officers' vehicles are not directly involved in collisions with those of the plaintiffs. In this regard, courts have refused to extend the zone of proximate cause beyond actual collisions with the litigants' vehicles.

The second approach reflects a growing trend among state courts, which have adopted a stance examining individual cases as they occur. Courts tend to analyze all intervening situational factors leading up to injuries or damage to innocent third parties. Officers, or other individuals, can be held liable as the proximate causes of accidents to the extent that their behavior and existing situational factors surrounding their accident contribute to the injuries or damage sustained in the accidents.

Wendy L. Hicks

Further Reading

Feinman, Jay M. *Law 101: Everything You Need to Know About the American Legal System.*

New York: Oxford University Press, 2001.

Kappeler, Victor E. *Critical Issues in Police Civil Liability*. Prospect Heights, Ill.: Waveland Press, 1993.

Roberts, Albert, ed. *Critical Issues in Crime and Justice*. 2d ed. Thousand Oaks, Calif.: Sage Publications, 2003.

See also Criminal law; High-speed chases; Motives; Police civil liability; Proximate cause; Sobriety testing; Traffic law.

Psychological profiling

Definition: Method of identifying probable offender characteristics, including behavioral, personality, and physical attributes, based on crime scene evidence

Criminal justice issues: Crime prevention; investigation

Significance: Media portrayals have fostered a growing public fascination with the budding field of psychological profiling. Although there is debate over whether this field is more of an art than a science, it has proven particularly useful in investigations of suspects who commit serial crimes. Research confirms that at this stage in the development of psychological profiling, it should be regarded as a valuable tool for investigators, rather than a crime-solving strategy.

Variously known as criminal profiling, crime scene analysis, and investigative analysis, psychological profiling is the technique of studying details of crimes in order to learn about the probable characteristics of the perpetrators. By examining all features of a crime, including time and location, victim characteristics, methods used, and other pertinent information, psychological profilers attempt to infer characteristics about the perpetrators. The profilers draw on their inferences to build models of possible perpetrators that include their likely psychological makeup, mental health, social adjustment, age, sex, race, height, and physical appearance. The profiles are provided to law-enforcement officials to assist in identifying potential suspects or to aid in interrogations of already identified suspects.

History of Psychological Profiling

What may have been the first employment of psychological profiling was used in the investigation of one of the most notorious murder sprees in history—London's Whitechapel murders of the late nineteenth century whose unidentified perpetrator was dubbed Jack the Ripper. However, psychological profiling did not begin to achieve acceptance in law enforcement until after the Federal Bureau of Investigation (FBI) established its Psychological Profiling Program within is Behavioral Science Unit in 1978.

The FBI program began with the classification of information gathered through intensive interviews of thirty-six convicted sexual murderers. In 1985, psychologist David Canter of the University of Surrey in England was asked to assist in the investigation of a criminal known as the Railway Rapist. The profile that Canter produced proved useful in apprehending the rapist-murderer and helped launch Canter on a search for psychological principles that would be useful in generating other profiles. Much of his research drew on what he could learn about interactions between perpetrators and their victims. Canter later established a graduate program in "investigative psychology" at the University of Liverpool. Canter's work was followed by that of private investigator Richard N. Kocsis and his colleagues in Australia, who have conducted studies on the accuracy of psychological profiling and the skills necessary to employ the method successfully.

The Process of Psychological Profiling

Although there is no single protocol, the process of developing profiles usually follows several steps. The first stage, profiling inputs, involves collecting all information that might help in solving the crimes. This information usually includes crime scene photos, police reports, autopsy results, and all information about victims, including age and sex.

In the second stage, known as the decision process models, collected information is organized so that preliminary analyses of the crimes are possible. In this stage, the nature of the crimes is considered, possible offender motives are inferred, and the amounts of time necessary to commit the crimes are considered.

In the third stage, crime assessment, profilers attempt to reconstruct the crimes in detail. They produce play-by-play reconstructions of interactions between offenders and their victims, while considering such matters as the amount of planning needed, the extent of gratuitous aggression, types of wounds, positioning of bodies, and lengths of time for crime scene staging.

Canter's research suggests that the "criminals' shadows" should be interpreted. He uses "shadow" to mean the story, or inner narrative, of the offender that is reflected in the degree of care the offender has taken to avoid capture, the degree of expertise needed to complete the crime, personal habits, and various peculiarities of an individual crime.

In the fourth stage, the criminal profile, actual psychological profiles are completed. Complete profiles may be so detailed as to include exact age, race, sex, body type, style of clothing, occupational history, capacity for emotional intimacy, and living arrangements. Profiles might also include relationships between the offenders and their victims; the offenders' behavior before, during, and after the crimes; and their personality makeup. The final stages, investigation and apprehension, ideally consist of successful identifications, location, and arrests of suspects who match the profiles.

Psychological profiling is based on several assumptions, including the belief that criminals' crime scenes reflect their personalities. Moreover, because personality traits tend to be stable and enduring, crime scenes should reveal similar consistency. This assumption is believed to be particularly true of serial offenders, such as murderers, rapists, and arsonists, whose behaviors typically reveal continuity and consistency. For example, many serial murderers leave identifiable marks, or "signatures," at their crime scenes. Some offenders collect items or "trophies." Body positioning and crime manipulations ("staging") are usually distinctive and consistent. Another assumption of psychological profiling is that while the methods, or modus operandi (MO), of serial criminals may change somewhat over time and in different situation, other behavior patterns, such as their signatures, generally do not.

Validity of Psychological Profiling

Part of the controversy over psychological profiling stems from misunderstandings of its purpose. The FBI's own Behavioral Science Unit cautioned that although profiles occasionally lead directly to identifications of suspects, such successes are the exception rather than the rule. The chief value of psychological profiles is the direction they give to investigations to help them focus on the most likely characteristics of suspects. A study of nearly two hundred FBI profiles found that they were deemed useful in 46 percent of the cases, and in 17 percent of cases they led to actual suspects. In a majority of cases, investigators felt that the profiles provided a better focus for the process of investigating a crime.

Critics of profiling have argued that although profiles may create a wealth of information, there is currently no way of knowing what part of that information is critical. Another criticism concerns the validity of the information in the databases used to develop profiles. No central database of information on criminals exists, and the few databases that do exist draw information almost exclusively from convicted felons. Information on perpetrators who evade arrest is therefore not included. Moreover, there is also concern about the accuracy of self-reported serial offenders, the majority of whom have antisocial personalities and are proficient at lying and impression management. Finally, the requisite skills for psychological profiling are debated. Some have argued that investigative experience is essential, but recent research suggests that objectivity and logical reasoning are more important.

Richard D. McAnulty

Further Reading

Canter, David. *Criminal Shadows: Inner Narratives of Evil*. London: AuthorLink Press, 2000. Summary of some of the findings of the pioneer English profiler who helped solve the Railway Rapist case and established a graduate program in investigative psychology in England.

Douglas, John. *The Anatomy of Motive: The FBI's Legendary Mindhunter Explores the Key to Understanding and Catching Violent Criminals*. New York: Pocket Books, 2000. A former criminal profiler for the FBI explains how understanding motive is essential for successful detective work.

Douglas, John, and Mark Olshaker. *Mindhunter: Inside the FBI's Elite Serial Crime Unit*. New York: Scribner, 1995. Memoir of a former FBI agent (Douglas) who specialized in tracking serial killers and made heavy use of psychological profiling.

Egger, Steven A. *The Need to Kill: Inside the World of the Serial Killer*. Englewood Cliffs, N.J.: Prentice Hall, 2003. A criminologist and former homicide investigator, Egger challenges myths about serial murderers and offers case descriptions of several, including Ted Bundy and Henry Lee Lucas.

Holmes, Ronald M., and Stephen T. Holmes, eds. *Contemporary Perspectives on Serial Murder*. Thousand Oaks, Calif.: Sage Publications, 1998. Collection of articles offering diverse perspectives on serial killers and investigation methods, including psychological profiling, with examples.

Kocsis, Richard N., Andrew F. Hayes, and Harvey J. Irwin. "Investigative Experience and Accuracy in Psychological Profiling of a Violent Crime." *Journal of Interpersonal Violence* 17, no. 8 (2002): 811-823. Attempt to support the findings of psychological profiling with empirical data.

Ressler, Robert K., and Thomas Schachtman. *I Have Lived in the Monster: Inside the Minds of the World's Most Notorious Serial Killers*. New York: St. Martin's Press, 1998. Memoir of a former agent who worked on the FBI's Behavioral Science Unit's psychological profiling system.

See also Crime scene investigation; Forensic psychology; Murders, mass and serial; Police powers; Police psychologists; Racial profiling; Restorative justice; Unabomber.

Psychopathy

Definition: Also known as sociopathy, a psychological disorder marked by a constellation of personality traits, including dishonesty, guiltlessness, and callousness

Criminal justice issues: Crime prevention; deviancy; mental disorders

Significance: Although not identical to either violence or chronic antisocial behavior, psychopathy is associated with increased risk for crime and recidivism.

Few individuals are of greater concern to the criminal justice system than psychopaths. Such people are also sometimes known as sociopaths—a term introduced by American psychiatrist G. E. Partridge in 1930. However, some authorities reserve the latter term for people whose antisocial behavior appears primarily psychosocial in origin.

Clinical Description

The term "psychopathy" has engendered considerable confusion. Psychopathy should not be confused with global mental disturbance (psychopathology) or with psychosis, which is marked by a loss of reality contact. Psychopaths tend to behave rationally, although their behavior may often strike others as outrageous. Psychopathy should not be confused with violence, either, as in the colloquial phrase "psychopathic killer," although psychopaths tend toward aggressiveness.

Although psychopathy has been described since at least the early nineteenth century, it was not until the 1941 publication of American psychiatrist Hervey Cleckley's book *The Mask of Sanity* that the features of psychopathy were formally delineated. Based on detailed clinical observations, Cleckley outlined sixteen criteria for psychopathy. Among these criteria are superficial charm, dishonesty, undependability, guiltlessness, callousness, failure to learn from punishment, poor foresight, and sexual promiscuity.

Cleckley's criteria formed the basis for the best-validated instrument for assessing psychopathy: the Psychopathy Checklist-Revised (PCL-R), developed in 1991 by University of British Columbia psychologist Robert Hare. Hare's checklist is a standardized interview that requires access to file information and is used extensively in forensic research. Cleckley correctly observed that psychopathy tends to be more common in male subjects than in female subjects, and that although many psychopaths are found in prison, other psychopaths (whom he termed "subclinical") function successfully in society.

Implications for Criminal Justice

The concept of psychopathy bears significant implications for criminal justice. A 1996 review by University of North Texas psychologist Randall Salekin and his colleagues demonstrated that high scorers on the PCL-R are at markedly increased risk for violence and both criminal and sexual recidivism, including rape. As a consequence of the documented association between psychopathy and recidivism, some prisons have begun to consider diagnoses of psychopathy in parole decisions, although this practice is controversial. There is also some evidence that psychopaths in prisons are at heightened risk for disciplinary infractions, although the findings in support of this possibility are mixed.

Despite the heightened risk of psychopaths for crime and violence, psychopathy must be distinguished from the diagnostic category of antisocial personality disorder (ASPD), which is characterized by the subjects' long-standing histories of illegal and irresponsible behaviors. Psychopathy and ASPD overlap only moderately, and only about 25 percent of incarcerated criminals meet PCL-R criteria for psychopathy. Psychopathy also overlaps with alcohol dependence (alcoholism) and other substance dependence disorders. This is especially important because the ingestion of certain substances may further amplify psychopaths' risk for crimes.

Research suggests that psychopaths may often "burn out" in middle age, meaning that their symptoms become less severe when they reach their forties and fifties. Nevertheless, this decrease is specific to the antisocial and criminal behaviors that sometimes accompany psychopathy, not to the core affective and interpersonal deficits of the syndrome. In other words, as psychopaths grow older, they generally remain guiltless and callous, while they typically become less dangerous.

The application of psychopathy to death-penalty determinations is controversial. Some authors maintain that psychopathy's well-documented association with recidivism argues for invoking this condition as an aggravating factor in death-penalty decisions. In contrast, others maintain that psychopathy's apparent biological roots argue for invoking this condition as a mitigating factor in such decisions. The outcome of this debate notwithstanding, psychopathy seems likely to play an increasingly prominent role in judicial decisions for the foreseeable future.

Scott O. Lilienfeld
Katherine A. Fowler

Further Reading

Bartol, C., and A. Bartol. *Psychology and Law.* 3d ed. Belmont, Calif.: Wadsworth/Thomson Learning, 2004.

Cleckley, H. *The Mask of Sanity.* 5th ed. St. Louis: Mosby, 1988.

Hare, R. D. *Without Conscience: The Disturbing World of the Psychopaths Among Us.* New York: Simon & Schuster, 1993.

Lykken, D. T. *The Antisocial Personalities.* Hillsdale, N.J.: Erlbaum, 1995.

See also Alcohol use and abuse; Capital punishment; Crime; Criminals; Defendant self-representation; Mental illness; Parole; Pornography and obscenity; Rape and sex offenses; Recidivism; Sex offender registries.

Public defenders

Definition: Government attorneys assigned to represent criminal defendants who cannot afford to hire private attorneys

Criminal justice issues: Attorneys; defendants; professional standards

Significance: By representing criminal defendants who cannot afford to pay for their own attorneys, public defenders play an important role in ensuring that the right of all defendants to counsel is satisfied.

Persons charged with a crime in the United States are entitled to have a lawyer represent them. Those who cannot afford to hire their own lawyer are entitled to representation by a lawyer appointed by the court and paid for by the government. In most U.S. cities and many states, this representation is provided by a lawyer or group of lawyers called public defenders. These attorneys are employed by the government specifically to represent those who cannot afford to hire their own counsel.

The Constitutional Right to Counsel

Before 1963 most persons charged with a crime who could not afford to hire a lawyer to represent them simply represented themselves. Even in very serious cases poor, and sometimes poorly educated, people presented their own cases to juries and judges. There was no nationally recognized right to have a lawyer appointed to represent indigent defendants. The U.S. Supreme Court held in 1942 that criminal defendants were entitled to the appointment of a lawyer at government expense only when special circumstances required a lawyer to make a defendant's trial fair. The Court held that the constitutional guarantee of "due process" required only that defendants have fair trials and that in most cases trials could be fair even though defendant did not have a lawyer.

The Supreme Court recognized two exceptions to this "special circumstances" rule, but these exceptions had limited applicability. First, persons charged with crimes against federal law in federal rather than state courts were entitled under the Sixth Amendment to the U.S. Constitution to have a lawyer appointed to represent them. The assistance of counsel clause of the amendment provides that "in all criminal prosecutions, the accused shall . . . have the assistance of counsel for his defense." Second, persons charged in federal or state courts with capital crimes, for which they could receive the death penalty, were entitled to the appointment of a lawyer. Because the vast majority of criminal charges did not carry a possible death sentence as punishment and most criminal offenses were (and still are) prosecuted in state rather than in federal courts, most people charged with most crimes were represented by a lawyer only if they had the money to hire one. Even persons charged with very serious crimes which could result in long prison terms were routinely tried without counsel.

These rules changed dramatically in 1963, when the U.S. Supreme Court decided in the case of *Gideon v. Wainwright* that having a lawyer represent an accused person was essential to ensuring that every criminal trial was fair. The source of this right was the Sixth Amendment's guarantee of the assistance of counsel. For the first time, the Court ruled that the Sixth Amendment's guarantee of the assistance of counsel was fully applicable to the states and required that all indigent persons charged with serious crimes or "felonies" in state courts, as well as those charged in federal courts, had to be provided with a lawyer at government expense.

The Creation of the Public Defender

The Supreme Court's *Gideon v. Wainwright* decision resulted in the creation of public defender offices and programs throughout the nation. Some jurisdictions established public defenders to handle most criminal cases against indigent persons, while others relied on the appointment of private lawyers to handle these cases. In 1972 the Supreme Court expanded the right to an appointed lawyer to include those persons charged with minor or less serious crimes (misdemeanors) as well as felonies. It later limited this right to those misdemeanor cases in which persons are actually sentenced to imprisonment, excluding cases in which punishment is limited to fines.

The right to have an appointed lawyer can begin at any "critical stage" of a case, even before it comes to trial, such as at an initial or preliminary hearing. This right can begin as soon as a person is arrested, when a person is questioned by police and given the Miranda warnings. These warnings include the right to speak with a lawyer, to have a lawyer appointed if an arrested person cannot afford to hire one, and to remain silent in order to avoid self-incrimination. Often the lawyer appointed is a public defender. Poor persons charged with a crime have a right to the services of a lawyer free of charge during trial, sentencing, and one appeal. The right does not provide for representation for further appeals or for representation in civil cases.

Modern Public Defenders

Although the Supreme Court has held that the U.S. Constitution requires that indigent persons charged with crimes be provided a lawyer at government expense, it has not specified how this must be done. Jurisdictions in the United States use three basic methods to provide such representation: public defenders, assigned counsels, and contract attorneys. Public defenders are lawyers who exclusively represent indigent criminal defendants. They may be organized by city, county, or state into offices, and they are usually employees of one of these units of government. Federal courts have a federal defender system, which provides representation to indigent persons charged with federal crimes. Assigned counsels are private lawyers who makes themselves available for appointment by the court on a case-by-case basis. They may or may not specialize in criminal defense, and they may or may not be screened or specially trained to handle criminal cases. They are paid a fee, which is usually fixed but can vary according to the time they spend on a case or on the type of case they are handling.

Under interpretations of the U.S. Constitution handed down by the U.S. Supreme Court, all criminal defendants are entitled to legal counsel. If they cannot afford attorneys of their own, they are usually defended by government-salaried public defenders. *(Brand-X Pictures)*

Contract attorneys are members of organizations, such as law firms or bar associations, which contract with cities, counties, or states to handle a certain number of appointed cases for a set period of time.

Most modern American criminal justice systems and virtually all urban ones rely on some combination of these options to provide representation to a large proportion of criminal defendants. A recent U.S. Department of Justice study found that in 1992 about 80 percent of defendants charged with felonies in the nation's seventy-five largest counties were represented by either a public defender or an assigned counsel. The estimated cost of these services to state and local governments was $1.3 billion in 1990, which was approximately double what these services cost in inflation-adjusted constant dollars in 1979. This rise in expenditures for the representation of poor defendants corresponds to the dramatic increase in incarceration rates in the United States during the 1980's and has led to concerns that increased caseloads and reduced funding may cause poor persons charged with crimes to have less fair trials than wealthy criminal defendants.

Problems of Public Defense

Although public defenders receive their salaries from the government, they are legally and ethically obligated to represent their clients, the accused persons, against the government. This has sometimes made the public, and even some clients, resentful or mistrustful of public defenders. Early studies of the system of public defenders during the late 1960's suggested that public defenders sometimes saw themselves as part of a team, which included the prosecutor and the judge, whose goal was to convince clients to plead guilty. Another strand of critical thinking challenged this critique, noting that effective public defenders could often obtain favorable plea bargains for their clients even if they did so through what appeared to be a less aggressive or less adversarial approach.

Whatever their views of themselves, public defenders have become essential components of the criminal justice systems in most densely populated U.S. jurisdictions.

During the 1980's and 1990's, many American jurisdictions experienced dramatic increases in the demand for public defender services. Between 1982 and 1986, for example, the U.S. Justice Department found that the caseloads of public defenders in the United States increased by 40 percent. This increase was caused in large part by increased prosecution of drug offenses, often characterized as the "war on drugs." In some jurisdictions, public defenders were each appointed to handle hundreds of cases a year, which raised questions about their effectiveness as defense lawyers and the quality of representation their clients received.

Some public defenders responded by going to court and refusing to accept additional cases without being provided with additional resources. All lawyers have an ethical obligation to represent clients competently, and some public defenders contended that no one could competently represent hundreds of different clients a year, with each case involving different facts and legal issues. Some courts responded to this demand for the services of public defenders by appointing private lawyers to represent indigent defendants *pro bono*, without compensation, as part of their obligation to serve the public. Because many of these lawyers had little experience practicing criminal law, this practice raised serious concerns about the quality of the representation they provided.

Standards for Criminal Justice

In an effort to establish uniform standards of practice for criminal defense lawyers, including public defenders, the American Bar Association (ABA), the nation's largest bar association, promulgated *Standards for Criminal Justice*. First published in 1968 and for the third time in 1992, the *Standards* set forth guidelines for effective and ethical conduct by both prosecutors and defense lawyers, as well as benchmarks for effective provision of defense services. They seek to provide to all eligible persons "quality" legal representation, as opposed to just competent counsel. They also stipulate that no public defender or ap-

pointed counsel should accept workloads that interfere with providing high-quality representation and that government must provide adequate funding for these services. Although these standards are only recommendations and have no legal weight, they have been influential in defining the role and operation of modern public defender offices.

David M. Siegel

Further Reading

Kunen, James S. *How Can You Defend Those People*. New York: Random House, 1983. Insider's view of what it is like to be a public defender, which sometimes requires defending reprehensible criminals.

Lewis, Anthony. *Gideon's Trumpet*. 1964. Reprint. New York: Vintage Books, 1989. Exciting account of the landmark Supreme Court case that firmly established the right to counsel of all criminal defendants.

McIntyre, Lisa J. *The Public Defender: The Practice of Law in the Shadows of Repute*. Chicago: University of Chicago Press, 1987. Detailed study of the structure and operation of the Cook County, Illinois, public defender's office, which serves Chicago. Provides a concise view of a busy modern public defender's office in a large city.

Smith, Steven K., and Carol J. DeFrances. *Indigent Defense*. Washington, D.C.: Office of Justice Programs, February, 1996. U.S. Department of Justice publication presenting statistical information on the use of public defenders throughout the United States.

Standards for Criminal Justice, Providing Defense Services. 3d ed. Washington, D.C.: American Bar Association, 1992. Professional guidelines for effective public defender services.

Wormser, Richard. *Defending the Accused: Stories from the Courtroom*. New York: Franklin Watts, 2001. Brief inside view of public defender work with many firsthand stories.

See also *Argersinger v. Hamlin*; Attorney ethics; Counsel, right to; Criminal justice system; Criminal procedure; Defendants; Defense attorneys; Effective counsel; Equal protection under the law; *Escobedo v. Illinois*; *Gideon v. Wainwright*; Privileged communications; Public prosecutors.

Public-order offenses

Definition: Acts that interfere with the operations of society and its ability to maintain order

Criminal justice issues: Morality and public order; substance abuse; victimless crime

Significance: Crimes against the public order comprise a collection of offenses, many of which are misdemeanors. The fact that these acts are considered crimes stems primarily from societal conventions.

Public-order crimes are often referred to as crimes against morality or vice. They typically include acts of prostitution, drug abuse, drunkenness, and gambling. Unlike common-law crimes such as murder or rape, which are evil in and of themselves (*male in se*), public-order crimes are crimes only because a particular law prohibits them (*mala prohibita*).

Public-order crimes supposedly reflect the prevailing norms, values, and opinions of the public at large. Because public-order offenses are socially constructed (not inherently wrong), they change throughout time and space. That is, ideas of what constitutes an offense may differ from one generation to the next and from one community to another. For example, narcotic drug use was not illegal until the Harrison Narcotic Drug Act of 1914. Likewise, some foreign countries, as well as the state of Nevada, allow sex for money.

The Public Debate

There is a major debate in the area of criminal justice as to whether vice crime is truly the result of a consensus of public values. As mentioned earlier, vice crime is characterized by immoral conduct, yet that conduct is also popular and considered pleasurable among a large segment of society. Many citizens partake in such activities and do not think they are truly wrong. In fact, many argue that public-order offenses are victimless crimes, saying that adults who seek to visit a prostitute or gamble away a paycheck are not hurting anyone. There is no complaining victim. Further, people so inclined will seek sexual pleasure or drugs no matter what the law dictates, and organized syndicates will supply the demand. Considering that these laws have failed to deter crimes for centuries, critics contend that the law should be more practical than moral.

Critics of public-order crimes also claim the laws regarding them are too arbitrary. They question why certain acts that cause great harm (like drinking alcohol) are permitted, while other acts (such as smoking marijuana) are outlawed. Similarly, they argue that the laws are too irrational. They question why a woman can pose nude for money, dance topless for paying customers, sell her voice for phone sex, and make erotic films for profit, but cannot directly take money for sex.

A final argument made by critics is a philosophical one: In a democratic society, people should be able to engage in self-destructive behavior if they choose to. It is hypocritical for society to legislate morality and force virtue on others. These critics feel that morals are a private matter and that moral offenses should be reserved for religious institutions, social condemnation, or individual conscience.

Supporters of public-order crimes argue that moral offenses do have victims. The loss of one's life savings at a roulette table or exposure to a sexually transmitted disease can destroy a family. Supporters also argue that vice crime victimizes the whole society. They believe that these "little" offenses can create a downward spiral into serious crime, as well as into urban decay and disorder. When society is disorganized, chaos ensues. Thus, morals act as the glue that ties society together and preserves social order.

Amy I. Cass

Further Reading

Best, Joel. *Controlling Vice: Regulating Brothel Prostitution in St. Paul, 1865-1883*. Columbus: Ohio State University Press, 1998.

Critcher, Chas, and David Waddington. *Policing Public Order: Theoretical and Practical Issues*. Brookfield, Vt.: Ashgate, 1996.

Meier, Robert, and Gilbert Geis. *Victimless Crime? Prostitution, Drugs, Homosexuality, and Abortion*. Los Angeles: Roxbury, 1997.

See also Antismoking laws; Breach of the peace; Commercialized vice; Disorderly conduct; Indecent exposure; Mafia; Neighborhood watch programs; Victimless crimes.

Public prosecutors

Definition: Attorneys serving as the public officials responsible for overseeing the prosecution of criminal cases by setting charges, conducting plea negotiations, and presenting evidence in court on behalf of the government

Criminal justice issues: Attorneys; political issues; professional standards; prosecution

Significance: The prosecutor is one of the most powerful actors in the justice system because of the office's broad discretionary powers to determine which cases will be pursued and which defendants will be permitted to plead guilty to lesser charges.

The prosecutor is the public official who acts as the attorney representing the government and the public in pursuing criminal convictions. The prosecutor possesses broad powers to determine which defendants to prosecute, what charges to pursue, and which cases to terminate through plea bargains. The prosecutor must oppose the defense attorney during trials and present sufficient and appropriate evidence to persuade a judge or jury to render a verdict of guilty.

The Prosecutorial System

The concept of the American prosecutor was drawn from English legal tradition, in which a representative of the king sought to persuade jurors that a particular individual should be charged and convicted of a crime. In the United States, prosecutorial responsibilities are divided among the various levels of government. Federal prosecutors are known as U.S. attorneys. They are appointed to office by the president and are each responsible for prosecuting federal crimes in one of the ninety-four federal district courts throughout the United States. Within each courthouse, they are assisted with their tasks by teams of assistant prosecutors. Their work is often coordinated by the attorney general of the United States and the U.S. Department of Justice.

At the state level, each state has an elected attorney general who, in most states, possesses the power to initiate prosecutions for violations of state laws. In three states—Alaska, Delaware, and Rhode Island—the attorney general oversees all local prosecutors. In most states, however, the focus of prosecutorial power is the local prosecutor. These local prosecutors are sometimes known as district attorneys, or states' attorneys. In all states except Connecticut and New Jersey, local prosecutors are elected officials who have primary responsibility for investigating and prosecuting violations of state criminal laws within their counties. In Connecticut and New Jersey, local prosecutors are appointed and supervised by state officials. By contrast, local prosecutors in other states are accountable to the voters within their counties. They are usually visible political figures who seek to please and impress the voters with their efforts to combat crime.

Many attorneys use the office of county prosecutor as a stepping-stone to higher offices as judges, state legislators, or members of Congress. The prosecutor's office serves this purpose especially well because of its high visibility in the local community and because the prosecutor can show tangible success in battling crime—an issue of widespread concern to voters. Moreover, prosecutors do not have to become involved in controversial issues that divide the community such as welfare spending or education. They can devote their time to publicizing their success in the battle against crime, which enjoys unified public support.

Because of the visibility and power of the local prosecutor's office, political parties frequently devote significant energy and resources to battling each other during election campaigns for the prosecutor's office. As a result, political leaders often select prosecutorial candidates based on their ability to raise campaign funds and their attractiveness to the voters rather than on their prior experience as attorneys. Attorneys who have never handled criminal cases before in their lives sometimes win elections as prosecutors. If their offices are anywhere but in rural areas, however, they usually have experienced assistant prosecutors who handle the steady flow of cases and teach them about criminal law. In small towns and rural counties, the local prosecutor may not have many assistant prosecutors, if any.

Because of prosecutors' involvement in politics, political considerations sometimes affect their decisions. They may use their offices to provide jobs (as assistant prosecutors and investigators) for loyal members of their political party. They may prosecute vigorously any questionable activity by political opponents while turning a blind eye to wrongdoing by influential citizens or by their political supporters. Because no official supervises or commands the local prosecutors in most states, it is up to the local voters to ensure that prosecutors perform according to professional standards. Voters are the only ones who possess the power to remove most prosecutors from office.

Prosecutor Decision Making

Prosecutors possess broad powers. They can use their discretion to determine which defendants are charged, what charges are pursued, which plea bargains to approve, and what strategies to employ during trials. Prosecutors even possess the power to drop charges against defendants without providing any reasons. This power to drop charges cannot be stopped or reversed by any other official, not even a judge or the governor. The primary pressure that keeps prosecutors from having unchecked power is the risk that the public will be unhappy with their decisions and vote them out of office in future elections.

Prosecutors are responsible for many key decisions in the criminal process. They must evaluate the evidence brought to them by the police in order to determine which charges, if any, to file against each defendant. Prosecutors make recommendations about whether defendants should be released on bail. Studies show that judges are usually very deferential to prosecutors' recommendations about whether bail is to be granted, the bail amount, and the conditions of release. Prosecutors also control the grand jury process by presenting evidence against the suspects that they have chosen without any defense attorneys in the courtroom to argue against the issuance of indictments. In states that do not use grand juries, prosecutors initiate charges against a defendant by filing an information describing the charges to be pursued based on the evidence thus far available. Prosecutors handle plea negotiations on behalf of the government and recommend sentences when defendants plead guilty.

Prosecutors also develop trial strategies and determine how evidence will be presented to the jury for those few cases that are not terminated through plea bargains.

Prosecutors' decision making is influenced by their need to please several constituencies. Because prosecutors' jobs depend on public support, prosecutors typically try to develop good relations with the news media. They want news reports to show them as making tough, intelligent decisions in identifying and prosecuting criminal suspects. Prosecutors must also have good relationships with the police, because they must rely on the police to do a good job in making arrests and gathering appropriate evidence. Prosecutors do not want to displease police officers by dropping charges or agreeing to light sentences during plea bargaining, because the police then may be less enthusiastic and cooperative in investigating subsequent cases. Prosecutors also rely on good relationships with the local county commission, city council, or state legislature that provides the annual budget for the prosecutor's office. If the prosecutors cannot please these elected officials, then they may receive inadequate resources in the following year's budget. Although prosecutors have broad discretionary power, their relationships with political constituencies influence their decisions and actions.

Prosecutors' decisions are also influenced by their need to process a steady flow of cases with their office's limited resources. For most prosecutors, this situation helps to encourage their participation in plea bargaining. Most offices do not have the time, money, or personnel to bring every case to trial. Moreover, prosecutors gain definite convictions when they can negotiate a guilty plea. If cases go to trial, there is always a risk that unpredictable juries might not render guilty verdicts. Through plea bargaining, prosecutors gain quick convictions with a minimal expenditure of resources.

Plea Bargaining

Prosecutors usually hold the upper hand in plea bargaining because they can initially charge defendants with multiple offenses, even if they are not sure that they can prove all the charges. This gives the prosecutor the ability to apply pressure to the defendant by scaring the defendant with the prospect of multiple convictions and punishments if a guilty plea is not forthcoming. The U.S. Supreme Court has decided that prosecutors can threaten defendants with additional charges during plea negotiations. Although the judge officially controls sentencing, most judges will routinely approve whatever sentence the prosecutor recommends as part of a plea agreement. Because more than 90 percent of cases terminate through plea bargains, the prosecutor effectively influences the sentences imposed on offenders in most cases.

The plea-bargaining process in many courthouses becomes streamlined through cooperative relationships that develop among prosecutors, public defenders, and judges. Frequently, the same assistant prosecutor, public defender, and judge are in the same courtroom day after day discussing plea bargains in one case after another. Before long, they come to understand one another's assessments of the seriousness of specific kinds of crimes and of the appropriate severity of punishment for each crime. Once they develop common understandings about the sentences to be imposed for specific offenses or repeat offenders, they can quickly develop consistent plea agreements in each new case that arrives before them.

Prosecutors and the Adversary System

Because the American justice process employs an adversary system that pits prosecutors against defense attorneys, many critics fear that prosecutors are encouraged to seek convictions at all costs rather than examine each case carefully to determine whether someone arrested by the police is, in fact, guilty. In an adversary system, attorneys can become too focused on simply defeating the opponent rather than ensuring that justice is accomplished through the conviction of guilty defendants. There is a risk that attorneys, including prosecutors, will attempt to hide

---

Prosecutors and Savvy Defendants

A Hollywood film that offers realistic insights into the complexities of prosecuting capital cases is director Harold Becker's *The Onion Field* (1979). Based on a book by novelist and veteran police detective Joseph Wambaugh, this film dramatizes the true story of Gregory Powell (James Woods) and Jimmy Smith (Franklyn Seales), who kidnapped two California police officers. Both men are eventually charged with the murder of one of the kidnapped officers.

The defendants are initially tried together, convicted of murder, and sentenced to death. However, the California Supreme Court reverses their convictions and orders them retried. In their second trial, the defendants wear the prosecution down with a variety of legal maneuvers. *The Onion Field* film is realistic in emphasizing the difficulties faced by prosecutors trying to convict defendants who are legally savvy. However, it ignores a corresponding reality: the government's powerful advantages over poor and uninformed defendants. Despite their legal maneuvering, both men are convicted again in their second trial. This time, however, they are sentenced to life imprisonment instead of execution, and one of them is eventually paroled.

Timothy L. Hall

---

information from their opponents, even when that evidence might cast doubt on the guilt of a defendant and thereby increase the probability that an innocent person receives unjustified punishment.

In other countries (in Germany, for example), prosecutors are appointed government officials who are under the supervision of a national office. They have secure positions, and their decisions are less susceptible to political pressures. They are obligated to reveal any evidence that questions the defendant's guilt, and their ultimate objective as professionals is to see that correct decisions are made. By contrast, as elected officials in an adversary system, American prosecutors are under pressure from the community to solve crimes. They may be blamed by the public and subsequently lose office if highly publicized crimes remain unsolved. This pressure may create incentives for prosecutors to pursue cases aggressively against defendants, even in instances in which the available evidence may be less than compelling. If prosecutors are unethical, their lack of the job security possessed by government-employee prosecutors in other countries may lead them to manufacture evidence against selected individuals simply to avoid public blame for unsolved crimes. Such problems are not widespread, but they have occurred with sufficient frequency over American history to raise questions about whether elected prosecutors in an adversarial system can make sufficiently objective decisions to avoid misuse of prosecutors' broad powers.

Christopher E. Smith

Further Reading

Cole, George F., and Christopher Smith. *American System of Criminal Justice*. 10th ed. Thomson/Wadsworth, 2004. General textbook contains a clear and up-to-date explanation of the prosecutor's role in each of the various stages of the criminal justice process.

Heilbroner, David. *Rough Justice: Days and Nights of a Young D.A.* New York: Pantheon Books, 1990. First-person account of a prosecutor.

Jacoby, Joan E. *The American Prosecutor: A Search for Identity*. Lexington, Mass.: Lexington Books, 1980. History and overview of public prosecutors in the U.S. justice system that offers a thorough social science analysis of several prosecutors' offices and the problems they face.

McDonald, William F., ed. *The Prosecutor*. Beverly Hills, Calif.: Sage Publications, 1979. Now somewhat dated but still useful collection of scholarly essays on different aspects of the work of government prosecutors.

Stewart, James B. *The Prosecutors*. New York: Simon & Schuster, 1987. Interesting account of major federal prosecutions.

See also Attorney general of the United States; Attorneys, U.S.; Attorneys general, state; Criminal justice system; Defense attorneys; Grand juries; Indictment; *Miranda v. Arizona*; Plea bargaining; Public defenders.

Punishment

Definition: Intentional infliction of harm by government on individuals for offenses against law

Criminal justice issues: Capital punishment; punishment; sentencing

Significance: Because punishment of criminal offenders usually involves inflicting harm on them in ways that would be considered unacceptable or immoral in other circumstances, competing theories attempt to justify or abolish the practice.

Punishment in the modern United States is a massive and costly enterprise. As of 2001, approximately 5.6 million adult residents of the United States had served at least some time in federal or state prisons. During that same year, federal, state, and local governments in the country spent $57 billion punishing these individuals. Moreover, that figure does not include the $72 billion spent on providing police protection and $38 billion spent on the court system.

Residents of the United States are more than eight times more likely to be incarcerated than residents of Germany—the most prosperous country in Europe—and they are nearly nineteen times more likely to be incarcerated than residents of Japan—the most prosperous country in Asia. Despite the fact that U.S. incarceration rates are so disproportionately high, compared to the rates of other wealthy democracies, the United States experiences far more violent crime per capita than other prosperous democracies. In 2001, the reported offense rate per 100,000 population for homicide in the United States was 5.6; in Germany the rate was 3.23. The disparity in rates for rape is even greater: 31.8 in the United States vs. 10.45 in Germany. Similar comparisons with Japan produce even more dramatic disparities, as Japan's homicide rate is only 1.10 and its rape rate 1.85 per 100,000.

Meanwhile, the United States invests more in punishing offenders than any other nation—both in financial outlays and in the loss of freedom for millions of incarcerated convicts—but even this price has not made for a safer society. All these disparities between crime and punishment rates raise fundamental questions about punishment: What justifies it? What are its objectives? How can those objectives be achieved? Finally, how important are those objectives compared to others, such as the preservation of civil liberties?

Philosophical Bases for Punishment

Until the eighteenth century, punishments for criminal offenses in Western societies typically consisted of sporadic public displays of spectacular corporal violence. Some of these punishments would now be considered forms of torture. A particularly gruesome example was known as "drawing and quartering": Ropes attached to each of a convicted criminal's limbs were tied to four draft animals, which pulled them in four dif-

ferent directions, eventually tearing the convict into four parts, hence, the "quartering." Severe punishments such as that served several objectives. They demonstrated the authority of the state, exacted revenge on criminal offenders, and issued warning to all those who might be considering committing similar offenses.

Punishment did not become a subject of serious systematic study until the mid-eighteenth century, when Cesare Beccaria published *On Crimes and Punishments* (1764). Beccaria argued that deterring offenders was the only legitimate function of punishment and it was best accomplished by standardizing penalties, publicizing them so that everyone understood and had notice of the harm they could suffer, and enforc-

Georgia chain gang breaking stones in a quarry in 1937. Until relatively recently in world history, making convicts suffer was a central idea behind punishments. *(AP/Wide World Photos)*

ing sanctions regularly and fairly. Beccaria further claimed that excessive punishments were inhumane and unnecessary to deter.

The late eighteenth-early nineteenth century English philosopher and reformer Jeremy Bentham developed Beccaria's insights into a comprehensive theory of law governed by the central premise of what has come to be known as utilitarianism. He argued that legislation should promote the greatest good, or utility, and the least suffering for the greatest number of people. According to his utilitarian philosophy, punishment should be forward-looking because its only legitimate purpose is preventing future crimes. From this perspective, three possible justifications for punishment arise: deterrence, incapacitation, and rehabilitation.

Deterrence functions as a disincentive to committing a crime. For example, it may be in the interest of students to steal books from libraries because they prefer having them exclusively to themselves and prefer not to have to return them. If no penalty exists for stealing books, the students have little reason not to steal them, other than their moral convictions. However, utilitarians believe it is foolish to rely on people's moral beliefs to prevent them from doing things that benefit themselves but decrease overall happiness for others. For utilitarians, threats of punishment shift the balance of incentives. If the book-stealing students risk paying burdensome fines or facing jail time, they are much less likely to steal books to avoid the minor inconvenience of having to return them. Criminal sanctions therefore alter incentive structures so that it becomes in each individual's best interest to obey the law. Breaking the law thus becomes unworthy of the risk.

To maintain this risk/reward deterrent ratio, the public must understand the laws and their sanctions, believe there is an adequate degree of likelihood that they will be apprehended and subjected to punishment, and agree that the punishment is not so extreme that its application would produce suffering that outweighs the happiness or utility it is intended to promote. For this latter reason, punishments designed to deter must not be too harsh—what in American constitutional language would be considered cruel and unusual—and must not violate rights of offenders by denying them due process or equal protection

under the law. The punishments must be proportionate to the crimes that are committed, so that perpetrators of more serious crimes receive more severe punishments. Finally, they must only be as severe as is required to accomplish the penological objective and therefore not be excessive. This argument presumes that a substantial portion of potential offenders engage in rational cost-benefit analyses to determine whether criminal activity is worth the risk of punishment, and some critics doubt whether potential criminals engage in such deliberations.

The Rationale for Incapacitation

Utilitarianism also regards incapacitation as a legitimate strategy for reducing crime. Incapacitation renders convicts incapable of committing further crimes against the general public, either by incarcerating the convicts or physically debilitating them. These ends may be achieved by such means as execution for murderers and chemical or surgical castration for sex offenders. The belief that individuals who commit crimes will continue to commit them unless incapacitated underlies this theory, which is the basis of recidivist statutes, such as "three-strikes" laws, that impose more severe punishments for repeat offenders.

The value of incapacitation is undermined if serving time actually increases the likelihood of the convicts committing more crimes upon their release. That might happen, for example, if their experiences of living among other convicts in prison conditions them to think of themselves as career criminals. Released convicts might also turn back to crime if they find that their opportunities for success in noncriminal life are worse after their release than they were before they entered the criminal justice system.

To some degree, warehousing convicts in prisons does prevent them from committing offenses against society. However, it is widely acknowledged that crime rates within prisons are higher than crime rates outside them. A consistent utilitarian cannot discount the pain caused by offenses committed inside prisons; however, most advocates of incapacitating criminals pay little attention to the consequences of segregating the most troubled populations in such brutal arrangements. Moreover, in the light of the fact that African American men are approximately ten times more likely than white men to be incarcerated, this concentration of violence raises troubling questions about fairness and discrimination.

The Goal of Rehabilitation

Rehabilitation is another legitimate means of preventing crime for utilitarians. It seeks to reform offenders so they no longer commit crimes, and under this theory, sentences may seem more like treatments than punishment. Rehabilitation can take many forms, including religious conversion, moral transformation, substance abuse therapy, vocational training, and education. Instead of conceiving of prison as a depository for offenders, rehabilitative theory seeks to use sentences as occasions to remove offenders who had strayed from law-abiding life from whatever social forces had corrupted them.

Early prisons practicing the rehabilitative model, such as those at Auburn and Sing Sing, New York, and Pittsburgh, Pennsylvania, during the 1820's, therefore isolated inmates from one another to prevent them from tempting one another to deviate from their paths toward the straight and narrow. Left to hard work, their conscience, and the Bible, reformers believed that the inmates' good natures would return. Rehabilitative ideals are committed to a belief that humans are good, equal, and redeemable and deserve the opportunity to correct their lives and restore their full citizenship. According to this position, governments are responsible for helping their citizens along this path.

In addition to rehabilitating individual offenders, utilitarianism also attempts to prevent crime by addressing the social causes of crime and "rehabilitate" the broader culture as well as individuals. If drug abuse, poverty, or racial discrimination cause crime, utilitarians would seek to uproot criminal behavior by eliminating the cultural forces that generate millions of criminals rather than simply incarcerating all of these criminals once they commit offenses. In this sense, utilitarian rehabilitation attempts to diagnose and cure the social diseases that cause crime rather than simply treating individuals once they have symptoms of criminal behavior.

Critics of the rehabilitative model question its effectiveness, doubting whether even the most thorough therapeutic treatment can reform incorrigible criminals. Others find rehabilitative objectives vague and difficult to measure, leaving too much of sentencing indeterminate and subjective. Further, some fear that rehabilitation blurs the line between treatment and punishment and thus results in extended criminal detention of those needing only therapy. The mentally ill, for example, will have difficulty ever leaving the criminal justice system.

Retributivist Theories

The most trenchant criticism of rehabilitation is leveled by those who disagree with the entire utilitarian view of punishment and find that "coddling" prisoners in this way suffers from a fundamental confusion: Criminals simply deserve to suffer punishment. By this view, it is morally imperative to punish murderers, for example, regardless of whether doing so might reduce crime rates.

The word "retribution," from a Latin word for paying back, traces its Western origins to the biblical *lex talionis* or "eye for an eye." Unlike the forward-looking orientation of utilitarianism, retributivism seeks to address the wrongs of the past by forcing offenders to pay their debts to victims and society. In other words, the retributivist believes that punishment should balance the scales of justice by causing offenders to suffer pain commensurate with that of their victims. In this sense, retribution exacts revenge in proportion to the moral desert of the offenders.

Immanuel Kant's late eighteenth century ethical writings provide the philosophical underpinnings for modern retributivism. The human ability to reason, Kant claims, enables each person to think freely and understand universal moral truths. By determining what is right from one's own reasoning, rather than from the authority of another, employing one's will to rise above the corrupting influences of culture and desire, and performing the good, one becomes self-governing and free. This understanding of humanity, wherein people use their reason to realize and live by objective ethical truth, provides the foundation for the Enlightenment's secular conception of human dignity. Because humans have dignity, Kant argues, they must always be treated as ends in themselves, rather than as mere means. He names this requirement that people not use others exclusively as tools the "practical imperative."

Utilitarian justifications of punishment violate the practical imperative because they use offenders merely to reduce crime rates. To preserve offenders' dignity, the justice system must hold them responsible for their crimes and treat them as if they were capable of freely making moral choices. Although this may seem odd, from a Kantian perspective offenders have a right to be punished. Otherwise they are but children or animals. In all utilitarian forms of punishment, offenders are denied dignity in this respect: rehabilitation seeks to cure them of their disease, deterrence treats them as rats that need shocks to keep them from eating cheese, and incapacitation simply denies them any ability to make moral choices. Anthony Burgess's novel *A Clockwork Orange* (1962), which was made into a controversial film by Stanley Kubrick, dramatically demonstrates these tensions between freedom and crime prevention.

Retributivists also claim that because preventing crime is the sole objective of utilitarian punishment, utilitarians would permit grievous injustices such as framing innocent people if such sacrifices furthered that goal. Although commentators repeat this criticism in most discussions about justifications of punishment, it does not appear to raise serious problems. Utilitarianism originated as a legal theory that demanded several institutional conditions for the public pursuit of utility, including security of person and property, legality, legislative supremacy, democratic accountability, publicity, and transparency. These utilitarian political procedures would preclude framing an innocent person.

Critics of retributivism find that its refusal to consider the objective of reducing future crime contradicts the most basic practical justification for punishment. Parents punish children, for example, to foster their development into moral citizens, rather than to balance metaphysical scales of justice. Society would surely find it reprehensible if parents were to assault a child physically and explain that they have administered corporal punishment as a vendetta because the child "deserves to suffer." Retributivism thus appears to offend the intuitive maxim that "two wrongs do not make a right."

To many, the retributive demand for "just deserts" provides a thinly veiled excuse for a lust for vengeance similar to the righteous indignation accompanying violence committed in the name of religion. As the Indian nationalist leader Mohandas K. Gandhi warned in his pacifist philosophy, "an eye for an eye makes the whole world blind." In addition, retributive theories claim that punishment must be proportionate with the offense, yet they offer no convincing explanation for how to go about matching offenses with crimes other than the bare assertion of *lex talionis*.

Sentencing decisions also raise problems of incommensurability. In what sense, for example, is any prison term proportionate with a drug offense? Even if society executes a murderer, the murderer's death is not in any meaningful way equivalent to the death of a particular victim. Death, suffering, and loss endure regardless of the pain that is inflicted on an offender.

Hybrid Theories

Debates between utilitarian and retributive theories of punishment have led some to adopt hybrid theories. The most common such theory calls for a consequentialism constrained by deontological boundaries. Attempts to synthesize the best of both theories, however, fail to resolve their incompatible foundations.

The "restorative justice" movement has recently been offered as a progressive alternative to retribution, as it emphasizes repairing the damaged relationships between offenders and victims through reconciliation programs rather than punishment. Still others advance the increasingly popular "restitution" theory of punishment. Following the principles advanced by the law and economics movement, it argues that offenders should pay their debts to society and their victims financially rather than through conventional penalties such as prison sentences. Some take the radical position that attempts to justify punishment will fail because such state-sanctioned violence is ultimately unjustifiable. The fact that punishment may make human affairs more orderly does not necessarily mean that it necessarily has ethical foundations, and if it does not, it should be abolished. In its place, abolitionists would understand crime as conflicts requiring resolution rather than the infliction of more pain. Abolitionists share many ideological commitments with pacifists and are subjected to similar criticisms, including the charge that abolishing punishments would fail to protect victims from aggressors.

Social scientists have become increasingly skeptical of the ability to deter or rehabilitate with punishment. This has led to a rebirth in the popularity of retributive arguments, which were thought to be barbaric only a few generations ago. This rise of retributivism, coupled with the brute efficacy of incarceration, has created a culture in which offenders are thought to deserve long sentences. The federal sentencing guidelines formalized these trends, requiring longer sentences and removing much of the discretion previously granted to judges to tailor individual sentences. Add to this situation lengthy mandatory sentences for drug offenders—who already constitute 25 percent of U.S. prison populations—and the staggering incarceration rates continue to grow.

Nick Smith

Further Reading

Beccaria, Cesare. *On Crimes and Punishments*. Indianapolis: Bobbs-Merrill, 1963. The eighteenth century Italian reformer's attempt to justify and regulate punishment by appeal to its social utility.

Bentham, Jeremy. *Introduction to the Principles of Morals and Legislation*. New York: Hafner Publishing, 1961. The original systematic and detailed theory of hedonistic utilitarian punishment that has been responsible for many philosophical and practical elements of modern democratic and criminal procedure.

Bianchi, J., and P. Pettit, eds. *Abolitionism: Towards a Non-Repressive Approach to Crime*. Amsterdam: Free University Press, 1986. Collection of essays arguing for the abolition of punishment and attempting to understand crime as conflicts needing resolution.

Binder, Guyora, and Nick Smith. "Framed: Utilitarianism and Punishment of the Innocent." *Rutgers Law Journal* 32 (2000). Defense of utilitarianism against the claim that it permits punishing the innocent.

Duff, R. A. *Trials and Punishments*. Cambridge, England: Cambridge University Press, 1986.
Argues that both deterrence and retribution are flawed justifications for punishments. Supports communicative theory of punishment, wherein offenders repent for their wrongdoing.

Duff, R. A., and David Garland, eds. *A Reader on Punishment*. Oxford, England: Oxford University Press, 1994. Collection of landmark articles, including papers on Marxism and retribution, expressive and paternalistic theories of punishment, sentencing, and abolitionism.

Foucault, Michel. *Discipline and Punish: The Birth of the Prison*. Translated by Alan Sheridan. New York: Vintage Press, 1995. Traces the migration of punishment from brutal public events to subtle exertions of power over individuals in everyday life. Although this trend away from corporal punishment appears to be motivated by humanism, Foucault explains how social control becomes much more efficient when it can control minds and private behaviors, rather than merely restrain or inflict pain on bodies.

Honderich, T. *Punishment: The Supposed Justifications*. Harmondsworth, U.K.: Penguin, 1984. Useful critical introduction to theories of punishment.

Kant, Immanuel. *Foundations of the Metaphysics of Morals*. Translated by Lewis White Beck. Indianapolis: Bobbs-Merrill, 1959. Kant's outline of the foundations of secular retributivism.

Kaplan, John, Robert Weisberg, and Guyora Binder, eds. *Criminal Law: Cases and Materials*. 5th ed. New York: Aspen Publishers, 2004. The leading criminal law casebook used in law schools. Provides statistics and well-chosen excerpts from historical and contemporary punishment theory.

Primoratz, Igor. *Justify Legal Punishment*. Atlantic Highlands, N.J.: Humanities Press, 1989. Accessible introductory explanatory analysis of competing theories of punishment. Argues for retributivism.

See also Capital punishment; Community-based corrections; Corporal punishment; Cruel and unusual punishment; Deterrence; Incapacitation; Just deserts; Punitive damages; Rehabilitation; Restorative justice; Sentencing; Sentencing guidelines, U.S.

Punitive damages

Definition: Money awarded in civil tort actions to punish intentional wrongdoers and to deter them and others from engaging in similar such behavior in the future

Criminal justice issues: Crime prevention; punishment; victims

Significance: Although awarded only in civil lawsuits, punitive damages share with criminal sanctions the purposes of punishing and deterring wrongful conduct.

Torts are civil wrongs committed by defendants against others, causing injury to the persons or property of the victims. Many crimes have civil counterparts in tort law. Plaintiff who win tort cases usually recover compensatory damages—money damages awarded by the courts as compensation for the harm the plaintiffs suffer due to the defendants' wrongful conduct. These damages cover losses suffered, such as medical expenses incurred due to injuries, lost wages and benefits, loss of privacy, harm to reputation, or emotional distress.

When the defendants' conduct is intentional and particularly egregious or reprehensible, injured victims can also recover additional awards known as punitive damages. Punitive damages do not compensate tort victims for their losses; rather, they are intended to punish deliberate wrongdoers and to deter them and others from committing such conduct in the future. However, punitive damages are awarded only for the worst kinds of wrongdoing and are not routinely assessed against losing defendants in tort actions.

The size of punitive damages awards is typically decided by juries and is subject to judicial review. Although punitive damages are most often awarded in cases in which injuries are due to deliberate misconduct, they are also awarded in product liability suits involving manufacturers who are aware of dangerous defects in their product and the potential for serious injury but fail to correct the defects.

Punitive damages are generally not recoverable in breach of contract cases, unless defendants have committed fraud or another tort at the same time. For instance, courts have awarded punitive damages when defendants have breached contracts in bad faith or have intentionally interfered with contracts between the plaintiffs and other parties.

Kurt M. Saunders

Further Reading

Blatt, Richard L., et al. *Punitive Damages: A State by State Guide to Law and Practice*. St. Paul, Minn.: West Publishing, 2002.

Schlueter, Linda L., and Kenneth R. Redden. *Punitive Damages*. Charlottesville, Va.: LEXIS Publishing, 2000.

Sunstein, Cass R., et al. *Punitive Damages: How Juries Decide*. Chicago: University of Chicago Press, 2002.

See also Boot camps; Deterrence; Fines; Punishment; Restorative justice; Sex discrimination; Sexual harassment; Verdicts.

R.A.V. v. City of St. Paul

The Case: U.S. Supreme Court ruling on hate crime

Date: Decided on June 22, 1992

Criminal justice issues: Constitutional protections; hate crime

Significance: This holding, invalidating an ordinance that made it a crime to burn a cross to harass African Americans, demonstrates how the Supreme Court affords a preferred status to First Amendment free speech, even reprehensible speech.

During the early morning hours of June 21, 1990, "R.A.V."—an unnamed seventeen-year-old, self-described as a white supremacist—and several other teenagers burned a makeshift wooden cross on the front lawn of the only African American family in their St. Paul, Minnesota, neighborhood. They were prosecuted for disorderly conduct in juvenile court under the city's "bias-motivated crime ordinance," which prohibited cross burning along with other symbolic displays that "one knows" or should know would arouse "anger, alarm or resentment in others on the basis of race, color, creed, religion, or gender."

The state trial court ruled that this ordinance was unconstitutionally overbroad because it indiscriminately prohibited protected First Amendment speech as well as unprotected activity. The Supreme Court of Minnesota reversed the lower court's decision and upheld the ordinance, which it interpreted to prohibit only unprotected "fighting words," face-to-face insults that are likely to cause the person to whom the words are addressed to attack the speaker physically.

The U.S. Supreme Court ruled unanimously in favor of R.A.V. and invalidated the ordinance, but the justices did not agree in their reasoning. Stating that they found the cross burning reprehensible, Justice Antonin Scalia, writing for the majority, nevertheless concluded that the ordinance was unconstitutional because it criminalized only specified "fighting words" based on the content of the hate message and, consequently, the government was choosing sides. He noted that the ordinance would prohibit a sign that attacked Roman Catholics but would not prohibit a second sign that attacked those who displayed such an anti-Catholic bias.

Four justices concurred in the ruling of unconstitutionality, but Justice Byron White's opinion sharply criticized the majority opinion for going too far to protect racist speech. He reasoned that the ordinance was overbroad because it made it a crime to cause another person offense, hurt feelings, or resentment and because these harms could be caused by protected First Amendment speech. Justices Harry Blackmun and John Paul Stevens also wrote separate opinions complaining that hate speech did not deserve constitutional protection.

This holding calls into question numerous similar state laws designed to protect women and minorities from harassment and discrimination. Some of these individuals and groups may still invoke long-standing federal civil rights statutes, however, which carry severe criminal penalties of fines and imprisonment. In 1993, *R.A.V.*'s significance was called into question by the *Wisconsin v. Mitchell* decision upholding a state statute that increased a sentence for a crime of violence if the defendant targeted the victim because of the victim's race or other specified status.

Eugene Larson

Further Reading

Bell, Jeannine. *Policing Hatred: Law Enforcement, Civil Rights, and Hate Crime.* New York: New York University Press, 2002.

Gerstenfeld, Phyllis B. *Hate Crimes: Causes, Controls, and Controversies.* Thousand Oaks, Calif.: Sage Publications, 2004.

Perry, Barbara. *In the Name of Hate: Understanding Hate Crimes*. New York: Routledge, 2001.

Streissguth, Thomas. *Hate Crimes*. New York: Facts On File, 2003.

See also Hate crime; *Virginia v. Black*; Supreme Court, U.S.; *Wisconsin v. Mitchell*.

Race riots in the twentieth century

The Events: Conflicts between members of racial groups, or disorders brought on by racial conflict that result in widespread illegal activities, including looting, arson, violence, and murder

Dates: 1901-1992

Criminal justice issues: Civil rights and liberties; morality and public order

Significance: Race riots both threaten the stability of society and, by their very occurrence, call into question the fundamental fairness of society.

Referring to racial violence in the United States as "race riots" is often misleading. Many race riots were actually one-sided white massacres of African Americans; this was particularly true of those prior to 1921. Nineteenth century race riots were often called "slave revolts" or "slave insurrections." These slave revolts were most frequent in the areas of the South where African Americans constituted at least 40 percent of the population. Fearing that slave revolts in one part of the South would trigger similar revolts throughout the South, slaveholders quelled such rebellions quickly and viciously.

Twentieth century race riots differ from nineteenth century riots in both motive and location. Whereas nineteenth century riots were primarily concerned with maintaining the institution of slavery, twentieth century riots—particularly those in the years before World War II—were often designed to maintain white supremacy over urban African Americans. Also, where nine-teenth century race riots were almost exclusively a southern phenomenon, twentieth century race riots took place in almost every major urban area of America.

1901-1945

Race riots prior to World War II often followed a consistent pattern. In almost all cases, the riots were initiated by whites against African Americans. In only two of the major riots—Harlem in 1935 and again in 1943—did African Americans initiate the riots. Second, most riots were caused by a white fear of African Americans competing for jobs that previously were held by whites. The rapid movement of African Americans from the South to the urban industrial areas of the North contributed to this fear. Third, most riots took place during the hot and humid summer months when young people were out of school. Finally, the riots were often fueled by rumors—allegations of police brutality against African Americans or allegations of black violence against whites heightened racial tensions.

One of the major race riots during this period occurred in East St. Louis, Illinois, in 1917. An automobile occupied by four whites drove through black areas firing shots. When a similar car was seen, African Americans opened fire and killed two occupants, both of whom were police officers. Whites invaded the black community, burning three hundred homes and killing fifty African Americans. The summer of 1919 saw twenty riots in communities such as Charleston, South Carolina; Washington, D.C.; Knoxville, Tennessee; and Chicago. The riots of 1919 were so bloody that the period was called the "Red Summer."

Post-World War II Riots

While post-World War II riots were fueled by rumor and also took place during the summer months, they differed from pre-World War II riots in two important ways. First, a majority of the riots were initiated by African Americans, not whites. Second, many of the post-World War II riots were not confined to the black community. In several cases, whites were singled out as victims of black violence.

The race riots of the 1960's threatened to destroy the fabric of American society. The 1964